Erik J. Zürcher is Professor of Turkish Studies at the University of Leiden. He is the author of 14 books on Turkish history, including *The Young Turk Legacy and Nation Building: From the Ottoman Empire to Atatürk's Turkey* (I.B.Tauris).

FOURTH EDITION

TURKEY
A MODERN HISTORY

ERIK J. ZÜRCHER

I.B. TAURIS
LONDON · NEW YORK

New paperback edition published in 2017 by
I.B.Tauris & Co. Ltd
London • New York
Reprinted 2017
www.ibtauris.com

First published in hardback in 1993 by I.B.Tauris & Co. Ltd

ISBN: 978 1 78453 187 4
eISBN: 978 1 78672 183 9
ePDF: 978 1 78673 183 8

A full CIP record for this book is available from the British Library
A full CIP record is available from the Library of Congress

Library of Congress Catalog Card Number: available

Typeset by Oxford Publishing Services, Oxford
Maps drawn by Russell Townsend
Printed and bound by CPI Group (UK) Ltd, Croydon, CR0 4YY

MIX
Paper from
responsible sources
FSC
www.fsc.org   FSC® C013604

Contents

PART III
A TROUBLED DEMOCRACY

PART IV
THE THIRD REPUBLIC: TURKEY SINCE 1980   281

Preface

Between the summers of 2015 and 2016, Turkey was in the news almost without interruption. The country was in turmoil and all manner of old, sometimes very old, tensions seemed to erupt into violent conflict. The national elections of June 2015 for a while looked like a watershed. The ruling Justice and Development Party (AKP) suffered significant losses in the polls, primarily due to the success of the Kurdish HDP, which, despite its strong links with the PKK guerrillas, proved able to attract many young secularist and liberal voters in the big cities. For the first time ever a Kurdish party crossed the 10 per cent threshold and entered parliament with no fewer than 80 seats; in fact, a coalition of opposition parties could theoretically have mustered a majority in parliament.

One reason for the HDP's success among the Kurds (it won nearly every seat in the southeast) was the latter's widespread anger at the way Turkey sat by and watched Islamic State militants encircle and assault the largely Kurdish town of Kobani within sight of the Turkish border between September 2014 and February 2015. The AKP government had refused to let Kurds from Turkey help in the defence of Kobani and was widely seen as sympathizing with the Sunni Arab Islamic State fighters. In June, the Kurds took their revenge at the polls.

President Erdoğan, whose party traditionally enjoyed strong support among conservative Sunni Kurds and who, since 2009, had supported the idea of a peaceful solution to the Kurdish problem, saw this as ingratitude, and, indeed, betrayal. In the run up to the elections, he started to campaign ferociously for the AKP (even though, as president of the republic, he was officially supposed to be above party concerns) and denounced the Kurdish politicians.

A month after the elections, on 20 July, a bomb attack killed 34 young people and wounded another 100 in the town of Suruç. The bomber was a Turkish Islamic State militant and the victims were young Kurds who were about to go to Kobani to help in the rebuilding. In revenge attacks, the PKK killed two Turkish policemen, whereupon Erdoğan ordered the Turkish Air Force to start bombing both IS positions in Syria and PKK positions in northern Iraq. This signalled the end of attempts to reach a peaceful solution to the Kurdish problem. PKK militants took up arms again and the Turkish army answered with an all-out offensive. In addition, the war was no longer limited to the mountains. Much of the fighting was done in the cities of the southeast, leaving whole neighbourhoods in a state of destruction reminiscent of contemporary Syria. After the offensive the war reverted to its familiar pattern of relatively low-level violence, with on average five to ten people killed every day.

After the June 2015 elections, in which it polled 41 per cent but lost its absolute majority in parliament, the AKP, on the orders of the president, successfully sabotaged all attempts to form a coalition government. Furthermore, because the three opposition parties were too far apart to find common ground, they could not exploit their theoretical majority in parliament. The biggest of the three, Atatürk's old Republican People's Party (RPP), got 25 per cent of the vote. This meant that it kept its core support base of Alevis (whose fear and mistrust of explicitly Sunni political parties would never induce them to vote AKP) but that it held very little attraction to a broader section of society. This was primarily because, as the old party of the Kemalist establishment, it could never choose between state-oriented secularist nationalism, which was its heritage, and an outward-looking social liberalism that could attract the urban youth. Some of that youth went over to the HDP, which managed 13 per cent. However, because the HDP failed to jettison its close relationship with the PKK and its imprisoned leader Abdullah Öcalan (a murderer in the eyes of most Turks), it was unacceptable as a coalition partner for the other two parties and, especially, for the ultranationalist Nationalist Action Party (NAP).

Erdoğan correctly estimated that a coalition without the Justice and Development Party (JDP or AKP) (Adalet ve Kalkınma Partisi) would be impossible and that the combined effect of the escalation of the Kurdish war, terrorist attacks and bickering between the political parties, would make the majority yearn for the stability that only he and the AKP could provide. New elections were held in November and Erdoğan's highly personalized campaign around the theme of *istikrar* (stability) brought the AKP to power once more, with an increased absolute majority in parliament and almost exactly 50 per cent of the popular vote.

Like the local and presidential elections the year before, the elections of 2015 were completely centred on the person of Recep Tayyip Erdoğan and, as a result, Erdoğan's grip on the AKP increased even further. In the six months after the November elections, he used his power to wage a war on four fronts at the same time, three of them at home and one abroad. The large-scale military operations against the PKK in the southeast continued unabated. Efforts to 'cleanse' the state machinery from members of Fethullah Gülen's 'Hizmet' movement, which had started when they released recordings of state ministers and members of their families discussing corrupt business deals back in December 2014, were intensified. Hizmet, which had been called 'the parallel structure' in the government press since early 2015, was now increasingly denoted the 'Fethullah Terror Organization' (FETÖ). Erdoğan had also not forgotten the resistance of the secularists during the Gezi protests in June 2013. Remnants of the independent media came under increased government pressure and social media and websites critical of the government were regularly closed down.

These three enemies were primarily internal to the country, but the fourth, Islamic State, was not. In the Syrian civil war that was continuing just south of the Turkish border, Turkey had always seen the Assad regime and its supporters as the main enemy. As the war progressed, a second strategic threat developed in the shape of the self-governing region in northwest and northeast Syria, in which the PKK offshoot Democratic Union Party (PYD) dominated with the help of its militias, the 'People's Protection Forces' or YPG. The idea that a virtually independent Kurdish state, similar to that in northern Iraq but ruled by PKK supporters, would come into existence on Turkey's southern border was a nightmare for Ankara. As a counterweight against Assad and the PYD, Turkey actively supported a range of Sunni Arab opposition movements, some of which had direct links with Al-Qaeda, as well as with Turkish speaking Türkmen groups. While IS was not one of the Turkish client groups, Ankara tacitly allowed the 'caliphate' to operate in Turkey. The country became a vital staging post for new IS recruits from all over the world and for bringing in armaments and exporting oil from the IS-held parts of Syria. From late 2014 onwards, Turkey came under increasing pressure from the United States to stop tolerating IS and to close the border. Ultimately, it complied and the border was closed. IS took revenge both on the Turkish government for its broken promises and on the Kurds for the American-supported and successful YPG attacks on IS in Syria through a campaign of bomb attacks in Turkey.

During the year, the rhetoric of the president, the governing party and the pro-government media became increasingly shrill and ever more anti-Western, with strong suggestions that the Gülen movement, the PKK and the liberal press were shielded by foreign powers and subservient to foreign interests. A particularly strong example was that, when a huge bomb explosion killing 41 people occurred at Istanbul's Atatürk Airport, the authorities blamed IS, but the popular press accused the CIA of masterminding it.

The Syrian refugee crisis exacerbated the anti-Western mood in the country. During five years of escalating civil war in Syria, 2.5 million refugees crossed the border into Turkey. A small minority lived in official camps near the border, but most of them lived a shadowy, undocumented life in the big cities. Turkey did not accord refugee status to non-Europeans, but it tolerated the presence of all these people. In Turkish eyes, their flight was caused by the West's failure to remove Bashar al-Assad; also, that Europe ignored the refugee situation in Turkey, Lebanon and Jordan was proof of its lack of interest in the fate of the peoples of the Middle East. President Erdoğan constantly harped on this point. It was not surprising, therefore, that Turkey was not too concerned when refugees started to use its western shore as a launch pad for crossing into Europe. The Greek islands were a short boat ride from the Turkish coast and, in the late summer and autumn of 2015, the number of people using this route exploded. Europe proved unable to devise a common policy for the distribution and resettlement of the hundreds of thousands of refugees in the EU. In desperation, it therefore decided to bribe Turkey to stop the flow. In March, an agreement was reached under which Turkey would take back any refugees who reached Greece in exchange for a promise that the EU would take in an equal number of refugees from Turkey. Other concessions included a promise to restart membership negotiations and the implementation of visa-free travel to the Schengen zone for Turkish tourists and business people. The EU added a sweetener of three, later six billion euros for Turkey, to be spent on improving the lot of the refugees. It was a cynical deal, but it worked: the flow of refugees turned into a trickle. In the eyes of the Turkish government and public, however, Europe had shown itself to be both immoral and weak.

By the spring of 2016, Turkey was in a familiar but paradoxical situation – a solid and stable one-party government with a complete power monopoly, but at the same time a deeply polarized society in which several groups (Kurds, Alevis, secularists and liberals), which together constituted half the population, were effectively disenfranchised. Political violence in the country was on the increase and the southeast was a war zone. Internationally, Turkey was isolated. In the Middle East, its support for opposition groups had led to a freeze in relations with Egypt, Israel, Syria and even Shi'i dominated Iraq. Turkey's only solid allies were Hamas and Qatar. Both the internal repression of Kurds, Gülenists and liberals and, externally, ambivalence over IS, made Erdoğan increasingly unpopular in the West. Relations with Russia had been a bright spot, but the Syrian crisis, in which both countries were on opposing sides, darkened even that: on 24 November 2015 Turkish fighter planes shot down a Russian warplane that had briefly trespassed into Turkish airspace and, when the pilots ejected, Turkish-supported fighters killed one of them from the ground. When Turkey refused to apologize, Russia declared a full economic boycott, which hit the Turkish economy hard. This was the situation when, on the evening of 15 July, military personnel took over key positions in Ankara and Istanbul, and Turkish state television announced that the Turkish Armed Forces had seized control of the government and that its members were under arrest. At first, the population was stunned and mainly stayed at home. In the early hours of the coup, confusion reigned. The president, who was on holiday in the house of a friendly businessperson in the southwest of the country, was invisible. After a few hours, however, it became clear that it was not the army as such, but a group of rebel officers who were executing a coup. The chief of general staff had been taken prisoner, but refused to join the rebels and the powerful commander of the First Field Army in Istanbul announced on a private television channel that the army did not support the coup and called on the troops to return to their barracks. The tide turned quickly against the rebels once President Erdoğan, who had narrowly escaped arrest, with the help of an iPhone managed to appear on the CNN Türk television channel and call on the population to come out onto the streets to resist the coup. The mosques broadcasted his message over their loudspeakers and, within a few hours, hundreds of thousands of citizens, supported by armed police units that had largely stayed loyal to the government, confronted the rebel soldiers. In the ensuing street battles, almost 300 people, mostly civilians, were killed, but when his supporters managed to reconquer the airport, President Erdoğan could return to Istanbul and rally the people around him. By early morning the rebellion had collapsed.

It is not at all clear who exactly was behind the coup, but Fethullah Gülen's followers in the officer corps seem to have played an important role in it, possibly in collaboration with the Kemalists. The gendarmerie and air force seem to have been deeply involved, whereas the navy and land forces played almost no part. Erdoğan and his government were in no doubt at all: they pointed the finger at the 'Fethullah Gülen Terror Organization' as the only force behind the plot. A state of emergency was declared and, in the weeks that followed, a purge of enormous proportions was undertaken. Anyone suspected of even the remotest link with the Gülen movement was purged and, in the next few weeks, more than 80,000 people were sacked, suspended or arrested. These included over one-third of the generals of the Turkish army and nearly 3000 judges. The rule of law was suspended and the government ruled by decree.

The coup once again damaged Turkey's relations with the West. Western leaders (unlike their Russian and Iranian counterparts) had been relatively slow to condemn the coup and contact Erdoğan, and this led him to believe that the West had adopted a wait-and-see attitude. The popular media went further and accused the USA of being behind the coup. The Americans' refusal to extradite Fethullah Gülen (who had been living in Pennsylvania since 1998) without hard evidence of his guilt, caused widespread indignation. In the months that followed, references to 'true' and 'false' friends became a stock item in Erdoğan's speeches and a chasm opened up between Turkey and the West in the perception of what had happened. Because the purges started immediately after the suppression of the coup, Western media focused on them rather than on what had been for the Turkish population an extremely traumatic event, in which members of the highly regarded armed forces had not hesitated to kill hundreds of their own citizens in an attempt to topple an elected government. It was a reminder of the darkest days of military dictatorship. At the same time, there was a lot of pride that unarmed but determined citizens had successfully defended democracy.

This book is not about the current affairs of Turkey. It makes no sense for the author of a history textbook to run out of breath trying to catch up with events as they unfold. This Preface apart, the book ends in the late summer of 2014. Even then, however, the trends that would dominate the last few years were already visible, as Chapter 17 shows. What this book tries to offer is a deeper historical insight to help the reader understand the roots of the current crisis in Turkey.

The protagonists of the conflicts in the country all build on a history of at least half a century. The AKP is the direct successor, and offshoot, of a series of parties founded, closed down and started again under different names between 1970 and 2000. All these parties were inspired by the 'National Vision' ideology, in which 'national' emphatically referred to an 'authentic' conservative Muslim Turkishness. The emergence of these parties was the work of a religious community, the Iskenderpaşa Cemaati led by Sheikh Mehmet Zahit Kotku. By the end of the 1960s, he had decided that the way to change the future of Turkey was to enter the political arena with a conservative Islamist party and one of his followers, the engineer Professor Necmettin Erbakan, was chosen as its leader. Erbakan would lead the movement for 30 years and the young Recep Tayyip Erdoğan, who was also a pupil of Kotku, was one of the energetic leaders of its youth wing.

The Hizmet movement, which Fethullah Gülen founded and which worked hand in glove with Erdoğan's AKP between 2002 and 2012, but which since early 2014 Erdoğan has vehemently persecuted, has equally deep historical roots. At the end of the 1960s, Gülen had been involved in the establishment of a number of boarding schools in İzmir, which would later develop into a huge international educational network. His vision of Turkey's future was not unlike the 'National Vision', but he differed in the strategy to achieve the goal of a modern, technologically well-informed, affluent and powerful, yet pious and 'moral' Turkey. Where Kotku and Erbakan opted for political struggle, Gülen's aim was to create new generations of followers that would infiltrate state and society and ultimately change Turkey's direction.

Both men, who clashed so violently between 2014 and 2016, therefore have a lot in common: they are both leaders of conservative and nationalist Sunni Muslim movements, which have a very different view of modernity from that of their secularist Kemalist predecessors.

Gülen, Erbakan and Erdoğan's roots go back even further. They are all ultimately linked to the Nakşibendi mystic brotherhood or dervish order – Erdoğan and Erbakan directly through Kotku, and Gülen indirectly. Fethullah Gülen is a *Nurcu*, a Follower of the Light, which means that he recognizes as his spiritual master the most important religious innovator active in Turkey in the twentieth century – Sait Nursi. Nursi, who was himself taught by Nakşibendi sheikhs in the east at the turn of the twentieth century, founded a religious renewal movement that offered an alternative to Kemalist modernization by accepting Western science and technology, but rejecting secularism.

The often fiercely anti-Western stance of the Turkish Islamists, who now run the country, can be traced to their historical roots. The poet Necip Fazıl Kısakürek first voiced the idea that Turkey should reject Westernization during the republican era in the 1940s and 1950s. He believed that Turkey should instead turn to its authentic roots and accept that its calling was to lead the people of the East, especially in the Muslim world, on an alternative path to modernity. It is no coincidence that the journal he published (and the circle around it) was called *The Great East* (*Büyük Doğu*). Many contemporary Turkish Islamists revere Necip Fazıl, a secularist Kemalist converted by a Nakşibendi sheikh in Istanbul, as a pioneer.

It was thanks to two broader historical developments that these Islamist movements achieved their dominance in Turkey from the 1990s onwards. One was the population explosion that Turkey underwent from the 1960s onwards and the consequent mass migration from the countryside to the big cities. The other was the IMF-enforced transition to a neoliberal economic system after 1980. The core constituency of the Islamists consisted of small family businesses, primarily in provincial towns and many of these expanded dramatically when the market opened up in the 1980s. A decade later, the vast immigrant proletariat in the big cities, which led a precarious existence, lacked basic security and felt alienated from the urban elites, proved a rich hunting ground for the Islamists with their slogan of a 'Just Order'.

The other protagonist in the violent conflicts that engulf Turkey today is the Kurdistan Workers Party, or PKK, which has historical roots that go back almost as far as the Islamists. For a generation, the Kemalist state had brutally suppressed any expression of Kurdish identity when, in the late 1960s, the first calls to recognize the Kurdish nationality problem (as opposed to just the economic backwardness of the East) were made. The calls came from both within the socialist Workers Party of Turkey (WPT) and from the radical left-wing student movement of the time. It was in this environment that Abdullah Öcalan, a student at Ankara University, founded the PKK in 1978. A year later, the PKK moved to Syria, where for the next 20 years it operated under the protection of President Hafez al-Assad, the father of the current president, Bashar al-Assad.

The historical roots of the current political struggles are also evident in the different protagonists' discourses. Ever since the AKP's electoral victories started in 2002, Kemalist secularists have seen the actions of Erdoğan's governments in terms of *irtica*, or religious reaction. Young Turks and Kemalists started to use the term in the first half of the twentieth century to refer to all those who resisted their particular brand of positivist and materialist modernity. Kemalists tend to see modern Islamist politicians as the direct successors of the bearded dervishes who resisted the republic in its early days. Conversely, Erdoğan's discourse on sinister foreign forces manipulating internal enemies and traitors to harm the country can only resonate so strongly with Turkish people because they have been reared on a diet of similar stories since their primary school history classes. Over time, however, the external forces and internal enemies have changed. At the beginning of the twentieth century, the Greek and Armenian citizens of the empire were accused of collaborating with Russia and Britain. In the early republic, it was the Kurds (and occasionally the Jews). During the cold war, it was communists working for the Soviet Union; and during the Cyprus conflict, it was the supporters of the Greek Orthodox Church of Istanbul. The narrative remains fundamentally the same, even as the actors change. Whether on the secularist side or on that of the Islamists, that people see current events through the prism of a traumatic history often leads to distortions and demonization of the other side.

These are just a few ways in which knowing something about the history of modern Turkey can improve our understanding of current events in the country. This is where this book, *Turkey: A Modern History*, can contribute. It is not about the events of today, let alone about trying to predict the future. Its aim is to explain how Turkey came to be what it is; how the history of Turkey in the last two hundred years has made it the country it is today.

This book is a new, and thoroughly revised, edition of a work that has been around since 1993. Its many reprints and translations into 11 languages (Dutch, Turkish, Greek, Italian, Polish, Albanian, Hebrew, Arabic, Indonesian, Chinese and Persian) indicate that it has had quite an impact. It has served to educate several generations of students in many different countries (and some of those students were not even born when it first appeared). Its central thesis on how the Republic of Turkey emerged from the Ottoman Empire, which was still highly controversial back in 1993, has now become mainstream.

All of this is of course very gratifying, but 23 years is a very long time. When the book was written, the world was still adjusting to the end of the cold war. The Berlin Wall had fallen, but the bloody dissolution of Yugoslavia had only just started. Bill Clinton was the new president of the United States. The European Community became the European Union. It had 15 members and the euro did not yet exist. The term 'Gulf War' could still be used without numerals – there had been only one.

Since 1993, Turkey has gone through deep economic and political crises, but after 2002 managed to achieve some stability and strong growth under the leadership of the AKP. The Turkey of today is completely different from that of 23 years ago: it is stronger and more affluent, but it is also dominated by a conservative Islamic worldview. Some things have remained the same – extreme polarization with respect to personal lifestyles, worldviews and ideals; an apparent inability to accommodate minorities like the Kurds within the framework of the unitary nation-state; and an ambivalent relationship with the West.

In terms of scholarship, the world in 2017 is also very different from that of 1993. The rise of the Internet, with its search engines and mass digitization of publications and archival documents, has opened up an enormous amount of information. Partly because of this, but also through the emergence of many bright, well-trained, young and largely Turkish researchers, many seminal studies have appeared over the past two decades, especially about the late Ottoman Empire. The output on the history of the republic has been smaller, but there too, very interesting and innovative studies have appeared. The emphasis has shifted from the study of the central state and its policies to local realities and daily life. We know much more than we did in 1993 and this has changed our interpretations of some events.

Already in 1997, *Turkey: A Modern History* appeared in a second edition in which a number of typos and factual errors had been corrected. In 2005, a well-revised third edition came out, which included a fuller treatment of the Armenian genocide (an area in which much new research was being done) and, of course, an overview of the history of the years between 1992 and 2002. Therefore, the book you hold in your hands is really the fourth edition and the revisions made to its text are far more radical than in any of the previous ones. There was a need to incorporate the findings of new historical research published in the past decade, but also to include the years of AKP rule in Turkey since 2002, as the country has changed so radically in that period.

New passages have been included, but existing sections have also been changed and, sometimes, deleted. Some events that seemed crucial in 1993 or 2002 turn out to be incidents rather than trends when one looks back from 2017. Fortunately, recent empirical research has confirmed the main arguments of the original book and analysis, especially concerning the period 1908–1950 and the transition from empire to republic.

I have learned a lot in the past 23 years. In 1993 I wrote that the best way to gain an understanding of a topic is by teaching it and that is still true. Critical students (and other audiences) sharpen the mind. Since 1993, I have had the privilege of supervising almost thirty Ph.D. students, nineteen of whom have now defended their theses. More than anything else, it has been discussions with this new generation of historians of Turkey, about their work and about mine, that have given me new perspectives. Therefore, it is only right that I should dedicate this new edition of *Turkey: A Modern History* to my Ph.D. students, past and present.

Erik Jan Zürcher
Leiden, February 2017

Glossary

Note: this glossary follows Turkish alphabetization.

adab	gentlemanly code of conduct and taste
adalet	justice; characteristic of a government that remains within its *hudud* (q.v.)
alaylı	officer who has risen from the ranks
Alevî	adherents of a syncretistic form of Shi'i Islam
altı ok	'Six Arrows'; principles of Republican People's Party
aman	safe conduct under Islamic law enabling non-Muslims who are not *dhimmi* (q.v.) to reside in Muslim countries
askeri	member of the arms-bearing, tax-exempt, ruling elite of the empire, consisting of the sultan's servants
aşar	tithe
ayan	provincial notables
bab-ı Ali	'Sublime Porte' or 'Porte', both the main building housing the Ottoman government and its collective name
berat	document recognizing someone as subject of a foreign power, entitled to *aman* (q.v.)
casus foederi	a case that comes within the provisions of a treaty or that causes a treaty to become operative
ciziye	poll tax payable by *dhimmi*s (q.v.)
çiftlik	privately owned farm
damat	son-in-law, a man who has married into the imperial family
dervish	member of a *tarikat* (q.v.)
divan	imperial council
dokuz umde	'Nine Principles'; 1923 programme of People's Party
dönüm	quarter of an acre

dragoman	translator, especially one in the service of a foreign embassy
evkaf	plural of *vakıf* (q.v.)
fetva	legal opinion based on *şeriat* (q.v.)
fitne	disorder, rebellion
gazi	'conquering hero', title for a successful soldier
gecekondu	'built at night'; squatter dwelling
halk evi	'People's House'; local educational establishment for disseminating Kemalist message in provincial towns
halk odası	'People's Room'; same as *halk evi*, but on a smaller scale, in villages
harbiye	military academy
hatt-i humayun	imperial decree
hatt-i şerif	see *hatt-i humayun*
hudud	bounds within which any individual or group had to remain in order not to trespass on others' rights
İdadiye	secondary school for boys
iltizam	tax farming
imam	Muslim prayer leader; also successor to the Prophet recognized by *Shi'i* (q.v.) Muslims
janissaries	see *yeni çeri*
jurnal	report by government spy
kadi	*şeriat* (q.v.) judge
kadi sicilleri	local court records
kâhya	steward of the grand vizier
kaime	Ottoman government bonds, used as banknotes
kanun	see *örf*
kariye	village
kaymakam	governor of a county
kaza	district
khedive	hereditary governor-general of Egypt
mabeyn	palace secretariat
medrese	religious college
mektep	traditional primary school
mektepli	officer who has graduated from military academy
millet	nation, community of *dhimmis* (q.v.)
mir	prince, specifically in Kurdistan

miri	state-owned real estate
muhassil	tax collector
mutasarrif	governor of a county (see also *sancak*)
müftü	expert of religious law, who pronounces *fetva*s (q.v.)
mülk	privately owned real estate
mülkiye	civil service academy
nahiye	rural community
nizam-i cedid	reform programme of Selim III ('new order'). Also the name of his new Western-style army
nizamiye	regular army
örf	legislation by sultanic decree
reaya	the tax-paying subjects of the Ottoman state
redif	army reserve
reisülküttab	chief scribe, secretary to the grand vizier
Rüşdiye	school for boys aged between 10 and 15
sadrazam	grand vizier, the sultan's chief minister
sancak	county
scribes	administrative corps of Ottoman central government before the transition to a modern bureaucracy
serasker	commander-in-chief (under the sultan)
Shi'i	Muslims who only recognize the male descendants of Ali, the Prophet's son-in-law and nephew, as legitimate leaders of the Muslim community
sipahi	member of semi-feudal cavalry
softa	student at *medrese* (q.v.)
Sufi	see dervish
Sultaniye	college (lyceum)
Sunni	Muslims who recognize the succession to the Prophet as leaders of the Muslim community of elected caliphs. The vast majority of Muslims in the Ottoman Empire
Şeriat	Islamic canon law
şeyhülislam	chief *müftü* (q.v.) of the empire
tanzimat	reforms, especially the centralizing and Westernizing ones of 1839 to 1873
tarikat	Islamic mystical order or fraternity
tekke	lodge of a *tarikat* (q.v.)

tercüme odası	translation office of the Porte (see also *bab-ı Ali*)
timar	fief
türbe	religious shrine, tomb of a Muslim saint
ulema	doctors of Islamic law
vakıf	religious charitable foundation
vali	governor-general of a province (see also *vilayet*)
varlık vergisi	discriminatory wealth tax, imposed during the Second World War
vekil	commissar, minister in the nationalist government between 1920 and 1923
vilayet	province
yeni çeri	salaried standing infantry, known in the West as janissaries
zülm	tyranny, oppression

Acronyms and Abbreviations

AFU — Armed Forces Union
AKP — *Adalet ve Kalkınma Partisi* (same as JDP)
AKUT — *Arama Kurtarma Derneği* (Search and Rescue Association)
ANAP — *Anavatan Partisi* (same as MP)
AP — *Adalet Partisi* (Justice Party)
ASALA — Armenian Secret Army for the Liberation of Armenia
BDP — *Barış ve Demokrasi Partisi* (Peace and Democracy Party)
CENTO — Central Treaty Organization
CHP — *Cumhuriyet Halk Partisi* (same as RPP)
CIA — Central Intelligence Agency
CUP — Committee of Union and Progress (*İttihad ve Terakki Cemiyeti*)
DeP — *Demokrasi Partisi* (Democracy Party)
DİSK — *Devrimci İşçi Sendikaları Konfederasyonu* (Confederation of Revolutionary Trade Unions)
DLP — Democratic Left Party (*Demokratik Sol Partisi*)
DP — *Demokrat Parti* (Democrat Party)
DSP — *Demokratik Sol Parti* (same as DLP)
DTP — *Demokratik Toplum Partisi* (Democratic Society Party)
DYP — *Doğru Yol Partisi* (True Path Party)
EOKA — *Ethniki Organosis Kyprion Agoniston*/National Organization of Cypriot Fighters
EU — European Union
FP — *Fazilet Partisi* (Virtue Party) (same as VP)
FRP — Free Republican Party (*Serbest Cumhuriyet Partisi*)
GAP — *Güneydogu Anadolu Projesi* (Southeast Anatolia Project)
GUP — Great Unity Party (*Büyük Birlik Partisi*)
HaDeP — *Halkın Demokrasi Partisi* (People's Democracy Party)
HDP — *Halkların Demokratik Partisi* (Peoples' Democratic Party)
İBDA — *İslamî Büyük Doğu Akıncıları* (Raiders of the Islamic Great East)
ICFTU — International Conference of Free Trade Unions

İHH   *İnsan Hak ve Hürriyetleri İnsani Yardım Vakfı*
           (Humanitarian Relief Foundation)
ILO   International Labour Organization
IMF   International Monetary Fund
IMRO   Internal Macedonian Revolutionary Organization
IS   Islamic State
JDP   Justice and Development Party (same as AKP)
JİTEM   *Jandarma İstihbarat ve Terörle Mücadele* (Gendarmerie
           Unit for Intelligence and Combating Terror)
JP   Justice Party (same as AP)
KADEK   Kurdish Freedom and Democracy Congress
KCK   *Koma Civakên Kurdistan* (Union of Communities in
           Kurdistan)
MDD   *Millî Demokratik Devrim* (National Democratic
           Revolution)
MGK   *Millî Güvenlik Kurulu* (National Security Council)
MHP   *Milliyetçi Hareket Partisi* (Nationalist Action Party)
MİSK   *Milliyetçi İşçi Sendikaları Konfederasyonu*
           (Confederations of Nationalist Trade Unions)
MİT   *Milli İstihbarat Teşkilatı* (National Intelligence
           Organization)
MP   Motherland Party (same as ANAP)
MÜSİAD   *Müstakil İş Adamları Derneği* (Society of Independent
           Businessmen)
NAP   Nationalist Action Party (same as MHP)
NATO   North Atlantic Treaty Organization
NDM   New Democracy Movement (*Yeni Demokrasi Hareketi*)
NDP   National Development Party (*Millî Kalkınma Partisi*)
NOP   National Order Party (*Millî Nizam Partisi*)
NSC   National Security Council (same as MGK)
NP   Nation Party (*Millet Partisi*)
NSP   National Salvation Party (*Millî Selamet Partisi*)
NTP   New Turkey Party (*Yeni Türkiye Partisi*)
NUC   National Unity Committee (*Millî Birlik Komitesi*)
OECD   Organization for Economic Cooperation and Development
OHAL   *Olağanüstü Hal* (State of Emergency); *Bölgesi*
           (Extraordinary Zone)
PDA   Public Debt Administration
PDK   Democratic Party of Kurdistan
PDL   Party of the Democratic Left (same as DSP)
PKK   *Partiye Karkeren Kurdestane* (Workers' Party of Kurdistan)
PLP   People's Labour Party (*Halkın Emek Partisi*)

PND	Party of Nationalist Democracy (*Milliyetçi Demokrasi Partisi*)
PP	People's Party (*Halk Fırkası*) (same as CHP and RPP)
PRP	Progressive Republican Party (*Terakkiperver Cumhuriyet Fırkası*)
PTP	Party of the True Path (same as DYP)
PUK	Patriotic Union of Kurdistan
PYD	*Partiya Yekîtiya Demokrat* (Democratic Union Party)
RPNP	Republican Peasants' Nation Party (*Cumhuriyetçi Köylü Millet Partisi*)
RPP	Republican People's Party (same as CHP)
SDP	Social Democrat Party
SP	*Saadet Partisi* (Party of Happiness)
SPO	State Planning Office
SPP	Social Democratic Populist Party (*Sosyal Demokrat Halkçı Parti*)
STFA	Name of Turkish construction firm
TEM	Trans-European Motorway
THKO	*Türkiye Halk Kurtuluş Ordusu* (People's Liberation Army of Turkey)
THKP/C	*Türkiye Halk Kurtuluş Partisi/Cephesi* (People's Liberation Army/Front of Turkey)
TİKA	Turkish Cooperation and Coordination Agency
TİKKO	*Türkiye İşçi Köylü Kurtuluş Ordusu* (Workers and Peasants Liberation Army of Turkey)
TİP	*Türkiye İşçi Partisi* (Labour Party of Turkey) (same as WPT)
TOBB	*Türkiye Odalar ve Borsalar Birliği* (Union of Chambers of Commerce and Industry and Exchanges of Turkey)
TKP	*Türkiye Komünist Partisi* (Communist Party of Turkey)
TMO	*Toprak Mahsulleri Ofisi* (Office for Soil Products)
TOKİ	*Toplu Konut İşletmesi* (Public Housing Administration)
TSP	*Türkiye Sosyalist Partisi* (Socialist Party of Turkey)
TSWPP	Turkish Socialist Workers and Peasants' Party
TÜSIAD	*Türkiye Sanaicileri ve İş Adamları Derneği* (Society of Turkish Industrialists and Businessmen)
UCPT	United Communist Party of Turkey
VP	Virtue Party (same as FP)
WP	Workers' Party (*İşçi Partisi*)
WPT	Workers' Party of Turkey (same as TİP)
YPG	*Yekîneyên Parastina Gel* (People's Protection Forces)

THE OTTOMAN BALKANS

Miles
0   100   200   300
0   100   200   300   400
Kilometres

CAUCASUS GEORGIA
Batum
Trabzon

BLACK SEA

CRIMEA

Dnieper
Bug
Dniester

Sebastopol

Odessa

MOLDAVIA

Jassy
(Iasi)

WALLACHIA

Danube

Ruscuk
(Ruse)

Plevna
(Pleven)

Kırkkilise
(Kırklareli)

Midye

İstanbul

San Stefano
(Yeşilköy)

Edirne
Lüleburgaz

E. RUMELIA

E. THRACE
Çatalca
Sarıköy
Gallipoli
(Gelibolu)

Enoz
(Enez)
W. THRACE

Maritsa

BULGARIA

Niş

SERBIA

Kumanova

KOSOVO

MACEDONIA

Seres
(Serrai)

Monastir
(Bitola)

Salonica
(Thessaloniki)

Kavalla

Imros
(Gökçe)

Tenedos
(Bozca)

Dardanelles

AEGEAN SEA

ALBANIA

Yannina
(Ioannina)

THESSALIA

GREECE

MOREA
(PELOPONNESOS)

Navarino
(Pylos)

MONTENEGRO
(CRNA GORA)

BOSNIA
HERCEGOVINA

Sarajevo

ADRIATIC SEA

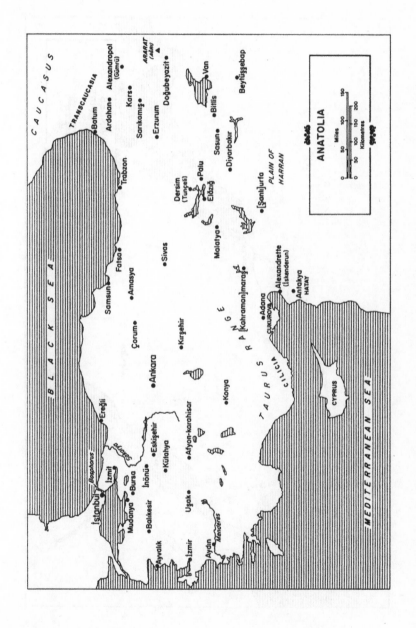

ANATOLIA

Miles 0 50 100 150
Kilometres 0 50 100 150 200

CAUCASUS

TRANSCAUCASIA

ARARAT
(Ağrı)

Batum
Ardahan• Alexandropol
(Gümrü)
Kars•
Sarıkamış•
Erzurum• Doğubeyazit•

•Van

•Bitlis

Beyrüşşebap•

Trabzon•

Palu•
Dersim •Elâziğ
(Tunçeli)

Sasun•
•Diyarbakır

[Şanlı]Urfa• PLAIN OF
HARRAN

BLACK SEA

Fatsa•
Samsun• •Amasya

•Sivas

Malatya•

•Çorum
Kırşehir•

[Kahraman]maraş•

•Ankara

Alexandrette
(İskenderun)
•Adana •Antakya
ÇUKUROVA HATAY

TAURUS RANGE

CILICIA

Ereğli•

•Eskişehir
•Kütahya •Afyon-karahisar

•Konya

CYPRUS

Bosphorus
İstanbul• Sakarya
İzmit•
Mudanya• •Bursa İnönü•
Balıkesir•
Uşak•

Ayvalık•
•İzmir
Aydın• Menderes

MEDITERRANEAN SEA

THE ARAB PROVINCES
OF THE OTTOMAN EMPIRE

Miles

0   100   200   300   400

0   100   200   300   400   500   600

Kilometres

PERSIA

(IRAN)

PERSIAN GULF

KURDISTAN

Mosul

Tigris (Dicle)

Baghdad

Euphrates (Firat)

MESOPOTAMIA

Basra

HEJAZ

Medina

Mecca

RED SEA

Nizip

Aleppo

Hama

Damascus

SYRIA

Accre

LEBANON

Beyrut

Sydon
(Saida)

PALESTINE

SINAI

Suez
Canal

CYPRUS

Cairo

EGYPT

Nile

PART I

Capitalism, Imperialism and the Growth of the Modern State

1 · The Ottoman Empire at the End of the Eighteenth Century

In the late eighteenth century, just before the upheavals caused by the French Revolution, the Ottoman Empire roughly consisted of the Balkans (with modern-day Serbia, Bosnia, Kosovo, Macedonia, Albania, Greece, Bulgaria and large parts of Romania), Anatolia (modern-day Turkey) and most of the Arab world (with the modern states of Syria, Lebanon, Jordan, Israel, Iraq, Kuwait, parts of Saudi Arabia, Egypt, Libya, Tunisia and Algeria). In large parts of his dominions, the sultan's real power was slight; in some parts (North Africa, the Arabian peninsula) it was practically non-existent.

The population of the empire

There are no reliable estimates of the population of the empire, but the number of inhabitants is often put at about 25 million, a low number for so large an area (about three million square kilometres).[1] Indeed, the lack of manpower constituted one of the main handicaps of the Ottoman Empire both economically and militarily throughout the nineteenth century, at a time when the population of Europe showed a high rate of growth. Of the Ottoman population, about 85 per cent lived in the countryside, while about 15 per cent lived in towns of 10,000 inhabitants or more. Both in population density and in the degree of urbanization there were great regional differences, with the Balkans being the most densely populated area. Around 1800, the Balkan provinces also held the majority of the population, but their share would decline sharply in the nineteenth century.[2] The population of the empire had probably been on the decrease during the seventeenth and eighteenth centuries, but the extent of this decrease is not known. The decrease, and the very low density that was the result, were the product of the classic Malthusian checks of war, famine and disease. Wars, and especially the small-scale internal conflicts that were the result of the existing lack of centralized control and maintenance of law and order, caused interruptions in the agricultural production process and in communications. The resulting famines in turn made the population vulnerable to epidemics, which usually attacked the weakened population in the aftermath of a food shortage. Lack of security caused the population in the countryside to withdraw gradually from the low-lying plains into the hills or the mountains. Over time this turned many former cultivated areas into malaria-infested marshes.

In the Asiatic provinces of the empire the large majority of the population was Muslim (mainly Turks, Arabs and Kurds), with significant Christian and Jewish minorities. In the Balkans, the majority was Christian (Greeks, Bulgarians, Serbs, Montenegrins, Vlahs) with significant Muslim minorities (Bosnians, most Albanians, Turks and Pomaks, namely Muslim Bulgarians). These religious divisions within the population were important because the empire, at least in theory, was an Islamic empire, ruled on the basis of religious law. It used to be the accepted truth that the Ottoman Empire knew no distinction between religion and state, but modern research tends to emphasize the extent to which the Ottomans did separate politics and religion, at least in practice. Theoretically, the holy law of Islam ruled supreme in the empire, but in practice by the eighteenth century it had been confined to matters of family law, of contract law and of ownership. According to Ottoman legal experts, the sultan had the right to rule by decree, *örf* or *kanun*, as long as his decrees could be shown not to contradict Islamic law. Public law, and especially criminal law, was largely based on these decrees.

Nevertheless, accommodating the non-Muslim communities within a dominant Islamic society did pose problems. As in earlier Islamic states, the Christian and Jewish groups had been incorporated into society by giving them *dhimmi* ('protected', in practice tributary) status. This meant that, in exchange for the payment of a special tax, they were allowed to continue to live within the Muslim state, without forced conversion but as second-class subjects. The *dhimmi* communities enjoyed a measure of autonomy in the conduct of their own affairs and were represented by their religious dignitaries in their dealings with the representatives of the state. As is the case with many aspects of the Ottoman state and society, the nature of this system, often designated as the '*millet* system' (*millet*: nation, community) has long been misunderstood. This is because scholars based their work on the writings of representatives of the central government, who wrote about the way things should be, not about how they really were. In the last 30 years, detailed research of local and regional realities has shown that the system did not consist of 'nation-wide' autonomous bodies headed by, for instance, the Greek patriarch in Constantinople, as had been supposed, but of local communities with a certain measure of autonomy *vis-à-vis* the local representatives of the government. Also, segregation seems to have been much less strict than had been assumed earlier.[3]

The Muslim majority of the indigenous population of the empire was by no means monolithic. The large majority belonged to the *Sunni* (Orthodox) version of Islam and according to its official ideology the Ottoman state was the protector of orthodox Islam in the world. Officially, it combated heterodox Muslims even more vehemently than it did Christians. This was logical because, while Islamic law could and did recognize the existence of other 'People of the Book' (Christians and Jews who were also the recipients of revealed religion), Islam was officially one and indivisible. In practice, important *Shi'i* (Heterodox) minorities lived in the Balkans, Anatolia, Syria and Mesopotamia, tolerated by the Ottoman authorities: Alevis, but also Nusayris and Druze.

Christian foreigners who resided in the empire enjoyed *aman* (mercy), a safe conduct under Islamic law. Their ambassadors and consuls, who had a measure of autonomy in dealing with cases that concerned only members of the expatriate community, represented them. These rights had been laid down in the so-called 'capitulations'. Originally, these were voluntary concessions the sultan granted to the subjects of friendly states, but in the second half of the eighteenth century, with the changing balance of power between Europe and the Ottoman Empire, the capitulations had acquired treaty status, with the European powers insisting the Ottomans could not change them unilaterally. Furthermore, in the eighteenth and especially in the nineteenth century more and more local Christians (mostly Greeks and Armenians but also Maronites and others) were granted the status of subject of a foreign power through the acquisition of a *berat* (decree of appointment) from the Ottoman government. They from then on fell under the capitulations of that power and with the growing strength of the European powers gained an ever-growing advantage over the sultan's Muslim subjects. At the same time, the influence of the foreign powers increased further because of the growth in the number of their subjects in the Levant.

The Ottoman system of government: theory and reality
According to the Ottoman ideology, society in the empire was organized around a – theoretically strict – distinction between a ruling elite, which did not pay taxes and was entitled to carry arms, and the mass of the population (in Ottoman terms: *reaya*, 'flocks') for which the reverse was true. The ruling elite consisted of two categories: the representatives of the sultan's power and the guardians of the moral order. The ruling elite,

which was designated as *askeri* (military), or 'Ottoman' *(Osmanli) par excellence*, consisted of all servants of the sultan: the military, the clerks of the scribal institutions and the royal household. The *ulema*, the religious scholars, who were entrusted with the keeping of the moral order and thus with most forms of formal education and justice, also belonged to the ruling elite. Although extremely privileged when compared with the mass of the people, the sultan's servants did not yet constitute a more or less autonomous bureaucratic/military elite such as they would become in the next century; they were instruments of imperial power, to be rotated, dismissed or executed at the sultan's will. This was even true for the highest dignitary of all, the grand vizier *(Sadrazam)*, who was regarded as the sultan's alter ego, and who was invested with all the powers of the ruler as long as he held the sultan's seal of office, but at the same time was completely dependent on the latter's whim.[4]

By 1800 the governmental system could still be characterized as 'patrimonial': it basically formed an extension of the sultan's own household. The pattern of rule through an extended household, of which not only family members but also servants, slaves and clients form a part, was characteristic of the Ottoman elite at all its levels. Seeking patronage through adhesion to such a household was a prerequisite for any governmental career.

The elite not only exercised power, it also was the keeper of a classic civilization, a 'great tradition', based on written Islamic sources (of which the *ulema* were the keepers and which was reproduced through the system of religious colleges called *medrese*s) and on a more secular code of conduct and taste called *adab* (which was characteristic of the military/bureaucratic elite and reproduced through informal education and training). This civilization, which was really the set of values and opinions that made an Ottoman an Ottoman, constituted a strong integrative force in an empire made up of so many diverse elements. There was an exceedingly wide chasm between this civilization and the outlook of the almost totally illiterate rural population, whose horizon was limited by the surrounding villages and, at best, the market town. One link between the elite civilization and popular culture was formed by the mystical orders or fraternities (*tarikat*), such as the *Mevlevi*, *Nakşibendi*, *Rifa'i* and the heterodox *Bektaşi* orders, which had established a closely-knit network of lodges (*tekke*s) all over the empire. Membership of these lodges cut across the different layers of society and the most important *şeyhs* had a great deal of influence even in the ruling circles.

Other links between the mass of the population and the ruling elite were formed by the rich merchants and bankers of the towns, who, while technically not members of the *askeri*, performed vital services to this group, and – for Muslims – by the *ulema*, who formed a body connecting the lowliest *kadi* (judge) in the provincial town to the highest religious dignitaries in Istanbul. An important category among the *ulema* was formed by the *müftüs*. These were legal experts who upon request and against payment gave legal opinions (based on Islamic canon law). Although these legal opinions (called *fetva*) were not binding (they were not verdicts), the *müftüs* enjoyed great respect. The fact that the Ottoman state legitimized itself as an Islamic state meant that the opinions of the doctors of Islamic law carried a great deal of weight. The most important of the müftüs was the Şeyhülislam, who was regularly asked to legitimize the acts of the government. In the event of rebellions against the palace or the grand vizier, the insurgents always made sure they received a *fetva* condoning their actions. For the Christians of the empire the churches with their own hierarchies constituted an important element linking the mass and the elite.

According to the official ideology, the main task of the ruler and of his servants was to defend the Islamic community against the outside world and to maintain justice within Islamic society. Justice (*adalet*) and the government's role in guaranteeing it was key to the Ottoman view of society. In the eyes of the Ottoman statesmen it, more than anything else, stood for stability and harmony. It meant that within society, each group and each individual should remain in his place (within his bounds or *hudud*), without trespassing on the rights of others. The government should rule within the bounds of law and enforce the *hudud*. A ruler (or his representative) who did not remain within the *hudud* was guilty of *zülm*, tyranny. The emphasis on the value of stability entailed a basically conservative political outlook in which any change in the social order had negative connotations. Ottoman writers were quick to label any social or religious protest *fitne* (mischief, disorder). According to nineteenth-century Ottoman sources, in the seventeenth and eighteenth centuries the Islamic scholars in particular had developed a very conservative, sometimes obscurantist attitude. This was blamed on the fact that appointments depended on nepotism, not scholarship.[5] It should be added, however, that very little research has been done on the *ulema* of this period.

Ottoman ideology emphasized the exclusivity of the relationship between the ruler (and his servants) and the subjects. The sultan represented absolute power and many of his servants, though powerful as delegates of his authority, were technically his slaves. The Ottoman system of government and of land ownership had always been geared towards preventing the emergence of competing centres of power, such as an aristocracy, which would be able to skim off part of the surplus production of the population, which would otherwise have reached the coffers of the state in the form of taxes. For a long time, the central Ottoman government was quite successful in this respect, but, as we shall see, by the end of the eighteenth century, this was no longer true.

Compared with governments of modern nation-states (but not with those of other eighteenth-century states) the Ottoman Empire, certainly in the eighteenth century, was very different in three respects. First, it was very small. This was true in an absolute sense: the central governmental apparatus in Istanbul (the *Bab-ı Ali*: 'Sublime Porte', or 'Porte' for short) employed between 1000 and 1500 clerks.[6] It was also true relatively speaking: the part of the national product that went to the central government in taxes is not known exactly or even approximately for this period, but it almost certainly did not exceed 3 per cent.[7] This does not mean that the tax burden on the population, especially the rural population, was light: quite the contrary. It does mean, however, that the revenue did not reach the central treasury, because intermediaries skimmed it off to an extraordinary extent. According to some estimates the central state received only the equivalent of between 2.25 and 4 million pounds sterling out of the 20 million that was levied in taxes in an average year. If this is true, the Ottoman state treasury held only between one tenth and one sixth of that of France.[8] Part of the explanation is that the empire by this time had a highly decentralized structure and provincial treasuries used a large part of the tax income to cover the costs of provincial government.[9]

The tasks performed by and expected of the government were, by modern standards, minimal. It concerned itself with the defence of the realm and the maintenance of law and order (including criminal justice); it supervised the markets, weights and measures; issued coins; provided the major cities, especially Istanbul, with food and built and maintained some major public works. In order to be able to execute these tasks, the government enforced, as much as it could, the collection of taxes. All kinds of things that are nowadays looked upon as normal tasks for a government, such as education, healthcare, welfare and housing, were of little concern to the imperial Ottoman government.

Second, the small scale of the government apparatus meant that, unlike a modern government, which deals directly with its citizens in many ways, the Ottoman government more often than not dealt (or had to deal) with representatives of communities: parish priests or imams represented the wards, grand masters the guilds, consuls the foreign residents and sheikhs their tribes. The main reason for this was, of course, that the state lacked the resources to deal with each individual, but it is also true that, as in most pre-modern societies, the individual was very much subordinate to the group, or the different groups, to which he or she belonged.

Third, there was no concept of equality before the law. Even in modern nation-states equality before the law is an ideal, not a reality, but in the Ottoman Empire it was not even an ideal. Inhabitants of the cities were treated differently from the rural population; Christians and Jews were treated differently from Muslims, nomads differently from settlers and women very differently from men. Towns, guilds, tribes or individuals jealously guarded old established privileges.

The Ottoman Empire was a very large pre-modern state and it had not undergone the centralization that France had experienced in the seventeenth century and that enlightened autocrats like Joseph II in Austria, Frederick the Great in Prussia and Catherine the Great in Russia had carried out in the eighteenth century. This meant that by the late eighteenth century the empire was in a weakened position, relatively speaking, with regards to its main European rivals. This weakness was expressed primarily on the battlefield. The two classical pillars of Ottoman military might since the fourteenth century, the salaried janissaries (originally *Yeni Çeri*, 'New Army') infantry and the semi-feudal *Sipahi* cavalry, had long since lost their value. The janissary troops, who by the eighteenth century were garrisoned in the major provincial centres as well as in the capital, were a numerically large (and expensive) but militarily largely worthless body, strong enough to terrorize government and population alike, but too weak to defend the empire, as a series of disastrous wars with technologically and tactically superior European armies had shown during the last hundred years. The janissaries had by now developed into a part-time militia. Through shared ownership of shops and protection rackets they had merged with the guilds in the bazaars. Their paper appointments in the regiments gave them and the shops they protected a privileged status. The number of appointment papers for a Janissary regiment was far higher than the number of soldiers actually serving and in some places had developed into a kind of informal currency. The *Sipahi*s, who during the heyday of the empire had been paid indirectly by the granting of fiefs (*timar*s), had been driven off the land by inflation because their income consisted of a fixed sum, while the real costs of going on campaign spiralled. Their number had greatly declined by 1800. Besides, the type of essentially mediaeval cavalry they represented was of course of little use in the wars of this time. In the wars of the late eighteenth century, the Ottoman army came to rely on levies of mainly Muslim Anatolian and Balkan peasants and of lawless young men from the towns, collectively called Levends. These militias were hired for a single campaign season or for the duration of a war and often dismissed in winter.[10]

Economic and financial developments

The military weakness was accompanied (and partly caused) by a permanent fiscal crisis. War, once an important source of income for the empire, had become a loss-making industry. Technological innovations (the growth of field artillery and the development of fortifications) combined with the increase in size of European armies had made warfare ever more expensive. Because war no longer provided booty, tribute and increased tax income for the state, it had to increase the pressure of taxation on the existing population.[11] Transit trade through the Ottoman lands had declined with the European overseas expansion since the sixteenth century and the government had lost control over many of the sources of tax revenue from the provinces. In the provinces, both Asiatic and European, the eighteenth century had witnessed the rise of the *ayan* (notables). These were influential people (or more often families) of diverse origin. Some were Ottoman governors who had established a local power base; some were rich merchants or bankers; others were landowners or religious dignitaries. In many cases members of an *ayan* family combined functions in all of these fields. The common denominator was that they had money and a regional power base, which forced the government, against its own official doctrine, to accept them as intermediaries between itself and the population of the provinces.

During the second half of the eighteenth century, the central government came to rely heavily on the *ayan* both for troops and for tax collection (many notables held official posts as tax collectors). In many cases the position of the great *ayan* families, such as the 'Azm in Hama and Damascus, Hasan Pasha and his son Ahmet Pasha in Baghdad, the famous Ahmet Cezzar Pasha of Akka (who was to defeat Napoleon) and the Karaosmanoğlu family in western Anatolia, verged on autonomy and central government's relations with them resembled those with vassal princes rather than those with subjects. Some of them, such as Ali Pasha of Yanina, who ruled Albania and northern Greece for a generation, even conducted independent foreign relations. In essence, the relationship between the political centre (Istanbul) and the notables was based on an ongoing process of negotiation. All the major notables had agents in the capital and the government often kept family members of the important notables in Istanbul as hostages, with the implied threat it could use them as an alternative to the provincial potentates. In spite of their local dominance the notables for their part also needed the sultan, because ultimately their power depended on their status as representatives of their lord.

Economically, the Ottoman Empire was a pre-capitalist state. The economic policies of the state, such as they were, were aimed at subsistence of the population, at provisioning the major population centres and at the collection of taxes in money and in kind. Not until the very end of the empire did the Ottoman government develop policies that could be described as mercantilist, actively protecting or stimulating certain sectors of the economy.

The Ottoman economy was an agricultural one, with the characteristic form of landownership in the more affluent parts of the empire being smallholdings. Large landowners and landless peasants predominated in the more arid parts of Anatolia and some of the Arab lands. Farmers in all areas were heavily dependent on people who could provide oxen and seed in exchange for part of the harvest. Nominally, by far the largest part of the agricultural land was owned by the state, while a smaller but still considerable part had the legal status of *vakıf* (plural *evkaf*, religious or charitable foundations), and was used for the upkeep of religious and public buildings (mosques, hospitals, libraries and schools but also fountains and bridges). Most of the *evkaf* were controlled by the *ulema*, which gave the latter considerable wealth and power. There had always been private ownership of land (*mülk*), but it had been largely confined to orchards, vineyards and kitchen gardens in the vicinity of the towns. After the decline of the *timar* system, private ownership spread more widely in the form of the *çiftlik* (farm), which had become the norm in the Balkans and western Anatolia. For the most part, the *çiftlik*s were not, as has been supposed, large-scale export-orientated farms (though by the end of the eighteenth century this phenomenon had begun to spread in the Balkans), but smallholders' plots that were not export-oriented.[12] Agricultural production was the main tax base of the state and collection of these taxes was now achieved everywhere through a system of tax farming (*iltizam*), a system that had been normal in the Arab provinces even in the classical age of the empire. Tax farming meant that the right to collect taxes in a given area during a certain period was auctioned off by the state and bought and paid for in advance by individuals. In turn, these tax farmers usually concluded a loan to finance their purchase with one of the Jewish or Armenian banking establishments in the big cities. For the central government, this system had many advantages: its income was assured, it was no longer dependent on the success of the harvest and tax was prepaid. For the peasants, the main disadvantage was that both the tax farmer himself and his creditors would want to see a return on their investment, thus increasing the burden on the peasants. Where taxation was in kind (the rule rather than the exception) tax farmers had added opportunities for speculation with the price of commodities such as wheat. In the eighteenth century lifelong leases of tax farms, called *malikane*, had become increasingly common. It was their stranglehold on the *iltizam* system that gave the *ayan* much of their strength.

Non-agricultural production was limited to small-scale enterprises in the towns, completely dominated by guild organizations. These guilds, like their late mediaeval European counterparts, prevented non-members from entering their profession and so protected the livelihood of their members. At the same time they guaranteed the quality of work and materials to their customers. The guilds maintained discipline and standards through a strict hierarchical system within which an apprentice could become a journeyman and – eventually – a master. Generally, the guilds looked askance at new products or production methods. Also, like their European counterparts, the guilds upheld a set of values and ethics, sanctioned by religion (the close links between the guilds and the mystical dervish orders have often been remarked upon), which strongly influenced society in the towns. The organization and the training systems of almost all of the army and the bureaucracy were modelled on those of the guilds. This is not to say that there was no non-guild labour: in fact there was quite a lot of it. Many guilds depended on semi-finished products supplied by women in surrounding villages and modern research has shown that towns with guilds were often surrounded by extensive networks of putting-out systems.[13]

Trade was overwhelmingly local: from the village to the market town or between adjacent districts. Long-distance trade overland was limited to expensive and relatively lightweight goods, as the cost of transport doubled every 100 kilometres. Lack of security made it imperative to carry these goods in caravans. Bulk goods (like grain and wood) were generally carried over sea. Of the total volume of trade, international trade constituted only a small part. Muslim merchants and shippers still played an important part in the Red Sea and Persian Gulf trade and, until 1774, the Black Sea trade, which was vital for provisioning the capital, was closed to foreign ships. In the Mediterranean, however, long-distance trade was in the hands of European nations, with the French merchant marine re-establishing its dominance in the eighteenth century at the expense of the Dutch and the English, who in turn had captured it from the French in the seventeenth century.

Because the Ottoman government experienced such a deep and intractable fiscal crisis, it has often been assumed that the eighteenth century was also a period of economic crisis for the empire. There is, however, no real evidence for this supposition. It is doubtful whether the empire as a whole can be described as an economic unit, as inter-regional trade was so insignificant. There were enormous regional differences and some areas, notably the Balkans, seem in the second half of the eighteenth century to have experienced economic growth that was partly export driven. This region and others, such as Syria and Palestine, had known a lively grain trade (more accurately, smuggling, since the Ottoman government strictly forbade the export of grain) for a long time. Halfway through the eighteenth century this trade was stimulated by a cyclical upturn in the price of wheat.

The emerging industries and growing populations of western Europe also stimulated demand for agricultural products such as cotton, which began to be planted especially for export. The main markets for Ottoman products were France and Austria (the export of cotton to France and of pigs across the border into Habsburg territory being especially important). The international political chaos of the end of the eighteenth century created new opportunities for Ottoman traders and shippers. Most of these were Greeks from the Aegean coast and islands. Their growing commercial interests led members of the Greek community to establish themselves in major trading centres outside the empire, such as Marseilles, Trieste and the recently founded Russian port city of Odessa on the Black Sea, thus creating an international network that further stimulated their business.[14]

The Ottoman state machinery did not profit from this economic upturn. Its lack of control over the provinces meant it lacked the power to improve its fiscal situation by taxing the new profits, while at the same time the export of foodstuffs endangered the provisioning of its cities.

The Ottoman Empire in international politics
By 1800, the position of the Ottoman Empire in international politics had been weakening gradually for two centuries. From the late sixteenth century onwards, European states, especially the newly emerging nation-states in western Europe, had surpassed it economically, technologically and militarily. The new technologies were transferred to the Christian empires of Eastern Europe more readily than to the Ottoman lands. This had become evident in a long series of wars, nearly all of them ending in serious Ottoman defeats and loss of territory. In the seventeenth and early eighteenth centuries the main enemy had been Habsburg Austria, but in the second half of the eighteenth century Russia under the Empress Catherine emerged as the main threat. Russia consistently tried to control – and later incorporate – the northern shores of the Black Sea and thus clashed with the Ottomans who regarded those areas, held by its vassals

the Crimean Tatar *khans*, as strategically vital. The war fought over this issue in 1768–74 ended with an Ottoman defeat and a peace treaty that is a watershed in Ottoman history in several ways. The treaty of Küçük Kaynarca (a village just south of the Danube in Russian-held Bulgaria) recognized the independence of the Crimea, gave Russia a secure foothold on the shore of the Black Sea, between the Dnieper and the Bug and gave the Russians the right of navigation in the Black Sea and ascribed to the Empress of Russia the right to establish a church under her protection in Istanbul. The Russians interpreted this clause to mean that Russia had the right to protect orthodox Christianity all over the Ottoman lands. These assumed rights were vigorously exploited both by the Russian government and by Greek Orthodox subjects of the sultan. The result was that in the next decades Russian consuls were appointed throughout the Balkans and on the Greek islands, who in turn extended Russian citizenship (under the *berat* system) liberally to the local Christians. After the opening of the Black Sea to Russian ships, it was Greek shippers flying the Russian flag who captured the Black Sea trade.

Both for the Russians, who had expected to gain more, and for the Ottomans, who found it hard to accept that the empire had lost Muslim territory for the first time in its history (which was very damaging to the credibility and legitimacy of the sultan's reign), the peace of 1774 proved unsatisfactory. First, Russian and Ottoman parties fought a proxy war in the Crimea, after which the Russians formally annexed the Crimea in 1779. The sultan's government reluctantly accepted this in 1784 but three years later declared war on Russia. The war of 1787–92, in which Russia was first supported then deserted by Austria, again ended in a great victory for Russia, whose hold over the northern Black Sea shore was confirmed and even extended towards the Dniester in the west and Georgia in the east. The Black Sea ceased to be an Ottoman lake.

2 · Between Tradition and Innovation: Sultan Selim III and the 'New Order', 1789–1807

In all the fields touched upon in the first chapter (territory, population, ideology, administration, economics and international relations) the period between the outbreak of the French Revolution and the close of the 1830s witnessed a quickening of the pace of change, most aspects of which in one way or another had to do with the changing relationship between the Ottoman Empire and Europe.

The first ruler to preside over these changes was Sultan Selim III, who acceded to the throne in 1789. Even before his accession, he had displayed interest in the world outside the palace and in Europe. It is known that, as a prince, he had corresponded with Louis XVI of France, his 'role model', and he had gathered around him a circle of friends and servants who shared his interest in things European. When he acceded to the throne, he appointed many of them to places of influence. During the first three years of his reign, Selim had to concentrate on the conduct of the war against Russia. In 1792, with the Ottoman military situation hopeless, Russia and the Ottoman Empire accepted British and Prussian mediation, which led to the Peace of Jassy, basically a confirmation of the Peace of Küçük Kaynarca (1774), with some additional territorial gains for Russia on the Black Sea shores.

Almost immediately after the conclusion of peace, the sultan launched the programme of reforms, which was officially called the *Nizam-i Cedid* (New Order). This programme aimed to increase the strength of the central state organization, against both external enemies (mainly Russia, which after two disastrous wars had emerged as the greatest threat to Ottoman power) and internal ones (the semi-independent *ayan*). These were problems that had plagued Selim's eighteenth-century predecessors and his attempts to solve them were essentially traditional: he attempted to strengthen the state apparatus (notably the armed forces and tax collection) by combating abuse and corruption and re-establishing the traditional system, and thus the *adalet* (justice). All groups and individuals were again forced within their *hudud* in an effort to show that the government was upholding the Islamic order. Selim's decrees enforcing traditional clothing and building restrictions, particularly on the non-Muslim *reaya*, clearly illustrate this side of his policies.

What makes Selim interesting as a transitional figure between the traditional attempts at reform since the time of the Köprülü *vezir*s, who had restored central authority in the mid-seventeenth century, on the one hand, and the nineteenth century *Tanzimat* (reforms), on the other, is the extent to which he was prepared to accept European practices (and European advisers) to achieve his goals and the way in which his reign opened up channels of communication between Europe and the Ottoman ruling elite.

The reforms of the 'Nizam-i Cedid'
The military programme started out with attempts to make the existing corps, the janissaries, the *Sipahi* feudal cavalry and the specialized units, for example gunners and wagoneers, more efficient. The programme separated the strictly military from the administrative functions of the officer corps to try to eliminate opportunities for corruption and reduced the ranks through the elimination of those people who held pay tickets (*esame*) but did not actually serve with the army, while enforcing stricter discipline and guaranteeing regular payment for the remainder. It soon turned out that obstruction from within the system rendered this type of reorganization almost totally ineffective. The sultan and his men then decided on a more radical solution: to create a new army outside the existing structure. The work on this new army began in 1794 and by the end of Selim's reign in 1807 it was close to 30,000 men strong and, according to contemporary observers, relatively well equipped and trained. The navy, too, was reorganized.

Of course, this programme demanded both a new system of training and education and a great deal of money. To meet the former need, the sultan tried to attract foreign officers as advisers and instructors. Most of them were French and they were recruited through the French government, interestingly both that of the *ancien régime* and those of the republic and the Napoleonic empire. A modern medical service and school were established, while the existing naval engineering school was modernized and an equivalent for the army established in 1795. When it came to financing the reforms, Selim III's government was ineffective. It did not try to create a regular budget in which income and expenditure could be balanced instead of the chaotic 'first come first served' financial regime, and its feeble attempts to reform the highly inefficient traditional system of taxation, or even to enforce the existing system, failed. The government employed traditional means to increase its revenue: confiscation and debasing the coinage, thus damaging the public's trust in the mint and in the long run only increasing the problems. Selim's attempts to increase the efficiency of the central scribal (administrative) institution consisted of efforts to reduce the chronic overstaffing of the offices (itself a source of corruption) and in 1797 to concentrate the work relating to important affairs of state in an 'office of important affairs' (*Mühimme Odası*), partly as an attempt to introduce a minimum of confidentiality. Overstaffing, favouritism and corruption, however, proved impossible to quash without regular payment of salaries and clear regulations defining positions and tasks; although the nineteenth-century reforms brought the latter into force, the Ottoman Empire continued to suffer from these problems almost until the end.

New channels of communication

More important, perhaps, than Selim's actual measures, were the increased opportunities he created for the flow of Western ideas into the Ottoman Empire. The European, mainly French, instructors attached to the different army corps that Selim had founded or reformed produced one channel of communication. Their students learnt French and eagerly started to discuss all kinds of new-fangled ideas with their foreign teachers. Besides, these foreigners were allowed much more freedom in Ottoman society than had been the case with their predecessors of the generation before them. They socialized regularly, not only with leading members of the local Christian communities, but also with members of the Ottoman ruling class.[1] The new Ottoman embassies in Europe provided a second major channel of communication. Sporadic Ottoman missions had been sent for specific purposes to European capitals earlier in the eighteenth century, but diplomatic business in the main was still conducted through Greek interpreters in Istanbul, as it had been in the heyday of the empire. Now Selim for the first time established permanent Ottoman embassies in London (1793), Vienna (1794), Berlin (1795) and Paris (1796). Many of the later reformers of the empire had their first experience of Europe while serving as secretaries at these Ottoman missions. The first ambassadors were by all accounts less than effective. After all, they brought no experience to their jobs and had to learn the European game of diplomacy from scratch. But however clumsy these first modern Ottoman diplomats may have been as Ottoman ambassadors to Europe, they and their successors a generation later most certainly were effective as ambassadors of European life in Ottoman society.

The fall of Sultan Selim III

Selim's policies had made him many enemies. He had alienated the military establishment by his efforts to create a new army and the majority of the *ulema* disliked the French influence at court and among the younger members of the elite. The sultan was also unpopular among the populace at large, which had not benefited from his attempts at reform but had been made to bear the burden of paying for the new army and navy through new taxes on, among other things, coffee and tobacco. In the provinces, the reign of Selim, despite his efforts to strengthen central authority, in fact saw an increase in the power and autonomy of the great *ayan* (notables). This was because the sultan not only depended on them for tax revenue and for provisioning the capital, but also because the notables provided the army with most of its troops in the Napoleonic wars. Even the original *Nizam-i Cedid* army was built up with contingents sent by a number of notables. The notables' attitude towards the sultan and his policies was ambivalent. On the one hand, they supported his attempts to weaken the position of the *ulema* and the janissaries, who were their main rivals for power in the provincial centres; on the other, they certainly did not want more effective control from central government. This showed in 1805, when the sultan issued an order for a new *Nizam-i Cedid* corps to be established in Edirne. When the troops arrived in Edirne in 1806, the notables from the European provinces threatened to march on the capital unless they were withdrawn. The sultan had to give in, so strengthening the notables' position even further.

It is doubtful whether any sultan like Selim, with his limited understanding of the European models he wanted to emulate, with insufficient funds and faced with the vested interests of powerful traditional institutions, could have achieved radical reforms. It is probably also true, however, that Selim lacked the necessary ruthlessness and cunning for the task. When in May 1807 the auxiliary contingents of the janis-sary garrison of Istanbul rioted (an uprising in all probability engineered by conservative court circles) and demanded the abolition of the *Nizam-i Cedid* corps and the sacking of important reformists, the sultan gave in without trying to use his new troops. He did not succeed in saving his position, however. He was deposed the same day, on the basis of a *fetva* (religious opinion) pronounced by the highest religious dignitary, the *Şeyhülislam*, which stated that his reforms were incompatible with religious law.

International relations: French Revolution and Napoleonic wars

Apart from internal opposition, the sultan was certainly hampered in his efforts at reform by the fact that his reign coincided with the international upheaval caused by the French Revolution and the Napoleonic wars.

The cornerstone of Ottoman foreign policy for over two centuries had been the empire's friendly relationship with France, the House of Habsburg's archenemy. As mentioned before, Selim himself had been in touch with the French king, but the relationship with France continued after the French Revolution and even after the execution of King Louis XVI – in fact until Napoleon Bonaparte suddenly landed in Egypt in 1798. Napoleon's expedition has been the subject of an extensive literature. It was a result both of the colonial and commercial rivalry between France and England, which was still being fought out in India, and of the realization in Paris that the available means did not allow a direct attack on England itself. Napoleon himself may well have entertained romantic dreams of conquering the Middle East as a new Alexander the Great, but French policy aims were more limited: indirectly to weaken the British position in the East by turning Egypt into a French base. The French invasion shocked the Ottoman government into concluding an alliance with Britain and with its old enemy Russia, but this expedient lasted only as long as the emergency itself. The Peace of Amiens in 1802 saw a restoration of the old warm relationship between France and the Porte. The refusal of the Ottomans, under Austrian pressure, to recognize Napoleon's coronation as emperor led to a breaking-off of diplomatic relations in 1805, but within a year the Ottoman Empire was allied to France once more and in a state of war with both Britain and Russia, a situation that led to a new Russian invasion. Napoleon's sudden reversal of policy during his negotiations with the tsar in Tilsit in 1807 left the Ottomans to face their enemies alone.

The ideological influence of the French Revolution

Although it is indisputable that the international complications of the French Revolution and its aftermath affected the Ottoman Empire a great deal, the extent of the revolution's ideological influence on Ottoman society is less clear.

The French Revolution had certainly not inspired Sultan Selim III when he launched the *Nizam-i Cedid*, even though the term itself may have been derived from the French.[2] He had admired the absolute monarchy of Louis XVI, whom the revolutionaries were to guillotine, and French military and administrative skills. It was the traditional Ottoman army's dismal performance in the Russian war that decided Selim in favour of military reform. The impact of the revolution and the ideas of the revolution in Ottoman Muslim ruling elite circles seem to have been limited. There is no evidence that the secular character of the revolutionary ideology made its ideas easier for a Muslim public to swallow than might have been the case with religiously tainted ideas. Ottoman observers who commented on the anti-religious character of the revolution without exception denounced it.[3] The French occupation of Egypt, too, though shocking as an attack on a Muslim heartland, created an awareness of French military strength, not of French philosophy. The exposure of members of the Ottoman ruling class to European ideas, caused by the opportunities of actually mingling with foreigners that Selim's regime allowed, certainly had an effect, notably in the tendency of the younger bureaucrats to look for rationally motivated solutions instead of traditional ones, and hence to new legislation. Especially those young Ottomans who served at the embassies in Europe were deeply impressed by the effectiveness of the bureaucracies they encountered there. Where Ottoman dignitaries had to sustain their way of life by supplementing their salaries (which were often months if not years in arrears) with an extra income consisting of 'appointment gifts', fees and fines, and had to ensure that they were reappointed each year, the servants of European states were already developing into the true bureaucrats they would become in the nineteenth century: salaried officials, secure in their jobs and with their tasks and prospects clearly defined by regulations. More abstract ideas like liberalism, constitutionalism and patriotism did not affect members of the Ottoman elite until the middle of the nineteenth century.

Where the ideas of the French Revolution had a marked effect was among the literate members of the Christian communities of the empire. The first to be influenced were the Greeks, thanks to their commercial connections with all the major European ports, and the Serbians, who were in constant touch with central Europe through their exports to Austria. Of the three catchwords of the French Revolution, 'liberty, equality, fraternity', it was 'liberty' that caught on among these communities; but to them liberty meant not the guarantee of civic rights but national independence. Nationalism was introduced into the Ottoman Empire in the aftermath of the revolutionary wars, but the nationalism of the Ottoman Christian communities was of a central European rather than a West European type. In search of a nation on which to build their states, the Balkan intellectuals constructed romantic visions of their historical past, defining Ottoman rule as an 'occupation' in the process.[4] The year 1808 saw the beginning of a Serbian insurrection, which at first was no more than a protest against the abuses of the local Muslim landowners and the janissaries, but which developed into a movement for autonomy and later independence. It was no coincidence that the movement's first leader was a rich pig exporter called Kara George. The birth of Greek nationalism can be traced to the founding by Greek merchants in Odessa in 1814 of the *Philiki Hetairia*, a secret society aiming for the reconstruction of the Byzantine Empire. During the nineteenth century the growth of nationalism, first in the Balkans and later also in the Asiatic provinces, was to prove the most important factor in the destruction of the Ottoman state.

Economic change
Economically, the main development of the revolutionary years in the Levant was the strengthening of the position of the Greek traders and shippers. The revolutionary and Napoleonic wars had seriously damaged the position of the French merchant navy in the eastern Mediterranean and its leading position in long-distance sea trade was taken over by the Greeks, whose business had already been booming in the late 1700s. At the same time, the British blockade of Napoleonic Europe and the counter blockade known as the 'continental system', introduced by the French, increased the importance of the Ottoman Empire for trade in and out of central Europe.[5] Selim III had actively tried to improve conditions for Ottoman merchants in their competition with the Europeans by establishing consulates in the major Mediterranean trading centres and by giving Muslim traders berats that would enable them to compete with the Europeans on equal terms. These initiatives were realized under his successor, but they failed to undermine European dominance in international trade.

Alemdar Mustafa Pasha: the provincial notables in power
After he was deposed, Sultan Selim III was kept prisoner in the palace. The coalition of conservative *ulema* and janissary officers that had staged the coup of 1807 brought to the throne his cousin, Mustafa IV. Their motivation having been a negative one (common loathing of Selim's policies), they failed to develop a coherent policy, however, and meanwhile a number of leading survivors of the toppled regime took refuge with one of the leading *ayan*, *Alemdar* Mustafa Pasha in Rusçuk. Mustafa Pasha, like many of the leading *ayan*, had had ambivalent relations with the deposed sultan, supporting him against the janissaries and the *ulema* but sabotaging his attempts to extend central control to the provinces. But he had drawn close to the sultan when in 1806 the Russian advance threatened his area of control on the Danube. His headquarters became the centre of opposition to the conservative coalition in power in Istanbul and a little over a year later, in July 1808, he marched on the capital, intending to restore Sultan Selim III to the throne. His captors assassinated Selim before he could be freed, but within a week *Alemdar*

Mustafa Pasha's troops were in complete control. They deposed Mustafa IV and raised to the throne Selim's other cousin, Mahmut II, a known partisan of the *Nizam-i Cedid.*

So, ironically, the reign of the first sultan who tried to re-establish central control in the empire ended with the provincial notables (the *ayan*) in power in the capital. *Alemdar* Mustafa Pasha's period in power lasted for barely four months but what he tried to accomplish in that time is interesting. Apart from trying to terrorize his opponents, the stagers of the 1807 coup, into submission, he tried to revive the reforms of Sultan Selim and even to reconstitute the *Nizam-i Cedid* under a traditional name, that of *Segban*s (Keepers of the Royal Hounds – later incorporated into the janissary corps as a division of 34 companies). Contingents sent to the capital by loyal notables formed the nucleus of this corps. Furthermore, he took the remarkable initiative of inviting all the major *ayan* of the empire to Istanbul, to take part in a conference, attended also by the highest dignitaries of the central government, on the problems of the empire.

Most of the leading Anatolian notables did come, but a number of the standard-bearer's Balkan rivals and Mehmet Ali Pasha of Egypt (of whom more anon) excused themselves, while Ali Pasha of Yanina, the most powerful notable in the western Balkans, sent only a representative. Those who attended the conference discussed a programme submitted by Mustafa Pasha and agreed on a 'document of agreement' (*sened-i ittifak*), signed in October 1808. In the document both the sultan and the notables promised to rule justly. Taxes would be justly imposed by the government and justly collected by the notables. The notables promised to support reforms and the creation of a new army. They declared their loyalty to the sultan and his government and promised to defend him against any rebellion. They also promised to respect each other's territory and autonomy. A remarkable document, the *sened-i ittifak*, has sometimes been presented as an Ottoman Magna Carta, or a first attempt at constitutionalism. The former is more accurate because the document is really a pact between the ruler and his barons, not a codification of the rights of citizens. As such, it constitutes the high-water mark of the influence of the *ayan* in the empire, who were here recognized officially as partners in government. The document, possibly for this very reason, was never personally signed by the sultan, but he gave permission to put the imperial monogram (*tuğra*) at its head.[6]

One month after its signature by the notables, the janissaries in the capital revolted once more over rumours that Mustafa Pasha intended to disband them. The pasha, who had had to send his best troops to Rusçuk to defend it against his rivals in Bulgaria and had no reliable support left

in Istanbul, had to take refuge in a powder magazine. When the janissaries entered, he blew himself up. The janissaries, in coalition with the
guilds and the *ulema* were once more masters of the capital. The sultan,
however, reacted swiftly: he had Mustafa IV, his only remaining male
relative, strangled and ordered the *Segban*s to the palace. A stalemate
ensued, which was eventually solved by compromise, the sultan
remaining on the throne but having to dissolve the *Segban* corps.

3 · The Early Years of Sultan Mahmut II: The Centre Tries to Regain Control

Mahmut II had been a witness both to the limited successes of the *Nizam-i Cedid* and to the fall and death of his cousin Selim. He seems to have learnt his lessons well and also to have been a much more adept tactician. He started from an extremely weak position. He had been put into power by the *Alemdar*, who himself was no longer there, and the only reason Mahmut II was left on the throne was that there was no other male successor available. He therefore had to move circumspectly and spent the first 15 years of his reign establishing a power base. This meant appointing trusted supporters to key positions in the scribal service, the *ulema* hierarchy and the army. His second aim was the reduction of the semi-independent *ayan* who had brought him to power. This he to a large extent accomplished. Between 1812 and 1817 the major Anatolian notables were brought under control, and between 1814 and 1820 the same happened in the Balkans. In Kurdistan the process took longer, but there too the power of the practically independent Kurdish princes, the *mir*s who had ruled over large tribal coalitions, was eventually broken. Here, the existing tribal structure of society meant that the removal of the princes and the inability of the central Ottoman government to replace them with effective central control led to a long period of anarchy, in which authority reverted to the tribal chiefs and to the religious leaders who built up their authority as mediators in inter-tribal conflicts.[1] In the Arab provinces the restoration of Ottoman government authority over the notables took place only later, in the 1840s.

The methods employed in subduing the *ayan*, in the age-old Ottoman tradition, were peaceful where possible (bribes were given, titles conferred, hostages taken, divisions among the notables ably exploited). Open warfare was used only as a last resort, and before 1826 it was that of the traditional military establishment: mainly the janissaries. It is important to understand that, while the sultan was slowly strengthening his hold on the government, he had not yet broken with the scribal or military establishment. While proponents of reform were put into more and more important positions, the most powerful politician of these early years of Mahmut's reign was Mehmet Sait Halet Efendi, a member of the *ulema* and former ambassador to Paris, with a generally conservative outlook. He was close to the janissaries and his efforts at, and success in, subjugating the *ayan* can also be seen as being motivated by a desire to strengthen the position of the janissary garrisons in the provinces, which were the great competitors of the notables.[2]

Lost territories: Serbia, Greece, Egypt

Mahmut and his servants succeeded in re-establishing control over most of the central Ottoman lands, but in a few important cases they failed. In 1804 the insurrection led by Kara George broke out in Serbia against the excesses of the local janissary garrisons. The government of Selim III, engaged in its own struggle with the janissaries, had condoned the insurrection, but after the elimination of the garrisons the movement developed into one aimed at Serbian autonomy. In spite of some modest Russian support for the Serbs, the Ottoman army suppressed the movement in 1813. Two years later, however, it flared up again and this time the new Serbian leader, Miloš Obrenovič, reached agreement with the Ottomans on autonomy for a Serbian principality between Belgrade and Nish. The Ottomans retained the right to garrison the major towns and to receive a yearly tribute (this, it should be remembered, amounted to the same degree of influence as the central government had enjoyed in, for instance, Kurdistan or some of the Arab provinces in the eighteenth century).

The Greek insurrection, which broke out in 1821, was more important for three reasons. First, the Greek community in the empire played a crucial role in the empire's external relations, both economic and diplomatic. Second, from the very beginning of the insurgency many of its leaders aimed at full independence; and third, the crisis that ensued directly involved all the major European powers.

The *Philiki Hetairia*, a Greek patriotic society founded in Odessa in 1814, had been busy over the next few years founding cells throughout the Balkans. Kara George was at one time a member. From 1820 the organization was led by Alexander Ipsilantis, a member of one of the elite Phanariote (so-called after the Phanar quarter in Istanbul) Greek families of the Ottoman Empire and himself a general in the Russian army. In 1821 Ipsilantis and his group considered the time ripe for a full-scale insurrection, which they hoped to trigger by an invasion of Moldavia and Wallachia (present-day Romania). Their aim was a general rebellion in the Balkans, in order to create a new Byzantine Empire under

Greek leadership, and not merely a Greek national state. The invasion that was supposed to bring about the realization of this ambitious scheme was, however, a disaster. The invading army was much too small (about 3000 men) and the peasant population in Moldavia and Wallachia was never likely to side with the invaders, since the great landowners and the governors of these provinces were traditionally from the same Phanariote families from which Ipsilantis stemmed. For their part, many of the influential and rich Greek families of the Ottoman Empire actually opposed the *Hetairia*'s nationalist aspirations.[3]

At the same time as the invasion failed, another and very different Greek insurrection began to spread in the southernmost parts of the Balkan peninsula and on the Aegean isles. Although the rebels were influenced by *Hetairia* propaganda, it was a genuine popular revolt against Ottoman misrule. The rebels were badly organized and divided among themselves, but nevertheless the Ottoman army in 1821–24 signally failed to defeat them. By 1824 almost the whole of the Morea (the Peloponnese) and many islands were in the hands of the rebels. It has been argued that the success of the rebellion was due in part to the fact that in 1820–22 the Ottoman government was engaged in the military suppression of the most powerful of all the Balkan notables, Ali Pasha of Yanina. In removing him, they also removed the only force that could effectively control the area.[4]

The most important territory lost to the empire in this period was the province of Egypt with about four million inhabitants. This loss was the work of one man, the Ottoman governor of Egypt, Mehmet Ali. In the years when Mahmut II was gradually strengthening his hold on the government apparatus by infiltrating it with his supporters, his governor in Egypt demonstrated what effective concentration of all power at the centre could accomplish. Mehmet Ali was an Albanian from Kavalla (now in northern Greece), who had come to Egypt as an officer in the Albanian contingent in the Ottoman expeditionary force against the French. In 1803 he had become the leader of that corps and had established himself as the de facto ruler of Egypt. In 1808, he was officially recognized as governor of Egypt by the sultan.

The French occupation had fatally weakened the position of the Mam-luks, the part-Circassian, part-Turkish military ruling elite of the country. They had been chased from lower Egypt by the French and during the Napoleonic wars had been unable to replenish their numbers by recruiting slaves in the areas north of the Caucasus, as had been their practice for hundreds of years. In a sense, therefore, the French occupation had provided Mehmet Ali with a clean slate. He used this opportunity to destroy the last vestiges of Mamluk power, massacring their leaders in the Cairo citadel in 1811. Thereafter, he embarked on an ambitious programme of reform aimed at the strengthening of his government.

As with Selim III's *Nizam-i Cedid*, the main element of the programme was to create a large, modern, European-style army. This brought with it the need for larger state income through taxation, the need for a more efficient bureaucracy to mobilize the resources of the country, and the need for modern Western-style education in order to create the cadres for the new army and bureaucracy. The Ottoman reformers from Selim III and Mahmut II onwards had faced the same dilemma; but they did not have the advantage of a situation, such as Egypt's, in which the old establishment had been destroyed by outside interference. Furthermore, Mehmet Ali took more drastic action than the early Ottoman reformers could or would undertake to solve the two main problems that modernizing the army entailed: lack of income and lack of dependable manpower from outside the military establishment (the janissaries and affiliated corps in the Ottoman case, the Albanian forces and the Mamluks in Egypt). At first, Mehmet Ali sought to overcome his manpower problem by recruiting Sudanese slaves in the years 1820–22, but when they proved incapable of enduring life in the army (they died in large numbers), he solved it by a radical innovation: the introduction of conscription among the Egyptian peasant population in 1822.[5] For the Ottoman ruling elite (of which Mehmet Ali himself was of course a member) this was a revolutionary notion, because it ran directly counter to the traditional concept of an unarmed population ruled by a distinct armed elite. The monetary problem was never completely solved, but Mehmet Ali was much more successful than the Ottomans of his era in increasing his income to pay for the expensive new army (and fleet). He replaced the tax farm system with direct taxation; and he encouraged the development of agriculture, investing in irrigation and road works and forcing the farmers to grow cash crops, of which cotton became the mainstay of the Egyptian economy. Also, Mehmet Ali enlarged the highly profitable state monopolies precisely at the time when, as we shall see, the Ottomans were forced to abandon them.

There can be no doubt that Mehmet Ali's example was highly influential in Istanbul, both as an inspiration and as a source of rivalry. In the early years of his reign, the sultan in his weakened position had no choice but to apply for help to his most powerful subject. When the tribal leader of the central Najd area in the Arabian peninsula, who had adopted the teachings of the fundamentalist *Wahabi* movement as the ideology of his political movement, extended his sway to the Hijaz and even occupied the holy cities of Mecca and Medina, it was Mehmet Ali who restored the sultan's authority there after a costly and difficult campaign against the *Wahabi*s between 1811 and 1818. When the Ottoman janissary army proved incapable of suppressing the Greek rebellion, the sultan turned to his Egyptian governor once more.

The last phase of the Greek rebellion, war with Russia again

At the request of the sultan's government, Egyptian troops landed in the Morea in 1825. Where the janissaries had failed, they were highly successful and over the next two years they conquered most of the mainland. Only the dominance of the Greek merchant navy, which was able to supply the rebels with arms and food, prevented a complete collapse of the rebellion. In the face of military disaster, the Greek insurrection was now saved by European intervention. There was a great deal of sympathy with the Greek rebels in Europe, most of all in Britain and in Russia. In Britain the sources of this philhellenism were liberal sympathy for Greek national aspirations and admiration for classical Greek civilization, with which the modern inhabitants of the southern Balkans were identified. In Russia, the main motive behind the sympathy for the Greeks was religious solidarity within the Orthodox Church. This public sympathy with the rebels did not translate into political support, except in one country: Russia. Tsar Alexander I tried to get the other great powers of Europe to agree to intervene in the conflict in support of the establishment of an autonomous Greece. The other powers, however, were not enthusiastic, fearing that an autonomous Greece would become a Russian puppet state. Tsar Alexander, one of the principal architects of the international order established in 1815, set too much store by the international 'system' and the principle of legitimate rule to intervene unilaterally against the wishes of the other powers.

This aspect of the situation changed with the death of Alexander and the accession by Nicholas I in December 1825. The new tsar let it be known that if no agreement with the other powers could be reached Russia would go it alone. This threat eventually had its desired effect for, rather than see Russia intervene on its own, first Britain agreed to autonomy for Greece (in 1826) and then in June 1827 Britain, France and Russia jointly decided to intervene to force a ceasefire on the parties (thus in effect saving the rebels).

When the sultan refused to accept the mediation of the powers, their fleets first blockaded the Ottoman and Egyptian navies in the harbour of Navarino on the western coast of the Morea (Peloponnese), and then on 20 October destroyed them completely, cutting off the Egyptian expeditionary force. This effectively decided the conflict, but even though Mehmet Ali agreed to withdraw his troops from the Balkans, the government in Istanbul refused to face facts, which led to full-scale war with Russia. After initial successes, Ottoman resistance collapsed in the summer of 1829. Russian troops occupied Erzurum and Edirne. At the Treaty of Edirne, concluded in September 1829, the Ottomans had to recognize the independence of Greece and the autonomy of the principalities of Moldavia and Wallachia and of a Serbia to which several Ottoman districts were added. That the Greece that emerged on the map was only a very small state, and fell far short of the designs of the Greek nationalists, was only due to the fact that Britain, France and Austria preferred a malleable Ottoman Empire to a strong Greece dominated by Russian influence.

4 · The Later Years of Sultan Mahmut II: The Start of the Reforms

The Egyptian crisis

At the time of the Treaty of Edirne (1829) the whole issue of Greek independence was already starting to be overshadowed by what developed into the most threatening crisis for the Ottoman Empire in the first half of the nineteenth century, the conflict between the sultan and his most powerful subject, the governor of Egypt.

Mehmet Ali had come out of the Greek crisis with precious little to show for his efforts and especially for the enormous expense he had incurred. In 1827 he had lost his fleet into the bargain. It is therefore understandable that he sought recompense in other areas. At first he tried to come to an agreement with the French government. Traditionally, Egypt had close ties with France. The French Catholic mission had been active in the country for a long time, Napoleon's occupation was still within living memory, and French officers had played a leading role in building and training Mehmet Ali's new army. Mehmet Ali discussed with the French consul, Drovetti, an Egyptian occupation of the North African Ottoman provinces (Tripolitania, Tunisia and Algeria) with French support and Ottoman acquiescence; in exchange the French would get political and economic concessions in the area. Nothing came of these plans. Instead France decided to occupy Algiers herself in 1830. Mehmet Ali now turned to Britain with similar proposals. When Britain refused to cooperate, he decided to move alone. He used a smouldering conflict with the Ottoman governor of Acre over the latter's refusal to return Egyptian peasants who had fled Egypt (primarily to escape conscription) as a pretext for a full-scale campaign to conquer Syria in 1831. After stubborn resistance by its governor, Acre fell in May 1832. In July Mehmet Ali's adopted son Ibrahim Pasha, who commanded the Egyptian army, twice defeated the Ottomans, completing the occupation of Syria. The Ottoman government now officially deposed Mehmet Ali and declared him a rebel. Mehmet Ali tried to open negotiations, but when the government refused, he ordered his troops into Anatolia, where, on 27 December 1832, they routed the Ottoman forces near Konya.

This disaster opened the road to the Ottoman capital for the Egyptians. Mehmet Ali now temporized while he tried to reopen negotiations. The Ottomans for their part desperately sought foreign support against him. Britain refused to give anything more than moral support. Austria's Chancellor Metternich was equally inactive. In desperation the sultan now turned to his traditional enemy, the tsar, for help. The Russians, who saw in Mehmet Ali a puppet of a detested French government (the July monarchy of Louis Philippe, which in the eyes of the rulers in St Petersburg was itself illegitimate), also saw a chance for a major diplomatic victory and offered the sultan diplomatic and military support.

When the negotiations between Mehmet Ali and the sultan broke down again and Ibrahim Pasha's forces started to march on Istanbul, Russian troops landed on the Bosphorus on 5 April 1833. They effectively forestalled any move by Ibrahim Pasha against the capital, but they were not in a position or in sufficient numbers to attack him. The sultan therefore had no choice but to accept the substance of the demands made by Mehmet Ali and to appoint him governor of Syria in May. In addition his son, Ibrahim Pasha, was made tax collector of the district of Adana. The Russians received the diplomatic prize they had aimed for in the shape of the treaty of Hünkar İskelesi, concluded in July 1833, which basically was an eight-year defensive alliance between Russia and the Ottoman Empire. The treaty consisted of six public articles and one that was kept secret. This excused the Ottoman Empire from the obligation to support Russia militarily, but stipulated that in case of war between the Russian Empire and a third state, the Ottomans would close the Dardanelles to all warships except Russian ones.[1]

The treaty made a deep impression in Britain, where Russophobia had already been mounting, especially in liberal circles. Now the cabinet, too, was deeply worried by the threat of Russian penetration in the Middle East. Combating the threat of Russian expansionism, as it was perceived in London, became one of the main determinants of British foreign policy for the next decades. At the same time, Britain became deeply hostile to the man who had caused all this trouble, Mehmet Ali.

Mahmut II never really accepted the loss of the Syrian provinces and sought an opportunity to take revenge. In 1838 he sent his influential Minister of Foreign Affairs, Mustafa Reşit Pasha, to London to try to get the British government's support for an attack on Mehmet Ali. This support was not forthcoming, in spite of the offer, and conclusion, of a free trade treaty that opened up Ottoman markets (including, presumably, the areas to be recaptured from the Egyptians) to British trade.

Nevertheless, in April 1839 the sultan felt strong enough to order an attack on the Egyptian forces in northern Syria. The result was a signal Ottoman defeat at Nizip on 24 June. To make matters worse, a few days afterwards the Ottoman admiral in command of the fleet in the Mediterranean, on hearing that one of his arch rivals had become grand vizier and that his fleet was being recalled, sailed to Alexandria and handed over the Ottoman fleet to the Egyptians. This incident shows the extent to which the conflict with Mehmet Ali was still seen as factional strife within the Ottoman ruling elite by its members.

The 'Eastern Question'

The later years of Sultan Mahmut II saw a marked increase in the major European powers' interest in the Ottoman Empire. The Greek and Egyptian crises had shown up the empire's weakness and had alerted Britain to the strategic threat of the Ottoman Empire coming within the Russian sphere of influence, which would enable the Russians to threaten the British position in the Mediterranean and in Asia. Austria, too, was increasingly afraid of Russian domination in the Balkans. Imperial rivalry between Great Britain and France was making itself felt again, a generation after Napoleon's expedition to Egypt.

The question of how to satisfy competing Balkan nationalisms and the imperialist ambitions of the great powers without causing the destruction of the Ottoman Empire, or, if this destruction was inevitable (something of which the majority of European statesmen were convinced), to dismember it without upsetting the balance of power in Europe and causing a general war, was known throughout the nineteenth century as the 'Eastern Question'.[2] It was high on the political and diplomatic agenda in every European capital – and quite rightly, too, for dissatisfied Serbian nationalism was to spark off the First World War in 1914 and lead to the destruction of not only the Ottoman but also the Austrian, Russian and German empires.

The international political developments sketched here form the background for the two partly contradictory developments that set the pace in the Ottoman Empire from the late 1820s onwards. On the one hand, the increasing incorporation of parts of the economy into the capitalist world-system and its attendant growth in trade strengthened the position of those who profited from this development, the Ottoman Christian traders, industrialists and bankers. On the other, the government of Mahmut II, faced with this process, under the personal direction of the sultan, increased its efforts to strengthen the state through military, administrative and fiscal reforms. Gradually, military and political power and economic strength were polarized between two distinct sectors of

Ottoman society: the predominantly Muslim military/bureaucratic elite and the emerging Christian bourgeoisie.

The role of foreign powers in this context was ambivalent: they, especially Britain from the 1830s to the 1870s, encouraged modernizing reforms aimed at strengthening the Ottoman state, but at the same time they jealously guarded their commercial interests and the rights of their Christian coreligionists, many of whom had become clients under the *berat* system. They pressed for equal rights for the sultan's Christian subjects as a touchstone for the sincerity of the reforms, yet supported the Christian communities' refusal to give up their traditional rights under the *millet* system in exchange for equality.

The sultan in control: the start of the reform movement

The policies of Sultan Mahmut II from 1826 onwards determined the direction that Ottoman reform efforts would take for the next 80 years. Like the policies of Selim III and those of his great rival and inspiration, Mehmet Ali Pasha, they were ultimately aimed at strengthening the central state through building a modern army. All his reforms can be understood as a means to that end: building a new army cost money; money had to be generated by more efficient taxation, which in turn could only be achieved through a modern and efficient central and provincial bureaucracy. Better communications were needed to extend government control and new types of education to produce the new-style military and civil servants the sultan needed. Where Mahmut II went much further than his predecessor (though not as far as Mehmet Ali) was in his efforts to uproot the existing establishment, abolishing or taming its institutions, and in the scope of his reforms. Where Selim III had mainly tried to combat abuse of the existing system, Mahmut created new administrative and legal structures.

The turning point in the subjugation of the establishment was the confrontation between Sultan Mahmut and the janissaries in 1826. Throughout the earlier part of his reign, the sultan had encouraged the further development of small, specialized military units (artillery, wagoneers, sappers), some of which had been founded even before Selim III came to the throne, but he had carefully refrained from repeating Selim's attempt to create a modern infantry. Disgusted by the behaviour of the janissaries in the Greek campaigns, in May 1826 he decreed what was in effect a revival of the *Nizam-i Cedid* army, although the new soldiery was now called *Muallem Asakir-i Mansure-i Muhammadiye* (Trained Victorious Soldiers of Muhammad). A hundred and fifty men from each janissary battalion were to be enrolled in the new corps. As was to be – and no doubt was – expected, the janissaries revolted against this undermining of their position, but the sultan was prepared and when the janissaries assembled to march on the palace, his artillery slaughtered them and set fire to their barracks. In 30 minutes the resistance of the janissaries, who apparently on this occasion were not supported by the mass of the capital's population, was broken. The corps was officially abolished the next day and in the following weeks the provincial garrisons, too, were disbanded, some after fierce resistance.

After this suppression of the janissaries, known in Ottoman history as the *Vaka-i Hayriye* (beneficial event), the sultan made sure of his future political control of the army by appointing the head of the new *Mansure* troops *serasker* (head soldier), or commander-in-chief, thus terminating the traditional autonomy of the different corps in the Ottoman army. In due course, the office of *Serasker* would develop into that of Minister of War. In the wake of the beneficial event, the Bektaşi order of dervishes, which had been closely linked to the janissaries since the fifteenth century, was officially closed down. Many of its convents were destroyed and the ones that survived were put at the disposal of the orthodox Sunni Nakşibendi dervish order. Later in the nineteenth century there would be a revival of Bektaşi faith and culture. But Sultan Mahmut very emphatically framed his government as an orthodox Sunni regime that would restore not only the power of the state, but also the true religion. After the defeat of the Janissaries he also brought the Islamic establishment under his control.

The *ulema*, who had so effectively opposed earlier reforming sultans through their coalition with the janissaries, had now lost their strong arm and the sultan made use of their weakened position to curb their power in two vital areas: he brought the holdings of the religious foundations, the *evkaf*, under government control through the institution of a separate directorate (later ministry) of religious foundations and he turned the *ulema* into a hierarchy headed by the *Şeyhülislam*, the chief *müftü* and highest religious functionary of the empire, thus centralizing control over the religious institution in the same way as he had done with the army.

Of course, the drastic solutions of 1826 left the empire with hardly any organized armed forces, so the sultan had to devote a great deal of attention to the building of a new army, the *Mansure* army he had announced in May. Supported by Husrev Pasha, the commander-in-chief at this crucial period, he did succeed in building a new Western-style army in spite of great difficulties. The greatest of these was finding suitable officers. Mehmet Ali had taken care to build up a small but effective cadre before he embarked on the expansion of his forces, but the sultan had been unable to do this in the political climate before 1826 and had to start practically from scratch. Immediately after the destruction of the janissaries, the sultan asked his Egyptian vassal to send him military instructors, but Mehmet Ali for obvious reasons politely refused. Therefore, as in Egypt earlier, foreign instructors were invited to train the officer corps. Because they were politically less suspect than French, British or Russian officers, the Ottoman government began to invite Prussians, thus starting the tradition of Prussian (and later German) influence in the Ottoman army, which was to last for nearly a century. Muslim sensitivities prevented the foreign officers from being put in command of Ottoman troops themselves, however, and limited their effectiveness. A major problem was that of dressing and equipping the new army. Large amounts of materials were imported from different European countries, but at the same time efforts were made to produce supplies within the empire.

All in all, it took a long time to build an effective army and militarily the empire in the 20 years after 1826 was probably weaker than ever before or after, something that clearly showed in the disastrous Russian war of 1828/9 and in the Egyptian crises of 1831–3 and 1839/40. An important step in the modernization of the army was the creation in 1834 of a military reserve (*redif*) after the Prussian model. The aim was to create a large pool of trained men in the provinces, both to strengthen law and order and to flesh out the regular army in times of war. Although poorly organized and equipped, later in the century the *redif* forces did develop into an important means of government control over the provinces.[3]

Mahmut II realized that a modern army was not enough, and that an effective bureaucratic machine was needed to control the country and to ensure the collection of revenues. At the central level, the sultan's attempts to achieve this consisted of three things. First, he took a number of measures to give his scribes, individually and collectively, a more secure status. In 1826 he abolished the age-old custom of confiscating the possessions of disgraced dignitaries. In 1834 he abolished the customary annual reappointment of all higher functionaries (with the attendant appointment fees that had been a heavy burden for most Ottoman scribes) and he replaced the fees (*bahşiş*) on which the income of the scribes had depended with regular salaries. The following year he introduced a modern hierarchical system of ranks and he also tried to replace the old guild-like system of on-the-job training in the departments with a formal system of instruction. This change took place gradually over the next half century. Second, he replaced the traditional, rather undifferentiated, system of government of the Sublime Porte with a division of labour compatible with the new ambitions of the central state.

In this process, the different tasks of the grand vizier, traditionally considered the sultan's *alter ego* to whom all the latter's powers were delegated, were parcelled out among the grand vizier's subordinates. His steward, the *kâhya*, became first minister of civil affairs and then in 1837 minister of the interior. The chief scribe (*Reisülküttab*) developed into minister of foreign affairs. Institutions resembling a treasury department and a justice ministry also evolved. Third, the sultan took the initiative in creating a set of advisory councils, both at the palace and at the Porte, to deal with the growing burden of legislation his reforms entailed. The most important was the *Meclis-i Vâlâ-i Ahkâm-i Adliye* (Supreme Council for Judicial Regulations), which together with a number of smaller more specialized bodies played an extremely important role in the reform policies of the next 30 years.

Financial problems
The reforms, especially the military reforms, cost money on an unprecedented scale. One of the most pressing problems for the sultan and his government was always raising the level of state income for the special treasury created for the army, the *Mansure Hazinesi* (Treasury of the Victorious). From 1826 onwards more and more revenue was diverted to this treasury: that from tax farms, from the religious foundations brought under government control, from confiscated property and from new taxes introduced for this purpose, the so-called *rüsumat-i cihadiye* (holy war taxes).

It is a clear indication of the military impetus behind the reforms that it was this *Mansure* treasure that eventually developed into the Ministry of Finance. The Ottoman government did not succeed in drastically raising the efficiency of the system of taxation during Mahmut's lifetime. Neither was it able to raise income through the efficient use of state monopolies or mercantilist policies like those Mehmet Ali employed in Egypt. On the contrary, towards the end of Mahmut's reign the existing monopolies were abolished. The government therefore resorted to the age-old practice of debasing the coinage (lowering the silver content) in order to finance the deficit. The result was, of course, galloping inflation. Against the major European currencies used in the Levant, the *kuruş* or Ottoman piastre, which had been fairly stable throughout the eighteenth century, fell by nearly 500 per cent during Mahmut's reign.[4] It goes without saying that this affected salaried officials severely. It was undoubtedly one of the reasons for the widespread corruption of which contemporaries complained and also of the continuous social unrest in Mahmut's later years.

Closely linked to the need for more tax revenue were the attempts to reform, or at least to combat the worst abuses of, the provincial administration. The sultan tried further to curb the military and financial power of the *ayan* through the appointment of officials directly controlled from Istanbul, notably tax collectors and military commanders. These policies were first put into operation in two experimental areas, the province of Bursa (called Hüdavendigâr at the time) and the county of Gallipoli; the other provinces were hardly affected during Mahmut's lifetime. To strengthen his hold on the provinces, the sultan also began the improvement of communications, through the introduction of a postal system and the construction of roads, though these, too, were limited to the areas closest to the capital. The same purpose was served by the launching of the first Ottoman newspaper, or more exactly official gazette, the *Moniteur Ottoman* with its Ottoman-language equivalent, the *Takvim-i Vekai* (Calendar of Events), in 1831.

In order to raise revenues through more efficient taxation and to be able to raise more troops, Mahmut ordered a census to be held. Started in 1828/9, this was severely handicapped by the war with Russia, so the census actually was held in a limited number of provinces. According to the data reported in 1831 the size of the population was 3.7 million. Because only males were counted this number has to be more than doubled, but even then it would probably only represent about half the population. The number of Muslims was in reality higher, because the main purpose of the census was to count the Christians who paid the poll tax (*ciziye*). In addition, the census officers limited themselves largely to the towns and easily accessible areas. A number of 23 million is probably a realistic minimum for the population of the empire, excluding North Africa. Over the following years there were several partial counts until in 1844 a completely new census was held, this time specifically aimed at the recruitment of army conscripts. Its results have come to us only indirectly, in the writings of contemporaries who had access to the data, but the total, this time including North Africa and Egypt, is given as 35,350,000.[6]

Education

The second most important condition, after the supply of funds, for the success of Mahmut's reforms was the creation of a cadre able to execute them. There was a desperate need for Ottomans with a knowledge of Europe, of European science and technology and thus of a European language.

Where formal education in a modern sense was concerned, the army was far ahead of the other Ottoman institutions. An army medical school, where modern medicine was taught, was founded in 1827: an innovation of revolutionary potential in a society where scientific medicine was still basically that of the ancient Greeks. Studying modern medicine, biology and physics almost inevitably induced a rationalist and positivist mentality in the students, and the army medical school spawned an extraordinary number of reformist thinkers, writers and activists later in the century. In 1831 a school of military music was established and in 1834 a military academy was founded in the Maçka district of Istanbul. This school, which was later moved to the district of Pangaltı and incorporated several other schools, played a momentous role in forming the cadres of the later Ottoman Empire and of the different nation-states that succeeded it. In all these new schools, the role of foreign instructors was crucial and knowledge of a Western language (usually French) was a prerequisite.

On the civilian side, too, the need for cadres with a knowledge of Europe and of a European language led to new types of education. Following the example set by Mehmet Ali, the sultan in 1827 for the first time sent a small group of students to Europe for training. It was, however, quite natural that the leading role in the creation of the new cadre should be reserved for the old office of the chief scribe (*Reisülküttab*), the new Foreign Office. Here there was at least a residue of knowledge about Europe from the time of Sultan Selim's ambassadors. Here, too, was located the 'Translation Office' (*Tercüme Odası*), where many of the leading Ottoman statesmen of the nineteenth century began their careers. As has been noted before, diplomatic transactions had traditionally been conducted in Istanbul through contacts between foreign embassies and the Porte. Because of the language problem, all negotiations were conducted between the official translator of the imperial council (the *divan*) and the translators, or *dragoman*s, of the various embassies. From the eighteenth century the post of translator to the imperial council had been held by members of the Phanariote Greek families of Istanbul. The Greek insurrection meant that the Porte no longer considered them loyal and reliable, and the last Greek translator was dismissed in 1821.

This left the Ottoman government with a serious communications problem at a time when diplomatic contacts were becoming more and more important to the survival of the empire. Between 1821 and 1833 the business of translation was conducted through makeshift arrangements, but in 1833 the new Translation Office was officially established. It was not only an office, but also an important training establishment, where young bureaucrats were taught to read, write and speak French – the diplomatic language of the day. In 1834, the sultan re-established the Ottoman embassies in the major European capitals. The new ambassadors took with them suites of younger Ottoman scribes and so also were instrumental in the creation of a modern outward-looking cadre. Two elements we encounter time and again when we scrutinize the curricula vitae of reformist Ottoman bureaucrats of the nineteenth century are service in the Translation Office and in one of the embassies.

The handicaps of the reformers

The reign of Sultan Mahmut II saw only the beginnings of the process of reform that was to transform the empire in the nineteenth century. It is certainly not true that the reforms were only window-dressing, that they were stillborn or that they stopped at the doorstep of the Porte. Eventually, with the creation of a European-style army and a bureaucratic apparatus, supported by modern educational facilities, a large measure of effective central control over the empire was established, but it took another 50 years to do it.

If we look at the problems that hampered efforts to reform, both during Mahmut's reign and during the reigns of his sons and successors Abdülmecit (1839–61) and Abdülaziz (1861–76), we can see that those efforts were undermined by five main factors.

First there was the lack of adequately trained and trustworthy personnel. The number of people with adequate knowledge of the new military and bureaucratic techniques could be counted in hundreds, even as late as 1850. The new training establishments could only gradually supply the state with suitable graduates, beginning in the 1840s. In the meantime, even the most radical innovations, like the abolition of the tax-farming system in 1840 or a new system of provincial administration had to be executed through the very people, such as the provincial notables, whose abuses the reforms were intended to terminate.

Second, the reforms were the result of a deliberate political choice at the top. They were based on the presumption on the part of the sultan and a number of his leading servants that the state had to be saved through the adoption of European methods. The reform policies were never the result of popular pressure and therefore lacked a secure basis in Ottoman society. This meant that it was always possible for those factions within the leading strata that disagreed with the Westernizing reforms to halt or sabotage them, even if only temporarily. Although reform-minded bureaucrats with close ties to Britain and France held the upper hand during most of the period up to 1878, they by no means had a monopoly of power. Sultan Mahmut used the competition between different factions to remain master of the situation, and in later years more conservative or anti-Western politicians were sometimes able to oust the reformists with the help of the Russian embassy or the palace.

Third, even though rational-legalism gradually replaced traditionalism in the workings of the bureaucracy, the patrimonial system,
which had been so characteristic of the 'classical' Ottoman system with
high officials who were at the same time patrons to numerous clients who
both depended on them for a living and supported them in the continuous
political infighting at the court, was still in place. This undermined the
rational working of the new institutions, especially in the 'hiring and
firing' department.

Fourth, apart from the breakthrough of 1826, the reforms of the
nineteenth century consisted of the creation of new laws, new regulations
and new institutions, rather than the abolition of old ones. In time this
created a dualism, with, for instance, the basically mediaeval scholastic
educational system of the *ulema* coexisting with modern teaching in
French in the new training colleges and regulations based on nineteenth-
century European law gradually replacing the Ottoman *kanuni* law, but
existing side by side with the holy law of Islam, the *şeriat.* The
jurisdiction of the older and the newer institutions was not always defined
very clearly.

Finally, it can no doubt be maintained that the Achilles' heel of the
reforms was their lack of an economic and financial basis. The reforms
were expensive, introducing as they did (though not by modern
standards) 'big government' in the empire for the first time. The stated
financial resources were simply insufficient and the attempts to increase
them were badly mismanaged. All through the period of the reforms, the
financial problem remained intractable. As a result, state servants were
badly and irregularly paid and corruption remained endemic.

Economic trends in the later years of Sultan Mahmut
The economic developments of Mahmut II and his immediate successors
must be understood in the context of worldwide economic trends. Great
Britain had emerged from the revolutionary and Napoleonic wars
without real rivals as a global trading nation and industrial power, but
faced with this economic hegemony of the British, their traditional
trading partners on the European continent and in America in the early
nineteenth century defended themselves by introducing protectionist
policies. These policies in turn forced Britain to intensify its efforts to
open up new markets in South America and Asia. For this purpose, it
concluded a series of free-trade agreements with a number of countries,
opening up their markets to British products and giving British industry
free access to their raw materials.

The old Levant Company had been disbanded in 1825. The ending of
its trading monopoly in the Ottoman Empire meant that British traders

were now free to try their luck as they pleased. In the Ottoman lands, they enjoyed the protection of the capitulations, which restricted import and export duties alike to 3 per cent. Moreover, at the Treaty of Edirne in 1829 the Russians had extracted a number of commercial concessions from the Ottomans, which other powers now also claimed. Nevertheless, a number of important restrictions on trade were still in force. They included Ottoman state monopolies on a variety of goods, internal customs duties paid on trade within the empire, and central government's ability to impose extraordinary duties, for instance in times of war. When the Ottoman government sought British support against the threat posed by Mehmet Ali in 1838, Mustafa Reşit Pasha, the architect of the British alliance, offered the British government a free-trade treaty that replaced all existing duties (including internal ones) for British traders with new tariffs of 12 per cent on exports and 5 per cent on imports.[7] The Ottoman merchants, meanwhile, continued to pay the additional internal duties of 8 per cent. In addition, all state monopolies were abolished, as was the right to impose extraordinary taxes. The treaty, known as the Treaty of Balta Limanı (after the village on the Bosphorus where Reşit Pasha had his palace) opened up the Ottoman market completely to British trade. As usual, all the other European states demanded the same rights, and similar free-trade treaties were signed with several other countries between 1838 and 1841.

Trade, especially exports of agricultural products, had already grown faster since the early 1820s. One reason was that the industrial revolution in England led to a fall in the prices of industrial goods and thus to more favourable terms of trade for exporters of agricultural goods to industrializing nations. Conversely, the falling prices of imported British industrial goods made life more difficult for local handicrafts.[8] One result of the free-trade arrangements of 1838–41, which coincided with the start of the rapid economic expansion in Europe known as the 'mid-century boom', was that the empire's external trade, which had already increased by roughly 80 per cent between 1780 and 1830, increased approximately fivefold in 1830–70.[9] The other result of the treaty was that the Ottoman government was deprived of exactly those mercantilist instruments (monopolies and discriminating taxes) that had been the financial basis of Mehmet Ali's reforms. All through the nineteenth century the empire's economic policy remained a classically liberal one without any attempts at protectionism. It is in any case doubtful whether such a policy would have been tolerated by the European powers.

Of course, the change in the empire's economic situation brought with it winners and losers. Winners were those groups directly involved in the expanding international trade. In general, these were not the producers of export crops themselves: large-scale export-orientated agricultural producers were relatively rare in the Ottoman Empire, where small- to medium-sized landholders prevailed, and small farmers could not export independently. On the other hand, the existence of many small farms made it difficult for foreigners to penetrate the economic networks. It was the intermediaries between the small farmers and European industry who profited.[10] In the Ottoman context, these intermediaries were predominantly Greek, and to a lesser extent Armenian, traders with contacts overseas. A network of largely Armenian bankers financed their expanding businesses. Many of the Greek traders and Armenian bankers held honorary foreigner status under the *berat* system and were thus practically untouchable for the Ottoman government. During the nineteenth century their position became strong, not only compared with the sultan's Muslim subjects but also compared with the foreign companies that tried to penetrate the Near Eastern markets on their own but whose attempts the indigenous Christians often successfully frustrated.

There were also losers. They were to be found in the traditional handicraft industries, organized in guilds, especially in those towns and cities, such as the major ports, that had direct links with the outside world. Evidence shows that at least some of these handicrafts, such as the very important production of cotton yarn, and to a lesser extent of cloth, were hit hard by the competition from industrially produced European goods. The results were falling incomes and unemployment.

The effects of the Ottoman Empire's incorporation into the European economic system should not, however, be overstated. Estimates suggest that even in 1870 foreign trade amounted to only about 7 or 8 per cent of total production (and to between 12 and 16 per cent of agricultural production).[11] The share of exports in the gross national product of the empire has been calculated at approximately 3 to 4 per cent in 1840.[12] Furthermore, the effects of incorporation were spread very unevenly, with the coastal regions and the big cities most affected while the inaccessible interior was affected much less. Even in the more remote areas the incorporation had its indirect effects: the price of wheat in the internal market, for instance, fluctuated with the price on the world market.

Foreign loans to the Ottoman Empire, or investments in the infrastructure or in industry, were not yet playing a role in the 1830s. Like other countries, the empire for centuries had had a number of institutions that produced on an industrial scale. These were all connected to the military: the imperial arsenal on the Golden Horn and the gun foundry of Tophane were among the most important. In Mahmut's reign new attempts were made at industrial production in the form of mills producing clothing, equipment and armaments for the new army. The mills worked exclusively or mainly as government contractors and were controlled by government bodies such as the mint or the office of the *Serasker* (commander-in-chief). The workers in these mills were regarded as part of the army. The most famous example of all was the *Feshane* (fez factory). The fez, a red felt brimless hat originating in Morocco, had been chosen as the official headgear for the new army and for the civil service after the destruction of the janissaries in 1826. For some time the fezzes were purchased from Tunisia, but in 1835 a number of Tunisian craftsmen were brought to Istanbul. In 1839 (after the death of Sultan Mahmut) the *Feshane* was enlarged and relocated in a wing of a palace at the top of the Golden Horn. At this time it also started to produce cloth, but it still depended on animal strength. In the mid-1840s steam engines were introduced. A few more mills of the same type were opened in the 1840s and 1850s but, like their early modern predecessors, they were suppliers to the military rather than commercial operations.

5 · The Era of the *Tanzimat*, 1839–71

Sultan Mahmut II died of tuberculosis on 30 June 1839, before the news of the Ottoman defeat by the Egyptians at Nizip had reached Istanbul. His elder son, Abdülmecit, who succeeded him, was to reign from 1839 to 1861. Mahmut's death did not mark the beginning of a period of reaction, as Selim III's death had in 1807. The centralizing and modernizing reforms were continued essentially in the same vein for another generation. Indeed, the period from 1839 to 1876 is known in Turkish historiography as the period of the *Tanzimat* (reforms) *par excellence*, although one could well argue that in fact the period of the reforms ended in 1871. The term *Tanzimat-i Hayriye* (beneficial reforms) had been used even before 1839, for instance in the imperial order establishing the Supreme Council for Judicial Regulations (*Meclis-i Vala-i Ahkam-ı Adliye*).[1] This illustrates the continuity between the period of Mahmut II and that of his successors. The main difference was that the centre of power now shifted from the palace to the Porte, the bureaucracy. In order to create a strong and modern apparatus with which to govern the empire, Mahmut had helped to start transforming the traditional scribal institution into something resembling a modern bureaucracy, thereby so strengthening it that his weaker successors lost control of the bureaucratic apparatus for much of the time.

The reform edict of Gülhane
Under Mahmud's successors foreign, especially British, influence on policy-making in Istanbul vastly increased. For a generation after the second Egyptian crisis, Britain supported the Ottoman Empire's continued existence as a buffer against what was perceived in London as dangerous Russian expansionism. The Russophobe Stratford Canning (from 1852 Lord Stratford de Redcliffe), who was British ambassador in Istanbul from 1841 to 1858 and was on close terms with many of the leading Ottoman reformers, played a crucial role in this British support.

The beginnings of the *Tanzimat* coincided with the attempts to solve the second Egyptian crisis. When Ottoman fortunes were at their lowest ebb, on 3 November 1839, an imperial edict written by the leading reformer and foreign minister, Reşit Pasha, but promulgated in the name of the new sultan, was read outside the palace gates (at the Square of the Rose Garden, hence its name *Gülhane Hatt-i Şerifi* (the Noble Edict of the Rose Garden) to an assembly of Ottoman dignitaries and foreign diplomats. It was a statement of intent on the part of the Ottoman government, promising in effect four basic reforms:

- The establishment of guarantees for the life, honour and property of the sultan's subjects;
- An orderly system of taxation to replace the system of tax farming;
- A system of conscription for the army; and
- Equality before the law of all subjects, whatever their religion (although this was formulated somewhat ambiguously in the document).[2]

Controversy has raged ever since its promulgation over the character and especially the sincerity of the edict and the *Tanzimat* policies based on it. It is undoubtedly true that the promulgation of the edict at that specific time was a diplomatic move, aimed at gaining the support of the European powers, and especially Britain, for the empire in its struggle with Mehmet Ali. It is equally true, however, that the text reflected the genuine concerns of the group of reformers led by Reşit Pasha. The promised reforms were clearly a continuation of Mahmut II's policies. The call for guarantees for the life, honour and property of the subjects, apart from echoing classic liberal thought as understood by the Ottoman statesmen who had been to Europe and knew European languages, also reflected the Ottoman bureaucrats' desire to escape their vulnerable position as slaves of the sultan. Taxation and conscription, of course, had been two of Mahmut's most urgent concerns. The promise of equal rights to Ottoman Christians, ambiguously as it was formulated, was certainly meant in part for foreign consumption. On the other hand, it is clear that Reşit Pasha and a number of his colleagues believed, or at least hoped, that it would halt the growth of nationalism and separatism among the Christian communities and that it would remove pretexts for foreign, especially Russian, intervention. Yet, the edict was much more than a series of European ideas and ideals. The way in which it was formulated reflected existing Islamic and Ottoman ideas on good and just governance.

In the short run the *Gülhane* edict certainly served its purpose, although it is hard to say how much it contributed to the decision of the powers to save the empire.

A solution to the Egyptian crisis

The defeat at Nizip had left the empire practically defenceless and it would have had to give in to the demands of Mehmet Ali (hereditary possession of Egypt, Syria and Adana) had not the great powers intervened. Britain reacted quickly, giving its fleet orders to cut communications between Egypt and Syria and taking the initiative for contacts between the five major powers (Russia, Austria, Prussia, France and Britain itself). Diplomatic consultations lasted for over a year, with Russia and Britain jointly pressing for an Egyptian evacuation of Syria, while France increasingly came out in support of Mehmet Ali. In the end, the other powers despaired of getting French cooperation and on 15 July 1840 Russia, Prussia, Austria and Britain signed an agreement with the Porte envisaging armed support for the sultan. Late in 1840 the British navy bombarded Egyptian positions in and around Beirut and landed an expeditionary force, which, in conjunction with widespread insurrections against his oppressive rule, forced Ibrahim Pasha to withdraw from Syria. Diplomatic haggling went on for some time longer, but basically the issue had now been settled. In June 1841 Mehmet Ali accepted the loss of his Syrian provinces in exchange for the hereditary governorship of Egypt, which remained nominally part of the Ottoman Empire until 1914.

Internal unrest and international politics

With the end of the second Egyptian crisis a noticeable lessening of tension in the Middle East set in. The fundamental problems of the empire, caused by rising tension between the different nationalities and communities, which the central government was unable to solve or control, had not gone away, but for about 15 years they did not lead to large-scale intervention on the part of the great powers of Europe.

The most violent inter-communal conflict of these years was fought out in the Lebanon. The strong man of the area was the Emir Bashir II, who belonged to the small religious community of the Druzes,[3] but had converted to Christianity and ruled the Lebanon from his stronghold in the Shuf mountains for 50 years. He had linked his fate closely to that of the Egyptian occupation forces, and when the latter had to leave Syria, his position became untenable and he was ousted by his enemies among the Druze tribal chiefs. After his demise in 1843, the Ottoman government introduced a cantonal system, whereby Lebanon north of the Beirut–Damascus highway was governed by a Christian *kaymakam* (governor), while the area to the south of the road was ruled by a Druze one, both under the jurisdiction of the governor-general of Sidon, whose seat was now moved to Beirut.

Because this division took no account of the mixed character of the population in the south and the north, tensions soon rose and in 1845 they erupted in large-scale fighting, with the Druzes burning down numerous Maronite Christian villages. Under pressure from the powers – the French had established a de facto protectorate over the Maronite Christians of the Lebanon (who were uniate, that is, they recognized the pope and were therefore officially regarded as Catholics), the British over the Druzes, and the Russians over the Orthodox Christians – the Ottomans severely punished the Druze leaders and set up consultative assemblies representing the communities in both cantons. This time the powers refrained from direct intervention.

The Crimean War
The one great international conflict of these years, the Crimean War (1853–56), had as its ostensible cause a dispute over whether the Catholic or the Orthodox Church should control the holy places in Palestine, especially the Church of the Nativity in Bethlehem. France interceded on behalf of the Catholics, while Russia defended the rights of the Orthodox. The Catholic Church had been granted pre-eminence in 1740, but the fact that many times more Orthodox than Catholic pilgrims visited the holy land over time strengthened the Orthodox Church's position. France, supported by Austria, now demanded reassertion of the pre-eminence of the Catholics. Russia wanted the status quo to remain in force. The bewildered Porte tried to please everyone at the same time.

The real reasons behind the aggressive attitude of France and Russia were almost wholly domestic. Both the newly established Second Republic in France, headed by Napoleon Bonaparte (soon to be Emperor Napoleon III), and the Russian tsar were trying to gain popular support by appealing to religious fervour.

A dangerous escalation began when, on 5 May 1853, the Russian envoy to Istanbul demanded the right to protect not only the Orthodox Church (a claim based on a very partisan reading of the privileges that had been granted in 1774) but also the Orthodox population of the empire, more than a third of its inhabitants. Supported by the French and British ambassadors, the Porte refused to give in. Russia announced it would occupy the principalities of Wallachia and Moldavia if the Porte did not accept its demands, and in July its troops crossed into the principalities. A last-minute attempt at mediation by France, Britain, Austria and Prussia failed. The Ottomans demanded the evacuation of the principalities and, when this was not forthcoming, declared war on Russia in October. Under pressure from violently anti-Russian public opinion and from the French government, the British cabinet now opted for war and on 28 March 1854 war was officially declared. None of the great powers wanted war, but all had backed themselves into a corner they could not leave without serious loss of face.

Austria's attitude in the conflict had been ambivalent from the beginning and gradually became more and more anti-Russian, so much so that the risk of an Austrian attack forced the Russians to withdraw from the principalities in July. So the French/British expeditionary force, which was sent to the Levant in the expectation of having to fight in the Balkans, was left without a target and landed in the Crimea instead, hence 'the Crimean War'. The war brought nobody much credit or profit. The allies' only major success was the taking of the Russian fortress city of Sebastopol, but the price paid in terms of suffering and casualties during the winter of 1854/5 (when Florence Nightingale reorganized the hospital the British army had established in the Selimiye barracks in the Istanbul suburb of Üsküdar) was very high. In 1855, therefore, all the belligerents were ready to talk. A peace conference was held in Paris in February–March 1856 and produced a treaty that embodied the main demands of France, Britain and Austria.

Although the war had been fought to defend the Ottoman Empire, it was not consulted officially on the peace terms and had to accept them as they were. The most important items in the peace treaty were:

- Demilitarization of the Black Sea (also on the Turkish side!);
- An end to Russian influence in Moldavia and Wallachia; and
- A guarantee of the independence and integrity of the Ottoman Empire on the part of all the major European powers.

As one of the signatories of the the Treaty of Paris the empire was officially admitted to the 'Concert of Europe', the system of great powers that had tried to preserve the balance of powers in Europe since the fall of Napoleon and the Congress of Vienna. The financial and military weakness of the Ottomans meant that they remained the object, or even the victim, of European diplomatic intrigue, rather than an active participant, however. A new reform decree elaborating promises made in 1839 and largely dictated by the French and British ambassadors in Istanbul, was published to coincide with the peace conference and to boost Ottoman prestige. The European powers officially took note of the declaration and stated that it removed any pretext for European intervention in relations between the sultan and his subjects.[4] This guarantee would prove a dead letter.

The Crimean War was to have far-reaching consequences for reforms within the empire and for its finances, but we shall come to those later.

For now, the integrity of the empire was indeed saved and it would be another 20 years before its existence was threatened again.

The Eastern Question again

In the meantime the old pattern of the politics and diplomacy of the Eastern Question took shape again. As in the Serbian, Greek and Lebanese crises, the pattern was basically always the same: the discontent of (mostly Christian) communities in the empire erupted into regional insurrections, caused partly by bad government and partly by the different nationalisms that were spreading at the time. One of the powers then intervened diplomatically, or even militarily, to defend the position of the local Christians. In the prevailing conditions of inter-power rivalry this caused the other major powers to intervene to re-establish 'the balance of power'. Usually, the end result was a loss of control on the part of the central Ottoman government.

This was what happened when the problems between Maronite Christians and Druzes in Lebanon developed into a civil war again in 1860. Maronite peasants, supported by their clergy, revolted against their landlords (both Maronite and Druze) and Druze fighters intervened, killing thousands of Maronite peasants. Shortly afterwards, in July 1860, a Muslim mob, incited by Druzes, killed more than 5000 local Christians in Damascus. This caused the Powers to intervene on the initiative of France. An expeditionary force, half of which France supplied, landed in Beirut, despite Ottoman efforts to pre-empt its arrival by draconic disciplinary measures. France's efforts to restructure the entire administration of Syria were then blocked by the Porte with British support. In the end, the mainly Christian parts of the Lebanese coast and mountains became an autonomous province under a Christian *mutasarrif* (collector), who had to be appointed with the assent of the Powers.

The pattern was repeated when a revolt broke out in Crete in 1866. What began as a protest against Ottoman mismanagement of affairs on the island, turned into a nationalist movement for union with Greece. The conflict aroused public opinion both in Greece, where volunteers were openly recruited for the struggle on the island, and among the Muslims in the Ottoman Empire (Crete had a significant Muslim minority) and by 1867 the two countries were on the brink of war. Russia, where solidarity with the Greek Orthodox subjects of the sultan was widely felt, urged European intervention on behalf of the rebels and the cession of Crete to Greece, but the hesitations of the other powers prevented the Powers from taking direct action. Their combined pressure forced the Porte to declare an amnesty for the rebels and to announce reforms in the provincial administration of Crete giving the Christians more influence, but foreign intervention went no further and by the end of 1868 the rebellion was at an end. Crete would only become a major problem for the Ottomans again 30 years later.

In the Balkans, meanwhile, nationalist fervour was also spreading, encouraged by the rise of the 'pan-Slav' movement in Russia (the influential Russian ambassador in Istanbul, Ignatiev, was an ardent supporter) and with Serbia as the epicentre of agitation. When revolts broke out among the Christian peasants of neighbouring Bosnia and Herzegovina against local Muslim landlords, Serbian and Montenegrin agitation turned these riots into nationalist movements. This was in 1853, in 1860–62 and again in 1875. In 1860 the Montenegrins actively supported a rebellion in Bosnia-Herzegovina. When the Ottoman governor of Bosnia suppressed the rebellion and then invaded Montenegro, the powers intervened to save the autonomous status of the small mountain principality. When the 1875 rebellion broke out, it set in motion a train of events that nearly ended the Ottoman Empire's presence in Europe.

The *Tanzimat*

There can be no doubt that the continuous external pressure was an important incentive for the internal administrative and legal reforms announced during the period of the *Tanzimat* (1839–71). This is especially true for those reforms that had to do with the position of the Christian minorities of the empire. The European powers pressed for improvements in the position of these communities, which in the classical Ottoman structure had been that of second-class subjects. Slowly but surely they achieved equality with the Muslim majority, at least on paper. This, however, never induced them (or the powers) to forgo the prerogatives they had under the older *millet* system. The powers were certainly motivated in part by the desire to extend their influence through the promotion of client groups – Catholics and Uniates (members of the Eastern churches who recognized the authority of the Pope) for the French and the Austrians, Orthodox for the Russians, Druzes and Protestants for the British – but genuine Christian solidarity played a role, too. The Victorian age saw a marked increase in piety and in the activity of missionary societies and Christian fundamentalist movements. The missionaries were increasingly active in the Ottoman Empire and they provided their supporters at home with – often biased – information on current affairs in the empire, so creating a great deal of involvement on the part of public opinion.

It would be wrong, however, to attribute the reforms to foreign pressure alone. Like the *Gülhane* edict of 1839, they were used to gain foreign support or to avert foreign intervention, but they were also the result of a genuine belief that the only way to save the empire was to introduce European-style reforms.

The post-1839 reforms covered the same areas as Mahmut II's programme: the army, the central bureaucracy, the provincial administration, taxation, education and communication. What was new was a much heavier emphasis on judicial reform and on consultative procedures.

Military reforms

The army, now called the *nizamiye* (regular) troops, was expanded and given modern European equipment throughout this period. Inspired by the Egyptian example, Sultan Mahmut had already tried to introduce conscription. Now, from 1845 onwards, it was officially introduced in most areas of the empire.[5] Christians, too, were now officially required (or, in Ottoman eyes, allowed) to serve, but since this was expected to create unmanageable tensions within the army, they were soon given the option of paying a special tax (the *bedel-i askeri*) instead, which by and large they preferred. Muslims, too, could opt for payment instead of service, but the sum demanded was very steep for most people. A number of categories, such as the inhabitants of Istanbul, Mecca and Medina, religious functionaries and students or nomads, were exempt, but for those communities that had to supply the army with recruits, conscription became a burden that was hated and feared. Normal service was for five years, but if the different categories of service with the territorial reserve were included, the total could amount to as much as 22 years. That made the chance that a conscript would ever come home rather small.

Organizationally, the most important development (apart from the new census described on page 37) was the institution of provincial armies with their own provincial commands in 1841. These were put under the command of the *Serasker* in Istanbul, ending the hold of provincial governors and notables over the local garrisons. Most spectacular in terms of hardware was the building of a modern navy with ironclad warships. During the reign of Sultan Abdülaziz (1861–76), who took a personal interest in everything concerned with military equipment, the navy was developed into the third largest in Europe. The quality of the naval personnel lagged far behind that of the major European navies, however, so the Ottoman navy never developed into an effective instrument of power.

Reform of the central bureaucracy

The main development in the administrative system at the central level in this period was ongoing rationalization and specialization, whereby a complete set of ministries and boards on the European pattern was gradually established.

As noted above, the centre of power within the government in this period clearly shifted from the palace to the newly emancipated bureaucrats of the Porte. Within the whole administrative structure of the Porte, the role and importance of the Ministry of Foreign Affairs are striking. The leading statesmen of the *Tanzimat*, Reşit Pasha and his pupils Ali Pasha and Fuat Pasha together, were appointed foreign minister 13 times and they held the post almost continually during the whole period (with the exception of the years 1841–45). The ministry not only conducted foreign affairs, but also took a leading part in formulating the internal administrative, judicial and educational reforms. There are several reasons for this. The normal function of the ministry, the conduct of foreign relations, had in itself been of growing importance since the eighteenth century because of the growing European pressure and the diminishing effectiveness of the empire's armed forces. Its dominant role in the reform movement stemmed both from the fact that the necessary expertise (knowledge of European languages, experience with European societies) was concentrated at the ministry, and also from the close relationship between foreign diplomatic pressure and intervention on the one hand and the attempts at reform on the other. This was especially evident in all problems related in one way or another to the position of the Ottoman Christians.

Apart from the growth of the new ministries, the one other important trend at the central level was the development of a system of consultative assemblies and commissions. Specialized bodies concerned with specific problems such as building or trade grew up in many ministries. Their task was to help prepare new measures and new legislation. A leading role was played by the *Meclis-i Vâlâ-i Ahkâm-i Adliye* (Supreme Council for Judicial Regulations), which in 1839 was given a new charter with a kind of parliamentary procedure (with decisions being taken by majority vote and the sultan promising to uphold its decisions). It is important, however, to point out that however 'parliamentary' its procedures were, the council and its successors were not embryo parliaments. They were consultative bodies of high dignitaries, not in any way elected, and their powers to control the government, let alone the sultan, were very limited indeed. The Supreme Council combined two functions: on the one hand it discussed and prepared new legislation, on the other it acted as a court of appeal in administrative matters. The amount of work involved soon became so great that the council became more and more bogged down as the years wore on. Furthermore, in the early 1850s divergences of opinion began to appear between the council, which was a stronghold of the first-generation reformers, led by Mustafa Reşit Pasha, and the statesmen of the second generation, led by his pupils and protégés Ali Pasha and Fuat Pasha, who wanted to move further and faster with the programme of Westernization.

For these reasons, a change was introduced in 1854. The judicial function remained with the council, while the legislative function now became the prerogative of a new body, the *Meclis-i Ali-yi Tanzimat* (Supreme Council of the Reforms), which was dominated by the second-generation reformers, with Fuat Pasha as president. The change removed some of the friction but did not solve the problem of the council's excessive workload. Therefore, in 1860 (after Reşit Pasha's death) the two bodies were once more merged, but the work was now divided over three subdivisions, one for legislation, one for administrative investigations and one that functioned as a court of appeal. Finally, in 1868, following the example of France and under French pressure, they were again split into a Council of State (*Şura-yi Devlet*) with legislative functions and a separate court of appeal.[6] The one important difference between the arrangement of 1868 and its predecessors was that the Council of State was a representative, though not an elected, body with Christian and Muslim members selected from lists provided by the provincial governors.

The provincial administration and the tax system
More important perhaps than the developments at the central level was the progress of the reforms in the provincial administration in conjunction with attempts to establish a fairer and more effective system of taxation (as announced in the *Gülhane* edict). In 1840 a major reorganization of the system of taxation was announced, with only three taxes remaining: the *ciziye* or poll tax on non-Muslims, the *aşar* or tithe, and the *mürettebat* or 'allocation taxes', in fact service taxes. At the same time, the custom whereby villages or communities had to provide board and lodging for passing or visiting officials and their entourage, and fodder for their horses – a major scourge on the countryside – was officially ended (something that had been attempted before more than once).

More important still, the system of tax farming was replaced by direct collection through centrally appointed and salaried *muhassils*. It was hoped that this would both increase central government's income and lessen the burdens on the farmers; but the result was a complete disaster. Reşit Pasha's government did not have enough competent officials to appoint as *muhassils*, the local notables who had held the tax farms sabotaged the collection, and lack of precise information made adequate collection impossible. In 1840 a completely new registration of all possessions (*temettuat*) of every household was introduced. Registration at the level of the individual household rather than at that of the village or ward was an innovation, but it could only be carried through in a part of the empire. In most areas there was no cadastre. In 1858 the surveying and registration of all landholdings in the empire was started, but it took until 1908 to complete. State income fell dramatically, just when a system of salaries had been introduced in the bureaucracy. As a result, Reşit Pasha fell from power and the system of tax farming was reintroduced. In most parts of the empire it was not replaced by direct taxation until the end of the nineteenth century. Even in the last days of the empire 95 per cent of the tithe was still collected by tax farmers.[7]

Of the other tax reforms that affected the mass of the people in the empire in this era, the first was the abolition of the *ciziye*, which was obviously incompatible with the declared policy of giving equal rights to non-Muslims. However, the military service exemption tax (*bedel-i askeri*), which in practice amounted to much the same thing, replaced it. The second was the reform of the sheep tax (*Ağnam Vergisi*), which was extended to all farm animals in 1856 and introduced differentiated taxation according to the animal's market value, not on their number. This was yet another sign that Ottoman society was gradually becoming more commercialized. The third change was the passing of the law on real estate property of 1858. This made possible private landholding on the basis of property deeds. Under the new law a lot of state land (*miri*) became private property (*mülk*). Land increasingly became a commodity that could be traded.[8]

Confronted with the complete failure of the introduction of direct taxation in 1840/1, the government resorted to military rule and handed provincial government over to the commanders of the provincial armies.[9] During the 1840s, the government aimed to centralize the empire's internal administration. It tried to reduce the governors' powers by appointing officials who were directly answerable to the Porte instead of to the governors, by sending out inspection commissions and by instituting county and provincial councils. In these councils, which were the first more or less representative institutions in the empire, the most important local representatives of the government (for example, the governor, the judge and the police chief) conferred with representatives of the local notables and of the most important *millet*s. In addition, during two months in 1845 an assembly of provincial notables was held in Istanbul, though it produced no concrete results. It is interesting that an assembly of notables should be held at all and it highlights an often-overlooked truth. While, since Mahmut II, the central state had increased its hold at the expense of the autonomous notables, these same notables and their families were sometimes able to strengthen their regional hold on power by monopolizing the new functions of the provincial bureaucracy. In some places the strengthening of the central state thus paradoxically meant a strengthening of regional power brokers as well.

In the 1850s, it became clear that centralization, aimed at undermining the autonomy of the provincial governors, was harmful to the efficient administration of the provinces. Accordingly, the new provincial regulation of 1858 restored the powers of the governors, subordinating all officials sent out by Istanbul to them. In 1864, a new law on provincial organization introduced a complete hierarchical system of provinces and subdivisions, from the *vilayet* (province) through the *sancak* (county) and *kaza* (district) to the *nahiye* (rural community) and the *kariye* (village). The system was largely based on French practice and it was refined further (under French influence) in 1871.

From Sultan Mahmut II's time onwards, most reforms were introduced as experiments in one or more model provinces or districts. The experience gained there in turn influenced the reforms formulated later on, like the 1864 law. The effectiveness of the reforms in taxation and administration differed hugely from area to area and from period to period, the main determinant seeming to be the ability of the man at the top. Some provincial administrators gained a reputation for efficiency and honesty wherever they went. Their administration could sometimes yield spectacular results in terms of public works programmes (roads, bridges, street lighting), improved health and safety and tax income for the state. Midhat Pasha in particular gained a reputation for honesty and efficiency during his stints as provincial governor in Nish (1861–64) and subsequently in the newly formed Danube province and in Baghdad.[10] They were, however, the exception rather than the rule.

Judicial procedures and secular laws

The *Tanzimat* era saw a number of important changes in the judicial system, many of them related to the changing position of the non-Muslim communities. The canon law of Islam, the *şeriat*, was never abrogated, but its scope was limited almost completely to family law (questions of ownership now also being brought under the sway of the secular law) and it was codified along European lines in 1865–88. The empire had always been ruled under a dual system with sultanic decrees functioning side by side with (though theoretically under) the Islamic canon law, but *Tanzimat* statesmen created new secular laws and institutions to replace this traditional *kanun* system, mainly where the changing position of the foreigners in the empire or the Ottoman Christians demanded it. In 1843 a new penal code was introduced, which recognized equality of Muslims and non-Muslims. At the same time, mixed tribunals were introduced for commercial cases in which foreigners were involved. In 1844, the death penalty for apostasy from Islam, a provision of the *şeriat*, was abolished. A new commercial code, copied from France, was introduced in 1850, followed in 1863 by a maritime trade code and in 1867 by a law enabling foreigners to own land in the empire for the first time. In 1869 a hierarchy of secular courts to deal with cases involving non-Muslims, the *nizamiye* courts, was created.

Not only the law and the institutions of the empire were secularized, so were those of the Christian *millets*. Within the Armenian and Greek communities the emerging commercial bourgeoisie was getting richer and more self-confident. At the same time its relations with Europe spread French political ideas among its members. This led to a movement for emancipation of the *millet* organizations from the exclusive control of the churches. This movement gained further impetus from the new Protestant Armenian *millet*, recognized (under British pressure) in 1850, which had a representative structure from the start. After long deliberations and struggles, the Gregorian Armenian *millet* adopted a constitution in 1863, which in turn served as an inspiration to the Ottoman constitutional movement. The Greek *millet* also achieved a measure of secular, representative administration in this period, although clerical control remained much stronger than among the Armenians. The Jewish community received its own constitution in 1865. An ironic consequence of this development was that due to this secularizing process the *millets* achieved a degree of formal institutionalization they had never had in the classical Ottoman Empire. Because representatives of the secular elites within the communities were empowered by the new legislation, the growth of nationalist currents, that had many supporters in these circles, was indirectly stimulated as well.[11]

Secular education

Secularization was also the most important trend in education in the *Tanzimat* era. As in the preceding period, priority was given to the creation of professional training colleges for the bureaucracy and the army, the most important being the *Mektep-i Mülkiye* (civil service school), founded in 1859. They formed the apex of the educational pyramid of the empire, because attempts to found a university, of which there were a number, were not successful until 1900. This reflects the essentially utilitarian educational ideals of the men of the *Tanzimat*.

Sultan Mahmut had already initiated the building of *Rüşdiye* (adolescence) schools, secular schools for boys between the ages of 10 and 15 who had graduated from the *mektep*, the traditional primary schools where children learned the Koran by heart and sometimes learned to read and write. The *Rüşdiye*s were meant as a bridge between the *mektep* and the professional schools or on-the-job training in the government departments. Fewer than 60 of these new schools were opened in the first half of the nineteenth century, however, due to the usual shortages of money and trained personnel. The slow development of modern education forced the army to develop its own network of military *Rüşdiye* schools from 1855 onwards, followed by secondary *İdadiye* (preparatory) schools in the major garrison towns.

In 1869, a new Regulation for Public Education was issued, based on the advice of the French Ministry of Education. This new regulation foresaw a three-tier system of education, starting with *Rüşdiye* schools in every large village or town quarter, civilian *İdadiye* secondary schools in every town, and colleges called *Sultaniye* (imperial) schools, modelled on the French lycées, in every provincial capital. These were all-male schools, but provisions for separate schools for girls were made in the regulation. In the 1870s progress was still very slow, but in the following era, the reign of Sultan Abdülhamit, the network of primary and secondary schools spread rapidly. Only two *Sultaniye* schools were established, both in the capital: one in the old palace school of Galatasaray in 1868 and one in the Aksaray district in 1873, the Darüşşafaka for Muslim orphans. Galatasaray especially was to provide the empire (and later the republic) with generations of well-educated outward looking administrators, diplomats, writers, doctors and academics, both Muslim and non-Muslim.

The result of the educational developments during the nineteenth century was that there were now four types of school in the empire. The first comprised the traditional Islamic schools, the *mektep*s, and the hierarchy of *medrese*s, which taught the traditional curriculum of Islamic sciences. Then there were secular state schools created during the *Tanzimat* and much extended during the reign of Sultan Abdülhamit II (1876–1909). Though they were often mediocre, these schools brought forth the reforming cadres that were to lead the empire (and the Turkish Republic). The third type was the schools founded and funded by the *millet*s, and the fourth was the schools run by foreign Catholic and Protestant missions and by the Jewish *Alliance israélite universelle*, which were attended by a small, but increasing, number of Muslim children too. It goes without saying that this was not an educational system designed to stimulate a feeling of national solidarity or even a common identity among the literate elite of the empire (still less than 10 per cent of the population).[12]

Increasing economic incorporation

As already noted, the period under consideration here coincided with the mid-century economic boom in Europe. After the free-trade treaties with the major European states in 1838–41, the incorporation of the Ottoman economy into the capitalist system progressed faster than before. The result of this and of economic expansion in the core countries of Europe was that Ottoman foreign trade expanded at a rate of over 5 per cent a year, doubling the volume of trade every 11 to 13 years. At the same time, Britain's share of this trade increased markedly; it was by far the most important source of industrial products for the empire.[13] France never came close in this respect, but remained important as a market for Ottoman agricultural products. Austria remained an important trading partner, but much of its trade was with those parts of the empire in the Balkans that seceded in the course of the century. Throughout the *Tanzimat* period, an important characteristic of the trade pattern was a large Ottoman trade deficit.

From the Crimean War onwards, European economic involvement in the Ottoman Empire expanded beyond trade into loans. Direct investment in enterprises was not yet important, but lending to the Ottoman government by European banks played a significant, indeed crucial, role.

Financial problems were and remained the Achilles heel of the reforming governments. On the one hand, the modernization drive was expensive. Replacing the old system of fees with salaries increased government expenditure, as did the purchase of military hardware for the new army and – especially – the acquisition of a modern navy. From the later 1860s onwards, the personal extravagances of Sultan Abdülaziz also became increasingly hard to control.

The governments of the *Tanzimat* period no longer tried to cover their deficits by debasing the coinage, as their predecessors had done since the sixteenth century. The reason was that, with the expansion of external trade, the rates of exchange had become much more important, and any debasing of the Ottoman coins was immediately reflected in a drop in its value against the major European currencies.

Local borrowing from Armenian bankers in Galata had been practised for some time, but these banks were relatively small and the rates they charged were high (often as much as 16–18 per cent a year). Therefore, the government had already begun to consider borrowing abroad during the 1840s. In fact, some of the borrowing actually involved Europe, as the Galata banks borrowed abroad part of the money lent to the state. Officially, borrowing abroad began in 1854, when the government faced acute financial difficulties because of expenditure for the Crimean War at a time when the alliance with the two major Western powers made conditions for borrowing on European markets relatively favourable – relatively because the terms under which this and successor loans were given were less attractive than they seemed. The nominal interest rate was always between 4 and 6 per cent, but, apart from the war loan of 1855, which Britain and France guaranteed, the bonds were sold on the European exchanges for prices far below their nominal value, often as low as 60–70 per cent. When the fees and commissions of the international banks were subtracted, the net income for the Ottoman treasury generated by these loans on the average was around 50 per cent of their nominal value. The Ottoman government had to pay back twice the amount it actually received, quite apart from the interest due.[14]

No wonder the loans soon became a millstone around the treasury's neck. In real terms, state income hardly grew and as a result servicing the debt became a serious problem. A default was narrowly avoided in 1861. Debt servicing took up one-third of treasury income by 1870 and this percentage was rising fast. A large part (half to two-thirds) of new borrowing was spent on paying interest and principal on earlier loans.

However attractive the loans might look to a government in need of money, to the bankers who earned huge commissions on them and to the small investors in Europe (most of all in France) as a high-yield investment, it was clear by the 1870s that any serious interruption in the availability of European loans would cause a disaster.

One loan of 1858 was specifically intended to restore stability to the Ottoman monetary system, which was very complicated. The continuous debasing had left in circulation coins with the same nominal value but with different silver contents and therefore different real values. The general lack of specie prevented the complete withdrawal of these coins from the market, even after the government had carried out a general monetary reform in 1844. With this reform, three units were introduced: the Ottoman pound, consisting of five *mecidiye*, each of which was worth 20 *kuruş* (or piastres). The new coins were linked to a mixed gold and silver standard after the example of France. But Ottoman coins were not the only ones in circulation in the empire. One of the results of the irresponsible monetary policies of different Ottoman governments had been that foreign coins, especially the Austrian Maria Theresa *thaler*, the French franc and gold *Napoleon* and the Russian *rouble*, were widely used, not only for foreign trade but also in internal transactions. On top of this, the Ottoman government in 1840 and again in 1847 tried to lessen its financial worries by issuing paper money, called *kaime*. Strictly speaking, these were not banknotes in the modern sense, but rather government bonds carrying an interest of 12.5 per cent, intended for use as legal tender. Confidence in the treasury's ability to pay was so low that *kaime*s were soon being discounted up to 40 per cent against the equivalent in gold and the only way to restore confidence was to withdraw the *kaime* altogether, something that the government, thanks to the 1858 loan, was largely able to do. Printing new *kaime* remained tempting to the Ottoman government however and it actually issued them again in 1861 and 1876. It took until 1885 before the last were withdrawn from the market altogether.[15]

One monetary problem that remained until the end of the empire was the fact that the same coins carried different values at different places within the empire, depending on local demand.

The complex monetary situation made banking a much needed and very profitable enterprise. So much so, in fact, that the rich Armenian, Greek and Jewish bankers showed a marked reluctance to invest in productive enterprises, which needed long-term investments. This was a serious handicap for the development of a capitalist economy in the empire. At the same time, the economic importance of banking was recognized and the government supported its development. In 1856 the Imperial Ottoman Bank was founded, which was to be by far the most important of the banks operating in the empire. At the start, this was a British enterprise, which was only marginally successful, but in 1863 the bank, faced with a challenge from French competitors, was reconstituted as the *Banque imperiale ottomane*, an Anglo-French firm with head-quarters in London and Paris.[16] It was this bank that gained the right to issue Ottoman banknotes later on.

Cultural changes

The period of the *Tanzimat* cannot adequately be understood if it is viewed only in terms of foreign political intervention, administrative reforms or economic incorporation. It was also in a sense a cultural revolution, albeit a limited one. The scribes, who were by now bureaucrats and who came to dominate the state during the *Tanzimat*, were a new breed. Their passport to preferment was their knowledge of Europe and of European languages, which many of them had acquired in the Translation Office and the foreign correspondence offices of the Porte and in the diplomatic service. Their knowledge was new, and so was their style. They wore frock coats and fezzes and liked the company of Europeans, with whom they now mingled frequently. The new lifestyle even affected the sultans, who now attended social and diplomatic gatherings, showed themselves to the population of the capital and even visited adjacent provinces. Sultan Abdülaziz's trip to France and Britain in 1867 was a complete novelty: the first time an Ottoman ruler ever set foot on foreign soil for peaceful purposes!

The best exponents of the bureaucracy, such as the 'father of the reforms', Reşit Pasha, and his pupils Ali Pasha and Fuat Pasha who directed the affairs of the empire in the 1850s and 1860s, the great provincial reformer Mithat Pasha or the legislator and educator Ahmet Cevdet Pasha, were extremely capable figures. But many of the lesser bureaucrats had only a superficial knowledge of the West, combined with a snobbish rejection of traditional Ottoman ways. That they, the representatives of a centralist state that made new demands on its subjects, were at the same time clearly the bearers of an alien culture, made them extremely unpopular in traditional Muslim circles. Westernized Ottoman Christians and certainly foreigners often ridiculed them as Orientals impersonating a civilization they did not understand.

Opposition to the reforms

The reform policies of the *Tanzimat* had never been based on popular demand. They were imposed on Ottoman society because the leading bureaucrats deemed them necessary or because they were forced to act by the representatives of the great powers. Support for the reforms was therefore never broadly based. The Christians of the empire, who might be expected to support them, did so to a certain extent but the reforms did very little to prevent the spread of separatist nationalism among these communities. The Muslim majority over time became more and more antagonized by what many Muslims saw as the surrender of a pre-eminence that their forefathers had established sword in hand. Especially after the edict of 1856, they saw the great pashas of the *Tanzimat* as subservient to the European powers and to the interests of the Christian communities whose wealth and power was rising visibly. A Muslim reaction set in during the 1870s, but this kind of feeling already played an important role in an attempt at a *coup d'état*, which broke out at the *Kuleli* barracks on the Bosphorus in 1859,[17] and also in the communal violence in Syria in 1860.

Another type of opposition to the reforms developed among the reformers themselves. A number of typical representatives of the reformist group of bureaucrats with Western-type training (most of them had served in the translation bureau of the Porte at one time or another) through their knowledge of French had become acquainted with the European currents of thought of their time, notably the ideas of '1848', liberalism and nationalism. They have been described as the pioneers of an Ottoman intelligentsia. They were also people who, after a promising start to their careers in the 1830s and 1840s as protégés of Reşit Pasha, had fallen out with Ali Pasha and Fuat Pasha and had therefore not progressed during the period when these two established their hold on the politics of reform. Because they were excluded from the centre of power, they had to look for other ways to make their mark and some of them found this in a trade that was new to the empire: journalism.

The first Ottoman newspaper, the *Takvim-i Vekai* was started in Sultan Mahmut's days, but was more an official bulletin than a newspaper in the modern sense. The first newspaper in Ottoman Turkish to be privately owned and published was the *Ceride-i Havadis* (Chronicle of Events) in 1840, which was the work of an expatriate Englishman called Churchill. It, too, largely reflected official policies but it gave more room to news about international developments than the government paper. The real beginnings of the Ottoman press can be traced to the early 1860s, when a new paper called the *Tercüman-i Ahval* (Interpreter of Situations) was published, which had as its chief editor, a man called İbrahim Şinasi.

Şinasi was a protégé of Reşit Pasha. He had studied in Paris during, or shortly after, the liberal revolution of 1848 and come back as a convinced modernist, imbued with liberal European ideas. In 1862 he left the *Tercüman-i Ahval* to publish a newspaper of his own, the *Tasvir-i Efkâr* (Illustration of Opinion). It soon became a vehicle for fairly moderate criticism of the government, attacking its authoritarian tendencies and its subservience to the European powers. In 1865 Şinasi, apparently fearing action on the part of the government, suddenly left the country for Paris, leaving his paper in the hands of a young functionary in the Translation Office of the Porte, who had already written a number of articles for his and other papers: Namık Kemal. Under his editorship, the *Tasvir-i Efkâr* became more radical. The editorials started to expound ideas that were to be more fully developed in the late 1860s.

The ideas of Kemal, who was the most articulate of the group of disgruntled young bureaucrats and writers, can best be described as a defence of liberal values with Islamic arguments. Kemal and the other 'Young Ottomans', as they became known, were both pious Muslims and Ottoman patriots, who looked back nostalgically both to a golden era of Islam and to the era of the empire's greatness. They decried the policies of Ali and Fuat Pasha as superficial imitations of Europe without regard for traditional Ottoman and Islamic values, and as subservient to European interests. They also saw the regime of the *Tanzimat* as a one-sided bureaucratic despotism, which had destroyed the older system of checks and balances that had supposedly existed in the empire when the *ulema* still had a more independent and powerful position. They were convinced that the *Tanzimat*'s policies would lead to the destruction of the state. The solution, in their eyes, lay in introducing representative, constitutional and parliamentarian government in the empire, thus instilling a true feeling of citizenship and loyalty to the state among all

Ottoman subjects, Muslim and non-Muslim. Although the empire would be following the example of liberal European states in doing this, the Young Ottomans believed it would at the same time mean a return to the principles of Islamic law, which recognized popular sovereignty. In the eyes of Kemal, the traditional practice of *baya*, for example, the oath of allegiance on the part of the leaders of the Islamic community to a new caliph when he ascended the throne, was essentially the sealing of a social contract between the people and the sovereign.

To expound his ideas to an Ottoman public, Kemal created a new vocabulary giving old words new meanings corresponding to the terminology of nineteenth-century liberalism. *Vatan*, the Arabic word for one's birthplace, became the equivalent of the French *patrie*, *hürriyet* (being a free man, not a slave) that of *liberty*, *millet* (community) that of *nation*. This new terminology would be the ideological instru-mentarium for later generations of Muslim liberals and nationalists.

Kemal did not content himself with public criticism and the exposition of new ideas in the press. He was also one of the six young bureaucrats who, in 1865, founded a secret society called the *İttifak-i Hamiyet* (Alliance of Patriotism), which was modelled on the *Carbonari* in Italy and aimed at the introduction of a patriotic, constitutional and parliamentarian regime. In the course of two years, a few hundred people seem to have joined the society, among them two nephews of the sultan, Prince Murat (the crown prince) and Prince Hamit.

Other members of the opposition movement who later made their mark through their writings in the emerging Ottoman press were Ziya Bey (later Pasha), a former member of the palace secretariat who had lost his position due to pressure from Ali Pasha, and Ali Suavi, a religiously trained teacher and preacher and editor of the short-lived newspaper *Muhbir* (Reporter). Ziya was generally more conservative than Kemal, advocating an Ottoman parliament with limited powers and opposing equal rights for non-Muslims, while Ali Suavi was a radical Muslim fundamentalist.

One more figure was of crucial importance to the opposition movement: Prince Mustafa Fazıl Pasha, a brother of the Egyptian khedive (viceroy) İsmail Pasha and a grandson of Mehmet Ali. Mustafa Fazıl Pasha was already known as a man of liberal opinions, but it was a personal grudge that induced him to take a public stand early in 1867. The succession in Egypt, as in the Ottoman Empire, was ruled by primogeniture and, according to this system, Mustafa Fazıl was next in line of succession, but his brother, the Khedive İsmail, had for some time been pressuring and bribing the Istanbul government to get the order of succession changed in favour of his own son. In 1866 he had finally succeeded in getting an imperial order changing the order of succession. Mustafa Fazıl thereupon took his revenge by leaving for France and sending the sultan an open letter in which he drew attention to the weakness of the Ottoman Empire and mercilessly attacked the government. Around the same time Mustafa Fazıl began to present himself in the European press as the representative of 'Young Turkey'.

The government, which had already introduced a press law and censorship in 1865, grew increasingly irritated by this criticism, notably of its handling of the Cretan crisis. It may also have been aware of the plotting of the *İttifak-i Hamiyet*. When Kemal and his friends printed and distributed Mustafa Fazıl Pasha's open letter to the sultan, it decided to crack down on its critics, sending them into internal exile, in the case of Ziya and Kemal exile disguised as appointments in the provincial administration.

When he heard of this, Mustafa Fazıl Pasha invited them to join him in Paris, which they did. By now they called themselves *Yeni Osmanlılar* (New Ottomans) or, in French, *Jeunes Turcs*, the phrase first used by Mustafa Fazıl. Supported by subsidies from the extremely rich pasha, they continued their broadsides against the policies of Ali Pasha and Fuat Pasha in journals published in London, Paris and Geneva, which reached the empire through the post offices operated by the European powers inside the Ottoman Empire. The most important was *Hürriyet* (Freedom), published by Ziya and Namık Kemal from 1868 onwards, but there were a number of others, often more radical in character. The activities of the Young Ottomans abroad continued even after their patron, Mustafa Fazıl Pasha, had used the occasion of the state visit of Sultan Abdülaziz to France in June 1867 to make his peace with the monarch and return to Istanbul. Before he returned, he made financial arrangements for the survival of the Young Ottoman organs.

He was by no means the last to return to Istanbul. The Young Ottomans were, with the possible exception of Ali Suavi, members of the ruling elite and former civil servants. They identified closely with the state they wanted to save through liberal reforms, and the temptation to return, given a chance to influence policy from within, was always great. Namık Kemal was the second to return, in 1870, and all except two (one of them Ali Suavi) of the Young Ottomans returned after the death of their old enemy Ali Pasha in 1871.

The Young Ottomans were a small group within the ruling elite, whose organized activities spanned no more than five years. They were never tightly organized and the ideas of the individual members of the group differed widely. Nevertheless, their influence in Turkey and beyond has been disproportionate. They certainly influenced, albeit indirectly, the introduction of the Ottoman constitution in 1876, and the Ottoman constitutional movement, which was to oppose the autocratic rule of the sultan after 1878, based itself on their writings. Their line of reasoning, especially that of Namık Kemal, with its attempt to merge European liberalism and Islamic tradition, was taken up by the Islamic modernists later in the century and has remained popular throughout the Islamic world.[18] Apart from their ideas, their major contribution was the creation of a new style of politics. They can be regarded as the first modern ideological movement among the Ottoman elite of the empire, and they were the first who, through their writings, consciously tried to create and influence public opinion, the Ottoman term for which (*Efkâr-i Umumiye*) was also of their making.[19]

6 · The Crisis of 1873–78 and its Aftermath

The Young Ottomans returned to Istanbul motivated by an astonishingly naive belief that with the deaths of Fuat Pasha (in 1869) and Ali Pasha (in 1871), the obstacles to democratic reform would disappear. They soon found out that, quite to the contrary, the death of Ali Pasha was the first stage in a development that in the course of a few years would lead to a crisis of unprecedented proportions in the empire.

A number of developments coincided to cause this crisis. Internationally, the empire's position had begun to change even before Ali Pasha's death. The opening of the Suez Canal in 1869 meant that Egypt, rather than the empire, became the focus of interest for the main liberal powers, France and Britain. The clear and unexpected defeat of France by Prussia in the war of 1870/1 meant a change in the balance of power in Europe; France, the power most closely associated with the Ottoman reformers since the Crimean War, was in temporary eclipse. This in itself strengthened the hand of the partisans of the authoritarian and conservative powers (most of all Russia) in Istanbul. At the same time, the sultan, who had already shown signs of impatience at the way Fuat and Ali kept him out of the conduct of public affairs, used Ali's death to exercise power himself, something for which he was by now ill-suited because of his increasingly idiosyncratic behaviour and emerging megalomania. One way he tried to exercise control was by not letting any official become entrenched in his post, shuffling them around at a frantic pace. The sultan's right-hand man in 1871/2 and 1875/6 was Mahmut Nedim Pasha, who went to extraordinary lengths in seeking the sultan's favour and who was so openly in the pay of the Russian embassy that he earned himself the nickname 'Nedimoff'.[1] Nedim Pasha had no experience of Europe nor did he know a European language and was thus ill equipped to lead the empire in times of crisis.

Economic causes and political effects
The crisis that developed in the 1870s was economic as much as it was

(or became) political. A combination of drought and floods led to a catastrophic famine in Anatolia in 1873 and 1874. This caused the killing-off of livestock and a depopulation of the rural areas through death and migration to the towns. Apart from human misery, the result was a fall in tax income, which the government tried to compensate for by raising taxes on the surviving population, thus contributing to its misery. As had become its practice since the Crimean War, it also looked to the European markets to provide it with loans, but they were not forthcoming. A crash on the international stock exchanges in 1873, which marked the beginning of the 'Great Depression' and which lasted until 1896,[2] made it impossible for dubious debtors like the Ottoman Empire to raise money. As a result, the empire could no longer pay the interest on older loans and had to default on its debt, which by now stood at £200 million.[3]

With the increased pressure of taxation, the unrest in the empire's Balkan provinces (which had not been affected by the famine) escalated into a full-scale rebellion of the Christian peasants, first in Bosnia and Herzegovina, and from April 1876 also in Bulgaria. When Ottoman troops suppressed the rebellion, killing 12,000 to 15,000 Bulgarians,[4] a shock wave swept through Europe, which virtually ignored the large-scale killings of Muslims by Christians that were also part of the picture. Especially in England, where Gladstone's Liberal opposition used the 'Bulgarian Massacres' as propaganda against the Conservative government of Disraeli (which was accused of being pro-Turkish and thus an accessory to the killings), the Turkophile atmosphere, which had prevailed since before the Crimean War, disappeared.

Russia and Austria-Hungary had been involved in intensive discussions on the 'Eastern Question' since late 1875. Austria still regarded the survival of the Ottoman Empire as a vital interest. Besides, its military authorities strongly advocated the occupation of Bosnia-Herzegovina in case Ottoman control there faltered. In Russia, on the other hand, pan-Slav solidarity with the southern Slavs was now widespread and the Russian ambassador in Istanbul, Ignatiev, was an ardent supporter of the movement. The Russian–Austrian discussions resulted in the 'Andrassy note' (called after the Austrian Foreign Minister) of 30 December 1875. This was a set of proposals for far-reaching reforms in Bosnia-Herzegovina under foreign supervision. The Porte accepted it in February, but the rebels refused to give up their fight. A short armistice in April was soon breached.

The constitutional revolution
In this ominous political and financial chaos, a group of leading Ottoman

politicians, including the provincial reformer Mithat Pasha (now minister without portfolio), the Minister of War, Hüseyin Avni Pasha, the director of the military academy, Süleyman Pasha, and the *Şeyhülislam* Hayrullah Efendi, carried out a coup d'état, deposing Sultan Abdülaziz on 30 May 1876. In his place, Crown Prince Murat, who was close to the Young Ottomans and who had been in touch with Mithat Pasha through Namık Kemal and Ziya Pasha, came to the throne as Sultan Murat V.

Before his accession, Murat had promised to promulgate a constitution as soon as possible, and it seemed as if the Young Ottoman programme (constitution and parliament) would now be implemented in full. Namık Kemal and Ziya Pasha were appointed as palace secretaries. Once on the throne, however, Murat listened to Grand Vizier Rüştü Pasha, who urged caution. Instead of a concrete promise of a constitution, as advocated by Mithat Pasha and the Young Ottomans, only a vague statement on reforms was included in the *Hatt-i Humayun* (imperial decree) after Murat's accession.

On 5 June 1876 ex-Sultan Abdülaziz committed suicide. Then, on 15 June, a Circassian army captain called Hasan shot and killed Hüseyin Avni Pasha, Minister of Foreign Affairs Reşit Pasha and several others during a cabinet meeting. This changed the balance of power in favour of the more radical reformers. On 15 July the first meeting of the new Grand Council decided to proclaim a constitution. His act was motivated by personal grievances (his elder sister was one of the concubines of Sultan Abdülaziz) but this could not be carried through, however, because of the rapidly deteriorating mental state of Sultan Murat.

Murat, who was by now an alcoholic, had shown signs of extreme nervousness when he was taken from the palace on the night of 30 May to take the oath of allegiance from the high dignitaries of state at the Porte (he was convinced that he was being taken to his execution).[5] The suicide of his uncle and the murder of several members of his cabinet seem to have led to a severe nervous breakdown. After having the sultan examined by Ottoman and foreign medical experts, the cabinet had to conclude that he was unfit to rule. It first tried to get his younger brother, Hamit Efendi, to act as regent, but when he refused had no choice but to depose Murat and replace him with Hamit, who ascended the throne as Abdülhamit II on 1 September 1876. Murat was taken to the Çirağan palace on the Bosphorus, where he was to live in captivity for nearly 30 years.

The Bulgarian crisis escalates: war with Russia
Meanwhile, the situation in the Balkans had gone from bad to worse.

Serbia had declared war on the empire on 30 June 1876 but, faced with the superior strength of the Ottoman army, it had to sue for an armistice by September. By this time, however, pan-Slav feeling in Russia had reached a fever pitch. Disappointed in Serbia, the Russian pan-Slavists now concentrated on the Bulgarians and the Russian government put pressure on Istanbul to introduce wide-ranging reforms and virtual autonomy in the areas inhabited by Bulgarians, threatening war if its demands were not met. Britain tried to defuse the growing crisis by proposing an international conference on the Balkans. When the conference met for the first time, in Istanbul on 23 December 1876, the delegates were startled by the Ottoman delegate's announcement that a constitution had now been promulgated. It was based primarily on the Belgian constitution of 1831, but a number of its articles (or omissions) gave it a more authoritarian character and left the sultan important prerogatives, which he was later to use to the detriment of the constitutional government. The authoritarian traits of the constitution were modelled after the Prussian constitution of 1850.

The promulgation of the constitution, from the Ottoman standpoint, made all discussions of reforms in the Christian areas of the empire superfluous, since all subjects were now granted constitutional rights. The Porte rejected all further proposals by the powers. As a result the conference failed and on 24 April 1877 Russia declared war, having first bought Austria's neutrality by agreeing to its occupation of Bosnia and Herzegovina. At first the Russian armies met little resistance, but then they were unexpectedly checked at Plevna in Bulgaria, where the Ottomans withstood a number of Russian assaults from May until December.

When the Russians finally broke through it meant the end of effective Ottoman resistance and, by the end of February, the Russians were at San Stefano (modern Yeşilköy), only 12 kilometres outside Istanbul. On 3 March 1878 a peace treaty was signed there, which was an unmitigated disaster for the Ottomans. It included the creation of a large autonomous Bulgarian state between the Aegean and the Black Sea, enormous territorial gains for Montenegro (which became three times its prewar size) and smaller ones for Serbia. Serbia, Montenegro and Romania became independent. Far-reaching reforms were to be carried through in Thessalia and Epirus. In Asia, Batum, Kars, Ardahan and Doğubeyazit were ceded to Russia and reforms were to be introduced in Armenia. Furthermore, the new Bulgarian state was to remain under Russian occupation for two years. Obviously, it remained under Russian influence even after that period.

The signing of the treaty produced the shock effect needed to prod the other European powers, notably Austria and Britain, into action, not because of any sympathy for the Ottomans, but because Russian domination of the Balkans and Asia Minor was unacceptable if the European balance of power was to remain in force. Pressure and sabre-rattling on the part of Austria and Britain led to the holding of a conference in Berlin in June 1878, to find an acceptable solution to the 'Eastern crisis' as the 'Eastern Question' had now become. It was to be the last in the series of great conferences attended by all the major European powers, which had started in Vienna in 1814. Needless to say, the influence of the Balkan peoples and governments at the conference was negligible.

The end result of the conference, the Treaty of Berlin, mitigated, but did not nullify, the provisions of San Stefano. Romania, Serbia and Montenegro still gained their independence, but the territorial gains of the latter two were much reduced. An autonomous Bulgaria was created, but it was much smaller than originally envisaged and it was split in two along the Balkan mountain ridge, the southern part remaining an Ottoman province under a special regime with a Christian governor. In Asia, most of Russia's acquisitions, including the port of Batum, remained in place. Moreover, both Austria and Britain had exacted a price for their intervention – Austria now occupied Bosnia-Herzegovina (which technically remained part of the Ottoman Empire) and Britain did the same with Cyprus. The sultan had no choice but to acquiesce.

7 · Reactionary Despotism or Culmination of the Reforms? The Reign of Sultan Abdülhamit II

By the time the Treaty of Berlin (1878) had been signed, the internal political situation in Istanbul had changed radically. As foreseen in the constitution, elections for an Ottoman parliament had been held in December 1876 and January 1877 and the parliament had been opened officially on 19 March. The provincial and county councils, and not the people, had elected the 130 representatives. Popular interest in the proceedings was almost totally absent and in some places there is evidence that appointments by the governor took the place of elections.[1] Nevertheless, the parliament, or rather the elected second chamber of the parliament, held two sessions during which its members acquitted themselves well. In spite of their inexperience and the lack of representative traditions in the empire, many members genuinely tried to represent the views of their constituencies responsibly. The parliament almost totally failed in its legislative functions, partly because the constitution allowed the sultan and his ministers to govern by decree, but it was an effective forum for criticism of the government's conduct of affairs – so effective and irritating, in fact, that on 14 February 1878 (with the Russian army almost at the gates of Istanbul and public criticism of the government mounting), the sultan prorogued it indefinitely.

This, to all intents and purposes meant the end of the constitutional regime and, from this time on, Sultan Abdülhamit II not only reigned but also ruled as an absolute monarch for 30 years (although the pretence of an imminent return to constitutional rule was kept up until 1880 and the constitution was never actually abolished).[2] His rule has been the subject of great controversy. Nineteenth-century Europeans came to see him, especially towards the end of his rule, as a bloodthirsty and reactionary tyrant. The bloody repression of the Armenians in the 1890s was instrumental in forming this image. The historians of the Turkish republic, which itself was the legacy of the Young Turks who forced Abdülhamit from power in 1908/9, likewise see him as a reactionary, who for a generation halted the regeneration of the empire. Modern historians of Turkey since the 1960s have drawn a different picture, emphasizing the way in which his reign marked a continuation, or even the culmination, of the *Tanzimat* and the benefits it brought to the empire and its population.[3] Among Islamic conservatives in Turkey (who have become the dominant current over the last 15 years) Abdülhamit is seen as an exemplary figure: the last truly powerful Islamic prince who was at the same time caliph.

Elements of continuity

The administrative centralization, which was the principal theme of the *Tanzimat* reforms, was only brought to fruition in the era of Abdülhamit, aided by a spectacular development of the means of communication in the empire. The most important was the telegraph. The first telegraph lines had been laid down during the Crimean War, connecting Istanbul to the European system. Thereafter, the network spread rapidly and in the era of Abdülhamit it reached every provincial town, thus giving the central government the means effectively to communicate with and exert control over its servants in the provinces for the first time. A well-trained army of telegraph operators came into being and, unlike the shipping lines and railways, the telegraph network from the beginning was in the hands of the state.

Railway construction, requiring as it does much greater investment, was far slower to develop, but still the mileage was greatly extended in these years. French and British companies had built the first railways in the Ottoman Empire. They consisted of short stretches connecting the agricultural hinterland with the main ports. The line from İzmit to Haydarpaşa (opposite Istanbul on the Asiatic side of the Bosphorus) was opened in 1873, as was the Bursa–Mudanya line. The lines running east from İzmir into the fertile valleys of the Lesser and Greater Menderes were even older, having been started in 1866. In the 1880s and 1890s, these few hundred miles of track were increased to several thousand. The French and British constructed railways inland from the Syrian and Palestinian coasts from 1888 onwards. Macedonia was connected to the capital, as was the interior of Anatolia with the building (by a German company) of the Anatolian railway, which reached Ankara in 1892 and Konya four years later. In 1903 a concession was granted to a German company to extend the line from Konya to the east, to Baghdad and Basra. This was the famous 'Baghdad railway', which caused a great deal of tension between the great powers in the years before the First World War. These lines were not simply connections between a productive area and the nearest port; they were powerful instruments for integration and central control (making possible, for instance, the faster movement of troops).

The railways caused a transport revolution. Before they were built, four-wheeled carts had been used in the Balkans, but these were unknown in Anatolia until the influx of refugees from the Balkans after 1877. In the Asiatic provinces freight was carried on the back of animals, particularly camels. Camels could carry up to 250 kilos and travel a distance of 25 kilometres per day. Transport was expensive. The costs of a caravan of camels doubled every hundred kilometres or four days. Now, a single railway box car could carry the load of 30–40 camels and move it with a speed of 25 kilometres an hour.

A similar transport revolution took place at sea. From the late 1870s onwards, steamships began to dominate the long-distance traffic in the eastern Mediterranean. In 1860, 75 per cent of the ships that docked in Istanbul or Izmir were sailing ships. In 1900 there were more sailing ships in absolute numbers, but their tonnage was only 5 per cent of the total. All the rest was steam. At the same time ships became much bigger. Average tonnage went from 100 for a sailing vessel to 1,000 for a steamship. The steamship made travel times predictable. In the early nineteenth century, a voyage from Istanbul to Venice could take 15, but also 80 days, depending on the prevailing winds. Now the journey was not only shorter, but also roughly of the same duration, which made possible the publication of timetables.[4] Like the railway companies, the steamship companies were almost exclusively foreign owned, except for the lines in and around the capital. In combination with the railway lines connecting the ports to the productive hinterland, the steamships speeded up the integration into the capitalist system of some areas and some sectors of the Ottoman economy. In terms of travelling time and economic activity, such areas were now more closely linked to European ports like Marseilles or Trieste than to places in the interior only a hundred miles away.

These improved technical means made the administration more efficient in collecting taxes, conscripting armies and keeping law and order. In addition, by the 1880s the modern schools had at last begun to turn out sufficient numbers of graduates to staff the bureaucracy at different levels. Both the number of schools and that of students more than doubled between 1867 and 1895, although the ratio of students to the population remained much higher among the Christian communities than among the Muslims. Improved education led to increased literacy, creating a market for the Ottoman press, which expanded rapidly under Abdülhamit in terms of both the number of publications and circulation figures.

In the years 1880–1900 the state also became much more visible in a literal sense. Every provincial capital and many district capitals acquired the typical buildings of the Hamidian period: barracks, schools, administrative buildings and clock towers that now showed uniform time all over the empire, both according to the European clock and according to the Ottoman one.

Contrasts with the preceding era

The press is the one area that clearly revealed the Hamidian era as both a continuation of the *Tanzimat* and a break with the past. Newspapers, when compared with the pioneering efforts of the 1860s, were now more professional and reached a much larger public. Between 1876 and 1888, nine to ten new periodicals appeared in Istanbul each year. When strict censorship was introduced in 1888, this number dropped to one a year on average. The censors now prohibited any discussion of political matters, especially anything related to liberalism, nationalism or constitutionalism. Debarred from discussing current affairs in any meaningful way, the newspapers and periodicals filled their pages with encyclopaedic articles about science, geography, history and technology and with literature. In this way, they served to acquaint the Ottoman reading public (still only a fraction of the population) with the outside world. The most important newspapers in Istanbul had a circulation of between 12,000 and 15,000 and of 30,000 on special occasions. The number of readers was far higher, however. This was due to the new fashion of the *kiraathane* that started in the 1870s. This 'reading house' was a coffee house that offered its guests all the important newspapers to read, while they were enjoying a cup of coffee or a hookah.[5]

The press of the period also shows the fundamental ideological switch of the regime, which represents a clear break with the preceding era. Not only was the sultan deeply opposed to what he saw as the disruptive forces of liberalism, nationalism and constitutionalism (Ali Pasha and Fuat Pasha in their time had been opposed to these movements too), but also he tried to counter them by emphasizing the traditional and Islamic character of his reign. This trend had already started in the last years of Abdülaziz, but more than any sultan before him, Abdülhamit appealed to Muslim solidarity, using the title and symbols of the caliphate. Not only was his choice informed by a desire to find a counterweight to disruptive ideologies but also it accurately reflected the new situation of the empire, which had become more Asiatic in terms of territory and more Muslim in terms of population as a result of the losses of 1878.[6]

The Islam the sultan supported was that of the more conservative *ulema* and *Sufi* sheikhs with whom he surrounded himself. Islamic modernists do not seem to have enjoyed much support at court. While foreign observers and members of the Christian communities saw it as an atavistic return to fanaticism, the appeal to Islam did strike a chord with Muslims inside and outside the empire who felt threatened by European imperialism and by the privileged position of the Christians. The greatest monument to the Islamist policies of Abdülhamit was the Hijaz railway from Damascus to Medina, built between 1901 and 1908 largely from voluntary contributions in order to serve pilgrims to Mecca.[7]

State ideology was not the only field in which the era of Abdülhamit differed from that of the *Tanzimat*. In the latter era, under weak sultans and strong pashas, the centre of power had been very much at the Porte, with the highest-ranking bureaucrats, but the relationship between the Porte and the palace had never been sufficiently defined and now, with a determined sultan at the top, the centre of power emphatically shifted back to the palace, where it had been under Mahmut II. The palace secretariat, the *Mabeyn* (intermediate office), already enlarged under Abdülaziz in his later years, grew into a formidable bureaucracy. At its summit stood the palace marshal. Until his death in 1897 this was *Gazi* (Hero) Osman Pasha, the defender of Plevna in the 1877 war, an authoritarian and conservative figure who for 20 years was the greatest power behind the throne. Some of the great bureaucrats of Abdül-hamit's era, such as *Küçük* (Little) Sait Pasha (grand vizier no less than seven times) and *Kıbrıslı* (Cypriot) Kâmil Pasha, were no less competent than the leaders of the *Tanzimat*, but their subservience to the palace meant that they never gained the same stature.

In a system as autocratic as this, the sultan's personality was of great importance and, through the 1880s and 1890s, this increasingly became a problem. In his younger years Abdülhamit (who was 34 when he ascended the throne) was frugal, hard-working and intelligent. But his background in Ottoman court politics, and especially the events of 1876, which had brought him to the throne, left him feeling insecure and suspicious of his servants. After all, if they could depose Abdülaziz and Murat, why not him? Over the years, this suspicion and his natural desire to remain master in his own house grew into a fear of grotesque proportions. The result was that the sultan came to rely more and more on the internal espionage networks he built up, with people of all ranks being encouraged to report on the activities of others. Tens of thousands of so-called *jurnal*s or reports accumulated in the archives of Abdülhamit's *Yıldız* (Star) palace.

With loyalty to his person becoming the sultan's overriding concern, the way was open to large-scale corruption and favouritism, something for which the vastly overstaffed government departments offered ample scope. In every department rational and efficient exercise of its functions was impaired: the navy was not allowed to leave its docks in the Golden Horn for fear it might train its guns on the palace; the army had to conduct its musketry training without bullets. The sultan was well aware of the liberal leanings of many of the graduates from the great military colleges. He therefore tended to rely on – and give preferment to – officers who had risen from the ranks and who had no inkling of modern military science (some of them were illiterate). Within the army, a sharp divide developed between the *mektepli* (from the school) and *alaylı* (from the ranks) officers. Demoralization within the army and the bureaucracy, especially among younger members, gradually became a serious problem. It is in this respect that the Hamidian era was not only a continuation of the *Tanzimat* but also its caricature.

To judge the character and the achievements of the Hamidian era, it is first of all necessary to realize that it was for a long time a period of recovery from a crisis that had come close to putting an end to the Ottoman Empire. The events of 1877/8 were a disaster for the empire. The loss of territory even after the Berlin conference was enormous, including as it did Romania, Serbia, Montenegro, Bosnia-Herzegovina, Bulgaria, Thessalia, parts of Anatolia and Cyprus, all in all about a third of the empire's territory and over 20 per cent of its population.

The disaster was not limited to a military, political or financial one; it was also a tragedy in human terms. Immigration of Muslims into the empire had been a feature of Ottoman life since the late eighteenth century. It was caused by the expansion of the Russian Empire along the shores of the Black Sea and in the Caucasus. After the Russian conquest of the Crimea (1771) and again after the Crimean War (1854–1856) large numbers, possibly up to half a million, of Muslim Tatars had migrated from the northern shore of the Black Sea. More to the east the Russians had been able to incorporate the uplands of the Caucasus in 1864, after a long struggle against Circassian guerilla groups. Again, many Muslims, sometimes including whole tribes, preferred migrating to the Ottoman lands to living under Christian rulers. Sometimes the Russian army and Georgian and Cossack bands had terrorized them into leaving. The total number of refugees from the Caucasus has been estimated as high as two million.[8]

The areas lost to the empire in central Europe up to now had not as a rule had large Muslim populations. In 1878, for the first time, areas where a considerable part of the population was Muslim and Turkish came under foreign occupation, a foreign occupation, moreover, that turned a blind eye to, or even assisted in, wholesale killings of Muslim villagers. The result was that about a million people were uprooted. Many of these returned home after the war, but about 500,000 became refugees (*muhacir*) permanently. Some 260,000 people died from diseases or hunger.[9] As many as 260,000 were killed or died of disease and starvation. Many of the survivors ended up in Istanbul, but many more were resettled in Anatolia, the Ottoman Balkans, Crete and even Syria, often with great difficulty, contributing to the anti-Christian feeling that became such a force in the late nineteenth century.

The international situation
The basic problems facing the Ottoman government were the same as earlier in the century – a combination of emerging nationalism among the different communities and pressure on the part of the great powers. What made the situation different was that these powers were now locked in an increasingly bitter inter-imperialist struggle, which enabled the Ottomans to play them off against each other more successfully than in the old days of the 'Concert of Europe'. The Ottoman government had very few other cards to play. One was the threat to arouse Muslim feelings of solidarity around the world, especially in the French, British and Russian empires. Many politicians of the great powers felt that this so-called pan-Islamic policy was a bluff, but they were never quite sure, and the colonial administrators of, for instance, India generally took the threat seriously. In fact, the future showed that the sultan did command a certain loyalty among Muslims outside the empire. The growth of communications (like for instance the steamships that now carried much larger numbers of pilgrims to Mecca) had increased contacts within the Islamic world and stimulated feelings of Muslim solidarity. The future would also show that converting these feelings into effective political or even military support was beyond the means of the Ottomans.

Within the international situation the role of the different powers changed. France, the dominant influence in Istanbul in the late 1850s and 1860s was still recovering from the blow of the lost war with Prussia and, in its search for revenge, also improved its relations with Russia, the arch-enemy of the Ottomans. For Britain, Egypt and Cyprus were now the main cards to play in the Levant, especially after the purchase of the Khedive İsmail's shares in the Suez Canal. Its occupation of Egypt in 1882 seriously strained relations with the Porte (after all Egypt was still nominally part of the Ottoman Empire). Its place in Istanbul was taken to a large extent by the growing influence of Germany, which the Ottomans saw as the least threatening of the European imperialist powers (and the only one not to have colonized Muslim lands). The Germans for their part saw prospects for the creation of a German sphere of economic and military influence in the Ottoman Empire. German military advisers, notably General von der Goltz, trained the Ottoman army and German military doctrine spread among the younger members of the Ottoman officer corps. German economic and diplomatic influence also steadily grew. The Germans supported the sultan's pan-Islamic policies. During his well-publicized state visit to the empire in 1898, Kaiser Wilhelm II declared himself 'the friend of the world's 300 million Muslims'.[10]

Intercommunal tensions and conflicts

The international situation thus prevented the great powers from effectively intervening in the communal conflicts of the empire. The two most intractable of these were the Macedonian and the Armenian problems. The area shown as Macedonia on European maps (actually the Ottoman provinces of Salonica, Kosovo and Manastır) had been largely incorporated into the new Bulgaria at San Stefano, but after the Conference of Berlin it had remained in the empire. Emerging nationalism caused more problems in Macedonia than anywhere else because of the composition of its population, which included Serbs, Bulgarians, Greeks, Vlahs and people who regarded themselves as a separate Macedonian nation. All of these were Orthodox Christians, but there were also large Muslim Albanian and Turkish minorities, as well as Jews. These groups' competing nationalist aspirations, and the struggle between Bulgarians and Greeks for control of the Orthodox Church, made the situation in Macedonia unmanageable. Secret committees used terrorism and guerrilla tactics to provoke the intervention of the powers. Most active among these was the Internal Macedonian Revolutionary Organization (IMRO), founded in Salonica in 1893, which wanted autonomy. There were also groups that strove for incorporation in Bulgaria.

The relationship between Bulgarians and Greeks was tense since the Ottomans, after long hesitations, had decided in 1870 to allow the foundation of a separate Bulgarian Orthodox church, the so-called Exarchate. Until then all Orthodox Christians, whatever their ethnicity, were under the sway of the patriarchate of Constantinople, which was completely dominated by Greeks. The founding of the exarchate was the fulfillment of Bulgarian nationalist dreams, but tore apart Macedonian society, as every village and every ward now had to decide whether it wanted to be Greek or Bulgarian. The stakes were high, because the Ottomans awarded the church possessions to the majority. Greek and Bulgarian militias exercised a bloody terror in the countryside to have the local population choose 'their' church, and by that act define themselves forever as Greeks or Bulgarians. The powers tried to intervene in the usual way, proposing reforms and a measure of autonomy under foreign control, but were thwarted by Ottoman procrastination and their own rivalry.

The other great communal problem was that of the Armenians. The Armenians, divided over a large Gregorian and smaller Protestant and Catholic *millet*s, constituted a sizeable minority in six of the eastern provinces of Ottoman Anatolia. Most of them were peasants in areas dominated by Turcoman and Kurdish tribes. Over the centuries they had migrated along the major east–west trade routes of Anatolia, so that by the nineteenth century there were also important Armenian settlements in many of the major Anatolian towns and in Istanbul itself. In the towns of Anatolia they were important as craftsmen and traders. The new nationalist ideology began to be felt among the Armenians in the 1870s. An Armenian delegation had demanded reforms in the eastern provinces of Anatolia under foreign control at the Conference of Berlin but only Russia had offered it lukewarm support. Article 61 of the Berlin Treaty stipulated that the Ottoman government would carry out reforms and guarantee the security of the Armenians, but there was no real control mechanism foreseen.

Then, in 1887 Armenian students in Geneva formed a radical nationalist organization called *Henchak* (the Bell), which was followed by a more moderate and larger social-democrat organization called *Dashnakzoutiun* (Armenian Revolutionary Federation), founded in Tiflis in 1890. These committees aimed at Armenian independence or at least far-reaching autonomy in both the Ottoman and the Russian Empire (something the majority of the Armenian community, especially the wealthier members, did not yet contemplate) and they aimed at attracting worldwide attention through terrorist attacks.

The government reacted by enrolling Kurdish tribes in new irregular regiments modelled on the Russian Cossack troops, the so-called *Hamidiye* units. In autumn 1894 a series of incidents led to a large-scale slaughter of Armenians by *Hamidiye* troops in the district of Sasun. A storm of indignation swept over Europe, but tentative negotiations between the great powers about how to force the Ottoman government to introduce reforms in the east failed because of inter-power rivalry. In 1895 and 1896 there were again widespread massacres in the east and now also in Istanbul, where an Armenian group occupied the headquarters of the Ottoman Bank and threatened to blow it up. Again, the powers did nothing effective. After 1896, the Ottoman government gradually re-established control and the fighting died down.

While Ottoman prestige in Europe was at its lowest due to the Armenian massacres, Ottoman self-confidence was suddenly raised in the spring of 1897, when the empire declared war on Greece (which had been openly supporting a new Cretan rebellion) and defeated it within weeks. The Ottomans were prevented from keeping their conquests by the European powers but Greece had to pay a large indemnity and cease supporting the rebellion. This latter point could be conceded fairly easily, as by this time England, France, Russia and Italy had jointly occupied Crete and appointed the crown prince of Greece as its governor. From then on, Crete was just as Ottoman as Eastern Rumelia (that was governed by the Bulgarian king as Ottoman governor) or Egypt (that was run by the British with a khedive – an Ottoman governor – as its titular head).

None of the problems with the nationalities (Macedonia, Armenia, Crete) had been solved, but after 1896 the acute political crises seemed to be defused somewhat and the Hamidian regime enjoyed relative stability for another decade.

Finance and economics

As problematic as the political situation Abdülhamit inherited was the financial situation. The state had defaulted on its debt in 1875 and the war against Russia had brought with it enormous expenses, so the empire was essentially bankrupt and its credit and credibility in the European financial markets, which were anyway much more tightfisted in the current depression, were completely gone. Negotiations about the debt crisis started as soon as peace was restored in 1878 and a solution was worked out gradually over the next few years.

As had earlier been the case in Tunisia and in Egypt, the solution was found in the creation, under the *Muharram* (a month in the Muslim calendar) decree of 1881, of a Public Debt Administration (the *Caisse de la Dette Publique Ottomane*), which was governed by a board on which sat representatives of the holders of Ottoman government bonds in Europe. At the same time, half of the outstanding debt of the empire was rescinded. The PDA built up a modern bureaucracy, which would eventually have more than 5000 employees, through which it directly managed a number of revenue sources, such as the tribute of some provinces, the salt and tobacco monopolies and taxes on things as diverse as silk, spirits and fisheries. After deduction of costs, these revenues were used for the servicing of the public debt. The PDA was much more efficient as a tax collector than the government and it controlled roughly one-third of regular state income. Over time this share grew as every time the empire contracted new loans, it had to mortgage new sources of tax income.

For a long time Abdülhamit's government borrowed very little abroad and paid off more of its old debt than it raised in new loans. Only at the beginning of the twentieth century did the pace of new borrowing accelerate. The growth of international trade, too, was slow in the first 20 years of the sultan's reign, which coincided with the 'Great Depression' in Europe. From 1896 onwards, the growth of trade resumed, in line with the recovery in the industrial economies of Europe, albeit at a slower rate than had been the case in 1830–75.[11]

The years 1888–96 saw the first wave of direct investment by foreign companies in the empire, most of it (two-thirds) in railways. This boom was partly motivated by profit seeking (especially since the Ottoman government was persuaded to give a kilometric guarantee payment that eliminated all real risk for the builders), but also to a large extent by the inter-imperialist rivalry and the desire to create spheres of influence around the new railways. After 1896, foreign investment contracted sharply. It picked up again at a much slower pace after 1905.

Britain remained the major trading partner of the Ottoman Empire, as it had been since the start of the century, taking about a quarter of all Ottoman exports (mainly agricultural produce) and delivering between 30 and 40 per cent of its imports. In investment, however, the British firms, which were much less strongly supported by their government than their continental counterparts, lost out to France and, especially, Germany. Britain's share of total investment fell from over 50 per cent to under 20 per cent during this period, while German investment increased sharply from around 1 per cent to over 25 per cent. It was France, however, that became the major investor, increasing its share from approximately 30 to 50 per cent.[12]

The traditional handicraft industry of the empire had been and continued to be severely affected by cheap industrial imports, especially in the coastal regions. At the same time, some industrial sectors restructured themselves and survived and some entirely new ones sprang up. By and large, these new industries (such as the silk factories built in Bursa by Armenian entrepreneurs, the carpet-making industry in Uşak that worked primarily for the American market, breweries, tobacco and tile manufacturers in Salonica) were based on extremely cheap non-guild labour, often women and children, working in small establishments.[13] Over 90 per cent of the industrial establishments with more than ten workers were owned by non-Muslims.

The growth of the new industries and the direct involvement of modern European companies created tensions in Ottoman society. The Ottoman authorities had traditionally protected the urban guilds. Now the authorities were often caught between the imperatives of rational practices, as the foreign companies understood them, and the traditional demands of the hard-pressed guilds. This was visible in the ports, for instance, where the construction of new quays made the many lightermen who had transferred passengers and goods between the ships and the land redundant.

The Young Turk movement

As we have seen, relations between the government and the Christian communities, especially the Armenians, grew more and more strained as the years wore on, but the sultan was not unpopular with the large majority of the empire's Muslim population. Nor was there any reason he should be because, while it would be an exaggeration to say that the peasants of the empire were well off, at least they were largely spared the major disasters of war, famine and epidemics. Bubonic plague had ceased to be a major problem by the middle of the century and typhoid and cholera receded after 1880. As a result, during Abdülhamit's reign, the population of the empire increased from about 20 million in the late 1870s to more than 27 million by the end of the century (without counting Cyprus or Egypt) – an increase of 37 per cent. In Anatolia the population grew even faster, by almost 50 per cent.[14]

Abdülhamit's major weakness was his failure to instil loyalty in the new generations of bureaucrats and officers, the Ottoman intelligentsia, which his own expanded educational institutions were producing. While it could be argued that his government succeeded remarkably well in keeping the remains of the empire intact, like the Austro-Hungarian Empire of his contemporary Francis Joseph II, it completely failed to provide inspiration and a sense of direction to its own servants.

The new generations being trained in schools like the *Mülkiye* and *Harbiye* (War Academy) continued to be attracted by the liberal and constitutional ideas, as well as the Ottoman patriotism, of the Young Ottomans, whose books they read and discussed clandestinely.

Directly after the suspension of parliament, there had been two armed attempts to remove Abdülhamit and replace him with Murat V, who was rumoured to have recovered completely. Former Young Ottoman Ali Suavi led one of the attempts, and Masonic friends of the former sultan another. Both failed. The next ten years saw no organized action of any significance, but in the schools low-level agitation continued despite tight government control. The first organized opposition group seems to have been established in the Military Medical College in 1889, when four students founded the *İttihad-i Osmani Cemiyeti* (Ottoman Unity Society), which aimed to reinstate the constitution and parliament. Interestingly, the four included an Albanian, a Kurd and a Circassian. Over the next few years this society slowly grew. Some of its members were arrested by the sultan's police and some managed to escape arrest by fleeing abroad, mostly to Paris, but also to Cairo and Athens. In Paris they found a small circle of Ottoman constitutionalist *émigrés*, who attacked the sultan in pamphlets and periodicals. The leading figure in this circle was Ahmet Rıza, son of a member of the Ottoman parliament and himself a former director of education in Bursa. The plotters in Istanbul approached Ahmet Rıza who agreed to accept the leadership of the organization in Europe in 1895. Rıza, who was a positivist, tried to have the society renamed the 'Society for Order and Progress' (the positivist motto), but this was rejected by the Istanbul group. Instead, the society was now renamed *İttihat ve Terakki Cemiyeti* (Society, or Committee of Union and Progress, CUP). The 'union' in its name of course referred to the unity of the (ethnic) elements, the old ideal of the Young Ottomans. Under Ahmet Rıza's leadership the Paris branch now published the newspaper *Meşveret* (Consultation), in both Ottoman and French, from 1895 onwards. In France the group called itself *Jeunes Turcs* (Young Turks), much as the Young Ottomans had done thirty years earlier.[15]

During the years of the Armenian crisis (1894–96) when Abdül-hamit's government became ever more unpopular and isolated internationally, CUP membership suddenly increased rapidly. The Istanbul branch of the Committee tried to organize a coup d'état in September 1896, but the plans were betrayed on the eve of its execution and the conspirators arrested. Most of them were sent into internal exile.[16]

The constitutional movement within the empire had received a serious setback and for the next ten years the centre of gravity of the opposition moved to the groups in Europe. From time to time Young Turks who had managed to flee from their places of exile joined them. Their arrival usually meant a new impetus for the movement. It also meant rivalry, because not all the Young Turks were prepared to follow Ahmet Rıza's lead, mainly because as a convinced positivist he went much further in his rejection of religion than most Young Turks were prepared to go. They were all of them influenced by European currents such as scientism, materialism and social Darwinism, but not positivists in the strict sense of belonging to the 'Church of Humanity'. Personality also played a part: Ahmet Rıza seems to have been an uncompromising and difficult man.

The first major challenge to Rıza's leadership was the arrival in Paris in 1896 of *Mizancı* Murat Bey, a former teacher at the *Mülkiye* who had become famous as editor of the liberal paper *Mizan* (Balance), first in Istanbul and then, in 1895, in Cairo. Although a liberal, Murat attached much greater importance to the caliphate and to the Islamic character of the empire than did Rıza. In this he was more in tune with the majority of the movement, which elected him president of the CUP in Ahmet Rıza's place after his arrival in Paris. Early in 1897, Murat and a group of followers moved the headquarters of the CUP to Geneva.

Six months later, however, Sultan Abdülhamit made use of his increased prestige (with the worst of the Armenian troubles over and the war against Greece of that year won) to deal with the internal and external opposition. In the capital, all known Young Turks were rounded up and after a mock trial sent into internal exile in Tripolitania, while at the same time agents of the sultan managed to persuade *Mizancı* Murat and a number of other prominent Young Turks to return to 'help him in his reforms'. Even though the CUP tried to portray this agreement as a truce, the credibility of many of the Young Turk leaders was destroyed when they accepted sinecures in Abdülhamit's government or diplomatic service. Their attitude vindicated Ahmet Rıza, who was now once again the undisputed leader of the movement in exile. But the movement had been dealt a serious blow, and the years 1897–99 were its nadir.

In December 1899 the movement received new impetus with the arrival in Paris of a rich Ottoman prince, Mahmut Celâlettin Pasha (a half-brother of the sultan), who had fled to France with his two sons, Sabahattin and Lutfullah. Until his death three years later, the pasha's role among the Young Turks was similar to that played by Mustafa Fazıl Pasha a generation earlier among the Young Ottomans. At the same time his elder son, Sabahattin, posed the most serious threat yet to Ahmet Rıza's authority. Sabahattin was unusual among the Young Turks in that he saw the engine for change and progress, not in the state, but in the individual, believing in minimal government and the power of free enterprise to regenerate the empire, while Ahmet Rıza was becoming more and more of an Ottoman nationalist. Between them they split the movement and this split became manifest at the first 'Congress of Ottoman Liberals', organized in Paris in 1902.

The reader should be aware of what the term 'liberal' actually meant in this context. The Young Turks were democrats only in a limited sense, even if they fought for the restoration of parliament against an autocratic sultan. Their allies in France were representatives of right-of-centre movements, mostly nationalist liberals who had been traumatized both by the loss of the Franco–Prusssian war and by the Paris commune of 1871. Like their French examples, the Young Turks were attracted by positivism (which in itself was elitist and authoritarian) and particularly by the works of Gustave Le Bon, whose ideas on crowd psychology were fed by a strong mistrust of popular movements.[17] The circles in which Prince Sabahettin moved, were a lot more right wing. They consisted of

French catholic aristocrats who idealized the role of the British aristocracy in creating and ruling a world empire. It is significant that none of the Young Turks felt seriously attracted by socialism, even though they must have witnessed the growth of socialist movements in Europe. This was an important difference with the Armenian nationalist movements, which were both nationalist and socialist.

At the congress, many nationalities of the empire were represented. The majority, including the Armenian organizations and Sabahattin's group, declared that both violence and foreign intervention in the empire were permissible as means to remove Abdülhamit. Ahmet Rıza rejected both, fearing for the empire's independence. After the congress, the split was formalized when the prince founded first the 'Society of Ottoman Liberals' and then in 1906 the *Teşebbüs-ü Şahsi ve Adem-i Merkeziyet Cemiyeti* (Society for Private Initiative and Decentralization). In line with the decisions of the congress, Sabahattin's faction attempted to organize a military coup d'état with the help of the Ottoman garrison in Tripolitania, but this remained stillborn.

For the more nationalist and centralist wing of the movement led by Ahmet Rıza, 1905 and 1906 were crucial years. Both Ottoman nationalism and constitutionalism received a boost from the outcome of the Russo–Japanese war of 1904/5 and its aftermath, the first Russian revolution. In the war, an Asiatic state had for the first time defeated one of the great imperial powers of Europe. Japan now became a role model for many Young Turks. Furthermore, in the following unrest in Russia, the tsar had been forced to grant Russia a legislative assembly and a measure of constitutionalism. Shortly after, in 1906, even backward Persia underwent a constitutional revolution. These events inspired the Ottoman opposition movement. At the same time, one of the prominent Unionists in Istanbul (and private physician to Prince Yusuf İzzettin, the second in line to the throne) was arrested and banished to Erzincan, from where he fled to Paris. Once in Paris, Dr Bahaettin Şakir was appalled by the lack of effectiveness he saw in Ahmet Rıza's organization and he set about reorganizing it almost from scratch. Ahmet Rıza had always been more of a theoretician than a practical politician, but Bahaettin Şakir, together with another leading figure from Ahmet Rıza's wing of the Young Turk movement, Dr Nazım, for the first time gave the CUP a sound organizational basis, with branches in many parts of the empire and adjacent countries and an effective secretariat and communications. The change was symbolized by a new name: the Committee of Union and Progress was now renamed Committee of Progress and Union (*Terakki ve İttihat Cemiyeti*).[18] Ahmet Rıza had always been more of a theoretician than an organizer but, together with another new arrival, Dr

Nazım, Bahaettin Şakır now for the first time gave the CUP a solid organizational framework with a secretariat, communication channels and cells in most parts of the empire and in neighbouring countries.

In 1907 a new attempt was made to unite the whole opposition movement at a second congress in Paris. This time the initiative came from the Armenian groups, and even the reorganized CUP now agreed to the use of violent means. The reason for this change of attitude lay in developments within the empire. There, small local groups, both at the great colleges in the capital and in provincial centres, had survived the crackdown of 1896, but contact between them had been lost. New groups were founded constantly, but none of them managed to establish a real network until the founding in September 1906 of the *Osmanlı Hürriyet Cemiyeti* (Ottoman Freedom Society) in Salonica. The founders were young bureaucrats and officers, of whom some had been connected to the CUP before 1896. The driving force behind the Committee was Mehmet Talât, a postal official from Edirne, who had been banished from there in 1896 because of his involvement in the old CUP and who had now become chief telegraph clerk at Salonica post office. Thanks to his organizational genius, the Ottoman Freedom Society spread rapidly in Macedonia. The crucial development was the involvement of officers from the Third (Macedonian) and Second (Edirne) armies, in which Major Enver of the staff of the Third Army played a leading role. In 1907, the Salonica group established contact with the *émigrés* in Paris and, finding the ideas of Ahmet Rıza much more to their liking than those of Prens Sabahattin, decided to demand a merger of their own group with his. After protracted negotiations this came about in October 1907. Eventually, the new organization reverted to the traditional name *İttihat ve Terakki Cemiyeti*.

Within the empire, and especially within the army, the years 1906 to 1908 seem to have witnessed increasing discontent, due to rising prices (inflation having picked up speed in the first years of the century) and to the fact that payment of salaries was even more in arrears than normal. Signs of discontent in the shape of strikes and small-scale rebellions, which have been documented for many different parts of the empire, set the stage, but the Macedonian problem was the direct cause of the revolution of July 1908.

In the early years of the twentieth century Macedonia was still the battle ground of rival nationalist movements. The Ottoman army was continuopusly engaged in counterinsurgency operations against Bulgarian, Serbian and Greek bands. In 1903 the conflict exploded when a part of the Bulgarian resistance started an armed rebellion against the Ottomans on 2 August 1903, the nameday of St Elias, or 'Ilinden' in

Bulgarian. The rebellion was suppressed with much violence but still in a way achieved its purpose. Austria and Russia started talks about a solution for the Macedonian question, which led to the 'Mürzsteg Agreement'. The Ottoman Empire was forced to carry out reforms under foreign supervision. European advisers were installed and a new gendarmerie manned by Muslims and Christians and commanded by European officers was created.

For the Young Turks all of this was extremely threatening. They were convinced that Macedonia would be lost if nothing was done. In June 1908, the Russian tsar and King Edward VII of Britain met at Reval (modern Tallinn) in the Baltic. Britain and Russia had gradually been drawing closer out of a common fear of Germany, and on this occasion statesmen from both countries tried to settle some of the remaining problems between them. One of the results was a proposal for the settlement of the Macedonian problem, based on foreign control that would leave the sultan with only formal suzerainty. When news of the Reval meeting reached Salonica (accompanied by rumours that Britain and Russia had agreed to partition the Ottoman Empire), the CUP decided to act. The timing of its actions was probably also influenced by the discovery that government agents were on the verge of uncovering parts of the organization.

In a coordinated campaign, officers who were members of the Committee (among them Enver) took to the hills with their troops and demanded the restoration of the constitution. In their eyes this would be the only way to restore unity among the different ethnic groups of the empire and so to forestall foreign intervention. The sultan tried to quell the revolt by sending first trusted officers and then Anatolian troops to Macedonia, but some of the officers were murdered and the troops, influenced by CUP agitators aboard their ships, refused to fight the insurgents. The sultan then gave in and on the night of 23 July 1908 announced that the constitution would henceforth be applied in full and parliament reconvened after an interval of 30 years.

PART II

The Young Turk Era in Turkish History (1908–50)

8 · The Second Constitutional Period, 1912–18

The constitutional revolution of 1908

The revolution of July 1908 was the result of the actions of the Unionist officers of the Third (Macedonian) and Second (Thracian) Army. In the European provinces of the empire this was clear enough, because the CUP sent delegations to every major town to announce the reinstatement of the constitutional regime and to explain its benefits to the population. The Unionist officers who headed these delegations took pains to explain that it was the Committee and not the sultan that was responsible for the change. In the Asiatic provinces and in the capital, Istanbul, the situation looked very different, however. The Hamidian regime's strict censorship had prevented the news from Macedonia from reaching the public. Hence, the sultan could successfully present his own version of events, which was that treacherous advisers had misled him into thinking that the country was not ready for constitutional rule, but that he now, and of his own accord, had come to the conclusion that the time was ripe.

Once the news had sunk in (this took some time because the first announcement in the capital was an unobtrusive, unheaded three-line item in the newspapers announcing new elections),[1] public reaction in Istanbul and Asia was similar to that in Macedonia – tremendous joy and relief, with people from all walks of life and every community, Muslim, Jewish and Christian, fraternizing and celebrating in the streets. There was a general, but unarticulated, expectation that somehow life would now change for the better. At the same time, in many places, including the capital, the people took revenge on the representatives of the old regime, forcing the dismissal of officials and hunting down known members of the espionage system.

The freedom of thought, expression and association the constitutional revolution brought about resulted not only in political demonstrations of either joy or anger but also in widespread labour unrest. Workers demanded wage rises to compensate for rising prices (inflation was a staggering 20 per cent in the first two months after the revolution) and, when their demands were not met, a wave of strikes swept across the empire: there were more than 100 in six months.[2] The government, which had been content for the public to let off steam in political demonstrations, was alarmed by the strikes and, with the CUP's support, enacted labour legislation that banned trade unions in the public sector, introduced compulsory arbitration and made strike action extremely difficult. This legislation effectively suppressed the labour movement and there were hardly any strikes for the rest of the second constitutional period. The role of the CUP in the defeat of the strikers is interesting because it shows that the Committee – the champion *par excellence* of constitutional liberty – sided unequivocally with the capitalists in suppressing the freedom, such as it was, of organized labour.

The leaders of the *émigré* movement, as well as those exiled within the empire, returned to Istanbul to a heroes' welcome. Except for Bahaettin Şakir and Dr Nazım, the two party organizers who had been most in touch with the internal movement in the empire before the revolution, they did not gain positions of real influence. Political power within the CUP remained in the hands of the men from Salonica.

Surprisingly, in this atmosphere of elation the CUP did not take power in its own hands or even depose the sultan whom it had so strenuously opposed and vilified for 20 years. One reason was that, because he manipulated public opinion, many people saw the sultan as the hero of the situation. Even though the CUP leaders distrusted him, they felt unable to remove him. They felt even less able to take the reins of government into their own hands. Age and seniority were important preconditions for authority in Ottoman society and the Young Turks, being for the most part captains and majors or minor bureaucrats in their late twenties and early thirties, had neither. The Committee therefore chose to leave politics in the hands of the existing cabinet under Grand Vizier Sait Pasha. In the meantime it set itself up as a watchdog with a mission to guard the newfound constitutional freedom, interfering in politics whenever it saw fit. In the following years the CUP's position as a secret society exerting pressure and holding political power without any formal responsibility was to prove a destabilizing factor.

The first conflict in which the CUP intervened was caused by the sultan's insistence on the right to appoint the ministers of war and the navy directly, instead of merely approving his grand vizier's choice for these positions. This was a clear violation of the letter, as well as of the spirit, of the constitution and when Sait Pasha supported the sultan, the Committee forced his resignation after only five days. *Kıbrıslı* (Cypriot) Kâmil Pasha, who had a reputation as a pro-British liberal, was appointed in his stead on 6 August.[3]

The main event of the months after the revolution was the first elections in 30 years. Before the revolution, the CUP had only had a strong provincial organization in the European provinces. It now endeavoured to spread its organization over the Asiatic provinces and North Africa. Sometimes new branches were established by converting existing local opposition groups, formed by people who had been sent into internal exile by Abdülhamit, into CUP organizations. Generally, the CUP's branches consisted of a coalition of professionals (teachers, lawyers, doctors), Muslim merchants and guild leaders and large landowners. While the Committee was almost exclusively Muslim and largely Turkish, it actively sought the cooperation of the other nationalities, guaranteeing them a number of seats in the new parliament. Eventually, Turks held slightly more than 50 per cent of the 288 seats.[4]

The only organization to contest the elections, besides the CUP was the new party founded by the followers of Prens Sabahattin (who had also returned) in September, the *Osmanlı Ahrar Fırkası* (Party of Ottoman Liberals). This, however, did not have a serious nationwide organization and managed to win only one seat.

Despite their complete victory, the Unionists' influence remained indirect rather than direct because in many parts of the empire they had to rely on local notables who allowed their names to be put forward as candidates on the Unionist list rather than on members of the CUP itself. This meant that party discipline in parliament was weak.

Thus, after the revolution and the elections the power of the palace was curbed but not eliminated and the leading bureaucrats of the Porte re-emerged as an independent political factor for the first time since 1878, while the CUP stayed in the background, relying on its majority in parliament to control the government.

The counterrevolution of April 1909
Although after the astounding success of the revolution, the CUP was the most powerful force in the country, increasingly through 1908 and the early months of 1909 it had to contend with two types of opposition. One was that of the *Ahrar Fırkası*, which had done badly in the elections and felt increasingly frustrated. Kâmil Pasha, who, like the Liberals, resented the pressure of the CUP, allied himself with this group and relations between him and the CUP became increasingly strained. On 14 February the CUP succeeded in having the pasha voted out of office in parliament and having him replaced with Hüseyin Hilmi Pasha, the former inspector-general of Macedonia, who was close to the Committee. The opposition launched a bitter press campaign, which was answered by the Unionist organs in kind. On 6 April Hasan Fehmi, editor of one of the

fiercest anti-Unionist papers, was killed, probably by a Unionist agent. His funeral the next day turned into a mass demonstration against the Committee.

The second type of opposition the CUP faced was from conservative religious circles, notably the lower *ulema* and sheikhs of the dervish orders. During the month of Ramadan, which coincided with October 1908, a number of incidents and at least two serious and violent demonstrations occurred, during which the closure of bars and theatres, the prohibition of photography and restrictions on the freedom of movement of women were demanded. On 3 April the religious extremists, who were already active as a group around the newspaper *Volkan* of the Nakşibendi sheikh *Derviş* Vahdeti, organized themselves as the *İttihad-i Muhammedi* (Muhammadan Union). This group organized large-scale propaganda against the policies and secularism of the Young Turks.

Despite all this political infighting and the rising tensions of the past months, it came as a complete surprise to Unionists and foreign observers alike, when, on the night of 12 April 1909, an armed insurrection broke out in the capital in the name of the restoration of Islam and *şeriat*. That night the battalions of Macedonian troops at Taşkışla barracks, which the CUP had brought in only a week before to replace the supposedly less reliable Arab and Albanian contingents, mutinied, taking their officers prisoner. The next morning, together with a large number of *softa*s, students from the religious schools, they marched to the parliament building. During the morning, more and more troops and *ulema* joined them. The government was in disarray. It dared not send in the loyal troops but instead sent the chief of police to listen to the mob's demands. The spokesmen of the troops presented six demands:

- dismissal of the grand vizier and the ministers of war and of the navy;
- replacement of a number of Unionist officers;
- replacement of the Unionist president of the Chamber of Deputies (Ahmet Rıza);
- banishing of a number of Unionist deputies from Istanbul;
- restoration of the *şeriat*; and
- an amnesty for the rebellious troops.

The most curious of these demands is that for restoration of the Islamic law. While the introduction of specific European-style laws and regulations had eroded the position of the *şeriat*, it had never been abolished and continued to hold sway in the field of family law.

Faced with these demands, the grand vizier went to the palace in the afternoon and tendered his resignation, which the sultan accepted. The next morning, it was announced that the colourless diplomat Tevfik Pasha (Okday) had been appointed grand vizier. The war minister in the new cabinet, Marshal Edhem Pasha, visited the soldiers, praised them and promised them that all their demands would be met. The troops and the *softa*s celebrated their victory extensively. At the same time, a pogrom against well-known Unionists developed, resulting in the deaths of at least 20 people, mostly officers, but also two deputies, who were mistaken for leading Unionists.

The Unionists went underground or fled the capital. As a result, the Chamber of Deputies, in which the CUP held the majority, did not have a quorum. Nevertheless, the deputies who did attend accepted the soldiers' demands and at the same time issued a proclamation saying that *şeriat* and the constitution would be maintained.

From the first day on, the leaders of the *Ahrar* tried without success to turn the rebellion into a purely anti-CUP affair and to prevent it from moving into a reactionary, anti-constitutionalist and pro-Abdülhamit direction. The higher-ranking *ulema* united in the *Cemiyet-i İlmiye-i İslamiye* (Society of Islamic Scholars), meanwhile never supported the insurrection and, from 16 April onwards, openly denounced it.

The CUP had been driven out of Istanbul, but it had kept its position in the provinces, notably in Macedonia, and it immediately started to take countermeasures. It organized public demonstrations in provincial towns and showered the parliament and the palace with telegrams. In Macedonia especially it easily won the propaganda battle, convincing the population that the constitution was in danger. From 15 April the CUP started the organization of a military campaign against the rebels. The Action Army (*Hareket Ordusu*) put together for this campaign consisted of regular units led by the commander of the Third Army, Mahmut Şevket Pasha, reinforced by volunteer units, mostly Albanians, led by Niyazi Bey, one of the heroes of the revolution of 1908. By train, these troops were moved to the outskirts of Istanbul.

The Chamber of Deputies sent a delegation to army headquarters to try to prevent it from taking the city by force, but meeting no positive response, the delegation members decided to stay with the army and issued a call to their colleagues to join them. From 22 April onwards both chambers of parliament sat together in San Stefano (modern Yeşilköy) as a general national assembly (*meclis-i umumi-i millî*).

In the early morning of 24 April, the Action Army occupied the city without encountering much resistance. Only around the Taksim and Taşkışla barracks was there serious fighting. After the suppression of the revolt, and under martial law, two courts martial were instituted, which convicted and executed a large number of the rebels, including *Derviş*

Vahdeti. A number of *Ahrar* leaders were arrested, but set free again under British pressure. On 27 April, the two chambers of parliament, still sitting together, deposed Sultan Abdülhamit, who was succeeded by his younger brother Mehmet Reşit, who now ascended the throne as Sultan Mehmet V, a name chosen to bring to mind that of Mehmet II (who reigned from 1451 to 1481), the conqueror of Istanbul, the new sultan being a 'second conqueror' of the capital thanks to the actions of the Action Army.

Several different causes for the events of April 1909 can be discerned. Different groups had become disenchanted with the constitutional regime for different reasons. The overthrow of the old regime had hurt those who had earned a living or enjoyed status as members of the Hamidian apparatus, including the thousands of government spies active in Istanbul, who had supplied the sultan with their *jurnal*s. The rationalizing policies of the new government aimed at ending the overstaffing of the government departments, which had been the result of the favouritism of the old regime. Thousands of civil servants of all ranks had already lost their jobs. In a city like Istanbul where government was the main source of income this had far-reaching consequences.

In the army, the main source of trouble was the friction between the *mektepli* officers, who had been trained in the military schools and academy, and the *alaylı* officers, who had risen through the ranks. The latter had been favoured by the old regime, being paid regularly and stationed in the First Army in and around Istanbul, while the former had been mistrusted (rightly so, because it was these modern educated officers who brought about the constitutional revolution of 1908). Now the *mektepli* officers had taken over. Many of the *alaylı* officers had been dismissed or demoted and worse: the whole system of promotion from the ranks was discontinued. The troops, too, had reason for discontent. They had been used to the slack discipline and relaxed atmosphere of the old army and were now confronted with young officers who wanted to impose Prussian training methods, among other things abolishing pauses for ablutions and prayers during exercises.

While no explicitly secularist legislation had been enacted in the eight months since the constitutional revolution, the change in atmosphere, which the constitutional revolution had brought about, clearly threatened the lower *ulema*. One particular measure that aroused feeling among this group was that students at religious schools who did not pass their exams in time were no longer exempted from military service.

The discord within the Young Turk ranks, with the *Ahrar* opposing what they saw as the Unionists' irresponsible policies and monopoly of power also helped to create the atmosphere in which the revolt could take place.

The counter-revolution of 1909 did not really spread to the provinces. There was, however, one instance of violence that can be linked to it. In the province of Adana a number of supporters of the *ancien régime* took the opportunity of the breakdown of central control to attack the Unionist representatives. The riot turned into a pogrom and a large number (possibly 20,000) of Armenian citizens were massacred. A parliamentary commission of enquiry was sent to Adana and 124 Muslims and seven Armenians were executed for their role in the riots.[6]

Political competition in 1909–13

The Committee had been badly shaken. The counter-revolution had shown up the fragility of the constitutional regime and of the type of modernizing policies the Committee stood for. In that sense it was both a traumatic experience and a lesson that would not be forgotten by the Unionists or by their successors after 1918.

The suppression of the counter-revolution left power in the hands of the army and more specifically in the hands of the commander in chief, Mahmut Şevket Pasha, who was made inspector of the three main armies, the First (Istanbul), Second (Edirne) and Third (Monastir). Neither the cabinet of Grand Vizier Hüseyin Hilmi Pasha, nor that of his successor from December 1909, Hakkı Pasha, nor even the CUP was in a position to challenge his authority. The result was that for the next few years to all intents and purposes the army stood above the law (which in any case was martial law until July 1912). On the other hand, the Committee was given a free hand to carry through the legislative changes it desired as long as it left the army alone.

As a result, the Unionist-dominated chamber embarked on a programme of legislation that aimed at the consolidation of the constitutional order. In August 1909 a number of articles in the constitution were changed, finally establishing a really constitutional and parliamentarian regime. From now on the sultan only had the right to appoint the grand vizier and the *şeyhülislam*. Parliament could now be dissolved only if the cabinet lost a vote of confidence and, in the event of dissolution, elections would have to take place within three months. Legislation and the conclusion of treaties became the prerogative of the parliament.

Following these constitutional changes, a number of laws were passed in the following months to strengthen central authority and to curb individual and collective freedoms. This was true of the new laws on public meetings, on associations, on brigandage, on strikes and of the new – and restrictive – press law. A new law on military service now imposed a duty to serve on all male Ottoman subjects, Muslim and non-

Muslim alike. Among the minorities, especially those of Greek descent, this change induced many young men to leave the country either physically or formally (by adopting foreign, mainly Greek, nationality).

The palace's diminished influence was apparent from the new budget in which expenditure on the royal family was cut by two-thirds. Finally, both the bureaucracy and the officer corps were trimmed and reorganized (the latter with Mahmut Şevket's consent), leading to cuts in salaries, early retirements and demotions. In the army, most of the officers who had risen from the ranks under Abdülhamit were now purged. All in all, more than 10,000, or roughly one-third, of the officers were removed over the next few years.[7] All ranks were also reconsidered and many officers demoted.

Two problems that kept cropping up between 1909 and 1913 were the role of the military, namely the officers, in politics and the relationship between the – still secret – committee and the parliament it dominated.

The fact that relatively junior officers wielded great political influence through their position in the CUP played havoc with army discipline because the political hierarchy cut right through the military hierarchy of the officer corps. Mahmut Şevket Pasha, who made it clear that in his view the army had intervened in April to save the constitution, not the Committee, urged the officers to devote themselves exclusively to their military work or else leave the army. In principle, the CUP agreed. Motions to the effect that officers should stay out of politics were adopted at CUP congresses more than once.

At the same time, however, the events of April had shown that the CUP eventually depended on its military members and its influence over the army for its political position. In spite of the fact that it clearly contravened the constitution, serving officers were allowed to sit in parliament. The interference of military men in politics and the politicization of the army were among the chief grudges of the opposition that re-emerged after 1910, but when it could not get its way, that same opposition organized an anti-Unionist movement within the army and threatened an armed insurrection. The dilemma was never solved during the second constitutional period. The same is true for the second problem, that of the relationship between the Committee and the parliament. The opposition reproached the CUP for exercising power without responsibility. In a reaction, the CUP decided to form a political party at its first congress in the autumn of 1908.

This party, however, which consisted of the Unionist members of parliament, did not replace the Committee but existed side by side with it. Because of its poor party discipline, the parliamentary faction was not fully trusted by the CUP leadership and as a result the CUP's internal regulations ensured that real power remained with the central committee and its secretary-general. The parliamentary party was given a greater say only after 1914, when parliament had anyhow become a rubber stamp institution.

The opposition, which had been crushed in April 1909, slowly re-emerged in the following years. Between 1909 and 1911 a number of new parties were formed, some by the CUP's old-established enemies and others by dissident Unionists who favoured a more liberal or more conservative line. In the first category were the *Mütedil Hürriyet-perveran Fırkası* (Party of Moderate Liberals) and the *İslahat-i Esasiye-i Osmaniye Fırkası* (Party of Fundamental Ottoman Reforms), founded towards the end of 1909. The second of these had its headquarters in Paris. The *Ahali Fırkası* (People's Party), founded in the spring of 1910 and the *Hizb-i Cedid* (New Party), founded early in 1911, belong to the second category. A former Unionist, Colonel Sadık, who had become disenchanted with the radical nationalist policies and secularist tendencies of the CUP, formed the last named party. Paradoxically, one of Sadık's main political demands was that the officers should refrain from interfering in politics. He also demanded that the CUP should cease to be a secret society.

This period also saw the first emergence of organized socialist activity in the empire. There was a small circle of leftist intellectuals in Istanbul who opposed the way in which the Unionists had suppressed the trade unions and strike action after the constitutional revolution. The main figure in this group was the editor of the periodical *İştirak* (Participation), *Sosyalist* Hüseyin Hilmi. It was he who founded the *Osmanlı Sosyalist Fırkası* (Ottoman Socialist Party) in September 1910. In spite of its name it was a progressive, liberal party rather than a real socialist one. It was a tiny group without representatives in parliament and without real influence. The Paris branch of the party, led by Dr Refik Nevzat, received some support from the French socialists.

The growth of opposition was given new impetus in 1910 with the outbreak of a large-scale insurrection in Albania and with the murder, on 9 June, of a prominent opposition journalist, Ahmet Samim. This was almost a repeat performance of the murder of Hasan Fehmi in 1909 and the Committee, fearing a repeat of the counter-revolution, had a number of leading opposition figures arrested in July on the pretext that a plot had been discovered. The opposition continued to grow, however, and by early 1911 the situation had become so serious that the CUP tried to placate the opposition by taking up a conciliatory position. A number of Unionist hardliners, among them Talât, resigned from the government and a new ten-point programme published on 23 April conceded the opposition's demands, as formulated by the increasingly influential Colonel Sadık. For the moment this seemed to placate the opposition and Hakkı Pasha's cabinet received a clear vote of confidence on 27 April, but the differences had only been papered over.

On 29 September Hakkı Pasha had to resign when Italy declared war and started to occupy Tripolitania, the last Ottoman province in Africa, and his cabinet had to shoulder the responsibility. He was succeeded by the veteran Sait Pasha, who now became grand vizier for the eighth time.

The opposition to the CUP was now gathering strength fast. In November almost all the opposition groups and parties united in one new party, called the *Hürriyet ve İtilâf Fırkası* (Party of Freedom and Understanding, or, by its French title, *Entente libérale*). This was a conglomerate of conservatives and liberals with hardly anything in common apart from their hatred for the CUP, but in the short term it was no less effective for that. Three weeks after its foundation, and to the surprise of all concerned, it managed to win a by-election in Istanbul, defeating the CUP candidate.

The Committee now decided that the time for action had come. Where it had relied on parliament as its main weapon to control the government, the palace and the bureaucracy since 1908, it now saw it was losing its grip on parliament and it engineered its dissolution. The elections that followed in the spring of 1912 are known in Turkish history as the *sopalı seçim* (election with the stick), because of the violence and intimidation with which the CUP made sure of its majority. As a result, the new chamber was an obedient instrument of the Committee, only a handful of opposition candidates being elected. It lacked any legitimacy in the eyes of the opposition, which now took extra-parliamentary measures. In May and June 1912, Colonel Sadık and his friends demanded the resignation of the government and threatened armed intervention by a group called the *Halâskar Zabitan* (Saviour Officers) unless it complied. The Unionist-dominated chamber gave Sait Pasha a vote of confidence, but the old statesman resigned anyway because, as he said, he no longer had any confidence in the chamber.[8] Almost simultaneously, Mahmut Şevket resigned in disgust over the continued political infighting within the army.

Sait Pasha was succeeded by a cabinet of national unity, also known as the 'Great Cabinet' because of the number of elder statesmen who figured in it. This new cabinet saw the political interference by officers and the CUP's irresponsible policies as the causes of the political chaos in the empire, and it made breaking the power of the Unionists, especially of the Unionist officers, its top priority. In this it was in agreement with

Colonel Sadık and when he demanded the dissolution of parliament, it went along with him. The chamber tried to forestall dissolution by adjourning of its own accord, but it was dissolved nonetheless. The following months saw the persecution of leading Unionists by the government, with many being sent into internal exile and others going underground or abroad. Bitter as they were, however, these party political struggles by the autumn of 1912 were completely overshadowed by the worst international crisis the empire had faced since 1878.

International politics: still the Eastern Question

The Young Turks had expected the re-establishment of the constitutional regime in the empire to earn it credibility and support in the liberal states of western Europe. Britain was still the great example for the Young Turks and immediately after the revolution there were popular demonstrations of support for the British ambassador. Their expectations, however, were dashed almost immediately. In the days after the revolution, Austria-Hungary announced it was formally annexing the Ottoman provinces of Bosnia-Herzegovina it had occupied militarily in 1876; Bulgaria announced the union of Eastern Rumelia (the autonomous province created in 1876) with Bulgaria proper, which now also abrogated its (entirely theoretical) links with the Ottoman Empire and declared itself an independent kingdom; and Crete was united with Greece. Britain cold-shouldered the Unionists and together with the other great powers declined to intervene on behalf of the Ottomans. There was little the Ottomans could do. In the event, they organized a boycott of Austrian goods, which was quite effective (although it hit the Greek and Armenian importers of Austrian goods as much as it hit Austria) and earned the Ottomans financial compensation. The boycott is also interesting because it is the first example of a new style of politics, in which the leaders tried large-scale mobilization of the civil population.[8]

After these first blows, the pressure continued unabated for the rest of the decade. As in previous decades the pressures were both external (the designs of rival imperialist powers on Ottoman territory and the irredentism of the new Balkan states) and internal (the separatist movements among the non-Turkish communities of the empire).

Regional insurrections were of course nothing new. Indeed, they had become part of the normal state of things in the nineteenth century. What made the new regime more sensitive to these troubles was its ideological character. It had come to power claiming to represent all Ottoman communities, and the fact that the agitation of the guerrilla groups in, for instance, Macedonia continued as before meant a further disillusion for the CUP.

The greatest setback in this respect was the series of uprisings that broke out from March 1910 onwards among the Albanians. This community had a Muslim majority and some of its members had played an important role in the Ottoman administration and in the CUP itself (one of the foremost heroes of the revolution of 1908 and of the Action Army in 1909 had been an Albanian, Niyazi Bey). The insurrections in Kosovo in 1910, around the southern border of Montenegro in 1911 and again in Kosovo in 1912 had to do with the traditional causes of resistance to taxation and recruiting, but they were also a protest against the centralizing policies of the CUP. One particular problem was that of Unionist opposition to the introduction of the Latin script in Albanian schools. The Unionists' attempts to disarm a population that regarded the firearm as an essential part of masculinity, caused a lot of resentment. Most Muslim Albanians did not want to cut the ties with Istanbul completely at this time, but they did want far-reaching autonomy. In an attempt to regain the loyalty of the Albanians, the CUP sent Sultan Mehmet on a goodwill tour of Macedonia and Kosovo, on which he was accompanied by Niyazi Bey, in June 1911. After the long years of seclusion of Sultan Abdülhamit, this type of public relations effort was quite a novel experience and one, which, as on the occasion of the new sultan's visits to the old Ottoman capitals of Bursa and Edirne the year before, was much appreciated by the public. Quite large numbers of Albanians turned up to meet the sultan and to pray with him at the gravesite of Sultan Murat I (who had died in 1389) in the plain of Kosovo,[9] but the trip did not change anything about the fundamentals. As events of a year later would show, the Albanians could not be turned into a buttress of Ottoman power in the face of separatist pressures.

The second major revolt was in the Yemen. This mountainous corner of the Arabian peninsula had been under nominal Ottoman sovereignty since the mid-nineteenth century. The empire's hold over this far-away province was always tenuous, however, and by 1904 the hereditary ruler Imam Yahya had again revolted. Many Ottoman soldiers lost their lives in the endless small-scale warfare in the Yemen (indeed, 'Yemen' became synonymous with the plight of the Ottoman soldier in folklore, as the many sad 'Yemen songs' show), but in 1911 the two parties reached an agreement whereby the Yemen returned to nominal Ottoman control and the imam kept his autonomy. Thereafter, the Yemen remained loyal to the empire until the very end.

The pressure of imperialist expansion made itself felt in the competing projects of the British, French and German governments for economic spheres of influence in Mesopotamia, Syria and Anatolia, respectively, but the most immediate threat was Italian ambitions in

North Africa. The province of Tripolitania (modern-day Libya) was economically and strategically insignificant, but it was also the last remaining part of the Ottoman Empire in Africa that had not been occupied by Britain or France. Expansion in Africa and in the eastern Mediterranean was seen in Italy as a precondition for the achievement of great power status and Italian diplomacy had persistently sought international approval of this expansion for two decades. By 1911 it had secured the tacit agreement of Britain, France and Russia and at least neutrality on the part of Germany and Austria and it went into action. On 28 September 1911 it presented the Ottoman government with an ultimatum, demanding Ottoman consent to the occupation of Tripolitania, on the pretext that Italian citizens there were being threatened by Muslim fanatics.

The Ottoman government rejected the ultimatum but gave a conciliatory reply. In spite of this Italy declared war the next day. The province was almost completely undefended and the Italian troops had little difficulty in occupying the coastal area. The Ottomans could not send an expeditionary force because of Italian control of the seas. While the government could or would do very little, the CUP demanded that countermeasures be taken, not so much because of any intrinsic value of Tripolitania because the loss of the province would seriously affect the credibility of the sultan's government in the eyes of its Arab subjects further east. When nothing was done, the Unionist officers within the CUP, led by Major Enver, decided to act. Some 50 officers went as volunteers (*fedai*) to Tripolitania via Egypt or Tunisia to galvanize the Arab resistance, which had already started under the leadership of the militant Sanusiya religious order. During the next year the Bedouin troops led by these officers successfully harassed the Italians and prevented them from making much headway inland.

In the ensuing stalemate the Italians tried to force the issue by enlarging the scope of the struggle. In April 1912 they bombarded the Dardanelles. When actions in this area alarmed the great powers, they occupied the islands of the Dodecanese in May. The war dragged on until the Ottomans agreed to conclude peace, leaving Tripolitania in Italian hands, on 17 October 1912, because by then a far more threatening situation had developed in the Balkans. The Dodecanese islands were to be returned to the Ottoman Empire after the conclusion of peace, but this never happened. The islands remained in Italian hands until 1943.

The point of no return: the Balkan War and the Bab-ı Ali coup
The new national states in the Balkans agreed on very little, but one thing they did agree on was the desirability of removing the Ottomans from

Europe. What had kept them from effective action in this direction was disagreement over the division of the spoils and fear of the Ottoman army (after all, the last war in the Balkans, that of 1897, had ended in a resounding Ottoman victory). But in 1911/12 this situation changed. In March 1912, Serbia and Bulgaria, on the initiative of the former, concluded an alliance that was officially defensive in character but in reality aimed at the conquest of European Turkey. In May 1912, a very similar agreement was reached between Greece and Bulgaria. Montenegro and Serbia concluded an alliance by the beginning of October. In the meantime, the Ottoman–Italian war had shown up the political and military weakness of the empire, thus encouraging the Balkan states to act.

On 2 October 1912 the allied Balkan states (Serbia, Montenegro, Greece and Bulgaria) issued a joint ultimatum to the Porte, demanding far-reaching reforms under foreign control in Macedonia. At the same time, they mobilized for war. The Ottoman government declared itself ready to implement all the reforms it had agreed to earlier, but it refused the kind of renunciation of its sovereignty the ultimatum implied. Thereupon Montenegro declared war on 8 October, followed by the other states. None of the great powers supported the war, but they were too divided to exert much influence in order to stop it.

In the Ottoman Empire the war was seen as one between an empire and four small states inhabited by former subjects. There was a great deal of confidence in the army, which was, however, anything but battle-ready. The Ottoman plan of operations in the event of an attack such as had occurred now envisaged a defensive war with the (heavily out-numbered) army withdrawing to eastern Thrace in the east and greater Albania in the west, while the troops in the Asiatic provinces were being mobilized. The new war minister, Nazim Pasha, however, was unfamiliar with the plans, while the former chief of staff who had drawn them up, Ahmet İzzet Pasha, was now serving in the Yemen.[10] As a result, the Ottoman army did not withdraw but fought the Serbians and the Bulgarians simultaneously and with disastrous results. After losing the battles of Kırkkilise (modern Kırklareli) and Lüleburgaz against the Bulgarians and Kumanovo against the Serbians, the army had to withdraw to the Çatalca lines just outside Istanbul. To the west, only a few fortress towns still held out: Yanina (modern Ioannina), Scutari (Üsküdar, modern Skhodër) and Edirne. Salonica was surrendered without a fight.

By November the situation was hopeless and on 3 December the Ottoman government agreed to an armistice. Ten days later two diplomatic conferences assembled in London, one of the belligerents and one of the great powers. The latter agreed on two points: the Ottomans were to remain in possession of Istanbul and the straits (both the Bosphorus and the Dardanelles), and a new independent state of Albania was to be created – mainly at the insistence of Austria, whose primary policy objective was to prevent Serbia from gaining an outlet on the Adriatic Sea. The conferences could agree on precious little else, however, least of all on the division of the spoils in Europe and the new boundaries in Macedonia and Thrace. Negotiations were therefore pretty much deadlocked when news reached London of an armed coup d'état in Istanbul on 23 January 1913.

The Bab-ı Ali coup and the second phase of the Balkan War

The inner circle of the CUP, led by Enver and Talât, had probably already decided by the end of 1912 to force the government out of office for purely domestic reasons.[11] The persecution of the Unionists by the government was gathering pace in November when Kâmil Pasha, the CUP's old enemy, had taken over as grand vizier and the Committee's continued existence seemed under threat. The London conference gave it the chance to act, not in the name of party political interests but for patriotic reasons. The great power proposals, communicated to the Porte on 17 January, included handing over the town of Edirne to the Bulgarians.

This was an issue of great emotional importance since Edirne was a largely Muslim town and a former capital of the Ottoman Empire. Furthermore, Bulgarians had been surrounding the town since October, but it was still holding out. When it became clear on 22 January that the government would give in to the great powers, the Unionists had found their justification and so launched their coup the next day. A group of Unionist officers rode to the Porte, burst into the room where the cabinet was in session, shot the war minister and took the members of the cabinet prisoner, forcing Kâmil Pasha to resign. A new cabinet was formed and Mahmut Şevket Pasha returned as grand vizier and war minister.

Almost immediately after the coup the Balkan states announced the resumption of hostilities. The CUP insisted on an aggressive policy with counter-attacks from the Çatalca lines, but the state of the army and the state of the roads in the winter made this impossible. An attempt to land forces in the rear of the Bulgarian army at Şarköy to coincide with a breakout from the Gallipoli peninsula (which was still in Ottoman hands) failed through lack of coordination, leading to bitter recriminations among the military.[12] A Bulgarian onslaught on the Çatalca lines was repulsed but on 26 March, starving Edirne fell. By May, even the Unionists had to recognize that the empire had no choice but to negotiate for peace. On 16 April, a new armistice was concluded. The Treaty of London, signed on 10 June, meant the loss of all territory to the north and west of a line from Enoz on the Aegean to Midye on the Black Sea, including Edirne.

In the meantime tension had been mounting between the different Balkan states. Romania, which had not taken part in the war, demanded compensation for the Bulgarian territorial gains. Serbia and Greece, dissatisfied with the division of the spoils in Macedonia, agreed on an anti-Bulgarian alliance. The Bulgarians, who were well aware of these combinations, decided on a pre-emptive strike against Serbia, which completely miscarried. It meant the start of a second Balkan war, in which Bulgaria was attacked from all sides. The CUP leadership pressed the government and the chief of staff to resume the offensive and when they hesitated and urged caution, a group of junior officers led by Enver, with the backing of the CUP, took the initiative and launched an attack on Edirne in July. Edirne was retaken and the Bulgarians were forced to sign the Constantinople peace agreement (29 September 1913), which restored the province of Edirne to the Ottoman Empire.

Nevertheless, the importance of the Ottoman losses in the Balkan War cannot be overstated. It was a disaster in human, economic and cultural terms. The empire lost nearly all its European territories, over 60,000 square miles in all, with nearly four million inhabitants. Again, as in 1878, Istanbul was deluged with Muslim refugees who had lost everything.[13] There were severe outbreaks of typhus and cholera and a very high mortality rate among the refugees. Their resettlement caused enormous problems and many spent the next few years in squatter towns. But the significance went even deeper: the areas lost (Macedonia, Albania, Thrace) had been core areas of the empire for over 500 years. They were the richest and most developed provinces and a disproportionate part of the Ottoman ruling elite hailed from them. Salonica, after all, had been the cradle of the CUP. A side effect of the losses was that now, for the first time in Ottoman history, ethnic Turks became a majority of the population.

Public reaction, at least among the Muslim part of the population, consisted partly of total bewilderment that something like this could have happened, partly of calls for vengeance and partly of harsh self criticism. In 1913/14 the newspapers were full of articles calling for revenge against the Greeks and Bulgarians, but at the same time Greece and especially Bulgaria were portrayed as exemplary states that had quickly gained strength thanks to the development of national consciousness and untiy – precisely the things that the Ottoman Empire lacked.

The Ottoman Empire was not in a position to embark on a new war at all. Therefore, the concrete expressions of feelings of revenge were not aimed at the neighbouring countries, but at the domestic Christian minorities, especially the Greek Orthodox. During the Balkan War many Ottoman Greek Orthodox (*Rum*) had sympathized with Greece and *Rum* soldiers in the Ottoman army ahd deserted in droves. Already in 1912 the Young Turks had reacted by organizing a strict trade boycott that had not just Greek but also *Rum* enterprises.

By the spring of 1914 peace had been restored but the relationship with Greece was still extremely tense, especially due to disagreement over the future of the big islands Chios (Sakız), Lesbos (Midilli) and Lemnos (Limni) that Greece had conquered but that were immediately adjacent to the Anatolian coast. The CUP feared a resumption of war and regarded the large *Rum* population there as unreliable. On Talât's infinitive some 150,000 Greek Orthodox were therefore expelled from the shores of the Marmara and the Aegean in a campaign of intimidation and sporadic violence in May–June 1914. Their houses and land were used to house part of the 400,000 Muslim refugees from the Balkans.

The Teşkilat-i Mahsusa

An important role in the liberation of Edirne was played by a group of officers who had been known within the CUP as *fedais* (volunteers) since before the revolution of 1908. They can be seen as the Unionist shock troops who did the Committee's dirty work (such as political assassinations) and rallied to its defence in times of crisis. They were prominent in the episode of the Action Army in 1909 and many of them had served in Tripolitania, organizing the Arab guerrillas against the Italians. This circle was very close to Enver, who seems to have acted as their leader.[14] After the retaking of Edirne, Enver directed members of the group to start a guerrilla movement in western Thrace, the area west of the Maritza River that was (and is) inhabited by Turkish-speaking Muslims. For this purpose they founded the Temporary Government of Western Thrace (*Garbi Trakya Hükümet-i Muvak-katası*). Although it lasted for only two months (the Ottomans used it to put pressure on the Bulgarians at the peace talks and it was terminated once the desired concessions had been received), it served as an important 'laboratory' for the national resistance movement that would develop in Anatolia after the First World War.

The group of volunteer officers around Enver seems to have been known informally as the *Teşkilat-i Mahsusa* (Special Organization) in 1913. Its organization was formalized under that name in 1914 and put under the direct control of Enver as minister of war (as he had become by then). In the First World War it played an important behind-the-scenes role both in the suppression of separatist movements, especially in the Arab provinces, and also in the terror campaigns against Greek businesses in western Asia Minor. Its role in the Armenian question will be discussed separately. The *Teşkilât* also operated outside the empire, where it tried to fan Muslim resistance to the Russian, French and British administrations in their respective colonial empires. Though romantic and adventurous, these activities of Ottoman 'Lawrences' seem to have had little effect.

The consolidation of Unionist power
After the January 1913 coup d'état the CUP was in complete control of the internal political situation. At first, the Liberal opposition was not persecuted. Its leaders were just told privately to stay out of politics. This changed when a supporter of the *Hürriyet ve İtilâf* assassinated the grand vizier, Mahmut Şevket Pasha, on 11 June 1913. There were widespread arrests and a number of people were sentenced to death. The Unionists now tightened their hold on the government even further: Talât entered the cabinet as minister of interior; Enver was promoted twice in quick succession and made a pasha and minister of war. Cemal, the military governor of the capital, was also promoted and given the rank of pasha. The new grand vizier was an Egyptian prince, Sait Halim Pasha, who was a member of the inner circle of the CUP but nevertheless wielded little real influence.

The regime that now developed has often been called the 'Triumvirate' of Enver, Cemal and Talât. This, however, is a simplification. The three men were certainly powerful: Enver controlled the army and Talât had great power within the Committee. Cemal was influential in national politics as long as he was governor of Istanbul, but less so after mid-1914. But Enver had his rivals in the army (not least of whom was Cemal). Within the Committee, local party bosses (called 'responsible secretaries' or 'inspectors') and Unionist provincial governors were often powerful and independent. The CUP was led by an inner circle of some 50 men, who belonged to a number of factions. In fact, Talât's great influence derived precisely from his recognized ability to reconcile the leaders of these factions.

During the period 1913–18, the inner councils of the CUP counted for much more in the conduct of policy than the cabinet, which was quite often faced with accomplished facts. Elections for a new parliament were held in the winter of 1913/14. The Liberal opposition party (the *Hürriyet ve İtilâf Fırkası*) had not been officially dissolved, but it did not participate and the parliament that emerged after the elections was a docile instrument of the CUP.

The entry of the Ottoman Empire into the First World War
Barely a year after the end of the Balkan War, the Ottoman Empire was at war again – for the last time. Ever since the First World War a debate has raged in Turkey over how and why the Unionist government of the day decided to join the central powers in that war. The facts (and chronology) of the matter are as follows.

In the atmosphere of quickly rising international tension after the murder of the Austrian crown prince, Archduke Ferdinand, by Serbian nationalists in Sarajevo on 28 June 1914, the Unionist government of the Ottoman Empire tried to interest the major powers in the conclusion of an alliance. The Balkan War had shown up the empire's diplomatic isolation and the Unionists were convinced that continued isolation would mean the end of the empire. Basically, they were prepared to accept any alliance rather than continued isolation.

First, Cemal Pasha approached the government in Paris, but was brushed off. France and Britain had good relations with Russia at the top of their agendas and, as far as the Levant was concerned, after the Balkan War they expected more from collaboration with an alliance of Balkan states than from an Ottoman connection. The Unionists then turned their eyes to the central powers. Austria-Hungary had sent out feelers about the possibilities of an anti-Serbian alliance with the Ottomans and both Talât and Enver had responded encouragingly. On 28 July Enver, in a conversation with German ambassador Wangenheim, openly proposed a defensive alliance with Germany. When relayed to Berlin, this proposal received Kaiser Wilhelm II's personal support.

In the days that followed a small circle of Young Turk leaders (Grand Vizier Sait Halim Pasha, Enver Pasha, Talât Pasha, President of the Chamber Halil) negotiated in deepest secrecy with the Germans on the details of an agreement. Not even the other cabinet members, including leading figures like Finance Minister Cavit, Cemal Pasha or *Şeyhülislam* Hayri Efendi were informed. On 2 August 1914 the agreement was signed at the private residence of Sait Halim Pasha on the Bosphorus. The eight articles of this momentous document are as follows:

1. Both parties would remain neutral in any Austro-Serbian conflict.
2. If Russia entered the conflict and forced Germany to do so too, the Ottoman Empire would join the central powers.
3. The German military mission would remain in Turkey and be given an effective role to play under the Ottoman high command.
4. Germany would protect Ottoman territory.
5. The agreement would enter into effect immediately and remain in force until 31 December 1918.

6. The agreement would automatically be renewed for five years unless one of the parties decided otherwise.
7. The sultan and the kaiser would ratify the agreement within a month.
8. The agreement would remain secret.[15]

It is important to note that this agreement was concluded one day after Russia had mobilized against both Austria and Germany. It must be assumed that the Ottoman leaders were aware of this, so the question arises of what induced them to sign an agreement that they knew must lead to war? Apart from the fear of isolation mentioned earlier, two other factors probably played a part. The first was that, alone among the great powers, the German Empire was ready to sign an agreement with the Ottomans as equal partners – a very important point for the Unionists who had been trying to emancipate the country from its semi-colonial status. The second was a miscalculation. The Ottomans were unaware that German strategic planning was dependent on knocking Russia's ally France out of the war first, by means of an enveloping movement through Belgium – something that would bring not only France, but almost certainly also Britain into the war. They probably expected a relatively short war with Russia only, and in that war they could expect Germany and Austria to win. Victory over Russia in turn could be expected to yield concrete results in the Caucasus and the Balkans. When the conflict turned out to be much wider and longer, the pro-German faction among the Unionists decided to take the plunge anyway.

The Ottoman Empire was in no condition to fight a serious war, militarily, economically or in terms of internal communications. The Germans were well aware of this, but for them the attraction of the Ottoman alliance lay not in the contribution of the Ottoman army to the war, which was generally expected to be over in a few months, but in its effect on Muslims in the colonial empires of France and Britain and on the Balkan states. In addition, the Ottomans could effectively block Russian ship movements through the Straits.

Immediately after the signing of the secret treaty, parliament was adjourned and the government began to prepare public opinion for war. In this, it was handed a trump card by the British government.

To counter the growing force of the Greek navy, the Ottomans had ordered two modern battleships from Britain in 1911. By mid-1914 the two ships, which had been paid for in part by popular subscription through the *Donanma Cemiyeti* (Fleet Society) all over the empire, were ready, but delivery was delayed because of extra tests and because of problems with the final payments. A party of Ottoman officers and seamen was already in England to take delivery and the final payments had been made when, on 1 August, the First Lord of the Admiralty, Winston Churchill, requisitioned them on behalf of the British government (something that would have been legal had Britain been at war, which it was not). This gave rise to intense indignation in the Ottoman Empire, something the Germans exploited adroitly by ordering their Mediterranean squadron, consisting of the battleship *Goeben* and the light cruiser *Breslau* to set sail for the Dardanelles. After an epic journey, being hunted by the whole French and British Mediterranean fleets, the ships reached the Straits on 10 August. On the orders of Enver Pasha they were let through the minefields. When Britain demanded their extradition (the Ottoman Empire after all was still neutral at this time), they were bought by the Ottoman government from the Germans for a nominal sum and incorporated into the Ottoman navy.

With the Russian entry into the war, the *casus foederi* had arisen and the Ottomans were under a clear obligation to join in the fighting, but the Unionist government managed to postpone a declaration of war on the grounds that the empire was unprepared and could not go to war without first receiving sizeable German subsidies and armaments. In fact, Enver Pasha would have preferred to delay the declaration of war until the spring of 1915 or even stay out of the war altogether, but when the German government increased its pressure and gave the necessary financial guarantees, the war could no longer be postponed. The decision to fight was taken on 25 October[16] and two days later an Ottoman naval squadron, led by the German admiral Souchon on the *Yavuz Sultan Selim* (as the *Goeben* was now called), set sail with explicit orders from Enver to attack the Russian fleet and achieve naval superiority in the Black Sea. By 11 November the Ottoman Empire was at war with Russia, France and Britain.

The Ottoman Empire during the First World War
When expectations of a short war proved unfounded and the campaign on the western front developed into trench warfare by late 1914, the importance of the Ottoman contribution in German eyes increased. The sultan officially declared Holy War (*Cihat*) after consulting the *Şeyhülislam* on 14 November. Expectations about the effect of this declaration on the Muslim inhabitants of the colonies of the Entente (and of Russian Central Asia) were very high among the Germans (though far less so among most Ottomans), but in spite of a considerable propaganda effort by the Ottoman government, mainly through the *Teşkilât-i Mahsusa*, its effect abroad was negligible. Where the Jihad declaration did have some effect was within the country, where it helped the mobilization effort.

Despite their doubts about the Ottomans' military strength, the Germans encouraged an offensive strategy. The operational plans developed by the German chief of the Ottoman general staff, Bronsart von Schellendorf, envisaged attacks on the Suez Canal and on Russian Transcaucasia. Enver Pasha enthusiastically embraced these plans.

On the Caucasus front, the Russians were the first to attack in November, but the Ottoman army managed to stop them. A counter offensive under the personal command of Enver Pasha started at the end of December. After a successful start, the Ottomans were heavily defeated at Sarıkamış, on the road to Kars, in January. Only a third of the 75,000 troops that took part in the offensive came back (the rest having died on the battlefield or through exhaustion and cold in the mountains or being taken prisoner). Of the survivors, many died in a fierce typhus epidemic in February. Among them was the commanding general, Hafız Hakkı Pasha, who had taken over from Enver after the defeat.

The Armenian question
This military fiasco left eastern Anatolia open to an advance, which duly materialized when the weather improved. It also marked the beginning of the suppression of the Ottoman Armenians, still a controversial issue 100 years later.

The Armenian community formed an important part of the population of the eastern Anatolian provinces although in no province did they constitute a majority or even a plurality (unless one counts Turks, Kurds and other Muslim communities separately, something the Ottomans never did). Estimates of the total number of Armenians in the empire vary, but a number of around 1,500,000, some 10 per cent of the population of Ottoman Anatolia, is probably a reasonable estimate.

After the troubles of 1896, the situation in the east had normalized to some extent, but relations between the local Armenians and Muslims, especially the Kurds, remained tense and there were frequent clashes mostly about land. In May 1913, representatives of the *Dashnakzutioun* had demanded the establishment of a foreign gendarmerie to protect the Armenians in eastern Anatolia. Russia, too, put pressure on the Ottomans after the Balkan War finally to implement the reforms that had been promised in 1878 in Berlin. The CUP government approached the British about this matter and the latter discussed it with the French and Russian governments. In February 1914 agreement was reached about the establishment of two inspectorates with far-reaching powers in eastern Anatolia and a Norwegian and a Dutch inspector were appointed in May. The outbreak of war prevented the scheme from being put into operation. The Unionists, however, had been deeply alarmed. For them the reform project was very reminiscent of what had happened in Macedonia ten years before. The fact that the Armenians had called for foreign intervention in their eyes constituted treason.

At the outbreak of the war, the leaders of the Armenian Revolutionary Federation (*Dashnaktsutyun*) decided that Armenians should stay loyal to the state in which they lived – Ottoman Armenians to the Ottoman, and Russian Armenians to the Russian Empire, but some Armenian nationalists saw in a Russian victory their chance to achieve the establishment of an Armenian state in eastern Anatolia. Russian propaganda encouraged these aspirations. Some 2,000 Armenians joined the Russian army; there were Armenian desertions from the Ottoman army and guerrilla activity behind the Ottoman lines. Confronted with this situation, the Ottoman army started with local deportations of Armenians from behind the frontlines. These were accompanied by a number of, relatively small-scale, massacres. On 25 February Enver Pasha ordered the disarmament of all Armenian soldiers and their transfer to labour battalions repairing roads and carrying supplies. By the end of March the CUP central committee probably took the decision to deport the entire Armenian population to the area of Zor in the Syrian desert. An armed insurrection by Armenians in the provincial capital of Van increased its urgency in the eyes of the CUP.

The measures were not limited to the east. On 24 April some 300 members of the Armenian elite in the capital were arrested and deported to Central Anatolia. Mass deportations started in May and they were retrospectively given a legal basis by a cabinet decisions of 27 and 30 May 1915. By the summer the Armenians had disappeared from Eastern and Central Anatolia. Then the deportation of Armenians from the West started and they lasted until the summer of 1916. Although the deportations generally adhered to a similar pattern, the details differed from place to place. In some places families were notified 24 hours before the deportation, in others several days or even a week. In some places they were allowed to sell their possessions, in others they were 'taken into custody' by the authorities. In some places carts and donkeys were allowed, in others everyone went on foot. The caravans were guarded by gendarmerie, which in many cases acted with great brutality. Even though the actual numbers of soldiers guarding the caravans was quite small, the victims seem to have been so intimidated that we know of very few instances of resistance. This was undoubtedly caused in part by the fact that adult males (roughly between 12 and 70) in many cases were separated from the rest at the start of the deportation and killed.

This relocation (*tehcir*), as it was officially called, resulted in the deaths of enormous numbers of Armenians. So much is undisputed historical fact. The controversies rage on three points. The first is the military necessity of the operation. Turkish historians and their supporters point to the treasonable activities of many Armenians during the war and to the difficulty of knowing which would remain loyal and which would side with the Russians. Some historians have even gone so far as to see the deportations as a justifiable form of counterinsurgency. The other side has – correctly – pointed out that the deportations were not limited to the war zone but took place all over the empire.

The second controversy is over numbers: Turkish historians have put the number of deaths as low as 200,000, while the Armenians have sometimes claimed ten times as many. The reason for the discrepancy, propaganda apart, lies in the differing estimates of the number of Armenians who lived in the empire before the war and of the numbers who emigrated. Between 600,000 and 800,000 deaths seems most likely. The Ottoman army itself mentioned 800,000 deaths, a number that is probably close to the truth.[17]

The third and most important controversy concerns intent, and whether genocide was committed. The Turkish side and its supporters claim that the situation in eastern Anatolia was one of inter-communal warfare, in which Armenian bands (supported by the Russian army) and Kurdish tribes (supported by Turkish gendarmes) struggled for control. They also recognize that the local Muslim population (especially the Kurds) subjected the Armenians sent to Syria to vicious attacks, but they attribute this to lack of control on the part of the Ottoman government rather than to its policies. They point out that the official records of the Ottoman government do not, as far as is known, contain any documents that demonstrate government involvement in the killings. The Armenian side has tried to demonstrate this involvement, but some of the documents it has produced (like some of the so-called Andonian papers) have been shown to be forgeries. Many of the British and American publications on this issue from the time of the First World War that purport to prove government involvement also bear a heavy stamp of wartime propaganda. On the other hand, the same cannot be said of wartime German sources that also report government involvement. Many Germans were shocked by what they saw and they called on the government in Berlin to intercede. In the event that the government prioritized the alliance, however, and faced with an Ottoman leadership that made it clear it would brook no intervention, it did nothing to stop the killings.

What are we to conclude from the evidence? On the basis of the memoirs of survivors and the descriptions of eyewitnesses, not just German, Austrian, American and Swiss missionaries, but also German and Austrian officers and consular officials who were in constant touch with the Ottomans; on the basis of the documentary evidence assembled by the Ottoman tribunal that investigated the Armenian massacres after the war, and, even, to a certain extent on the basis of the memoirs of Unionist officers and administrators we have to conclude that the Committee of Union and Progress under the direction of Talât wanted to 'solve' the Eastern Question by the extermination of the Armenians and that it used the relocation as a cloak for this policy. Some provincial governors, like Dr Mehmet Reşit in Diyarbakır, were themselves instigators of large-scale persecutions, but there were also governors and army officers who refused to cooperate. These, however, were overruled or replaced. The party bosses took the real decisions 'on the ground' in this matter.

Talât's own notes show that he kept stock of the deportations in great detail and his telegraphic instructions show that he ordered that Armenians could not constitute more than 5 per cent of the population anywhere.

The deportation into the Syrian desert of hundreds of thousands of people was in itself a death sentence, as no food or shelter was available there. Apart from this, however, there were mass killings of deportees along the trails, particularly in some specific 'killing fields' like the gorges of Kemah.

The policy of extermination was directed by Dr Bahaettin Şakır, who was based in Erzurum and made use of the members of the 'Bureau of Eastern Affairs', as the Special organization was now called. The agents of this organization in turn nobilized militias that were largely composed of three groups: Kurdish tribes, refugees from the Balkans and the Caucasus, and freed prisoners. Some provincial governors, like Mehmet Reşit Bey in Diyarbakır, Cemil Azmi Bey in Trabzon or Abdülhalik Bey in Bitlis were themselves the architects of large-scale massacres, but there were also governors and officers who refused to cooperate. These were generally removed from office. The real decisions were generally taken by the local party bosses, on instructions from Istanbul.

It is quite hard to determine the precise links between local actions and decision making in the capital, not just because the archive of the CUP does not exist anymore, but also because much of the confidential communication within the CUP was oral and not written down. All in all though, there is enough evidence to be able to say that in 1915/16 there was a conscious, centrally orchestrated policy to end the thousand-year-old Armenian presence in Anatolia. In our modern terms this is a genocide, but that is a term invented in 1944. Contemporaries used different terms: horrors, massacres and – even at that time – holocaust.

The attitude of the population in the areas through which the caravans moved to the desert, varied from time to time and from place to place. Sometimes Armenians were attacked by villagers or tribes and robbed of their last possessions, raped or killed. But sometimes poor villagers shared bread with the deportees or tribes saved them. Those who managed to make it to the isolated and mountainous Alevi stronghold of Dersim were generally sheltered. A large number of Armenian girls ended up in Muslim families and were forcibly converted. Although the motives for adoption were often very far from altruistic, this undoubtedly saved many lives.[18]

If we assume that there was at least a group within the CUP that was intent on the extermination of part of their own population, the question remains: why? The most important motive undoubtedly was nationalist ambition, but not – as many Armenian scholars have long believed – Panturkism. For some the idea of opening up the way to Central Asia may have played a role, but at least until 1917 Panturkism remained a fairly marginal intellectual movement. An Ottoman Muslim nationalism on the other hand had been on the rise since the early years of the century and it had been strengthened enormously since 1912. The fact that by the start of the First World War at least a quarter of the population of Anatolia consisted of refugees, or children of refugees, from the Balkans, the Black Sea shores or the Caucasus, increased existing ethnic tensions. These people remembered the way they or their families had been pushed out of their ancestral homes, often more than once, and they were determined not to let this happen again. The Armenians' decision to call for foreign intervention in 1913 and their refusal to call for an Armenian insurrection against Russian rule acted as catalysts for the radicalization within the CUP.

The massacres were not motivated by some bogus scientific theory on race (and this is an important difference with the persecution of the Jews by the Nazis in the Second World War). On the other hand, it is true that many of the Young Turks had come under the influence of biological materialism and social Darwinism. Their worldview was that of a struggle for survival between nations. In order to survive a nation needed to prove itself through ruthlessness. In this worldview it was easy to see the Ottoman Armenians or Greeks as 'microbes' or 'tumours' that endangered the healthy body of the nation and indeed this kind of terminology can be found in the writings of those who were involved in the persecutions.[19]

Attacks on the Suez Canal

In January 1915 there was a first attempt to take the Suez Canal when 20,000 troops crossed the Sinai desert in ten days, but their attempt to cross or cut off the canal was defeated. Nor was there an anti-British insurrection in Egypt to support the 'holy war', as had been expected. The Ottoman army withdrew to southern Palestine with relatively light casualties. A second attempt to attack the canal, in 1916, also failed.

Offensives by the Entente

After these first Ottoman attempts, the initiative lay squarely with the Entente. The first offensive action by the British was the landing of two Indian divisions at the top of the Persian Gulf to protect British oil installations in the Gulf (which had gained in importance after the British navy started its conversion from coal to oil). On the Sinai front, the Ottoman attempts on the Suez Canal had awakened the British government to its vulnerability and 1915/16 saw a gradual building-up of the forces there in preparation for an offensive.

The main thrust of the Entente, however, was aimed at the Dardanelles. The – strategically undoubtedly correct – assumption was that forcing the Straits and occupying Istanbul would at one stroke cut off the Ottoman Empire from German aid and make it possible to supply and strengthen the Russian front. It would also probably convince the wavering Balkan states to join the Entente. After deadlock had been reached on the western front, this seemed a golden opportunity to defeat Germany through the back door.

A first attempt to force the Straits was made during February and March of 1915. This was a purely naval operation, in which French and British warships tried to silence the Ottoman batteries and then to sweep the minefields in the Dardanelles. But when heavy losses were sustained on 18 March, the operation was cancelled and it was decided to launch an amphibious attack, involving landings on the coast of Asia Minor and on the Gallipoli peninsula. The first landings took place on 25 April. British and Australian troops occupied a number of beaches but they were fought to a standstill before they could reach the top of the ridges that dominate the peninsula. New landings in August brought no breakthrough either and, by January 1916, the Entente troops had evacuated their positions. For the Ottomans this victory over Britain was a source of tremendous national pride, but at the same time the battles at Gallipoli were by far the most costly of the war for them. They had perhaps as many as 300,000 casualties.[20]

The other major success for the Ottoman armies also came in 1916. The British Indian expeditionary force, which had been moving up the Tigris in the direction of Baghdad, was surrounded and forced to surrender at Kut al-Amara in July and 13,000 prisoners of war were interned. The commander, General Townshend, spent the rest of the war in Istanbul; his soldiers spent it in prisoner camps in Anatolia, where they were often employed in forced labour.

Ottoman divisions did not only fight on Ottoman territory. At the request of the German general staff they were also sent to assist the Germans and Austrians in Romania and Galicia and the Bulgarians in Macedonia. Sending these troops to Europe was a luxury the empire could ill afford, because from the second half of 1916 things began to go wrong on all fronts. The Russians continued to advance into Anatolia, eventually taking Trabzon, Erzurum and Van and supplies of weapons and gold and promises of independence from Britain induced the hereditary Ottoman governor of Mecca, Sharif Huseyn, to start an Arab war of independence. At first this was no more than a nuisance, but with the help of British officers and equipment it gradually grew into a serious menace over the next two years; at the same time, British armies were methodically building up their strength in Mesopotamia and on the Palestinian front.

In March 1917, the British expeditionary force took Baghdad and moved on upstream. In Palestine, two attempts by the British to break through at Gaza failed in the spring. The Ottoman army suffered from hunger and disease. In winter, lice in hair and clothing carried typhus. It could be eradicated, but only through effective cleaning of the men and heating of the clothes, for which both water and fuel were often lacking. Malaria struck in summer, particularly in the wetter coastal plains or in places with stagnant water. In late summer and early autumn, cholera, caused by contaminated drinking water, was the greatest killer. In addition, lack of vitamins caused widespread scurvy. The army on the whole was relatively well armed (by the Germans, partly with Belgian and Russian weapons), but otherwise its equipment was dismal. By 1917, the soldiers were dressed in rags and they often went barefoot. Conditions were so bad that soldiers deserted in droves. For the civilian population the situation was often worse, especially in Palestine and Lebanon, which were hit by an unusually severe locust plague and the worst famine in centuries. It was not unusual for divisions to lose half their strength or more on the way from Istanbul to the front (often a journey of a month and a half) and by the end of the war there were more than half a million deserters.[21] The army reached a maximum strength of 800,000 in 1916. By 1917 its strength was halved and by October 1918 only 100,000 men remained in the field. Its main problem was the complete lack of transport facilities. The railways were single-track and they did not yet run through the Taurus and Amanos ranges, so there was no direct rail link between Anatolia (and the capital) and the front. This meant that, to take one example, ammunition imported from Germany had to be loaded and unloaded a total of twelve times to reach the front in Palestine. Instead of strengthening the existing fronts, the German reaction to the reversals was to prepare a counter offensive against Baghdad, for which a new army group called *Yıldırım* (Lightning) was formed in Aleppo under the former German chief of staff, von Falkenhayn. More than 13,000 German troops were sent to Aleppo, but by the time they arrived, the situation in Palestine had become so threatening that they were sent there instead of to Baghdad. Despite this, the British army broke through the lines at Gaza in December and took Jerusalem just before Christmas 1917.

The only positive development of the year from the Ottoman point of view was that after the Russian revolution of November 1917 the Russian government asked for an armistice. At the following peace negotiations in Brest–Litovsk (December–March 1918), the Russians agreed to evacuate eastern Anatolia, including the areas they had conquered in 1878, but while negotiations were going on at Brest, the Russian army in Anatolia was collapsing and Turkish forces retook the area. The most stubborn resistance was offered by Armenian troops, whom the Russians had now deserted. Thousands of other Armenians retreated with the Russian troops to the east.

After the Russian revolution, in December 1917, anti-Bolshevik groups in Georgia, Armenia and Azerbaijan had formed the Republic of Transcaucasia with its capital in Tblisi. This republic refused to recognize the restoration of the border of 1876, whereupon Ottoman troops forcibly occupied the area and the Ottoman government raised its territorial demands beyond what had been agreed at Brest–Litovsk. The Russian revolution had given a new impetus to pan-Turkist ideas, and Enver Pasha himself now strongly favoured the idea of a new empire built on a union with the Turkic areas in Central Asia to replace the areas lost in the Near East. In spite of the dangerous situation on the Mesopotamian and Palestinian fronts, he sent the divisions that returned from Galicia to the Caucasus instead of to the south. When the Transcaucasian republic collapsed in May 1918, the Germans, who were primarily interested in access to the Baku oilfields, tried to restrain the Ottomans, but Enver pressed on and Ottoman troops occupied Azerbaijan in September. The Bolsheviks repudiated the Brest–Litovsk treaty in protest, but there was little they could do in practice.

By the time the Ottoman army entered Baku, the war had already been lost. From 8 August onwards the German army in France was slowly but relentlessly forced to retreat. On 20 September the British army made its decisive breakthrough on the Palestinian front in the battle of Megiddo and the remnants of the Ottoman army retreated to the north.

A British–French expeditionary force from Salonica defeated Bulgaria, which had joined the central powers in 1915 and had formed a vital link between Germany, Austria and the Ottoman Empire, on 29 September. It surrendered on 2 October.

The Unionist government now realized that it had no choice but to sue for an armistice. It also foresaw that negotiations involving the wartime leadership (whose members the Entente had branded as war criminals) would be difficult. The cabinet therefore resigned and was replaced with one led by General Ahmet İzzet Pasha. After some preliminary talks in which General Townshend was the intermediary, an armistice was signed between an Ottoman delegation led by navy minister Hüseyin Rauf (Orbay) and the commander of the British squadron anchored in Moudros in the Aegean, Admiral Calthorpe, on 31 October 1918. This took place aboard the British flagship HMS *Agamemnon* in the bay of Moudros on Lemnos. The fact that the ship was named after the conqueror of Troy gave the setting a curious symbolism.

Reform policies 1913–18: social and cultural change

The CUP used the monopoly of power it acquired in January 1913 and the fact that, through the abolition of the capitulations in October 1914, it was master in its own house for the first time during these years, to force through a programme of political and social reforms.

Part of this programme was concerned with administrative reform, first of all in the army. As we have seen, in January 1914 Enver, the hero of the liberation of Edirne, was promoted twice, given the title of pasha and made war minister. As soon as he was appointed he embarked on a massive reorganization of the army. A large part of the older officer corps was purged and a German military mission of 70 officers led by General Liman von Sanders was given the task of reforming the army. In contrast to earlier military missions, the members of this one were given actual commands and, especially during the First World War when their number increased tenfold to more than 700 officers,[22] they wielded great influence. A German officer, Bronsart von Schellendorf, was even appointed chief of general staff directly under Enver.

There were also renewed attempts to reform the provincial administration, making it more effective, while introducing a measure of decentralization. In this respect, the policies of the CUP in 1913/14 contrasted with those of the previous five years. The decentralization policies were aimed primarily at winning over the Arabs, now by far the largest minority of the empire, to the side of the regime. These policies were only partly successful. While many Arab notables supported the

Unionists, Arab separatist groups, such as *al-Ahd* (the Oath), led by former Unionist officer Aziz Ali al-Misri, continued their agitation.

Another aspect was the further secularization of the judicial and educational systems and the further undermining of the position of the *ulema*. In 1916, the *şeyhülislam*, the highest religious dignitary, was removed from the cabinet and during the next year his jurisdiction was limited on all sides. In 1917 the *şeri* (religious law) courts were brought under the control of the (secular) Ministry of Justice, the religious colleges (*medreses*) were brought under the Ministry of Education and a new Ministry of Religious Foundations was created to administer the *evkaf* (charitable foundations). At the same time the curriculum of the higher *medreses* was modernized, even the study of European languages being made compulsory.

Family law remained the territory of the *şeriat*; but inroads were made even in this stronghold of the Islamic state. In 1913 a new law on inheritance, based on the German code, was introduced. In 1911 a law regulating the court procedure in religious courts was introduced and a decree had laid down a uniform family law for all Ottoman subjects, based on a modernist selection of regulations from all four of the orthodox Muslim schools of law. The law included a number of special arrangements for non-Muslims.

Partly due to the policies of the CUP and partly as a result of the effects of the First World War, the position of women changed, at least of middle and upper class women in the cities. Their right to take the initiative for divorce was expanded, but polygamy was never prohibited. Under the family law of 1917, marriages had to be concluded before a magistrate and brides had to be aged over 16 (although the magistrate could grant exemptions). The Young Turks encouraged women to take part in social life and middle and upper class women started to appear in public with their husbands and to go to theatres and musical performances. At the Turkish nationalist clubs of the Turkish Hearth movement (see ideological debates on page 126 below), women not only listened to speeches, but also gave them. Most important of all perhaps were the educational opportunities the Unionist regime created. Girls profited from the growing number of schools on different levels. Furthermore, primary education was made compulsory for girls in 1913. With respect to higher education, this was at first limited to teacher training colleges (which were expanded rapidly after 1913), though from 1914 onwards a number of courses were opened to women at the University of Istanbul.

Before the First World War few Ottoman women had paid jobs, though a relatively high percentage of the small industrial labour force consisted of women and children. As in other belligerent countries, the lack of manpower caused by the mobilization of the men had to be compensated for by women and this hastened the entry of women into the labour market. The Unionists even founded a Society for the Employment of Women (*Kadınları Çalıştırma Cemiyeti*), which tried to recruit women for service in industry and to regulate their working conditions.[23]

Quite apart from the content of their policies, the whole style of politics was much altered during these last five years of CUP rule. The Unionists tried to mobilize all the country's available resources through the establishment of nationalist organizations – with the word *millî* (national) in their names – the most important of which was the Committee of National Defence (*Müdafaa-i Milliye Cemiyeti*) established in 1913 to create a strong 'home front' during the Balkan War. Participation in politics became much wider. The political game became less elitist. At the same time it also became more brutal. Finally, an important part of the reform programme executed after 1913 consisted of efforts to free the economy from the control of foreigners and Ottoman Christians.

Finance and economics: from liberalism to nationalism
It was no coincidence that the first real Unionist to enter the cabinet was the financial expert Mehmet Cavit Bey, who became minister of finance in June 1909. One of the reasons for the emergence of the Young Turk movement had been the anger of younger members of the ruling elite at the almost colonial economic situation to which the empire had sunk. The CUP was very conscious of the need to attain economic independence if the revolution was to yield meaningful results. In the period between the revolution and the Balkan War, they tried to achieve this through reforms and negotiations.

The Unionists approached the economic situation from a classically liberal point of view. They aimed to encourage the growth of trade and industry by removing traditional barriers and modernizing legislation on transactions and ownership (for instance the land law of 1911 and the inheritance law of 1913). The CUP supported free trade and did not yet see the Ottoman Empire's position as a peripheral producer of raw materials, in a fundamentally weaker situation than the liberal states of western Europe or America, as a reason for protectionism. In Cavit's eyes foreign investment and imported foreign management skills were crucial and he did his best to encourage them whenever he could, even approaching the Japanese government (Japan being the great example for many Young Turks) with a request for experts.

Internally the CUP sided with the capitalists. This is clear from the way it suppressed social unrest and strike actions in the years after 1908 and from the labour-relations legislation it enacted, which favoured the entrepreneurs. In the countryside, the Unionists protected the property rights of the landowners and while they actively encouraged modernization and investment in agriculture (through irrigation projects, infrastructural works and credit facilities), they never attempted to redistribute land or to end the practice of sharecropping.

While encouraging foreign trade and investment, the government also tried to put its own financial house in order, improving the inspection and collection of taxes. As a result government revenue went up by nearly 25 per cent. In December 1909 Cavit published the first realistic and modern budget of the Ottoman Empire, without any attempt to disguise the country's financial problems. This meant, of course, that estimates of expenditure also had to go up. The Unionists hoped and even expected that the combination of liberalism and responsible financial policies would earn them the respect and cooperation of the European powers, which would then be prepared to relinquish the privileges they had under the capitulations and deal with the Ottomans on equal terms.

In these expectations they were disappointed. Foreign investment did not rise spectacularly with the introduction of the constitution. On the contrary, foreigners were frightened by the nationalism of the new regime. Negotiations with the European powers on modification or gradual abolishment of the capitulations led nowhere and even attempts to raise the customs tariffs by 4 per cent were at first frustrated by the powers. The greatest setback was the refusal of France and Great Britain to grant the Ottoman Empire a loan on acceptable terms in 1910. Most of the Ottoman loans had been placed in the European markets, primarily that of Paris, by consortia led by the Anglo–French Ottoman Bank. Since 1881 all of them had been guaranteed by the board of the Public Debt Administration, which was considered much more reliable than the Ottoman government.

In 1909/10 the Ottoman government again needed to borrow money. Pensioning off of large numbers of civil servants, which accompanied the reduction of the overstaffing in government departments, was expensive in the short run and Mahmut Şevket Pasha's unassailable position as *generalissimo* meant that Cavit was powerless to curb the steeply rising military expenditure. So he went to France to seek a loan of about 11 million Turkish pounds, but he refused as contrary to the dignity and independence of the empire the conditions of the Ottoman Bank, which meant having the loan guaranteed by the Public Debt Administration and allowing French supervision of the Ottoman finances. As a result, the negotiations with the Ottoman Bank broke down. Shortly afterwards,

Cavit managed to reach agreement with another French consortium, but the French government wanted to make a point of putting the Young Turks in their place and refused to let the loan be floated on the Paris stock exchange. In this, it was backed by Britain. At this crucial moment in the showdown the Deutsche Bank, on instructions of the German government, intervened to let the Ottomans know that they were prepared to offer a loan without strings attached. An agreement was duly signed, saving Cavit's position and earning the Germans a great deal of goodwill in Istanbul.

There were a few people who drew attention to the semi-colonial position of the Ottoman Empire and to the naiveté of Young Turk economic policies, advocating a much more nationalist economic policy. Chief among them was Alexander Helphand (Parvus), also known by his pen name Parvus. Helphand was a Russian Jew who had emigrated to Germany as a young man and joined the socialist movement there.

After the 1905 revolution in Russia, he had returned and served on the St Petersburg soviet together with Trotsky. After 1912 he combined the functions of journalist, German agent, arms dealer and Marxist intellectual, settling in Istanbul. As an orthodox Marxist, he did not advocate a socialist revolution for the empire (seeing it as irrelevant for a country without an industrial proletariat), but he advocated nationalist economic policies and the building of an indigenous merchant and industrial bourgeoisie in a number of influential articles in the journal *Turk Yurdu* (Turkish homeland).

Parvus's ideas gained in influence from 1913 onwards. In the context of the national mobilization after the Bab-ı Ali coup, the state, now completely dominated by the CUP, began to intervene more actively in the economy. In the following years this new direction evolved into the policies of *Millî İktisat* (National Economy), in which nineteenth century German industrialization served as an example. Any nationalist economic programme could, of course, be fully implemented only if the government were master in its own house first and abolished the capitulations that kept it in a subordinate position to Europe. This chance came with the outbreak of the First World War in 1914. Immediately after the signing of the secret Ottoman–German pact, on 2 August 1914, the Ottoman government announced that it had suspended payment on the national debt.

With the great powers occupied elsewhere, the Unionist government announced in September 1914 that it would unilaterally abolish the capitulations from 1 October. The powers reacted furiously, but there was little they could do about it. Germany first joined in the protest, but later reached an agreement with the Ottomans, recognizing the abolition. Two years later the government unilaterally changed the system of import duties, finally replacing the old method of *ad valorem* taxation, based exclusively on the money value of the imported goods, with specific tariffs for the different imported goods – a further protectionist measure that gave the government more room to pursue an economic policy.

Even before the war, in June 1914, a Law on the Encouragement of Industry had been promulgated, which stipulated that products of Ottoman industry would be preferred, even if they were as much as 10 per cent more expensive than the imported equivalent. A national consumer society was also founded. Echoing Parvus's ideas, the government sought to build a strong national bourgeoisie by forming entrepreneurial cadres; candidates for these cadres were recruited from among Muslim traders in the provincial towns, from the guilds and even from among bureaucrats. The government encouraged the members of this embryonic bourgeoisie to accumulate capital by making use of the exceptional market conditions during the war, which made profiteering possible.

The victims of these policies were the consumers in the cities and above all the Greek and Armenian entrepreneurs, who were not only obliged to use Turkish in their administration and on their shop windows and to take Turks onto the boards of their companies, but were also subjected to discrimination. A campaign of threats and intimidation, orchestrated by İzmir's CUP secretary (and later president of the Turkish republic) Mahmut Celâl (Bayar) drove at least 130,000 Greeks from the Western coastal regions into exile in Greece.[24] Their companies were given to the new Muslim entrepreneurs, who in many cases proved incapable of making a go of them, deprived as they were of overseas contacts, markets and management skills.

The programme of the National Economy gained impetus after the unexpected triumph at Gallipoli, which, of course, gave Turkish morale – and nationalism – a great boost. Its architect was the Unionist party boss in Istanbul and former steward of the guild of bearers, *Kara* ('Black') Kemal Bey, who controlled the newly formed 'national' companies through the *Heyet-i Mahsusa-i Ticariye* (Special Trade Commission). Over 80 new joint stock companies were founded between 1916 and 1918 with active support from the CUP.[25] One of the most important developments in this respect was the establishment of the *Esnaf Cemiyeti* (Society of Artisans and Shopkeepers), in which a number of important trades in the capital were united. They were encouraged to invest their profits in the new companies. This was in a sense a reversal of official policy because as recently as 1913 the government, in an effort to liberalize the economy, had announced the abolition of the old Ottoman guilds.

The war created an extraordinary demand for all kinds of goods, especially foodstuffs. Traditionally the Ukraine, Russia and Romania had been the sources of Istanbul's wheat. Now it had been cut off from these sources and Anatolia, the Turkish heartland, had to replace them. Besides, the empire's allies, Austria and Germany, were also in need of food. The rising demand created new wealth in the countryside, but not through the operation of market forces alone.

After mobilization, the CUP government had a monopoly of railway transport, so it was provincial merchants with good CUP connections who managed to get the necessary freight cars to transport their wheat to Istanbul or to the army. Through the Committee of National Defence and the Artisans' Society, CUP trustees controlled the sale and distribution in the towns and the sale of wheat to the allies was also government-controlled. This led to the intended capital accumulation by the Muslim traders, the large landowners and the guilds, but also to favouritism and corruption on a grand scale. The 'rich of 1916', in other words the war profiteers, became infamous. The wage earners in the towns, of course, bore the cost and at hugely inflated prices (these rose by more than 400 per cent during the war on the official market and even by 1885 per cent if one counts unofficial prices on the black market).[26] Government attempts to ban profiteering and to set up distribution systems were half-hearted and unsuccessful.

In another sense the small farmers and sharecroppers of Anatolia paid the price, for they were not in a position to profit from the higher prices for their products. This was because they not only depended on the large landowners and town merchants for transport and access to the market and but also had to provide the manpower for the Ottoman armies. Manpower shortages became an ever more acute problem as the sons of Anatolia's farmers died in the hundreds of thousands in Mesopotamia, the Caucasus, the Dardanelles and Palestine. By the end of the war, the empire's economy was in ruins.

Ideological debates

The year 1913 marked a turnaround in the influence of ideological currents in the empire, just as it did in political and economic developments. After the suffocating atmosphere of the later years of the reign of Sultan Abdülhamit, with its censorship and intolerance, the start of the constitutional period in 1908 witnessed an explosion of public debate on all kinds of political and social questions. The intensity of the debate was reflected in the number of new publications that appeared. The number of periodicals, which by the end of the old regime had dwindled to barely a dozen, increased thirtyfold in the year after the revolution.

The political and social debate has often been described as going on between three competing ideologies: Ottomanism, the old Young Ottoman ideal of a union of the different communities around the Ottoman throne; (pan) Islamism, which sought to regenerate the empire on the basis of Islamic practices and of solidarity within the Islamic *Ümmet* (Community); and (pan) Turkism, which sought the union of the Turkic peoples under the Ottoman flag. Later authors have sometimes added a fourth current in their descriptions of the intellectual life of the period: Westernism, the movement to adopt European techniques and ideas, which they contrast with Islamic traditionalism.

Such a description fails to bring to life the reality of the debates, which were much more multi-faceted. The basic problems that concerned the publicists of the second constitutional period were the regeneration of state and society. For most of the Young Turks, being the bureaucrats and officers that they were, the state was the logical, indeed the only, means to achieve change. Those who emphasized society rather than the state and who saw in decentralization, private initiative and education the means for regeneration were a much smaller group, centred on Prens Sabahattin.

Two constantly recurring themes in the debates on this fundamental problem of regeneration were the measure of Westernization needed or acceptable and the question of what was to be the basis for identification with and loyalty to the future Ottoman state. It was on this second aspect that Ottomanists, Turkists and Islamists differed. On the first, the divisions were less clear-cut and ran through the three main currents. Some extreme Westernizers, such as Dr Abdullah Cevdet, were in favour of discarding traditional Ottoman civilization completely and adopting the ways of Europe in *toto* in its stead. On the other hand, some religious activists rejected any adoption of Western techniques or ideas. They, however, were the exceptions. The large majority of intellectuals favoured adopting what was seen as the useful elements of European civilization. They believed deeply in the power of science and technology and, for most of them, the most difficult and urgent question, and the one on which most of their debates centred, was the one that Namık Kemal had tried to answer: how to bring about a synthesis of these European elements with Muslim Ottoman civilization; in other words how to become modern while remaining oneself.

The ideological currents were not mutually exclusive either: many Young Turks rationally supported the idea of Ottomanism, were emotionally attached to a romantic pan-Turkish nationalism and were devout Muslims at the same time.

Ottomanism, the idea that all subjects, irrespective of creed or language, would become loyal citizens with equal rights in the new constitutional state, was the official ideology of the revolution of 1908 and it remained so until all Ottomanist illusions were shattered in 1913. Although there were a number of people, for instance in the circle around Prens Sabahattin, who genuinely believed in the concept, its fundamental weakness was that nationalism had already established its hold on all the major communities of the empire. After the euphoria of the revolution, it was soon clear that Greeks, Macedonians, Bulgarians and Armenians continued to further their particularist goals. From 1910 onwards, it became evident that even most Muslim Albanians preferred Albanian rather than Ottoman identity, if the latter implied giving up the autonomy most of Albania had enjoyed in practice under the old regime. At the same time it is true that the CUP itself was already in the grip of Turkish or at least Muslim nationalism, even before the revolution of 1908. While the Committee officially supported Ottomanism (and, indeed, how could it have done otherwise, without voluntarily shedding two-thirds or more of the empire's territory), its interpretation of Ottomanism came close to Turkification of the non-Turkish elements. This did not go unobserved and undermined the credibility of Ottomanism even further.

Turkish, as opposed to Ottoman, nationalism, was a relative late-comer. It had first emerged as a cultural movement in the last two decades of Sultan Abdülhamit's rule. Its origins went back to the work of European Orientalists, such as the Frenchmen de Guignes and Cahun and the Hungarian Vambery, who had started to study the Turks of Central Asia in the nineteenth century, and to the influence of Turks from the Russian Empire, notably the Tatars and the Azeris (also known as 'Tatars' at the time).

Among these peoples a native bourgeoisie had come into being in the latter half of the nineteenth century, sending its sons to Russian schools and universities, where they became acutely aware of the Russian and pan-Slav threat to their own communities. Chief among the Turkists from Russia who were active in the Ottoman Empire were the Azeris Hüseyinzade Ali (Turan) and Ağaoğlu Ahmet and the Tatar Yusuf Akçura, whose family had emigrated to Istanbul.

Akçura studied at the War Academy in Istanbul, where like so many of his contemporaries he was caught disseminating Young Turk propaganda and banished to Tripolitania in 1897. From there he escaped to Paris, from where he went back to Kazan on the Volga, his native city. He became active in Russian politics, but at the same time he published a long article in the Young Turk émigré paper Türk (The Turk), which appeared in Cairo in 1904. This article, which has been called the 'Communist Manifesto of Turkism', was titled Üç Tarz-i Siyaset (Three

Types of Policy). It compared the relative merits of Islamist, Otto-manist and Turkist policies, advocating the last. It can be considered the first coherent statement of pan-Turkist political aims. It pointed out that forging an Ottoman nation out of the diverse elements of the empire was an illusion, that the colonial powers would block any attempt at political union by the Muslims of the world, but that, by contrast, pan-Turkism – the union of the Turkish and Turkic peoples – would have the support of all the Turkic peoples of Asia and would encounter opposition only from Russia.

Pan-Turkism gained a certain amount of support among Young Turk intellectuals, but it received no official blessing until the Balkan War of 1913 had made Ottomanism a dead letter anyway. Even then, however, it remained more of a romantic dream offering an escape from the disasters of day-to-day politics than a concrete policy. From 1911 onwards, the (pan) Turkist movement's platform was the Unionist social and cultural organization *Türk Ocağı* (Turkish Hearth). This organization founded clubs all over the empire, where lectures, discussions, theatrical and musical performances and exhibitions spread Turkish nationalist ideology. Its journal *Türk Yurdu* (Turkish Homeland) was widely read.

During the First World War the Unionists stimulated pan-Turkism in the context of the struggle with Russia. It received a boost with the collapse of the Russian army in 1917 and the occupation (or liberation) of Azerbaijan. A booklet entitled *Türkler bu Muharebede Ne Kazanabilirler?* (What can the Turks win in this struggle?), which Unionist writer Tekin Alp (a pseudonym of Moise Cohen of Seres) published in 1914, was the best-known formulation of pan-Turkist political aims in this period. Under the title *Turkism and Panturkism* it gained fame in Europe as a supposed statement of Ottoman war aims, but Tekin Alp was never influential in CUP circles. At the same time a second type of Turkish nationalism, which concentrated on Anatolia as the Turkish heartland and idealized the culture of the Turkish peasant population, developed side by side – and in competition with – pan-Turkism. It was a city-bred romantic movement that did nothing to improve the appalling living conditions of the Anatolian peasants, but its doctrine of populism (*halkçılık*) aimed to create national solidarity at a time when the economic developments of the war years were creating social tensions that had to be subdued. Not surprisingly, therefore, the organization that represented this type of nationalism, *Halka Doğru* (Towards the People), which was founded in Izmir in 1917, was a creation of the CUP itself.

The (pan) Islamic current had of course had its heyday during the

second half of Sultan Abdülhamit's reign. During the second constitutional period, and especially after the failed counter-revolution of
April 1909, the Unionists were deeply suspicious of Islamic activism.
They saw it as a threat, both to the continued existence of the multi-
national empire and to themselves. Only when political expediency
demanded it, were the Unionists prepared to emphasize the Islamic
character of the state, as they did in 1914–16 in an effort to gain the
loyalty of the Arabs and the support of Muslim inhabitants of the
colonies. This policy, the clearest expression of which was the declaration of holy war (*Cihat*) in 1914, in the end failed in both its aims.

It would be wrong, however, to identify the Islamic current of this era
solely with conservatism or reaction. There were Islamic reactionaries
such as the group that had gathered around the newspaper *Volkan* and
participated in the counter-revolution of 1909, but much more important
was the large group of Islamic modernists or reformists who supported
the constitution. The leading organ of this group, which included people
like Sait Halim Pasha, Mehmet Akif (Ersoy) and Eşref Edip (Fergan),
was the *Sirat-i Müstakim* (the Straight Path), from 1912 known as the
Sebilürreşat (Path of Righteousness). For them, social regeneration was
to be found in a return to Islamic values. Many advocated a return to the
şeriat law, arguing that it was compatible with the adoption of
modernization (as Namık Kemal had done). In their view, the solidarity
of Muslims outside the empire, but in the Islamic *ümmet* (community),
could be an added strength to the empire.

One important Islamic movement that had its roots in the second
constitutional period was that of Nurculuk (the adherents of *Nur* or the
Light), founded by a Kurdish *alim* and member of the modernist wing of
the Nakşibendi mystical order, Sait Nursi. He had joined the
Muhammadan Union in 1909, but at the same time was close to leading
Unionists and later served as a CUP propagandist with the *Teşkilat-i
Mahsusa* and commanding a militia unit on the Caucasus front. The real
growth of his movement belongs to a later period, however, and is best
treated there.

Mehmet Ziya (Gökalp) made the most creative and consistent attempt
at a synthesis of the various elements of the Ottoman heritage (Islam,
Turkish ethnicity, Ottoman state) with European-style modernization.
Gökalp was a follower of the French sociologist Durkheim, whose ideas
on the supremacy of society over the individual he took up, though he
replaced 'society' with 'nation'. An ardent nationalist, Gökalp believed
the nation (*millet*) to be the natural social and political unit. Gökalp's
most influential contribution, however, was not owed to Durkheim.
Drawing on the ideas of the German sociologist Tönnies, he made a

distinction between 'culture' (*hars*), the set of values and habits current within a community, and 'civilization' (*medeniyet*), a rational international system of knowledge, science and technology. According to Gökalp, the Turkish nation had its own strong culture, which had become submerged within a mediaeval civilization that was partly Islamic/Arabian and partly Byzantine. The road to salvation lay in replacing this civilization with a modern European one, while holding on to Turkish culture (of which he considered a purely religious Islam a part). The fault of the *Tanzimat* reformers in his eyes was that in joining European civilization they lost touch with the culture of their own people. In this he echoed the ideas Young Ottomans such as Namık Kemal had put forward fifty years earlier.

Whatever the merits of Gökalp's ideas as theories, their great attraction was that they allowed national pride to be reconciled with the adoption of European ways. Both in the Turkish Hearth movement and in the CUP itself (where he was for a time a member of the central committee and more or less the party ideologue), Gökalp enjoyed considerable influence.

In reviewing these intellectual currents of the second constitutional period it is remarkable that, like the CUP itself, which had its origins in the ethnically mixed region of Macedonia, most of the important thinkers and writers who took part in the debates were from peripheral or mixed areas. Apart from those who came from the Turkic areas of the Russian Empire (Akçura, Ağaoğlu, Hüseyinzade, the nationalist poet Mehmet Emin), the most ardent Turkish nationalist Tekin Alp was a Jew from Seres, the Westernizer Abdullah Cevdet a Kurd from Arapkir, Ziya Gökalp half Kurdish and from Diyarbakır, and Sait Nursi a Kurd from Bitlis. It seems that direct confrontation with the multiethnic character of the empire in these regions made them more acutely aware of the fundamental problems of Ottoman society.

While it is important to have an understanding of the ideological debates of the Young Turks, it is also important to remember that the men who actually wielded power, the leaders of the CUP, were not ideologues but men of action. They were ideologically eclectic and their common denominator was a shared set of attitudes rather than a common ideological programme. Important elements in this set of attitudes were nationalism, a positivist belief in the value of objective scientific truth, a great (and somewhat naive) faith in the power of education to spread this truth and elevate the people, implicit belief in the role of the central state as the prime mover in society and a certain activism, a belief in change, in progress, which contrasted sharply with the cautious conservatism prevailing in the Hamidian era. The Young Turks really were young (aged

30 on average in 1908) and they were the first movement in the Ottoman Empire to see youth as an advantage. In Ottoman culture, which had always privileged age and experience, the whole idea that youth might have a better understanding of the future was in itself revolutionary.

9 · The Struggle for Independence

The armistice of Moudros

The armistice concluded on 31 October 1918 at Moudros between Admiral Calthorpe, commander of the British Black Sea squadron, and an Ottoman delegation under Hüseyin Rauf Bey, the Navy Minister, really amounted to an Ottoman capitulation. The 25 articles contained provisions such as the military occupation of the Straits, control by the Entente of all railway and telegraph lines, demobilization and disarmament of the Ottoman troops, except for small contingents needed to keep law and order, surrender by all Ottoman troops in the Arab provinces and the freeing of all Entente prisoners of war in Ottoman hands (but not the other way round). All German and Austrian military personnel had to leave the country within two months. The most dangerous clause from the Ottoman point of view was article seven, which stipulated that the Entente had the right to occupy any place in the Ottoman Empire itself if it considered its security to be under threat. Article 24 gave the Entente the right to intervene militarily in the 'Armenian' provinces if law and order should break down there. These articles could (and did) allow the Entente to use force more or less as it pleased. Harsh though they were, the conditions were accepted – sometimes even greeted with relief – by the Ottomans. When a resistance movement developed in the years after the war, its leaders did not protest against the armistice agreement as such, but against the way the Entente abused its conditions.[1]

The armistice went into effect the next day and on the whole was effective. The only major problem arose over Mosul, the main town in northern Mesopotamia. On the day of the armistice, the British forces were still some 60 kilometres to the south of Mosul, but the British command insisted on the occupation of the town under article seven of the armistice. The local Ottoman commander refused and referred the matter to Istanbul, which told him to comply, and between 8 and 15 November the Ottoman troops evacuated the town. The fact that Mosul was occupied after the armistice caused controversy over the possession of the province in later years. The same situation applied in the *sancak* (district) of Alexandrette (İskenderun) on the Syrian coast. Who held exactly what in the inland desert of Syria was also completely unclear. This would lead to conflicting claims in years to come.

The postwar situation: an overview

The wartime leaders of the CUP, who had already handed over power to a new cabinet under Ahmet İzzet Pasha on 14 October, left the country as soon as the armistice was concluded. On the night of 1 November, Cemal, Enver, Talât, Bahaettin Şakir, Dr Nazım and three others left aboard a German warship for Odessa, for fear that they would be held to account for their treatment of the Armenians. As far back as 1915 the Entente had announced that it intended to do so and there is no doubt that it would indeed have brought them to trial. In the event, these Unionists never appeared in court but Armenian assassins killed them all, apart from Enver, in 1920/21.

After the war the former leaders spent most of their time in Berlin, where they engaged in complex political schemes and intrigues, which took them to places as far apart as Rome, Moscow and Afghanistan. Only one of them, however, Enver Pasha, played a significant role in postwar Turkish politics.

The flight of the main Unionist leaders left a power vacuum in Istanbul. The parties who were in a position to compete for power were:

- The palace: Sultan Mehmet V had died in July 1918 and been succeeded by his brother Vahdettin Efendi, who ascended the throne under the name of Mehmet VI. Intelligent and headstrong, the new sultan fully intended to use the opportunity to escape from the role of puppet he had had to play under the Unionists.
- The Liberals: the Liberal opposition, united in the *Hürriyet ve İtilâf Fırkası* which had been silenced in 1913, now reorganized around a number of its pre-1913 leaders, notably *Damat* ('son-in-law' because he was married to a member of the royal family) Ferit Pasha.
- The Entente: representatives of the Entente soon arrived in the capital amid great pomp. A fleet of allied warships anchored off the imperial palace on the Bosphorus. The main concern of the Entente representatives was supervision of the execution of the armistice terms, but they also tried to influence Ottoman politics. However, soon after the armistice the first differences of opinion between the French, the British and the Italians started to appear.
- The Unionists: even though their leaders had left, the Unionists still controlled parliament, the army, the police force, the post and telegraph services and many other organizations. The new regime

started purges in 1919, but neither it nor the Entente had enough manpower to replace the majority of Unionist officials.

While these were the main players in the political game in the capital, increasingly from late 1918 onwards and completely after the British occupied Istanbul in March 1920, the real political struggle was fought in Anatolia. The wartime CUP leadership had prepared the ground before it left the country. It based its plans on establishing a national resistance movement in Asia Minor, drawn up when everyone, including the CUP leaders, expected the British and French navies to break through the Dardanelles in March 1915. Had that happened, the Ottoman government would have left Istanbul for Konya.[2]

Though several leaders played a role in 1918, Enver seems to have been the driving force. He was convinced that only the first phase of the war had been lost and that, as in the Balkan War in 1913, the opportunity would come for a second round in which the Ottomans could return to the offensive. By the end of the war, pan-Islamist and, especially, pan-Turkist ideas had taken hold of Enver and he expected the Turkic areas of Central Asia, especially recently liberated Azerbaijan, to play a vital role in the continued struggle. It was for this reason that he decided to order the Ottoman divisions that had returned from Europe in 1918 to proceed to the Caucasus. He himself had intended to go to Baku from Odessa in November 1918, but illness had prevented him from doing so. At the same time, both he and Talât had ordered the *Teşkilât-i Mahsusa* to store guns and ammunition in secret depots in a number of places in Anatolia. The *Teşkilât* – which was reconstituted in October 1918 under the name of *Umum Alem-i İslam İhtilâl Teşkilâti* (General Revolutionary Organization of the Islamic World) – sent out emissaries with instructions to start guerrilla bands in the interior. This was not a particularly difficult thing to do since many such bands were already in existence and had played a gruesome part in the maltreatment of Armenians and Greeks. They lived in fear of retribution should they give up their arms and disband.

The most important step taken by the Unionist leadership before the end of the war was the creation of *Karakol* (the Guard). Again, the initiative was taken by Talât and Enver the week before they left. The actual founders were Colonel *Kara* (Black) Vasıf (an important member of the inner circle of Unionist officers) and *Kara* Kemal, the Unionist party boss in Istanbul. The name of the organization was a pun on their surnames, and its purpose was to protect Unionists in the postwar situation and shield them from the revenge of the Entente, the Liberals and the Christian communities. It also aimed to strengthen the resistance in Anatolia and the Caucasus by sending able people, money, arms and supplies there from the capital.[3]

While it prepared an armed resistance movement from Anatolia, the CUP also prepared for a public defence of the rights of the Turkish Muslim parts of the population in areas perceived to be in danger of occupation by the Greeks, Armenians, French, Italians or British. This initiative took the shape of the formation of regional 'societies for the defence of the national rights', which were to play a vital role in the establishment of the national resistance movement in Anatolia (and Thrace) after the war. The first such society was founded as early as November 1918.[4]

When the national resistance movement in Anatolia developed, its main adversary turned out to be not Britain or France but Greece. With strong support from Britain, Greece was granted the right to occupy the area around İzmir in May 1919. In the following years, the Greek invasion of Asia Minor would take on massive proportions. The reason for this can be found in the way the Entente powers conducted the peace negotiations after the war. Negotiations were conducted not with the defeated countries – the victors dictated the peace terms – but between the Entente powers, who faced a number of partly conflicting agreements and promises made during the war that had to be sorted out. This took time. So much time, in fact, that when the Entente finally imposed its extremely harsh peace terms on the Ottoman Empire in August 1920, the continuous demobilization of its troops since the war had left it without the means to enforce them. The Greeks, led by their Prime Minister Eleutherios Venizelos, exploited this situation; they offered to act as the strong arm of the Entente and to force the Turkish resistance movement in Anatolia to accept the peace terms. The result was a bloody war that ended with a complete Greek defeat in 1922.

Istanbul, November 1918–March 1920

The palace

Throughout this whole period Sultan Mehmet VI Vahdettin, who was destined to be the last Ottoman Sultan, pursued policies aimed at appeasing the Entente, and especially Britain, in order to get a more favourable peace treaty. As with other advocates of this line, he lost all credibility when, despite his efforts, the peace treaty turned out to be extremely harsh in the summer of 1920.

The sultan, like his predecessors, thought along dynastic and religious lines. What mattered for him was the preservation of the dynasty, of Istanbul as the seat of the caliphate and of his own authority over the

Muslim population of the Middle East, for which he felt a strong responsibility. He was not a nationalist (indeed, he saw nationalism and the Unionists who had succumbed to that ideology as responsible for the disaster that had befallen the empire) and he cared little for the complete independence of Anatolia or any other region.

In contrast to his direct predecessor, who had been a puppet in the hands of the Unionists, Sultan Vahdettin actively intervened in politics to promote the anti-Unionist, anti-nationalist, pro-British line. His main weapon was of course the appointment of grand viziers (and cabinet ministers) of his choice. In this respect, the period up to April 1920 can be divided into three sub-periods.

The cabinets

The first period was one of transition. When the wartime leaders handed over power in October, the sultan had wanted to install a nonpartisan cabinet under the old diplomat Ahmet Tevfik Pasha (Okday), but the Unionists had insisted on a moderate CUP cabinet led by the former chief of staff Field Marshall Ahmet İzzet Pasha (Furgaç), not a Unionist but nevertheless trusted by the Committee. With the wartime leaders out of the way and the armistice concluded, the sultan replaced İzzet Pasha with Tevfik Pasha, who headed two cabinets, of an increasingly anti-Unionist character, from 11 November 1918 to 3 March 1919.

On 4 March his cabinet was replaced with the first headed by *Damat Ferit Pasha*, a key figure in Ottoman politics after the war who headed no less than five cabinets. He was close to the palace, being the sultan's brother-in-law and the only person the monarch really trusted. He was also a leading member of the revived *Hürriyet ve İtilâf Fırkası*. The three Ferit Pasha cabinets of March–September 1919 constitute a second sub-period. They were confronted with increasing activity from the nationalist resistance, both in the capital and in Asia Minor, especially after the Entente had granted Greece permission to occupy İzmir and surrounding areas in May. They reacted with increasingly determined efforts to suppress the resistance and punish the Unionists.

By late September the pressure of the resistance movement forced Ferit Pasha to step down. Unlike Ferit Pasha's governments, the two cabinets that succeeded him under Ali Rıza Pasha (until 3 March 1920) and Salih Hulusi Pasha (until 2 April) tried to cooperate with the nationalist resistance and to heal the increasing rift with Anatolia.

The parties

Although the revived Party of Freedom and Understanding was the dominant force in official politics for most of this period, the Unionists' activities were not limited to underground resistance. For a while Unionist parties continued to function. At its last congress at the beginning of November, the CUP dissolved itself and founded the *Teceddüt Fırkası* (Renewal Party). A group of dissident Unionists under Fethi (Okyar) founded the *Osmanlı Hürriyetperver Avam Fırkası* (Ottoman Liberal People's Party). Apart from these, a plethora of smaller parties led an ephemeral existence in the postwar period.

After the dissolution of parliament in December, pressure on the Unionists began to rise. Increasing numbers of prominent committee members were arrested (more than 100 had been arrested by the beginning of April), partly on the initiative of the Liberal government and partly at the request of the British, who intended to try 'war criminals' for their assumed role in the persecution of Armenians, for maltreating British prisoners of war, or for undermining the terms of the armistice. A special Ottoman tribunal dealt with a number of cases, but the British later deported many of those arrested to Malta, where most of them stayed until late 1921.

Political activity, which the dissolution of parliament had anyway impeded, was further curtailed when the Renewal Party was closed down in May 1919. The government resisted the pressure for new elections because it did not consider the situation stable enough, but in the end it yielded to demands from the Anatolian resistance. Elections were held in the autumn of 1919, but by then the Unionist-led resistance movement was in control of most of Anatolia and the chamber, when it met in January 1920, bore a decidedly Unionist and nationalist stamp and acted as a mouthpiece for the resistance. The nationalist majority in the chamber organized itself as the *Felâh-i Vatan Grubu* (Salvation of the Fatherland Group).

On 28 January 1920 it adopted a manifesto called the National Pact (*Misak-i Millî*), which was the resistance movement's official statement of aims and this remained so throughout the independence war that followed. The text, which was based on the earlier resolutions of the congresses organized by the nationalists in Erzurum and Sivas (see pp. 149–50), consisted of six articles.

1. The territories inhabited by an Ottoman Muslim majority (united in religion, race and aim)[5] formed an indivisible whole, but the fate of the territories inhabited by an Arab majority that were under foreign occupation should be determined by plebiscite.
2. A plebiscite could determine the fate of the 'three *vilayet*s' of Batum, Kars and Ardahan, which were Russian from 1878 to 1918.

3. The same should hold true for the fate of western Thrace.
4. The security of the capital, Istanbul, and of the Sea of Marmara must be assured. The opening of the Straits to commercial shipping would be a subject for discussion with other interested countries.
5. The rights of minorities would be established in conformity with the treaties concluded between the Entente and European states.
6. The economic, financial and judicial independence of the empire should be assured and free from restrictions (in other words, a return of the capitulations would be unacceptable).

This was the fundamental statement of the nationalist programme. It is significant that it advocated not Turkish national sovereignty but that of all Muslim Ottomans.

There was an attempt to bridge the party differences and to present a unified front to give the Turks a voice at the peace conference in Paris by establishing a 'National Congress' uniting 63 different groups and parties. The congress was active intermittently between November 1918 and November 1919, but although it published a number of brochures and even sent a delegation to Paris, it received no hearing.

Open political activity ended with the British occupation of Istanbul on 16 March 1920, which was intended both to stop collaboration with the nationalists from within the Ottoman government institutions and to put pressure on the nationalists. The nationalist leaders in parliament were aware that action on the part of the British was impending, but they decided to stay in session rather than go underground and leave for Anatolia because they wanted to show up clearly that British policy was suppressing the national rights of the country. And, indeed, British security officers arrested both Hüseyin Rauf and *Kara* Vasıf, the most prominent leaders of the Felâh group in the parliament building. The last Ottoman parliament thereupon prorogued itself in protest on 2 April.

Efforts to arouse public opinion

Whereas the different parties and political groups – both Unionist and anti-Unionist – failed to make a significant impact either on public opinion or on politicians in Europe, a number of social and cultural organizations that had been closely linked to the CUP during the war but that were not openly political, made an important contribution to winning over Muslim opinion to the nationalist cause. In the first months after the armistice the atmosphere among the Muslim population in general was one of despair and resignation, but the Greek occupation of İzmir in May 1919 was a turning point. Immediately after the occupation, mass demonstrations, led by students and professors from the University of Istanbul, took place in protest.

The Entente

The conditions of the armistice and the presence of over 50,000 Entente troops (30,000 of them British) always meant that the representatives of the Entente would be the dominant political influence in the capital, even before the official occupation of Istanbul in March 1920. Even during the periods when a compliant Ottoman government was in power, Entente control was complicated by several factors.

The fact that the empire was still formally independent gave Ottoman officials sympathetic to the nationalists all kinds of opportunities to aid the Anatolian movement by sending information, supplies, arms and people. The Entente had no means of checking what went on in every government department. Its information on what went on in the Turkish Muslim part of Ottoman society was limited by having to rely (certainly in the case of the British) almost exclusively on members of the Greek and Armenian minorities, which led them to underestimate both the numerical strength and the abilities of the underground resistance.

The administrative structure the Entente introduced was extremely complicated. The British Black Sea army, commanded first by General Milne and later by General Harington, was responsible for the occupation of the Straits zone, while it had been agreed that European Turkey, as part of the Balkans, would be under the control of the French commander of the *Armée de l'Orient*, which had originally been based on Salonica and had defeated Bulgaria in 1918, General Franchet d'Esperey. In Istanbul, which was both on the Bosphorus and in Europe, this of course made for continuous friction. The military authorities were not, however, in complete control. The Entente states also had their diplomatic representatives, called high commissioners and not ambassadors while a state of war continued to exist formally between the Entente and the empire. Officially, the military commanders were subject to their authority. In reality, they often acted independently. After the military occupation of the capital in March 1920, the influence of the military commanders naturally increased even further.

The high commissioners not only represented their governments diplomatically, but also shouldered a large and increasing part of the actual administration of the capital through the 'Allied Commissions of Control and Organization', which dealt with things like food supplies, medical facilities, refugee problems and financial affairs. The Ottoman government lacked the means to pay its servants or to feed the population, so the Entente was more or less forced to step in and it did so quite efficiently. Even so, life was difficult enough in Istanbul in the postwar years. The cost of living, which had already gone up by a staggering 1800 per cent during the war (1400 per cent of which was between 1917 and 1918), peaked in February 1919. The capital experienced a severe shortage of coal and wheat, which was eventually solved by imports from Britain and the USA respectively, primarily by relief agencies. Prices dropped by about 35 per cent and then stabilized.[6]

The large number of refugees in the city aggravated the situation. Apart from the mass of displaced persons one would expect in the capital of a defeated country after a war, there were the Russian fugitives. Some had come early in 1920 and in November of that year the French navy evacuated some 150,000 anti-Bolshevik White Russians under General Wrangel from the Crimea and settled them in the Straits area. About half of the refugees lived in the Istanbul area, adding to a housing problem that was compounded by the Entente's requisitioning of buildings.[7] The complicated administrative structure could have been made to work if trust and goodwill had characterized relations between the Entente powers, but this emphatically was not the case. While British policy towards the Ottomans remained hawkish and Britain's conduct in its zone of occupation was harsh and even vindictive, the Italians from 1920 and the French from 1921 began to court the nationalist resistance – a cause for frequent clashes between the high commissioners.

The Unionist underground

The Unionist underground in Istanbul exploited this disunity. Between November 1918 and March 1920, *Karakol* managed to smuggle a considerable number of Unionist officers – many of them wanted men – to Anatolia. In addition, it supplied the emerging resistance movement in Anatolia with large quantities of arms, supplies and ammunition stolen from Ottoman stores under Entente control. Some 56,000 gun locks, 320 machine guns, 1500 rifles, 2000 boxes of ammunition and 10,000 uniforms are reported to have been smuggled to Anatolia in this way.[8] Apart from former *Teşkilat-i Mahsusa* agents, the bearer and boatmen's guilds – still under the control of *Kara* Kemal – and the Unionist officials in the War Ministry and in the telegraph service played a vital role in these operations. Finally, *Karakol* provided the resistance with information gained from its espionage network in government offices. The realization of the extent of collaboration with the Anatolian nationalists from within the Ottoman bureaucracy was the prime reason for the formal occupation of Istanbul by the British in 1920.

When more and more officers left for Anatolia in 1919 and a resistance movement started to emerge, the need was felt for someone with authority and an untainted reputation to head the movement. First, the underground seems to have approached Ahmet İzzet Pasha (Furgaç), the former Chief of General Staff and grand vizier – not a Unionist but trusted by the Unionists as an ardent patriot. When they could not get his agreement, leading *Karakol* members approached Mustafa Kemal Pasha (Atatürk). According to some sources Enver's uncle Halil had been approached first, when İzzet Pasha refused.[9]

Mustafa Kemal Pasha had been an early member of the CUP, having joined the organization in February 1908.[10] He had been one of the inner circle of activist officers who took part in the revolution of 1908, and in the 'Action Army' of 1909, and he had served in Libya in 1911. Within the CUP he seems to have belonged to Cemal Pasha's faction. Within that, he was particularly close to Ali Fethi (Okyar), an influential Unionist officer and a rival to Enver. During 1912/13, personal relations between Enver on the one hand and Fethi and Mustafa Kemal on the other had become very strained. As a result, Mustafa Kemal was left outside the centre of power once Enver had emerged as the foremost military leader after the Bab-ı Ali coup of January 1913. This meant that in 1919 he was not associated with the wartime policies of Enver and Talât. During the First World War, Mustafa Kemal had made a name for himself as commander of the Anafarta front during the Dardanelles campaign and afterwards he had fought with distinction on the eastern Anatolian and Palestinian fronts, ending the war as a brigadier in charge of all the troops on the Syrian front. In the army he had a reputation as an extremely able but proud and quarrelsome officer. After the armistice, he moved to Istanbul and for a time tried to gain a position in politics, associating himself with the Ottoman Liberal People's Party of his friend Ali Fethi and giving press interviews to raise his profile. By the spring of 1919 it was clear that this led nowhere and he considered leaving for Anatolia, as increasing numbers of his colleagues were doing.

Mustafa Kemal's combination of high standing within the army and, politically speaking, clean hands made him an ideal candidate for the leadership of the resistance. Once he had agreed, an opportunity to launch him was soon found. The *Damat* Ferit government was alarmed at the amount of inter-communal violence in eastern Anatolia and the Black Sea region (which could provoke Entente intervention under article 24 of the armistice agreement) and it wanted to appoint a military inspector to pacify and disarm the region. The interior minister, Mehmet Ali Bey, was related to Ali Fuat Pasha (Cebesoy), one of Mustafa Kemal's closest officer friends, who had himself already left for Anatolia. A meeting with Mehmet Ali Bey, and then with the grand vizier was arranged, and Mustafa Kemal was appointed inspector of the Third Army in the east.

Friends at the War Ministry then drew up his brief, giving him very wide powers, including the right to communicate directly with all military and civil authorities in the region of his inspectorate, which encompassed all of eastern Anatolia. Armed with these wide-ranging powers and accompanied by a staff of 18, he then left Istanbul, arriving in the Black Sea port of Samsun on 19 May 1919. His activities once he had arrived there are best treated within the context of the developments in Anatolia.

The peace negotiations

Even during the war, the Entente powers had concluded a number of agreements concerning the division of the Ottoman Empire, once it was defeated. Basically, they fall into two categories. In the first are agreements between the powers that aimed at a division of the spoils without upsetting the balance of power between them. The diplomatic activity concerned with these agreements can be considered the final act in the drama of the 'Eastern Question'. In the second are the promises made to inhabitants or would-be inhabitants of the region under a more modern type of arrangement in which self-determination, albeit under tutelage, played a role.

The first treaty was the so-called Constantinople agreement of March 1915, in which France and Britain recognized a number of Russian demands. After the victory Russia would be allowed to occupy parts of eastern Anatolia, Istanbul and the Straits. This of course constituted a major gain for the Russians and subsequently France and Britain started negotiations on their claims for compensation for this disturbance of the balance of power. In the meantime, the Entente promised southwestern Asia Minor to Italy, as part of its price for joining the Entente, under the Treaty of London of April 1915.

The Franco–British negotiations about compensation, which took place at the French embassy in London eventually led to an agreement between their representatives on 16 May 1916. This so-called Sykes–Picot agreement (named after the two negotiators – Mark Sykes of the British Arab Bureau in Cairo and François Georges-Picot, a French diplomat) handed the coastal strip of Syria to France, with a sphere of influence in the interior, that also included the oil-rich province of Mosul. Britain would receive the provinces of Baghdad and Basra and a sphere of influence to the west, including access to the Mediterranean at Haifa and Jaffa. Apart from these two port cities Palestine would come under international administration, but its exact form remained unclear.

The interior areas would be handed over to an Arab kingdom or kingdoms, whose territory would overlap with the spheres of influence. The agreement was approved by the British and the French cabinet in

February 1916 and laid down in an exchange of letters between the British foreign office and the French ambassador. It was later also agreed to by the Russian government, but the agreement remained secret until the Bolshevik government published it after the Russian revolution.

The August 1917 agreement of St Jean de Maurienne redefined Italy's claims on southern Asia Minor, including İzmir and its hinterland in the Italian zone, but the revolution in Russia prevented its ratification. France and Britain later used this fact to oppose Italy's claims.

These were all agreements between the powers, but in the meantime promises had been made to others too. Contacts between the British high commissioner in Egypt and the Sharif of Mecca, which would eventually lead to the Arabian rebellion, had first been laid in the spring of 1915. They developed into a long-drawn-out exchange of letters (between July 1915 and March 1916) in which, in exchange for an Arab revolt, the British promised the sharif support for the establishment of an Arab kingdom stretching to the 37th parallel in the north, with the exception of the Syrian coast and the holy places in Palestine. The promise was only valid insofar as it did not conflict with existing agreements.

In November 1917, the British foreign secretary, Arthur Balfour, in an effort to gain the support of influential Jewish circles at home and – especially – in Germany and Austria, promised the leader of the Zionist movement in Britain, Lord Rothschild, that Britain would support the establishment of a Jewish 'national home' in Palestine. Finally, in January 1918, President Wilson clarified the American war aims with his 'Fourteen Points'. These recognized the right to self-determination of nations – something that made them intensely unpopular with the French and British governments. Wilson's programme raised the hope of national independence movements all over the world – hopes which would largely remained unfulfilled after the war.

The situation was further complicated for the statesmen of the Entente when, immediately after the Bolshevik revolution, the new Russian government denounced all 'imperialist' treaties and – worse – made them public. The Ottoman government seized this propaganda opportunity to distribute the Sykes–Picot agreement, which clearly contradicted the promises made to Sharif Husayn in Syria. The sharif protested to the British high commissioner but received a noncommittal reply. Only in June 1918 did the British government clarify its position on the matter. It made a distinction between two groups of territories. Areas that had been independently Arab before the war and those liberated by Arabs would gain independence, while the areas liberated by the Entente or still in Turkish possession would be brought into the sphere of influence of one of the Entente powers.

This was the situation with regard to treaties, agreements and promises when Ottoman resistance collapsed in October 1918. Now the peace
conference that gathered in Paris was faced with the task of reconciling
them. Basically the work of this conference consisted of negotiations
among the major Entente powers and between them and their client states
such as Greece and Serbia. Russia of course was no longer an Entente
power and the United States withdrew from the conference for domestic
reasons in 1919. There was never any question of serious negotiations
between the victors and the defeated states. The latter were simply
presented with a final text that they could either sign or – theoretically –
refuse.

The decision-making on the Near East was delayed because a settlement of the German and Austrian questions had priority. It was also made
more difficult by the fact that the representatives of the powers were
literally beleaguered by delegations representing the different ethnic
groups in the Near East: Greeks, Armenians, Turks, Kurds, Arabs and
Jews, all pressing their conflicting claims.

The main conflict between Britain and France concerned Syria.
Britain had made commitments to the Arab rebels and was ready to
modify the Sykes–Picot treaty in favour of the independent Arab
kingdom proclaimed in Damascus by Faysal, son of Sharif Husayn. This
state had been recognized by Britain, but not by France, which demanded
full execution of the Sykes–Picot agreement. When the negotiations had
reached deadlock, the Americans took the initiative to send a commission
(the so-called King–Crane Commission) to Syria in June 1919 to find out
the views of the population. The Arabs pinned their hopes on this
commission, but France and Britain never took it seriously and ditched it
after the American withdrawal from the peace conference. Faced with a
choice between France and the Arabs, Britain finally opted for France in
September 1919. France would acquire the Syrian coast outright and a
mandate on behalf of the League of Nations over the hinterland, which
Faysal would govern. In return, France agreed to a British mandate for
Palestine and inclusion of Mosul and its oilfields in the British mandate
of Iraq. This arrangement, which was confirmed at the session of the
peace conference in San Remo in the winter of 1919/20, led to an Arab
revolt in Syria. It was brutally suppressed by French troops, and France
occupied all of Syria in July 1920.

The three main problems with respect to a settlement in Anatolia
were: the Armenian question; the conflicting claims of Greece and Italy
in the West; and the position of Istanbul and the Straits. As regards
Armenia, the conference eventually decided to establish an independent
Armenian state in eastern Anatolia, which went a long way to fulfilling

the Armenian nationalists' expansionist demands. The determination of the precise borders of the new Armenia was left to US president Wilson. The reason for this was the hope that the United States might take upon themselves a mandate for Armenia. In September 1919 Wilson sent the Harbord commission (a sister of the King–Crane Commission) to Anatolia to investigate the feasibility of such a plan. Harbord advised an American mandate for all of Anatolia, but because of the growing American isolationism, his plan was never formally discussed in congress. The idea of an American mandate appealed to many Ottoman Turks, who pinned their hopes on the twelfth of President Wilson's Fourteen Points, which assured the Turkish portions of the Ottoman Empire a 'secure sovereignty'. A number of Turkish intellectuals even founded a 'Wilsonian League', but the idea was never seriously taken up by the Entente, or indeed by the nationalist leadership in Anatolia.

By late 1919 the agreement on the establishment of an independent Armenia was a dead letter anyway, because of Turkish opposition. The geographical location of the area meant that enforcing the decision in the face of Turkish armed opposition would have necessitated a large-scale military invasion, for which the Entente by now had neither the means nor the stomach.

The second problem revolved around the fact that both Italy and Greece (which had joined the Entente towards the end of the war) claimed the same area in southwestern Asia Minor. Italy had the older claims, but its simultaneous pursuance of territorial claims on the eastern shores of the Adriatic weakened its position at the conference, while Greece received ever-stronger backing from Britain. This was due partly to the remarkable psychological ascendancy of the Greek prime minister, Venizelos, over his British colleague, Lloyd George,[11] but partly also to cool political reasoning: Britain saw in Greece a valuable counterweight to France and Italy in the eastern Mediterranean. The result was that Greece received permission to occupy İzmir and its environs in May 1919.

The Entente was faced with a dilemma over Istanbul and the Straits. The strategic and political importance of these areas in the eyes of the British government meant that if they were to be left inside the Ottoman Empire, the whole empire would have to be under some sort of foreign control, possibly in the shape of a mandate. If, on the other hand, the areas were to be severed from the Ottoman Empire, the latter would be so insignificant that it could be left to its own devices. The British took up a hard-line position, but the French were much more conciliatory to the Turks, wanting them to remain in possession of Istanbul. In December 1919 the French – in exchange for getting their way on Syria

– accepted the British demands, but strangely enough the British cabinet itself then changed its mind under pressure from the India Office, which feared a violent reaction among British Indian Muslims and and from the War Office, which regarded Istanbul as indefensible against a future Turkish attack.[12]

All the major decisions concerning the peace settlement had been made by the beginning of spring 1920 and the terms were submitted to the Ottoman delegation on 11 May. Istanbul remained in Ottoman hands, but, that apart, the terms were extremely severe. So severe in fact that the Ottoman delegation refused to accept them and the treaty was only signed after Istanbul had sent a new and more compliant delegation.

The Treaty of Sèvres, signed on 10 August 1920, left the Ottoman Empire only a rump state in northern Asia Minor with Istanbul as its capital. Eastern Thrace and the area around İzmir were given to Greece, while the Straits were internationalized. An independent Armenian republic was created in eastern Anatolia. France established mandates in Syria and Lebanon and a sphere of influence in southern Anatolia. Britain established mandates in Palestine, southern Syria (now called Transjordan) and Mesopotamia (Iraq), including the oil-rich province of Mosul. Italy received the southwestern part of Asia Minor as a sphere of influence. Kurdistan to the north of the province of Mosul was left with the Ottoman Empire, but was to receive autonomy and the right to appeal for independence to the League of Nations within a year.

By the time the treaty was signed, it was clear that the signature of the sultan's government in Istanbul counted for little and that the terms would have to be imposed on a country that was already mostly in the hands of a militant national movement. As we have seen, the Entente, anticipating resistance to the terms of the treaty, had occupied Istanbul in March, but it could and would not consider a full-scale military occupation of the interior. Instead, and under strong British pressure, it accepted the Greek offer to enforce the treaty by military means. The result was a full-scale Turkish–Greek war, which lasted from 1920 to 1922.

Anatolia, November 1918–spring 1921

Apart from their underground activities, the Unionists took the initiative in activating public opinion in the provinces. The twelfth of President Wilson's 'points' promised the Turkish areas of the empire secure sovereignty, so the first task of those who wanted to prevent Turkish areas from being separated from the empire was to show that areas in danger of being cut away at the peace conference were indeed overwhelmingly Turkish-Muslim and that they wanted to stay united with the motherland. To this end CUP branches in provincial capitals, often in conjunction with representatives of their province in the capital, founded societies for the 'defence of national rights' (*müdafaa-i hukuk-u milliye* – the phrase most often used at the time).

This type of political agitation was of course most urgent in those regions that were in obvious danger of being handed over to the Greeks or the Armenians. In Thrace a 'Society for the Defence of Rights' was founded in November 1918 at Edirne, and a separate one for western Thrace began around the same time. İzmir followed with its own regional organization in December. In the east, the first organization was that founded in Kars (in November 1918), followed by Trabzon and Erzurum (both in February 1919 after earlier preparations). In the south, one was founded in Urfa in December.

There were many smaller organizations and they all acted similarly: the Unionists behind the organization usually tried to get local notables and religious dignitaries (often *müftüs*) to act as titular heads of the society in order to emphasize its 'national' character and to attract wide support. Then they set about organizing a congress to prove its representative character. In fact these congresses were generally packed with officials of the provincial CUP organization, who were invited not elected. The congresses, 28 of which were held between December 1918 and October 1920, would then pronounce on the Turkish and Muslim character of the area and its determination to stay united with the motherland. In the towns of Anatolia, the Muslim landowners and traders generally supported the 'Defence of Rights' organizations. Many of them had become wealthy through government contracts and by taking over the land, property and businesses of the deported or emigrant Greeks and Armenians for next to nothing; they thus had a very strong incentive to resist the Greek and Armenian claims. Leaders of the public 'Defence of Rights' groups were often also involved in the underground resistance.

This pattern can be discerned all over Anatolia and Thrace between November 1918 and June 1919; while initially the organizers had problems motivating a war-weary and decimated population, they received an enormous boost with the Greek occupation of İzmir in May 1919. Greece had joined the Entente near the end of the war and had never defeated any Ottoman troops, so the fact that the Entente rewarded it in this way was perceived as a great injustice. Furthermore, the Greeks did not stop after the occupation of İzmir and Ayvalık (as had been agreed beforehand) but moved on. The Entente recognized the Greek occupation of a much larger area in October by the drawing of the 'Milne Line', a demarcation line between the Ottoman and the Greek sectors.

In the course of 1919, it became ever more evident that the Turks would have to fight for the possession of the disputed provinces in the east and the west and their ability to do so depended on the military.

Defeats, epidemics and desertion had depleted the Ottoman army, but it still functioned as one entity. Its command structure was still intact and its leading officers – the Young Turk officers who had made their careers in the past ten years – almost uniformly supported the resistance. They sabotaged the disarming and demobilization of their troops and secretly supplied the regional resistance organizations with arms and ammunition. Even so, the army's strength in most of Anatolia was unimpressive. Thrace, the Straits area and all of western Anatolia had about 35,000 troops, spread along a 500-mile coastline, and many were in Entente-controlled areas. The regular army units were so weak that until 1921 the nationalists had to rely on bands of Turkish and Circassian irregulars for resistance to the Greek invaders. While they could, and did, harass the Greek army a great deal, they could not possibly be a deciding factor.

In the south the military situation was little better, with about 18,000 troops (the remnants of the Ottoman Syrian armies) in Cilicia and the north of the Syrian desert and 8000 further east in Kurdistan. The atmosphere in Cilicia – with the capital Adana – and in the towns of Urfa, Maraş and Antep was very tense from the beginning. Not only were these predominantly Muslim areas occupied by the French, but also there were strong suspicions that Armenian claims on the area would be honoured when the French recruited and armed local Armenians. Fighting started here in January 1920.

The only place where sizeable Ottoman forces were concentrated was in the east. The troops that had been ordered back from Azerbaijan after the armistice were now also garrisoned here and their total strength (when mobilized) was about 30,000. These troops, now called the XVth Army Corps, were also much better equipped than those in the west and they operated in an inaccessible area. Militarily speaking, their commander, Kâzım Pasha (Karabekir), was the key figure in Anatolia, followed by Ali Fuat Pasha (Cebesoy), the commander of the XXth Army Corps in Ankara who moved back from Cilicia to central Anatolia at the end of 1918.

This was the situation when Mustafa Kemal Pasha landed in Samsun on 19 May 1919 (four days after the Greek landing at İzmir). He immediately contacted the major commanders and started attempts to draw together the different regional organizations into one national one. On 21 June he, together with Rauf (Orbay), Ali Fuat and Refet (Bele) – the highest-ranking member of his own staff – met in Amasya and drew up a circular, which, after telegraphic consultation with Kâzım Pasha who was in Erzurum, was sent to all civil and military authorities in Anatolia. It stated that the country was in danger, that the government in Istanbul was unable to protect it and that only the will of the nation could save it.

It was announced that a national congress would be held in Sivas (considered the safest place in Anatolia) and that each province should immediately send three delegates who 'possessed the confidence of the nation'. Mustafa Kemal had wanted to hold this congress straightaway,[13] but in the east a regional congress was already being organized by the *Şarkî Anadolu Müdafaa-i Hukuk Cemiyeti* (Society for the Defence of the National Rights of Eastern Anatolia), a union of regional and local societies. It was well known that the Armenians claimed the six eastern Anatolian provinces and that their demands found a sympathetic reception in Paris. Political agitation was therefore fiercest in the east.

The congress met in Erzurum on 23 July, the eleventh anniversary of the constitutional revolution. It agreed on a ten-point declaration, reaffirming the determination of the six eastern provinces to stay within the empire but also demanding the territorial integrity and national sovereignty of all lands within the armistice lines as well as of other regions in which Muslims formed a majority. It stated that the national forces must be put in charge to preserve the national independence and to protect the sultanate and caliphate and announced that it would resist any attempt to separate parts of Ottoman territory from the empire, even if, under foreign pressure, the government in Istanbul were forced to abandon them. The congress, before dispersing, elected a 'representative committee' (*heyet-i temsiliye*) with Mustafa Kemal Pasha as its president.

By the time of the congress, Mustafa Kemal was once again, as he had been three months before, an unemployed officer on half-pay. The government in Istanbul as well as the Entente representatives had become increasingly alarmed by his activities. It had recalled him on 5 July and three days later, when he refused to return, dismissed him. Warned beforehand, Mustafa Kemal resigned his position just before he was sacked. This was potentially a very dangerous development, since it could have ended Mustafa Kemal's hold over the army. But his position was saved when the military strongman of the east Kâzım Pasha (Karabekir), who had been ordered to arrest him and send him to the capital and had been offered his job as inspector, refused to obey and made it clear that he still regarded Mustafa Kemal as his superior. The great majority of the army followed his example.

The national congress in Sivas took place from 4 to 11 September. Only 31 provincial representatives had managed to reach Sivas, but a number of military and civil authorities not officially designated as representatives also attended the meetings. All in all 38 people attended.[14] The congress, presented as the *Anadolu Rumeli Müdafaa-i Hukuk-u Milliye Cemiyeti* (Society for the Defence of the National Rights of [all] Anatolia and Thrace), discussed a number of options, including an American mandate, but in the end reaffirmed the resolutions adopted at Erzurum. Again a representative committee was elected and again Mustafa Kemal was made its president. This committee from now on functioned as the national executive of the resistance movement.

The *Damat* Ferit government in Istanbul made a crude and unsuccessful attempt to get the governor of Malatya, Ali Galip Bey, to suppress the congress with the help of Kurdish irregulars. The initiative now clearly lay with the resistance. Ferit Pasha, whom the Entente had treated very rudely when he visited Paris in the summer and who had nothing to show for his policy of appeasing the Entente, had to resign. The government of his successor, Ali Rıza Pasha, immediately adopted a much more pro-nationalist line and attempted to reach an accord with the resistance. Indeed, negotiations in Amasya in October between Mustafa Kemal and the navy minister, Salih Pasha, resulted in an agreement by which the government adopted the nationalist programme as formulated in Erzurum and Sivas, while the nationalists recognized the government as the highest authority. Neither party, however, proved able to execute the agreement under diverging pressures.

In December the Representative Committee moved to Ankara, chosen for its central location and because it was at the head of a railway line directly linked to Istanbul. In the final months of 1919, the last general elections of the Ottoman Empire took place. The new members of the Ottoman parliament were elected throughout Anatolia under the complete control of the Defence of Rights Society (at Amasya, the government had agreed that only candidates approved by the society could stand); the Anatolian representatives conferred with Mustafa Kemal in Ankara before travelling to Istanbul for the opening of parliament.

For the next few months the parliament, which decided to publish the 'National Pact' (see above) on 17 February as a statement of official aims, acted as the mouthpiece of the resistance movement. The nationalist leaders in the chamber were constantly in touch with Ankara, though they did not always follow directions from Ankara, especially in tactical matters. When it became clear that the British occupation of Istanbul was imminent, Mustafa Kemal agreed that parliament should remain in session, but he urgently asked the leaders, especially Hüseyin Rauf Bey, to come back to Ankara. They decided to stay on, however, and 14 leading members of parliament were among the 150 prominent Turks arrested on and immediately after 16 March. As soon as the news of the occupation reached Ankara, Mustafa Kemal invited the parliamentarians to come to Ankara to take up their seats in a 'national assembly'. Some 92 members managed to do so over the next few weeks and, together with 232 representatives elected by the local branches of the Defence of Rights movement, they formed the *Büyük Millet Meclisi* (Great National Assembly), which met for the first time on 23 April 1920.

The National Assembly was not a normal parliament. The assembly itself functioned as government and it individually elected *vekils* (commissars) from among its members, who were charged with the different executive tasks. The commissars were chaired by a *başvekil* (head commissar) but it was not a cabinet with collective responibility as had been the case with the Ottoman government. It was not a classic system founded on the separation of powers, but a revolutionary one, based on the unification of legislative and executive.

With the convening of the national assembly, the resistance movement had turned a corner. While it formally continued to recognize the authority of the sultan-caliph, the headquarters of the nationalist movement in Ankara now took on the character of a complete government (all legislation by the Istanbul government after 16 March was officially declared void).[15] At the same time, it was clear that a confrontation was now imminent, as the nationalists would never accept the peace terms on which the Entente had now agreed.

The Independence War, 1921/2

With Ferit Pasha's return to office in Istanbul in April 1920, the rift between Istanbul and Anatolia widened fast. The *şeyhülislam*, the chief *müftü* of the empire, at the request of the government, issued a *fetva* (legal opinion) in which he declared the nationalists rebels, whom every true believer should endeavour to kill. Shortly afterwards, Mustafa Kemal and a number of other prominent nationalists were officially condemned to death in absentia. The nationalists countered with a *fetva* by the *müftü* of Ankara, declaring the government traitors. The nationalists emphasized that they were fighting for the preservation of the sultanate and caliphate and put the blame on the cabinet and the Entente. They also stressed the Islamic character of their struggle. Mustafa Kemal Pasha took great care to get the public support both of the orthodox Sunni religious dignitaries of Anatolia and of the leaders of the Alevi (Shi'ite) community and the related Bektaşi order of dervishes.

The Istanbul government also tried to organize armed resistance to the nationalists, with support from the somewhat sceptical British. They used exactly the same kind of bands of irregulars as the nationalists did.

Circassian Ahmet Anzavur led the most important of these in the region of Balıkesir, but they were suppressed, though with some difficulty, by *Çerkez* (Circassian) Edhem's bands on behalf of the nationalists.

The Istanbul government also tried to bring into the field a regular army called the *Kuva-yi İnzibatiye* (Disciplinary Forces). This force of two regiments (about 2000 men strong) was deployed in the area of İzmit in May, but its morale was low and the leadership incompetent and it never developed into an effective fighting force.

There were a number of other local or regional rebellions against the nationalists in different areas of Anatolia in 1920, but all were suppressed, sometimes with difficulty. Among the nationalists' counter-measures were the adoption of the High Treason Law (*Hiyanet-i Vataniye Kanunu*)[16] and the institution of revolutionary courts, the so-called 'independence tribunals' (*İstiklâl Mahkemeleri*), which dealt very severely with Ankara's opponents, as well as deserters.

In the summer of 1920, the Greek army extended its zone of occupation over all of western and northwestern Asia Minor and over Thrace, where only intense Entente pressure prevented them from occupying Istanbul itself. The Turkish nationalist army was still very weak in the west and had to resort to guerrilla warfare by bands of irregulars under leaders like Edhem in the northwest and *Demirci* (Blacksmith) Mehmet in the southwest. In the east, the army had for some time been ready to go on the offensive to recapture the provinces of Kars, Ardahan and Batum (which had been evacuated at the end of 1918 and was ceded to the Armenian republic in the Treaty of Sèvres), but it had been told to wait while the leadership in Ankara tried to reach an agreement with Soviet Russia.

Negotiations with the Bolsheviks about military and financial aid to Turkey and about the opening of a direct route between the two countries (through independent Georgia and Armenia) had been going on since July. Soviet support was absolutely vital for the nationalist movement, so the Turkish emissary, Bekir Sami Bey (Kunduh), pushed hard for a treaty, but the Bolsheviks temporized and demanded the cession of the areas of Van and Bitlis to Armenia. This was unacceptable for the Turks. The negotiations broke down and on 28 September Kâzım Karabekir's army advanced on Sarıkamış taking the town two days later. Fighting was then halted for a month, while the Turkish army redeployed. It resumed on 27 October, and by the end of November Armenia was decisively beaten. The peace concluded at Alexandropol (Gümrü) on 2 December 1920 was a Turkish dictate.

Soon after the signing of the treaty the Bolsheviks toppled the nationalist and social democrat *Dashnakzoutiun* government in Armenia and by the beginning of 1921 negotiations between the Turkish nationalists and the Bolsheviks were resumed. They led to a treaty of friendship (16 March 1921), the first diplomatic treaty concluded by the nationalists. In this the Turks agreed to cede Nachicevan and Batum and to give the Bolsheviks a say in the future status of the Straits.[17] The gold and military supplies they hoped to receive in exchange were somewhat slow in coming. It was really only after the nationalist victory on the Sakarya (September 1921, see below) that they started to flow in, but then they played a crucial role in rearming the nationalist forces. The peace agreement with Armenia and the treaty with the Bolsheviks also enabled the nationalists to transfer troops from the eastern to the western front, where the situation was still very threatening.

A first attempt by the Greek army to push eastward from Bursa to Eskişehir was thwarted when Turkish troops under Colonel İsmet (İnönü) managed to beat them back at İnönü on 10 January 1921. This was the regular army's first success in the west. As a result of the victories over Armenia and at İnönü, the nationalists' diplomatic position was considerably strengthened. The two most ardent supporters of the Entente, Venizelos in Athens and Ferit Pasha in Istanbul, had both by now fallen from power. Venizelos had lost the Greek elections of December 1920 to the royalists and Ferit Pasha's position had become untenable because of the nationalists' successes and the severity of the peace terms of the Entente. The French, and even the British, now began to see that a revision of the Treaty of Sèvres was inevitable. The Greek and Ottoman governments were invited to have talks in London starting on 21 February on a possible revision of the treaty. It was left to the Ottoman government to reach an understanding with the nationalists – a procedure that was unacceptable to the latter since they regarded themselves as the only legitimate representatives of the 'national will'. In the end a formal invitation was extended to a nationalist delegation through the Italian government. At the conference, the grand vizier, Ferit Pasha's successor Ahmet Tevfik Pasha, made a short opening speech, after which, in a gesture of national solidarity, he gave the floor to Bekir Sami (Kunduh), Ankara's commissar of foreign affairs.

The two sides first took up extreme positions: the National Pact bound the Turks and the Greeks demanded that the terms of the peace treaty be made even harsher as a punishment for Turkish resistance. The powers tried to find a solution based on an investigation by an international commission of neutral experts in the disputed areas, but the Greek side turned it down. Proposals to establish an autonomous province around İzmir with a Christian governor broke down over the Turks' refusal to accept even a token Greek force in the area.

During the conference it became clear that the French and the Italians had begun to have strong reservations about the Greek expansion, which they now saw as a British attempt to establish a vassal state in the eastern Mediterranean to counter French and Italian influence there, and were quite eager to reach separate understandings with the Turkish nationalists. On 11 March the French foreign minister, Briand, reached an agreement with Bekir Sami, based on a French withdrawal from Cilicia in exchange for economic concessions. Italy's Count Sforza reached a similar agreement with the Turks two days later. With the British, only an agreement about the exchange of prisoners of war was reached. They still strongly supported the Greeks and coordinated their activities with them behind the scenes. When the Greeks asked for an assurance that they were free to resume the attack in spite of the conference being held, Lloyd George, who was informed that the Greek army was ready to strike, insisted that this assurance be given.

When Bekir Sami returned to Ankara with what he thought were quite encouraging results, he found that the majority in the national assembly thought he had deviated too far from the National Pact. Even his separate agreements with the French and the Italians were thrown out and he himself had to resign. The Greek army now returned to the offensive. They were halted once again at İnönü (7 April 1921), but during the summer they broke through and occupied Afyon-Karahisar, Kütahya and the important railroad junction of Eskişehir. The fall of this last-named town caused considerable panic in Ankara, where the assembly prepared to leave the town for the safety of Sivas. Mustafa Kemal, at the request of the assembly, took personal command of the army and for three months all powers of the assembly were invested in him. The government requisitioned one-third of all foodstuffs and farm animals and all available arms and munitions in the countryside. Every last available recruit was called up.

The army took up positions on the Sakarya river, about 50 miles to the west and southwest of Ankara. There, in typically bare and hilly Anatolian steppe country, the decisive battle of the war was fought. It lasted for over a fortnight and ended with a Turkish victory when the Greek forces started to withdraw from 13 September onwards. The exhaustion of the Turkish army prevented it from pursuing its enemy. The front remained static for almost exactly a year, with the Greeks still in possession of western Asia Minor up to the line Afyon-Karahisar–Eskişehir.

During that year the political situation changed fundamentally in favour of the Turkish nationalists. In October an agreement on the return of Cilicia to Turkey was reached with a French representative in Ankara,

Franklin-Bouillon. Despite Greek appeals, the Entente powers now declared their neutrality as Lord Curzon, the British foreign secretary, tried to reopen negotiations, first along the lines of the proposals made in London, and then based on a complete Greek withdrawal from Asia Minor. These attempts were, however, unsuccessful and, after meticulous preparations, Mustafa Kemal ordered his forces to attack the Greek army on 26 August 1922. For the Greek army, which was poorly led by an officer corps divided by political squabbles between Venizelists and monarchists, the main thrust of the attack, coming as it did to the south of Afyon-Karahisar, was a complete surprise. They were routed everywhere and large parts of the army, including its commander-in-chief, were captured to the west of Afyon. On 30 August (now celebrated as 'victory day' in Turkey), the battle was won and after that the retreat of the Greek army to the coast – and beyond – became a flight. On 9 September Turkish cavalry entered İzmir. Out of anger and frustration the Greeks had torched and destroyed many villages and even some towns like Manisa during their retreat. On 13 September a fire broke out in the Armenian quarter of Izmir – now under Turkish control. There is strong historical evidence that this fire was started by elements in the Turkish army. Aided by a wind from the south it fully destroyed the Armenian, Greek and European parts of the city, while leaving the Muslim and Jewish ones untouched.

With the Greek army defeated, there was nothing left between the Turks and British forces, which still occupied the Straits zone. A confrontation seemed imminent. The Turks demanded the right of passage into Europe. The British government decided to stand firm and defend the Straits and called for support from the Entente partners and Dominions. When no support was forthcoming (except from New Zealand), the British government decided to fight on its own, if necessary, rather than suffer a loss of face, which it considered would endanger its hold over the Muslim populations of the empire. In the end, the sensible behaviour of the local commanders General Harington and İsmet Pasha (İnönü), who managed to avoid confrontations, defused the dangerous situation. On 10 October, after a week of negotiations in Mudanya on the Sea of Marmara, agreement was reached on an armistice. This left Istanbul and the Straits under British control for the duration.

Political developments within the National Resistance Movement
The story of the development of the Turkish national resistance movement from the regional congresses of 1918 and 1919 to the victory of 1922 is at the same time the story of the emergence of Mustafa Kemal Pasha (Atatürk) as the clear leader of the movement. His authority was

far from unchallenged, however. His authority over the armed forces was maintained throughout, despite his dismissal by the Istanbul government, because the leading commanders remained explicitly loyal to him. Political authority was another matter. The Unionist cadres who had organized the regional resistance movements with their congresses, and who had contributed decisively to the success of the movement through the activities of *Karakol*, were aware of the fact that they had been first on the scene and their loyalty to Mustafa Kemal was far from automatic. Their independence (*Karakol* even conducted its own talks with Bolshevik representatives in January 1920) caused serious friction with the pasha, such as when he had a public row with the *Karakol* leader Colonel Vasıf at the Sivas congress.

The Unionist officers in the War Ministry in Istanbul, who supported the nationalist resistance, basically saw the latter as an instrument to put pressure on the Entente and to get it to revise the peace terms. They were displeased with the increasingly independent line of the Anatolian movement: at one point, they seem to have considered replacing Mustafa Kemal with the more tractable Kâzım Karabekir. What really finished them off as competitors were the British occupation of Istanbul in March 1920 and the deportation of leading *Karakol* members to Malta. The underground in Istanbul continued to function, but from now on it was effectively controlled from Ankara.

In the period between the occupation of Istanbul and the final victory of 1922 two types of opposition emerged, which can roughly be classified as left wing and right wing. The left-wing opposition consisted not of hard-line communists but of people who supported a mixture of Islamic, anti-imperialist, corporatist and socialist ideas. Their common denominator was their anti-Western attitude. Their first serious organization was the *Yeşil Ordu* (Green Army), which was set up in May 1920 (with the approval of Mustafa Kemal Pasha). It was not a real army, but a political organization designed to improve morale within the nationalist forces and to counter the activities of the sultan's propagandists who operated under the name of 'Army of the Caliphate'. When Çerkez Ethem, at the head of his Circassian fighters, joined it, it became a force to be reckoned with and a potential threat. Mustafa Kemal Pasha had it disbanded in July. But the radicals in the assembly reorganized as the *Halk Zümresi* (People's Faction) the same month. Mustafa Kemal Pasha reacted by getting a number of people he trusted from among the People's Faction to found an officially approved 'communist' party (the *Türkiye Komünist Fırkası*), which was tightly controlled by people close to himself.

Neither the radicals nor the Third International, however, recognized the party because a real Communist Party already existed, founded in the spring of 1920 in Baku. In May 1920 it had been taken over by a group led by Mustafa Suphi, a former high-school teacher (and Unionist) who had fled to Russia in 1914 and had been interned there during the war. After the revolution he had helped to spread communist ideas among the 60,000 Turkish prisoners of war in Russia. His supporters, together with a number of like-minded people from among the 'People's Faction' in November formed the *Halk İştirakiyun Fırkası* (People's Socialist Party) in Ankara.

Mustafa Kemal Pasha took steps to crush this left-wing movement in January 1921. First he ordered *Çerkez* Ethem to disband his troops and let them be integrated in the regular army. When he refused, troops were sent against him, most of his men were taken prisoner and he himself fled and went over to the Greek side. With the strong arm of the left thus cut off, Mustafa Kemal dissolved the Popular Socialists. When Mustafa Suphi tried to enter Anatolia through Trabzon, he was forced to return and then drowned at sea, with a number of supporters, at the orders of the local nationalist commanders.[18]

It was not that the extreme left constituted a real threat to Mustafa Kemal's leadership: in fact, until the 1960s, the extreme left was a marginal phenomenon in Turkey. But its existence might have jeopardized vital Soviet support for the nationalists. This was especially dangerous as long as the former Unionist war leader Enver Pasha was around as an alternative to Mustafa Kemal. Enver still had a high reputation in the army and among some of the local and regional Unionist groups on which the nationalist movement had been built.[19] After his failed attempt to reach the Caucasus in 1918 to continue the struggle from there, he had spent the next year and a half in Berlin, building up his contacts with the Bolsheviks. He tried to build a kind of Islamic Comintern on the basis of a group of former *Teşkilât-i Mahsusa* agents from different parts of the Islamic world who were living in Europe, and he visited the Soviet-sponsored 'Congress of the Peoples of the East' in Baku in September 1920 as a representative of North Africa. After the congress, he drew up a radical partly Islamic, partly socialist programme and founded a party (which was to be the Turkish affiliate of his worldwide Islamic revolutionary network), called the *Halk Şuralar Fırkası* (People's Soviets Party). At the same time he tried to get Soviet support by posing as a more reliable left-wing alternative to Mustafa Kemal.

What he really wanted was to raise a Turkish army in the Caucasus with Soviet money and arms and then to enter Anatolia at the head of this army. In the spring and summer of 1921 this idea might have been successful in view of the critical situation on the western front and the criticism within the assembly in Ankara of Mustafa Kemal's conduct of the war, but Soviet support was not forthcoming. The Bolsheviks kept Enver dangling for some time, using him as an implicit threat against Ankara. When they finally signed a friendship treaty with Ankara and it became clear that they would not support his scheme, Enver decided to go to Anatolia alone, relying on his reputation to pick up a following.

On 30 July he left Moscow for Batum on the Turkish border. He was refused entry into Turkey, but supporters from Anatolia met him in Batum and he was in constant touch with leading members from the nationalist organization across the border in Trabzon. Early in September his group even held a 'congress' in Batum, not as the People's Soviets Party, but as the Party of Union and Progress. This shows that he now no longer banked on Soviet support but aimed at the support of the Unionists in the nationalist organization. He was too late, however. While he was busy on the border, the battle on the Sakarya was at its height. The victory of 13 September saved not only Ankara but possibly also Mustafa Kemal's position. Enver stayed on for two weeks and then left for good. He never gave up his dreams of a new Islamic/Turkic empire, however, and he died in June 1922, fighting the Red Army at the head of Turkic guerrilla bands near the Afghan border.

The left-wing (or Enverist) threat was, however, not the only hurdle Mustafa Kemal had to overcome in 1921. His conciliatory policies towards the Soviet Union had caused anxiety among conservative deputies from the east. In March they formed the *Muhafaza-i Mukad-desat Cemiyeti* (Association for the Preservation of Sacred Institutions), led by *Hoca* Raif (Dinç), a cleric and one of the organizers of the Congress of Erzurum in 1919. This movement stressed the importance of religion and of the sultanate and caliphate.

It will be apparent from the above that the first national assembly was quite a heterogeneous and unruly body. It was to strengthen his hold on it and to make its actions more predictable that Mustafa Kemal organized his more dependable followers into the *Müdafaa-i Hukuk Grubu* (Defence of Rights Group) in May 1921. After the Greek threat had receded in the autumn of 1921, the opposition, temporarily silenced during the emergency, reorganized. It received a boost when by the end of the year the prisoners the British held on Malta were released and returned to Ankara.[20] A number of them (including the former *Karakol* chief Vasıf) joined the opposition and founded the *İkinci Grup* (Second Group) early in 1922. The group was ideologically very heterogeneous and really only bound together by joint opposition to what was perceived as Mustafa Kemal's growing autocracy and radicalism. While the Defence of Rights Group generally had a majority in the assembly, neither group was very disciplined and the number of adherents of each fluctuated.

The victory in the independence war of September 1922 immensely strengthened Mustafa Kemal's position. He was now the *Halâskar Gazi* (Saviour and Conqueror – the traditional Ottoman title of Gazi (victor, conqueror) had been granted to him by the National Assembly after the victory on the Sakarya) and he was determined to use this situation to consolidate his position in the postwar era. On 1 November the Ottoman sultanate (but not the caliphate) was officially abolished. In the decision to separate the religious caliphate from the sultanate Kemal played a decisive role, but the future would show that for him this was just an intermediate stage in the process. On 6 December he announced for the first time his intention to convert the Defence of Rights Group into a political party, to be called the *Halk Fırkası* (People's Party). In conversations with a number of leading journalists, he also talked for the first time about abolishing the caliphate and establishing a republic.

At the end of March, in a situation that was very tense because of the murder of one of the leaders of the Second Group by the commander of Mustafa Kemal's bodyguard, an amendment to the High Treason Law of 1920 was introduced in the assembly, declaring it illegal to campaign for a return of the sultanate. On 1 April, Mustafa Kemal announced his intention to dissolve the assembly and to hold new elections. A week later, he presented a nine-point manifesto for his new party. This was a curious mixture of general statements ('sovereignty belongs uncon-ditionally to the nation') and specific items ('measures to improve the marketing of tobacco') taken from different sources.[21] On 15 April, the amendment to the High Treason Law was passed and the next day the assembly was dissolved.

While all this was going on in Ankara, in Istanbul the final congress of the Committee of Union and Progress took place. It was convoked by *Kara* Kemal Bey, the former Unionist party boss in Istanbul and one of the founders of *Karakol*, who had had secret discussions about the future role of the Unionists with Mustafa Kemal Pasha in İzmit in January. The congress, which was held at the house of Cavit Bey, drew up its own nine-point programme and offered the leadership of a revived CUP to Mustafa Kemal – an honour he declined.

The two-stage elections for a new assembly were held in June and July and, since Mustafa Kemal himself had thoroughly vetted the can-didates, hardly any former Second Group members entered the new assembly. It met for the first time on 9 August 1923 and then – but only then – the Defence of Rights Group (now encompassing the whole assembly) reconstituted itself as the People's Party (PP). The new party took over all the assets of the Association for the Defence of the National Rights of Anatolia and Rumelia, which gave it a nationwide organization in one go. It was this new, much more tightly controlled, assembly that debated and ratified the peace treaty that was concluded in Lausanne between Turkey and the Entente powers.

The Peace Treaty of Lausanne
Soon after the cessation of hostilities, the Entente invited the Turks to start negotiations. The Turkish side wanted them to take place in İzmir (in which case Mustafa Kemal himself would lead the delegation) but the Entente refused to negotiate on Turkish soil and eventually Lausanne was chosen. Britain, France, Italy and Greece were the hosts, while on the Turkish side both the government in Ankara and that in Istanbul were invited to send delegations. In reaction to this, the last grand vizier of the Ottoman Empire, Ahmet Tevfik Pasha (Okday), sent a telegram to Ankara suggesting that a joint delegation be sent. This caused a furore in the national assembly and led directly to the adoption, on 1 November 1922, of the motion to abolish the sultanate. Four days later, Tevfik Pasha handed over his seal of office to the nationalist representative in Istanbul, Refet Pasha (Bele), who ordered the Ottoman ministries to terminate all activities and, on 17 November, the last Ottoman sultan sought refuge on a British warship, which took him to Malta. His cousin Abdülmecit succeeded him, but only as caliph, not as sultan.

To the surprise of everyone, including himself, İsmet Pasha (İnönü) was appointed leader of the Turkish delegation in Lausanne. Mustafa Kemal chose him partly because İsmet was his most loyal and dependable supporter, but also because the prime minister, Hüseyin Rauf (Orbay), was known as an Anglophile, while the commissar for foreign affairs Yusuf Kemal (Tengirşenk) was too pro-Soviet. İsmet duly left for Lausanne, armed with strict instructions not to deviate from the National Pact in any way. The conference opened on 20 November. Represented were Great Britain, France, Italy, Greece and Turkey, while the Soviet Union, Ukraine, Georgia, Romania and Bulgaria were invited to those sessions in which they had a direct interest. It was clear from the start that the negotiations would be extremely difficult because of the different perspectives of the two sides. The Entente, among whom the British foreign secretary Lord Curzon was by far the most dominant figure, saw themselves as the victors of the First World War. In their eyes the conference was meant to adjust the terms of the Treaty of Sèvres to the new situation. In the eyes of the Turks, they themselves were the victors in their national independence war and Sèvres for them was past history. They came to Lausanne with a maximalist interpretation of the National Pact, and had instructions to demand the inclusion of the district of Alexandrette (İskenderun), the Syrian inland up to the Euphrates, the province of Mosul and the Aegean islands that were adjacent to the Anatolian coast in the new Turkey and to demand a plebiscite for Western Thrace.

The Turkish delegation had a very hard time at Lausanne, especially in the beginning. They were not considered equal partners. Curzon adopted an extremely patronizing and arrogant attitude, which contributed to the bad-tempered atmosphere. The Turks were severely handicapped by their lack of diplomatic expertise. For fear of being tricked into major concessions, they remained almost totally inflexible, refusing to give direct answers or to be drawn into impromptu discussions. İsmet's deafness often served as a useful excuse. The Turkish delegation continually consulted Ankara, unaware that British intelligence intercepted all their messages.

The problems discussed came under three headings: territorial and military; economic and financial; and the position of foreigners and minorities. Little was achieved on any of these fronts in the first two months. Early in February all the main territorial problems (the border in Thrace, the future regime of the Straits) had been solved, with the parties agreeing to postpone the discussion of the Mosul question until later. The problems in the other two areas, however, proved insuperable. The Entente presented the Turks with a draft treaty, which it considered its final offer. The Turks refused to sign. The conference broke down and the delegations went home.

Extreme nationalist fervour now reigned in Ankara and at the beginning of March both İsmet and the government were vehemently attacked in the assembly for the few concessions they had made.

Mustafa Kemal had to intervene personally to get the assembly to empower the government to continue negotiations.

The Turkish side handed over 100 pages of amendments to the draft treaty it had been given in February. At the end of March, after its experts had studied the amendments, the Entente invited the Turks to reopen negotiations and, on 23 April, the parties reconvened. The Greek and Turkish delegations soon solved their bilateral problems, Turkey receiving a small border correction in Thrace in exchange for renouncing its claim to war reparations, but the main problem remained the Entente countries' insistence on economic and judicial concessions in exchange for recognition of the abolition of the capitulations. The Turkish side refused anything that amounted to an infringement of the complete sovereignty of the new Turkish state. The Entente position was weak because in none of its countries was the population prepared to go to war over these issues. Therefore, agreement was eventually reached on 17 July. İsmet asked the government in Ankara for permission to sign. When no answer was forthcoming, he asked for permission from Mustafa Kemal and got it. The treaty was signed on 24 July 1923.

Basically, though not in every detail, the goals of the National Pact had been attained and within the borders of the National Pact the Turkey that emerged was a completely sovereign state. The province of Mosul, which Turkey claimed but Britain occupied, remained part of Iraq pending a decision by the League of Nations; the *sancak* of Alexandrette remained with French Syria and, except for Imroz (Gökçe Ada) and Tenedos (Bozca Ada), the Aegean islands adjacent to Asia Minor, which the Turks had claimed, remained with Greece and Italy.

But Anatolia and eastern Thrace became part of the new state and there was no mention of Armenia or Kurdistan. The Straits zone was internationalized under a commission chaired by a Turk and demilitarized, except for a garrison of up to 12,000 men in Istanbul. The capitulations remained abolished, but Turkey had to honour all existing foreign concessions and it was not free to change its customs tariffs until 1929. All attempts by the powers to establish supervision over the Turkish judicial system had failed and all inhabitants of Turkey, including foreigners, were now subject to the Turkish courts. The only concession was that foreign observers were to be admitted to the Turkish courts. All wartime reparation claims were renounced. As far as the minorities were concerned, a clause was inserted, in which Turkey bound itself to protect its citizens, regardless of creed, nationality or language, but there was to be no supervision of Turkey's handling of its minorities. One should note that whenever there was talk of 'minorities' in Lausanne, religious minorities, that is: Christians and Jews, were meant, not ethnic or linguistic minorities.

The Entente had wanted a general amnesty to be part of the treaty. Proposals for this were discussed in the sub-commission on minorities, but the Turks did not want to grant a general amnesty to opponents of the nationalists and, since no lists of 'undesirables' had been prepared, they were unable to specify who should be excluded from any amnesty. In the end, the Turkish government accepted the amnesty but reserved the right to make 150 – as yet unnamed – exceptions. The amnesty was announced on 16 April 1924, but the exceptions were still undetermined. A list was finally submitted to the assembly in June and, shortly afterwards, those of 'the 150' (*yüzellilikler*) who were still in the country were ordered to leave. The assembly accepted the peace treaty (although not unanimously) and it was ratified on 21 August. The Entente immediately began withdrawing its occupation forces. On 1 October 1923, the last British troops left Istanbul.

Turkey in 1923

It is hard to envisage the condition of the country that had won its continued survival and its independence in Lausanne. After ten years of almost continuous warfare it was depopulated, impoverished and in ruins to a degree almost unparalleled in modern history. Demographically, it showed the effects of large-scale migration and mortality. Mortality among the Anatolian population had been incredibly high. The Ottoman army had always recruited most of its soldiers among the peasant population of Asia Minor (the 'soldier mines of the empire') and the countless casualties of the campaigns in the Caucasus, Gallipoli, Palestine and Mesopotamia turn up in the population statistics of Anatolia. Furthermore, from early 1915 onwards, eastern Anatolia had become a war theatre itself. This had led to great suffering among the Muslim population, which had partly followed the retreating Ottoman armies. It had also led to the deportation and partial extermination of the Armenian community. The First World War was followed by the independence war, during which campaigns had been fought both in the east and in the west. On the western front the retreating and fleeing Greek forces had committed large-scale atrocities among the Muslim population and some of the advancing Turkish troops had acted with comparable brutality against the Greek Orthodox population. Some 2.5 million Anatolian Muslims lost their lives, as well as between 600,000 and 800,000 Armenians and up to 300,000 Greeks. All in all, the population of Anatolia declined by 20 per cent through mortality, a percentage 20 times as high as that of France, which had been the hardest-hit country among the large European protagonists in the First World War. Only Serbia had lost a larger part of its population in the war. Even this number is deceptive, however. In the war zones the number was higher: in some eastern provinces half the population was dead and another quarter had become refugees. There were 12 provinces, most of them in the west, where the number of widows among the female population exceeded 30 per cent. Anatolia's high mortality rate was not due only to warfare and atrocities. The wars had led to disruption of the infrastructure and a shortage of labour in agriculture. These in turn had led to famine and famines usually had epidemics, notably of cholera and typhoid, trailing in their wake.

Next to mortality, migration was the major demographic phenomenon. It has already been noted that the war of 1878 and the Balkan War of 1912/13 had brought hundreds of thousands of Muslim (mainly

Turkish) refugees into the country. During and after the First World War several hundred thousand surviving Armenians emigrated from Anatolia, mainly to the Soviet Union, France and the USA. Their example was followed by large numbers of Greeks from western Anatolia. Finally, under the provisions of the Treaty of Lausanne, the remainder of the Greek Orthodox population of Anatolia (but not that of Istanbul), about 900,000 people, was exchanged against the Muslims from Greece (except the community in western Thrace) who numbered about 400,000. In actual fact, the large majority of the Greek population had already fled the country in 1922. The communities that were exchanged under the agreement were the inhabitants of the Black Sea coastal region and the Turkish speaking Greek Orthodox from Karaman. The migratory movements meant a net loss to the population of Anatolia of about 10 per cent, which should be added to the 20 per cent loss due to mortality.

The population changes meant that, culturally also, Anatolia in 1923 was a completely different place from what it had been in 1913. The larger Christian communities were practically gone (the Armenian community had shrunk to about 65,000 and the Greek community was down from around two million to 120,000); and Anatolia, which had been 80 per cent Muslim before the wars, was now approximately 98 per cent Muslim. Linguistically, only two large groups were left: the Turks and the Kurds, with a number of smaller groups (Greek, Armenian and Syriac-speaking Christians, Spanish-speaking Jews, and Circassian, Laz, Albanian, Bosnian, Bulgarian and Arabic-speaking Muslims) as well as immigrants from the Balkans. The city population had shrunk even further than the rural population. As a result of this ruralization of the country, 18 per cent of the people now lived in the towns, as opposed to 25 per cent before the wars started in 1912.[22]

In economic terms the havoc wrought by the wars was also considerable. The actual physical damage was limited: there were relatively few industrial installations that could be damaged and most of those were in the Istanbul region, which had not been directly afflicted by the war. The major structural damage was to the railways and bridges in western Anatolia and to housing. It was caused both by the fighting and by deliberate destruction by the withdrawing Greek army. Large parts of the Greek and Armenian quarters of the great port city of İzmir were burnt to the ground in September 1922. It is still unclear who was to blame for this catastrophe. Far more serious was the fact that the emigration of the Greeks and Armenians also meant the exodus of the large majority of entrepreneurs and managers. With them went an irreplaceable stock of industrial and commercial know-how. And it was not just highly skilled personnel that was now lacking in Turkey. It went much further. There were whole regions where not a single welder or electrician could now be found. International trade in 1923 was one-third of what it had been ten years earlier. By far the most important sector of the Turkish economy was agriculture, which recuperated relatively quickly after 1923. Nevertheless, it took until about 1930 for the gross national product to reach pre-First World War levels.[23] The development for a new class of entrepreneurs and managers would take a generation.

In one respect Turkey was lucky. Like other protagonists, the Ottoman government had incurred heavy war debts, but in the Ottoman case these debts were not to the United States, a victor, but to Germany, a defeated country. Therefore, the debt, which totalled about 160 million Turkish gold pounds, or 720 million US dollars, was informally written off.[24] This was not the case with the old consolidated Ottoman public debt. At Lausanne, it was decided that this should be apportioned to the successor states or territories of the empire and five years later an agreement was reached under which 65 per cent (a total of £78 million) of the debt fell on Turkey. Turkey would repay the last of the Ottoman debt in 1954.[25]

10 · The Emergence of the One-Party State, 1923–27

The republic and the caliphate

As we have seen, Mustafa Kemal Pasha had started to consolidate his political position even before the independence war had formally come to an end with the signing and ratification of the Treaty of Lausanne. The means he had employed were: a change in the High Treason Law; the dissolution of the assembly and tightly controlled elections; the creation of a new party, the People's Party, and the takeover by this party of the whole Defence of Rights organization. This process of consolidation, of gathering power in the hands of Mustafa Kemal and an assembly and party that were both under his complete control, continued after the coming of peace.

The exact nature of the emerging new Turkish state was still somewhat indeterminate at this time. The Ottoman sultanate had been abolished nearly a year before. The country was ruled by the national assembly, which elected not only the president but also every minister or rather 'commissar' (*vekil*) directly. The constitutional relationship between the assembly and the caliph, Abdülmecit Efendi, was unclear. The caliphate as conceived in 1922 was a purely religious function, but it was inevitable that many people continued to see the caliph as the head of state, even if only in a ceremonial sense. Furthermore, as caliph, his jurisdiction transcended the boundaries of the Turkish state and – at least in theory – encompassed the whole Muslim world.

In his interviews with the Turkish press in January, Mustafa Kemal had already hinted that he intended to change this confused situation and declare a republic, and he reaffirmed this in an interview with a Viennese daily in September. An opportunity arose when, in October, the assembly elected Hüseyin Rauf (Orbay) and Sabit (Sağıroğlu) to the posts of vice-president of the assembly and home secretary respectively, in preference to the government candidates. Mustafa Kemal persuaded the government of Prime Minister Ali Fethi (Okyar) that this constituted a motion of no confidence, upon which the government resigned. The assembly was automatically charged with replacing it with a new council of *vekil*s, but once Mustafa Kemal had instructed his more prominent followers not to accept posts, this proved impossible. When the assembly then decided to consult the president, he submitted a proposal to proclaim a republic, with an elected president, a prime minister appointed by the president and a conventional cabinet system. The majority in the assembly accepted the proposals and, on 29 October 1923, the Turkish Republic was proclaimed, with Mustafa Kemal as its first president and İsmet (İnönü) as its first prime minister.

The decision was taken while a number of celebrities from the independence war, Hüseyin Rauf, Ali Fuat (Cebesoy), Adnan (Adıvar), Refet (Bele) and Kâzım (Karabekir) were not in the capital. They reacted angrily to the proclamation in interviews in the Istanbul press, calling the decision premature, and stressing that calling the state a republic did not in itself bring freedom and that the real difference was between despotism and democracy, whether under a republican or a monarchic system. The Istanbul papers took up their criticism with relish. The government was highly unpopular in Istanbul at the time, not so much because of the proclamation of the republic as because it had officially made Ankara the new capital of Turkey a fortnight earlier. This was something that not only hurt the pride of the inhabitants of the old capital, but it also meant continuing unemployment for the tens of thousands of civil servants among them. Rauf's critical remarks (with their implied accusation that the government was despotic despite its new name) led to a row within the PP parliamentary faction, which came close to splitting the party in December.

The anti-republican feeling was partly fuelled by concern over the future of the caliph. Many people, certainly in Istanbul, were emotionally attached to the dynasty, but it was also felt that the caliph was the only possible counterweight to Mustafa Kemal's dominance of the political scene. It was – rightly – feared that the proclamation of the republic sounded the death knell of the caliphate. In November the president of the Istanbul bar association, Lûtfi Fikri, sent an open letter to the press in which he pleaded for a more influential position for the caliph; and in December two eminent Indian Muslims, Ameer Ali and the Aga Khan, sent a similar letter both to the prime minister and to the press. Because of the difficulty of communications with Ankara, the letter was published in Istanbul before it had been delivered to Prime Minister İsmet, which was something that angered him and his followers in the assembly. It was decided to send an Independence Tribunal to Istanbul to investigate whether Lûtfi Fikri or the newspapers had committed treason. The newspaper editors were acquitted but Fikri was sent to jail for five years.

All this indicated growing tensions within the People's Party and between Ankara and Istanbul. In February talks between the president and the leading editors of the Istanbul newspapers failed to heal the rift.

Immediately after the opening of the new parliamentary year on 1 March the expected blow fell: the caliphate was abolished and all members of the Ottoman dynasty were ordered out of the country. After extensive discussions, a new republican constitution was adopted in April. This replaced the old Ottoman constitution of 1876, which had been modified in 1909 and again in January 1921 when the first assembly adopted the Law on Fundamental Organization (*Teşkilât-i Esasye Kanunu*), the de facto constitution of the resistance movement, which had allowed it to function to all practical purposes as a republic within the legal framework of the Ottoman Empire.

The nationalist movement is split: the establishment of the Progressive Republican Party

All through the winter and spring of 1924, the radical wing of the People's Party led by Mustafa Kemal and İsmet continued to increase the pressure on the smaller moderate group led by Hüseyin Rauf, which had objected to the way in which the republic had been proclaimed. Continued opposition to this group from within the party became stronger and stronger and by late summer it was clear that the minority had no option but to found a separate opposition party. The actual split took place in the context of a debate over how the government had handled the resettlement of Muslims from Greece, especially with respect to the possessions of the Greeks who had had to leave, which was something that had given rise to widespread corruption. When, after a heated debate in the assembly, İsmet asked for a vote of confidence and easily won it, 32 deputies around Hüseyin Rauf left the party and founded the Progressive Republican Party (*Terakkiperver Cumhuriyet Fırkası*) on 17 November. The rumour that the new party would use the adjective 'Republican' led the People's Party to change its name to 'Republican People's Party' (RPP).

When the new party published its manifesto and its programme, it became evident that it was a party in the western European liberal mould. It stood for secular and nationalist policies, like the majority party, but it clearly opposed its radical, centralist and authoritarian tendencies. Instead it advocated decentralization, separation of powers and evolutionary rather than revolutionary change. It also had a more liberal economic policy, accepting foreign loans as necessary.

It was clear that the mood in many parts of the country, certainly in the conservative east, in Istanbul and in the areas where resettlement problems were particularly bad (such as the area around İzmir), favoured an opposition party. The leadership of the RPP recognized the danger and took countermeasures. Discipline within the parliamentary party was tightened (deputies being bound to vote in the assembly according to the majority decision in the closed session of the faction), and an accord was reached with a group of conservative representatives from the east. Most importantly, İsmet, who had had a personal feud with Rauf since Lausanne and who was considered an outspoken radical, was replaced by the much more conciliatory Ali Fethi (Okyar) on 21 November. These measures prevented mass desertions from the RPP.

The conciliatory line was only a temporary expedient, however. A number of hardliners, led by Recep (Peker), the interior minister, were put into the cabinet as watchdogs and by the beginning of 1925 it was clear that the radical wing was putting more and more pressure on Fethi to deal with the opposition, which was gradually building up a grassroots organization in Istanbul and the east. For a time Fethi resisted the pressure, but outside events gave the radical wing its chance.

The Sheikh Sait rebellion and Kurdish nationalism
The event that the hardliners and the president used to put an end to political opposition was the eruption of Kurdish discontent into an armed rebellion to the north of Diyarbakır in February 1925.

Kurdish nationalism was a relative newcomer among the ideologies of the region. The Kurds had always been divided along tribal lines and since the suppression of the Kurdish emirates under Sultan Mahmut II their society had been increasingly fragmented. Sultan Abdülhamit had exploited the divisions among the Kurds, and at the same time used their martial qualities when he created his Cossack-like *Hamidiye* regiments out of some (but by no means all) of the tribes after 1891. The Young Turks had abolished the *Hamidiye* but law and order problems had soon forced them to reinstate them in the form of a militia. Regiments of this militia fought in the Balkan War and in the First World War.

After the constitutional revolution in 1908, members of the Kurdish elite in the capital had founded the *Kürt Teavun ve Terakki Cemiyeti* (Society for Support and Progress of the Kurds), of which Sait Nursi, the religious reformer, had also been a member. This, however, had social and not political aims and it kept aloof from the mass of the population in the southeast. In 1912 a number of Kurdish students in Istanbul formed *Hevi* (Hope), a society with a more pronounced nationalist tendency.

During the war, the removal of the Armenian population from the eastern Anatolian provinces left the Kurds masters of the terrain, but this and the collapse of the Russian front also meant that the Kurds' and

Turks' common enemies disappeared and that the two communities were left in competition with each other. In 1918, the *Kürdistan Teali Cemiyeti* (Society for the Elevation of Kurdistan) was founded in Istanbul, with branches in Kurdistan itself, both among the Kormanci-speaking majority and among the Zaza-speaking groups to the northwest of Diyarbakır and both among Sunnis and Alevis.

During the independence war there was one major Kurdish insurrection against the nationalists in the east of Sivas province and the adjacent Dersim (now Tunceli) area, led by tribal chiefs who demanded autonomy, but it was easily suppressed. By and large, the Kurds supported the resistance movement, despite the efforts of British agents to influence them and despite the fact that they were granted autonomy under the Treaty of Sèvres. There were Kurdish representatives at Erzurum and at Sivas and even on the nationalists' representative committee.

Within the new borders of the republic (which, incidentally, in the southeast ran right across traditional pasture areas of the tribes) about 20 per cent of the population was Kurdish, but they were not mentioned in the peace treaty of Lausanne and promises of autonomy made by the nationalist leaders, including Mustafa Kemal himself, during the independence struggle,[1] were forgotten. This was a great disappointment to the Kurdish nationalists. In 1923 former militia officers founded the *Azadi* (Freedom Society), which held its first congress in 1924. One person at that congress whose performance drew attention was Sheikh Sait of Palu, who was very influential among the Zaza tribes.

That a sheikh, a religious leader, exerted great political influence was not at all extraordinary in Kurdistan, where the two great dervish orders of the Kadiriyya and – especially – the Nakşibendi were the only organizations that transcended tribal differences. The leaders of these dervish orders were often called in to decide quarrels between different tribes and this brought them prestige, connections and, often, considerable wealth. Sheikh Sait was himself an influential member of the Nakşibendi order.

Relations between the Kurds and the predominantly Turkish republican government deteriorated in 1924. The abolition of the caliphate removed an important religious symbol that bound the two communities together. The first sign of resistance against these policies was an abortive rebellion by the garrison in Beytüşşebap in the extreme southeast in August 1924.

The great rebellion, which the *Azadi* and Sheikh Sait planned for May 1925, broke out prematurely when a shooting incident with the gendarmes in the little town of Piran got out of hand on 8 February. Nearly all the Zaza tribes and two large Kormanci tribes took part in the insurrection, but the divisions between the Kurds showed themselves again: the Alevi Kurds fiercely attacked the Sunni insurgents. That they did so is understandable given the dual character of the rebellion. While the leadership was undoubtedly motivated by the desire for an autonomous or even independent Kurdistan, the rank and file acted from religious motives, demanding the restoration of the holy law and the caliphate. The Alevis, as a heterodox community, generally supported the republic's secularist tendencies against the partisans of the caliphate and orthodox establishment – for good reason because prejudice against the Alevis was and is deeply rooted among the Sunnis.

Although at one time they threatened Diyarbakır, the only town the rebels managed to seize was Elazığ and that only for a short time. The government in Ankara took strong countermeasures as soon as the extent of the insurrection became clear. The assembly was informed about the situation on 25 February. The same day, martial law was declared in the eastern provinces for one month and the High Treason Law was amended to include the political use of religion among the treasonable offences. Around this time the prime minister, Fethi, asked the PRP leaders to disband voluntarily. This they refused to do, but the party chairman, Kâzım Karabekir, did support the government policy in the east very emphatically, both in the assembly and in the press.

Meanwhile, the pressure of the hawks within the RPP on Fethi was rising, İsmet had already returned to Ankara and attended the cabinet meetings. On 2 March Fethi lost a vote of confidence by the RPP faction, when Mustafa Kemal himself sided with the hardliners who demanded stronger measures.[2] He resigned and the next day İsmet became prime minister. His first act was to have the assembly pass the *Takrir-i Sükûn Kanunu* (Law on the Maintenance of Order). This empowered the government for two years to ban by administrative measure any organization or publication it considered might cause disturbance to law and order. The law, which the PRP opposed as being too elastic, would be in force in the whole country, not only in the southeast. At the same time two independence tribunals were reinstated, one for the eastern provinces and one for the rest of the country.

The Kurdish rebels were now rapidly pushed back into the mountains. The capture on 27 April of Sheikh Sait really marked the end of the rebellion, although small groups continued a guerrilla war all through the summer. In 1926, a new Kurdish insurrection broke out on the slopes of Mount Ararat, which lasted for four years and can be considered a direct sequel to the Sheikh Sait rebellion, but it did not spread. After the rebellion was over, the government through the military authorities and the independence tribunals dealt very harshly with the Kurds. Many of their leaders were executed and large numbers of Kurds, more than 20,000 in all, were deported from the southeast and forcibly settled in the west of the country.[3] The government now ordered a rethink of its entire policy towards the Kurds. This resulted in the 'Plan for Reforms in the East' (*Şark İslahat Planı*). Under this plan, which was approved in 1927 and put into operation over the next few years, a very strict and militarized regime was introduced in the east. The use of the Kurdish language in public spaces was banned and Kurds were no longer allowed to serve in the judiciary in the east. From the 1930s the policies grew even more extreme and existence of a separate Kurdish identity was officially denied. Kurds were now officially seen as formerly Turkish tribes that had lost their Turkishness under the influence of Persian culture.

The Law on the Maintenance of Order was not, however, only used to suppress the Kurds. Eight of the most important newspapers and periodicals (conservative, liberal and even Marxist) in Istanbul were closed down, as were several provincial papers, leaving the government organs *Hâkimiyet-i Milliye* (National Sovereignty) in Ankara and *Cumhuriyet* (Republic) in Istanbul as the only national papers. All the leading journalists from Istanbul were arrested and brought before the Independence Tribunal in the east. Eventually they were released, but they were not allowed to resume their work. With the press out of the way, on the advice of the Independence Tribunal the government closed down the Progressive Republican Party on 3 June. According to the tribunal, members of the party had supported the rebellion and tried to exploit religion for political purposes.

Reforms and executions

With complete domination of the political scene assured, Mustafa Kemal and his government embarked on an extensive programme of reforms.

In September 1925 the religious shrines (*türbes*) and dervish convents (*tekkes*) were closed down and in November the turban and fez, the red felt cap that had been the Ottoman gentleman's traditional headgear since the days of Sultan Mahmut II, were prohibited and replaced by the Western-style hat or cap. These measures met with stubborn resistance from the population. *Tekkes* and *türbes* played an important role in everyday Muslim life and the hat was considered a symbol of Christian Europe. The independence tribunals played their part in suppressing this resistance. Under the Law on the Maintenance of Order nearly 7500 people were arrested and 660 were executed.[4]

In the first half of 1926, the European calendar was adopted, as were the Swiss civil code and the penal code from Mussolini's Italy. A number of laws restructuring the banking sector were passed and, except in the army, all courtesy titles (like *Bey*, *Efendi* or *Paşa*) were abolished.

Together with the abolition of the sultanate and caliphate and the proclamation of the republic, these measures form the first wave of the Kemalist reforms. It is clear that they constituted an extension of the *Tanzimat* and Unionist reforms, which had secularized most of the legal and educational systems. With the relegation of the sultan-caliph to the role of ornament and the removal of the *Şeyhülislam* from the cabinet, the state itself had been secularized to a large extent already. Islam had been the state religion of the empire, but so it was under the early republic.

The major new step of the Kemalists was the complete secularization of family law, which, through the abolition of religious marriages and polygamy, touched the daily life of the population. They also went much further in the secularization of society (see below).

Like the Unionist reformers before them, the Kemalists stopped short of unleashing a real socio-economic revolution or reform programme. There was no attempt to change the ownership relations in the country.

The day of reckoning: the İzmir conspiracy

The political opposition and its press had been silenced in 1925, but Mustafa Kemal, being well aware of the capabilities of his opponents and of their expertise in underground organization (going back to the days before the revolution of 1908), still felt insecure. As long as the former leaders of the CUP and the PRP were still around, with their prestige as heroes from the independence war intact, they could exploit the prevailing discontent arising from the continuing bad economic situation and the unpopularity of the reforms.

Mustafa Kemal spent May and June 1926 on an extended inspection tour of the south and west of the country. When he was about to arrive in İzmir on 15 June (he was unexpectedly delayed), a plot to assassinate him was uncovered. The plotters were arrested and turned out to be a small band of professional gunmen, led by a former representative in the national assembly (and secretary of the Defence of Rights Group), Ziya Hurşit. The Ankara Independence Tribunal was sent to İzmir and immediately after its arrival on 18 June waves of arrests began.

Almost all the surviving prominent Unionists were arrested, as well as the former PRP members of the assembly, except for Hüseyin Rauf (Orbay) and Adnan (Adıvar), who were abroad at the time. During the trial, held from 26 June to 12 July, the arrested politicians were accused of having supported the assassination plot and of having planned a coup d'état. Of the accused, 16 were condemned to death, despite the fact that most of them had not been proved to be involved. The military heroes associated with the PRP, Kâzım Karabekir, Ali Fuat (Cebesoy), Refet (Bele), and Cafer Tayyar (Eğilmez), were released under the pressure of public opinion and of signs of discontent from the army. It was clear, however, that their position in politics had been irretrievably lost.

A second trial opened in Ankara in August against more than 50 important former Unionists. Even more than the first, this was a show trial during which the policies of the CUP leaders when in power and their opposition to Mustafa Kemal were the real themes and the conspiracy of June 1926 was a side issue. Four of the accused were hanged, while a number of others received prison sentences. Hüseyin Rauf, who was officially regarded as the main culprit, was sentenced *in absentia* to ten years imprisonment. *Kara* Kemal, whom the prosecution regarded as the brains behind the actual assassination attempt, had been sentenced to death *in absentia* during the first part of the trial. When his hiding place in Istanbul was discovered, he shot himself.

The fundamental reason for the purges of the summer of 1926 was undoubtedly that Mustafa Kemal himself knew very well that his movement was in many respects a continuation of the CUP and that its success was in part due to the party cadres of the CUP and the Unionist officers in the army. The people involved were, of course, just as well aware of this. That is why for them Mustafa Kemal's leadership was not self-evident. Challenging his leadership was still conceivable and it was this danger that he sought to suppress in 1926.

End of an era: 'The Speech'
The troubled postwar period was symbolically closed with Mustafa Kemal's 36-hour speech before the congress of the Republican People's Party from 15 to 20 October 1927. This is a remarkable and hugely influential text, which deserves consideration.

He presented it as a report on the history of the Turkish national movement from 1919 to 1927 and generally the historical character he claimed for his text has been accepted, although later generations in Turkey have debated whether it should be considered a historical source or as a piece of historiography. The author's prestige and the political climate of the period have seen to it that the text has become the basis for nearly all Turkish historiography on the period to the present day. It was translated into German, French and English in 1928/9 and has been deeply influential in foreign historiography as well.

In reality, the *Nutuk* (Speech), as it is simply known, is not a history of the period from 1919 to 1927, but it ends with the emergence of the Progressive Republican Party in November 1924. Only 1.5 per cent of the text is concerned with later events. The reason is that the speech is not really a survey of modern Turkish history at all. It is a vindication of the purges of 1925/6, and criticizing the former leaders of the PRP is its main theme, just as criticism of the old CUP leaders had been the theme of Mustafa Kemal's 'memoirs' published in March 1926. In his attempt to disgrace his former colleagues, he presents them throughout as doubters, incompetents and traitors, and depicts himself as the one who led the movement from the outset. It is significant that the speech begins with his arrival in Anatolia in May 1919, disregarding the earlier phase of the national resistance movement. In what is obviously a distortion of the historical truth, it presents the independence struggle not as one to preserve parts of the Ottoman Empire, but as a movement for the establishment of a new Turkish state.

The context in which the speech was given also served to distort the historical picture. The RPP called its 1927 congress – and it is generally described as such – the 'second congress of the RPP' though in fact it was the first. The RPP called it the second because it retrospectively adopted the congress at Sivas in 1919 as its first, thus emphasizing the (false) identification of the RPP with the national liberation movement and monopolizing its heritage. While the period from 1923 to 1926 decisively influenced political life in Turkey in an authoritarian sense for the next 20 years, the congress of 1927 and Mustafa Kemal's speech determined the historical vision of the genesis of the new Turkish state for generations.

11 · The Kemalist One-Party State, 1925–45

The political system of Kemalist Turkey: party and state

From the promulgation of the Law on the Maintenance of Order in March 1925, Turkey's government was an authoritarian one-party regime and, not to put too fine a point on it, a dictatorship. We have seen how the law and the tribunals established under it were used in 1925/6 to silence all opposition and how, in his great speech of 1927, Mustafa Kemal Pasha vindicated this repression. The Law on the Maintenance of Order remained in force until 1929, when the government felt secure enough to allow it to lapse. To all intents and purposes, the Republican People's Party had established a power monopoly and, at the party congress of 1931, Turkey's political system was officially declared to be that of a one-party state.[1]

Apart from an experiment with a 'tame' opposition party in 1930, no legal opposition was active in Turkey until after the Second World War. Underground opposition was limited to an insignificant communist movement and more important actions of Kurdish nationalists. There were almost continuous small uprisings in the mountains of the southeast and one major insurrection in Dersim (Tunceli) in 1937/8. This was again suppressed with the utmost severity and again tens of thousands of Kurds were forcibly resettled in the west of the country. Small groups of *émigrés* of different political colours (royalists, liberals, Islamists and socialists) continued to attack the regime in pamphlets and periodicals from places as far apart as Paris, Sofia, Damascus and Cairo, but none carried any real weight.[2]

According to the 1924 constitution, all power resided in the Great National Assembly of Turkey, which was the only legitimate representative of the nation's sovereign will. But one of the reactions of the RPP leadership to the emergence of opposition in 1924 had been to tighten party discipline to the extent that free discussion was only allowed in the (closed) meetings of the parliamentary party. After a decision on any topic had been reached in these meetings, delegates were bound by the majority decision and were required to vote for it in the assembly. This meant that even before March 1925 the assembly votes were a foregone conclusion. During the one-party era they became a mere formality. Discussion was restricted, even within the meetings of the parliamentary party, which served as the forum in which the cabinet announced and explained its decisions. Although the leeway of the faction varied according to the field of policy concerned (the economy being debated much more freely than foreign affairs, for instance, which were left almost completely to the cabinet), the function of its meetings was essentially to ratify and legitimize cabinet decisions.

While the RPP had a rank-and-file organization throughout the country, which its secretary-general led, the members of the national assembly, the cabinet, the prime minister (who was also executive chairman of the party) and the president (who doubled as party chairman) dominated it. State and party were closely identified. One important result was that the party itself never developed an independent ideological or organizational 'personality' and became heavily bureaucratized. Attempts by the party's long-serving secretary-general, Recep (Peker), to make the party more independent and to develop an independent 'Kemalist' ideology failed when, at the 1936 congress, İsmet (İnönü) declared the congruency between the state apparatus and the party organization to be official policy. This meant that, to take just one example, the governor of a province would automatically be the head of the RPP branch in his province.

In the 1930s and 1940s the very powerful 'inspectors' (*müfettişler*) formed an administrative layer between the centre and the governors of the provinces. The inspectorates were part of the state's reaction to the Kurdish insurrection of 1925. In 1927 the 'Reform Plan for the East' was adopted and the first inspectorate was formed in the Kurdish southeast. From 1934 onwards they were also introduced in the rest of the country. The inspectors, whom the minister of the interior appointed, had wide-ranging powers, particularly in the field of security. Ultimately, there were five inspectorates and they remained in being until 1 January 1948.

Four-yearly parliamentary elections were held throughout the one-party period, but they served only a ceremonial function. The slates of candidates for parliamentary seats were drawn up by the chairman of the party, the executive chairman and the secretary-general and then ratified by the party congress and there was no way in which citizens, even if they were active party members, could stand for parliament on their own initiative. Even if elections were tightly controlled, the fact that women were given the right to vote and to be elected on 5 December 1934 was still an important step in the emancipation of Turkish women. From

March 1935 onwards, 18 women deputies took their places in the Great National Assembly in Ankara. In this respect at least Turkey had caught up with the most advanced countries of Europe.

Tutelary democracy: the Free Republican Party

The monolithic political system established after 1925 left very little room for the ventilation of competing ideas within the leadership, and none at all for the expression of social discontent from without. At the same time, the authoritarian behaviour of the RPP and of its regional and local representatives, the attendant favouritism and corruption, the lack of civil liberties, and the reform policies of the government, created widespread resentment. By the end of the 1920s, the world economic crisis, which hit Turkey very hard as it did other agricultural producers, had compounded this situation. The RPP had no real means of managing this discontent (other than suppressing its expression) since its authoritarian structure left it without the means of communication with the mass of the population. The crisis in the country was not reflected in more lively debates in the assembly at all. At the opening of the 1931 party congress party chairman İsmet not once mentioned the economic crisis.

In 1930, Mustafa Kemal, who was aware of the existence of discontent (though probably not of its scale) through reports and through his frequent inspection tours in the country, decided to allow and even encourage the founding of a loyal opposition party, with the twin aims of channelling the social discontent and of shaking up the lethargic RPP. He may also have wanted to put pressure on İsmet who, after five years in power, had gradually built up his own power base and was no longer only the president's puppet.

Mustafa Kemal approached his old friend Fethi (Okyar) with an offer to found a new party. Fethi had recently returned from a tour of duty as ambassador in Paris (where he had been sent after his defeat as prime minister in March 1925) and he had submitted a highly critical report on the state of the country and İsmet's policies to the president. The two men discussed the proposal for a few days. Fethi asked for guarantees that the government would allow his party to function and that Mustafa Kemal himself would remain impartial. For his part, Mustafa Kemal demanded that the new party remain faithful to the ideals of republicanism and secularism. When they agreed, Fethi proceeded to found the *Serbest Cumhuriyet Fırkası* (Free Republican Party). Mustafa Kemal ordered a number of his closest collaborators, among them his oldest friend Nuri (Conker), to join the new party. To prove his good faith, he also announced that his own sister, Makbule, had joined it.

In the end, only 15 representatives joined the FRP but they were all eminent members of the Kemalist establishment. The party produced an 11-point manifesto, which echoed that of the Progressive Republican Party of 1924 in that it advocated a liberal economic policy and encouragement of foreign investment, as well as freedom of speech and direct elections (Turkey still had a system of two-tier elections).

The new party was greeted with widespread enthusiasm. Its branch offices were literally inundated with applications for membership. Huge and ecstatic crowds met Fethi when he visited İzmir early in September. There were skirmishes with the police, and when the police fired into the crowd a number of people were wounded and a boy was killed. This was a turning point in the party's short history. The RPP leaders were alarmed and demanded that Mustafa Kemal should state openly that he was and would remain at the head of their party, which he did on 10 September.[3]

In October 1930, local elections were held and the FRP managed to win in 30 of the 502 councils.[4] Even though this was only a small minority of the seats, the governing party was surprised and alarmed. Then, in an assembly debate directly after the elections, Fethi accused the governing party of large-scale irregularities and electoral fraud. This in turn led to fierce attacks on the FRP, in which it and its leader were accused of high treason. Mustafa Kemal now told Fethi privately that, in this atmosphere, he could no longer retain his impartiality. Unwilling to conduct political opposition against the president himself, Fethi felt that he had no choice but to close down the FRP on 16 November 1930. For the rest of his life he remained bitter about what he felt to be Mustafa Kemal's desertion at this juncture.[5]

A month later, on 23 December, an incident occurred in the town of Menemen, not far from İzmir. A group of young dervishes from Manisa, led by a certain Mehmet, walked into town, unfurled a green banner and called for the restoration of the şeriat and the caliphate. When word of this reached the headquarters of the gendarmerie, it sent out a company of soldiers under reserve lieutenant Mustafa Fehmi Kubilay. When he demanded the surrender of the dervishes, they attacked him and cut off his head, which they then paraded on a stick. A gendarmerie unit arrived and opened fire, killing three of the ringleaders, including Mehmet. It was a relatively small incident, but what made it really shocking to the Kemalist leadership was not so much the action of the dervishes but the fact that over a thousand bystanders had watched these events unfold without anyone raising his voice in protest. This could be, and was, interpreted as tacit support by the public for the rebels. The government took stern action, with martial law being declared and over 2000 arrests made (among them many former FRP supporters). Some 28 people were executed, but the bill envisaging the razing to the ground of Menemen and the deportation of its inhabitants, though initially supported by Mustafa Kemal, was eventually dropped.[6]

The RPP's totalitarian tendencies

The extent of resentment and opposition to the RPP regime, which the Free Party episode had brought to light were a sobering experience for Mustafa Kemal and his followers, who thereafter tightened their hold on the country by bringing under their direct control all the country's cultural and intellectual life, suppressing those independent social and cultural organizations that had survived from the CUP era. There were no more experiments with opposition, although Mustafa Kemal tried to combat the lethargy of the assembly by having a number of seats (30 in the 1931 elections, 16 in 1935) reserved for independents. In the prevailing climate, however, this was not very effective: in 1931 not even the 30 seats left vacant by the People's Party for independent candidates could be filled and in 1935 the number of independents dropped to 13.[7]

First and foremost among the social and cultural institutions to be suppressed was the *Türk Ocakları* (the Turkish Hearth movement). It had been reactivated under the leadership of the minister of education, Hamdullah Suphi (Tanrıöver), and it tried to spread nationalist, positivist and secularist ideas in the country through lectures, courses and exhibitions. When it was closed down in 1931, it had more than 30,000 members and 267 branches.[8] From 1932 it was replaced by the so-called *Halk Evleri* (People's Homes) in towns and by *Halk Odaları* (People's Rooms) in large villages; they served essentially the same function but were tightly controlled by the provincial branches of the party. By the end of the Second World War there were nearly 500 of these People's Homes in all parts of the country.

Another organization to be closed down was the *Türk Kadınlar Birliği* (Turkish Women's Union), which women who had been active in the national resistance movement had founded in 1924. At an extraordinary congress in May 1935 it decided, at the request of the RPP leadership, to disband officially because its aims (equal rights for Turkish women) had been achieved with the granting of the vote to Turkey's women. The Turkish Freemasons' lodges, whose members had often been prominent in the Young Turk movement from the beginning of the century, were 'temporarily' closed down in the same year on the orders of the interior minister Şükrü (Kaya), himself a prominent mason. Another organization to be disbanded was the union of journalists.

All newspapers and periodicals leaning towards the liberal or socialist opposition had been closed down in 1925. From then on only government-controlled newspapers appeared. The last media that were even slightly critical, were silenced with the adoption, in 1931, of a new press law that gave the government powers to close down any paper that published anything contradicting the 'general policies of the country'.

Finally, in 1933, the old *Darülfünun* ('House of Sciences', the university) in Istanbul was given a new charter and reconstituted as the University of Istanbul. In the process two-thirds of its teaching staff, more than 100 people, lost their tenure and only the most dependable followers of the Kemalist line were kept on. It was the first of many purges the Turkish universities were to experience in the following 50 years. Starting in 1933, however, academic life in Turkey was also strengthened by an influx of German scholars and scientists, who left Germany after Hitler came to power. The Turkish government invited 63 German professors to come and teach in Turkey, where they raised the level of academic learning dramatically and provided a formative influence on several generations of students.[9]

It is significant that all of the organizations that were banned or closed in these years were ideological allies of the RPP. Unlike the dervish orders that had been banned in the 1920s they all represented modernist, nationalist and secularist ideas. The repression, therefore, was not motivated by ideological quarrels but by the Kemalists' desire to establish complete control over society.

Both the press and the educational institutions were mobilized to spread the Kemalist message. The stifling political and intellectual climate that resulted has often been overlooked in traditional historiography and needs to be given due attention. Nevertheless, it should also be pointed out that the Kemalist leadership did inspire a great many people – mostly writers, teachers, doctors and other professionals and students – with its vision of a modern, secular, independent Turkey. These people, who saw themselves as an elite, with a mission to guide their ignorant compatriots, often worked very hard and with great personal sacrifice for their ideals. This 'noblesse oblige' attitude of the Kemalist elite is something that modern revisionist writers of the right and the left tend to overlook.

The Kemalist message
The set of ideas or ideals that together formed *Kemalizm* (Kemalism) or *Atatürkçülük* (Atatürkism) as it came to be called in the 1930s, evolved gradually. It never became a coherent, all-embracing ideology, but can best be described as a set of attitudes and opinions that were never defined in any detail. As we have seen, Recep Peker's attempts to do so

failed. As a result, Kemalism remained a flexible concept and people with widely differing worldviews have been able to call themselves Kemalist. The basic principles of Kemalism were laid down in the party programme of 1931. They were republicanism, secularism, nationalism, populism, statism and revolutionism (or reformism).

Secularism and nationalism had of course been among the distinctive characteristics of Young Turk ideology at least since 1913. During the 1930s both were carried to extremes, secularism being interpreted not only as a separation of state and religion, but as the removal of religion from public life and the establishment of complete state control over remaining religious institutions. An extreme form of nationalism, with the attendant creation of historical myths, was used as the prime instrument in the building of a new national identity, and as such was intended to take the place of religion in many respects.

Republicanism had been a basic principle since 1923 (when, it will be remembered, political activity in favour of a return of the monarchy had been outlawed). 'Populism' meant the notion, first emphasized during the First World War, of national solidarity and putting the interests of the whole nation before those of any group or class. In a negative sense it entailed a denial of class interests (according to Kemalism, Turkey did not have classes in the European sense) and a prohibition of political activity based on class (and thus of all socialist or communist activity). Revolutionism – or reformism, as Atatürk's more conservative followers have preferred to interpret the Turkish term *İnkılapçılık* – meant a commitment to ongoing (but orderly and state-led) change and support for the Kemalist reform programme. Statism was a new concept that recognized the pre-eminence of the state in the economic field; and it was probably the most widely discussed issue in Turkey in the 1930s and 1940s. It is treated in more detail below.

These six principles, symbolized in the party emblem as six arrows (the *Altı Ok*), were incorporated into the Turkish constitution in 1937. Together they formed the state ideology of Kemalism and the basis for indoctrination in schools, the media and the army. Sometimes Kemalism was even described as the 'Turkish religion'. Nevertheless, as an ideology it lacked coherence and, perhaps even more importantly, emotional appeal. This ideological void was filled to some extent by the personality cult that grew up around Mustafa Kemal during and even more so after his lifetime. From 1926 onwards statues of him were erected in the major towns. He was presented as the father of the nation, its saviour and its teacher. Indoctrination in schools and universities (where 'History of the Turkish Revolution' became a compulsory subject in 1934) focused on him to an extraordinary degree. The fact that he was not associated with a very definite ideology that could be discredited, as fascism, national socialism and Marxism–Leninism have been, has meant that his personality cult could survive changes in the political climate. At the time of writing it is still very much part of the official culture of Turkey.

Friction within the leadership

While the political leadership was in complete control over both party and parliament, tensions gradually built up within the leadership, notably between İsmet, who served as prime minister for 12 consecutive years from 1925 to 1937, and the president, Mustafa Kemal. In his later years the president largely withdrew from politics and left the day-to-day running of the country in İsmet's hands, while he interested himself in specific reform projects such as that of the script and language. He surrounded himself with a small group of supporters and friends with whom he spent most nights eating, drinking and discussing the coun-try's problems and future. Experts from different walks of life were often invited to these sessions in the presidential villa in Çankaya, which as a rule lasted from late in the evening until the break of day. Suggestions were made, criticisms voiced, plans drawn up and decisions taken.

What made the situation potentially dangerous was Mustafa Kemal's relative isolation from the daily affairs of the government. His plans and decisions therefore tended to become increasingly poorly coordinated with those of the prime minister, İsmet. The fact that, even in semi-retirement, Mustafa Kemal remained the undisputed master of the country meant that he could overrule the prime minister and his cabinet if he chose to do so under the influence of his circle of friends and advisers. Over the years there were several instances of this happening, in internal, economic and foreign affairs. Twice the president forced a cabinet minister to resign without consulting İsmet. His interference irritated İsmet, who became increasingly wary of what he saw as the president's kitchen cabinet in Çankaya.[10]

Finally, in September 1937, there was an open row between the two men, which led to Atatürk (as he had become in 1934 with the intro-duction of family names) demanding İsmet's resignation. İnönü duly resigned, ostensibly for health reasons. Mahmut Celâl (Bayar), a former CUP secretary and *Teşkilât-i Mahsusa* chief in İzmir, first head of the Business Bank of Turkey (*Türkiye İş Bankası*) created in 1924 and minister of economic affairs since 1932, replaced him.

Atatürk's death and İsmet's return to power

Some of Atatürk's irritability and erratic behaviour during 1937/8 may have been due to his deteriorating health. Apart from two heart attacks, in 1923 and 1927, which seem to have left no permanent damage, he was generally healthy until early in 1937, when the symptoms of advanced cirrhosis of the liver, due to excessive consumption of alcohol over many years, started to become apparent. The illness was officially diagnosed only at the beginning of 1938 and from March onwards his condition deteriorated quickly. His illness was kept a secret from the public (even in October a newspaper that mentioned it was immediately closed for three months), but leading political circles were well aware of the impending end and a struggle for power began.

Despite the events of the previous year, İsmet İnönü was clearly the leading candidate for the succession, but he had made many enemies during his years in office, the most determined being the members of Atatürk's 'kitchen cabinet'. They attempted to remove him (by having him appointed ambassador to Washington) and to engineer new elections for the assembly, which would have to elect Atatürk's successor and which was still packed with İsmet's supporters. There was even talk of a verbal political testament of the president, in which he pronounced himself against İsmet's succession.[11]

All these attempts, however, proved fruitless. Mustafa Kemal Pasha Atatürk died on 10 November 1938 in the Dolmabahçe Palace in Istanbul, where he had been lying ill for the past few months. On 11 November the national assembly elected İsmet İnönü the second president of the republic. His succession was due to four factors: the refusal of the prime minister, Bayar, to cooperate with his adversaries (Bayar had kept in touch with İnönü throughout this period); his adversaries' inability to come up with a credible candidate; the fact that the parliamentary deputies, as well as the party bureaucrats, were people who had been picked by İnönü himself years before; and the decision of the military leaders to support İnönü and of the Chief of General Staff, Marshal Fevzi Çakmak, not to stand as a candidate, even though it was made clear to him that his candidacy would have considerable support in the assembly.

Atatürk's body was brought to Ankara amid widespread demonstrations of grief and mourning and laid to rest temporarily in the Ethnographic Museum. In 1953 it was finally interred in an imposing purpose-built mausoleum on what was then a hill on the outskirts of the capital but is now right in its centre.

An obituary

Under the influence of the official historiography of the Turkish Republic (and ultimately of Atatürk himself in his great speech), historians have depicted the emergence of modern Turkey as the single-handed achievement of one man. The reader will have noticed that in this book an attempt has been made to paint a different picture. Nevertheless, it remains true that it is doubtful whether Turkey would have survived as an independent state without his unique combination of tactical mastery, ruthlessness, realism and sense of purpose. Up to 1919 he had been a member of the military inner circle of the CUP with a reputation as both a brilliant staff officer and commander and a quarrelsome and over-ambitious personality. His rule after 1925 may be regarded both as a daring attempt at achieving a modernization leap for Turkish society and as a regressive phase in the development of mature and democratic political institutions in Turkey, but there can be hardly any doubt that he was absolutely the right man on the right spot during the greatest crisis in the history of his country and that he contributed more than anyone else to its survival.

İsmet İnönü as 'National Leader'

Around the time of Atatürk's death there had been widespread specu-lation about whether there would be a change in policy and even about whether the republic would endure. It was soon clear, however, that İsmet İnönü meant to continue the basic policies of his predecessor. His position as leader was formalized at an extraordinary party congress in December 1938, at which the party statutes were changed to make Atatürk the 'eternal party chairman', while İnönü was made 'permanent party chairman'. The term *millî şef* (national leader), which from time to time had been used for Atatürk in the 1930s, now became İnönü's official title.

For a few months İnönü kept Bayar as prime minister, but on 25 January 1939 the latter handed in his resignation. The main reason was the basic difference of opinion between the president and the prime minister over economic policies, but İnönü had also made life difficult for the cabinet by inspiring a number of press campaigns, inquiries and lawsuits aimed at the administration that had been in power in 1937/8. At the same time İnönü tried to broaden his political base by a policy of reconciliation with the old leaders of the independence movement who had been purged in 1926. Two of these, Ali Fuat Cebesoy and Refet Bele had made their peace with Atatürk during his last years, but the rest had remained in limbo. A number of them had lived abroad since 1926. They now returned to the country and were given parliamentary seats.

Celâl Bayar was succeeded by Dr Refik Saydam who served as prime minister until his death in July 1942. He in turn was succeeded by the foreign minister, Şükrü Saraçoğlu, who remained in power until 1945, but during these years, which were of course entirely dominated by the Second World War, İsmet İnönü was in complete control and his prime ministers (who were always at the same time vice-chairmen of the party) executed the policies determined by the president.[12]

Turkey's place among the other authoritarian states of the interbellum
The Turkish regime of the 1930s and 1940s, of which the main characteristics have been outlined above, thus in many ways resembled the other authoritarian regimes that sprang up all over eastern and southern Europe in this era (such as the regimes of Horthy in Hungary, Salazar in Portugal, Franco in Spain and Metaxas in Greece, and, of course, Mussolini in Italy). It differed from them, however, in that it was not culturally and religiously conservative, but on the contrary attempted a far-reaching cultural revolution in a conservatively religious society. The example of the most important dictatorship in the Mediterranean, fascist Italy, was certainly important to the Turkish leadership. The way in which Mussolini seemed to forge national unity and to energize Italian society impressed many in Turkey (as, indeed, it did in many other European countries), and a number of new laws promulgated under the republic were straight copies of Italian legislation.

There were many similarities between the Italian fascist regime and the Kemalists: the extreme nationalism, with its attendant development of a legitimizing historical mythology and racist rhetoric, the authoritarian character of the regime and its efforts to establish a complete totalitarian monopoly for its party of the political, social and cultural scene, the personality cult that developed around both Mussolini on the one hand and Atatürk and İnönü on the other, and the emphasis on national unity and solidarity with its attendant denial of class conflicts.

Nevertheless, the differences between the two regimes are greater than the similarities. Fascism came into being as a genuinely (albeit orchestrated) popular movement, in reaction to the disruption of traditional society brought about by the industrial revolution and to the threat posed by the socialist movement to the middle class; the Young Turk regimes in Turkey imposed their policies from above on an indifferent population. Unlike the fascists, the Kemalists never attempted any large-scale or permanent mobilization of the population for its goals. It has been pointed out that of all the speeches made by Atatürk in these years not a single one took place before a mass rally in the fascist style. Also, while the Kemalist state was undoubtedly authoritarian and totalitarian, the existence of an all-powerful leader was not made into a guiding political principle with its own legitimacy, a 'leader principle'. Atatürk intensely disliked being called a dictator.[13] The semblance of a democratic system with a parliament and elections was carefully left in place. It legitimized the regime, where in Fascist eyes liberal democracy with its parliamentary procedures was an obsolete system. Finally, one great, and possibly decisive, difference from the Italian example is the lack of militarist rhetoric and expansionist (or irredentist) propaganda and policies in the Turkish case and the cautious, defensive and realistic policies of Turkey's leaders.

Reform policies 1925–35: secularism and nationalism
In the secularist drive, which was the most characteristic element of Kemalist reform, three areas can be discerned. The first was the secularization of state, education and law: the attack on the traditional strongholds of the institutionalized Islam of the *ulema*. The second was the attack on religious symbols and their replacement by the symbols of European civilization. The third was the secularization of social life and the attack on popular Islam it entailed.

It can be argued that the first wave of Kemalist reforms had finished the process of secularization of state, education and law, which had begun under Sultan Mahmut a century before and which had been almost completed under the CUP during its rule from 1913 to 1918. The abolition of the sultanate and caliphate, the proclamation of the republic and the new constitution in 1922–24 were the final stages in the secularization of the state, and the seal was set on this development with the removal from the 1928 constitution of the clause that made Islam the state religion of Turkey.

Even before the birth of the republic, the role of the *şeriat*, the holy law, had been limited almost exclusively to the realm of family law. Now this sector too was taken from the jurisdiction of the *ulema* with the adoption of the Swiss civil code. The penal code adopted from Italy in 1926 prohibited the forming of associations on a religious basis. The educational system, which had already been brought into the control of the Ministry of Education under the CUP, was now completely secularized through the Law on the Unification of Education in March 1924. At the same time the *medreses*, or religious colleges, were abolished, and their place was taken by schools for preachers and by a theological faculty established at the University of Istanbul.

The year 1924 also witnessed the abolition of the venerable function of *Şeyhülislam* and of the Ministry of Religious Affairs and Pious Foundations. Two directorates were created in its place, the *Diyanet İşleri Müdürlüğü* (Directorate for Religious Affairs) and the *Evkaf Umum Müdürlüğü* (Directorate-General for Pious Foundations). Both were attached directly to the prime minister's office. The establishment of these directorates clearly shows that the Kemalist perception of secularism meant not so much separation of state and religion as state control of religion.

The second area in which secularization took place was that of religious symbols. This was the most important aspect of measures like banning traditional headgear (such as the fez and turban) for men in 1925 and restricting religious attire to prayer services in the mosques, which was ordered in September of that year. It also inspired the attacks made by Atatürk and his followers on wearing the veil (although this was never actually forbidden)[14] and, for instance, the decree of 1935, which made Sunday the official day of rest instead of Friday.

It is clear from Atatürk's own statements that measures such as the ban on religious attire were motivated as much by the desire to claim all visible expression of authority as a monopoly of the state (and its uniformed servants) as by the wish to secularize society.

A number of other reforms, which were not specifically aimed at religion, were nevertheless symbolic. The adoption of the Western clock and calendar in 1926, of Western numerals in 1928 and of Western weights and measures in 1931 not only gave Turkey a more European image, but also made communication with the Western world much easier. It was also one more measure designed to cut links with the Islamic world. The changes in the position of women also have religious connotations, or at least were felt to do so by many people. These changes, after all, consisted not only of formal emancipation (the right to vote), but also of the active promotion of new and very different role models: professional women, women pilots, opera singers and beauty queens.

The introduction of family names in 1934 was a great step forward insofar as registration was concerned. The assembly voted to bestow on Mustafa Kemal Pasha the family name Atatürk (Father-Turk). The name was exclusive to him and his descendants, but since he died childless no other Turk has ever been called Atatürk.

Perhaps the most drastic measure was the adoption of the Latin alphabet in 1928. Ottoman Turkish was written with a version of the Arabic/Persian alphabet. While this suited the Arabic and Persian vocabulary, which made up three-quarters of written late Ottoman, it was highly unsuitable for expressing the sounds of the Turkish part of the vocabulary, Arabic being rich in consonants but very poor in vowels while Turkish is exactly the opposite. The result was that Ottoman Turkish sometimes had four different signs for one single sound, while it could not express other sounds at all. When the written language became an important means of communication with the advent of new media such as the press and the telegraph in the mid-nineteenth century, reform of the alphabet was needed. The first attempt was made by Münif Pasha, one of the statesmen of the *Tanzimat*, in a lecture in 1862.[15] During the second constitutional period several Young Turk writers – Hüseyin Cahit (Yalçın), Abdullah Cevdet, Celâl Nuri (İleri) – had advocated the adoption of the Latin alphabet, while Enver Pasha had experimented with a reformed version of the Ottoman script, which the army had tried out. From 1923 onwards there had been sporadic discussions of the matter, at the İzmir economic congress and – in February 1924 – in the assembly. At that time there was still much opposition to the adoption of the Latin script in conservative and religious circles, but from 1925 the opposition was silenced. Furthermore, in 1926 the Turkic republics of the Soviet Union decided to adopt the Latin alphabet, which gave added impetus to the discussions in Turkey.

In the summer of 1928, a commission under the personal direction of Mustafa Kemal drew up a report on the matter and on 9 August the president officially announced for the first time that the Turkish script would replace the Ottoman alphabet. An 'alphabet mobilization' was proclaimed and in the following months Mustafa Kemal toured the country explaining the new letters and exhorting everyone to learn them quickly and to teach them to their compatriots. On 1 November a law was passed that made the use of the new alphabet in public communications compulsory from 1 January 1929.

While there were good rational arguments for the change, the reason Mustafa Kemal and his followers pushed it through so energetically was undoubtedly ideological: it was yet another way to cut off Turkish society from its Ottoman and Middle Eastern Islamic traditions and to reorient it towards the West. The change was carried through with amazing speed and eventually gained widespread acceptance, but its effect on the struggle against illiteracy was disappointing. There was a huge effort to spread literacy (in the new script) through the *millet mektepleri* (schools of the nation) for adults, but the lack of primary education in the villages meant that illiteracy has remained relatively high, even compared with other developing countries. In the early 1990s it was still over 35 per cent. Under those people who had received their education before 1928, the old script remained in use in private correspondence, notes and diaries until well into the 1960s.

The success of the alphabet reform encouraged those who wanted to reform the language itself. By the nineteenth century the chasm between the written Ottoman of the literate elite and the vernacular of the Turkish population had become very wide. Attempts to bring the written language closer to the spoken one dated from the middle of the nineteenth century

– the Young Ottomans, as the first Ottoman journalists, had played a pioneering role. During the reign of the CUP this trend had been reinforced. Ziya Gökalp and his circle advocated the replacement of Arabic and Persian grammatical elements in the language with Turkish ones and the discarding of 'superfluous' synonyms, but unlike the purists they accepted Arabic and Persian words that had become part of everyday language.

After the alphabet reform, for several reasons the more extreme purists came to the fore. In the first place, the success of the alphabet reform encouraged the idea that this type of 'revolution by decree' was possible. In the second place, the nature of the new script encouraged purism. It had been designed to reflect the actual sounds of spoken Turkish, not to transcribe the shape of the old Ottoman writing in new letters. As a result, many of the originally Arabic and Persian words looked alien and even unintelligible in the new script. In the third place, the radical solutions of the purists – to remove all Arabic and Persian words from the language and create a pure Turkish one – were in tune with the extreme nationalism of the 1930s.

In 1932 Mustafa Kemal took the initiative in convening the first Turkish linguistic congress. During it there was a showdown between the purists and the moderates, and the former won. The moderates argued that language could not be changed by revolution or decree, which was held to be an indirect attack on the revolutionary changes the president had pushed through and a sign of a counter-revolutionary mentality. A reform programme was drawn up and a Society for the Study of the Turkish Language (*Türk Dili Tetkik Cemiyeti*, later *Türk Dil Kurumu*) was founded. Its members enthusiastically started to collect words from dialects, ancient literary sources and even Turkic languages from Central Asia to replace the Ottoman vocabulary.

The movement soon ran into difficulties. The population only adopted some of the new words and these often existed side-by-side with the word they were intended to replace, acquiring a different meaning. A kind of artificial language, intelligible only to insiders, came into existence. Mustafa Kemal himself gave a number of perfectly unintelligible speeches in the 'new language' in 1934, but by 1935 he had reverted to more conventional usage.[16] The language reform movement was temporarily saved from deadlock by the launching in 1935 of the *Güneş-Dil Teorisi* (Sun-Language Theory). This theory held that all languages derived originally from one primeval language, spoken in Central Asia, that Turkish was closest of all languages to this origin and that all languages had developed from the primeval language through Turkish. The theory, concocted by a Viennese 'Orientalist' by the name of Kvergic, was greeted with scepticism among Turkish linguists, but it gained the support of Mustafa Kemal, who ordered the Society for the Study of the Turkish Language to study it in detail. The society's third congress in 1936 officially adopted the theory, and courses in it were made obligatory at the Arts Faculty in Ankara. There was one very good practical reason for the success of the theory: if all words came from Turkish originally, there was no need to purge them now: they could simply be 'nationalized' through a fake etymology. Nevertheless, it is clear that many Turks, along with their president, were actually fascinated by the doctrine. After Atatürk's death in 1938 the language reform movement lost much of its *élan*. After the Second World War it was continued, but the government no longer actively promoted it.

While it lasted, both the existence and the theorizing of the linguistic society owed much to the work of the Society for the Study of Turkish History (*Türk Tarihi Tetkik Cemiyeti*, later *Türk Tarih Kurumu*), which had been founded slightly earlier, in 1931. At its first congress, held in Ankara in 1932, the 'Turkish historical thesis' was propounded for the first time. This theory, which Mustafa Kemal emphatically supported, held that the Turks were descendants of white (Aryan) inhabitants of Central Asia, who had been forced by drought and hunger to migrate to other areas, such as China, Europe and the Near East. In doing so, they had created the world's great civilizations. In the Near East, the Sumerians and the Hittites were really proto-Turks. (It is no coincidence that the two major state banks founded in the 1930s were called *Sümerbank* (Sumerian Bank) and *Etibank* (Hittite Bank). Attila and Genghis Khan were described as executing civilizing missions. The theory aimed to give Turks a sense of pride in their history and national identity, separate from the immediate past, that is to say the Ottoman era. Declaring the Hittites (and the Trojans) proto-Turks had the added advantage of proving that Anatolia had been a Turkish country since time immemorial, thus extending the roots of the citizens of the republic in the soil they inhabited beyond those of the Armenians and the Greeks. It was one of the means whereby the Kemalist leadership tried to construct a new national identity and strong national cohesion. That is not to say that it was a purely cynical form of indoctrination. As with the linguistic theories, there is every indication that Mustafa Kemal himself, and many in the national political leadership and educational establishment, believed in it.

From 1932 onwards, the historical thesis formed the mainstay of history teaching in schools and universities. Its more extreme claims were quietly dropped from the late 1940s onwards, but traces remain even in the schoolbooks of today.[17]

The extreme nationalism of which the historical thesis was a part seems to contradict the admiration for and imitation of Western ways that was the other characteristic of Kemalist policies, but in fact it served to facilitate the adoption of Western ways. On the one hand, the emphasis on the Turkish heritage, even if it was largely mythical, as something separate from the Middle Eastern and Islamic civilization of the Ottoman Empire, made it easier to exchange elements from traditional Middle Eastern civilization for those of the West. On the other hand, it instilled in the Turks, especially those of the younger generations, a strong feeling of national identity and national pride, sometimes bordering on a feeling of superiority, which in a sense psychologically counterbalanced the need to follow Europe.

The most significant step in the secularization of social life was the suppression of the dervish orders (*tarikat*s), announced in September and put into operation in November 1925. These mystical brotherhoods had served vital religious and social functions throughout Ottoman history. On a psychological level they offered a mystical, emotional dimension that was lacking in the high religion of the *ulema* and at the same time they served as networks offering cohesion, protection and social mobility. As part of the reaction against Western economic, political and cultural penetration, they seem to have become even more active in the late nineteenth and early twentieth centuries. As had been the case with the Ottoman state, the relations between the Young Turks and the orders had been unstable. On the one hand, the heterodox (close to Shi'ite Islam) Bektaşi order seems to have supported both the CUP and the Anatolian resistance movement. The Mevlevi order (the followers of the mystic Celâleddin Rumi) had contributed its own battalions during the First World War. On the other hand, members of the Nakşibendi order had led both the anti-constitutionalist uprising in 1909 and the Kurdish rebellion of 1925. Whatever their political position, their widespread networks of convents and shrines, the obedience their followers owed to their sheikhs and the closed and secretive culture of the brotherhoods made them independent to a degree that was unacceptable to a modern centralist national government.

By extending their secularization drive beyond the formal, institutionalized Islam the Kemalists now touched such vital elements of popular religion as dress, amulets, soothsayers, holy sheikhs, saints' shrines, pilgrimages and festivals. The resentment these measures caused and the resistance put up against them was far greater than, for instance, in the case of the abolition of the caliphate, the position of *şeyhülislam*, or the *medrese*s, which was only important to official 'high' religion.

While the government succeeded in suppressing most expressions of popular religion, at least in the towns, this did not, of course, disappear. To a large extent, the *tarikat*s simply went underground. But through the simultaneous imposition of an authoritarian and – especially during the 1940s – increasingly unpopular regime and suppression of popular Islam, the Kemalists politicized Islam and turned it into a vehicle for opposition. One could say that, in turning against popular religion, they cut the ties that bound them to the mass of the population.

During the 1930s, there were government-inspired attempts to nation-alize and modernize Islam, but interest in this 'Turkish reformation' was limited to a small part of the elite, and its most obvious manifestation was the replacement of the Arabic *ezan* (call to prayer from the minaret) with a Turkish one, recited to a melody the state conservatory had composed in 1932.[18] This was introduced after earlier state-induced experiments with the reading of the *mevlut*, the text recited on the Prophet Muhammad's birthday and with completely Turkified Friday sermons.

Much more important in the long run was the movement the Islamic modernist Sait Nursi, whom his followers called *Bediüzzaman* (Marvel of the Time), founded in the 1930s. Nursi had had a chequered relationship with the Young Turks, taking part in the counter-revolution of 1909, but also serving as a *Teşkilât-i Mahsusa* propagandist in the First World War, supporting the national resistance movement but warning against its secularist tendencies in 1923. From the early years of the century, Sait had acquired a reputation as a religious scholar, especially in the east. After the Sheikh Sait rebellion, he was arrested along with many other prominent Kurds and resettled in the town of Isparta in the west. From the 1920s onwards, he laid down the ideas he preached in brochures and booklets, which were later collectively known as the *Risale-i Nur* (Message of Light). In it, he enjoined Muslims to take God's unity as the basis of their lives, but also to study modern science and technology and to use them in the cause of Islam, which in his eyes was the only true basis for social cohesion.

Between 1935 and 1953, Sait Nursi was arrested and tried a number of times for alleged political use of religion. But while he preached social mobilization and rejected both secularism and nationalism, Sait did not indulge in direct political activity until the late 1950s. During the Kemalist period, his writings were banned, but his growing circle of disciples copied them by hand. After his death the *Nurcu* movement, as it is called, continued to grow and became very influential in Turkey and among Turkish migrant workers abroad.

Taken together, the Kemalist reforms literally altered the face of Turkey. The fact that a non-Western and Muslim country chose to discard its past and seek to join the West made a huge impression in the

West, where the fact that an entirely new, modern and different Turkey had sprung up was generally accepted (witness the titles of well-known books about Turkey which appeared in the 1930s, 1940s and 1950s: *The Turkish Transformation* (Henry Elisha Alien, 1935), *The New Turks* (Eleanor Bisbee, 1951), *The Old Turkey and the New* (Sir Harry Luke, 1935), *Die neue Turkei* (Kurt Ziemke, 1930), *Modern Turkey* (Geoffrey Lewis, 1955) and many more).

Generally, these writers overestimated the extent to which Turkish society had changed. By the late 1930s the provincial towns had begun to change visibly. The old town centres more often than not were still in bad repair, but the Kemalists had begun to build new towns, often along the road to the (often equally new) railway station, with 'rational' modern architecture, public parks, tea gardens, cinemas and statues of Atatürk. Most provincial centres now had their own electricity plant. In the towns and cities the Kemalists succeeded in dramatically enlarging the group that supported their positivist, secularist and modernist ideals. Typically, the backbone of the Kemalist 'revolution' in the towns consisted of bureaucrats, officers, teachers, doctors, lawyers and entrepreneurs of larger commercial enterprises. The craftsmen and small traders formed the backbone of the suppressed traditional culture.

At the same time, the reforms hardly influenced the life of the villagers who made up the great mass of the Turkish population. A farmer or shepherd from Anatolia had never worn a fez, so he was not especially bothered about its abolition. His wife wore no veil anyway, so the fact that its use was discouraged did not mean anything to him or her. He could not read or write, so the nature of the script was in a sense immaterial to him, although the fact that the only man in the village who was able to read and write was the local imam tended to strengthen the religious connotation of the Arabic alphabet. He had to take a family name in 1934, but the whole village would continue to use first names (as is still the case) and the family names remained for official use only. The new family law made polygamy illegal, but those farmers who could afford it would still quite often take into the house a second woman, without marrying her, ascribing her children to his legal wife, if need be.

There were attempts to extend the reforms to the villages, to spread modern techniques and to instil a secular and positivist attitude. The 'People's Rooms' constituted one such attempt. Another was the creation of the 'Village Institutes' (*Köy Enstitüleri*). In 1935, an alphabetization drive was begun to combat illiteracy in the Turkish countryside. At that time only about 5000 of the 40,000 Turkish villages had schools (mostly with three classes). Most of them were very primitive and had only one teacher. The man responsible for the campaign was Ismail Hakki

Tonguç, Turkey's leading pedagogue, who had studied the educational ideas of Dewey and Kerschensteiner in Germany.

The first attempt to solve the illiteracy problem was to take young villagers who had learnt to read and write in the army, to have them follow a six-month course and then to send them to their villages as 'educators' (eğitmenler). When this solution proved unsatisfactory, Tonguç was given the chance to execute his own ideas and to experiment with institutes in which village youngsters trained as primary school teachers, and at the same time acquired modern technical and agricultural skills. The idea was to supply the villages with people who could not only teach their children to read and write, but who could also introduce the villagers to twentieth-century science and technology on a practical level. The village institutes were very successful while they lasted, but with the advent of political pluralism after the Second World War they became a liability to the government, when the opposition accused them of spreading communist propaganda. In 1948, the government turned the institutes into ordinary teacher-training establishments. When the Democratic Party came to power in 1950, it abolished them altogether.

Economic developments in the one-party era
The one subject that dominated Turkish politics and public opinion in the 1930s was the economy. That the Turkish leadership realized the importance of economic problems is shown by the convening as early as February 1923 of the 'First Turkish Economic Congress' in İzmir. Mustafa Kemal opened the congress with a speech in which he emphasized the importance of economic independence now that political independence had been won. In this he no doubt addressed the French and British delegates at the peace conference over the heads of his audience. At the congress, 1100 delegates of farmers, traders, workers and industrialists discussed economic policies. Its resolutions were partly incorporated in the *dokuz umde* (nine principles), the nine-point programme of the People's Party, which was published in April.[19] Much of the debate at the congress was devoted to the same issue that had divided the Young Turks of the prewar era: the choice between liberalism and the state intervention of the 'National Economy' programme. The congress did call for protection of local industry, but it did not oppose foreign investment, provided foreigners were not given preferential treatment. The leadership took the rather disparate resolutions of the congress to mean that it called for a mixed economy, with the state being responsible for major investments.

The minister of economic affairs at the time, Mahmut Esat (Bozkurt), announced that Turkish economic policies would be based on the 'New

Turkish Economic School', which was neither capitalist nor socialist. What the new school amounted to never became very clear, however. Basically, the economic policies pursued in the 1920s were liberal, in the sense that they were based on private ownership and initiative. They were not liberal, however, in the sense of non-interference on the part of the state. The state did interfere where major investments were concerned. By far the most important investment concerned railway building. Eight hundred kilometres of track were laid between 1923 and 1929, and in 1929 another 800 kilometres were under construction. In 1924 the government decided to buy out the foreign-owned railway companies, which dominated the west of the country. By 1930, 3000 kilometres of track had been bought and another 2400 still remained in foreign hands. Eventually, all would be bought by the Turkish state.

In 1925, the other major foreign presence in the economy, the old Ottoman tobacco monopoly, was bought out. It was turned into a state monopoly into which a number of other sectors (alcohol, sugar, matches and explosives) were integrated. The state then partly farmed out these monopolies to private companies.

In line with the 'National Economy' programme of the First World War the early republic took measures that aimed to strengthen the position of Muslims and Turks in the world of business. The fact that Turkish was now imposed as the sole language of business created a problem for the many Armenian, Greek and Jewish employees in Istanbul who had very little Turkish. At the same time, foreign companies were put under pressure to hire Turks (meaning Muslims) and dismiss non-Muslims. The quota that were imposed varied between 50 and 100 per cent. The government announced that it would only award contracts to firms with Turkish personnel. In some branches that were heavily dominated by non-Muslims, such as pharmacists and lawyers, the existing permits were withdrawn and new ones were given almost exclusively to Muslim Turks. Non-Muslim Turks lost their jobs, but for Muslim Turks new avenues were opened up in sectors where until then they had played almost no role. The policies led to large numbers of conversions to Islam. As before, the categories 'Turk' and 'Muslim' were barely distinguishable. Both in public opinion and among the Kemalist Young Turks who now held power, the two were connected. This would be proved time and again over the next decades, the first time in 1934 when vicious anti-Jewish pogroms broke out in Thrace.

The state also tried to improve the financial infrastructure. The largest bank in the country was still the Ottoman Bank, but in 1924/5 the old Agricultural Bank was reorganized and two new banks were founded; the Business Bank (*İş Bankası*) and the Industrial Bank (*Sanayi Bankası*),

Mustafa Kemal took a personal interest in the Business Bank. He invested the donations sent to him by Indian Muslims during the national struggle, but the main impetus for the new Business Bank came from the forced merger with the much bigger National Credit Bank (*İtibar-i Millî Bankası*), which the CUP had founded as part of its National Economy programme during the First World War.[20]

Turkish industry was still very weak and took a long time to recover from the effects of the departure of the Greeks and Armenians. Until 1929, the provisions of the Lausanne treaty prevented Turkey from raising its import tariffs and it has been pointed out by some historians that the disappearance of the Greek and Armenian traders actually made it easier for foreign companies to penetrate the Turkish markets directly, with their main competitors out of the way. By 1927, Turkey had slightly over 65,000 industrial firms, employing a total of 250,000 workers, but of these firms only 2822 used mechanical power; the overwhelming majority were artisans' workshops.[21] In 1927, the 'Law on the Encouragement of Industry', which built on the similar law adopted in 1913, was passed. It provided tax exemptions for new and expanding industrial firms. When the restrictions imposed at Lausanne lapsed in 1929, the import tariffs were immediately raised drastically (which hit many Turkish trading firms harder than it did the foreign producers). The lack of entrepreneurial know-how and the lack of a prosperous market, however, prevented a quick expansion of the industrial sector.

By far the largest sector of the Turkish economy was still the agricultural one. Here, recovery in the first postwar years had been spectacular (90 per cent during the years 1923–26). The farmers were helped by the abolition of the tithe (*aşar*) in 1925 and its replacement by a sales tax. In 1927 and 1928 agriculture was hit by a long drought and over the period between 1927 and 1930 growth in this sector was only 11 per cent.

The government's financial policies were conservative, aiming at a balanced budget, low inflation and a strong lira through a tight monetary policy, but Turkey had a trade deficit with the outside world throughout the 1920s and this gradually forced down the exchange rate of the Turkish lira. Then in 1929 and 1930 the world economic crisis reached Turkey and, like all agricultural producers, it was hit very hard. The price of wheat declined by two-thirds in a few years and if the terms of trade for wheat producers (against industrial producers) are set at 100 for 1929, they had gone down to 30 by 1933.[22] There was as yet no system of buffer stocks to regulate prices so the producers felt the full impact of the crisis. As a result of the loss of the population's purchasing power and of government-imposed quotas and restrictions, imports declined from 256 million liras in 1929 to just 85 million in 1932. The import of consumer goods declined even faster. As a result, despite falling agricultural producer prices Turkey's trade deficit turned into a surplus in the 1930s, but many of the small luxuries to which Turkish citizens had become accustomed simply disappeared from the market. It also meant that autarky was no longer a political ideal but became a practical necessity. There had been successes in the building of an autonomous Turkish industry to replace imports, but they were limited to the production of sugar and textiles.

Like many governments around the world the Turkish government was at a loss over what to do about the crisis. The years from 1929 to 1932 were a period of searching. The debate between the RPP and the opposition party created by the regime in 1930, the FRP, was almost exclusively about economic policy, with the opposition advocating liberalism (for instance criticizing the government's programme of buying out foreign railway companies) and the RPP under İnönü demanding a greater role for the state in the economy. At the 1931 RPP congress 'statism' (*devletçilik*) was officially adopted as the new economic policy and one of the pillars of Kemalist ideology. What this term meant exactly was never clearly defined. It was certainly not a form of socialism: private ownership remained the basis of economic life. Rather, it meant that the state took over responsibility for creating and running industries for which the private sector could not accumulate the necessary capital. A major influence on the formulation of Turkish statist policies was the Soviet Union, which had started its own first five-year plan in 1927. In 1932 a Soviet delegation visited Turkey and drew up a report on the development of Turkish industry. It recommended concentrating on textiles, iron and steel, paper, cement, glass and chemicals. The Soviet Union also made available $8 million in gold to aid the Turkish industrialization programme.[23] In 1933 the first Turkish five-year plan was announced, which largely followed the Soviet recommendations. One result was the building of an enormous textile '*kombinat*' in Kayseri, which significantly lessened the dependence of Turkey, a raw cotton producer and exporter, on imported cotton cloth.

In Turkey, the most enthusiastic supporters of the policy of statism (apart from İnönü who was very committed to this line himself) were a group of young Kemalist writers who published the journal *Kadro* (Cadre) from 1932 to 1934. The Kadro group went much further than the party leadership. It wanted to transform the RPP into a trained elite, a cadre that would act as a vanguard of the Kemalist revolution. They advocated state planning in all areas of social, economic and cultural life and saw statism as a viable alternative to communism and capitalism, a sort of 'third way'. In the end, their wider ideas were not taken up by the leadership, which limited planning to the economic field.

Within the leadership itself there were two conflicting currents. One, led by İsmet İnönü, saw statism as a permanent solution and as preferable to liberal capitalism in the Turkish situation. The other, headed by Mahmut Celâl Bayar, the president of the *İş Bankası* saw it as a transitory stage, necessary until Turkish industry could fend for itself. The friction between the two groups was aggravated because both the Ministry of Economic Affairs and the Business Bank were faced with limited investment opportunities, so both ended up pursuing the same projects. The conflict was resolved when Mustafa Kemal intervened and had Celâl appointed minister of economic affairs in İsmet's cabinet in 1932, thus assuring coordination of economic policies. When İsmet İnönü was ousted and replaced by Celâl Bayar in 1937, a more liberal approach was adopted, but from 1939 onwards the more statist approach of İnönü dominated once more.

Under the five-year plan two large holding companies were founded: the *Sümerbank* (Sumerian Bank), responsible for industry, in 1933, and the *Etibank* (Hittite Bank), responsible for mining, in 1935. Most state-owned economic enterprises were brought under the umbrella of these two holdings. They were given all kinds of advantages. Among other things, they were allowed to borrow from the Central Bank against 1 per cent interest. A law of 1938 regulated their operations. In theory the state economic enterprises, as they were called, were supposed to operate in a businesslike manner with as much autonomy as possible. In practice their decision-making was heavily influenced by political considerations, which were often irrational from a strictly commercial point of view. While the contributions of the state sector to the Turkish economy have been fiercely criticized over the last few decades, it should also be pointed out that a whole new generation of managers and engineers, who later played an important role in the development of private industry, learned its trade in the state economic enterprises.

The state also intervened in the agricultural sector. In 1932, the Agricultural Bank was ordered to regulate prices by building up and selling off stocks, a responsibility transferred in 1938 to the newly created Office for Soil Products (*Toprak Mahsulleri Ofisi* or TMO). This, however, could only intervene effectively from 1938 onwards when enough silos had been built to stock produce.

During the second half of the 1930s, there was a steady increase in Turkey's GNP in line with the recovery of the world economy. Trade recovered, too, although much of it now took place within the bounds of bilateral agreements between governments. Nearly 50 per cent of

Turkey's trade in the years before the Second World War was with Germany or its allies, which offered more scope for this type of trade than the more liberal economies of the West. Nevertheless, the economy was still very vulnerable when the Second World War broke out.

As we shall see, Turkey managed to remain neutral and stay out of the war until the very end, but in order to do so, it increased its army from a peacetime strength of 120,000 to 1.5 million (although without official mobilization). Feeding and equipping this army brought tremendous economic strains. The Ministry of Defence's share of the national budget went up from 30 to 50 per cent. Basically, the government had no option but to finance this expenditure by raising taxes and by having the Central Bank print money, thus encouraging inflation. The official consumer price index went from 100 to 459 during the war,[24] and this took no account of the black market prices. The war occasioned a new wave of state intervention in all sectors of the economy, which was legitimized by the 'National Defence Law' (*Millî Korunma Kanunu*) passed in January 1940, giving the government almost unlimited powers to fix prices, requisition materials and even to impose forced labour. Forced labour was widely used during the war, especially in the mining industry.

The fact that the government used its powers to combat inflation by fixing prices at unrealistically low levels while stimulating inflation through its monetary and budgetary policies led to a booming black market economy, while fewer and fewer products were available through regular retail channels. In the second half of the war the government bowed to this reality and more or less relinquished price controls between 1942 and 1944. Turkey's GDP, which had been rising steadily throughout the latter half of the 1930s, dropped sharply during the war. It did not reach its 1939 level again until 1950. The standard of living also went down and only recovered in the early 1950s.

While for the great majority of Turkish citizens the war meant a sharp drop in their standard of living, there were exceptions. The black market on the one hand and the large degree of government intervention on the other gave those who were in a position to exploit them (big farmers, importers and traders and those officials who handled government contracts and permits) huge profit opportunities. There was a great deal of resentment against these war profiteers and the government reacted by introducing the 'wealth tax' (*varlık vergisi*) in November 1942. But the way in which this law was applied was scandalous: local committees consisting of local government officials and representatives of the local councils and chambers of commerce made the tax assessments. There was no fixed rate. The result was that the tax was almost wholly paid by traders in the big cities, notably Istanbul, and that the small non-Muslim communities, who were subjected to rates ten times higher than those of Muslims, paid 55 per cent of the total tax revenue. In addition, non-Muslims were not allowed to spread their payments and as a result often had to sell their businesses or properties to Muslim businessmen in order to pay. Those unable to pay were deported and sentenced to forced labour. The wealth tax was withdrawn in March 1944, under the influence of criticism from Britain and the United States, but by then irreparable damage to the confidence of the minorities in the Turkish state had been done.[25]

Five months after the passing of the wealth tax law a tax on agricultural produce was introduced to tax the new wealth in the countryside (which was concentrated in the hands of the large commercial land-owners). The power relations in the countryside were such, however, that this tax (which in practice meant a return of the tithe abolished in 1925) failed to skim off excess profits from large farmers and fell relatively heavily on small subsistence farmers whose standard of living was already low and falling.

Although there are no dependable figures available, up to the early 1950s there probably was a shortage of labour in towns and countryside alike. Widespread unemployment would become a scourge in Turkey in later years, but not yet. According to the laws of economics, this should have meant that the labour force was in a good position to demand better wages and working conditions. The opposite, however, was true. In line with the Young Turk tradition the Kemalist state sided with the traders and entrepreneurs, whom it saw as the standard-bearers of a new and modern society, and it suppressed the labour movement. The Labour Law of 1936 was a direct copy of that of fascist Italy and, while it brought some safeguards to workers in industry, and promised some forms of workers' insurance (the introduction of which was actually begun in 1946), it also prohibited the formation of trade unions and the calling of strikes. When a Trade Unions Law was introduced in 1947, it still did not allow strikes. Real wages in Turkish industry declined throughout the 1930s and 1940s.

Foreign relations

The Turkish Republic's foreign policy throughout the period from 1923 to 1945 can be characterized as cautious, realistic and generally aimed at the preservation of the status quo and the hard-won victory of 1923. Until the end of the 1920s, its relations with the western European democracies were dogged by the aftermath of Lausanne, where a number of problems had not been solved. Most important was the quarrel with Britain over Mosul, an oil-rich province, largely inhabited by Kurds, though with

Arab and Turkish minorities. The British army had occupied Mosul after the armistice of 1918, so the Turks included it among the areas whose independence they claimed in the 'National Pact'. In negotiations during 1923 and 1924 the British insisted on including Mosul in Iraq, rejecting the Turkish proposal of a plebiscite. When the parties could not agree, the issue was submitted to the League of Nations in Geneva, of which Turkey was not yet a member. The League started its discussion of the matter in September 1924. At the same time there were skirmishes between Turkish and British troops in the north of the province and on 9 October the British government issued an ultimatum in which it demanded the withdrawal of the Turkish troops. Turkey backed down and a temporary border was established. A year later, in September 1925, a commission of the League investigated the situation on the spot and, to the surprise of no one at all, announced that it favoured the inclusion of Mosul in Iraq. The League of Nations took a decision to this effect in December 1925 and in June 1926 Turkey formally acquiesced. In return it received 10 per cent of the province's oil revenues over the next 25 years. This claim was then relinquished in return for a payment by Britain of £700,000.

A similar problem existed between Turkey and France, but over the district (*sancak*) of Alexandrette/İskenderun. This, too, had only been occupied after the armistice and in this case, too, Turkey failed to get its claims recognized at the Lausanne Conference. Until 1939 the area remained part of the French mandate of Syria.

Apart from these major diplomatic wrangles, in the first years after Lausanne there were continuous irritations between Turkey and the powers. Turkey made a point of asserting its sovereign rights to the full, while France and Britain showed that they had difficulty shedding old habits acquired during the regime of the capitulations. Frictions arose over the European powers' refusal to move their embassies to Ankara, over the jurisdiction of the Turkish Ministry of Education over mission schools, over the degree of independence of the International Straits Commission established at Lausanne to supervise shipping through the Bosphorus and Dardanelles, and over the supranational character of the Orthodox patriarchate in Istanbul. All these matters were eventually settled to Turkey's satisfaction.

The late 1920s and early 1930s saw a gradual improvement in Turkey's relations with its neighbours. A non-aggression pact was concluded with Italy in 1928 and, partly through Italian diplomatic efforts, reconciliation with Greece took place. In October 1930 a friendship treaty with Greece was signed, motivated by shared fear of Bulgarian irredentism. After a number of Balkan conferences, a Balkan Pact was concluded in 1934 with Greece, Yugoslavia, Romania and Turkey as its members. In 1937 the Sadabad Pact linked Turkey to its eastern neighbours, Iraq, Iran and Afghanistan, in a similar fashion.

Throughout the period after the war of independence, when distrust of the West was still rife, the cornerstone of Turkish foreign policy had been the maintenance of good relations with the Soviet Union. In the 1930s relations with the Soviet Union remained excellent (a ten-year friendship treaty was signed in 1935) but it was no longer the sole pillar of Turkish foreign policy. Apart from the rapprochement with its neighbours, Turkey's relations with the Western powers improved markedly. At the root of this improvement lay the fact that, together with France and Britain, Turkey now definitely supported the status quo and rejected the aspirations of the 'revisionist' powers such as Nazi Germany and fascist Italy, which wanted to redraw the map of Europe. Turkey maintained good relations with Hitler's Germany in spite of this, but saw Italy's expansionism in the eastern Mediterranean as a great threat.

The fact that its ally, the Soviet Union, too, joined the anti-revisionist camp, facilitated Turkey's rapprochement with the West. In 1932 Turkey joined the League of Nations. In April 1936 it sent the signatories of the Treaty of Lausanne a note in which it asked for a change in the demilitarization of the Straits, in view of the increasingly tense international situation, and received a sympathetic hearing. A conference was held in Montreux and in the resulting treaty Turkey regained full control of the Straits. The Straits Commission was abolished. All parties accepted a number of restrictions on the passage of warships through the Straits, but commercial traffic would be free for countries not at war with Turkey itself.

The one issue over which Turkey and France clashed in the 1930s was that of the *sancak* of Alexandrette, the ethnically extremely mixed area known to Turkish nationalists as 'Hatay' (Land of the Hittites, who it will be remembered were considered proto-Turks at the time) with the towns of Antakya (Antioch) and İskenderun (Alexandrette). In the Franco–Turkish agreement of 1921 and at Lausanne this area had remained outside the borders of the new Turkish state, but cultural autonomy was extended to its Turkish community, which had close links with Turkey and followed developments in Turkey closely. A *Hatay Halk Fırkası* (People's Party of Hatay) was formed and it even carried through such things as the 'hat' and 'alphabet' reforms.

In September 1936 France announced that it would grant independence to Syria and that it intended to include Hatay in the new Syrian state. This was unacceptable to the Turkish community. The issue was brought before the League of Nations, which sent a mission to the district in January 1937. The mission concluded that the Turks constituted a majority. Britain, anxious to avert a breach between France and Turkey in view of the Italian threat, now mediated and an agreement was reached whereby Hatay would become an 'independent entity', represented in external matters by Syria. An international committee of lawyers drew up a constitution and elections were held in April 1938. During the elections there were bloody riots all over the *sancak*, so the elections were annulled. By now the international situation was so threatening that France was ready to come to terms with Turkey and secure its support against Nazi Germany and Italy at almost any price. In July, new elections were held under joint Franco–Turkish military control and they produced a narrow Turkish majority of 22 in the 40-seat parliament. In its first session, the new parliament proclaimed the independent Republic of Hatay. Almost exactly a year later, on 29 June 1939, it announced the union of that state with Turkey – to the great anger of the Syrians, who even today depict the area as Syrian on their maps.

Turkey in the Second World War
Possible aggression by Italy remained the foremost concern of the Turkish leadership in the late 1930s. Concern was intensified by Italy's occupation of Albania in April 1939, which brought Turkey, France and Britain closer together.

Discussions about a treaty of mutual assistance between Turkey, France and Britain went on all through 1939. They proceeded only slowly because Turkey demanded large amounts of military and financial assistance in view of its own weakness and because it was determined to preclude any possibility of becoming embroiled in a war with the Soviet Union. The Turkish government very much hoped to include the Soviets in the alliance. The sudden announcement of the Molotov–Ribbentrop pact in August 1939, in which Hitler's Germany and Stalin's Russia more or less divided eastern Europe between them, therefore came as a tremendous shock to Ankara. France and Britain now became even more anxious to secure Turkish support and on 19 October 1939 the Anglo–Franco–Turkish treaty of mutual support was signed. With it, the Turks got most of what they wanted. A loan of £16 million in gold and a credit of £25 million for the purchase of military equipment were granted. In a separate protocol attached to the treaty, Turkey was excused from any obligation that could involve her in a war with the Soviet Union.[26]

The treaty stipulated that Turkey would 'collaborate effectively' with France and Britain in the event of an act of aggression of a European power leading to war in the Mediterranean (a clear reflection of the importance attached to the Italian threat). A *casus foederi* had clearly arisen after Italy declared war on France and Britain on 10 June 1940. By then, however, the collapse of France had drastically changed the balance of power and, despite its obligations, Turkey devoted all its energy to staying out of the war, invoking the separate protocol as a pretext. The British government saw Turkey as a valuable source of manpower and exerted pressure to get it to enter the war, but Turkey resisted and Britain had no choice but to accept. After the German occupation of Greece and Bulgaria's siding with the Axis in 1941, the war had reached Turkey's borders. As a consequence, in June 1941, almost simultaneously with the German invasion of the Soviet Union, it concluded a treaty of friendship with Germany. Throughout the next year and a half, the period of the greatest German expansion, Turkey kept up a scrupulously neutral position, pleading lack of preparation and the need for supplies with the British government. At the same time, however, and until quite late in the war, Turkey supplied Germany with large amounts of chromite ore for its arms industry.

After the German defeat at Stalingrad (November 1942) allied pressure gradually increased, but Turkey was still very exposed to a German attack. The allies' requirements had changed and they now regarded Turkey as a forward base for allied troops and aircraft rather than as a source of manpower, but the Germans threatened that the arrival of even a single allied fighter plane would mean war. In January 1943, Churchill and İnönü reached agreement over a programme of preparations for the arrival – in due course – of allied warplanes, but the preparations were subsequently sabotaged and the building of installations intentionally slowed down by the Turks.[27] The pressure increased even further at a conference of İnönü, Churchill and Roosevelt in Cairo in December 1943. The allies now clearly held the winning hand and they pointed out that, if Turkey stayed out of the war for much longer, it risked being completely isolated after the war. The implied threat was that it would have to face the Red Army and any demands Stalin might make on its own. İnönü now finally accepted that Turkey would become an active belligerent on the allied side, but he asked for an overall campaign plan for the allied conquest of the Balkans first. This was a clever ploy because the allied powers differed widely about the desirability of a Balkan campaign, Stalin objecting to any British or American interference in the area and the Americans tended to listen to him.

Throughout 1944, the Turks kept stalling, although they did break off diplomatic relations with Germany in August. Their attitude led the British and the Americans to lend a more sympathetic ear to Soviet demands. In February 1945, at the Yalta conference, they agreed to future changes in the Montreux convention. Shortly afterwards, on 23 February

1945, Turkey officially declared war on Germany in order to qualify as a founding member of the United Nations. This was a purely symbolic act and no shot was ever fired in anger by a Turkish soldier during the Second World War.

Throughout the war both domestic politics and the press were kept under tight control and they were both manipulated in Turkey's effort to stay out of the conflict. When Germany seemed to be on the verge of defeating the Soviets, there was a resurgence of pan-Turkist propaganda. A pan-Turkist committee was founded in July 1941 with German encouragement, a number of Turkish generals toured the eastern front at the invitation of the Germans and some pan-Turkist sympathizers were taken into the cabinet – all as a sort of insurance policy in the event of a German victory. When the impending German defeat had become clear, in May 1944, the pan-Turkist organizations and propaganda were suppressed.

Turkey's policies during the war have often been seen as immoral and as reneging on the treaty of 1939. The country's international reputation was damaged, but keeping out of the war was a great success in the eyes of politicians like İnönü and his successive foreign ministers (first Şükrü Saraçoğlu, then Numan Menemencioğlu, and then Saraçoğlu again), who had a clear memory of how the Ottoman Empire had allowed itself to be used as a German tool during the First World War, and the disasters that this had brought upon their country.

12 · The Transition to Democracy, 1945–50

Within a few years of the end of the Second World War, Turkey's political system, economic policies and foreign relations all underwent a fundamental change. In this chapter I will examine the factors behind the change and the way in which it came about.

Socio-economic pressure for change

By the end of the Second World War, İsmet Pasha İnönü's government had become deeply unpopular, even hated, by the large majority of the Turkish population for a variety of reasons. In analysing this discontent, one should make a distinction between the mass of the population (the peasants and industrial workers) and the segments of the coalition on which the Kemalist regime had been built (the officers and bureaucrats, the Muslim traders in the towns and the landowners in the countryside).

The regime had never been popular with the masses. The small farmers in the countryside, who at the time still made up about 80 per cent of the total population had not seen any great improvement in their standard of living, in health, education or communications. If we take something like electrification as a measure of modernization, we note that as late as 1953 the total number of villages that had been linked up to the electric grid was ten, or 0.025 per cent of Turkey's 40,000 villages![1] While total production of electricity had grown tenfold between 1923 and 1943, it was still a phenomenon of city life, since Turkey had a grand total of nine miles of power lines in the latter year. Of the total energy capacity of 107,000 kilowatts available in 1945, 83,000 kilowatts went to Istanbul, Ankara and İzmir. And even so, the trolleybuses in Ankara had to stop when the lights went on.[2]

On the other hand, the one characteristic of the modern state with which the villagers had become familiar during the 25 years of Kemalist rule was the central state's effective control over the countryside. The gendarme and tax collector became more hated and feared than ever. Resentment against the state, in itself a traditional feature of country life, became more acute because the state became more effective and visible. It was also exacerbated because the state's secularist policies, especially the suppression of expressions of popular faith, severed the most important ideological bond between state and subject.

Industrial workers were still a very small minority in Turkish society, some 330,000 in a population of around 20 million, but the exact number depends on what is understood by 'industrial'; the number mentioned includes many who were really employed in artisanal production.[3] Their socio-economic position was weak. Until June 1945, organizations based on class, and trade unions were regarded as such, were still prohibited in Turkey, as were strikes. The workers, like the other wage and salary earners, had been badly hit in their purchasing power by the rising cost of living during the war.

Discontent among the mass of the population was not new and in itself would probably not have led to political change. More immediately important in this respect was the fact that İnönü's government lost the support of important elements of the 'Young Turk coalition' on which the Kemalist movement had been built. During the war, the government, faced with the necessity to feed and equip a large army, had paid for its needs by having the Central Bank print money, thus encouraging inflation. On the other hand, it had tried to mitigate the social effects of this policy by establishing price controls and by punitive taxation on excessive profits through the wealth tax and the tax on agricultural produce. The inflation had led to a sharp drop in purchasing power for the civil servants, who numbered about 220,000. For lower-ranking civil servants the drop was about one-third; for senior civil servants it was as high as two-thirds, which was something that led to tensions within the bureaucracy.[4]

Although its main victim had been the non-Muslim business community, the *varlık vergisi* (wealth tax) of 1942 had caused unrest and suspicion among the Turkish bourgeoisie in general. It had shown that the Kemalist regime, dominated as it was by bureaucrats and the military, was not an entirely dependable supporter of the interests of this group, whose essential vulnerability it had demonstrated. The position of the indigenous bourgeoisie, whose growth had been such a high priority for Unionists and Kemalists alike, had by now become so strong that it was no longer prepared to accept this position of a privileged, but essentially dependent and politically powerless, class.

Large landowners had been an essential element in the 'Young Turk coalition' since the First World War, but they had been alienated by the government's policy of artificially low pricing of agricultural produce to combat inflation during the war, by its 'tax on agricultural produce' and especially by the introduction of a land distribution bill (the *çiftçiyi topraklandırma kanunu* or 'law on giving land to the farmer') in January 1945. This last bill, which President İnönü strongly promoted, played a crucial part in the emergence of political opposition in postwar Turkey. Widespread discontent prevailed. Because of the Republican People's Party's close identification with the state apparatus under the one-party system, this resentment was directed at the party as much as it was at the state. İnönü was aware of these tensions and, remembering Atatürk's experiment with the Free Party in 1930, he decided to allow a degree of political liberalization and the formation of a political opposition as a safety valve. That he and his government moved in this direction also owed something to international developments.

External pressures for democratization
In a very general sense, the defeat of the Axis powers in the Second World War was in itself a victory for democratic values. The USA, a pluralist, capitalist democracy, emerged from the war as the dominant world power and its example could not fail to impress many in Turkey, just as it did in countries all over the world. In April 1945, Turkey took part as a founding member in the San Francisco conference and, in signing the UN charter, committed itself to democratic ideals. There were, however, more immediate reasons why the Turkish government felt compelled to move closer to the West and especially to the United States.

A close relationship with the Soviet Union had been the cornerstone of Turkish foreign policy throughout the 1920s and 1930s, but the relationship had been soured first by the Molotov–Ribbentrop pact and then by Turkey's neutral stance during the war. The Soviet Union had announced that it would not renew the friendship treaty with Turkey after it lapsed in 1945 and in June that year, in conversations with the Turkish ambassador, Molotov formulated a number of conditions that would have to be met before a new friendship treaty could be signed. They included a correction of the border between the two countries, returning to the Soviet Union the areas in northeastern Anatolia that had been Russian between 1878 and 1918, and the establishment of a joint Turkish–Russian defence force in the area of the Bosphorus and Dardanelles, in order to guard the Black Sea.[5]

These conditions were, of course, completely unacceptable to the Turks, but when the Soviets tabled their proposals at the inter-allied Potsdam conference in July, neither the British nor the Americans immediately rejected them. After all, Turkey's wartime policies had not exactly endeared it to the Western allies. Gradually, however, the United States became more supportive of the Turkish position. When the Soviet demands were communicated officially to Turkey in August 1946, the USA advised the Turkish government to take a firm line. Thus encouraged, Turkey refused the Soviet demands, but it did so in conciliatory terms, trying to keep down the tensions.

With concern about Stalin's policies in eastern Europe increasing with every communist regime established there, Washington began to re-evaluate the strategic importance of Turkey. Although theoretically the United Nations was the forum to which international conflicts could and should be referred, the constant use of the veto by the Soviet Union in the security council made working through the UN impossible, and the United States administration decided to act unilaterally. On 12 March 1947, President Truman launched his so-called 'Truman doctrine'. This stipulated that the USA should and would help defend 'free nations' whose existence was threatened by foreign pressure or by militant minorities inside their borders. The occasion for the promulgation of the doctrine was a proposal by President Truman to the US congress for military and financial support for Greece (where the civil war between communists and monarchists was raging at the time) and Turkey. It was the start of the American commitment to the defence of anti-communist regimes throughout the world. Shortly afterwards, in June 1947, the Marshall Plan, envisaging financial support on a gigantic scale to the European countries to help them rebuild their economies, was put forward. This plan had three complementary aims: to help the Europeans help themselves; to sustain lucrative export markets for US industry; and to eliminate poverty as a breeding ground for communism.

It was clear to the Turkish leadership that, in order to profit fully from the American political and military support and from the Marshall Plan, it would be helpful for Turkey to conform more closely to the political and economic ideals (democracy and free enterprise) cherished by the Americans. Thus we can say that the political and economic change in Turkey after 1945 had both domestic and international roots.

The process of democratization
The first sign that the government was considering a change of direction came even before the end of the war, when İnönü strongly emphasized the democratic parliamentary character of the Turkish political system in his speech at the opening of the parliamentary year on 1 November 1944. On 19 May 1945, he elaborated this theme and promised measures to make the regime more democratic, without as yet specifying what these measures would be.

Also in May, the Land Distribution Law, which had first been put forward in January, came up for discussion in the national assembly.

Turkey was still overwhelmingly a nation of small farmers. Some 99.75 per cent of the landownership consisted of farms with fewer than 500 *dönüm* (125 acres) of land. Properties of more than 5000 *dönüm* comprised only 0.01 per cent; most farmers held far fewer than 125 acres. There were great differences between the regions but in the more affluent agricultural areas a holding of between 25 and 50 *dönüm* (6–12 acres) was typical.[6] Many of the small farmers led a marginal existence. There was not enough arable land to sustain the approximately three million peasant families and a holding of between six and twelve acres meant existing on, and in many cases below, the poverty line. As a result a great many farmers had long since become sharecroppers with a very low standard of living. As a rule a large landowner or an affluent city dweller supplied them with seeds and equipment and took from a quarter to a half of the harvest in return.

The law introduced in the assembly in May 1945 aimed to provide adequate land for farmers who had none or too little by distributing unused state lands, lands from pious endowments (*evkaf*), reclaimed land, land without clear ownership and land expropriated from landowners who owned more than 500 *dönüm*. Under article 17 of the law even up to three-quarters of the land owned by farmers with more than 200 *dönüm* (50 acres) could be expropriated in densely populated areas. The peasants would also be given 20-year interest-free loans.

The discussions of this bill in the assembly were the first occasion when the government was openly and vehemently criticized. The opposition came from members with landowning connections and their spokesman was Adnan Menderes, himself a large landowner from Aydın. The opposition first focused on economic arguments (contending that the proposed land redistribution undermined the security of property, would impede investment and would lead to inefficient farming) but the autocratic way in which the government handled the debate also led to protests about the lack of democracy in the country, which were again led by Menderes.

In the end, the law was passed unanimously, despite the acrimonious debates – a clear indication of the discipline that still governed the RPP – but very soon after, on 7 June, Menderes, with three other deputies, Celâl Bayar (the former prime minister), Refik Koraltan and Fuat Köprülü (a famous historian) submitted a memorandum to the parliamentary party demanding that the Turkish constitution be implemented in full and democracy established. This *Dörtlü Takrir* (Memorandum of the Four), as it has become known, seemed to aim at a reform of the RPP rather than at the establishment of an opposition party, but it nevertheless marked the beginning of organized political opposition after the war.

The parliamentary party rejected the proposals of the four, but the four were not themselves in any way punished for their temerity. This was generally interpreted as a sign that the government was prepared to allow a certain relaxation of the political climate. There were other signs that pointed in this direction. Some newspapers, notably the liberal (and American-orientated) *Vatan* (Fatherland) of Ahmet Emin Yalman and the leftist *Tan* (Dawn) of Zekeriya and Sabiha Sertel began to support the 'Four', giving them room in their columns to express their ideas. When, a week after the submission of the *Dörtlü Takrir*, by-elections were held in Istanbul, the government for the first time allowed a free choice between different candidates of the RPP.

Strictly speaking, the multi-party period began in July when a prominent Istanbul industrialist, Nuri Demirağ, founded an opposition party, the *Millî Kalkınma Partisi* (National Development Party), which was officially registered on 5 September. The NDP's platform consisted of a call for liberalization of the economy and the development of free enterprise. The party had no experienced politicians among its members and no representation in the national assembly. It was therefore not very effective and drew little support. The real breakthrough came slightly later when Adnan Menderes and Fuat Köprülü, followed shortly afterwards by Refik Koraltan, were officially ousted from the Republican People's Party on 21 September because of the critical articles they had written in *Tan* and *Vatan*.

In a speech on 1 November, İsmet İnönü declared that the main shortcoming of Turkish democracy was the lack of an opposition party (apparently disregarding the National Development Party) and he announced that the general elections scheduled for 1947 would be free and direct – as opposed to the two-stage system with electors that was still in place at the time. At the beginning of December, Celâl Bayar resigned from the RPP. All four signatories of the 'Memorandum of the Four' had now left or been forced to leave the governing party and it was clear that the establishment of a new party was in the offing. In the preparations for launching the new party Bayar and İnönü worked closely together. The fact that Bayar was a veteran Young Turk, and trusted as someone who subscribed to the fundamental tenet of secularism, undoubtedly eased the acceptance of the existence of an opposition party by the Kemalist bureaucracy and party. For the new party it created a problem. While it was clear that the 'Four' would be dependent on İsmet İnönü's goodwill during the embryonic phase of the new party, the collaboration between Bayar and İnönü gave the impression that the creation of the party was the result of collusion and this would prove an accusation the new party would have difficulty in living down.

The *Demokrat Parti* (Democratic Party) was officially registered on 7 January 1946 and it was at first welcomed by the RPP and its organs, which took their lead from İnönü. Once the DP started establishing branches it became clear that it met with an enthusiastic response all over the country. The RPP leadership, which had been aware of the existence of discontent, was still shocked by its extent. An extraordinary congress was called for May 1946. It took a number of liberalizing measures: it accepted direct elections and the position of permanent chairman of the party was abolished, as was the title of *millî şef* (national leader). İnönü still remained chairman, of course, but he would now have to be re-elected. Soon after the congress, the press law was liberalized and the universities received a degree of autonomy, but national elections were brought forward from July 1947 to July 1946, clearly in the hope of catching the Democrats before they were fully established. The Democrats protested and even considered boycotting the elections (as they had boycotted the municipal elections earlier in the year), but in the end they took part and managed to win 62 of the 465 seats in the assembly.

On the face of it, this was a considerable, but not a spectacular success for the new party, but the reality was different. One reason the RPP was returned with a majority was that there had been massive vote rigging. The electoral procedures were far from perfect: there was no guarantee of secrecy during the actual voting; there was no impartial supervision of the elections and, as soon as the results were declared, the actual ballots were destroyed, making any check impossible. It has to be remembered that at this time all local and provincial administrators were RPP party members, who had great difficulty in discriminating between political opposition and high treason. The scale of the fraud was so obvious that there was an outcry in the country. Celâl Bayar stated that, according to a DP inquiry, the real number of seats won by the party was much higher and that there had been 'wickedness involved in the election'. His statement to this effect was published in the newspapers in disregard of a government notice that strictly forbade any criticism of the elections.[7]

Faced with widespread support for the DP, the RPP had a choice: either to suppress the opposition as it had done in 1925 and 1930, or to go further down the path of liberalization. For a year after the elections of 1946, the party seemed to hesitate between these alternatives. İnönü selected Recep Peker, who was considered the most prominent hard-liner in the party and a supporter of the one-party state, as his new prime minister in August. Peker tried to intimidate the opposition into conducting itself as junior partner of the government and refraining from the constant attacks it launched against the RPP. This, however, the DP refused to do. The fraudulent behaviour of the RPP bureaucrats during the elections had thoroughly poisoned the atmosphere, but another reason why the opposition kept up its acrimonious criticism of the government was because its own programme differed less and less from that of the RPP. The DP subscribed to the basic Kemalist tenets of nationalism and secularism, so it could not differentiate itself from the government on that score. The points on which it had originally differed from the RPP (political and economic liberalization) were to a large extent taken over by the governing party between 1947 and 1950. So the DP needed an atmosphere of constant high tension to mobilize public opinion. It therefore introduced new complaints in the assembly almost on a daily basis.

Another way in which both parties tried to distinguish themselves from the other was by tarring each other with the brush of communism. The end of the Second World War had ushered in a period of relative tolerance for the left, while the government saw fit to suppress the extreme (and pan-Turkist) right. Even in this immediate postwar period there were elements in the RPP that identified the emerging opposition with a 'communism' it detested. On 4 December 1945, a crowd of nationalist students, who had been aroused by inflammatory articles in the RPP press, sacked the offices of the leftist newspaper *Tan*, which had been publishing articles by the future DP leaders, and destroyed its printing presses. Police were present but did not intervene. Nevertheless, in June 1946, a socialist party and even a communist one, *Türkiye Sosyalist Emekçi ve Köylü Partisi* (Turkish Socialist Workers and Peasants' Party) led by the veteran communist Dr Şefik Hüsnü Değmer were founded.

But the effects of the cold war soon began to be felt and, in December 1946, martial law regulations were used to close down these parties. The DP and the RPP now started mud-slinging campaigns in which they accused each other of being soft on communism. The DP was even accused of being in the pay of Moscow. The years 1948 and 1949 saw a witch-hunt against the left. Prominent pan-Turkists like Nihal Atsız and Zeki Velidi Togan, who had been prosecuted at the end of the Second World War, were rehabilitated and their most vocal opponent, the socialist novelist Sabahattin Ali was murdered by one of Atsız's supporters.

Relations between the parties went from bad to worse. The discussions on the 1947 budget were extremely hostile and at one time the prime minister described Menderes as a psychopath, whereupon the Democrats left the assembly and boycotted its meetings for a few days.

In January 1947, the DP held its first congress, at which the representatives adopted the *Hürriyet Misaki* (Freedom Pact), a term that not coincidentally echoed the famous *Millî Misak* (National Pact) of 1920. The DP saw itself as the new political wave that would finish what Atatürk had begun. He had brought national independence and reformed Turkish society; they would now complete his reforms by introducing democracy. The Freedom Pact authorized the DP members of parliament to leave and boycott the national assembly unless the government withdrew a number of undemocratic laws. This was a serious threat because the Peker government, whose legitimacy was doubtful because of the ballot rigging in 1946, could not afford to be seen as anti-democratic by the people and the outside world – certainly not with the growing importance of American aid.

The DP and the RPP were clearly on a collision course, but in July 1947 İnönü intervened. He held separate talks with Peker and Bayar and then gave out a statement to the press. This so-called 'Twelfth of July Declaration' legitimized the existence of the opposition and called upon the state apparatus to be impartial and to deal even-handedly with both parties. It was the decisive intervention by the president that made it clear that multi-party politics were there to stay. Within the RPP it meant the defeat of the hard-liners led by Recep Peker, who had to resign and was succeeded as prime minister by Hasan Saka, significantly the minister of foreign affairs who had headed the Turkish delegation at the San Francisco conference.

At its congress in November 1947, the RPP moved even closer to the DP programme. It advocated free enterprise and decided to retract article 17 of the Land Distribution Law (something the assembly eventually did in 1950). It also tried to counter the way in which the Democrats played the religious card and decided to allow religious education in the schools and to reform the Village Institutes, which DP propaganda had targeted and depicted as centres of communist agitation.

It is a measure of the discipline within the RPP that the party did not split after İsmet İnönü had so emphatically sided with the reformists and disavowed the hard-liners. The new conciliatory line of the People's Party did cause serious problems for the Democrats, however, who were essentially bound together by their joint opposition to the RPP, not by a coherent political programme of their own. Several groups of representatives, who considered the DP leadership too moderate and wanted a more uncompromising opposition to the RPP, split off from the main body. One group founded the *Millet Partisi* (Nation Party) with Marshal Fevzi Çakmak (who had been an implacable enemy of İnönü ever since the latter had dismissed him as chief of staff in 1944) as its figurehead. The result was that by 1949 the DP faction in parliament had been halved, but at the same time it had become a much more coherent body. Hasan Saka reshuffled his cabinet once, in June 1948, and in 1949 someone who was even more of a compromise figure, Şemsettin Günaltay, a university professor with known Islamist leanings, replaced him.

The main bone of contention between the two parties remained the election law that was changed several times under pressure from the opposition, which threatened to boycott the national elections scheduled for 1950 if completely free and fair elections could not be guaranteed. It specifically demanded supervision of the elections, not by the administration but by the judiciary. Finally, in February 1950, a compromise was reached, just in time for the elections of 14 May 1950.

Social and economic reform

As in the process of political reform, 1947 was the turning point in the adoption of new economic policies. Up to then, the RPP was still wedded to the policy of 'statism' (*devletçilik*) introduced in the 1930s. This policy increasingly came under attack, both from indigenous business circles and from the Americans. The DP made itself the voice of the indigenous criticism. Menderes sometimes went so far as to depict statism as a discredited relic of fascism. The more moderate leaders of the DP, such as Celâl Bayar, wanted to change the role of the state in the economy from direct intervention to coordination and support of private initiative. In their eyes, private enterprise should have absolute priority and the state should only intervene where private enterprise failed or could not hope to succeed through lack of capital. In January 1947 a number of Istanbul businessmen founded the *İstanbul Tüccar Derneği* (Association of Istanbul Traders), the first such group not to be controlled by the government. It criticized statism, which it held responsible for the lack of economic progress in the country, and supported the ideas put forward by the Democrats.

At the same time, Turkey, impoverished as it was after the years of wartime mobilization, was desperate for American financial assistance. In order to facilitate this, the Turkish government had already applied for membership of the International Monetary Fund (IMF) and in order to qualify for membership, it took the so-called '7 September Decisions' of 1946. Essentially, these meant a devaluation of the Turkish lira by 120 per cent (the first of many devaluations of the republican era) and a number of liberalizing measures aimed at integrating the Turkish economy into the world economy.

In 1946, the RPP drew up a new economic five-year plan. It was similar to prewar plans, with an emphasis on autarky and state control (its authors came from the *Kadro* circle, which had been active in the 1932–34 period), but in 1947 it was ditched and a new 'Turkish Development Plan' was adopted, which echoed the wishes of the Istanbul businessmen and of the DP. It emphasized free enterprise, the development of agriculture and agriculturally based industry (instead of heavy industry), roads instead of railways and development of the energy sector (oil). The RPP congress of November 1947 embraced the plan wholeheartedly. From this time onwards, there was hardly any difference between the economic policies of the DP and of the RPP, the one exception being that the DP wanted to sell off the state industries, while the RPP did not. An 'economic congress' held in Istanbul in November 1948 (following the one held in İzmir in 1923) was even more emphatic in its support for liberal economic policies. Significantly, it was organized by a civil organization, the Association of Istanbul Traders (*İstanbul Tüccar Derneği*) and not by the state or a party.[8]

From 1948 onwards, the Democratic argument was much reinforced by the activities, and later the reports, of American fact-finding missions that reported on possibilities for economic development in Turkey and on how American aid should be given and used. These commissions, the best known of which was headed by industrialist Max Thornburg for the World Bank, whose report came out in 1949, were very influential in government circles, both in Turkey and in the USA. Their recommendations were entirely in line with the Turkish Development Plan of 1947.

For the Turkish economy, the years between 1945 and 1950 were years of explosive growth (roughly 11 per cent growth in GDP per year), but it should not be forgotten that this was partly a recovery from the very low level of economic activity of the Second World War. Two indications that the relative autarky of Turkey was coming to an end, and that incorporation was speeding up, were the fact that most of the economic growth was in the agricultural sector and that from 1947 onwards, the trade surplus changed into a persistent trade deficit, due to fast-rising imports of machinery. This means that the economic trends that were to be characteristic of DP rule after 1950 actually started before the takeover of power by that party.

The government's social policies did not change as much as its economic policies during this time. When the ban on organizations with a class base was lifted in 1946, a number of trade unions sprang up, just in time for Turkey to be able to join the ILO, the International Labour Organization (which was linked to the UN). But most of the unions were small-scale affairs and the most active among them were linked to the communist TSWPP or the socialist TSP. In December 1946 the martial law regulations were invoked to close them down along with the two parties.

In 1947, a new 'Law on Trade Unions' was passed, giving the right of organization in trade unions to the workers, but at the same time forbidding political activity by trade unions, as well as strikes. Despite the ban on political activity both the DP and the RPP actively sought the support of the unions, which were founded in 1947, and the DP promised to grant them the right to strike once it took power. In reality, it took another decade for Turkish workers to gain that right. Apart from the restrictive policies of the different governments, the position of these embryonic unions was fundamentally weak because of the small number of industrial workers, their low level of education and their extreme poverty, which made it well nigh impossible to collect sufficient union dues.

The elections of 14 May 1950

The climax of the whole period of transition came with the elections of May 1950. They went off without major incident and by all accounts were indeed free and fair. The turnout was very high, with 80 per cent of the electorate casting its vote. When the results were announced, public opinion was stunned: the Democratic Party, which had campaigned with the slogan 'Enough! Now the people have their say', had won 53.4 per cent of the vote against the RPP's 39.8 per cent. Under the Turkish electoral system this meant that the DP received 408 seats in the new parliament against the RPP's 69. The RPP did not win a single province in the more developed west of the country – all the provinces it won were to the east of Ankara and that it did manage to hold on to them was largely because power brokers loyal to the RPP such as notables, tribal chiefs and large landowners controlled the vote in the less-developed regions.

The results were celebrated in an atmosphere of liberation all over the country, but they were a bitter disappointment to İnönü. In spite of his efforts to cut the ground from beneath the DP by introducing far-reaching political and economic liberalization, the memory of the years of repression, of which İsmet Pasha himself was very much the symbol, weighed too heavily with the electorate – it did not trust the RPP's 'new look'. It is probably correct to say, however, that the victory of the DP would have been even more comprehensive, had the elections been held two years earlier.

Although the details have never been established, some elements within the military seem to have offered to stage a coup for İnönü and nullify the elections. To his eternal credit, İnönü stuck to the course he had set five years earlier. He had wanted to establish a loyal – but basically powerless – opposition. He had miscalculated, but now he accepted the consequences and handed over power with good grace and, after 14 years as prime minister and 12 as president, devoted himself to the duties of a leader of the opposition.

The DP now about to rule Turkey was an entirely new phenomenon in Turkish politics, not because of its programme (which it has been noted closely resembled that of the RPP, certainly after 1947) but because the party, which had its roots in a split within the ruling 'Young Turk' coalition, was the first political organization in the country's modern history with a genuine mass following that had been able to express its support in a free election.

It has often been said that the peaceful transition from a dictatorship to multi-party democracy in Turkey in 1946 and the equally peaceful handover of power four years later is a unique experience in the developing world. However, one should not overlook the fact that Turkey, though socio-economically in many ways a developing country, had had a heritage of experiments with parliamentary election since 1876, and of multi-party democracy between 1908 and 1913, between 1923 and 1925 and in 1930. Although democracy had only shallow roots and had been easily repressed, it did not have to be built from scratch.

PART III

A Troubled Democracy

13 · The Rule of the Democratic Party, 1950–60

The new assembly and the new cabinet

There is widespread consensus among historians that the Democratic Party's landslide election victory in May 1950 is a watershed in modern Turkish political history. The character both of the new assembly, in which the DP held an overwhelming majority (408 seats against the RPP's 69), and of the new government was very different from the old.

When one looks at the social characteristics of the DP representatives, one is struck by a number of differences from those of the Kemalist period. The DP representatives were on average younger, more often had local roots in their constituencies, were less likely to have had a university education, and far more likely to have a background in commerce or in law. The most striking difference from the RPP was the virtual absence of representatives with a bureaucratic and/ or military background. It was clear that a significantly different section of Turkey's elite had come to power.[1]

One of the first things the new assembly did was to elect Celâl Bayar president of the republic. There was very little debate about his candidature: he was the founder of the new party, he had a record as a statesman going back to the days of Atatürk and he was widely regarded as a moderate. There was more competition for the post of prime minister, but the post went to Adnan Menderes, who was backed by Bayar because of his popular appeal. Menderes became not only prime minister but also party chairman, a position the president had always held under the RPP.

Under the RPP the state apparatus and the party machine had been merged (even officially) to the extent that one could say that the party was just one of the instruments through which the state controlled and steered society. When the DP came to power the link was broken. The Democrats mistrusted the bureaucracy and the military they inherited from the old regime, and devoted a great deal of effort to getting them under their control. Over the years, therefore, state and party tended to coalesce again, especially at the higher levels, but the difference from the Kemalist era was that the party dominated the bureaucracy, not the other way around.

Relations between the parties

Relations between the two parties were strained almost from the start. Both had difficulty adjusting to their new roles after, respectively, 27 years in power and four years of fierce opposition.

The DP saw itself as the representative of the popular will (*millî irade*, a term used endlessly by the DP leaders), with a mission to transform the country and, like the RPP before it, it expected the opposition to be a junior partner in this process. But while the RPP, certainly after 1946, suspected that it did not have widespread support in the country, the DP felt that it represented the majority, and in its vision of democracy this majority gave it absolute power and legitimacy to do whatever it deemed necessary. Under the 1924 constitution there were no checks such as a second chamber or a constitutional court to counterbalance the power of the assembly and, especially after 1954, the government used this situation to make life hard for the opposition.

The RPP, on the other hand, was in disarray. In the first few years after its defeat, when the Turkish economy was booming and the Democrats seemed to make all their promises come true, the RPP had no political alternatives to offer. At its 1951 and 1953 congresses, the party decided to conquer its ideological confusion and to restore its prestige with its traditional supporters by emphasizing its Kemalist traditions. It redefined the 'Six Arrows' with more emphasis on social policies, but the RPP remained on the defensive because this programme held no attractions for the great majority of the voters.

Without being able to present credible alternatives, the RPP subjected the government to a constant barrage of criticism of anything and everything it did, often changing its own position in the process. The government grew increasingly irritated at what it saw as the RPP's refusal to accept the legitimacy of the DP regime. But there was more than irritation: there was a deep-seated fear that İnönü, whose position at the head of his party had not been in dispute despite the election defeat, had not really accepted the situation and was still supported by the bureaucracy and the army. This fixation on İsmet Pasha (the *paşa faktörü* or 'Pasha factor' to which many references are made in the press of the period) made the Democrat leaders feel insecure in spite of their electoral successes.[2]

The DP increased its share of the vote in the municipal and provincial elections, held later in 1950, and gained control of the administration at all levels. Nevertheless, the increasingly irritated government saw a need to hit back at the opposition through intimidation and by excluding the RPP from the decision-making process in the assembly. A tour of the country by İnönü in September 1952 saw violent demonstrations by DP supporters and it was abruptly cancelled by İnönü when the governor of Balıkesir refused him permission to speak in that town.

The RPP might have lost its hold on the electorate, but through its long monopoly on power and the way it had been intertwined with the government it had over the years become a powerful – and rich – organization. Among its possessions was the material legacy of Atatürk himself, consisting of land, money and a large minority stake in the *Türkiye İş Bankası*. It was against this organizational base of the party that the government decided to strike next. In December 1953, the DP-dominated assembly requisitioned all the RPP's material assets and handed them over to the treasury. The *Halk Evleri* (People's Homes) and *Halk Odaları* (People's Rooms), which were closely linked to the RPP, had already been closed down in 1951, their assets also being turned over to the treasury.

The 1954 elections: increased DP majority

The DP's basic insecurity also showed in the adoption in 1953 of a number of amendments that increased government control of the press and the universities (banning political activity on the part of professors). Two months before the elections scheduled for May 1954, the press law was again tightened.

As it turned out, all the anxiety was completely unnecessary. The DP's economic success guaranteed it the support of the mass of the population, especially in the countryside and the central theme of the RPP campaign – the lack of freedom and the government's authoritarian tendencies – lacked credibility coming, as it did, from a party so closely identified with the authoritarian regime of the past. On 2 May 1954 the DP increased its share of the vote (from 53.6 to 58.4 per cent – still the highest number ever recorded by a Turkish party in free elections), while the RPP share dropped from 39.9 to 35.1 per cent. In the assembly this meant 503 seats for the DP, while the RPP was left with only 31. Again, the only areas where support for the opposition had held up were the underdeveloped areas in the east, where landowners and tribal chiefs were still able to deliver blocks of votes.

The third party of any importance, the reactionary *Millet Partisi* (Nation Party), which had won one seat in 1950, had been banned in July 1953 because of its political use of religion. It was soon reconstituted, however, as the *Cumhuriyetçi Millet Partisi* (Republican Nation Party).

In 1954 it had only limited success: 4.8 per cent of the vote and five deputies, all from the province of Kırşehir, whence its leader (and the only NP deputy from 1950 to 1954) Osman Bölükbaşı hailed.

With the benefit of hindsight one can say that the 1954 elections were the high-water mark of the DP's fortunes. That its fortunes began to deteriorate in the following years was due to two main factors: the growing economic crisis and the disaffection of parts of the ruling elite, notably the intellectuals and the army.

Economic developments
As far as the changeover from a statist, strictly controlled and autarkist economy to a liberal free-market economy is concerned, the crucial turning point was not the DP's coming to power in 1950, but the decisions taken by İnönü's government in 1947 (the first consignments of Marshall Plan tractors arrived in May 1949). It is, however, true that the Democrats had been the most vocal supporters of free-market economics since 1946 and that they implemented liberalization policies with vigour once they were in office. More than the RPP, they realized that in a country like Turkey any serious modernization drive would have to start from an agricultural base (a point emphasized in a number of American reports).[3] Under the direction of Menderes, they, for the first time in Turkish history, put the interests of the farmer first, and they continued to do so until the very end. The basic instruments for this policy were to provide cheap credit to the farmers and to maintain – artificially – high prices for agricultural products through the government buying agency, the TMO.

Supported by large-scale American aid, the progress in these first years was impressive. The credits were used to buy imported machinery. The total number of tractors for example grew from 1750 to more than 30,000 in the years 1948–52. This allowed the acreage under cultivation to be drastically enlarged, from 14.5 million hectares in 1948 to 22.5 million in 1956 – far outstripping the population growth. Combined with excellent weather in the first three years of Democrat rule, this resulted in bumper harvests, which meant that farmers' incomes rose noticeably. Although it is true that the terms of trade for agricultural produce against industrial products declined during this period, the sheer volume of the agricultural production made up for it. Led by this expansion of the agricultural sector, the economy as a whole grew at a rapid rate of between 11 and 13 per cent. Incomes in the towns also rose, although profits rose much more rapidly than wages.

The Democrats' economic ideas were rather unsophisticated. They trusted implicitly in the workings of the market once it was allowed a free rein. Under strong American influence, in 1951 the government introduced a law to encourage foreign investment in Turkey. It expected the Turkish bourgeoisie to start investing the profits it had accumulated in the 1940s and foreign capitalists to queue up to invest in the Turkish economy. The contribution from these sectors was disappointing, however. With few exceptions, the Turkish industrialists of this period were still people who ran relatively uncomplicated family businesses that they could fully control, and they hesitated to invest on the scale the Democrats desired. Despite all the encouragement, foreign investment also remained extremely limited. During the Democrat decade no more than 30 firms invested in Turkey and their share never exceeded 1 per cent of total private investment. As a result, between 40 and 50 per cent of investment had to come from the state, all the liberal rhetoric notwithstanding. Total investment rose by 256 per cent between 1950 and 1954. The most important areas in which this investment was concentrated were the road network, the building industry and agro-industries.[4]

New roads tied the country together for the first time and opened up access to the villages. In 1950, Turkey had only about 1600 kilometres of hard-surfaced roads. With American technical and financial assistance, another 5400 kilometres of hard-surfaced two-lane highways were built during the decade. Together with significant improvements in the loose-surfaced roads, the new roads and the fast-rising number of (imported) cars and trucks (from 53,000 to 137,000), allowed more effective marketing and distribution. By contrast, the building of railways, which had been such an important part of the Kemalist modernization scheme, came to an almost complete halt. The switch to road transport also meant a changeover from public to private transport, since most of the trucks and buses were in private hands while the railways had all either been built by, or taken over by, the state.

The reluctance on the part of private investors and the limited capital they had for investment also meant that the privatization of the large state enterprises, which the Democrats had demanded so vociferously during their years in opposition, was an almost completely dead letter. Much of the government investment was made within the framework of the state industrial sector.

The effectiveness of the massive investments of these years was lessened in three ways. First, because the Democrats aimed to jump-start the economy and wanted quick and tangible results (their professed aim being to reach the level of western Europe within 50 years), the use of their subsidies, cheap credit facilities and investments was often short-sighted, aimed at a high level of growth rather than at longterm improvements in the productive capacity of the country. It has sometimes been said that they confused development with growth, but to a large extent their policies were dictated by the unsophisticated views of the villagers who supplied the DP vote. Second, the DP leadership, Prime Minister Menderes in particular, was allergic to anything resembling economic planning, which they associated with the evils of statism. Menderes even denounced planning as synonymous with communism. The investments, at least until 1958, were therefore uncoordinated. Third, investment decisions were often politically inspired, which resulted in factories being put up in economically unpromising locations and in the wrong sectors, leading, for instance, to a disastrous overproduction of sugar, which had to be dumped on the world market at a loss.

Income distribution and social policies
Most people were better off under the Democrats, though not all to the same degree. Exact numbers are hard to come by, but it is certain that agricultural incomes grew fastest, with the larger farmers profiting most. Profits grew faster than wages and salaries in the towns, so traders and industrialists were relatively better off. From 1955 onwards, worsening inflation began to hit the wage- and salary-earners. Still, it is probably correct to say that by the end of the decade even their real incomes had grown considerably when compared with the immediate postwar years.

In spite of the money invested directly and indirectly in the agricultural sector, which gave even relatively inefficient farms a chance to survive and kept many people on the land who were not essential to the upkeep of agricultural production, the 1950s saw the start of mass migration from the countryside to the towns and cities. Over a million people left the land and by the end of the decade the major cities were growing by 10 per cent a year. Labour migration was not a new phenomenon but the pattern changed in that, whereas earlier the migrants would have been essentially village-based while working part of the year in for instance the mines of Ereğli, now they increasingly moved permanently to the city and went back to the farms only for seasonal work if at all. They came in search of work in the new developing industries, but in the 1950s the capacity of these industries to accommodate this fast-growing but unskilled workforce was limited and as a result only a small proportion of the migrants found permanent jobs in industry, while most of them ended up as casual labourers or as street vendors. The cities were not equipped to receive large numbers of new inhabitants in a regular fashion and most of the new settlers had to fend for themselves, building their own houses on unused land on the outskirts of town. Whole satellite towns of these so-called *gecekondu*s (built at night) sprang up, lacking an infrastructure: they had no water, electricity, roads or sewers. Over the years the *gecekondu*s were gradually incorporated into the cities. Because they became a much more prominent feature of Turkish life in the 1960s and 1970s with the explosive rate of urbanization of those decades, the phenomenon will be treated more extensively in the next chapter.

Population growth

The urbanization cannot be dissociated from the overall growth of the population. The most spectacular and far reaching change that Turkey underwent from the 1950s onwards was the explosive growth of its population. This was due to the coming of peace from the mid-1920s, but also due to better communications (first railways, later roads) that made it possible to balance local food shortages with surplus from other areas. The most important development from the 1950s was the fall in child mortality caused by better hygiene, basic medical care in the countryside and primary education for girls (which also led to better childcare). That made Turkey a classic example of demographic transition. In the 1950s adult Turkish women on average gave birth to six children of whom two died. When child mortality went down, so did fertility – eventually. It took until the 1970s and 1980s before people adjusted to the new reality. Then the number of children per woman started to decline sharply: five in 1970–75, four in 1980–85 and two in 2010. The combination of high fertility and declining child mortality was what caused the fast population growth. From about 20 million in 1950 the population grew to 28 million in 1960 and 40 million in 1975. The gradual increase in the life expectancy was another factor that stimulated growth. In 1960 life expectancy was only 48 years but in the next half century it would increase to 73 years.

The most explosive growth of the population took place in the 1970s and 1980s but its basis was laid in the Menderes years.[5]

Organized labour

Most of Turkey's workers were still unorganized when the DP came to power, even in the industrial firms with more than ten employees, which fell under the Labour Law. Of about 375,000 workers some 78,000 were members of a trade union in 1950.[6] In the years between the Trade Unions Law of 1947 and the elections of 1950, most unions were closely linked to the RPP through its 'Workers' Bureau' (*İşçi Bürosu*). Actually, the party forced quite a number of these unions on the workers. In competing with the RPP for the workers' allegiance the Democrats' most powerful weapon had been the promise to grant them the right to strike.

After the elections this promise was forgotten, however, and the DP's attitude towards the trade unions became almost as repressive as that of the old regime.

In 1952, a trade union confederation called *Türk-İş* was founded with moral and material assistance from the ICFTU (International Conference of Free Trade Unions), but the position of the unions remained weak. The extremely low living standards of their members meant that contributions were insufficient for running the organizations. In fact, the main source of the unions' income was the fines employers paid to the Ministry of Labour for transgressions of the Labour Law. Part of these fines was handed over to the unions as the government saw fit. Especially from 1957 onwards, the government acted heavy-handedly in preventing the unions from establishing contacts between different industrial sectors or with international organizations.

The economic problems accumulate

The Democrats' basic problem, pointed out by many foreign observers at the time, was that they tried to do too much too quickly and with insufficient means at their disposal. The modernization programme meant importing huge quantities of materials and machinery and Turkey suffered a trade deficit from 1947 onwards. This deficit rose, even during the boom years of 1950–53, when Turkey had a wheat surplus and for a short time became a major wheat exporter. By 1954, the boom was over. Agricultural growth had been achieved by a combination of extension of the sown area with exceptionally good weather, not by improved agricultural techniques, irrigation or the use of fertilizers. When the weather turned bad, the agricultural sector's vulnerability was exposed and Turkey had to import wheat once again. Economic growth fell from around 13 per cent to around 4 per cent and, as a result, the trade deficit in 1955 was eight times that of 1950. Nevertheless, the government kept up the rate of imports and investment. It used Turkey's strategic position in the cold war to the utmost to get financial aid and easy borrowing terms. It borrowed on the international markets and from its suppliers (by delaying payment). As a result, in 1960 the total external debt of the country stood at $1.5 billion, or a quarter of the GNP.

The Democrats could have solved at least some of their financial problems by introducing a more effective system of taxation, specifically by taxing the new wealth in the countryside. The rich landowners and substantial farmers who together earned more than a fifth of the GDP, paid only 2 per cent of the total tax revenue. But political considerations always prevented DP governments from using this option. Instead, they borrowed from the Central Bank, which basically meant printing extra money. As a result inflation gradually went up from 3 per cent in 1950 to 20 per cent in 1957, hitting wage and salary earners and consumers in the towns.[7]

The weakness of the Turkish economy was first reflected in the measures taken in September 1953, when import and foreign-exchange controls were established, ending the five-year period of gradual opening up and rapid integration into the world economy. From 1954 onwards, the international financial institutions began to caution the Turkish government, prescribing what would later become known as the classic 'IMF package': devaluation, an end to artificial prices and to subsidies, and an end to import and export restrictions – all measures aimed at complete incorporation into the capitalist world system. For some years, the DP resisted these pressures. It stuck to the official fixed exchange rate of the Turkish lira (2.80 to the dollar), while the deteriorating economy and growing inflation steadily widened the gap between the official rate and the real value of the lira. Instead of recognizing the economic realities, the government revived the National Defence Law of 1940 to enforce price controls. Needless to say, the result was a thriving black market, where everything that had disappeared from the shops could be bought – at a price. By 1958 the black-market rate of the lira was approximately ten to the dollar.

In August 1958 the government was so desperate for further foreign loans that it finally agreed to the demands of the IMF. The lira was devalued, the debts rescheduled and prices were raised. In exchange, the country received a new loan package, paid for partly by the USA, partly by European countries and partly by the IMF.

The debit side of the economic policies of the DP during its ten years in office is fairly clear: they were financially and fiscally unsound, creating huge deficits, debts, inflation and a black market. But the credit side should not be forgotten: the Democrats succeeded in modernizing Turkish agriculture to a certain extent and they vastly increased the industrial base of the country. The majority of the large industrial firms of present-day Turkey have their roots in the 1950s. The new road network opened up the country and the villages came into contact with the outside world for the first time. The result was a sense of mobility and a dynamism that were entirely new.

The culture of the 1950s
The 1950s saw the emergence of a modern, American oriented lifestyle among the urban bourgeoisie. Its members embraced consumerism. They started to dress more fashionably, wore sunglasses, drank soda, drove American cars and attended cocktail parties. Comic strips (often with

Wild West themes) and illustrated magazines modelled after *Life* became popular among broad swathes of the population. The epicenter of this new lifestyle was the hypermodern Hilton Hotel that was built from 1952 in Istanbul's Elmadağ neighbourhoud with the help of Marshall Aid, and which opened in 1955. It was more than a hotel – it embodied the style and ambitions of the Menderes years.

This was also true for the wide new avenues that were now built by Istanbul municipality and that cut mercilessly through whole neighbourhoods. The plans were originally from the 1930s, but now they were actually carried through and thousands of houses were bulldozed to the ground. New apartment blocks for the middle class were built, in an international modernist style, helped by new legislation that made it possible for the first time to own part of a building. Over the next few decades the apartment would become the standard dwelling for the vast majority of the population in all Turkish cities.

Increasing opposition and a return to authoritarian politics

The 1954 elections had been a tremendous success for Menderes. The economic boom had vindicated his policies and the peasants now massively supported him. Over the next few years, however, the economic downturn slowly began to erode support for the Democratic Party. This was due partly to a real deterioration in standards of living (caused by the limits put on the imports of consumer goods, for instance), but it was also true that there had been an explosive rise in the average villager's expectations of material improvement, which the government could not meet. The 1957 elections showed a certain loss of support for the DP in the countryside, but nevertheless the party unquestionably kept the support of the majority of the village population.

A far more serious problem was the crumbling of support among intellectuals, members of the bureaucracy and the armed forces. This was brought about to some extent by the growing economic difficulties and especially the inflation (which of course hit salaried people like civil servants, teachers, university professors and officers more than other groups in society), but a more important factor was the growing authoritarianism of the government. It had been brought to power on a programme of economic and political liberalization but from 1954 onwards the latter was to a large extent sacrificed to save the former.

The election victory had very much been the personal triumph of Prime Minister Adnan Menderes. People selected by him had replaced many of the locally powerful representatives in the last assembly. After the election, he consolidated his position further – in the months after the elections many dissidents were expelled from the party. The changed circumstances were also reflected in Menderes's behaviour. He had always found it very hard to accept criticism; now he became positively allergic to it.

In 1954, a number of measures were taken against the bureaucracy, which the DP still suspected of loyalty to İnönü and his party. The government increased its hold over the bureaucracy by introducing a new rule that any civil servant with more than 25 years of service could be suspended and then sent into early retirement. This applied also to judges and university professors and completed the establishment of political control over the executive and even over the judiciary. Academic freedom, always weak in Turkey, was restricted even further.

In 1955 opposition to the DP's authoritarian line and also opposition to Menderes within the DP started to grow. While the DP, almost from its inception, had been a broad coalition, with supporters in every conceivable section of society, parts of the coalition gradually became estranged from the party over its authoritarian policies *vis-à-vis* the press, the universities and the judiciary.

The extent of the tension in Turkish society first showed in the riots of September 1955. In August and September negotiations between Great Britain, Greece and Turkey over the future of Cyprus led to rising nationalist fervour, fanned by the press. A Greek citizen of Turkish origin (and with links to Turkish security) placed a bomb in the Turkish consulate in Salonica, Greece, by way of provocation.[8] On 6–7 September, large-scale riots took place in Istanbul. In all probability, Menderes and his foreign minister, Zorlu, had decided to have a limited 'spontaneous' demonstration by students in Istanbul to express public feeling on the Cyprus issue in Turkey, but the demonstrations got completely out of hand and developed first into a pogrom against Greek businesses and then into a general attack on visible wealth by the inhabitants of the *gecekondus*. Greek shops in Istanbul's main shopping streets were ransacked and trucks came even from Anatolia to collect the loot. The police, who had apparently been instructed not to act in the original planned demonstration, watched without interfering. The government declared martial law in the three big cities (Istanbul, Ankara and İzmir) and the interior minister had to resign. All in all, 5,622 houses owned by Christians and Jews in Istanbul had been ransacked.[9]

The main bone of contention within the DP, which led to a split in the party, was the demand made in October by a number of liberal representatives that journalists who were taken to court under the restrictive press law should have the right to prove the truth of what they had written and that this should be admitted as evidence in the courts. Later that month, under great pressure from Menderes, the parliamentary group rejected the proposal after acrimonious debates. The mounting criticism forced Menderes himself to seek a vote of confidence from the party parliamentary group. This he got, but dissent within the party had now become so great that in December the liberal wing, under the leadership of Fevzi Lûtfi Karaosmanoğlu broke away from the DP to form the *Hürriyet Partisi* (Freedom Party), which at one stroke became the biggest opposition party in the national assembly. The Freedom Party seems to have had the support of big business, which by now wanted a more sophisticated economic policy with a degree of planning that Menderes would not provide.

During 1956 the trend towards authoritarianism continued. It was the year in which the 'National Defence Law' of 1940 was revived to control prices and supplies. In June the press law was again changed, not to liberalize it (as Menderes had promised during the December crisis) but to strengthen further government control of the media. Another law prohibited political meetings except during an election campaign.

Elections were not due until 1958 but when the government announced that base prices for agricultural products would be raised and that there would be a ten-month moratorium on farmers' debts, it was clear to everyone that elections were imminent. They were duly announced for 27 October. The major opposition parties (RPP, Freedom Party and Republican Nation Party) had for some time been holding discussions on cooperation. These had not been very productive, resulting only in a joint declaration of principles on 4 September, but all effective cooperation among the opposition parties was made impossible by a law enacted on 11 September that banned the use of combined lists in elections.

The elections produced a major setback for the Democrats, despite some vote rigging in their favour. They remained the largest party, but lost their absolute majority in the country. With 47.3 per cent of the vote they had 424 seats in the new assembly, while the RPP increased its percentage of the vote by nearly six points to 40.6, but dramatically increased its number of seats from 31 to 178. The result for the Freedom Party was extremely disappointing, showing that it was a head without a body, that is to say a party without grassroots organization. They got only 3.8 per cent of the vote and four seats. After the elections, in December 1958 the party decided to merge with the RPP. There, they provided a much-needed infusion of new ideas, which helped to reorient the RPP's policies in the direction of social justice and democratic safeguards. The ultra-conservative Republican Nation Party, which received 7 per cent of the vote but also only four seats, merged after the election with the small Peasants' Party (*Köylü Partisi*) to form the Republican Peasants' Nation Party (*Cumhuriyetçi Köylü Millet Partisi*).

The issue of secularism

In the 1957 elections the DP, confronted with an extremely hostile opposition, a worsening economic crisis and crumbling support among the city-dwellers and the more educated, sometimes resorted to an appeal to religious sentiments, describing the Republicans as communists and unbelievers and boasting about the number of mosques and religious schools opened under the Democrats.

This laid the DP open to the charge of using religion for political purposes and of reneging on the secularist principles of the state. The RPP had been harping on about this since the early 1950s and more and more intellectuals were now taking up the theme. In reality, the DP's attitude towards religion was ambivalent. Menderes used appeals to Islamic sentiments, especially during election campaigns. At the DP's party congress in 1958, he said: 'Without paying heed to the outcry of the zealots of the revolution, we Arabicized the call to prayer. We accepted religious teaching in schools. We had the Koran recited over the radio. Turkey is a Muslim state and it will remain so.'[10] At the same time, the DP did not try to give Islam a greater role in the administration or legislation of the country.

To understand the argument we have to remember what the Kemalist concept of secularism had been. The Kemalists, like the Unionists before them, were the executors of a modernization strategy based on a positivist world vision, in which religion was seen as a hindrance to progress in the modernization of state and society. Their secularism meant not so much the separation of church and state as the subjugation and integration of religion into the state bureaucracy.

In the 1930s and 1940s the regime's attitude towards religion had become extremely repressive, but after the introduction of multi-party politics both parties started to court the Muslim vote and the RPP itself became more tolerant of religion after the seventh party congress in 1947. It reintroduced elective religious education in schools and training establishments for preachers. Ankara University announced the establishment of a Faculty of Divinity and in 1949 the tombs and shrines (türbeler) were allowed to reopen. At the same time the RPP tried to guard against any religious reaction in politics by enacting article 163 of the penal code, which strictly prohibited propaganda attacking the secular character of the state.

In the years before 1950 the Democrat leaders took great care to emphasize that they would not allow any fundamental change in the secular basis of the state. This earned them the scorn of Islamic currents such as that represented by the journal Sebilürreşat, which started to attack the DP, and it led to the formation of a number of more radical opposition parties, the most important of which was the *Millet Partisi* (Nation Party).

After they had come to power, the Democrats continued the RPP's policy of relaxing restrictions on expressions of religious feeling and making concessions to the feelings of the Muslim population, while at the same time combating anti-secularist tendencies. The prayer call in Arabic was made legal again (and adopted overnight in every mosque in the country);[11] religious education was expanded and parents now had to opt out instead of having to opt in (social pressure of course saw to it that hardly anyone opted out). The number of preacher schools was increased. There was a marked rise in the number of mosques being built (as much through increased wealth in the countryside as through any government policy) and the sale of religious literature was allowed again. But the DP's understanding of the secularist character of the state was not significantly different from that of the RPP in the 1950s. When activists of the *Ticani* dervish order started to smash busts of Atatürk after the DP's election victory, their leader Kemal Pilavoğlu was arrested, sent to prison and then placed under house arrest. A law against defaming Atatürk's memory was passed in 1951.

The Democrats did not end the integration of the religious establishment into the bureaucracy (through the directorate of religious affairs) and every preacher remained a civil servant. They did, however, accept the existence of autonomous religious organizations, such as the brotherhoods, and even legitimized them when they accepted the support of the *Nurcu* movement in the 1954 and 1957 elections. What the Democrat leadership was tacitly admitting by its attitude towards Islam was that religion was not necessarily incompatible with development. To the majority of the educated elite (including civil servants, teachers and academics and officers) who had internalized the Kemalist dogmas and who themselves owed their position in the ruling elite to the fact that they represented the positivist, Western-orientated outlook, this admission threatened their cultural hegemony and their monopoly of the political scene and the state machinery. This explains why their reaction to expressions of even non-political Islamic feeling, was little less than hysterical. Within the army, which regarded itself as the keeper of Atatürk's heritage, the feeling that the DP was betraying the Kemalist traditions was especially strong. As we shall see, this would prove fatal for the government.

The relaxation of secularist policies under the DP made Islam much more prominent in everyday life in the cities, where the culture of the countryside was anyway becoming more visible through massive urbanization. Turkish intellectuals at the time – and later – saw this as a resurgence of Islam, but although there were fundamentalist groups at work, it was really only the existing traditional culture of the mass of the population, the former subject class, reasserting its right to express itself.

Foreign relations: Atlantic Turkey

The postwar era, and especially the Democrat decade, was a period of intensified incorporation of Turkey into the world capitalist system, not only in the economic field, but also in the realms of foreign policy and defence. Turkey in these years became a solid – albeit peripheral – part of the political and military structures the United States and its allies built up to safeguard the continued existence of democracy and free enterprise in their countries. This was a major break with the Kemalist foreign policy of cautious neutralism.

Turkey's foreign relations in the postwar period were, of course, dominated by the cold war. We have already seen how the Truman doctrine was formulated in part with Turkey in mind. When the Democrats came to power in 1950, Turkey was already a member of the Organization for European Economic Cooperation and of the Council of Europe. After the creation of NATO in 1949, the RPP government had already started to sound out the major NATO countries on the possibilities of joining the organization. In August 1950 the new government officially applied for membership. Menderes knew that several NATO countries, notably the Scandinavian ones, were opposed to Greek and Turkish membership, arguing that these countries were neither Atlantic nor democratic, but he thought he had a trump card: when the United Nations sent an international expeditionary force to Korea to counter the invasion from the north and asked for contributions from member countries to stop the invasion in June 1950, Turkey was one of the few countries that immediately offered to contribute troops. The first, a brigade of 4500 men, were sent in October and before the war was over some 25,000 Turkish soldiers had fought in Korea, suffering more than 6000 casualties.[12] This action gained Turkey a great deal of credit among NATO governments, but even so it was another year before Denmark and Norway, which blocked Turkish entry, were finally persuaded to drop their objections. On 18 February 1952 Turkey became a full member of NATO.

The entry into NATO was celebrated as a great success in Turkey by the Democrats and the opposition alike. The reasons for the enthusiasm for NATO were both rational and emotional. Rationally, it was seen as a guarantee against Soviet aggression and as guaranteeing the flow of Western aid and loans that would make the modernization of Turkey possible. Emotionally, it was taken as a sign that Turkey had finally been fully accepted by the Western nations on equal terms. This feeling seems to have been fairly widespread. Even in the 1970s one could still buy 'NATO wine' in Turkish restaurants.

Regional alliances

Turkey's membership of the Western bloc in the cold war largely determined its position in the two regions of which it formed part: the Balkans and the Middle East. The country was a key element in Secretary of State Dulles's attempts to encircle the Soviet bloc with regional alliances based on NATO.

In the Middle East, the first American attempt to construct a regional alliance was by bringing together Turkey and Egypt in 1951/2, but there was very little enthusiasm for this option in either country. Relations between Turkey and the Arab countries were strained by Turkey's stance in the Israeli–Palestinian conflict.

Turkey had at first backed the Arab countries because the leadership in Ankara expected the Jewish state to be pro-Soviet. With the warming of American–Israeli relations from 1949 onwards, Turkey also shifted its position. It sat with France and the United States on the Palestine Conciliation Commission in 1949 and recognized Israel diplomatically.

After the failure of the Turkish–Egyptian alliance, the second attempt to form a regional bloc was a treaty of cooperation with Pakistan, concluded in August 1954. In February 1955 this was followed by a treaty of cooperation and mutual assistance with Turkey's only friend in the Arab world, the Kingdom of Iraq under its strongman Nuri al-Said. Great Britain, Iran and Pakistan also joined this 'Baghdad Pact' while the USA received observer status.

The years after 1955 saw a rising tide of Arab nationalism sweep through the Middle East, led or at least inspired by the Egyptian president Gamal Abdel Nasser. When the USA blocked his attempts to raise money for building the Aswan dam, in 1956 he nationalized the Suez Canal. This led to an attack by Israel, France and Britain. Even though they were militarily victorious, these nations were forced to retreat by the United States, which saw their action as irresponsible, old-fashioned colonialism that might endanger Western interests in the region. The results were that Nasser, although defeated militarily, came out of the conflict with great prestige in the eyes of the Arab world and that his brand of Arab socialist nationalism became popular throughout the Arab Middle East. Turkey's DP government intensely disliked Nasser and saw him as a communist agent. During the Suez crisis, it felt it had to support Egypt verbally, but it did so in rather equivocal terms and Turkey and the Baghdad Pact continued to be regarded as puppets of Western imperialism in much of the Arab world. Tension between Turkey and Syria rose so high in 1957 that for some time the Turkish army threatened to cross the border and Egyptian troops landed in Syria to help defend the country against possible Turkish aggression. The same year British troops had to intervene in Jordan to suppress a Nasserite uprising and to keep King Hussain on his throne. In 1958, Syria and Egypt, at the request of the Syrian leadership, joined forces to form the short-lived United Arab Republic. A civil war between conservative Christians and Nasserites broke out in Lebanon and, at the request of the Christian Lebanese President Chamoun, American marines landed in Lebanon, making use of bases in Turkey. From the point of view of the Turkish government, the worst news of 1958 was a nationalist coup in Baghdad, which left the king and Prime Minister Nuri al-Said dead. Menderes took the decision to intervene militarily in Iraq and Turkish troops were moved to the border. Only strong American pressure, and promises of more money, prevented a Turkish invasion.

In 1960, the Baghdad Pact, or what was left of it after the new regime in Iraq had withdrawn, was changed into the Central Treaty Organization (CENTO), of which the United States was a full member. Like its predecessor, however, CENTO accomplished very little. Unlike the NATO countries, the members of CENTO lacked the mutual trust necessary to exchange military secrets and ciphers and to integrate their forces effectively in a supranational structure and without that its military effectiveness was bound to remain minimal.

In the Balkans, Turkey's main problem was with its neighbour, the Soviet puppet regime in Bulgaria. In revenge for the sending of Turkish troops to Korea, the Bulgarians suddenly expelled some 250,000 of their Turkish-speaking Muslim citizens. The Turks were totally unprepared for this immigration and closed the border. The conflict was finally resolved in 1953 when the border was reopened, but now the Muslim Bulgarians were forbidden to leave the country altogether. Curiously, nearly 40 years later the Bulgarians provoked a second crisis that was almost a carbon copy of this first one.

In the Balkans, too, the USA encouraged the formation of a regional alliance between Turkey, Greece and Yugoslavia. This Balkan Pact, concluded in February 1953, was as ineffective as the Baghdad Pact, but it did allow the Americans indirect access to the communist, but anti-Soviet, regime in Yugoslavia.

It is perhaps surprising, in view of the bloody history of the years between 1913 and 1923, that the one country with which relations were good and stable in the postwar years (and had been since the early 1930s) was the old enemy, Greece. The relationship stayed good, with both countries joining NATO, until the growing crisis in Cyprus, which started to erupt in 1954, shook it to its very foundations.

On the former Ottoman island of Cyprus a Greek-speaking Orthodox majority of some 80 per cent and a Turkish-speaking Muslim minority of some 20 per cent had lived together under British administration since 1878. Agitation by Greek nationalists of the EOKA movement escalated in 1954 into riots and terrorist attacks on the British. The Greek media and government supported these actions, the aim of which was the union of Cyprus with Greece. The idea of union ('*enosis*') also found growing support in circles of the British Labour Party.

For the Turkish government it was totally unacceptable, not only out of solidarity with the Cypriot Turks, but also for strategic reasons: it would effectively double the Turkish–Greek border. In August 1955, Greece, Great Britain and Turkey met for discussions on the future of the island, but these did not produce any conclusive results. Turkey supported maintaining the status quo. In the next few years the discussions centred on the idea of partitioning the island. Turkey supported this idea as the next best solution, but the idea was unacceptable to the Greek Cypriots, now led by Archbishop Makarios, a Greek nationalist and an astute politician, whom the British authorities had imprisoned and banned but set free in 1957.

Further discussions in 1958 and 1959, first in Zürich and then in London again, led to an agreement whereby Cyprus would become an independent republic and its independence, territorial integrity and constitutional order were guaranteed by Greece, Britain and Turkey. The agreement provided that the three countries would jointly uphold the guarantees and that, if they were unable to act together each of the guarantor countries could act unilaterally. Article 3, in which these provisions were made, formed the legal basis for Turkish intervention in later years. On 16 August 1960 Cyprus became an independent republic, with Archbishop Makarios as its first president.

The Cyprus problem has proved to be almost intractable, souring relations between Turkey and Greece up to the present day, and we shall return to the subject in the next chapters. At the same time, the Cyprus issue is an example of the way in which Turkish foreign policy, which on the whole had been governed by pragmatism, could still be influenced by the emotional issue of the 'outside Turks', the Turkish communities living outside Turkey. These communities, either remnants of the Ottoman Empire such as those in Bulgaria, Greece and Iraq (and in the prewar *sancak* of Alexandrette), or of the Turkic empires in Central Asia, have often had to live under – at least cultural and religious – repression and, even though the main body of Turkish politics, the Republicans and

Democrats (or their successors) have always emphatically rejected irredentism, the fate of the 'outside Turks' is an emotive issue in public opinion, which can, and sometimes does, exert pressure on the politicians.

The DP and the military

The year 1958 also saw the first signs that all was not what it should be between the government and the armed forces. In December 1957, nine army officers were arrested for plotting against the government. The arrests were made public on 16 January 1958.

The Democrats had always distrusted the army, because of the close links of its leading officers with the old regime and İsmet Pasha in particular, but after a purge of the military leadership in 1950 they felt more at ease and, indeed, for the most part of the decade, the top echelon of the armed forces seems to have been loyal to the elected government. The trouble was that by the late 1950s this no longer guaranteed the government the loyalty of the whole officer corps. The reason lay in the fundamental changes wrought by NATO membership and US assistance in the armed forces.

At the end of the 1940s the Turkish army was a huge (700,000 strong) manpower-based force led and organized according to Prussian doctrines of pre-First World War vintage. Unbridgeable chasms existed between the recruits, the NCOs and the officers. Because the level of technical equipment within the army was extremely low, there was no need for large numbers of people with special skills. In the 1950s, all this changed. More than \$2 billion of military aid was spent on modernizing and mechanizing the Turkish army, and American teams assisted in the training of personnel. Younger officers with expertise in engineering or communications took up the most vital positions in the army. They often received part of their training abroad through NATO exchange programmes and so had a chance to see how far behind the Western allies the Turkish army and Turkish society really were. We now know that from 1955 onwards plots against the government were hatched in these circles.[13]

The accusations against the nine officers involved, who were arrested in 1957, were investigated by a military tribunal, but it did not probe very deeply – the army was not prepared to wash its dirty linen in public. The officers were acquitted and only the informer was convicted. Nevertheless, the government had been alarmed and the military takeover in friendly Iraq in July 1958 was another warning of what could happen.

The final years of Menderes

Meanwhile, the opposition, buoyed up by the result of the 1957 elections, kept up its campaign of rejecting and criticizing absolutely everything and anything the government did. The DP now gave signs that it was no longer prepared to put up with this. It hinted at repressive measures and in October, with a lot of pomp and circumstance, Menderes launched the *Vatan Cephesi* (Fatherland Front), an effort to broaden the DP's base and to mobilize the mass of the population. The main element in the campaign was the daily reading on state-controlled radio of endless lists of people who had joined the Front. They included babies, deceased people and even entirely fictitious names and the campaign, which continued for a year and a half, so disgusted many people that 'Societies of Those who Refuse to Listen to the Radio' (*Radyoyu Dinlemeyenler Cemiyetleri*) were founded in many towns.[14]

In late 1958 and early 1959 two factors strengthened Menderes's hand in the countryside, if not in the cities. First the acceptance of the IMF stabilization programme led to the release of $359 million in aid. Together with reasonably good harvests this improved the situation of the farmers, while the price rises connected with the programme hit the cities hard. Then, on 17 February 1959 Menderes survived a plane crash at London's Gatwick Airport in which most passengers were killed. Fully exploited by Turkish radio and the party, his miraculous escape convinced many religious Turks that Menderes was a superhuman figure, chosen by God to lead his people.

Tension between the parties remained high. İnönü was attacked during a tour of the DP heartland on the Aegean, and early in April 1960 troops were used to stop him holding a meeting in Kayseri. When he refused to turn back, the troops were withdrawn. On 18 April the Democrats in the assembly decided to establish a committee with wide powers to investigate the activities of the opposition. The committee, composed exclusively of hard-line DP members, would report on its findings within three months and during this period all political activity outside the assembly would be banned. Even newspaper reports of assembly debates were now forbidden.

The establishment of the investigatory commission was denounced as unconstitutional by law professors at Istanbul and Ankara universities. When disciplinary action was taken against the professors (for engaging in politics) there were student demonstrations and riots. The government now decided to use the army to suppress the student riots and the universities were closed down. One student was killed (although in the tense situation wildly exaggerated numbers were generally believed). The use of troops to suppress demonstrations in turn led to a large silent demonstration by cadets of the War Academy through Ankara on 21 May. The press, which under the censorship restrictions could not report on the riots, instead gave extensive coverage to the student demonstrations in Korea, which brought down President Syngman Rhee around this time.

Prime Minister Menderes, meanwhile, was trying to strengthen his support, or maybe only his nerve, by addressing large crowds of supporters in the Aegean provinces before returning to Ankara for the visit by Prime Minister Nehru of India between 20 and 24 May. On 25 May Menderes suddenly announced that the investigation committee of the assembly had finished its work in one month instead of the projected three, and that it would shortly report its findings. The commission is known to have looked into possible links between the RPP and the army and Menderes's announcement may well have moved the conspirators in the army to act. Whether or not that was the reason, in the early morning of 27 May 1960 army units took over all government buildings in Ankara and Istanbul and arrested all DP ministers and deputies, including Menderes and the president of the republic, Celâl Bayar.

14 · The Second Turkish Republic, 1960–80

The military takeover of 27 May 1960

The general public became aware that a military *coup d'état* had taken place at three o'clock in the morning of 27 May 1960 only when a declaration read by Colonel Alpaslan Türkeş was broadcast on Turkish radio later that morning. The statement announced that the Turkish armed forces had taken over the administration of the country 'to prevent fratricide' and to 'extricate the parties from the irreconcilable situation into which they had fallen'. The declaration emphasized the non-partisan character of the coup.[1]

The military takeover was greeted with explosions of public joy in Ankara and Istanbul, notably among the large student population in both cities and in general among the intelligentsia. The rest of the country showed no such reaction. The countryside especially remained ominously silent. The upheavals of the past months had been almost completely limited to Ankara and Istanbul and there is no evidence of any sharp drop in Menderes's popularity elsewhere.

It is now known that the coup was the result of years of planning on the part of the conspirators, a number of radical colonels, majors and captains in their early forties. Two things were crucial to the success of their takeover. One was the posting of their members to command positions (such as that of the garrison in the capital), which were essential for the takeover of power, and the other was finding a senior officer to head their movement in order to gain the support of the rest of the armed forces. Eventually they were successful on both counts. By May 1960 they were in a position to strike and, after a few failed attempts, they had found the senior officer they needed as a figurehead. It was General Cemal Gürsel , a former commander-in-chief of the land forces, who had been sent on permanent leave on 3 May, after writing a memorandum to the minister of defence in which he commented on the political situation. Gürsel, an easy-going and fatherly figure, was well known and well liked throughout the armed forces. He had agreed to head the *coup d'état* but he was not involved in the details of its organization. When the coup had succeeded, he was brought to Ankara by air force plane from his home in İzmir.

The military announced that power was now in the hands of a 'National Unity Committee' (*Millî Birlik Komitesi*) headed by General Gürsel, but for some time neither the exact functions nor the membership of the committee were clear. The day after the coup it was announced that Cemal Gürsel had been appointed head of state, prime minister and minister of defence, in theory giving him more absolute powers than even Atatürk had ever had.

From coup to revolution: the role of the professors

From the beginning the military were convinced that more was needed than a simple change of government. On the very day of the military coup, five law professors from the University of Istanbul, headed by its rector Siddik Sami Onar, were summoned to Ankara and given the task of drawing up a new constitution. The next day they issued a declaration, which has been likened to a modern-day *fetva*. In it, they justified the military intervention on the grounds that the DP government had acted unconstitutionally (notably in establishing the investigatory commission) and had thus itself become illegal. This interpretation, when accepted by the NUC, brought the military into direct confrontation with the Democratic Party and put an end to its pretensions of being above party politics. On 31 August the DP was suspended and on 29 September it was dissolved.

On 12 June the NUC, assisted by its team of professors, issued a provisional constitution, which gave a legal basis both to the coup and to the existence of the NUC. The cabinet of technocrats, which the military had installed after the coup, was a purely executive organ. All important policy decisions were made by the NUC itself.

Factions within the NUC

The NUC at this time consisted of 38 officers (one died in September and was not replaced). Ostensibly, Cemal Gürsel was the leader of the junta, but in reality Colonel Alpaslan Türkeş, who held the position of adviser to the president, was the most influential member in the early period. A Turkish Cypriot by birth, Türkeş was a charismatic figure, much more widely read than most of his colleagues and with an excellent command of English. He was not well known to the public at large, but he had gained some notoriety 15 years earlier, at the end of the Second World War, when he was accused of pan-Turkist, and possibly pro-Nazi, sympathies (he was later acquitted). He was a representative of the most radical wing within the NUC, which wanted a thorough reform of the political system and had no confidence at all in political parties.

It was undoubtedly Türkeş's group that forced through the NUC decision of 3 August to retire 235 out of 260 generals and some 5000 colonels and majors. Although it is true that the Turkish armed forces were notoriously top-heavy, the main reason for the retirements was doubt about the political reliability of those concerned.

After the army, it was the turn of the universities. Although Türkeş had to resign from his official position as counsellor to the president when his influence became too great in the eyes of his colleagues, the radical group was still powerful enough to push through a measure whereby 147 university professors and lecturers were sacked in October. The criteria for selection, however, were unclear and there followed an outcry during which the rectors of all the Turkish universities resigned. The extent of the academic protest clearly embarrassed the military leaders and soonnegotiations about reversing the measure were started. Eventually, the university teachers were restored to their positions, but only in March 1962. The retired officers, united in the organization of 'Retired Officers of the Revolution' (*Emekli İnkılâp Subayları* or *Eminsu*), were unsuccessful in their attempts to achieve the same for themselves.

Despite the opposition to the purges, the radicals in the NUC launched an even more ambitious scheme in October. This was a plan, clearly inspired by Türkeş, for a Turkish Union of Ideals and Culture (*Türkiye Ülkü ve Kültür Birliği*), which was to take over the functions of the Ministry of Education, the Directorates of Religious Affairs and Pious Foundations and the press and the radio, thus establishing a totalitarian hold on the whole cultural life of the country. This went too far, both in the eyes of the civilian politicians and in those of the more moderate members of the NUC, including General Gürsel. On 13 November 1960 he suddenly announced that the NUC had been disbanded and that a new one had been founded, excluding 14 of the best-known radicals, among them Türkeş. The seemingly complicated way of sacking these officers from the NUC was necessitated by the provisional constitution, according to which NUC members could not be removed except in cases of grave misconduct. The 14 were posted as attachés to Turkish embassies abroad and flown out of the country. Türkeş himself became military attaché in New Delhi.

The NUC and the army

Originally, the NUC had consisted of the conspirators and a number of people, among them senior officers such as Gürsel, who commanded the respect of the army. Even though it had been successful and the armed forces as a whole had sided with the coup, the committee did not represent the armed forces as such. Increasingly, during 1960/1 the army's highest-ranking officers became worried about the interference of the NUC in purely military matters and about the way it undermined the army hierarchy. To prevent any future independent action by junior officers, the army top brass itself founded the Armed Forces Union (*Silâhli Kuvvetler Birliği*), which interfered in politics repeatedly during 1961 and 1962 with memoranda warning the civilian politicians not to return to the politics of before 27 May. They did this in order to keep the initiative and forestall independent action by radical officers who opposed any return to civilian politics.

That fear of such independent action was not completely unfounded was shown by the actions of Colonel Talât Aydemir, one of the original conspirators in the mid-1950s and now commander of the War Academy in Ankara. Twice, on 22 February 1962 and on 21 May 1963, he executed an abortive *coup d'état*. The first time he was granted a pardon; the second time he was executed.

All through the period 1960–63 there were rumours of unrest and plotting within the armed forces and a new military takeover was still considered likely. The military takeovers in Iraq on 8 February 1963 and in Syria exactly a month later were seen as danger signs, the more so as the return to civilian politics in Turkey was far from smooth.

Return to democracy
The purge of the NUC in October 1960 was a clear sign that power was in the hands of those who favoured a return to parliamentary democracy. After that date, the structures of the Second Republic began to be put in place fairly quickly. The commission of professors charged with drawing up a new constitution had originally planned to finish its work within a month, but the work progressed more slowly than expected, mainly because of differences of opinion within the commission. Three of its members, led by the chairman, Onar, had little faith in the politicians and were in favour of a detailed document that would bind them hand and foot, while two others (Tarık Zafer Tunaya and İsmet Giritli) favoured a constitution that would leave maximum scope to the political parties to develop the system. Early in September, Onar had Tunaya and Giritli removed from the commission. Thereafter, a draft constitution was submitted to the NUC on 17 October.

In the meantime, however, a separate group of law professors from the University of Ankara had drawn up its own draft constitution under the leadership of Professor Yavuz Abadan. At the insistence of this group, the task of finalizing the text of the constitution was given to a constituent assembly that consisted of two chambers, an upper house – the NUC – and a lower house consisting of 272 representatives of the remaining political parties (Republican People's Party and Republican Peasants' Nation Party), of professional groups and of the provinces. The constituent assembly convened for the first time on 6 January 1961. Thereafter its constitutional committee of 20 members, chaired by Professor Enver Ziya Karal and Professor Turhan Feyzioğlu, did most of the work.

The text that resulted from these deliberations was markedly different from the 1924 constitution. The main aim of the authors of the new constitution was to prevent a power monopoly such as the DP (and the RPP before it) had held, by counterbalancing the national assembly with other institutions. Under the old structure the party that held a majority in the assembly had an almost free hand. A second chamber, called the senate (*senato*), was created and all legislation would have to pass both chambers (with a mechanism to overrule a senate veto with a two-thirds majority in the assembly). The senate was to be elected, apart from a contingent to be appointed by the president. An independent constitutional court was introduced, which could throw out legislation it regarded as unconstitutional and the judiciary, the universities and the mass media were guaranteed full autonomy. In addition, proportional representation was introduced to lessen the chance of one party holding an overwhelming majority in the assembly. A full bill of civil liberties was included in the constitution.

Significantly, the military were given a constitutional role for the first time through the establishment of a National Security Council (*Millî Güvenlik Kurulu*) mentioned in the constitution. The council was actually established by law in March 1962. Chaired by the president (or in his absence the prime minister), the council advised the government on internal and external security. The service chiefs, the Chief of General Staff and the ministers concerned were *ex officio* members of the council, which had its own secretariat and a number of departments. In the two decades that followed its establishment, the NSC gradually extended its influence over government policy and became a powerful watchdog, sometimes replacing the cabinet as the centre of real power and decision-making.

On 13 January the ban on political activity was lifted and new parties were given a chance to register for the elections that were to take place later in 1961. Eleven new parties were registered (in addition to the RPP and RPNP). Most were ephemeral, but the most important new party was without doubt the Justice Party (*Adalet Partisi*), which had as its primary goal full rehabilitation of the retired officers and arrested democrats. It was seen, both by its supporters and by its adversaries, as the continuation of the DP. Its relations with the NUC were therefore extremely delicate from the beginning. Until his death in 1964 Ragip Gümüşpala, one of the retired generals who by his moderate stance did much to alleviate the tension between the NUC and his own more radical supporters, headed the party.

The first chance for the Turkish population to express itself politically came with the referendum on the new constitution on 9 July 1961. This turned out to be a severe setback for the forces of 27 May: the constitution was accepted with 61.7 against 38.3 per cent of the votes cast, but the latter percentage must be – and was – regarded as remarkably high considering the government's propaganda effort on behalf of the constitution. It showed that even without any organization, the pro-Menderes vote held up to a large extent. This was confirmed by the fact that the constitution was rejected outright in the 11 coastal provinces in the west where the DP had been strongest before 1960.

The trend was confirmed in the parliamentary elections held on 15 October 1961. By all accounts the elections were free and honest. The only restriction on the parties was a protocol the NUC had forced them to sign in September, in which they promised not to make the 27 May coup or the trials of former Democrat politicians then being held an issue in the campaign. İnönü's Republican People's Party was deeply disappointed to gain just 36.7 per cent of the votes (173 seats), only slightly more than the Justice Party, which polled 34.7 per cent (158 seats). The New Turkey Party (*Yeni Türkiye Partisi*), which can be regarded as a continuation of the Freedom Party founded by dissident Democrats in 1955, got 13.9 per cent of the vote, while the conservative RPNP polled 13.4 per cent. Taken together, the parties that were considered heirs to the Democrats were clearly still the strongest force in the country.

The new constitution was more liberal than the old one in the sense that it tolerated a wider spectrum of political activity than before, both to the left and to the right. The first party to emerge, which was clearly outside the old Kemalist mould was the Workers' Party of Turkey (*Türkiye İşçi Partisi*), which was founded in February 1961 by a number of trade unionists, but whose driving force for almost its whole existence was to be the publicist, lawyer and former university teacher, Mehmet Ali Aybar. The party modelled itself after the British Labour Party.

The importance of the WPT lay not in its political power or in the votes it attracted – it never managed to attract more than 3 per cent of the vote in a general election and it never entered a governing coalition – but rather in the fact that it was the first really ideologically based party to compete in elections. By its existence it forced the other parties to define themselves more clearly in ideological terms, too. During the 1960s, the WPT attracted the support of many young intellectuals and it served as a kind of laboratory for the Turkish left, which would later split up into innumerable factions. It also served as a legal home for quite a few important cadre members of the outlawed Turkish Communist Party, although it would go much too far to call it a communist front organization.

The greater political freedom under the new constitution did not immediately lead to the formation of parties of an outspoken rightist or Islamist signature; that came later. To the surprise of many observers, however, who had noticed the way in which Menderes and his government had been fiercely attacked by both the military and the RPP for the political use they made of religion, there was no return to the strict secularist, or even anti-Islamic, policies of the years before 1945. On the contrary, efforts were made to cut the ground from under the feet of the Islamist currents by increased attention to the building of mosques and the restoration of shrines and to religious education in schools. To combat religious bigotry, the early governments of the second republic tried to propagate a modern, rationalist version of Islam, very different from that practised by the average villager. The curriculum of the colleges for preachers was changed to include sociology, economy and law. The Directorate for Religious Affairs started publication of 'enlightened' sermons and the Koran was published in Turkish translation. At the same time, the new regime, like İnönü's government after the war, guarded itself against the risks this greater tolerance of religious expression might entail: the prohibition of the political use of religion, which had been incorporated into the High Treason Law in 1925 and into the penal code in 1949, was now made an article in the new constitution.

The trial of the old regime

The one issue dominating public opinion in Turkey during this time was not that of the constitution but that of the fate of the former leaders of the Democratic Party, who had all been arrested in the aftermath of the coup. The trials took place on a heavily guarded island in the Sea of Marmara, off Istanbul, and were conducted by a nine-man tribunal of judges, appointed by the NUC and chaired by Judge Salim Başol.

Opinions vary on the legality and fairness of the trials.[2] It is true that the only changes in the existing procedures were those that made the verdicts of the tribunal irrevocable and suspended the rule that death sentences on people over 65 years old would not be executed (a change clearly aimed at Celâl Bayar). For the rest, the procedures took place under the existing laws of the republic. On the other hand, there was no legal basis for the existence of the tribunal itself and its members were clearly biased politically against the DP. The proceedings seem to have been reasonably fairly conducted, although the judges made no effort to hide their distaste for the accused.

The charges were a rather strange mixture. The cases brought against the defendants consisted of three criminal cases, nine cases of corruption and seven cases of violation of the constitution. The criminal cases and the corruption charges – some of which were bizarre, such as the one in which Menderes was accused of killing his illegitimate baby, or in which Bayar was accused of forcing a zoo to buy a dog he had received as a gift – were clearly brought in a largely ineffectual effort to tarnish the reputations of these men. The constitutional cases were based on Article 146 of the penal code, making it an offence to attempt to alter the Turkish constitution by force or forcibly to silence the national assembly. The Democrats were deemed to have done this when they instituted the investigatory commission on the activities of the RPP and sections of the press in 1960. Article 17 of the former constitution, however, stated that deputies could not be held accountable for their votes. Furthermore, the constitution also stipulated that it itself could be altered by a two-thirds majority of the assembly (which the DP had had).

In the end, 123 people were acquitted, 31 were sentenced to life imprisonment and 418 to lesser terms, while 15 were sentenced to death. Of these, 11 were sentenced by majority vote and the NUC commuted their sentences. The four other death sentences, those of Bayar, Menderes, Foreign Minister Zorlu and Finance Minister Polatkan, were unanimous. Bayar's death sentence was commuted because of his advanced age (he was 77 but lived for another 26 years) and ill health (and possibly under the influence of his strong showing during the trial, which contrasted sharply with Menderes's behaviour), but Zorlu and Polatkan were hanged on 16 September 1961 and Menderes the next day after a failed suicide attempt. In confirming the sentences, the NUC disregarded pleas from many foreign governments and from İnönü. It has been speculated that the disappointing result of the referendum on the constitution, showing as it did the extent of the following Menderes still had in the country, decided his fate. Since then Turkish public opinion has generally regretted the killing of these politicians who had certainly not acted with less legality or abused their power more than either their successors or their predecessors. Menderes, Zorlu and Polatkan were eventually reinterred at a state funeral in Istanbul in September 1990.

Politics: a period of transition

Parts of the army wanted to intervene after the disappointing election result of September 1961, but the army's most senior officers and the AFU prevented it. Instead, heavy pressure was put on the two parties to collaborate in a coalition to be led by the veteran İsmet İnönü. The parties bowed to the pressure and a 20-member cabinet was formed on 20 November but it was a marriage of convenience, not love. There was inevitably a lot of bad blood between İnönü and the Republicans on the one hand, and the JP, which claimed to be the heir to İnönü's old enemies in the DP, on the other. Many JP members suspected İnönü of collusion with the military. The coalition's failure was brought about by the delicate problem of an amnesty for the former DP politicians – where the cabinet had to tread warily because of the sensibilities of both the military and the old DP supporters in the JP – and by the project for a planned economy, which was supported by the RPP and the military but bitterly opposed by the JP.

In May 1962, the JP rejected as insufficient a proposal to reduce the sentences of the imprisoned Democrats and withdrew its ministers from the cabinet, whereupon İnönü formed a new cabinet, this time based on a coalition of the RPP with the two smaller parties (RPNP and NTP). A partial amnesty was agreed upon but this coalition did not work any more smoothly than the first one. There were many frictions and the worst was the proposal, sponsored by İnönü as part of the reforms demanded by the constitution, for a land tax. When the local elections of November 1963 produced a clear victory for the opposition Justice Party, the fate of the coalition was sealed. The two smaller parties wanted out and when they withdrew their ministers from the cabinet, İnönü had no choice but to resign. He did so on 2 December after his return from President Kennedy's funeral in Washington.

Now, for the first time, President Gürsel (with the backing of the Chief of General Staff, General) asked the JP leader, Gümüşpala, to form a government, a highly significant development since it showed that the military now regarded the JP as a normal and acceptable part of the political landscape and no longer required it to be held under tutelage by İnönü. Gümüşpala, however, failed in his attempt and once again, for the last time, İsmet İnönü, who was by now nearly 80, was charged with forming a government. On 25 December 1963 the third İnönü coalition, this time a minority one of RPP and independents, took office. Like its predecessors it was weak. During 1964 it was kept in office because of the serious international crisis that developed over Cyprus in that year, but when the crisis had passed the JP lost no time in bringing it down. On 13 February 1965 İnönü resigned when he failed to get his budget approved in parliament. A caretaker cabinet headed by a former diplomat and independent deputy, Suat Hayri Ürgüplü, then ruled the country until parliamentary elections were held in October.

By this time General Gümüşpala no longer headed the Justice Party, for he had died suddenly in 1964. After his death there had been a bitter struggle for the succession, during which some contenders tried to whip up feeling with attacks on the military *coup d'état* of 27 May 1960. The Chief of General Staff, Sunay, had reacted with a stern warning, which tipped the scales in favour of the moderates within the JP. Their candidate, a 44-year-old hydraulic engineer called Süleyman Demirel, was elected party chairman in November. Demirel was a self-made man, born in a village in the province of Isparta, who had been in charge of dam building under Menderes and had had a successful career in private enterprise (working for an American firm) after 1960. He proved, if not the most important, certainly the most enduring Turkish politician of the postwar era. The emergence of Demirel as party leader was at the same time the symbol of the emergence of an entirely new elite. The DP had managed to capture the vote in the more developed parts of the countryside, but it had its origins in a split within the Unionist/Kemalist elite, which had, it is true, always co-opted members of the traditional landowning elite, but was itself city based. The JP by contrast was a party in which, and through which, self-made men from the countryside and from the smaller (but fast-growing) provincial towns became a dominant force.

Demirel in power

The JP won a landslide victory in the elections of October 1965, gaining an absolute majority of the votes cast (52.9 per cent) and of seats in the assembly. The RPP was down to 28.7 per cent. All the other parties (RPNP, NTP, WPT and the new Nation Party, which had split off from the RPNP) gained less than 7 per cent of the vote. It was clear from the distribution of the votes that the JP had managed to capture the old DP support. Demirel proved to be a first-rate vote catcher in the countryside, where people could identify with his background and see his career as the embodiment of their hopes. Like Menderes before him, Demirel was an orator who could speak the language of the mass of the people – something İnönü and the other Kemalist political leaders, or for that matter socialists such as Aybar, had never been able to do.

With a solid majority in the assembly, Demirel had no problem getting a vote of confidence for his cabinet. For the next five years he dominated Turkish politics. As we shall see, the mid- and later-1960s were good years for Turkey. Economic growth was high and real incomes went up almost continually, by an average of 20 per cent in the years between 1963 and 1969. One of Demirel's most important achievements was to reconcile the army with rule by civilians who were clearly heir to the Democrats the military had toppled only five years before. He had to pay a price, however: the armed forces were granted almost complete autonomy, their submission to the authority of the Minister of Defence and the cabinet being no more than a formality. At the same time he had to keep in check the more radical members of his following who were still bent on vengeance for the 27 May coup.

Keeping his cabinet and his party together was Demirel's main problem, which occupied far too much of his time. The JP was a coalition of industrialists, small traders and artisans, peasants and large landowners, religious reactionaries and Western-oriented liberals. It had very little ideological coherence. Besides, Demirel was a relative new-comer on the political scene and he lacked legitimacy in the eyes of the old DP cadres, who saw him as no more than a caretaker for the real leaders who were still in prison at the time. This aspect of the matter was emphasized, when, after the promulgation of an amnesty law in August 1966, the DP leaders, including former president Celâl Bayar, were set free. From 1968 onwards a pressure group called *Bizim Ev* (Our Home) formed around Bayar to influence the policies of the JP. Nevertheless, Demirel – against the expectations of most observers – managed to preserve the unity of the party and his own position at the top of it throughout the 1960s.

To do so he had frequent recourse to two tactics. He emphasized the Islamic character of the party and the way it stood for traditional values, especially during elections (openly flirting with the leaders of the *Nurcu* movement, for instance); and he kept up a constant campaign of anti-communist propaganda and of harassment of leftist movements. With the backing of the National Security Council and with the help of the infamous MİT (*Millî İstihbarat Teşkilâti*, or National Intelligence Organization), which had succeeded the older Bureau for State Security in 1963, continuous pressure was exerted on left-wing organizations and individuals. In 1966/7 there was an attempt to purge the schools and universities of leftist teachers. Translators of foreign socialist or radical literature were brought to trial, even if the translated texts were eighteenth-century tracts. People were arrested for publishing communist propaganda, which, in the most famous case, turned out to consist of quotes from an early speech by Atatürk himself.

Demirel's position was, however, fundamentally different from that of Menderes because of the checks and balances built into the con-stitution. The independent judiciary, including the constitutional court, in many cases did its job of protecting the rights of individuals and ensuring the constitutionality of new legislation in defiance of the government. The state radio and television were autonomous and often very critical of the government (as was a large part of the press) and the autonomy of the universities meant that the police could now enter a campus only at the invitation of the rector. Demirel's hands were therefore tied in many ways and he never had the two-thirds majority in the assembly required to change the constitution and curb civil liberties, although many in his party were in favour of such a change.

Because of these policies, Demirel became as unpopular among intellectuals as Menderes had ever been, but that his support held up well in the countryside was shown in the elections of 1969. The JP suffered slight losses (its percentage of the vote was down to 46.5 per cent) but it kept its majority in the assembly and the RPP was unable to profit from its decline, polling only 27.4 per cent. Demirel formed a new cabinet, slightly more centrist than the old one.

Demirel's problems lay not with the electorate or the opposition but within his own party. In spite of all his efforts, he eventually lost the support of the most conservative wing, representative of the interests of the Anatolian landowners and small traders and artisans over his proposals for new taxation to help pay for the industrialization of the country. In February 1970 the right wing of the JP voted with the opposition and forced Demirel to resign. There was no alternative to Demirel, however, and in March he was back at the head of a new cabinet. But the rift had only been healed superficially and in June the right wing started talking openly about leaving the party. Some of its members were forced out by Demirel and some resigned of their own accord. In December 1970, 41 representatives and senators who had left the JP, led by the former president of the national assembly, Ferruh Bozbeyli, founded the *Demokratik Parti* (Democratic Party), its name, of course, recalling the banned *Demokrat Parti* of Menderes and Bayar.

The Republican People's Party moves left of centre

The RPP had gone into the 1965 elections with a new manifesto, written by the two coming men of the party, Turhan Feyzioğlu and Bülent Ecevit, which emphasized social justice and social security without being explicitly socialist. Ecevit defined the position of the party as 'left of centre' (*ortanın solu*), a definition that was used – and thus endorsed – by party chairman İnönü for the first time in a speech on 28 July. Ecevit had managed to convince İnönü that the future of the RPP lay in mobilizing the votes of the proletariat, the inhabitants of the *gecekondus*. This meant that the RPP would have to compete with the Workers' Party, something the new slogan was meant to help achieve. The RPP's new stance did not profit it in the 1965 elections, however. It still lacked credibility as a progressive party (certainly with İsmet İnönü at the helm) and anyway the people in the squatter towns were still villagers who had moved to the big city, taking their village values with them. As in the villages, they voted JP. The real party of the left, the Workers' Party, fared just as badly in the elections as did the RPP. Besides, the 'left of centre' slogan offered JP propagandists every opportunity to use the crudest scare tactics against the Republicans. The slogan 'Ortanın solu, Moskova yolu' (left of centre is the road to Moscow) was much used during the campaign.

After the defeat an acrimonious debate started within the party and there were many who blamed the 'left-of-centre' tactics for the defeat. İnönü stood by Ecevit and the new programme, however, and the latter was elected secretary-general of the party in 1966. The infighting continued until the Fourth Extraordinary Congress, which met on 28 April 1967. Ecevit, backed by İnönü, proposed measures to increase central office's hold over the party and its parliamentary representatives and to increase party discipline. When they were adopted, a group of 47 representatives and senators who opposed the 'left-of-centre' line left the party to found the *Güven Partisi* (Reliance Party). They were led by Turhan Feyzioğlu, who had been Ecevit's main competitor for the position of 'crown prince' of the RPP. He had always belonged to the progressive wing of the party and it is hard not to believe that personal jealousy of Ecevit was one of his motives for splitting the party.

The 1968 local elections, in which the RPP improved its share of the vote in the big cities, seemed to indicate that the new line was beginning to have an effect. Yet, the 1969 elections were again a big disappointment, possibly due to the still ambiguous position of the RPP, for, while Ecevit and his supporters enthusiastically embraced the party's new orientation, İnönü seems to have had second thoughts – while not actually disavowing Ecevit, in declarations and interviews he strongly emphasized the RPP's Kemalist traditions and anti-communist character.

The political landscape of the late 1960s, however, can no longer be described in terms of the activities and ideas of the two major parties alone. The 1961 constitution offered opportunities for much more political diversity, opportunities that were only fully exploited from the mid-1960s onwards.

The growth of political radicalism
The 1960s were years of rapid change. People became more mobile, both socially and physically. There was a growing student population and a

growing industrial proletariat, both of which could have been the natural stamping grounds of a modernized RPP, had it not been for the fact that this party, in spite of the rhetoric about being 'left of centre' remained a coalition with a broad base, and did not dare to opt for radical policies. This left an opening for the Workers' Party and, later, for the militant left.

The Justice Party in turn was vulnerable on the right. Its electoral base consisted of farmers and small businessmen, but its policies increasingly served the interests of the modern industrial bourgeoisie, of big business. This left many of its voters disgruntled and they became the prime targets of both the Islamic and the ultra-nationalist parties that were founded.

The left

The oldest party on the left was, of course, the Turkish Communist Party. Despite having been banned for nearly 50 years, it still had a small but devoted following inside Turkey. Its influence among those interested in left-wing politics, however, was declining. This was both because of its hard-line pro-Moscow stand (which discredited it in the eyes of many when the horrors of the Stalin era became known and certainly after the suppression of the Hungarian independence struggle in 1956) and because of its doctrinaire concentration on the industrial proletariat as the moving force of the revolution. The industrial proletariat, although growing, was still relatively small. The main legal party of the left was the Workers' Party, which also aimed at the proletariat (especially the trade unions) for support, but at the same time was very influential among intellectuals.

The 1960s saw a lively intellectual debate about all kinds of political and social issues, which found expression in a host of new periodicals whose publication was made possible by the new constitution. The first was the journal *Yön* (Direction), which started to appear in 1961. It was not a narrow Marxist publication but a broad-based forum for the expression of different radical and leftist views. Its editor, Doğan Avcıoğlu, saw socialism as the only viable model of development in a semi-colonial country and he advocated state planning and protectionism. Later journals, such as *Devrim* (Revolution) or *Aydınlık* (Enlightenment) were as a rule more narrowly committed to one specific brand of Marxism. The groups that formed around these publications often developed into factions or parties.

This growth of a new left consisting of students and intellectuals during the 1960s was not, of course, unique to Turkey. It happened all over the world, but there were two reasons why its development in Turkey was especially important. The universities had played an important part in toppling Menderes and in formulating the constitution of the second republic. It was only logical therefore that students and teachers began to see themselves as the moving force of society. It was, moreover, an idea that tallied perfectly with the Kemalist concept of a revolution from above carried out by an enlightened elite.

Political debating societies (*fikir kulüpleri* or 'idea clubs') sprang up at all the major universities, the most prominent being the one at the political science faculty of Ankara University (the successor to the old imperial *mülkiye* as the breeding-ground of Turkey's civil servants), where Professor Sadun Aren, one of the leaders of the Workers' Party, was a formative influence. In the mid-1960s this and other debating societies were taken over by student activists of the WPT who now founded a national network, the *Fikir Kulüpleri Federasyonu* (Federation of Debating Societies).

The major debate in Marxist circles in the mid-1960s was about which historical phase Turkey was in. Mehmet Ali Aybar and the main faction of the WPT maintained that it was ripe for a socialist revolution, which could be brought about by democratic means. They expected success to come from a growing class-consciousness and political awareness among Turkey's workers, whom they tried, with considerable success, to organize in a new trade unions confederation led by WPT members. Another influential group, led by Mihri Belli, held that Turkey was an Asiatic society with feudal characteristics, that the proletariat was too weak and that revolutionary change could only be brought about by a coalition of intellectuals and officers. This current, which was called *Millî Demokratik Devrim* (National Democratic Revolution) took over the Federation of Debating Societies in 1968 and turned it into the organization 'Revolutionary Youth', known by its Turkish acronym as *Dev Genç*.

From 1968 onwards, student movements in Germany, the United States and especially France (where students had come close to launching a revolution and toppling General de Gaulle in May 1968) influenced the youth movement in Turkey. At the same time, the Soviet invasion of Czechoslovakia caused a crisis of consciousness among the Turkish left, as it did in socialist circles around the world. The WPT split when Mehmet Ali Aybar's condemnation of the invasion was not supported by a number of other party leaders, such as Sadun Aren and Behice Boran. At the same time, the *Millî Demokratik Devrim* group also split, over the rather more esoteric question of whether Turkey was a feudal society or rather one in which the 'Asiatic mode of production' dominated. This seemingly arcane discussion was not without political relevance. Those who defended the feudalism thesis saw the state (for state read army) as a potential ally in a progressive coalition to fight feudal and 'compradore' interests. The supporters of the Asiatic mode of production thesis on the other hand saw the struggle as being between an oppressive state (including the armed forces) and the population. Thus the historical analysis was also a coded discussion about a vital question: the possible role of the army in any revolution. One part of the radical wing of the movement, led by Doğu Perinçek, later turned Maoist.

From 1970 onwards some radicals from the MDD circle decided that agitation was not enough and that only 'armed propaganda' (in other words terrorist attacks) and an armed guerrilla struggle could bring about a revolution. The Maoist splinter group TKP–ML (*Türkiye Komünist Partisi–Marksist/Leninist*) spawned the TİKKO (*Türkiye İşçi Köylü Kurtuluş Ordusu* – Turkish Workers and Peasants Liberation Army), while other groups were the THKO (*Türkiye Halk Kurtuluş Ordusu* – Turkish People's Liberation Army) of Deniz Gezmiş and the THKP/C (*Türkiye Halk Kurtuluş Partisi/Cephesi* – Turkish People's Liberation Party/Front) of Mahir Çayan. These groups began a campaign of terrorism, or urban guerrilla warfare, aimed at destabilizing the country.

In radical left circles some people began to demand that attention be paid to the plight of the Kurdish minority. When the majority felt that ethnic identities should be submerged in class solidarity, Kurdish intellectuals founded the 'Revolutionary Culture Clubs of the East' (*Doğu Devrimci Kültür Ocakları*).

The hopes of the National Democratic Revolution for a coalition with progressive officers received a blow on 15 June 1970, when large-scale demonstrations of workers in Istanbul were dealt with heavy-handedly by the troops. With both the WPT and the other groups of the new left having suffered serious setbacks, the old Turkish Communist Party regained some of its influence among intellectuals around this time.

The right

The conservative Republican Peasants' Nation Party had done badly in the elections of October 1965, gaining no more than 2.2 per cent of the vote. Nevertheless, the party was destined to play a major role in Turkish politics in the following 35 years. That it would do so was wholly due to one man, Colonel Alpaslan Türkeş, who had returned to Turkey announcing his intention to enter politics. After an unsuccessful attempt to found his own party in 1964, he had, together with ten of the 'fourteen', the officers dismissed from the NUC in 1960, joined the RPNP in the spring of 1965. Shortly afterwards, in August, Türkeş managed to be elected chairman of the party. After ousting the old leadership, he turned it into a hierarchically organized, militant party with an ultra-nationalist programme.

The RPNP's new ideology was laid down in a booklet written by

Türkeş and published late in 1965, called *Dokuz Işık* (Nine Lights). The basic principles were nationalism, idealism, morality, social responsibility, scientific-mindedness, support for freedom, support for the peasants, developmentalism and industrialization/technology. In many ways Türkeş's programme was not far removed from the Kemalism of the 1930s, but in practice a violent nationalism (also in a pan-Turkist sense, meaning the reunification of all the Turks of Asia) and anti-communism were the elements emphasized. In 1969 the party's name was changed to *Milliyetçi Hareket Partisi* (Nationalist Action Party). As well-known as the party itself was its youth organization, officially called the 'Hearths of the Ideal' (*Ülkü Ocakları*), whose members called themselves *Bozkurtlar* (Grey Wolves), after a figure in pre-Islamic Turkish mythology and who in December 1968 began a campaign to intimidate leftist students, teachers, publicists, booksellers and, finally, politicians. The Grey Wolves received paramilitary training in specially designed camps and, like Hitler's SS, their mission was to conquer the streets (and the campuses) on the left.

Until 1969, Türkeş was an outspoken supporter of secularism, but in the run-up to the elections that year he changed course and began to emphasize Islam as a part of the Turkish national heritage. For Türkeş, although not necessarily for his followers, this was clearly a tactical move, intended to catch votes. The other major party of the right, which emerged around this time, went further. In 1969, Professor Necmettin Erbakan was elected president of the Union of Chambers of Commerce and Industry after a campaign in which he had made himself the voice of the smaller businessmen who criticized Demirel and the JP for being subservient to big business and, especially, foreign capital. A religious flavour entered into Erbakan's argument when he denounced the JP for being an instrument of Freemasons and Zionists that had turned its back on Islam. The same year he left the JP and was elected to the national assembly as an independent member for Konya, the stronghold of religious conservatism in Turkey. In January 1970 Erbakan, with two other independents, formed his own party, the National Order Party (*Millî Nizam Partisi*). Behind the scenes the founding of this party had been orchestrated by a religious current, the İskenderpaşa community in Istanbul, which was a branch of the Nakşibendi dervish order. The leader of this community was a man with a large network in business circles, Şeyh Mehmet Zahit Kotku. Kotku was a mystical sheikh from an immigrant family from the Caucasus, who had been active as a preacher and religious leader in Istanbul since 1952. Several other important political figures besides Erbakan, such as the later presidents Özal and Erdoğan, would be among his pupils.

Together, the NAP and the NOP posed a serious threat to Demirel's power. This was not because either of the new parties was able to replace the JP as the mass party of the right, but because, together with the dissidents within the JP who were later united in Bozbeyli's new Democratic Party, they could endanger his hold on the assembly. There is little doubt that left-wing groups started political violence in the late 1960s. There were violent clashes with police and troops during visits by the American Sixth Fleet in July 1968 and February 1969, during which people were killed. There were bombing attacks, robberies and kidnappings. But from the end of 1968 onwards, and increasingly during 1969 and 1970, the violence of the left was met and surpassed by violence from the militant right, notably Turkeş's Grey Wolves.

The military ultimatum of 12 March 1971
By early 1971, Demirel's government, weakened by defections, seemed to have become paralysed. It was powerless to act to curb the violence on the campuses and in the streets and it could not hope to get any serious legislation on social or financial reform passed in the assembly. This was the situation when, on 12 March 1971 the Chief of General Staff handed the prime minister a memorandum, which really amounted to an ultimatum by the armed forces. It demanded that a strong and credible government be formed that would be able to end the 'anarchy' and carry out reforms 'in a Kemalist spirit'. If the demands were not met, the army would 'exercise its constitutional duty' and take over power itself. Soon rumours circulated that the high command had in fact acted to forestall a coup by junior officers on the pattern of that of May 1960. We now know that a coup was indeed planned for 9 March 1971. The originators were retired general Cemal Madanoğlu (who had been one of the original plotters in 1960) and the editor of the MDD journal *Devrim*, Doğan Avcıoğlu. Even more alarming for the army leadership was the fact that the chief of the airforce, General Muhsin Batur, was aware of the plans. He had first expressed, but then withdrawn his support, without, however, betraying the plotters. The army top reacted by forcibly retiring all officers below the rank of four star general whose names had been mentioned in connection with the plot. Three days later the memorandum was issued.

The politicians' immediate reaction to the ultimatum was negative. Demirel immediately resigned and İnönü sharply denounced any military meddling in politics. But both party leaders soon took up more conciliatory positions. Demirel cautioned his party to remain calm and adopted a wait-and-see attitude, while İnönü announced his support for the new government installed by the generals once it became clear that

that government would be headed by Nihat Erim, a member of the right wing of the RPP and a close associate of İnönü's for many years. İnönü's support for Erim so infuriated Ecevit that he resigned as secretary-general.

Many on the left at first greeted the ultimatum with hope, interpreting it as a 1960-type coup against a right-wing government. This soon proved to be a dreadful mistake. It was a 'coup' by the high command, not by a radical group of officers and the high command by this time was mesmerized by the spectre of a communist threat.

Erim formed a cabinet, which consisted largely of technocrats from outside the political establishments. He announced that his government would restore law and order and enact a number of long overdue socio-economic reforms. Atilla Karaosmanoğlu, a leading progressive economist who had worked for the World Bank, drew up a reform programme. The programme included land reform, a land tax, national-ization of the mineral industry and measures to protect Turkish industry by demanding that joint ventures be at least 51 per cent Turkish owned. This reform programme met with stubborn opposition from vested interests in business and agriculture. Only the largest and most sophis-ticated industrialists, men like Vehbi Koç and Nejat Eczacıbaşı, supported the reform proposals, which they saw as necessary if Turkey was to join the industrialized countries in the foreseeable future.

With unequivocal backing from the military, Erim might have been able to push through his programme in spite of the resistance from the right, but the military's attention was elsewhere. In April there were renewed terrorist attacks and on 27 April the National Security Council decided to proclaim martial law in 11 provinces, including all the big cities, from the next day; it was to be renewed every two months for the coming two years. Under martial law the military began to round up people who were suspected of terrorism. This in itself might have been justified, but the military, which had a free hand under the Erim govern-ment, used the situation to institute a veritable witch-hunt against anyone with leftist or even progressive liberal sympathies. The perse-cution of the left became very serious after members of the THKP/C (Turkish People's Liberation Party/Front) kidnapped and killed the Israeli consul in Istanbul, Ephraim Elrom, on 22 May. About 5000 people were arrested, among them many leading intellectuals (writers, journalists and professors), all the leading members of the WPT and many prominent trade unionists. There were widespread reports of torture, both in the prisons and in so-called 'laboratories', torture chambers of the MİT.

A role in the suppression of the left seems also to have been played by the 'contra-guerrilla', an underground organization of rightist civilians who were paid and armed by the army. It had been founded in 1959 with American help to organize resistance in the event of a communist takeover. Its existence became known to the public at large 20 years later, when Ecevit was prime minister (in the 1980s the existence of similar operations in other NATO countries, such as 'Gladio' in Italy, received much publicity).[3]

The Workers' Party was closed down on 20 July, when at its fourth party congress a motion was carried, expressing support for the 'democratic aspirations of the Kurdish people'. The National Order Party of Necmettin Erbakan had met the same fate in May. The closure of the NOP was adduced as proof of the even-handedness of the anti-terror campaign, but in fact Erbakan himself was not brought to court and he was allowed to resume his activities in October 1972, when he restarted the NOP under a new name, *Millî Selâmet Partisi* (National Salvation Party). The terrorists of the right and the NAP, under whose aegis they worked, were left conspicuously alone.

The Erim government in the meantime made very little progress with its reform programme. When Erim showed himself ready to compromise with the conservatives in the assembly and accept some of Demirel's old ministers in his cabinet, 11 of his reformist technocrats resigned from the cabinet in December. Politicians from the right took their places. Erim's cabinets did, however, propose a number of amendments to the constitution, aimed at making it less liberal, which the national assembly adopted with the support of the parties of the right. All in all 44 articles were changed. The opportunity was created to limit by law the civil liberties mentioned in Article 11 of the constitution; the autonomy of the universities and of radio and television was ended; the freedom of the press was limited, as were the powers of the constitutional court. By contrast, the powers of the National Security Council were increased to include giving unsolicited advice to the cabinet, advice that, in the circumstances, was binding. In addition, special 'state security courts' (*Devlet Güvenlik Mahkemesi*) were instituted, which were to try more than 3000 people before they were abolished in 1976.[4]

Some of these changes were carried through by Erim's successor. He himself resigned in April 1972 when the assembly refused to give him the right to rule by decree as he and President Sunay demanded. He was succeeded by Ferit Melen, one of the leaders of the Reliance Party, who collaborated even more closely than Erim had done with Demirel and the JP. The only party not to subscribe to the policies of the Erim and Melen cabinets was the RPP. Within the RPP, Ecevit's principled stance was rewarded when he ousted İnönü from the party chairmanship and succeeded him at a tumultuous party conference in May 1972. In November, İnönü resigned from the party he had helped to found almost 50 years earlier.

The reason that the politicians in general, and Demirel in particular, could slowly but surely re-establish their hold over the cabinet and its decision-making from 1971 to 1973 lay in the dilemma with which the army was faced. It did not want to take over power itself, having seen the damage that that course of action had caused to Greece after the takeover by the military junta there in 1967. On the other hand they could hardly intervene with memoranda and ultimata on a daily basis to keep the politicians in line without losing their credibility, so the politicians' leeway gradually increased.

The parties showed their teeth during the presidential elections of 1973. The term of office of President Sunay, who had succeeded Gürsel in 1966 (because of the latter's ill health), came to an end in 1973 and the army put forward the chief of general staff, General Faruk Gürler, as his successor. The parties, however, agreed that it should not become traditional for a president automatically to be succeeded by the chief of staff (as had happened with Sunay), and Gürler was defeated. Finding an alternative candidate proved more difficult. After 15 ballots the main parties finally managed to agree on a candidate, senator and retired admiral Fahri Korutürk. He in turn appointed the economist Naim Talû to lead a caretaker government to take the country to the first free elections after the 12 March coup, those of October 1973.

The elections produced a surprise result. Ecevit's new look RPP became the biggest party, polling 33.5 per cent against 29.5 per cent won by Demirel's JP (down nearly 15 per cent). None of the parties had an absolute majority – a situation that continued throughout the decade – so coalition or minority governments were inevitable. After long-drawn-out negotiations, in January 1974 a cabinet was formed, based on the surprising combination of Ecevit's RPP with Erbakan's NSP, a marriage of convenience that nevertheless had some common basis in a distrust of European and American influence and of big business.

The coalition had only been in power for a few months when the Cyprus crisis broke out. Ecevit became a national hero overnight through his successful handling of the crisis and the invasion of Cyprus. He wanted to use his new popularity to gain an absolute majority in early elections and he therefore resigned on 16 September 1974. This was a major miscalculation. The other party leaders, well aware that Ecevit had eclipsed them all, were prepared to go to any lengths to avoid early elections. After months of rather undignified haggling, and the installation of a caretaker cabinet under Professor Sadi Irmak, Demirel was finally able to put together a coalition of the JP, the NSP, the NAP, the RRP and a number of defectors from the DP, which announced itself to the public as the 'Nationalist Front' (*Milliyetçi Cephe*).

Demirel had only been able to get the parties to cooperate by bribing them with cabinet posts. As a result the new team included 30 cabinet ministers. The parties in the coalition, especially the NSP and the NAP, knowing full well that Demirel depended on them, wielded disproportionate influence. They set about colonizing 'their' ministries in an unprecedented way: thousands of civil servants were discharged or demoted and replaced with party loyalists. The coalition held together until the 1977 elections. These elections, held in an atmosphere of increasing violence and economic crisis, seemed to show a return to a two-party system in Turkey. The RPP, profiting from Bülent Ecevit's personal popularity, got 41.4 per cent of the vote, its highest share ever in a free election. The JP also went up to 36.9 per cent. Again there was a stalemate. An attempt by Ecevit to form a coalition of his party and independents soon failed. Demirel then formed a second 'National Front' coalition, in which the influence of the NSP and NAP was even greater than in the first, and which held out amid increasing chaos until December, when defections by JP representatives brought about its fall.

The defectors were rewarded when in January 1978 Ecevit formed a cabinet of RPP and independents. The independents were all given cabinet posts. Ecevit's cabinet survived until October 1979, but it accomplished little. It clearly could not master the rising tide of violence. The military leadership grew increasingly disillusioned with what it saw as Ecevit's 'soft' attitude to terrorism and Kurdish separatism, and there are strong indications that the army top brass decided in the summer of 1979 to start preparations for a coup, which it now regarded as inevitable.[5] Life was made extremely difficult for Ecevit's cabinet by the savage attacks of the opposition, notably Demirel, who denied the very legitimacy of the government and even refused to call Ecevit 'prime minister'. The administration was partly paralysed by the cabinet's efforts to purge the ministries and services, which the 'Nationalist Front' coalitions had parcelled out among themselves. Nor could Ecevit muster much support from the left. His relationship with the left and the trade unions deteriorated because of the way the government had to emphasize law and order and austerity.

In October 1979 elections for the senate showed a drop in support for the RPP. As a result defections began in the assembly. Ecevit lost his majority and had to resign. Demirel returned to power, but to the relief of many he did so with a minority government supported by his own party and independents but without the NSP or NAP.

The coalition governments of the period between 1973 and 1980 were without exception weak. The one solution that would have yielded a government with a large and stable majority, a JP–RPP coalition, proved impossible to realize. The political system gradually became paralysed because the two major parties, the JP and RPP, were unable to cooperate after the restoration of democracy in 1973, thus giving small extremist groups disproportionate influence. The polarization of the big parties was due partly to ideological factors (the parties were now far more 'ideological' than for instance the DP and RPP during the 1950s), and partly to personal rivalry between the leaders. Besides, each party felt that it was just one step away from an absolute majority and that cooperation would only harm its chances in the next election. The paralysis of the political system this produced was shown clearly when the assembly proved utterly incapable of electing a successor to President Korutürk when his term ended in 1980, even after 100 rounds of voting. This paralysis meant that no government was able to take effective measures (and even more importantly see them carried out) to combat the two overwhelming problems Turkey faced in the 1970s, political violence and economic crisis.

Political violence
During the late 1970s political violence became a real problem. A number of extremist youth groups on the left, and the Grey Wolves and fundamentalists on the right, fought for control of the streets and the campuses. They had no trouble with recruiting youngsters who had few or no career prospects due to the economic crisis that hit Turkey in the 1970s and to the system that made higher education available to only 20 per cent of the 200,000 potential students who graduated from high school each year.

The struggle between right and left was an unequal one. During the Nationalist Front governments of the years between 1974 and 1977, the police and the security forces had become the exclusive preserve of Türkeş's NAP, and even under Ecevit's government of 1978/9, they had remained heavily infiltrated by fascists who shielded and protected the Grey Wolves. The splinter groups of the left enjoyed no such protection. Not only did Ecevit, as leader of the only left-of-centre party, reject the policies and methods of the extreme left, but also he could not afford to leave the RPP open to accusations of fostering political violence.

The number of victims of political violence rose quickly: from around 230 in 1977 (39 of them the victims of unknown gunmen who opened fire on a 1 May demonstration organized in Taksim Square in Istanbul) to between 1200 and 1500 two years later. What made the political extremism in Turkey so exceptionally violent was the fact that it overlay a traditional culture in which honour and shame, an extreme contrast between one's own family or clan and outsiders, and vendetta played a prominent role. Traditional conflicts were given political connotations. The most notorious case was in Kahramanmaraş in December 1978, when the worst in a series of pogroms of Alevis (Turkish Shi'ites, who generally supported the political left), organized by the Grey Wolves, left more than 100 people dead. Even Ecevit, though he opposed military interference under any circumstances, had no alternative but to declare martial law in 13 provinces (it was later extended to 20 provinces), but he did his best to control the military authorities and presented his measures as 'martial law with a human face' – hardly a likely combination.

Another instance of traditional divisions coalescing with the right–left divide was the founding of the neo-Marxist Kurdish Workers' Party (known as PKK from its Kurdish initials) by Ankara University student Abdullah Öcalan in 1978. Its aim was the establishment of a socialist Kurdish state in the southeast of the country.

In 1979/80, the character of the violence changed in that increasingly it no longer consisted exclusively of reciprocal killings by left-wing and right-wing extremists, but that they started to kill public figures. In May 1980, the deputy chairman of the NAP was killed, followed in July by former prime minister Nihat Erim and Kemal Türkler, former president of DİSK (Confederation of Revolutionary Trade Unions). In spite of the proclamation of martial law the military felt that they lacked a free hand to deal with the problem.

The authorities seemed unable to restore order. Whole neighbourhoods, especially in the squatter towns, came under the control of one or the other of the competing groups and were declared 'liberated areas'. The most famous example was the small Black Sea town of Fatsa, where a left-wing mayor and his supporters officially repudiated the authority of the government and proclaimed an independent Soviet republic. Eventually, this peculiar experiment was ended when the troops were sent in.[6]

The rising tide of political violence was not, however, the only, or even the most important, factor to lead to the breakdown of the political system of the second republic and to armed intervention. This development must be seen against the background of an escalating economic crisis, which had a deeply destabilizing effect on the society. To understand this we must now look at the economic and social developments of the 1960s and 1970s.

The economy: planning and import substitution

The NUC and the RPP had both placed the blame for the economic and financial chaos at the end of the 1950s on the Democrats' lack of planning (which in the case of Menderes had developed into a pathological aversion to the word itself). Both had a natural affinity with the concept of planning. The Republicans had their statist heritage and to the officers, many of whom were or had been staff officers, planning was a way of life. A more planned approach to the economy was also supported by the modern industrial bourgeoisie, whose political representation had been the Freedom Party, which split off from the DP in 1955. This group was still too weak in the early 1960s to impose its own policies, but the developmentalist ideals of the bureaucrats (with their RPP background) and the military gave it support.

The wish for planned and coordinated development found expression in the creation, in Article 129 of the constitution and later in Law 91 of September 1960, of the State Planning Office (*Devlet Planlama Teşkilâtı*), which was given extensive powers in the fields of economic, social and cultural planning. Together with foreign consultants the SPO started to formulate five-year development plans. From the beginning there was a large measure of disagreement, however, on the role and position of the SPO. The RPP took a statist view of its role and saw the SPO policies as binding for all sectors, but the other parties found this unacceptable and İnönü had to make a number of concessions on the SPO's powers.

Under the Justice Party government after 1965, the SPO's influence was curbed further. The second five-year plan, which went into operation in 1968, was declared binding for the state sector, but only indicative for the private sector. Where the RPP, true to its statist traditions, saw the role of the state as one of guidance, the JP as keepers of the DP tradition, saw the state as subservient to private enterprise.

The development policies of the governments of the second republic, almost until the very end, were aimed at the substitution of imports through industrialization. Turkey was still dependent on imports for almost all industrial goods apart from processed foodstuffs, textiles and iron and steel: almost all consumer durables had to come from abroad. On the other hand, the growing wealth of the population during the 1950s had created increased demand for precisely these consumer durables. A greater awareness of the outside world and Western (especially American) lifestyles had given status to the possession of goods like cars, refrigerators and vacuum cleaners.

Apart from direct investment incentives, such as subsidies and tax rebates, successive governments stimulated the creation of a homegrown industry in three main ways: through extensive import restrictions and high tariffs designed to keep out European and American industrial products; through manipulation of the exchange rate (by keeping the rate of the Turkish lira artificially high firms that were allowed to purchase dollars or Deutschmarks from the government were able to buy foreign materials comparatively cheaply); and by creating a buoyant internal market. The latter was done by paying high guarantee prices to farmers (far above the world price) and by allowing industrial workers high wage rises.

As a rule, the import-substituting industrialization took the form of a joint venture, with the foreign company supplying technological know-how (and the necessary licences) and most of the time (part of) the components and raw materials. The Turkish partner supplied (part of) the capital, the workforce, the distribution system and, at least as important, the influential contacts. In the 1960s and 1970s, the army, through the *Ordu Yardımlaşma Kurumu*, the Army Mutual Help Society, the pension fund of the officer corps, became a major investor in the new industries.

The inward orientation and import restrictions saw to it that there was no real competition between the foreign firms and their Turkish partners. There was also very little competition between Turkish producers. In almost every sector oligopolies were established, with two or three rival holding companies each founding one car factory, one firm producing appliances, one soft-drink distribution network, and dividing the market between themselves. Under this cosy arrangement, industries that would never have been able to compete on an open world market made handsome profits on the home front. The new industries were spread very unevenly among the regions, the vast majority being established in the Istanbul area, with smaller concentrations around İzmir and Adana.

In terms of economic growth, the import-substitution strategy was quite successful for some time. After a hesitant start subsequent to the 1960 coup and the period of uncertainty that followed it, the economy picked up in 1962 and between 1963 and 1976 the annual rate of growth averaged 6.9 per cent.

In the industrial sector the role of the state economic enterprises (SEEs) was still important. About 40 per cent of total industrial production came from this sector, though it was far from efficient. In spite of all professions to the contrary, business decisions in the state sector, including the pricing of products, remained politically influenced and together with huge overstaffing (the workforce doubled to 650,000 in the 1960s and 1970s) resulted in heavy losses, culminating in a loss of nine billion Turkish liras for 1977 alone. The state sector's inefficiency also shows in the fact that, while between half and two-thirds of fixed capital investments were in this sector, its share in total value added declined from over half to one-third in this period.

The Achilles heel of this development policy was that new industries were heavily dependent on imports of foreign parts and materials for production, and thus on the availability of foreign reserves to pay for them. This meant that access to these (largely government-held) funds, rather than industrial or commercial qualities, tended to determine whether a firm could survive. Given that Turkey had a persistent balance of trade and balance of payments deficit throughout these two decades (as one would expect with an economy that was industrializing but that was not export-orientated), making available the necessary dollars and Deutschmarks was a major problem. It was partly met by foreign, especially American, aid, which totalled $5.6 billion over 20 years. Increasingly, however, huge transfers from Turkish workers who had moved to Europe covered the deficit. These peaked in 1974 with a total of $1.462 million.[7]

The economic crisis of the later 1970s
It has already been pointed out that, more than the social unrest or even the violence in the streets, it was the growing economic crisis that derailed the governments of the later 1970s.

The combination of a persistent balance of payments deficit and an industry that depended on foreign inputs, and thus on the availability of foreign reserves, made the Turkish economy extremely vulnerable. The oil crisis of 1973/4 led to a quadrupling of the price of oil on the international market. For Turkey, which since the 1950s had become increasingly dependent on oil as a source of energy, this meant a steeply rising import bill, which had to be paid in dollars. By the end of the 1970s, and after a second oil price shock in 1979/80, two-thirds of Turkey's foreign currency earnings went to meeting the oil bill. At the same time the Western market for Turkish products declined because of the recession in Europe. For a little while it was possible to keep up economic growth by depleting the Central Bank's foreign reserves and by using the transfers of the Turkish workers in Germany. These began to decline steeply after 1974, however, as the situation of the workers in Europe deteriorated and at the same time as they lost confidence in the situation in Turkey. Increasingly, they kept their money in Germany.

The National Front coalition governments tried to meet the problem by concluding extremely costly short-term Euro-dollar loans (by the end of the decade more than half of Turkey's debt consisted of this type of loan) and by printing money. They also tried to conserve precious foreign reserves by imposing import restrictions. Oil for industry and for generating electricity became increasingly scarce and by 1979 power cuts of up to five hours a day were the rule, even in mid-winter.

The rising price of energy and the irresponsible financial policies of successive governments fuelled inflation. Inflation had been running at around 20 per cent a year during the early part of the 1970s, but by 1979 it was at 90 per cent and rising. The government tried to keep inflation down by controlling prices through the price-control board (which existed from 1973 to 1980). The result was a huge black market. Another measure to keep down inflation was an artificially high rate of exchange for the Turkish lira. There were a number of devaluations but they always came too late, the result being that the black market was extended to money. Import restrictions imposed to save foreign exchange fuelled the black market even more and gave rise to large-scale smuggling, while the shelves in the shops were emptier and emptier.

It was clear that radical measures were needed to extricate Turkey from its financial and economic quagmire. In 1978 Ecevit's government began negotiations about new credits with the IMF, World Bank and OECD. The negotiations dragged on because of the drastic demands for economic reform made by the creditors, but in July 1979 an agreement was reached that would release $1.8 billion in new credits. This was dependent on the Turkish government introducing a reform package that included abolishing import and export controls; cutting subsidies; freeing interest rates; raising prices; and cutting government expenditure.

When Süleyman Demirel returned to power in October 1979, his new government made implementation of this programme its highest priority. The task was given to the under-secretary for economic affairs in charge of planning, Turgut Özal. In January 1980 he launched the reform package, after which the credits began to arrive. Part of the package was a drastic 48.6 per cent devaluation of the lira. During the spring of 1980, however, it became clear that there was widespread resistance to what was called the 'Chilean solution' (a reference to the policies General Pinochet had introduced in Chile after his coup against President Allende). The continued activity of the unions, and especially DİSK, made it impossible to implement Özal's economic package. Members of DİSK occupied a number of factories between January and April and there were strikes everywhere, often accompanied by clashes with the police or the army.

The end of the second republic

The developments that led to the end of the second republic and to the third military intervention in Turkish politics in 20 years were thus manifold: increasing law and order problems, Kurdish separatism, a political system that seemed completely deadlocked and an economy in tatters. To this was added what seemed to many, including many in the army, the threat of Islamic fundamentalism. The Islamic revolution in Iran in January 1979 encouraged the NSP and other Islamist groups that may also have been receiving assistance from Iran. They were increasingly visible and, on 6 September 1980, held a mass demonstration in Konya. During it they called for a return to the *şeriat*, the Islamic holy law, and refused to sing the Turkish national anthem although, curiously enough, its text had been written in 1921 by Mehmet Akif (Ersoy), a Pan-Islamist poet who is greatly revered in fundamentalist circles.[8]

The fundamentalist threat was generally considered to be the immediate cause of the military intervention, but in all probability it was a mixture of the above-mentioned factors that induced the general staff to take power after they had gradually lost confidence in the politicians' ability to run the country effectively. As we have seen, preparations for a takeover had been started in the summer of 1979 and in December of that year, at a meeting in Istanbul, the country's most senior generals decided to draw up an ultimatum to the politicians (very much in the vein of the ultimatum of 12 March 1971). It was made public on 2 January 1980, but from the point of view of the generals the first six months of 1980, with the endless charade of the presidential elections, showed that the politicians would not listen. At three o'clock in the morning of 12 September 1980, therefore, the Turkish army took power again.

Social change: squatters and 'guest workers'
For most Turkish citizens, the squabbles between the different political parties were a long way off. Their lives were affected by different things: the violence in the streets, of course, but also growing wealth in the 1960s and early 1970s, shortages and price rises thereafter, and industrialization and large scale migration throughout the period.

Turkey's rapid population growth, a lack of opportunities in agriculture, and the attraction of the new industries combined to increase the flow of people from the countryside to the big cities, which had started in the 1950s. Huge numbers of people migrated to Istanbul, Ankara, İzmir and Adana. There, the squatter towns of *gecekondu* (built at night) dwellings, the emergence of which was described in chapter 13, soon assumed gigantic proportions and their growth has continued. By the 1990s over half of the built-up surface of Ankara, the capital, consisted of *gecekondu*s, and over half its inhabitants lived in them.

Although the *gecekondu*s have sometimes been called slums, the description is misleading. The houses were small and primitive, but not more so than the average village house, and they were usually surrounded by a small garden. In the beginning the *gecekondu* neighbourhoods lacked any kind of infrastructure. The first links to the 'official' town usually consisted of bus services (first privately owned, later also municipal) and of postal deliveries. The inhabitants of the neighbourhoods, organized in their own societies, made quite effective use of the competition between the parties before elections to extract promises from local politicians, with the result that gradually the squatter towns were connected to the municipal electricity grid and water supply, the road system and – sometimes – the sewers. The municipalities made repeated but feeble attempts at zoning and often tried to get the squatters to move to newly constructed high-rise buildings, but the supply of housing always lagged behind the demand.

Another reason why the appellation 'slums' is misleading is that, unlike the inhabitants of the slums in major Western cities, who have reached the end of the line and often do not feel part of society any more, the people in the Turkish squatter towns were, and are, upwardly mobile and integration-orientated. Another difference is that the social fabric of the squatter communities on the whole remained quite strong, helped by the fact that the population of a neighbourhood usually consisted of people from one area in the country (even if that area lay 500 miles away). Ties between the squatter town and the original villages remained close, with people going back to marry, for instance, or to invest in land.

As was pointed out earlier, only a minority of the migrants found regular work in the new industries. Many more had to make a living in temporary jobs, as day labourers, street vendors or janitors. As a rule, several members of one household would contribute to the family income. Vast numbers of women from the squatter towns worked as domestics in bourgeois neighbourhoods. Nevertheless, the migrants usually decided to stay in the city, only returning to help with the harvest.

Many people who had left their ancestral village to go to the city left on an even bigger adventure during the 1960s. The first Turks to go to work in Germany (in 1957) were graduates of technical schools on training courses, but from the beginning of the 1960s Turkish workers started to move to Germany in ever-increasing numbers. In the beginning this movement was caused by a 'pull' rather than a 'push' factor. Germany's booming industry had an acute labour shortage from the early 1950s onwards. Large numbers of German men had been killed in the war and the iron curtain made it impossible to recruit migrant workers in Poland, as Germany had done since the late nineteenth century. Hence, it had been recruiting in the poorer Mediterranean regions of Europe (Italy, Yugoslavia and Greece) for some time. In Turkey initial reactions to the

German recruitment drive, which began in earnest after a bilateral German–Turkish agreement was signed in 1961, were rather hesitant. The first to go to Germany were skilled workers from the cities, but later recruitment took place increasingly among new city dwellers who had recently migrated from the countryside (thus establishing a pattern of two-stage migration). Later still, recruitment took place directly in the provincial towns. The numbers tell their own story: in 1962 there were 13,000 Turkish workers in Germany; by 1970 there were 480,000 and, by 1974, the total had reached 800,000. While the main drift of the migration continued to be to Germany, Turkish workers also went to Belgium, the Netherlands, France, Switzerland and Britain. By the end of the 1970s more than 2.5 million Turks were living in western Europe.

At first, the overwhelming majority of the migrants intended to return to their country within a few years. They came alone, without wife or children, stayed in what were often dismal hostels and saved every penny. Gradually, however, the prospect of an impending return to Turkey faded; as life in Europe proved unexpectedly expensive, their expectations (and those of their families) rose and unemployment in Turkey made a return there almost impossible. From the early 1970s onwards, more and more workers moved their families to Germany. After the oil crisis of 1973, when the economic recession hit Europe, regular recruitment in Turkey stopped. The number of Turks in Europe kept on rising, however, as more and more relatives joined their husbands or fathers. Illegal immigration, which had been a feature as early as in the 1960s, continued after 1973. With rising unemployment in Turkey, many people were easy prey for unscrupulous middlemen who arranged, or pretended to arrange, illegal entry into European countries. The illegal workers (euphemistically called *turist* in Turkey) mostly did low-paid menial work without any social security. Their illegal status made them vulnerable to all kinds of pressures. Still, the success stories of those who made good in Germany ensured that for many in Turkey it remained the Promised Land.

The effects of labour migration on Turkey, and especially the Turkish countryside, were many and varied. There was undeniably an injection of wealth, visible in new and grander houses, tractors, cars and appliances (sometimes before electricity had arrived in the village). The emergence of new wealth disturbed power relationships and social systems in the countryside. It also introduced a more materialistic out-look and established new mass consumption patterns. The migration also introduced a new awareness of the outside world, although not necessarily a deeper understanding of it. The migrant communities in Europe tended on the whole to become more rather than less traditional when confronted with the unfamiliar surroundings of an industrial society. This tendency grew stronger when relations between the migrants and the host populations began to deteriorate. When recruitment started, both industries and governments had tried to create a positive image for the migrants (calling them *Gastarbeiter* or 'guest workers' – a term that later acquired extremely negative connotations in the eyes of the migrants themselves), but when unemployment rose after the oil crisis, resentment began to grow among the host populations. This resentment became much stronger in the 1980s.

Trade unions and social security

That so many of the most active and highly skilled workers emigrated was a handicap for the Turkish labour movement. Nevertheless, the 1960s not only saw the emergence of home grown industry, but they also saw the growth of a serious labour movement. The constitution had promised the workers the right to strike and to conduct collective bargaining. In July 1963 a new law spelled out these rights in more detail. The unions were quite successful at defending workers' incomes. The protection of the Turkish market meant that relatively high wage rises could be granted to buy off social unrest, because they could be easily translated into price rises for industrial goods. Real wages in industry rose by approximately 50 per cent in the 1960s and 1970s, something that would have been impossible had Turkish industry been export-orientated and subject to competition from other newly industrializing countries (for instance in the Far East).

It has to be said, however, that these gains were reserved for a limited part of the workforce: the workers in the modern part of the economy with its large industrialized firms. During the 1960s and 1970s they developed into a kind of labour aristocracy. The far larger proportion of the workforce, which worked in small establishments, was largely unorganized and earned much lower wages. The small industrialists' lower profit margins simply did not allow them to offer the kind of wage rises that big industry paid. After 1975, even the bigger employers were no longer in a position to pay real wage increases. Union pressure did not let up, however, and the result was a rising tide of labour unrest, with strikes and lockouts, in the late 1970s.

The number of jobless at that time is very hard to estimate: since there was – and is – no system of unemployment benefits, there is no inducement to register the unemployed. But there are indications that the number of unemployed as a percentage of the labour force, which was relatively stable at around 10 per cent in the 1960s and early 1970s through mass emigration, went up steeply in the later 1970s.

Türk-İş, the confederation of trade unions, under American influence was geared to gaining material benefits for its members. It was politically mixed, with some unions and union leaders supporting the WPT, some the RPP and some the JP. As a rule, the confederation did not interfere in politics, but sought good relations with whoever was in power. In 1967 a number of trade unions led by people connected to the Workers' Party broke away because they rejected the cooperation of *Türk-İş* with Demirel's increasingly rightist government. The actual split occurred over the refusal of *Türk-İş* to support a strike at the glass factories in Istanbul and soon the trade union movement was deeply divided between *Türk-İş* and a new confederation, DİSK (*Devrimci İşçi Sendikaları Konfederasyonu*, or Confederation of Revolutionary Trade Unions). Competition between the two organizations was fierce from the beginning, each competing for the favour of the workers by setting higher wage demands than the other. By the late 1970s *Türk-İş* was estimated to have had between 1 million and 1.3 million members, while DİSK had between 300,000 and 400,000.[9]

The constitution of 1961 had declared Turkey to be a 'social state' (a contemporary reinterpretation of the old Kemalist principle of populism) and during the 1960s the politicians made some efforts to make good this promise and to improve the working and living conditions of the mass of the people. In 1965, the 'Social Securities Society' (*Sosyal Sigortalar Kurumu*) was founded as a first step in the development of a welfare state. It provided insurance for medical care, insurance against work accidents and life insurance. Two years later a new Labour Law replaced the one of 1936. It was extended to cover all wage earners, not only those in establishments with ten employees or more, as had been the case with the older law. The working week was limited to 48 hours and restrictions (but not a ban) on child labour were introduced.

Government employees already had their pension fund and a pension scheme for the self-employed was introduced with the founding of *BaE-Kur* in 1972. Nevertheless, even at the end of this period the coverage of the social security system was still very patchy. Only about 70 per cent of the industrial workforce and about 60 per cent of the self-employed in the towns had any social security. For more than half the Turkish population, agricultural workers and their families, there was no social security at all.

Foreign relations during the second republic

The foreign policies of all governments of the second republic were firmly linked to the principles laid down after the Second World War. Close ties with the United States and an orientation towards the Western democracies remained the cornerstone. The policies of successive governments were aimed at increasing Turkey's strategic value in the eyes of the Western alliance, both to have them remain committed to Turkey's defence and to extract from them military and economic aid. The underlying continuity was punctured, however, by crises over missiles, opium production, Cyprus, human rights and the Armenian question. Furthermore, during this period the policies the foreign policy strategists pursued in Ankara were less and less in tune with public opinion.

Turkey was tied to the United States not only by its membership of NATO, but also by 56 separate agreements, of which three were concluded before 1950, 31 under Menderes and 22 during the early 1960s.[10] An umbrella agreement concluded in 1969 served partly to supplant these agreements and partly to update them. The 1954 treaty on military facilities granted the Americans the right to build military installations and bases in Turkey. The Turkish army met the cost of the building and upkeep of the installations and they remained Turkish territory, but the Americans ran them. From 1957 onwards, Jupiter nuclear missiles were based in Turkey.

During the 1960s there were two contradictory developments: on the one hand the rising cost of weaponry and higher pay for the officer corps made Turkey more dependent on foreign financial assistance; on the other, the new liberal constitution allowed left-wing intellectuals, such as those connected to the journal *Yön* and to the Workers' Party, to criticize Turkey's dependence on America and NATO with increasing vehemence. They protested against the bases and against the prerogatives of the American servicemen: immunity from the Turkish law and law courts while on duty, their own postal service and tax-free imports through the PX stores. These reminded nationalist Turks (and in Turkey many left-wingers were ardent nationalists) of the system of capitulations in force during the Ottoman Empire. During the 1960s and 1970s the cry for an 'independent Turkey' or a non-aligned Turkey (*bağımsız Türkiye*) grew louder and louder, and there were mass demonstrations against visiting ships of the American Sixth Fleet.

Successive Turkish governments generally stayed loyal to the alliance and defended it at home. They were put in a difficult position when developments seemed to show that NATO was an organization that served American strategic interests and not those of Turkey. The first time this happened was in 1962/3. During the negotiations following the Cuban missile crisis President Kennedy gave in to Russian demands that the missiles based in Turkey should be withdrawn in exchange for the USSR not basing missiles in Cuba. This was no great sacrifice since the Jupiter system was obsolete anyway and about to be replaced by the submarine-based Polaris system, but the withdrawal of the missiles gave Turkey the feeling that it was no more than a pawn in the American game.

Another irritation was opium production. By the end of the 1960s hard drugs were beginning to be a major problem in the United States and a sizeable proportion of the opium and heroin used in America was produced in western Anatolia. The American government put pressure on Turkey to ban the growing of poppies, but Demirel's shaky government could not afford to be seen to be giving in to pressure. When democracy was temporarily suspended in 1971, however, Nihat Erim's government did conclude an agreement to ban the growing of poppies after 1972 in exchange for financial help for the peasants. This decision was very unpopular: no other crop could yield the peasants anything like the income derived from opium. Turkey itself did not have a drugs problem, so it was felt that Turkish interests were being subordinated to American ones. Reversing the decision was one of the first things Ecevit did when he came to power in 1974.

Cyprus again

By far the most serious crises in Turkey's foreign relations were linked to the problem of Cyprus. In 1964 President-Archbishop Makarios of Cyprus and his government made moves to change the island's constitution, limiting the autonomy of the Turkish minority. The Turkish population was put under pressure and a number of Turkish villages were besieged. İnönü's government responded by having the air force make demonstration runs over Cyprus and threatening an invasion if Makarios did not back down. It is doubtful whether the Turkish navy at that time had the technical capability to execute such a landing, but in any case it was prevented by American reaction in the form of a letter from President Johnson to Prime Minister İnönü. In it he warned that a Turkish invasion might bring the Soviet Union into the conflict and that NATO countries would not automatically side with Turkey if that were to happen. He also pointed out that he would not permit the use of war *matériel* donated by the USA in any invasion. The letter was leaked to the press and caused a wave of anti-Americanism. Once more it seemed that NATO did not see fit to protect Turkish interests.

The crisis, which had died down in 1964, flared up again in 1967 when the newly installed colonels' junta in Athens encouraged the Greek nationalists in Cyprus to step up the agitation for *enosis*, the union of the island with mainland Greece. The Turks put pressure on the Greek government – for a few days in November war seemed imminent, but the junta backed down and the crisis was again defused. But when the Greek junta was in its death throes in 1974, it engineered a *coup d'état* against

Makarios in Cyprus by the Cypriot national guard, which went on to proclaim *enosis*. Ecevit's government in Ankara demanded intervention by the powers that had guaranteed the independence and the constitutional order of Cyprus in 1960 (Turkey, Great Britain and Greece). Ecevit was determined to show that Turkey could act independently and when the other two countries refused to act he ordered military intervention by the Turkish armed forces alone. Turkish troops landed in northern Cyprus on 20 July and established a bridgehead around Kyrenia (Girne). Two days later a ceasefire was agreed, but when communal violence on Cyprus continued, the troops began a second offensive on 14 August, during which about 40 per cent of the island was brought under Turkish control.

After these actions (which Turkish government propaganda called *barış harekâtı* or 'peace operations') the island was to all intents and purposes partitioned. The Greeks living in the north and the Turks living in the south fled their homes. Some Greek villagers were driven out at gunpoint by the army. All of the refugees had to be resettled in the other sector. In 1983 a formally independent Turkish Republic of Northern Cyprus (*Kuzey Kıbrıs Türk Cumhuriyeti*) was proclaimed, though only Turkey recognized it.

In the eyes of the vast majority of Turks Ecevit had successfully protected the rights, and perhaps saved the lives, of the Turkish minority in Cyprus, but internationally the action put Turkey in an isolated position. The USA declared an arms embargo, which was only gradually lifted after 1978. In reaction, the Turkish government closed down a number of American installations. In the United Nations there were consistent majorities for calls for a withdrawal of Turkish troops and reunification of Cyprus.

Attempts at reorientation
There were attempts to lessen dependency on the American connection by developing ties with Europe, the Soviet Union and, to a lesser extent, the Islamic world. Turkey had become an associated member of the European Community in 1964. The agreement, signed a year earlier, foresaw a preparatory phase (in two stages) of 17 years, after which Turkey would be in a position to apply for full membership. While the road to membership proved considerably longer than foreseen (and perhaps endless), economic relations blossomed and the EC replaced the USA as Turkey's most important trading partner in the 1960s. Ecevit was particularly keen to reorient Turkish foreign policy towards Europe (the EC and the Scandinavian countries ruled by socialists), which made him extremely unpopular in Washington. Relations with the Islamic, and

especially the Arab, world were always problematic because of Turkey's relations with Israel. The Six Day War of 1967 resulted in a surge of support for the Palestinians among the Turkish left, but government policy continued as before. The oil crisis of 1973/4, which brought such difficulty for the Turkish economy and such wealth to the Gulf countries, encouraged the government to explore the possibilities of Turkish–Arab cooperation. This was also desired by the ministers of Erbakan's NSP for ideological reasons, but the policy yielded very little. Turkey's industry was not export-orientated and there was little tradition of trade with the Arab peninsula, so schemes for joint ventures (Turkish know-how and Arab money) nearly all came to nothing. Real development in this sphere took place only after the second oil price shock in 1979/80.

Armenian terrorism
A separate headache for the Turkish Foreign Ministry, and the government in general, was the emergence in the 1970s of Armenian terrorism, aimed primarily at Turkish diplomats. The first attack was on the Turkish consul-general in Los Angeles (a city with a large Armenian community) on 27 January 1973. This seems to have been an individual act of revenge by a survivor of the genocide of 1915, but in 1975 the 'Armenian Secret Army for the Liberation of Armenia' was founded in Beirut. Its founder was Bedros Ohanessian, a 28-year-old Armenian from Mosul in Iraq who used the pseudonym Hagop Hagopian. In the following ten years the ASALA murdered more than 30 Turkish diplomats all over the world and wounded many more.[11] It also carried out terrorist attacks on travellers at Orly airport near Paris and at Ankara's Esenboğa airport (both in 1982) and on Turkish tourist and airline offices. The ASALA was not motivated only by revenge for the 1915 killings. It also demanded Turkish recognition that genocide had been perpetrated and the establishment of an Armenian state in northeast Anatolia. From the beginning, the ASALA had close connections with Palestinian terrorist groups (which trained its men) and with the drugs trade (which supplied it with money to buy arms). Until the Israeli invasion of Lebanon in 1982, its headquarters were in Beirut. Thereafter, it seems to have been based in Cyprus.

At the same time as the ASALA was murdering diplomats, the Armenian communities in France and the United States (the two countries with by far the largest Armenian communities) pressed their governments for recognition of the 'Armenian genocide' of 1915. In both countries they had considerable success, which soured Turkish relations with the French government of President Mitterrand and with the United States Congress.

PART IV

The Third Republic:
Turkey since 1980

15 · The State of Kenan Evren and the Economy of Turgut Özal

The coup and its aftermath: uprooting the existing political system
The first communiqué read in the name of the junta at 04.30 hours on the morning of 12 September 1980 announced that the armed forces had taken over political power because the state organs had stopped functioning.[1] It also said that parliament had been dissolved, that the cabinet had been deposed and that the immunity of the members of the national assembly (the parliament) had been lifted. Immediately afterwards, all political parties and the two radical trade union confederations (the socialist DİSK and the ultra-nationalist MİSK – *Milliyetçi İşçi Sendikaları Konfederasonyu*, or Confederation of Nationalist Trade Unions) were suspended. The political party leaders were arrested, with the exception of Alpaslan Türkeş who had gone underground but who turned himself in two days later. A state of emergency was declared throughout the country and no one was allowed to leave.

Almost from the start it was clear both that the military envisaged an eventual return to a democratic system (an eight-point scenario for this was announced on 1 November though, significantly, without a timetable) and that they intended to enforce radical changes in the political system before handing power back to the civilians. In many ways, the changes they wrought consisted of undoing the work of their predecessors, the perpetrators of the coup of 27 May 1960. Significantly, 27 May was abolished as a national holiday, along with 1 May.[2]

The generals saw their task as saving democracy from the politicians and as purging the political system. In this, they went much further than on previous occasions. Not only were the parliamentarians sent home and the parties abolished, but also all mayors and municipal councils (over 1700 in all) were dismissed. All power was concentrated in the hands of the military, more specifically in those of the National Security Council headed by the chief of staff, General Kenan Evren, who was officially declared head of state on 14 September. A week later, the NSC, which now consisted of its military members only, appointed a 27-member cabinet under retired admiral Bülent Ulusu, but it was composed of bureaucrats and retired officers and there were no active or even former politicians among its members. Its only functions were to advise the NSC and execute its decisions, and the NSC reserved the right to fire individual ministers. The NSC acted not only through the cabinet but also through regional and local commanders, who, under martial law, were given very wide-ranging powers. They were put in charge of education, the press, chambers of commerce and trade unions, and they did not hesitate to use their powers. Especially in Istanbul, the centre of intellectual life and of the press, this led to a continuous series of closures of newspapers and arrests of journalists and editors. Even the venerable *Cumhuriyet* (Republic), founded in 1924 at the instigation of Atatürk himself, was closed at one time.

General Evren made it very clear that as far as he was concerned there was no place for the former politicians in the Turkey of the future. Demirel and Ecevit were released in October. Erbakan and Türkeş were brought to trial (on charges of planning to change the constitutional order of the Turkish Republic), but in both cases a verdict of not guilty was eventually returned. In June 1981 all public discussion of political matters was prohibited. In 1982, an NSC decree forbade the old politicians, in almost Orwellian fashion, to discuss publicly the past, the present or the future. The old parties, which had been suspended after the coup, were officially dissolved on 16 October and their possessions were confiscated. In their zeal to enforce a radical break with the past, the generals even tried to destroy that past itself: the archives of the parties, including those of the Republican People's Party of the last 30 years (the earlier parts had already been confiscated by the Democrat Party government in the 1950s and their whereabouts are unknown) disappeared and were probably destroyed.

Suppression of terrorism – and of dissent
In the meantime, a wave of arrests swept the country. As we have seen, the *coup d'état* had been prepared for over a year before it actually took place and lists of 'undesirables' had no doubt been drawn up beforehand. In the first six weeks after the coup 11,500 people were arrested; by the end of 1980 the number had grown to 30,000 and after one year 122,600 arrests had been made. By September 1982, two years after the coup, 80,000 were still in prison, 30,000 of them awaiting trial.[3]

The positive effect of this policy was that the number of politically motivated terrorist attacks diminished by over 90 per cent. Although still strongly biased against the left, the anti-terrorist campaign was somewhat more even-handed than it had been during the period between 1971 and 1973: many members of Türkeş's murderous street gangs, the 'Idealists' (*Ülkücüler*) commonly known as the Grey Wolves, were also arrested.

The negative side was that it was achieved at great human and social cost. It was not only suspected terrorists who were hunted down and arrested. Respectable trade unionists, politicians, university professors, teachers, journalists and lawyers, in short anyone who had expressed even vaguely leftist (or in some cases Islamist) views before September 1980, was liable to get into trouble. The universities were put under tight centralized control through the establishment of the *Yüksek Öğretim Kurulu* (Higher Education Authority), which directly appointed all rectors and deans.[4] Late in 1982 more than 300 academics were dismissed, followed by a second wave of dismissals early in 1983. Many others resigned of their own accord because those fired also lost their pensions and the right ever again to hold a job in the public sector.

Both during the interrogation of detainees directly after their arrest and later during their imprisonment, torture was widespread and often applied as a matter of course. The international human rights organization Amnesty International repeatedly drew attention to the widespread use of torture and its sometimes fatal effects and Turkish governments, especially the civilian cabinets after 1983, under international pressure made moves to improve their country's record in this respect. A number of officers and policemen were brought to trial. The civilian government's grip on the security apparatus however, remained tenuous. Torture has been endemic primarily during the period during which people can be held in custody before charges are brought. After the coup this period was 90 days, but during the 1980s and 1990s the problem was recognized and the period of detention was gradually brought down.

Apart from the huge number of individual cases, a number of mass trials were organized against the *Millî Selâmet Partisi* (NSP), the *Milliyetçi Hareket Partisi* (NAP), the WPT, DİSK, the extreme left-wing organization *Devrimci Sol* and the Kurdish PKK.

In most cases the trials were held before military courts and under martial law. All in all, over the two years following the coup nearly 3600 death sentences were pronounced, though only 20 were actually carried out.[5] There were also tens of thousands of lesser sentences.

The new constitution
As far as the reconstruction of political life was concerned, the military more or less followed the procedures of 1960/1. A consultative assembly (*danışma meclisi*) of 160 members met for the first time on 23 October 1981. Its members were appointed by the NSC, 40 of them

directly, 120 after nomination by the new governors, who had themselves been appointed by the military. It elected a 15-member constitutional committee, headed by Professor Orhan Aldıkaçtı, which
produced a first draft for a new constitution on 17 July 1982.

The document was in many respects a reversal of the constitutional
developments of 1960. It concentrated power in the hands of the
executive and increased the powers of the president and the National
Security Council. It also limited the freedom of the press, the freedom of
trade unions (banning political strikes, solidarity strikes and national
strikes) and the rights and liberties of the individual. The usual rights
and liberties (such as freedom of speech and freedom of association)
were included in the constitution, but it was stipulated that they could be
annulled, suspended or limited on the grounds of a whole series of
considerations, including the national interest, public order, national
security, danger to the republican order and public health.

The new constitution was subjected to a referendum on 7 November
1982. Approval or rejection was linked directly to the figure of General
Evren because a temporary article of the constitution (during the
transition from military to civilian rule) stipulated that he would automatically become president for a seven-year term if the constitution were
adopted. Evren was still quite popular with the mass of the population for his
suppression of political terror, so this linkage was supposed to engender a
certain enthusiasm for an issue, the constitution, which otherwise would have
been rather abstract in the eyes of the man in the street.

Nevertheless, the generals took no chances. Voting was made
compulsory and anyone who chose not to – or neglected to – vote, not
only had to pay a fine but also lost his or her right to vote for five years.
Furthermore, a decree of 20 October banned all criticism of the
constitution, its temporary articles or of the speeches General Evren
made in favour of a yes vote. Thus prepared, the referendum yielded the
expected result – a 'yes' vote of 91.4 per cent. Only in the Kurdish
southeast were relatively high percentages of 'no' votes recorded.

Democracy on a narrow road
After the adoption of the constitution and Evren's installation as
president, the generals duly embarked on the next stage of their political
reconstruction programme. In March a new Law on Political Parties was
promulgated. Politicians who had been active before September 1980
were banned from politics for ten years. New parties could now be
formed, but their founders needed the approval of the National Security
Council. Students, teachers and civil servants were barred from party
membership and the new parties were not allowed to form roots in

society because they were not allowed to found women's or youth branches, to develop links with trade unions or to open branches in villages. Some 15 parties were founded, but the military deemed 12 of them unacceptable, even after several changes had been made to the lists of founders. The obvious successors to Demirel's Justice Party (the 'Great Turkey Party' and the 'Party of the True Path') and to the Republican People's Party (the 'Social Democrat Party') were among those banned. In the end, the three parties that were allowed to take part in the elections of 6 November 1983 were:

- The *Milliyetçi Demokrasi Partisi* (Party of Nationalist Democracy), a party closely identified with and supported by the generals and led by retired general Turgut Sunalp;
- The *Halkçı Partisi* (Populist Party), led by Necdet Calp, the party that came closest to the traditional Kemalist wing of the RPP; and
- The *Anavatan Partisi* (Motherland Party), led by Turgut Özal, the man behind the economic reform programme launched in 1979/80, who had served also as 'super minister' in charge of the economy under the military regime until he was forced out of office as a result of financial scandals.

The military leadership came out fairly clearly in support of the PND and to a lesser extent the PP. Ironically, this turned out to be one of Özal's main assets. It enabled him to pose as the only genuine democrat and thus to attract the votes of those who, after three years, wanted the military out of politics. In the elections his MP scored an overwhelming victory, polling over 45 per cent of the vote. The PP did reasonably well to poll 30 per cent, while the generals' party, the PND, came a very poor third with only slightly over 23 per cent. The new electoral system was heavily weighted in favour of large parties because the lawmakers had seen the disproportionate influence of the small parties before 1980 as one of the reasons for the breakdown of the system. As a result, the 45 per cent gave the MP an absolute majority in the new assembly.

After this surprise result, Özal duly became prime minister, although the military, now represented as the 'presidential council' (as the NSC had become after the elections) kept a close watch. The new cabinet became known as the 'cabinet of engineers'. Özal himself had been trained as an engineer (like Demirel before him) and there were nine others in the cabinet.

The MP, on which the new government depended for support, was a strange coalition of ideological currents and interest groups that had joined the party partly because they had nowhere else to go under the

military's restrictive policies. The party attracted the support of the old
Justice Party, which itself had been a coalition of the modern industrialized bourgeoisie, the farmers and the small-time businessmen of
Anatolia, of the fundamentalist National Salvation Party and of the
fascist Nationalist Action Party.

Turgut Özal's personality was crucial to the party; indeed, it is
doubtful whether the coalition would have kept together for long without
him. He had a foot in both camps: he had been a successful manager in
private industry in the 1970s and was very well connected in big business
circles, which liked his liberalization of the economy. On the other hand,
he was known to have connections with the *Nakşibendi* order of
dervishes and his brother Korkut had been a leading member of the NSP
(Turgut Özal himself had at one time tried to become a representative
for that party, too). Özal was to prove adept at playing off the factions
within the MP against each other.

Above all, like Demirel he was the kind of politician with whom the
average Turk could identify: he hailed from Malatya, a provincial town
in a backward area and he was a self-made man, whose own career
embodied the hope and ambition of countless peasants, squatters and
small traders and other self employed, whom he could address in their
own language. His election slogan, which depicted this section of society
as the *orta direk* (centre pole of a tent, in other words a pillar of society),
was devised to flatter them.

Gradual liberalization

Under Özal, the slow process of further democratization (or of
'broadening the road') went on. However much Özal might have
cooperated with the junta, he was determined to re-establish the primacy
of civilian politics over the military. Before the municipal elections of
March 1984 the MP majority in the assembly voted to allow some of the
parties that had been banned the year before to participate. This was in
part a stratagem to divide the opposition (which opposed the move), but
it would also hurt the MP. The results of the local elections were as
follows: The MP did only marginally less well than five months earlier,
polling 41.5 per cent. Second place was taken by the new *Sosyal
Demokrat Parti* (Social Democrat Party) led by Professor Erdal İnönü,
the son of the late İsmet Pasha, with 23.5 per cent. Third came the new
Doğru Yol Partisi (Party of the True Path), which everyone knew to be
Demirel's party, although, with Demirel himself still being banned from
political life, other politicians were fronting it. It polled 13.5 per cent.
The *Refah Partisi* (Welfare Party), which was a reincarnation of
Erbakan's National Salvation Party, received 4.5 per cent of the vote.

The two other parties that had participated in the 1983 national elections were now clearly shown up as artificial constructions, with the PP polling less than 9 per cent and the PND only 7 per cent.

The elections created a very strange political landscape in which the opposition parties in parliament had clearly lost their legitimacy, while a number of parties that demonstrably had a sizeable portion of the electorate behind them were not represented on a national level at all. On the left, this problem was solved when the Populist Party and the Social Democrat Party merged in November 1985, but at the same time a new challenger for the inheritance of the old Republican People's Party emerged with the founding of the *Demokratik Sol Partisi* (Party of the Democratic Left), which was led from behind the scenes by Bülent Ecevit, but fronted by his wife, Rahsan, who became party chairwoman. The Ecevits rejected any resurrection of the old RPP, depicting the SPP as elitist and old fashioned. Instead, they favoured starting from scratch with a new party, the PDL, which they tried to position as the only true workers' party. In May 1986, the leadership of the PND drew its conclusions from the election result and dissolved the party. Most of its representatives joined the MP though some preferred the PTP. In December 18 members of İnönü's faction deserted to Ecevit's PDL, thus giving that party representation in parliament too.

The return of the old guard
In the meantime, the old political leaders themselves were casting an increasingly long shadow over political life, not only by running a number of parties from behind the scenes, but also by making political statements (still officially illegal). Özal decided to accept their challenge. He announced a referendum on a change in the constitution, which would allow the old politicians to take part in politics once more. At the same time, he and the MP actively campaigned against any such return. In the referendum (on 6 September 1987) he lost by the narrowest of margins: 50.24 per cent 'yes' against 49.76 per cent 'no'.

The result of the referendum led Özal to announce early national elections, to be held in November 1987. He had one very good reason for doing this: over two million people who had not voted in the constitutional referendum of 1982 would not be eligible to vote until 1988. They might reasonably be expected to vote for the opposition. Before the elections, the MP again altered the election law. The electoral system already included provincial and national thresholds. A party that did not pass the threshold in a given province lost all its votes in that province, and they were proportionally distributed between the larger parties. Now the d'Hont system of proportional representation was tinkered with again in favour of the largest parties; this way the MP managed to retain its absolute majority in the national assembly, even though, in the elections of 29 November it polled only 36.3 per cent. The SPP did rather well. Its leader, Erdal İnönü, was generally considered a nice and honest man, but a disastrous politician, so it came as a surprise when a clever, hard election campaign, built around the symbol of a squeezed lemon (to indicate the position of the majority of the population after seven years of a 'stabilization programme'), earned the SPP 24.8 per cent. Demirel's PTP came third with 19.2 per cent. All the other parties failed to pass the threshold; Ecevit's PDL did best with 8.5 per cent. On the right and left the new politicians (Özal and İnönü) seemed to have beaten off the challenge of the old guard (Demirel and Ecevit). As the future would show, however, these two old warhorses were down, but not out.

The year 1987 saw a further broadening of the political spectrum with radical and 'green' parties being founded. They attempted to put issues like care for the environment and women's and gay rights on the political agenda, but in a country such as Turkey these were bound to remain playthings for members of the elite. The more traditional left, still in exile in Europe, also showed signs of life. On 6 October the old Turkish Communist Party, now led by Nabi Yağcı (better known under his *nom de guerre* Haydar Kutlu) and the reconstituted Workers' Party of Turkey, led by Behice Boran, merged at a meeting in Brussels to form the United Communist Party of Turkey (*Türkiye Birleşmiş Komünist Partisi*). Only four days later, Prof. Boran died and was succeeded by Nihat Sargın.

Articles 141 and 142 of the penal code still made communist politics illegal in Turkey, but Prime Minister Özal hinted that the restrictions might be lifted. The leaders of the UCPT, Kutlu and Nihat Sargın, decided to test the waters and they returned to Turkey on 11 November. On their arrival at the airport of Ankara, they were immediately arrested, despite being accompanied by a planeload of journalists and Euro-parliamentarians. The arrests were probably ordered not by the government but by the army. It was one of the signs of increasing friction between the military leaders and Özal, which had already come to light in June when the prime minister overturned the military hierarchy by appointing General Torumtay, and not the senior general Öztorun, as new chief of staff.

The decline of the MP

At the MP party congress of June 1988, a young man armed with a pistol made an attempt to kill Özal as he was making a speech from the rostrum, apparently for personal reasons. Özal suffered only a sore thumb and remained master of the situation. Less than a year after the national elections, and for reasons that are not altogether clear, he decided to hold another referendum, this time on the relatively trivial question of whether the 1989 municipal elections should be held earlier. He linked his personal prestige to the question, saying that he would consider resigning if he did not get a majority 'yes' vote. When the referendum was held, on 25 September, the result was a clear defeat for Özal (65 per cent 'no' against 35 per cent 'yes'). Nevertheless, the prime minister stayed on, declaring that 35 per cent was only slightly less than the 36.3 per cent the MP had gained in the last elections and that his power base was therefore still intact.

When the local elections were held (at their scheduled time) in March 1989, the results showed that support for the MP had been severely eroded. The SPP now came out on top, with 28.2 per cent of the vote. The PTP came second, with 25.6 per cent and the MP managed only third place with 21.9 per cent. Again Özal had staked his position as prime minister on the outcome, and again he stayed on regardless of the result, even announcing – to the fury of the opposition – that he intended to stand as presidential candidate when President Evren's term came to an end in November 1989. The opposition boycotted the session of the assembly in which the new president was elected, but the MP's majority assured Turgut Özal of his election as the eighth president of the Turkish Republic, only the second civilian (after Bayar) to hold that post.

The main reason why the popularity of Özal and his party declined was undoubtedly continuing high inflation (which was back at its pre-1980 level of around 80 per cent) and the erosion in purchasing power it had caused. The average wage earner's purchasing power had declined by 47 per cent since 1980. Another reason was the nepotism and corruption that surrounded the regime. It is undoubtedly true that the MP had brought a new dynamism to both the economy and the administration. The new men Özal had brought in, often with a background in business, many of them with American or German management degrees, had gained a reputation for 'getting things done', which contrasted sharply with the almost total paralysis of the governments of the later 1970s. The debit side was that, like his contemporaries in office Ronald Reagan and Margaret Thatcher (both of whom he greatly admired), Özal believed in an unrestricted capitalist free-for-all. As in the United States and the UK, only more so, this resulted in a number of business scandals. Over the years, a whole series of MP ministers and party leaders were forced to resign because they turned out to be involved in these scandals. Increasingly, the Özal family itself was criticized for nepotism and corruption in its business activities, which ranged from commercial television to airlines and imports of Jaguar cars. When one of the president's sons made vast sums of money on the Istanbul stock exchange, dealing in stocks of firms that were given government contracts soon afterwards, there was a suspicion that more than just foresight was involved. After the 1989 elections, Özal countered some of the criticism by removing his family members from the cabinet.

His majority in the assembly meant that the opposition parties did not unduly worry Özal. His main problem was with factionalism within the MP, which increased when the party's standing in the polls went down (hitting its lowest point of only 8 per cent early in 1990). In 1988, the Islamist faction and the ultra-nationalist faction in the party had reached an accord, which they publicized as the 'Holy Alliance' (*Kutsal İttifak*). This had enabled them to gain a majority of the seats on the party central committee, where Minister of State Keçeciler from the fundamentalist wing was their main spokesman. The liberal wing of the party, which represented the modern business sector, was led by Mesut Yılmaz, who sat in the cabinet as foreign minister, but resigned in February 1990 because of Özal's continued interference in foreign policy matters.

When Turgut Özal was elected president, he appointed Yıldırım Akbulut, a political (and intellectual) nonentity with a long history of service to the party, as his successor as prime minister. It was clear to everyone, however, that real control lay with the president. At the same time, Özal began to inch away from the 'Holy Alliance' and strengthen the MP's liberal wing. The president's influential wife Semra supported the liberals (openly smoking cigars and drinking whisky to make her point). Against fierce opposition from the alliance and even from members of his own family, Özal forced through the appointment of his wife as chairwoman of the crucial Greater Istanbul branch of the MP in April 1991. At the same time, Mesut Yılmaz bounced back and with the support of the president took the position both of party leader and (on 17 June 1991) of prime minister from Akbulut.

Coupled with this edging away from the conservatives between 1989 and 1991 were further liberalizing reforms. One suspects that this partial change in policy may have been inspired by the realization on Özal's part that with first the 'perestroika' and then the disintegration of the Soviet bloc the left was no longer a threat (if, indeed, it ever had been) and that the Islamic political movements that were gathering strength in many parts of the Arab world and in the Turkic republics of Central Asia might be more dangerous. The increasing Islamic militancy in Turkey itself may well have given rise to concern, even to a government as sympathetic to religion as that of the MP. It certainly worried the army, which more than once issued thinly veiled criticism of the government and admonished it to guard Atatürk's secular legacy.

The Hearths of the Enlightened

Many in the MP, including Özal, were influenced in their ideas by the ideology of the *Aydınlar Ocağı*, the 'Hearths of the Enlightened', an organization founded in 1970 by influential people from the business world, the universities and politics. Its aim was to break the monopoly of left-wing intellectuals on the social, political and cultural debate in Turkey. It held seminars and sponsored publications, proposing solutions for all kinds of questions in the realms of culture, education, social life and economics.[6] The system worked out by its leading ideologue and chairman, İbrahim Kafesoğlu, was called the Turkish–Islamic Synthesis (*Türk İslam Sentezi*). Its basic tenet was that Islam held a special attraction for the Turks because of a number of (supposedly) striking similarities between their pre-Islamic culture and Islamic civilization. They shared a deep sense of justice, monotheism and a belief in the immortal soul, and a strong emphasis on family life and morality. The mission of the Turks was a special one, to be the 'soldiers of Islam'. According to this theory, Turkish culture was built on two pillars: a 2500-year-old Turkish element and a 1000-year-old Islamic element.

In the late 1970s, this ideology had become very popular on the political right, in the National Salvation Party, but even more in the Nationalist Action Party of Turkey. Notwithstanding the secularist traditions of the Turkish officer corps, the Turkish–Islamic Synthesis also appealed to prominent military leaders, among them general/president Kenan Evren. The army had been conditioned to see socialism and communism as Turkey's most deadly foes and it saw indoctrination with a mixture of fierce nationalism and a version of Islam friendly to the state as an effective antidote. It is no coincidence that it was under the military government after 1980 that 'religion and ethics' became part of the basic curriculum of all schools. This religious teaching was exclusively Sunni in content, and patriotism and love for parents, the state and the army (in the shape of the Turkish 'Tommy Atkins'–*Mehmetçik*) was presented as a religious duty. After 1983, the synthesis became a guiding principle in Özal's MP. There it was linked to a strong belief in technological innovation to catch up with the West (or, in Özal's phrase, 'to skip an age').[7]

The growing influence of unofficial Islam

From 1984 onwards the press, both Kemalist and socialist-oriented, constantly drew attention to the growth of Islamic currents as manifested in the building of new mosques; the enormous growth in the number of *imam-hatip* (preacher) schools, whose graduates were now allowed to enter university; the growing religious content of school books and of the state-controlled radio and television; the growing number of Islamic publications and bookshops and incidents during the month of fasting, *Ramazan*, during which people who were smoking or drinking were attacked. The fiercest criticism was reserved for the explicit way in which members of the cabinet took part in religious ceremonies. All these developments were seen as so many attempts to undermine the secular character of the state, but legally and institutionally Turkey remained a secular republic.

In the late 1980s, the debate about secularism concentrated on one issue in particular: the ban on wearing a *türban* (a scarf that completely covers a woman's hair) in public buildings, especially in the universities. Islamist students, most of them female, agitated against this ban. The MP, whose 'Holy Alliance' wing sympathized with the agitators, passed a law that would allow the wearing of a scarf, but President Evren referred it to the constitutional court, which declared the law unconstitutional. Finally, in December 1989, a decree was issued that lifted the ban and left it to the rectors of the universities to decide whether to allow the wearing of the *türban*. But the debate left much tension and bitterness and in 1990 fundamentalists murdered two prominent secularists, Professor Muammer Aksoy (the president of the Turkish Law Society), and Bahriye Üçok, both members of the SPP.

In the early 1990s the polarization between secularists and Islamists continued apace. On the side of the Islamists, other more radical groups besides Erbakan's *Refah Partisi* were active, such as that of the followers of the 'Black Voice', Hoca Cemalettin Kaplan, a cleric who propagated the establishment of an Islamic state from Germany, where he lived, using the methods earlier employed with such success by the Iranian leader Ayatollah Khomeini and pronouncing himself caliph in the process. In the mid-1980s, when the memories of Khomeini's campaign to bring down the shah were still fresh, Kaplan for some time was taken quite seriously, but his movement never developed mass appeal. Other more secretive groups that operated in Turkey were the İBDA (*İslamî Büyük Doğu Akıncıları* or 'Raiders of the Islamic Great East') and the *Hizbullah* (Party of God).

In January 1993 a car bomb killed Turkey's most famous living journalist, Uğur Mumcu, who had reported extensively on the connections of the fundamentalists with Iran and Saudi Arabia. This last murder especially brought the secularists out onto the streets. The public's indignation not only concerned the murders themselves, but also the seemingly half-hearted attempts of the police and the state prosecutors to find the killers. Feeling themselves threatened in their way of life by the Islamists, many former liberals and even socialists among

Turkey's intellectuals reacted by reconverting to classic Kemalism in the early 1990s.

Sunni-Alevi tensions

The polarization between the Sunni majority and the Alevi minority, which had traditionally supported secular politics, also increased. Alevis felt increasingly threatened by the militant Sunni movements and some Alevis decided to make a stand for secularism and for the rights of non-believers. The occasion was the Alevi Pir Sultan Abdal festival in Sivas on 2 July 1993, where a speech by the writer Aziz Nesin (who was involved in the translation of parts of Salman Rushdie's *Satanic Verses* into Turkish), in which he said that he personally did not believe in the Qur'an, was used by local fundamentalists to inflame the feelings of the Sunni community. Spurred on by the Islamist mayor of Sivas, a crowd set fire to a hotel, burning to death 36 Alevi singers and writers and a Dutch female anthropology student. Again the state took up an ambivalent position. Those who had incited the crowd to violence (and who were clearly visible on videos shot by the police) were prosecuted, but at the same time the prosecutor asked for an investigation of Aziz Nesin, who was accused of provocation. Under threat from extremist Sunni currents, the Alevis, both in Turkey and in Europe, increasingly identified themselves primarily along religious, rather than political lines. This showed in the increasing number and strength of Alevi organizations, whose growth coincided with the erosion of the traditionally Alevi-supported parties, notably the RPP. That tensions between the Alevis and the Sunni majority were on the rise was demonstrated late in 1994 when Alevis attacked a commercial television station after a quizmaster made some derogatory remarks and, more seriously, on 12 March 1995, when an attack on a teahouse in the Alevi district of Gaziosmanpaşa in Istanbul led to widespread rioting. The area calmed down only after the army had replaced the police (whom the Alevis deeply distrusted) in the streets.

An Islamic current that grew quickly in importance in the early 1990s was that of *Hoca* Fethullah Gülen, the leader of the modernist wing of the *Nurcu* movement. This was not a political movement, but one that promoted its ideas primarily through education. Fethullah had built up a large network of schools, high schools and even universities that sought to further the adoption of Western technology coupled with Islamic morals. The network had spread to Central Asia and to the Balkans as well, and it possessed its own media, such as the newspaper *Zaman* (Time) and the television channel *Samanyolu* (Milky Way). Fethullah Gülen emphatically supported the secular state and while his relations with the Islamist Welfare Party had been strained, he had become very influential in other political circles, such as the MP and the PTP, whose leaders actively courted him.

Özal's final years: further democratization
In the period from 1989 to 1991 (which was of course dominated to a large extent by the Gulf crisis, of which more anon), the government embarked on a gradual liberalization of the political system. In April 1989 a number of reforms were announced, the most important being a reduction (from 15 days to 24 hours) of the period people could remain in police custody without being charged – which was when most torture took place. The measures, however, got no further than their announcement. More effective were those actually taken two years later, in March and April 1991. The cabinet introduced a package of constitutional amendments that dealt partly with the political system (enlargement of the assembly, direct presidential elections, lowering the voting age to 18), but also partly with human rights. At the government's request the assembly decided to allow the use of the Kurdish language in private and it approved the deletion of Articles 141, 142 and 163 (which banned politics on the basis of class or religion) from the penal code. These restrictions, however, remained part of the constitution.[8] This, among other things, led to the rescinding of the ban on the DİSK trade unions confederation after 11 years (on 17 July). Only the use of terrorism to foster political ideals was now an offence. It has to be said, though, that the new anti-terrorism law, which was adopted at the same time, defined the concept of 'terrorism' very broadly. Under article 8 of the new law verbal or written statements could also be regarded as an act of terrorism. In following years countless trade unionists, lawyers, human rights activists, journalists and writers would be prosecuted on the basis of this article.

The elections of 1991: Demirel's return to office
There had been speculation over early elections for some time and the opposition parties had pointed out over and over again that the government's majority in the assembly was built on a highly inequitable election law and that, anyway, every poll showed it had lost most of its support. That elections were impending was clear when generous (and irresponsible) wage increases for government employees and high guarantee prices for agriculture were announced. The elections were held on 20 October 1991.

As expected, the MP's main rival, Demirel's PTP, won the elections with 27 per cent of the vote. To everyone's surprise, however, the MP was not far behind with 24 per cent, a result at least twice as good as that predicted by most polls in 1990/1. The SPP had a disappointing result with 20 per cent of the vote. This included the votes for the Kurdish *Halkın Emek Partisi* (People's Labour Party – PLP) whose candidates had contested the elections on the SPP slate because the PLP could not participate, not having candidates in every province. Of the other parties, Erbakan's *Refah Partisi* did best, with 17 per cent, but this was due to a tactical alliance with the ultra-nationalists of Türkeş. If this was taken into account, the support of the far right did not show much growth.

Before the elections, both opposition leaders had made it known that they would seek the impeachment of President Özal if they won the elections. After the elections this subject was quietly dropped and the president stayed on. Relations between him and his cabinet were strained from the start because the parties that supported Demirel's new cabinet were united first and foremost by their desire to dismantle the heritage of the 1980 coup. The new government's programme bore a very liberal stamp and promised constitutional change and more academic freedom, freedom of the press, democratization and respect for human rights (thus in fact continuing the liberalization Özal had already set in motion).

During its first months the new cabinet enjoyed a veritable honey-moon with the press and public opinion, but it was not to last. Six months later the cabinet was beleaguered. It had taken a few 'confidence-building measures' soon after coming to office, such as the closing down of Eskişehir prison, the most notorious political prison in Turkey, but its liberalization package foundered on stubborn opposition from the right wing of the PTP. To prevent the package from being defeated in parliament, the cabinet even had to take it off the agenda for the time being.

Arguments against liberalization were not hard to find. The death toll in the campaign of political murders conducted since 1989 by the urban guerrilla movement *Devrimci Sol* (Revolutionary Left, generally known as *Dev Sol*) had risen steadily, reaching over ten a month. The victims were generally judges, policemen and retired officers who had been involved in intelligence work or in the martial law administration. The Kurdish insurrection in the southeast was escalating at frightening speed and the economy was increasingly fragile, with high inflation. The cabinet was further handicapped by President Özal's continual interference and obstruction. He constantly blocked legislation and cabinet decisions by refusing to sign new laws or decrees. He also constantly and openly criticized the cabinet's policies.

But Özal had his problems, too. Within the MP he was engaged in a power struggle with Mesut Yılmaz, who acted more and more independently. At an extraordinary party conference at the end of 1992 Özal tried to have him removed as party leader, but that attempt miscarried. From that moment onwards the MP was in a state of ferment and rumours that the Özal family would found a breakaway party with the support of the 'Holy Alliance' abounded. Perhaps, if Turgut Özal had lived longer than he did, something along these lines could have taken place. In the event, as we shall see, it did not.

The early 1990s were years in which more and more cracks appeared in the Turkish political landscape. The Nationalist Action Party saw its religious wing, the people closely associated with the ideas of the Turkish–Islamic Synthesis, break away to form the *Büyük Birlik Partisi* (Great Unity Party) and in the SDP a split occurred when second man Deniz Baykal, who had tried in vain to topple Erdal İnönü, reconstituted the Republican People's Party. A number of veterans of the Democratic Party of Menderes came together to relaunch their party 32 years after it had been banned, while Menderes's son Aydın Menderes launched his own party, the 'Party of Great Change'.

The death of Turgut Özal

Far more shocking to the Turkish public than this political sectarianism, which anyway had more to do with personal differences than with ideas, was the sudden death (of a heart attack) of President Turgut Özal on 17 April 1993. In spite of his great unpopularity in the late 1980s, in spite of all the scandals and of all the conflicts during the two years of his presidency, there was a general feeling that he had a unique place in the modern history of Turkey and in many commentaries he was called the second great modernizer (after Atatürk) of the country. It has to be said that the years since his death have tended to confirm this view. While the corruption that was a legacy of the Özal era has become more and more apparent, it is also true that the kind of courage and decisiveness displayed by Özal in his best moments was sadly missed since his death.

Exactly a month after Özal's death, Süleyman Demirel was sworn in as the ninth president of the republic. Not everyone thought it a wise move on Demirel's part to accept the post. He was a political street fighter through and through and, with the memory of Özal's use of the presidential privileges fresh in their memory, many people would have liked a more clearly 'above-party' and representative figure for president. Furthermore, Demirel's move left a power vacuum at the head of the party he had led directly or indirectly for 28 years. The election of his successor as party leader, and thus automatically as prime minister, developed into an exciting struggle when the obvious candidate, the speaker of parliament Hüsamettin Cindoruk, withdrew his candidacy, ostensibly because he feared President Demirel would interfere with his functioning as prime minister. The election was won by Tansu Çiller, a woman, former professor of economics and minister of state for the economy in Demirel's last cabinet.

Çiller's election gave a new, young and modern image both to her party and her country. Together with the takeover of the MP by Yılmaz, it seemed to herald a changing of the guard in a political landscape still dominated by figures such as Demirel, Ecevit, Erbakan and Türkeş who had come to the fore more than 30 years earlier. Although Çiller had gone into politics at the prompting and under the guidance of Demirel, her politics were closer to those of Özal, both in content (extremely pro-American with an almost blind faith in the workings of the free market) and in style (dramatic, adventurous and publicity seeking). Just as had been the case with Yılmaz and Özal, her relationship with president Demirel quickly deteriorated.

There was also a changing of the guard for the other partner in the coalition, the SDP: Erdal İnönü retired from politics and was succeeded in September 1993 by Murat Karayalçın, a former mayor of Ankara, who thus also became vice-premier (but not a member of parliament).

Tansu Çiller's time in government was dominated by three themes, all of which will be dealt with in more detail below: the economy, the Kurdish question (with its attendant human rights problems) and the relationship with the European Union. As was the case with all coalition governments in Turkey, this one too was constantly in danger of falling apart. On the left, the SDP was constantly challenged by Ecevit's PDL and Baykal's RPP to prove its social-democratic credentials, something that was virtually impossible in a coalition dominated by the conservative PTP; on the right there was pressure both from business circles, the army and from certain political circles to merge the two, programmatically almost identical, right of centre parties, MP and PTP, under something called the 'Motherpath formula' (from 'MOTHER-land Party' and 'True PATH Party'). This, however, was only possible if Çiller and Yılmaz were ready, or forced, to step down.

Özal's economy

The Özal government devoted the lion's share of its attention to an all-out effort to restructure the economy. Özal had been the architect of the IMF-inspired economic reform package of the last Demirel cabinet, announced in January 1980. The suppression of the trade unions and the political left by the military after September 1980 made it possible to execute this so-called 'stabilization programme'.

The international business world and financial community the IMF,

World Bank and OECD represented had renewed confidence in Turkey and the flow of credits, denied to pre-1980 governments, resumed. As a consequence, the national debt grew from $13.5 billion in 1980 to $40 billion in 1989. By 1994 it stood at $70 billion. By the end of the decade yearly repayments amounted to $7 billion (10 per cent of export earnings) but repayment posed no real problems.

The programme's aims were threefold: to improve the balance of payments, to combat inflation and to create an export-orientated free market economy. The means employed to attain these goals were drastic (ongoing) devaluation of the Turkish lira to make Turkish exports competitive in foreign markets; a large rise in interest rates to reduce consumption and thus inflation; freezing wages (to increase competitiveness and lower inflation); and raising prices through the abolition or reduction of state subsidies. Exports were encouraged through a set of specific measures: subsidies for exporters, simplification of notoriously complicated bureaucratic export procedures and abolition of the customs duties on imported inputs for export-orientated industries.

The rise in interest rates was accomplished by removing all restrictions and controls on rates in July 1980. But it did not bring about an increase in investment and venture capital for Turkish industry, which was anxious to expand. Most banks were either government-owned and bound to strict regulations or owned by holding companies, which invested the banks' funds only in their own production companies. Brokers (confusingly called *banker* in Turkey) seized the opportunity to float stock and bond issues the big banks would not touch; members of the public in search of a 'second income' bought them enthusiastically.

The brokers also entered the banking business, trying to gather funds by offering extremely high rates of interest (up to 140 per cent). When the government, at the end of 1981, tried to impose some order on the market and introduced minimum standards of credit worthiness, over 300 brokerage firms collapsed. A panic broke out, with a number of brokers being killed by their customers and many more fleeing the country. On 22 June 1982, even *Banker Kastelli*, the eleventh largest bank in Turkey, collapsed and its owner, Cevher Özden, fled abroad. As a result, Turgut Özal and several other ministers had to resign.

One reason why the shady brokers were so successful (for a short while) is that ordinary people were searching desperately for a means to beat inflation. It is clear that the burdens of the new economic policy fell on the wage earners, both in industry and in the civil service. Price rises, a freeze on wages and high interest rates together caused a drop in real purchasing power of between 40 and 60 per cent for most wage earners in the years from 1979 to 1989.

The main winners of the decade were the big family holdings. Some of these, such as the Koç group or the Eczacıbaşı group, had roots that went back to the 1920s; some, like the Çukurova group and the Sabancı group (which was particularly close to Özal) had begun their rise in the 1950s. Building firms such as Anka and STFA, which had profited enormously from the building boom in the Arab oil-producing countries in the early 1980s, formed a third 'generation' of holdings and used the opportunity to branch out into other sectors. Nearly all these firms were family owned and were structured as holding companies, with their own banks, insurance companies, trading companies and production companies. Imports and joint ventures with foreign firms for the production of goods under licence had been the main business in the age of import substitution. Now, the holdings increasingly became export-oriented, without halting their earlier activities.

The government tried to keep down prices for industrial goods by encouraging competition on the home market through the abolition of import restrictions. In the shops the difference was immediately apparent, especially after the shortages of 1979/80. The latest European, Japanese and American consumer goods were now available in Turkey. Luxury items could be freely imported, but were subject to a special tax, the revenue of which was used for the housing programme. The result was a consumer-led boom. The consumption of luxury goods was not limited to those whose wealth increased in these years (the people who worked in the fast-growing import and export, banking, communications and tourism sectors). Those parts of the middle classes whose income decreased in real terms (everybody in the state sector, for instance) also went on a buying spree. They were enabled to do so through a very extensive system of hire purchase and credit. There was a tremendous hunger for the technology, luxury and trappings of modern life in general, a feeling (as it was often expressed) of 'not having lived' (*bir yaşamamışlık duygusu*) and having to catch up.

Foreign investors were encouraged. They no longer faced discriminatory measures; the repatriation of invested capital and export of profits were made possible; investors were given preferential treatment over import duties; and in four different places (around the ports of İzmir and Mersin and near Adana) free trade zones were instituted. Many firms that set up factories in these areas re-exported their products.

The government promoted investment in the infrastructure and in utilities too. The telecommunications and road networks were modernized (with a second Bosphorus bridge and a ring road around Istanbul helping to ease the congestion in the traffic between Europe and Asia), a modern highway, curiously called TEM or 'Trans-European Motorway', replaced, or at least relieved pressure from, the old two-lane road between the metropolitan areas of Istanbul (with nearly ten million inhabitants at the time) and Ankara (with perhaps five million), the construction of natural gas pipelines from the Soviet Union to Turkey began to have a significant impact on air pollution in the big cities by the late 1980s, replacing the inferior coal and lignite used previously.

Because the government was strapped for cash it tried to get contractors to agree to work on the basis of 'build-operate-transfer' formulas. This meant that a foreign investor would build a facility (a bridge, a hotel or a power plant) and operate it until its costs had been recovered and a profit margin achieved. The facility would then be handed over to the Turkish government for further operation. This technique was often used in the tourism sector. The Özal government recognized that one of Turkey's major natural resources, its coast and scenery, had hardly been exploited and the building up of a Turkish tourism industry was energetically pursued during the 1980s. By the late 1980s, Turkey had captured a sizeable part of the Mediterranean holiday market and had become a popular destination for package tours from northern Europe. That the coast and the scenery suffered as a result goes without saying. The Gulf crisis of 1990/1 hit the Turkish tourist trade hard, but it recovered quickly in 1992, helped this time by the civil war in the former Yugoslavia. When the first plans for the expansion of the tourism sector were made, it was stipulated that Turkey should aim for the top end of the market and that strict zoning regulations should be enforced to preserve the natural beauty of the coastline. In the event, the opposite happened. Turkey went in for low to medium budget mass tourism and large parts of its coasts were commercialized and covered with areas of hotels, holiday villages and resorts identical to those in Spain, Greece and Cyprus with which it competed mainly on price. By the mid-1990s Turkey attracted over seven million tourists a year and tourism had replaced workers' transfers as the main source of hard currency. By the end of the decade the number of tourists had doubled again and Turkey had emerged as the third largest holiday destination in the Mediterranean, after Spain and Greece.

Another project that was energetically pursued by the government was the gigantic Southeast Anatolia Project (*Güneydogu Anadolu Projesi* or GAP), originally devised in the 1960s. The plan envisaged the building of a whole complex of dams on the Euphrates and Tigris rivers including hydroelectric plants and irrigational works to produce energy for Turkish industry and to irrigate 1.6 million hectares in the plain of Harran, doubling the area under irrigation in Turkey. The main part of the project, the enormous Atatürk dam on the Euphrates northwest of Urfa, was opened in 1992. For political reasons (to avoid having to reach agreement with the downstream countries, Syria and Iraq, about sharing the water), the project and the dam were built without financial assistance from international agencies.

After a difficult start (in 1980/1 the economy actually contracted), the stabilization programme achieved many of its aims. Exports grew by an average of 22 per cent per annum during the years from 1980 to 1987. In 1979 exports had totalled $2.3 billion; by 1988, however, they totalled $11.7 billion. The nature of Turkish exports changed over the decade. In 1979, nearly 60 per cent of exports had consisted of agricultural products. In 1988 this figure was down to 20 per cent. Over the same period the percentage of industrial products in total exports grew from under 45 to over 72. Among the industrial goods, textiles were of special importance, contributing more than a quarter of the total value of the exports.

Export destinations changed too. The early 1980s coincided with the second boom in world oil prices. Unlike in 1974, this time the Turkish exporters, supported by the government, managed to profit fully from the new wealth in the Arab oil-producing countries. Between 1982 and 1985 Turkish exports to the Middle East and North Africa exceeded those to the European Community, with Iran the single biggest market. Thereafter, the older pattern re-established itself and the EC, later EU, once again became the main Turkish export market. Gross national product grew by an average of 4.5 per cent during the first few years (until 1985). In 1987 growth was even higher (7 to 8 per cent). From 1988 onwards the growth figures became erratic and unpredictable. Until the crisis of 1994 (about which more below), the growth rate varied between 1.5 and 9 per cent. Imports also went up (from $5 billion in 1979 to $14.4 billion in 1989) and consistently exceeded exports all through the period. The balance of payments gap was closed by remissions from Turkish workers in Europe. Political stability and attractive interest rates above the rate of inflation encouraged the workers to put their money in Turkish banks.

High interest rates and the wage freeze combined to lower inflation to between 30 and 40 per cent in the first half of the 1980s. Then inflation rose again and in 1988 it reached its pre-1980 level of around 70 per cent. The reason was not primarily excessive consumer demand but the continuing high government deficit. This was caused by a number of factors: a failure to curb the growth of the large civil service; inefficient taxation, which left the huge profits of the industrial holdings and, especially, of the self employed, almost untouched; and, most import-antly, the continued existence of a huge state industrial sector, which was inefficient and largely loss-making. The Özal government publicly declared its intention to privatize the public sector industries many times (as, indeed, had all governments since the early 1950s), but its privatization programme progressed only very slowly. Most of the state industries were so old-fashioned and overstaffed that investors were not interested in them. More effective was the abolition of a number of government monopolies, leading, for instance, to a large number of private airline companies and television stations. In both sectors members of the Özal family were among the pioneers. The position of the commercial radio and television channels was really rather extraordinary. The first TV stations, such as Star-1 (later Interstar) broadcast from Germany and could be received in Turkey via satellite dishes. Soon all the major holdings and especially the large newspaper publishers had their own channel. This was tolerated, although the article in the constitution that gave a broadcasting monopoly to the state was only changed years later in 1993.

The year 1989 was in many ways a turning point in the Özal era's economic development. This was partly because of a serious drought, which hit agricultural producers (and exporters) hard. Agriculture had received relatively little attention in the Özal years and the drought showed just how technologically backward the sector still was. It employed 60 per cent of the Turkish labour force but its contribution to the national product, even in good years, was only between 15 and 20 per cent. Other factors that slowed growth were an increase in interest rates (exceeding even the rising inflation), cutbacks in government investment and a high exchange rate for the Turkish lira. The lira's gradual devaluation had dropped behind inflation, so that by 1990 it was overvalued by some 40 per cent. The reason was that large numbers of Turkish workers in Europe deposited their money in Turkish banks (attracted by the high interest rates) and as a consequence changed marks, francs and guilders into liras. In 1991/2 the speed of devaluation picked up again and the lira reached a more realistic level.

One point that should be borne in mind when considering the budgetary policies of the Özal era is the extraordinary extent to which Özal managed to siphon off state income into separate 'funds' (*fon*). The system consisted of levies with a very specific purpose, which were imposed as a surcharge on many different items and activities. One example was the *Konut Fonu* or 'Housing Fund'. This fund was not only fed from import duties on luxury items, but also from the $100 charge levied on all Turkish citizens travelling abroad. This fund and many more like it were kept outside the budget and therefore were not subject to parliamentary control. In this way Özal created a 'shadow budget', which he and his aides could use as they saw fit.

The economic policies of the 1980s had greatly increased the differences between rich and poor. On the one hand, a whole new class of often very wealthy entrepreneurs had arisen. Fortunes were made in imports, exports and construction. The new rich also flaunted their wealth in ways that had been unthinkable in Turkey before and that were reminiscent of Latin America. On the other hand, by the end of the 1980s, the purchasing power of the majority of the population had been drastically reduced and there was very real poverty in many Turkish homes. Added to this was a steep rise in the number of unemployed (although, as has been noted, any estimate of the number of unemployed in Turkey is of necessity tentative because there is no official registration or unemployment benefit).

The growing liberalization of the political system gave the trade unions more clout from 1988 onwards. Labour unrest increased, especially in 1990/1. In January 1991 a million and a half employees held a general strike. The unions managed to make good their members' loss of purchasing power since 1980, but, as before, only for those in the large modern industrial sector and in the state economic enterprises. The small family businesses, which made up the core of the Turkish economy, were still largely outside the reach of the unions. Unfortunately for the organized workers, the 1980s saw more and more work being farmed out to small subcontractors, who worked with increasingly narrow margins. From 1989 onwards, the number of bankruptcies in this category rose steeply. Turkish civil servants were still barred from trade union membership.

Confronted with the growing economic crisis, the MP government chose to close its eyes. The sixth five-year plan (for the period 1990–94), officially adopted in 1989, was totally unrealistic, envisaging high growth, 15 per cent inflation and a lower deficit. With the slowdown in the world economy at the end of the 1980s, the projected growth figures proved unattainable (Turkey by now being much more sensitive to global economic trends because of its export-orientated economy) and the country entered a period in which economic growth was highly erratic, while inflation, the deficit and unemployment were on the rise.

Özal's successors in the Demirel–İnönü coalition of 1991–93 had less clear-cut economic policies. Both the PTP and the SDP tried to protect the interests of their traditional following. To a certain extent the SDP defended the interests of the civil servants and the workers, especially in the state sector, while the PTP, even more than the MP, represented the traditional small businesses and the farmers. The rivalry between the two big right of centre parties, the PTP and MP, also led to increasing tension between the two large employers' organizations of Turkey – the

TÜSIAD (Society of Turkish Industrialists), which represented big business and hence was closer to the MP; and the TOBB (Union of Chambers of Commerce and Industry), which represented small and medium businesses and therefore was more PTP-oriented.

The Kurdish problem: war against the PKK

The political problem that came to dominate the Turkish agenda more and more as the years wore on concerned the rights of the Kurdish community. After the coup of September 1980 the suppression of expressions of Kurdish identity was intensified. Even the use of Kurdish in private conversation was officially forbidden. People were constantly being indicted for 'weakening national sentiments', the most famous cases being those of the writer Ismail Beşikçi (not a Kurd himself) and of the popular singer İbrahim Tatlıses ('Sweet voice'), who was prosecuted for 'separatist propaganda' when he declared that he regretted not being able to sing a folk song in his native Kurdish.

Despite the military regime's draconian measures, leaders of the most radical Kurdish movement, the *Partiya Karkeran Kurdistan* (Workers' Party of Kurdistan, universally known as PKK), founded in November 1978 by Abdullah Öcalan, managed to flee the country. The PKK was not the first Kurdish political organization to emerge in the 1970s. Up to 1980 other organizations were more important and more ideologically sophisticated, but the PKK was the only one that consciously aimed at the poor and ill-educated village and town youths who felt left out of society, with a simple programme and strong emphasis on (armed) action. In September 1980 Öcalan settled in Damascus and, with Syrian government help, established training camps in the Beqa'a valley, where Syrian and Palestinian officers trained his followers. In July 1981 the PKK's first official congress was held on the Syrian–Lebanese border.

From 1982 onwards, the Iran–Iraq war gave Kurdish organizations in northern Iraq, Mahmut Barzani's Democratic Party of Kurdistan and Jalal Talabani's Patriotic Union of Kurdistan, a free hand because Iraq needed its troops on the front in the south. Relations between the Marxist PKK and Barzani's conservative PDK were never very cordial, but the latter nevertheless allowed Öcalan's followers to operate from PDK-controlled areas south of the Iraqi–Turkish border. This gave the PKK two routes of infiltration into Turkey: directly from Syria and through Iraqi Kurdistan. The (banned) celebrations of the Kurdish New Year (*Nevroz*) on 21 March 1984 signalled the start of the PKK's guerrilla activity in the southeast. Since then, *Nevroz* has every year been the occasion for intensification of the PKK's guerrilla warfare. The actual attacks on Turkish military posts started on 15 August 1984 with simultaneous strikes on Eruh and Şemdinli, two places 200 kilometres apart.

Gradually, the scale of PKK actions increased. From 1986 onwards countermeasures by the Turkish authorities included paying and arming some villagers (the so-called 'village guards') to resist PKK attacks. This was not an unqualified success. Local tribal chiefs put forward the candidates for recruitment and these often had a violent or criminal past. All in all some 18,000 village guards were recruited, but when in 1987 the PKK conducted an intensive campaign against them, the village guards, with their Second World War vintage rifles, proved no match for the PKK's kalashnikovs. Many were killed and in many cases their whole families, women and children included, were massacred. Demoralization became a big problem and the army had to threaten with sharp counter-measures in order to forestall mass deser-tions.[9] The Turkish army's efforts to close the border and to hunt down the guerrillas in the mountains were not very effective. The main problems on the Turkish side were the lack of equipment for counterguerrilla warfare (helicopters, telecommunications) and the lack of coordination between the intelligence services, the army, the gendarmes and the police. To solve these problems and improve coordination, a former MİT (intelligence) officer, Hayri Kozakçıoğlu, was appointed as 'super governor' (*süpervali*) in eight, and later in 11 provinces – a system reminiscent of the inspectorates of the 1930s.[10] Coordination remained a problem, however, and over the next few years, the super governor gradually lost most of his powers to the military authorities. Tactics began to change significantly from 1992 onwards when the Turkish army established a permanent presence in the inhospitable mountain ranges instead of working from town garrisons. This allowed them gradually to gain the initiative in the mid-1990s.

The PKK did not have a monopoly over Kurdish nationalism in this period. There were other organizations and parties that strove for the independence of Turkey's Kurds, but rejected the PKK's brutality, both against the Kurdish villagers who cooperated with the Turks and against other Kurdish organizations. Eight of these organizations concluded an anti-PKK alliance (called *Tevger*) in 1988. *Tevger* was strengthened by defections from the PKK leadership, but its influence was restricted to the *émigré* communities in Europe and the PKK remained the only organization with grassroots support inside Anatolia.

Abdullah Öcalan's image in Turkey underwent a change through a sensational interview with the Istanbul daily *Milliyet* (Nationality) in June 1988. The man who had been depicted for years as Turkey's public enemy number one (which in a sense he was) and as a true demon, turned out to be a man of flesh and blood who was a fan of the Galatasaray football club. The PKK prestige also increased because after 1988 it dropped its terror tactics against the villagers in the southeast, which Öcalan now recognized had been a mistake. In 1989, the PKK concluded an alliance with a number of extreme left-wing urban guerrilla groups (*Dev Sol*, TİKKO, THKP/C and others), which increased its ability to strike in Turkey's big cities. Old habits died hard, however. There was a return to terror tactics in 1993/4, when Öcalan himself ordered an assassination campaign against village teachers in the southeast. Dozens of teachers were killed. They were caught between a rock and a hard place: either they had to live in constant fear of their lives or they had to risk prosecution for 'deserting their post'. This campaign did long-term damage to the image of Öcalan and his movement.

For a long time the Turkish authorities kept up the fiction that the PKK operated from over the border, but when the number of incidents kept growing despite all efforts to close the border, they had to recognize that the PKK could draw on local support and that the 'kidnappings' that were constantly reported in the press were really instances of people joining the guerrillas. This presented the Turkish army with the classic guerrilla situation. It was clear that most of the local population supported the PKK and that the guerrillas simply merged into the village population. Like many armies in this position, it vented its anger and frustration on the local civilians.

The most infamous incident of this type took place in October 1993, when army units carried out an artillery bombardment on the town of Lice as revenge for the killing of the commander of the gendarme force of Diyarbakır, Bahtiyar Aydın. Another traditional anti-guerrilla tactic the Turkish army used more and more in the early 1990s was that of 'scorched earth': villages in the mountains were evacuated and then destroyed in an effort to cut off the PKK from its bases. Some 500 villages were emptied by the end of 1993 and, in 1994, 900 more followed. By 1996 the total was 3000. The villagers were sometimes resettled in 'safe villages' or camps, but more often they were just sent packing. Most of them ended up in the big cities. Diyarbakır had to accommodate more than half a million refugees and was completely overwhelmed.

The manpower employed in the struggle by the Turkish army kept on increasing – from 150,000 in 1991 to 250,000 in 1994 – but the number of casualties rose even faster. Between 1984 and 1990, according to official figures, some 2500 people had died, by 1994 the number was 7000 and by the end of 1996 the official number stood at over 17,000. By the time the conflict was suspended in 1999 it was generally put at around 30,000.

In an attempt to cut the PKK's supply and infiltration routes, the battle was regularly carried over the border into Iraq. Turkish warplanes bombarded and strafed camps in northern Iraq. The government in Ankara also tried to forge more effective alliances with the Kurdish movements in Iraq, Barzani's PDK and Talabani's PUK. Since the Gulf war of January 1991, these two movements controlled the northern parts of Iraqi Kurdistan; the PDK the area immediately adjacent to the Turkish border and the PUK the area more to the southeast. In November 1992 Turkish troops carried out a joint offensive against the PKK with the Iraqi Kurds. It temporarily drove the PKK from northern Iraq, but the effect was very limited, which was proved by the fact that the Turkish army carried out a large-scale invasion of the area in March 1995 (the so-called 'Operation Steel') in order to remove the PKK once more; 35,000 troops and 13 generals took part in these operations. After these troops had been withdrawn, negotiations were opened with Barzani about the creation of a security zone on the pattern of the Israeli security zone in southern Lebanon, but while Barzani was ready to accept Turkish money and arms he was against any Turkish military presence in his domain. In the meantime, the PKK fighters quietly returned to the border area and the war went on as before.

The Kurdish problem and national politics

The escalation in the southeast placed the Kurdish question on the political agenda in Ankara. In November six SPP representatives were suspended because they had attended a conference on Kurdistan in Paris. In protest, nine SPP representatives resigned from the party. Ten of the fifteen founded the *Halkın Emek Partisi* (People's Labour Party), which campaigned for Kurdish rights, in June 1990. The chauvinist majority in Turkish politics considered the representatives of the PLP to be traitors and from the start they were targets for all kinds of petty harassment. The inauguration ceremony of the new members of the assembly in 1991 turned into a scandal when a number of PLP representatives spoke in Kurdish. They also answered 'Turkish' when asked which foreign languages they knew in a questionnaire. The constitutional court was asked to ban the PLP on the grounds of separatism. This eventually happened – in July 1993 – but by then all the members of the party save one had transferred to a new party, the *Demokrasi Partisi* (DeP), thus avoiding losing their seats when the PLP was banned. The DeP was persecuted as much as its predecessor. One of its parliamentary representatives was murdered in September 1993 and in February 1994 the party's headquarters in Ankara were blown up. Ankara's chief prosecutor, Nusret Demiral, in December 1993 opened a case against the

DeP at the constitutional court and in March 1994 the immunity of the parliamentarians was lifted at the insistence of Prime Minister Çiller, who, during the election campaign of that month, would boast of 'having chased the PKK out of the assembly'. Immediately afterwards they were arrested inside the National Assembly building. The party was banned in June 1994. Six DeP representatives had already left the country for Europe; the seven who were arrested in March were tried and in December 1994 they received prison sentences of up to 15 years. Former members of the DeP in the country went on to found a successor party again, the HaDeP (*Halkın Demokrasi Partisi* – People's Democracy Party), which did very well in the southeast in the 1995 elections, but failed to make any impression on the Kurdish electorate in the big cities. The DeP members who had gone to Europe played a central role in the formation of the 'Kurdish Parliament in Exile', which convened for the first time in The Hague on 12 April 1995. HaDeP was not banned (not for want of trying on the part of the public prosecutors) but a number of its leaders received heavy prison sentences in June 1997.

The war in the southeast had a traumatic effect on the whole of Turkish society. Quite a few people in politics, in the business world and in intellectual and academic circles recognized that a political, peaceful solution to the Kurdish problem was the only way out. President Özal, himself half Kurdish, had been the first member of the political establishment openly to advocate concessions to the Kurds. Without consulting the cabinet, he even issued a decree lifting the ban on the use of Kurdish in speech and music. Shortly before his death he seems to have considered political concessions. Shortly after her succession to the premiership, Tansu Çiller talked about 'seeking a Basque solution' (referring to the devolution process in Spain where a large measure of autonomy has been granted to regions such as Catalonia and the Basque country in the post-Franco era). TÜSIAD's president Halis Komili called for talks, as did Cem Boyner. Nonetheless, the supporters of a political solution were powerless in the face of the pressure from the security establishment, the army top brass, the rightist majority in parliament, the chauvinist media and an increasingly polarized public opinion. The official line, which Demirel and Çiller endlessly repeated, was that the PKK had first to be beaten militarily before any discussions could possibly take place.

Of all the major parties, the WP seemed most inclined to take a more conciliatory line. Erbakan indirectly hinted at talks, and when a WP deputy for Van went to northern Iraq to try to free Turkish soldiers in the hands of the PKK, the party supported him, even though the media denounced him as a traitor and an investigation was started against him.

But Erbakan, too, had to recognize that for the time being he was unable to influence the military's handling of the situation.

International relations in the 1980s and 1990s: Turkey, the United States and the European Union

The coup of September 1980 was greeted with understanding (and a great deal of relief) in American government circles. Over the next few years political relations between the USA and Turkey developed in a completely different direction from those between Turkey and Europe. In Europe, more specifically in the EC (of which Turkey was an associate member) and in the Council of Europe, attention focused on the human rights situation in Turkey, while in the USA security was the main issue. That the European organizations focused to such a large extent on human rights was due partly to the relative proximity of Turkey and partly to the fact that so many Turks lived in Europe, especially when Turkish political refugees tried to influence public opinion. However, the harsh attitude of the European Community institutions was primarily the work of a coalition of social democrats (with whom Ecevit had a very high standing) and Greek representatives. In May 1981 Turkey's membership of the Council of Europe was suspended and in July 1982 an official inquiry into human rights in Turkey was announced.

Turkey's trade relations with Europe were, however, in no way affected and trade with the EC continued to be vastly more important than it was with the United States. From 1983 onwards, political relations with the EC improved, for the EC had grown impatient with Greek policies of obstruction. Turkey officially applied for full membership of the EC in April 1987. While the EC did not completely shut the door, its reply to the Turkish application amounted to a rejection, at least for the time being. What was offered instead of full membership was a customs' union between Turkey and the EU. The negotiations about the customs' union progressed slowly and with difficulty because the EU demanded full compliance with European regulations on intellectual property, cartels and free trade. In return, Turkey demanded financial compensation. These problems were largely solved in 1993/4, but then the Turkish economy was hit by the recession following the 5 April measures. At the same time, the whole process was thrown into doubt by the trial of the Kurdish parliamentarians. Unlike the European governments, the European parliament, like many of the parliaments of the member states, was highly critical of Turkey's human rights record and this trial was the final straw. In October 1994, the assembly of the Council of Europe started exclusion procedures against Turkey. The negotiations over the customs' union were suspended until March 1995. Then, finally, the necessary protocols were signed, but ratification by the European parliament was made dependent on further political liberalization, which, as we have seen, was long in coming. The constitutional changes of July 1995 opened the way for ratification. The European parliament still hesitated, but both the Turks themselves and the Americans on their behalf lobbied intensely for ratification, with their prime argument being that it would anchor Turkey firmly in Europe and prevent the 'fundamentalists' from gaining power. Ironically, two weeks after the European parliament ratified the customs' union on 13 December, the 'fundamentalists' emerged as the biggest party in Turkey's elections. Within six months they were in power.

Regional relations

In the years 1980–88 first the Iranian revolution and then the Iran–Iraq war dominated the situation in the Middle East. The Turkish military government of 1980–83 regarded the Islamic Republic of Iran with suspicion, fearing its influence on Islamic groups within Turkey. Iranian attacks on Atatürk and his policies did not help and Turkish opinion was offended when visiting Iranian representatives refused to lay the customary wreath at Atatürk's grave. Nevertheless, Turkey maintained a scrupulously observed policy of neutrality during the war, which broke out when Iraq invaded southern Iran in 1982. Iran, which was suffering from an American trade embargo, became Turkey's foremost export market in 1983/4, but at the same time Turkey allowed Iraq to pump oil through the double pipeline over its territory to the terminal on the Mediterranean.

In the late 1980s, Turkey's relations with Iran gradually improved, while those with Iraq and Syria deteriorated. The reason for the latter was a simmering conflict about the use of the water resources of the Euphrates and Tigris rivers, which was becoming more acute as the GAP (Southeast Anatolia Project), with its huge new dam on the Euphrates, neared completion. As a downstream country, which needed water for its own agricultural projects, Syria was in a vulnerable position. It tried to put pressure on Turkey by supporting the Kurdish guerrilla war of the PKK, which was allowed to operate from its territory, the implied bargain being that it would cut off the PKK if guarantees about the water supply were received. Ultimately, this policy miscarried and Syria was forced to sacrifice the PKK without getting anything in return.

During the 1980s, Turkey's relations with the other region of which it forms part, the Balkans, remained strained as before. More than once the United Nations started up negotiations about a solution to the Cyprus problem, but they remained deadlocked over the extent of Turkish autonomy in any future federal state. This continued to sour Turkish–Greek relations, which were also strained by differences over oil rights on the continental shelf in the Aegean. Both countries started exploration for oil in disputed waters in 1982, protected by their respective navies. The conflict also extended to the airspace over the Aegean, which Greece claimed but Turkey saw as international. Turkish jets made demonstration flights to support the Turkish claim. From 1987 onwards, after a sudden reconciliation between Özal and Greek Prime Minister Papandreou, relations seemed suddenly to improve, but the relationship did not warm much further until a new generation of politicians came to power in Greece in the mid-1990s.

A crisis with Bulgaria, Turkey's other European neighbour, suddenly developed in 1989, when the communist Bulgarian government stepped up its policies of forced assimilation of the Turkish-Muslim minority and 344,000 Bulgarian Turks fled across the border into Turkey. This caused a tremendous upsurge in nationalist fervour in Turkey, but the country was hardly in a position to accommodate so many refugees. When they could not find work or housing, most of the refugees trickled back to Bulgaria during the next year.

Desert Shield and Desert Storm

When Iraq occupied Kuwait in August 1990, Turkey became one of the most active and enthusiastic supporters of the American-led United Nations coalition, which first imposed sanctions on Iraq and then in January 1991 waged war on that country. The ardent support for the coalition (which involved stopping all traffic to Iraq and cutting the flow of oil through pipelines on Turkish soil) was very much the personal policy of President Özal (who was given emergency powers on 17 January 1991 to deal with the crisis). He realized that Turkey had lost most of its strategic significance as a bastion against the Soviet Union, which had been its most important bargaining chip in seeking membership of the EC and generally in securing Western support. He saw Turkish participation in the coalition as a way of emphasizing Turkey's status as a Western stronghold in the Middle East and perhaps even of forcing Turkish entry into the European Community, very much in the way Menderes had secured Turkey's membership of NATO by sending his troops to Korea. Neither the opposition parties nor Turkish public opinion supported this policy. Opposition to Özal's extremely pro-American line increased when he gave the Americans the right to use their major military installation in Turkey, İncirlik airbase to the east of Adana, for bombing raids on Iraq. This put Turkey in the front line and made it a potential target for the Iraqi air force. Despite this, to great public indignation, Turkey's NATO allies made hardly any moves to help to defend it. Belgium, Germany and Italy sent a number of completely outdated and lightly armed warplanes that had already been marked for retirement. Only the Dutch sent units of modern Patriot ground-to-air missiles.

In the event, Turkey escaped Iraqi attacks. Its real problems started when the war was virtually over. During the war, US President Bush had encouraged the Kurdish leaders in Iraq to revolt against Saddam Hussain's regime in Baghdad. When the allied forces had crushed the Iraqi army in the south, the Kurds did as they were asked and Barzani and Talabani together launched an insurrection in the north. At the insistence of its Middle Eastern allies (including Turkey), who did not want to see Iraq dismembered and a Kurdish state established, the Americans halted their offensive, leaving Saddam Hussain's regime in place. This enabled him to suppress the Kurdish rebellion with his remaining troops.

The result was that huge numbers of Kurds fled across the border into Iran and tried to flee across the northern border into Turkey. This Turkey did not want. It already had a serious problem on its hands with its own Kurdish community and it was convinced that if it let in half a million Kurdish refugees the world would leave it at that and forget all about it. Turkey had some experience to show that this might happen: 36,000 Kurdish refugees who had fled from Iraq when Saddam Hussain bombarded them with poison gas in 1988 were still in camps near Diyarbakır. So Turkish troops were ordered to stop the Kurds a few kilometres from the Turkish border, which was something that gave rise to a great deal of – gratuitous – criticism of Turkey in the West.

Instead of opening the border, Turkey's president launched a plan (quickly adopted by Britain's prime minister, John Major) to establish a security zone in northern Iraq, where the Kurds would be protected and the Iraqi air force would not be allowed to fly. The United Nations organized relief operations for the Kurdish refugees and in June 1991 Turkey agreed to the establishment of an intervention force (first called 'Poised Hammer', later 'Provide Comfort II'), consisting of American, British and French troops, to ward off any Iraqi attempt to suppress the Kurds in the security zone. The air force units used bases in İncirlik and Batman, while the ground troops were located in Silopi. After 30 September the force consisted of air force units only.

The Gulf war had cost Turkey a great deal (more than $6 billion in lost revenue) and, although this loss was partly made up by contributions from Germany and Japan, the political dividends President Özal had imagined did not materialize. The achievement of full membership of the EU continued to be as elusive as it had been before.

Turkey and the fall of the Soviet empire

The collapse of the Soviet bloc during the years from 1989 to 1991 held both promises and dangers for Turkey. Relations between Turkey and the Soviet Union, especially in the economic field, had developed quickly during the era of 'perestroika', the opening up started by President Gorbachev. Between 1987 and 1990 30 different agreements were concluded and trade grew from $350 million to $1.9 billion a year. The acute economic crisis that developed in the USSR and its successor states from 1990 onwards could endanger one of Turkey's most promising export markets.

The changes held great promise as well. The non-Russian republics of the Union declared their independence one after another and one of the results was the emergence of five new Turkic republics: Azerbaijan, Turkmenistan, Uzbekistan, Kazakhstan and Kirghizia.

The first reactions in Turkey, both on a political level and in public opinion were euphoric. President Özal talked about the coming of a 'Turkic century' and about the 'Turkic [or Turkish, for the Turkish language does not differentiate between the two] world, stretching from the Adriatic to the Great Wall of China'. Turkey was the first country to recognize the republics diplomatically. In 1991 and 1992 delegations from Central Asia and the Caucasus came and went and received massive media exposure. The West, and especially the Americans, encouraged Turkey to develop an active Central Asian policy. The perception in Washington was that the disintegration of the Soviet Union created a political vacuum in the area, which could only be filled either by Turkey or by the Islamic Republic of Iran. The Americans saw the latter eventuality as a major catastrophe and therefore encouraged and supported Turkey in its efforts to develop ties with the new states and to pose as a role model (a secular state with a multi-party political system and a market economy).

In response, Turkey has indeed developed an active Central Asian policy. Over 300 agreements of all types have been concluded between Turkey and the different Turkic republics covering such diverse subjects as civil aviation and prevention of double taxation; three 'Turkic' summits have been organized; a special agency for Turkic cooperation and development (TİKA) has been created in the Ministry of Foreign Affairs; joint ventures in banking and financing have been created; and over 7000 students from Central Asia and Azerbaijan have received scholarships to study in Turkey – despite the desperate overcrowding at

Turkish universities. The private sector is heavily involved as well. Hundreds of Turkish firms operate in the new republics, especially in the building sector, but also as shopkeepers and restaurant owners and the Russian market continued to be at least as important as the combined Central Asian markets for Turkey in the decades after the fall of the Soviet Union. Russia also developed into a very important export market for Turkish goods and services. Side by side with the state and private enterprise, Turkish religious groups, competing with missionary organizations from Saudi Arabia, Iran and Pakistan, have become very active in Central Asia. The modernist 'Fethullahcılar' branch of the *Nurcu* movement alone is rumoured to have founded nearly 300 educational centres there.

Nevertheless, there has been a gradual realization that there are clear limits to what Turkey can achieve in Central Asia as well. In the first place, the whole idea of a 'vacuum' created by a Russian withdrawal may have been a mirage. The economies and the transport and communication networks of the Central Asian republics have been integrated with the Russian Federation to such an extent that loosening these ties too quickly would be disastrous. In 1990 between 80 and 86 per cent of the import trade and between 85 and 98 per cent of the export trade of the Central Asian republics was with the rest of the Soviet Union. Furthermore, some of the Central Asian republics have large Russian minorities (in Kazakhstan the Kazakhs themselves constitute a plurality, but not a majority) and Moscow has trained the political elites of these countries, resulting in a political culture that is much closer to that of Russia than to that of Turkey. Even in its present difficult circumstances Russia remains a much greater financial and military power than Turkey can hope to be. All this has meant that gradually Russia has been able to reassert its position as an important power in the region. The main competition over the last decade has come, not from Turkey, but from China.

Furthermore, although there is some sentimental attachment to Turkey, it is clear that in the longer term its position and prestige in Central Asia depend on its effectiveness both as a source of economic aid (or a channel of Western aid) and as a regional political power. In both these respects it has been less than successful. No great influx of aid has materialized and even in the area directly adjacent to its borders, Turkey has proved itself unable either to stop the Armenian offensive against Azerbaijan or to protect Elchibey's pro-Turkish government in Baku against its pro-Moscow opponents.

The project that had the highest priority in the eyes of the Turkish government and that was seen to be of vital national interest was the building of oil and gas pipelines from the Caspian to the Mediterranean over Turkish soil. These pipelines should in the future be able to transport oil from the fields in the Caspian Sea and gas from the huge Tengiz field in Kazakhstan to Western consumers. Russia and Turkey promoted rival projects of pipelines over Russian territory to the Black Sea terminal at Novorossisk and over Georgian territory to Batumi. Turkey hoped that the latter option would eventually lead to the construction of a branch line to the Turkish Mediterranean coast. This would give Turkey a hold on what could become a vital energy supply route for the West and at the same time relieve the congestion in the Bosphorus, where serious accidents with oil tankers are becoming more and more frequent. With strong support from the US government and from the American participants in the Caspian Sea oil consortium, Turkey eventually won the battle. The agreement between Turkey, Georgia and Azerbaijan on the construction of the 'Baku–Ceyhan Pipeline' was finally concluded under President Clinton's watchful eye in Istanbul on 18 November 1999. Work was started in September 2002 on this line, which was to become the main outlet for Caspian oil. It was a triumph for the Americans at least as much as for the Turks because it broke Russia's stranglehold on the energy sources in the Caspian basin and isolated the United States' old enemy Iran. A pipeline over Iranian territory to the Persian Gulf would have been cheaper and shorter, but it was rejected anyway. All this happened at a time when it was becoming clear that the Caspian basin could develop into an alternative energy source to the Middle East, which would make Europe and the USA less dependent on the Gulf states with their actual or potential political problems.

The Turkic republics have made it clear that they value their newfound independence, but that they are not prepared to antagonize Moscow by making moves towards pan-Turkist unity or by subjecting themselves to Ankara's tutelage. Movements advocating political pan-Turkism have existed in most parts of the Turkic world for nearly a century. They have flowered to a certain extent in the context of both world wars (in both cases with German support) and during the cold war (with American support), but they have never been able to become a dominant force anywhere.

Different sections of the Turkish political establishment reacted differently to the disappointing developments of the years after 1992. For the elected politicians, the opening towards Central Asia had been a godsend, diverting attention from the deteriorating economic situation and the increasingly violent conflict with the Kurdish PKK. Both President Turgut Özal, between 1990 and 1993, and Prime Minister Tansu Çiller, from 1993 to 1995, played the pan-Turkist card with relish. In September 1993 and again in 1995 Turkey claimed that its position as (self appointed) spokesman for the Turks entitled it to a semi-permanent seat on the security council of the United Nations. While Özal's successor Süleyman Demirel adopted a somewhat more cautious stance, he too constantly harped on the theme of the 'brotherhood of the Turks'. Many of these elected politicians made rather grandiose claims for the future of pan-Turk cooperation and accordingly found it very hard to come to terms with the continued influence of Russia and what they saw as the timidity of the Turkic states.

There was, however, a second strain within Turkish foreign policy making – the professionals at the Ministry of Foreign Affairs and, to a certain extent, the leadership of the armed forces. This second strain was influenced far more by a realistic appraisal of the Turkish national interest than by any vision of pan-Turk unity and thus formed a continuation of the traditional policies of the republic. In the minds of the strategists of the Ministry of Foreign Affairs, the number one priority for Turkey remained its relationship with the West, the European Union in particular. The relationship with Central Asia was seen in this context: quite apart from defending Turkey's economic and security interests in Central Asia, presenting Turkey as Europe's window on Central Asia was a bargaining chip that gave the country added leverage in its struggle to be accepted as an equal partner by the Europeans.

16 · Years of Crisis, 1994–2002

The Islamists take control

By far the greatest challenge challenge to the established parties that
competed for power after Özal's death came from the Islamist *Refah
Partisi* (Welfare Party). The size of the challenge became clear in the
municipal elections of 27 March 1994. The PTP just managed to remain
the biggest party, with 21.4 per cent, only a fraction more than the MP
with 21 per cent. The true winner, however, was the WP, which scored
19.1 per cent. In 1991 the party had also scored 17 per cent, but that had
been on a joint list with the extreme rightist NAP, which now took part
independently and managed to get 8 per cent in its own right. If was,
therefore, clear that support for the Islamists had nearly doubled. This
success was due as much to the excellent grassroots organization of the
party as to its message, which was summarized by its election slogan *adil
düzen* (just order). The WP's electoral gains were greatest in the
metropolitan areas. The WP took over six of the 15 largest Turkish cities,
including Istanbul and Ankara. This showed that the party had achieved
a breakthrough. It was no longer predominantly a party of small
businessmen, but had become the voice of the poorest sections of the
population in the enormous conurbations as well. It was also an
indication that in Turkey, as in many other European countries, the
phenomenon of the 'floating voter', who no longer had strong ideological
allegiances but could be won over from one party to another in each
election, was gaining importance. This trend would become even clearer
over the following decade. The secularist intelligentsia, which was of
course also based in the big cities, was in a state of panic after the urban
takeover by the WP, but after a few excesses in the immediate aftermath
of the elections, which were mainly due to young hotheads making the
point that 'it was now their turn', the situation calmed down and an
uneasy *modus vivendi* was gradually found in the cities, if not on a
national level.

The left of centre, in large part because of the traditional support it
received from the Alevi community, had always been able to count on a
minimum of 25 per cent of the vote, but internal divisions within the left

took their toll: the three 'social-democrat' parties polled 13.6 (SDP), 8.8 (DLP) and 4.6 (RPP) respectively. It was clear that the egos of Karayalçın, Ecevit and Baykal made a reunification of the left very difficult, but after the election disaster a grassroots movement started within the RPP and the SDP to force the leadership into a merger even if the two party leaders would have to step down to achieve it. A year later, on 18 February 1995, this movement was crowned with success when, after acrimonious debates with much mud slinging, the two leaders stepped down (at least temporarily) and the parties were reunified under the venerable banner of the Republican People's Party. Former foreign minister Hikmet Çetin led the unified party. The DLP, however, was so completely the party of Bülent Ecevit (people joked that whenever Ecevit had a cold the party headquarters stayed closed) that a similar movement in that party proved impossible.

The elections did not change the position of the government. The coalition and, above all, the discipline of the parties within the coalition, remained very weak. This showed in the problems the government faced on the two most important laws it wanted put on the statute book: the privatization law (which after a number of false starts was finally passed on an evening in November 1994 when about a third of the members of the assembly were glued to the television watching the European Cup football match between Galatasaray and Barcelona) and the political liberalization package, which had been on the agenda since 1989. It proved extremely difficult to get the statutory two-thirds majority for this package, which consisted mainly of the removal of a number of restrictive measures from the constitution that the junta had imposed in 1982. Conservatives in the ruling PTP joined the NAP and MP in opposition against measures such as the granting to civil servants of the right to join unions or the right of political parties to found youth organizations, while the WP and the religious wings of the MP and PTP made their support conditional upon scrapping article 24, which guaranteed the secular character of the political system. This in turn was totally unacceptable to the Social Democrats. Liberalization acquired more urgency when the European Union made the conclusion of a customs' union with Turkey explicitly dependent on it. Finally, and after a great deal of bargaining behind the scenes, the necessary two-thirds majority in the assembly passed a package on 23 July 1995. It contained changes to the preamble and 14 articles of the 1983 constitution. The change to the preamble meant that the passage praising the military takeover of September 1980 was deleted. The changes to the articles gave associations and trade unions the right to engage in politics, allowed civil servants to join trade unions and parties to establish youth and women's branches.

The voting age was brought down from 21 to 18. At last the legacy of the military coup was being discarded, but the package was a compromise and the people who had held power during the period of military rule still had immunity. The infamous article 8 of the anti-terrorism law was also kept in being after the army had let it be known that it considered it 'inappropriate' to scrap it.

A new phenomenon in the political landscape was the emergence of the *Yeni Demokrasi Hareketi* (New Democracy Movement) founded and led by a textile tycoon, Cem Boyner. Emulating other Mediterranean business tycoons such as Bernard Tapie in France and Silvio Berlusconi in Italy, he went into politics and drew a lot of attention with his unconventional informal style, his modern communication techniques and his sometimes rather daring opinions. That he was in favour of free market liberalism was less surprising than his advocacy of full religious freedom and a political solution to the Kurdish problem. Boyner, somewhat like Özal a decade earlier, managed to attract people from varied backgrounds, but his main support came from the modern business sector. At first Boyner said he wanted the NDM to remain a broad movement for change, not a party, but in the run-up to the elections of 1995 it was changed into a regular party. Little attention was paid to organizational matters and the building of grassroots support, however, and after its poor showing in the elections of December 1995 the movement petered out. Nevertheless, Boyner was a trendsetter in the sense that his exploits encouraged wealthy members of Turkey's civil society to take the initiative into their own hands and not to leave politics to the professional politicians and wait for them to solve the country's problems.

The reunification of the SDP (junior partner in a coalition with the right) and RPP (an opposition party) increased the tensions within the coalition. The RPP at first demanded that a new government be formed. Çiller was prepared to reshuffle the cabinet but would not hear of forming a new government, which would have implied renegotiating the coalition protocol. Over the summer and into the autumn, tensions kept on rising within the coalition, particularly when the trade unions began mass action for higher wages. In line with her austerity programme, Tansu Çiller at first offered increases that lagged far behind the galloping inflation, but the social democrat wing of the government could not afford to take such a hard line with what was after all its natural electoral base. The coalition finally broke up in early October, but decided to stay on as a caretaker government until elections could be held.

The elections of 24 December 1995 confirmed the trends that had surfaced in March 1994. The Islamist Welfare Party had further increased its strength and now became the biggest party with 21.4 per cent of the

vote – a true watershed in modern Turkish history. The Motherland Party
came second with 19.7 per cent, but this included the share of the Islamic
ultra-nationalists of the Great Unity Party with which it had a joint list.
After the elections the GUP split off and had seven seats in the new
assembly (out of 550). Çiller's Party of the True Path did far better than
expected, with only slightly fewer votes (19.2 per cent) but more seats
than the MP.[1] The left just managed to hold on to its core constituency
of 25 per cent, with 14.7 per cent going to the Democratic Left Party of
veteran Ecevit and Baykal's Republican People's Party just managing to
cross the electoral threshold of 10 per cent. The Nationalist Action Party
did not make the threshold (due to the split off of its Islamic wing as the
GUP) and neither did the pro-Kurdish People's Democracy Party
(HaDeP) and Cem Boyner's New Democracy Movement. HaDeP did
well in the southeast where it came second in most places, after the WP,
and first in some, but it failed to attract the votes of the Kurds living in
the big cities.

After the elections, a Mother–Path coalition seemed the logical way
out, but the personal differences between the leaders Yılmaz and Çiller
rendered it extremely difficult. President Demirel stuck to parliamentary
custom by giving WP leader Necmettin Erbakan, as leader of the largest
party, the first chance to form a government. Although all the other large
parties had emphatically declared that they would never join forces with
the Islamists, Yılmaz's MP actually came very close to a deal with
Erbakan. It miscarried at the last moment under tremendous pressure
from the military and the business community, after which an extremely
uneasy MP–PTP coalition was formed. This short-lived coalition was
almost completely paralysed by internal differences during its four
months in office. Its end came when the MP decided to support a
parliamentary investigation into alleged corruption on the part of Tansu
Çiller, which was demanded by the Welfare Party. Incensed by this 'treason
on the part of her partners', Çiller then announced that she was pulling her
party out of the coalition. Prime minister Yılmaz finally resigned on 6 June.
It was now clear that no stable government could be founded without the
participation of the Islamists and Erbakan was once more instructed to form
a government. This time it was Tansu Çiller who proved vulnerable to the
lure of power. She had excellent reasons to listen to Erbakan's overtures
because the WP offered to suspend the parliamentary investigations into her
financial dealings in exchange for her support. A cabinet was formed on 28
June. Erbakan would be prime minister for the first two years before
handing over to Çiller. In Turkey there was far less of a panic in secularist
circles than there had been after the March 1994 elections. Even the
Western-oriented business circles now gave priority to a stable government

over a secularist one. The army grumbled and signalled its alertness by firing officers it considered 'unreliable' (because of their Islamist tendencies), but showed no signs of open rebellion. The fact that supposedly secular Turkey was now ruled by an Islamist prime minister – so soon after the conclusion of the customs' union that was supposed to prevent it – sent shock waves through the Western world, however, which adopted an anxious wait-and-see attitude.

In its first months, however, the new cabinet (in which sensitive posts such as internal affairs, foreign affairs and economy were manned by people from the 'secular' PTP) went out of its way to avoid confrontation and acquire respectability. The strong Islamist rhetoric employed by the WP in opposition, which had called for the abolition of interest, a halt to integration with the EU (which was depicted as a Jewish–Masonic–Catholic conspiracy) and the breaking-off of relations with Israel was seemingly forgotten.

After six months the coalition seemed quite strong and stable. It was tolerated, rather than supported by the business community; suffered grudgingly by the military; and fiercely and constantly attacked by the mass circulation press, which in Turkey is dominated by two conglomerates (the Doğan group publishing *Milliyet* and *Hürriyet*, and the Bilgin group, which publishes *Sabah* and *Yeni Yüzyıl*), which hold 66 per cent of the market and own important television channels as well. The reasons why the coalition held together so well were not hard to find: Tansu Çiller could not afford to break it up with the accusations of corruption hanging over her head like a sword of Damocles and Erbakan could afford to wait while his support in the country continued to increase. By-elections in 1996 consistently gave him more than 30 per cent of the vote.

28 February 1997: Kemalist restoration

The apparently unassailable position of Erbakan and his party led them into a false sense of security. Not so much the party leadership, but some radical parliamentarians and mayors were tempted to make inflammatory statements and by New Year 1997 relations between the government and the army had begun to deteriorate rapidly. The first confrontation came when the Islamist mayor of Sincan (near Ankara) organized a 'Jerusalem Night' in support of the Palestinians, at which the Iranian ambassador to Turkey gave an anti-Western speech. The ambassador was called in to receive a formal protest, but three days later on 4 February a long column of armed personnel carriers slowly drove through the centre of Sincan, ostensibly on their way to manoeuvres. Shortly after, the army announced that it had formed a 'Task Force West' (*Batı Çalışma Grubu*) in the naval staff to collect evidence about fundamentalist threats to the state. Then, on 28 February, it presented the cabinet with a long list of demands (officially 'advice') aimed at curbing the influence of the Islamists in the economy, in education and inside the state apparatus. The most conspicuous demand was about the introduction of compulsory eight-year primary education in state schools. The idea behind this was that this would put the schools for preachers and prayer leaders (*imam-hatip okulları*) at middle school level out of business. These schools were very popular among the poorer sections of the population because they offered free and (in the eyes of conservative Muslims) safe education. Graduates of these schools had access to college-level education and ultimately the universities and, since the schools produced many times the number of graduates than could be employed in the religious estab-lishment, most of these graduates found places in other branches of the 'secular' state apparatus. In the eyes of the military and many secular Turks this created a danger that people with an Islamist agenda might infiltrate and gradually take over the state. The cabinet officially accepted the 28 February recommendations on 13 March, but did not do much about them. After six weeks the patience of the military had run out and in a nine-hour meeting of the National Security Council, the army top brass put forward its demands again, this time as an ultimatum. By now there was almost open warfare between the WP and the army. A general in Erzurum made derogatory remarks about Erbakan's pilgrimage to Mecca and about the Saudi government and when the government demanded that the army investigate his behaviour, it refused.

Erbakan survived a motion of no confidence on 20 May, but the army went on to mobilize different sections of society against the government. Trade unions and employers' federations got together in a 'front for secularism' on 21 May and on the same day the fanatically secularist prosecutor at the supreme court in Ankara, Vural Savaş, demanded the closure of the WP because 'it had become the focal point of criminal activity'.[2] Five days later the army dismissed 161 officers and NCOs on suspicion of Islamist leanings. In June the army started briefings for journalists and members of the judiciary on the fundamentalist threat. As a result of the pressure applied, increasing numbers of Tansu Çiller's PTP, the junior coalition party, started to desert the party. By mid-June it was clear that this flow could no longer be stemmed and on 18 June Erbakan stepped down. His assumption and that of the coalition was that Çiller would now be allowed to take over, but instead President Demirel, to the fury of Erbakan and Çiller, asked MP leader Mesut Yılmaz to form a government. Under enormous pressure from the military, Yılmaz formed a coalition with Ecevit's Democratic Left Party and the

Democratic Turkey Party of Hüsamettin Cindoruk, the grouping of Demirel's supporters who had broken away from the PTP. Thus the army had succeeded in executing what was called in Turkey at the time the 'first postmodern coup'.

The new government's main task obviously was to implement the reforms demanded by the army. This it did to a certain extent (a new education law introducing eight-year primary education was passed on 16 July),[3] but soon rifts started to appear. Throughout 1998 both Yılmaz and Ecevit gave vent to their irritation at the continued interference of the army in politics. Each time this happened, however, the Chief of the General Staff General Karadayı rebuked them and they were forced to express their support for the army publicly.

Measures to suppress the Islamists continued in quick succession. On 16 January 1998 the constitutional court banned the WP and Erbakan personally was banned from politics for five years, a sentence later increased to a life ban. In February, a case was opened against the popular WP mayor of Istanbul, Recep Tayyip Erdoğan. He was accused of inciting religious hatred because during an election rally he had quoted from an 80-year-old poem by Ziya Gökalp, in which Turkey's minarets were compared with bayonets. Two months later he was sentenced to ten months in prison. A number of other WP mayors were also prosecuted and a case was opened against MÜSİAD, the society of Muslim (officially 'independent') businessmen.

In the meantime the Islamists reorganized. On 23 February 1998 41 former WP deputies founded the Virtue Party (*Fazilet Partisi*) and when most of their colleagues joined them, the VP emerged as the largest group in parliament with 140 seats. Yılmaz's cabinet had its hands full with the attempts to satisfy the military without, at least in the case of the MP, estranging an important section of its following. At the same time it had to take urgent measures to rescue the economy. Inflation in July 1997, the month it took office, had been the highest since the founding of the republic and in August 1998 the Russian financial crisis hit Turkey hard. The cabinet sought part of the solution in urgent privatizations and it was over one of these that a corruption scandal erupted, involving Yılmaz himself. As a result he was forced to resign on 25 November and to announce new elections for 18 April 1999.

As these were the first elections after the coup of 1997, everybody was anxious to see if there would be an Islamist backlash. President Demirel had already made what can only be termed a shocking statement for the elected leader of a democratic country when, on 24 August 1998, he had said that if the VP and PTP won the next election, 'the state would act'.[4] But there was no backlash. The VP lost about a quarter of the old

WP's support and polled 15.4 per cent in April 1999. This was still considerable, but it meant a wholly unexpected third place behind Ecevit's DLP (22.1 per cent) and the NAP (18 per cent). The classical parties of the centre-right, MP and PTP, polled 13 and 12 per cent respectively. Geographically, there was a clear division: the developed west voted DLP, the Anatolian heartland NAP and the VP held on to most of the underdeveloped east. With the benefit of hindsight, two factors would seem to have determined the outcome. One was the sensational capture of PKK leader Abdullah Öcalan in February, which gave immense prestige to Ecevit who presided over the action as acting prime minister. That, combined with the generally recognized personal integrity of Ecevit, which contrasted sharply with the corruption scandals surrounding Yılmaz and Çiller, accounted for the DLP's success. The doubling of the votes of the NAP was more surprising. The man who had founded the NAP almost thirty years earlier, the 'leader' (başbuğ) Alpaslan Türkeş, had died on 4 April 1997 and, after a long drawn-out and acrimonious battle for the succession, Devlet Bahçeli, a veteran member of the violent 'idealist' (ülkücü) movement had become party leader. He moved at once in two directions. On the one hand he strove to give the NAP a more modern and civilized image, distancing himself from the radicalism and violence of the past, but on the other hand he consciously flirted with the Islamist vote, defending for instance the right to wear headscarves in schools and universities – something that was and is anathema to the Kemalists. This, plus the fact that the NAP was untainted by the scandals of either the Erbakan–Çiller days or of those of Yılmaz, made the party attractive to floating voters, of whom Turkey now had more than ever.

The cabinet formed after the elections was a coalition of DLP, NAP and MP under the leadership of veteran Bülent Ecevit, by now in his seventies. It may seem surprising that ultra-right and democratic left could join forces in a coalition, but in fact there was a lot of ideological common ground. Both parties were fiercely nationalistic and believed in a strong state.

The new government was totally preoccupied with the efforts to save Turkey's economy. A letter of intent was signed with the IMF on 2 July in which the government committed itself to tight fiscal policies and privatization in exchange for loans. Some newspapers drew attention to the fact that this was the seventeenth time Turkey had concluded such an agreement. The government was still concentrating on this issue to the exclusion of almost everything else when, at 3.02 a.m. on 17 August 1999, a huge earthquake (7.4 on the Richter scale) hit the densely populated area around the Gulf of İzmit east of Istanbul. The devastation was enormous and the official death toll was 15,000. In reality, probably at least double that number died, for registration of the population was very defective in the endless suburbs where immigrants from the countryside lived in an amorphous jungle of apartment blocks.

In the first days after the disaster, the state and the government seemed to be at a loss as to what to do. While politicians in Ankara gave out reassuring platitudes, the disaster affairs agency remained passive. No organized relief operation was launched in the crucial first 24 hours. The army took care of its own people (at the naval base in flattened Gölcük) but it was not put to work to save civilian lives. A host of countries – among them Greece and Israel – offered to help and sent specialized teams and medical supplies, but their efforts met with little cooperation on the part of the state. Supplies were held up at the customs and Osman Durmuş, the ultra-nationalist minister of health, tried to block foreign aid, saying that true Turks did not need a foreigner's blood. Significantly, the only organization that acquitted itself well, indeed performed heroics, was AKUT, which was not linked to the state. After a few days state agencies began to work in a more coordinated and efficient manner, but by then it was of course too late for many victims. The very visible failure of the state organs in the aftermath of the earthquake angered the population and brought forth an avalanche of criticism in the media. Uniquely for Turkey, the army was not exempt from the public's anger.

The recovery from the disaster was hampered by a second, slightly less lethal but still serious (7.2 on the Richter scale) earthquake more to the east, at Düzce on 12 November.

While the government struggled with the economy and with the human and material cost of the earthquakes (put at more than $25 billion), the Kemalist restoration continued unabated. The Virtue Party was accused of being a direct continuation of the Welfare Party and, in May, the indefatigable Vural Savaş opened a case against it. A little over two years later, on 22 June 2001, the constitutional court indeed banned the party. This brought to a head the debates within the VP between the conservatives, who were in favour of a strict Islamist line, and the modernists who wanted to turn the party into a broad right of centre movement and jettison the Islamist rhetoric. When the modernists lost out, they broke away under the leadership of Abdullah Gül and Tayyip Erdoğan to form the Justice and Development Party (*Adalet ve Kalkınma Partisi* or *AK Parti*)[5] on 14 August 2001. The Islamists went under a new name yet again, this time that of Party of Happiness (*Saadet Partisi*). This split was something the army probably had been aiming for all along, but it would come to rue it.

Memories of a darker Islamic past were rekindled in January 2000 with the discovery of a series of 'houses of horror' in which the bodies of dozens of missing businessmen and intellectuals were dug up. They were the work of the *Hizbullah*, a radical fundamentalist group inspired by Khomeini's revolution in Iran and the Muslim Brethren in Egypt. This organization had been started in the early 1980s by a man called Hüseyin Velioğlu and had operated in competition with the PKK in the southeast. The *Hizbullah* had split up and one section, with its epicentre in Batman, had developed close ties with the security apparatus, which had used it in its war against the PKK. As early as 1993 the *Hizbullah* organization in Diyarbakır had been dismantled in a wave of arrests, but the police commissioner responsible had immediately been transferred. A parliamentary commission of inquiry, which was formed in 1995, came under pressure to restrain itself and its report was subsequently buried, but when the war against the PKK seemed to be won in 1999, the *Hizbullah* had outlived its usefulness and there followed a crackdown in early 2000, during which the killing fields were discovered and Velioğlu was killed.[6]

The long drawn-out struggle to establish the rule of law over political considerations and the *raison d'état* received a boost with the election on 5 May 2000 of Necdet Sezer, the president of the constitutional court, as tenth president of the republic. Ecevit had tried his best to get his old rival Süleyman Demirel re-elected because he saw Demirel as a stabilizing factor, especially in the relationship with the army, but this needed a change in the constitution. His coalition partner Mesut Yılmaz, who had ambitions of his own, was not ready to support this. Sezer was nominated as someone with prestige but without a political power base, but the politicians soon discovered they had landed themselves with a problem. Sezer introduced a new style: he instructed his chauffeur to respect traffic lights, a novelty that yielded him tremendous positive publicity, but there was substance to his style as well. He had only been in office for a few months when he refused to sign the presidential decree that would allow the dismissal of public servants on political grounds (suspicion of fundamentalist leanings). This set the tone. In the years that followed, president Sezer again and again would refuse to sign laws and decrees that in his judgement ran counter to the rule of law. He took up an independent and critical attitude towards the cabinet. This culminated in an enormous row in February 2001, when the president confronted the prime minister with files on corruption in government circles and accused him of neglecting this for political reasons during a meeting of the National Security Council. Ecevit was enraged and – in a quite unprecedented manner – informed the press about what had been said in the NSC. This row between the president and the prime minister triggered a massive economic crisis because investors lost their confidence in the stability of the cabinet that had signed the IMF accords.

During the years 2001 and 2002 the cabinet was focused completely on its efforts to stem the economic and financial crisis. It brought into the cabinet Kemal Derviş, a Turkish director of the World Bank with a strong international reputation and gave him extensive powers. Derviş in many ways was quite successful in his efforts and he laid the foundation for long-term stability, but the credibility of the ruling coalition in the eyes of the Turkish population was gone and could not be restored in time.

The return of the Islamists

In the end it was not the economic or financial crisis that led to the demise of Ecevit's cabinet, but the prime minister's behaviour. There had been strong suggestions that he was physically unfit and at times emotionally unbalanced even at the time of his row with Sezer in February 2001, but in the year that followed the state of his health became more and more of a problem. By early 2002 he was clearly barely able to stand or speak for any length of time. When he refused to be hospitalized or to stand down and hand over the premiership, a revolt started in his party, which led to the unravelling of his coalition. The DLP dissidents split off to found a party of their own (the New Turkey Party) and Ecevit was left with no other option than to call for early elections. Derviş (who had so far stayed out of party politics) first threw in his lot with the DLP, but quickly recognized that it was a head without a body and changed sides to Deniz Baykal's opposition RPP.

The elections were held on 3 November 2002 and the results were spectacular. Polls had already indicated that the parties in the government coalition were unlikely to cross the 10 per cent threshold and so it was. The polls had also indicated that the modernist wing of the Islamist movement, the JDP of Tayyip Erdoğan, would be the main winner, but the size of its victory, when it came, was astonishing. The party polled more than 34 per cent and gained the absolute majority in the National Assembly. Deniz Baykal's RPP was the only other party to get into the assembly, with just over 19 per cent of the vote. Ecevit's support had shrunk by 95 per cent, but the dissidents of the New Turkey Party fared almost as badly. Of the other traditional parties only the Party of the True Path came close to the 10 per cent threshold.

It was a political earthquake and it had several causes. One was the rejection by the voters of the parties in the government coalition. These were held responsible for the collapse of the financial system. Another was the existence of a floating vote. This had already become clear in

1995 and 1999, but now traditional party loyalties seemed almost completely to have disappeared. Voters were prepared to follow anyone who could offer hope. There the figure of Tayyip Erdoğan was crucially important. Not only was he a charismatic leader with a working class background who could appeal to the masses, but he had also proved himself to be a very successful and popular mayor of the Istanbul metropolitan area in the years from 1994 to 1998. So in 2002 he was 'outside the system' (with his conviction for 'inciting to religious hatred' he could not even stand as a candidate himself) and at the same time he had credibility as an administrator.

The Turks voted for Erdoğan because they believed he could put an end to *yoksulluk* (poverty) and *yolsuzluk* (corruption), not because they wanted an Islamic state. This was shown convincingly by the fact that the JDP trounced the 'real' Islamists of the *Saadet Partisi* even in Konya, their heartland, where they had polled over 30 per cent in 1999.

Recurrent financial crises: 1994–2002
Economic policies were less important to the coalition government than they had been to Özal. It was Tansu Çiller who again put the economy at the top of the agenda. Her first priority was privatization of the state industries, not only because, as a confirmed Thatcherite, she was ideologically opposed to state intervention, but also because she saw it as a solution to the inefficiency of the state sector and to the mushrooming budget deficit. Çiller showed more than once that she clearly saw what the weak spots were in the Turkish economy. Nevertheless, her cabinet did not take any drastic measures during her first six months in office. By keeping the interest rates relatively low and at the same time supporting the exchange rate of the lira, the government tried to keep economic growth going. In this it was successful: GNP growth was 7.3 per cent in 1993, but the fundamental imbalances in the economy created an underlying tension. Sooner or later something would have to give and at the start of 1994 it did. Two American firms whose job it was to determine the credit ratings of countries and firms and whose judgement the international banks generally followed, both lowered their rating for Turkey twice in succession, down from 'investment grade' to 'risky'. The result was that the lira crashed (from 17,000 to the dollar to 30,000 in a matter of days) and interest rates shot up. It was the beginning of the first of three major economic recessions Turkey was to experience in the next seven years. Until the local elections of 27 March the government remained passive, but immediately after, on 5 April, a drastic stabilization programme was announced. It consisted largely of immediate short-term measures (tax raises, cuts in expenditure, rises in interest rates,

and sharp price increases for government services and state products) and in part also of plans for tax reform, an independent Central Bank, increased exports and a faster rate of privatization.

The short-term measures reduced (but did not eliminate) the budget deficit. At the same time the free fall of the lira ended the import boom, which also redressed the trade balance. The measures satisfied the IMF, which was ready to resume lending money to Turkey, but no emergency aid was forthcoming from either the IMF or the World Bank. This was in sharp contrast to Mexico's experience, for when it went through an almost identical crisis at this time it was bailed out under strong American pressure. Turkey had to face the crisis on its own.

The lira did not lose much further ground during the rest of 1994. Inflation by the end of the year stood at 150 per cent (mainly because of the government's price rises) but started to go down in early 1995. The other side of the coin was that the measures plunged the Turkish economy, already showing signs of stagnation at the start of the year, into a deep recession. GNP decreased by 6 per cent and more than 600,000 people lost their jobs. Those who kept their jobs faced a sharp drop in purchasing power. The trade unions, both *Türk-İş* and the smaller DİSK, hemmed in as they were between restrictive legislation, dwindling membership and lack of funds, offered no serious resistance. The most combative trade union was the Islamist confederation *Hak-İş*, which became more influential in the 1990s, but ultimately it was as powerless as the rest. For the moment, the labour movement seemed entirely demoralized and, even the fact that the social security system could no longer meet its obligations because employers had not paid their premiums, did not bring them out onto the streets.

While the government's immediate countermeasures brought some success, the structural reforms agreed with the IMF progressed hardly at all. The privatization law was finally passed in November 1994, but after that the actual selling off of state assets moved at a snail's pace. The state airline, ground handling facilities, tourism operations, petrochemical industries, electricity generators and telecommunications were all earmarked for speedy privatization, but between December 1994 and May 1995 only $65 million worth of assets were sold off. Some privatizations, like the sale of a tyre factory to an Iranian and of the state meat and fish suppliers to the Islamist trade union *Hak-İş* were politically so sensitive that they had to be cancelled. Nevertheless, the Turkish economy once more showed its resilience in the face of mismanagement and a gradual recovery began in late spring 1995. By the end of the year growth was quite strong again and the recovery continued throughout 1996. None of the fundamental problems, however, had been addressed.

Inflation stayed above 80 per cent and the trade deficit ballooned as soon as the recovery got underway. A programme to curb tax evasion was announced in May but never materialized and when the new Islamist-led government came to power, it embarked on populist policies that formed a clean break with Çiller's policies of 1994/5. As soon as Erbakan was in power, he announced a 50 per cent pay rise for the country's 1.8 million state employees and rises for pensioners of up to 130 per cent. That there was no room in the budget for this kind of generosity was clear to all, but the government blithely announced that it would raise $50 billion of extra revenue through privatization, the eradication of the black market and the sale of state land. Clearly, this economic policy lacked credibility. The structural problems of the Turkish economy (debt, inflation, state sector inefficiency) were not addressed and in 1998 the country suffered a sharp downturn. The immediate cause was the Russian financial crisis of that year. This, coming as it did after the financial crisis in East Asia, undermined confidence in the so-called 'emerging markets' in general, but it hit Turkey more severely because Russia was such an important market for Turkish business. GDP declined by 6.4 per cent in 1999.[7]

The Ecevit government, which came to power after the elections of April 1999, launched a far-reaching economic reform programme with the help of the IMF and the World Bank (which, unlike in 1994, was forthcoming this time). The programme, agreed in December 1999, consisted of a curb on government spending, privatization and a pre-announced exchange rate. The target for inflation was set at 25 per cent for 2000, dropping to 10 per cent in 2002. Wage increases were linked to the expected instead of the real inflation. For a time this programme worked. Inflation and the interest rate fell sharply, investment rose and there was an atmosphere of optimism. But it did not last for long. The consumers used the new environment to go on a buying spree. The current account deficit rose and the government had to borrow at increasingly unfavourable rates. It became clear that the fixed exchange rate of the lira to the dollar would be untenable and foreign banks, afraid of a sudden collapse, stopped lending to Turkish banks. For some of the Turkish banks this was the last straw. They had been irresponsible both in their lending and in their borrowing. The banks had borrowed heavily abroad to buy government bonds with high real interest rates, but they had also lent out money indiscriminately because after the 1994 crisis the state had introduced a blanket guarantee for all bank deposits. The state banks had the added problem (which had been around for decades) that the political bosses used them to provide cheap credit to politically interesting sectors, such as agriculture, small business and house building.

In November 2000, a full-scale flight out of the lira was narrowly avoided, but with a public row between President Sezer and Prime Minister Ecevit about the latter's alleged refusal to combat corruption in February 2001, confidence disappeared overnight and the programme collapsed. The lira halved in value and in 2001/2 the economy contracted by perhaps as much as 9 per cent. As the elections of November 2002 showed, the political elite was not forgiven for this failure. In purely economic terms, though, the Ecevit government's legacy was far from wholly negative. Under the guidance of the minister for the economy, Kemal Derviş, important steps had been taken to restructure the financial system. The Central Bank was made independent and political influence in the banking sector was reduced. The law on tender procedure was changed. All these measures were intended 'to increase transparency' (IMF jargon for reducing corruption).

Victory over the PKK?
Combined military and political pressure eventually gave Turkey the victory over the PKK it so desired. After the removal of Erbakan (and Çiller) from office, the new Ecevit–Yılmaz cabinet, which in security matters clearly was under tutelage of the army, began to make threatening noises in the direction of Syria. This country, after all, still gave shelter to Abdullah Öcalan and the PKK headquarters and training camps. Syria probably already saw Öcalan as something of a liability. After all, the Syrian leadership had been left out in the cold after the collapse of the Soviet Union and now realized it had to improve its relations with the United States, a close ally of Turkey. At the same time Syria was hemmed in between Israel and Turkey, and military cooperation between these two countries was increasing all the time. So, when Turkey was threatening war in October 1998, the Syrians told Öcalan that he had outstayed his welcome and put him on an aeroplane. After a stay of about a month in Moscow, some left-wing Italian parliamentarians brought Öcalan to Rome. There he was put under house arrest while his application for political asylum was being dealt with. An attempt to go to Germany or the Netherlands having failed, Öcalan left Rome for the Greek island of Corfu. The Greek government, fearing a confrontation with Turkey, in turn shipped him off to its embassy in Nairobi (Kenya). Somehow he was persuaded to leave the embassy compound, however, and Turkish commandos captured and kidnapped him on 16 February 1999, most probably with the help of the CIA, which had its largest station in the region in Nairobi.

After his return to Turkey, Öcalan was imprisoned on an island in the Sea of Marmara, which is also where he was tried and ultimately convicted to death by hanging (a sentence changed to life imprisonment in 2002). Öcalan's behaviour during the trial was remarkable and a source of disillusionment for many of his supporters. He was anything but defiant and heroic. Rather, he gave the impression of a broken man, meek and at times depressed. He asked for understanding and forgiveness and more than once declared his great love for the Turkish people.

Öcalan had already declared during his stay in Rome that the PKK would seek a peaceful solution to the conflict. This line was now reaffirmed by the PKK leadership, which declared that it continued to regard 'Apo' as its leader, but also that the cease-fire declared in August 1998 would remain in force. The changeover from military to political struggle was symbolized by changing the name PKK into KADEK (Kurdish Freedom and Democracy Congress) in 2002. Turkey reacted by gradually abolishing the state of emergency in the southeast. The 'Extraordinary Zone' (OHAL) was diminished from 2000 onwards and completely abolished by 2002.

Human rights and the 'deep state'
The years 1994–2002 were not just years of crisis because of the political instability, corruption scandals, military intervention and economic crises, but also because of a breakdown in the relationship between the state and sections of society. The polarization caused by the Kurdish conflict put the civil rights of the citizens of Turkey under increasing pressure. More and more people were persecuted under the anti-terrorism legislation. Even worse, perhaps, were the 'executions without due process' (*yargısız infaz*) – the shooting of suspects who, according to the police, had resisted arrest – and the mounting number of murders whose perpetrators remained unknown.

The connection between the rightist mafia and the state was an issue that touched on both the Kurdish question and human rights. Organized crime in Turkey (mainly drugs and arms smuggling) had become increasingly important during the 1980s and early 1990s. It was in the hands of two distinct groups of mafia families. One was Kurdish. Some of its leading 'businessmen' supported and subsidized the PKK, some did not and most played both sides against the middle. The other group consisted of former 'idealists' (*ülkücüler*), the armed gangs attached to Alpaslan Türkeş's Nationalist Action Party. These had always had close links with the security apparatus. They were now rumoured to serve the government in its 'dirty war' against the Kurds. The relations between mafia and state hit the headlines first in 1995 when Uğur Kılıç, daughter of a famous mafia godfather (and ex-wife of another), was shot dead after she had testified that Semra Özal, the wife of the former president, had been behind the shooting of a former director of a state bank by mafia members. Then, in the spring of 1996, Tansu Çiller was accused of illegally siphoning off money from the budget for unspecified 'security expenditure' in the last weeks before the 1995 elections (this was one of the accusations that caused the fall of her coalition with Yılmaz). According to an intelligence report leaked by the MİT (possibly to undermine the new coalition of Çiller and Erbakan), this money was spent on an unofficial 'state gang' engaged in secret operations against the PKK and its sympathizers and led by Çiller and the interior minister (and former police chief) Mehmet Ağar. The existence of close links between the state and organized crime seemed to be confirmed when, on 3 November, a car was crushed in a road accident in the western town of Susurluk. There were four people in the car: a senior police officer, a pro-government Kurdish chief (and PTP parliamentarian), a former beauty queen and Abdullah Çatlı, a former *ülkücü* terrorist who had killed seven leftist students before 1980 and had been indirectly involved in the assassination attempt on the Pope. He was supposedly on the run, but turned out to be holding an official VIP passport. It also turned out that the four had just returned from a seaside resort, where Interior Minister Ağar had also been staying. Both the opposition and large sections of public opinion now began to clamour for an Italian-style 'Operation Clean Hands'.[8] But the mafia's arm reached far: when opposition leader Yılmaz demanded a full investigation, he was attacked by another former Grey Wolf during a stopover in Budapest on his way back from Berlin, and suffered a bloody nose. Particularly frightening was the fact that this 'warning' came during an unscheduled stop, implying help from inside.

In the second half of the 1990s *derin devlet* ('the deep state') became a frequently used codeword for this whole complex of links between the security services, the politicians, the ultranationalists and the mafia. Investigations into the existence of these links did not lead to any convictions of high ranking persons. The key figure in Çiller's 'dirty war', former police chief and minister Mehmet Ağar continued his political career and was elected into parliament as an independent member for Elazığ both in 1999 and 2002.

Luxemburg, Helsinki and Copenhagen: or does Turkey belong in Europe?

If the Europeans had hoped that the customs' union would satisfy Turkish ambitions for the foreseeable future, they could not have been more wrong. The customs' union was seen in Turkey as the penultimate step towards full membership (as indeed had been foreseen in the 1963

Ankara treaty) and they continued to press the EU to recognize this. By the second half of the 1990s, the EU had to come up with some answers about its future shape and size, for the eastern European countries, which had shaken off communist rule in 1989–90, now wanted to start concrete negotiations on membership. The accession process was started at the EU summit in Luxemburg in December 1997, but its decisions were a bitter pill for the Turks. The summit decided to open negotiations with ten east European countries and Cyprus, but not with Turkey. It continued to recognize Turkey's right to accede to the Union, but negotiations would start only when the political conditions had been met. These conditions consisted of the so-called 'Copenhagen criteria' formulated by the EU in 1993[9] and of the demand that Turkey cooperate with the UN over Cyprus and submit its differences with Greece on the Aegean Sea to the International Court of Justice in The Hague.

The summit decision did not come as a complete surprise. Politicians of the Christian Democrat right, including Germany's long-serving Chancellor Kohl, had said publicly that they did not consider Turkey a European country. On 4 March 1997, the Christian Democrats in the European parliament had even declared officially that Turkey was not a candidate for EU membership. Nevertheless, Turkish public opinion was infuriated by the different treatment meted out to itself, the EU's oldest associate member, and the new candidates from eastern Europe. The Turkish government broke off contacts with the EU and, in 1998, EU–Turkish relations reached an all-time low. Prime Minister Yılmaz contributed to the bad-tempered atmosphere by stating on different occasions that Germany was in search of 'living space' (*Lebensraum* – a term used by Hitler) in eastern Europe and that Chancellor Kohl was an enemy of the Turks. The ferocity of the Turkish reaction made an impression. After Kohl's departure from office, Germany under the new Social Democrat chancellor Schröder, took the initiative for a rapprochement and, at the Helsinki summit of December 1999, the EU reaffirmed its commitment to Turkey's future membership. It also gave Turkey access to the so-called pre-accession programmes, from which the east European countries profited. In the following years, Turkey concentrated on meeting the Copenhagen criteria, changing its legislation and even its constitution in the process, but it could not catch up with the other candidates. At the EU summit in Copenhagen in December 2002, ten new countries were offered membership by 2004. The most Turkey could achieve was an agreement that its candidature would be reviewed in December 2004 and that negotiations would then start 'without delay' if it met the criteria.[10]

Regional relations after 1991

Turkey remained relatively isolated in the Middle East. Relations with the Arab world remained cold because of Turkey's increasingly close relationship with Israel, which included military cooperation. When Erbakan came to power, foreign relations was the one field where the Islamist prime minister, who had to make far-reaching concessions to the military and to his coalition partners at home, could show that the WP in government really did make a difference. Accordingly, his first foreign visits were to Muslim countries, including – to the Americans' fury – Iran and Libya. Erbakan did not and almost certainly could not move to weaken the ties with NATO and the EU. The army even pressured him into signing a military cooperation agreement with Israel. His foreign policy was largely symbolic.

If Turkey has had to face rebuffs in its relations with the Turkic states of Central Asia, it is also true that Turkish foreign policy has achieved some real and concrete successes in its own back yard – in the Balkans and the Black Sea area – since the end of the cold war. The good and even warm relations with post-communist Bulgaria, Macedonia and Albania, as well as later Bosnia and Kosovo, have put an end to Turkey's isolation in the Balkans and the founding of the Black Sea Economic Cooperation Organization with ten member states in 1992 – a brainchild of Ministry of Foreign Affairs *éminence grise* Şükrü Elekdağ although President Özal poached the idea – gave Turkey the initiative in the development of relations in the Black Sea region. Significantly, the organization includes both Muslim and non-Muslim states.

Turkey emphasized its role as a Balkan power by taking part both in the peacekeeping operations in Bosnia and in the war with Serbia over Kosovo. Relations with the old enemy Greece improved dramatically in the late 1990s. Contacts between the artists and intellectuals of the two countries had been on the increase for some time (Yılmaz had met the Greek prime minister Simitis in November 1997 and the Turkish Chief of the General Staff had met his counterpart in April 1998), but it was the earthquake of 17 August 1999 that really caused a breakthrough. The Greek government grabbed the chance to force an opening to Turkey. The Greek Red Cross and volunteer organizations were among the first to offer help and their generosity received a lot of attention in the Turkish press. Contacts in the realm of sports followed, with Turkey and Greece putting in a joint bid to host the European football championships in 2008. In 2002 Greece came out strongly in support of Turkey's future membership of the EU.

17 · Justice and Development, 2002–14

Together with Europe against the Kemalist state

The outcome of the elections of 3 November 2002 started an earthquake of a magnitude that was comparable only to the elections of 1950 that ended the power monopoly of the Republican People's Party. The new *Adalet ve Kalkınma Partisi* (Justice and Development Party, or AKP) won the elections with more than 34 per cent of the vote and thereby gained an absolute majority in parliament. It achieved this success even although its real leader, the charismatic mayor of Greater Istanbul Recep Tayyip Erdoğan, had been unable to take part in the campaign (or stand as a candidate) because he was still in prison. He had been given a prison sentence because, at a meeting early on in the campaign, he had read a poem by the Young Turk nationalist Ziya Gökalp, which spoke of 'minarets used as bayonets'. Soon after the elections he was released and, in March 2003, he was appointed the 25th prime minister of the Republic of Turkey. In the next decade, he would put his stamp on the country in a way that only Atatürk and to a certain extent Özal had done before him.

The election result of November 2002 was an earthquake, not only because of the AKP's success, but also, and even more so, because of the complete collapse of the parties that had been in power until then. Ecevit's party, the DSP, lost 95 per cent of its following and was left with slightly more than 1 per cent of the vote. Its place was taken over by Deniz Baykal's CHP, which after years in the wilderness now became the only opposition party in parliament, with 19 per cent of the vote. Of the major right-wing parties, the MHP and DYP remained just under the 10 per cent threshold, and the ANAP was stuck on 5 per cent. With only 2.5 per cent of the vote, Erbakan's conservative Islamist Necmettin Saadet Partisi was thrashed. The new Kurdish party, the HDP, did well in the southeast, where it became the largest party in every province, but countrywide it only managed to get 6 per cent of the vote, so it too was excluded from parliament. On the map it was now very clear how Turkey was divided – the southeast was Kurdish; the south and west coasts, as well as European Turkey, were secularist Kemalist; and all the rest, including the big cities of Ankara and Istanbul, were AKP.

There were several reasons for the AKP's success. Above anything else, the Turkish people wanted to punish the established political parties, which they held responsible for the deep economic crisis of 2000/1, which had hit many Turks directly, and for years of political instability and impotence. Struggles between the army and Islamists, between the ANAP and DYP on the right, and the CHP and DSP on the left, the rivalry between President Sezer and Prime Minister Ecevit – had all destroyed public respect for the political system. Electoral surveys showed that the AKP drew its support not only from former supporters of the Islamist SP, but also from the traditional parties of the right, ANAP and DYP, and even from the CHP and MHP.

The personality of Recep Tayyip Erdoğan was important for the success of the AKP. In him the party had a charismatic leader, with whom the mass of the population could identify. He was a son of migrants, who had moved to Istanbul from the eastern Black Sea coast, and he had grown up in a poor migrant neighbourhood, Kasımpaşa, where he gained experience as a street seller and semi-professional football player. He was someone who represented the aspirations of millions of new city dwellers. Ever since his days as an Islamist student activist in the 1970s, he had supported the values with which the mass of the people could identify, which were religious, conservative, nationalist and anti-Semitic. After the Islamists' electoral victory in 1994, he became mayor of the Istanbul metropolitan area and, in that position, made himself popular by markedly improving the administration and public services.

The AKP could form a government on its own, first with Abdullah Gül as prime minister and, from March 2003 onwards, under Erdoğan. The government had little to fear from the opposition, but with the 'postmodern coup' of 1997 still fresh in everyone's memory, it nevertheless felt insecure. Paradoxically, even when in power, the AKP had the mentality of an underdog. The reason for this was that, although government and parliament were in AKP hands, the state machinery, judiciary, police and army were not. Chipping away at the autonomy of the state and establishing political control over its organs, particularly the army, would become the most important theme of the next five years. In this struggle, the AKP found a strong partner in the European Union. Ever since the 1999 summit in Helsinki, Turkey had been recognized as a candidate for EU-membership, but in the next few years its prospects of membership had not really improved, partly because of the severe financial crisis in Turkey. At the 2002 summit in Copenhagen, the EU announced that it would admit ten new members in 2004, but Turkey was not among them.

The best that Turkey could achieve was an assurance that its membership prospects would be discussed again at the summit in The Hague in December 2004 and that, if by then it met the so-called 'Copenhagen criteria', membership negotiations would start without further delay. This promise came to be known as the 'date for a date'. In the meantime, the debate in Europe about the borders of Europe and Turkey's European credentials intensified, but the December 2004 summit gave the green light after all and, on 3 October 2005, membership negotiations actually started.

To gain access to the EU, Turkey was obliged to carry out far-reaching political and judicial reforms aimed at establishing democratic controls, transparency and legislation that took human rights and civic freedoms into consideration. At the same time, becoming part of Europe was an ambition with widespread support among the Turkish public. For the elite, it was partly an ideological issue because anchoring Turkey in Europe would guarantee its Western orientation. For the mass of the population, however, it was a more pragmatic desire for a better and more affluent lifestyle, but it meant that the AKP could now defend its own political agenda – bringing the state under control – by referring to the demands of the EU.

Between 2002 and 2006, the pace of reform was breathtaking. From October 2003 to July 2004, parliament passed 261 new laws,[1] many of which concerned the position of the military in the political system, legal procedures and human rights. In the next parliamentary year, another 166 laws were passed. Thereafter, the pace slackened, but the cumulative effect of these legal changes in the first years of the AKP government was enormous. Changes in the role of the National Security Council (MGK) fundamentally altered the position of the army. The MGK now became what, on paper, it had been from the beginning – an advisory body. The cabinet's legal obligation to act on its advice was dropped and its powerful secretariat lost its right to do research, collect information from all state organs at all levels, as well as to monitor the execution of its own recommendations. For the first time, a civilian was appointed secretary to the MGK. Important parts of the defence budget were brought under parliamentary scrutiny for the first time. In May 2004, the infamous state security courts (*devlet güvenlik mahkemeleri*) with their military judges were abolished and the General Staff lost the right to appoint its own members to the councils controlling higher education, radio and television.

A completely new criminal law was passed in January 2005 that replaced the old one of 1934 (which had been derived from Mussolini's criminal code). Together, with new laws on judicial procedure, the creation of a new level of courts between the courts of first instance on the one hand and the supreme and constitutional courts on the other, made the judiciary much more accessible for citizens and gave them better protection against arbitrariness and torture. The death penalty was abolished. New laws on press freedom and the right of association increased citizens' liberties. To give just one example, in case of a violation of the press law, it was no longer possible to confiscate the printing presses where the publication had been produced.

Overall, this wave of reforms in the years between 2002 and 2006 changed the relationship between the state, its citizens and their elected representatives in a fundamental way. At least on paper, Turkey had quickly become an essentially European country.

The policies of the AKP, which positioned itself as the party fighting the almighty authoritarian state on behalf of 'the people', were overwhelmingly endorsed when the Turkish population next went to the polls for the local elections of 2004. In these elections, which were for mayors as well as municipal and provincial councillors, the party won almost 42 per cent of the vote, up 8 per cent from 2002. The CHP remained the biggest opposition party with 19 per cent (the same as two years earlier), but it only won in towns and cities along the west coast and in Thrace, where there was strong resistance to the conservative Islamic ideas of the AKP. Perhaps the most telling result was that the three main opposition parties (the MHP, CHP and DYP) together received fewer votes than the AKP on its own. Undoubtedly, the AKP's success was primarily due to the economic recovery after the 2000–2 crisis, but essentially the opposition, both left and right, stood empty handed. The AKP reformed, brought economic growth and closed the gap with Europe. The opposition's hollow rhetoric on the 'danger of Islamization' or 'betrayal of Cyprus' (see below) could not counterbalance that.

With the opposition essentially powerless, in its early years President Necdet Sezer became the AKP cabinet's main hurdle. Sezer was a committed secularist and primarily interpreted the AKP reforms as attempts to undermine the secular republic. As a former judge in the constitutional court, he frequently used his powers to refer legislation passed in parliament to that same court, where it was often ruled unconstitutional. This is not surprising given that the constitution was still the one imposed by the military junta back in 1982. He refused to sign more than three hundred appointment decrees that the cabinet had submitted to him and strictly applied the ban on headscarves in public service. In fact, he refused to receive the spouses of AKP politicians who wore headscarves in the presidential palace. No wonder the AKP counted the days until the end of Sezer's seven-year term in 2007. The issue of his succession led to the biggest – and in many respects most decisive – test of strength between the AKP and its enemies.

In the spring of 2007, there was a lot of speculation about who the AKP would present as its presidential candidate – Prime Minister Erdoğan or Foreign Minister Gül. Even before there had been an official announcement, the secularists mobilized their forces. Their nightmare was that with Sezer's departure the last counterweight against the AKP would be removed and that this would open the door to the far-reaching Islamization of Turkey. The secularist Kemalists felt abandoned by the EU and the United States. The EU continuously praised the AKP for its reforms and in Washington the idea gained traction that Turkey, as a moderate Islamic state with a market economy and democratic politics, could be an attractive example for the rest of the Middle East. The Kemalists saw this as an insult – Turkey after all was part of the West! Sezer played an active role in this mobilization with speeches in which he showed his concern about the future of the secular order. On 17 April, more than 300,000 Kemalists demonstrated in Ankara. In the end, Erdoğan withdrew his own candidacy and supported Abdullah Gül as the AKP's sole candidate for the presidency.

The first vote was on 27 April 2007. According to the constitution, a two-thirds majority was needed in the first round, but because the whole opposition boycotted the session, this could not be attained. In the second round a simple majority would be enough, but the opposition asked the constitutional court to declare the vote void because there had been no quorum. During this stalemate, shortly before midnight a proclamation appeared on the general staff website under the heading 'fundamentalist activities and the duties of the army'. In the statement, the army top brass said that 'nobody should forget that the army was a participant in the debates about the secular nature of the state and that it would clarify its position when needed.' Of course, this was strongly reminiscent of the start of the military intervention against the Islamist Prime Minister Erbakan, ten years before, but this time the government, which had much more self-confidence after two successive electoral landslides, hit back. The next morning, 28 April, the AKP reacted with a sharply worded statement in which it said that the general staff was subordinate to the prime minister and that in a democracy it was unacceptable for a general staff to criticize its own government.

Meanwhile, the tension rose. The secularists held daily mass demonstrations in all the major cities and, on 1 May, the constitutional court, on advice from the army and president, declared the election void. However, this time, too, the cabinet reacted swiftly and decisively. Prime Minister Erdoğan called for new elections and proposed a number of amendments to the constitution. The most important of these were a reduction of the president's term from seven to five years (with the option of re-election) and a proposal that in future (but not this time) the president should be elected directly by the people and not by parliament. For the time being, the parliamentary term was reduced from five to four years. There was an outcry from the opposition and the president refused to sign the amendments that parliament had passed, but the constitutional court turned down his request to declare them unconstitutional. Instead, it ordered a referendum, which was to take place three months later.

The early election on 22 July made power relations in the country abundantly clear. The AKP continued its rise and now polled 46.5 per cent of the vote. The CHP recovered somewhat with 21 per cent, but because the MHP now also crossed the threshold with 14 per cent, the AKP ended up with fewer seats (341) despite its bigger share of the vote. Nevertheless, the outcome of the election was a resounding endorsement of the AKP and a snub to the army. Nearly all 27 of the independents who entered the new parliament were linked to the Kurdish DTP. They had made use of a loophole in the electoral law that allowed independents to be elected without a threshold. The attempts of the traditional centre-right parties (ANAP and DYP) to merge, in the end failed.

On 21 August, Abdullah Gül was elected the eleventh president of Turkey. The referendum on the constitutional amendments took place on 21 October and once more was a resounding victory for the AKP. All the protests and 'republican marches' of the secularists notwithstanding, a silent majority of 69 per cent of the population proved to support Erdoğan and Gül.

The last act in this confrontation between Kemalists and Islamists, between the old and new power in Turkey, was the case that the highest public prosecutor, Abdurrahman Yalçınkaya, brought before the constitutional court in March 2008. He requested the closure of the AKP on the grounds of a claim that the party had become a centre of anti-secular activities. In the end, the court let the AKP off with a warning: six judges voted for closure and five against. As seven votes were required for a closure decision, a further confrontation was narrowly avoided and the party could continue to rule the country.

The year 2007 marked a very important turning point – a struggle for power with no holds barred between the old Kemalist establishment and the AKP. The AKP decided to stand its ground and, with backing from nearly half the population in the elections and two-thirds in the referendum, it was so strong that neither the army nor the constitutional court dared confront it. With the opposition parties as impotent as they ever were, the AKP could now consolidate its hold on the country and settle its accounts.

Ergenekon and Balyoz

The means the government chose to eliminate the army as a political actor was a criminal investigation that had been running since June 2007 and that would dominate the headlines in Turkey for the next six years.

It was an investigation into the 'deep state'. As we have seen, people had been aware of an underground network of militias, security services and military officers, known collectively as *kontragerilla*, since the 1970s and that it had been involved in the persecution and suppression of the radical left in Turkey. In the 1980s, a gendarmerie officer, Veli Küçük, secretly reorganized this group and named it JİTEM (*Jandarma İstihbarat ve Terörle Mücadele* – Gendarmerie, Intelligence and Counterterrorism) and, in the 1980s and 1990s, it was primarily deployed in the 'dirty war' against the Kurdish PKK. In 1997, the Susurluk scandal brought to light the ties that connected right-wing militants with a background in the circle of the 'Idealists' with JİTEM and the government of Tansu Çiller. In the months that followed, more and more details about the illegal network of militias and security services emerged and the whole complex became known collectively as *derin devlet*, 'the deep state'. The deep state was also held responsible for the disappearance of thousands of Kurdish citizens in the southeast.

In 1997, Ergenekon – the ultranationalist, pan-Turkist name for the Turks' mythical homeland in Central Asia – was first used to describe the illegal network.[2] The word resurfaced in June 2007 when police searching a retired subaltern officer's house in the Ümraniye neighbourhood of Istanbul found a stash of hand grenades and explosives. The public prosecutor investigating the case linked it to an older file from 2001 on Tuncay Güney. At the time, Güney, a young Jewish Turkish journalist, had been arrested for fraud, but during his interrogation it transpired that he was an undercover agent working for JİTEM under the code name *İpek* (Silk). That was not all. He was also a double agent who had infiltrated JİTEM on behalf of the national security service, MİT. In his statement, Güney said that there was a widespread network of ultranationalists called Ergenekon and that this state within the state had been responsible for murders and disappearances. In 2001, the file was put aside and MİT helped Güney slip out of the country on a false passport to settle in New York. It is impossible to judge the veracity of his statements, but the Susurluk case four years earlier had shown that there was in fact a secret underground war going on between JİTEM and MİT.

In 2007, the prosecution concluded that the discovery of the hand grenades and explosives was connected to Ergenekon and that this network was involved in one or more conspiracies aimed at a *coup d'état* against the AKP government. The network was also linked to two shock-ing murders in 2007, that of the Armenian Turkish chief editor of the weekly *Agos*, Hrant Dink, on 18 January and that of three owners of a Christian publishing house in Malatya on 18 April.

Wave after wave of arrests followed, in which ever-larger groups of increasingly prominent people were arrested, including retired officers, journalists, police constables, a mayor and a number of academics. In 13 separate waves in 2008 and 2009, 275 people were arrested and charged and, in the meantime, several arms caches were discovered. Ultimately, three separate cases were brought to court and Hrant Dink's murder was added to one of these three files.

While the police and public prosecution services were undertaking these actions, the media, or at least some media, were also playing an important role. Some of the left-wing liberal media, like *Nokta* (Point) and *Taraf* (Side), which were strongly antagonistic to the Kemalist state's army and security services, acquired important and explosive inform-ation. For example, diaries ascribed to a former naval commander sug-gested that the armed forces had been finalizing plans to destabilize the government and execute a *coup d'état*. Their planned operations, which had evocative names like 'Blondie' (*Sarı Kız*), 'Moonlight' (*Ay Işığı*) and 'Cage' (*Kafes*), included murdering non-Muslims in Turkey and mis-informing the public about government plans to turn Turkey into an Islamic state.

The whole process entered a new phase when, in January 2010, *Taraf* was handed a suitcase containing 8000 documents pertaining to a coup called 'Operation Sledgehammer' (*Balyoz*) that the Turkish army had been planning since 2003. These documents showed that the army intended to orchestrate fundamentalist attacks in the country and, as an excuse for taking over power, even considered blaming Greece for a planned downing of a Turkish fighter jet. The army, which denied the existence of the plan, claimed that some of the documents referred to regular army exercises. Although numerous people at the time doubted the authenticity of the documents and, indeed, many of them were later shown to be falsifications, the public prosecutors brought two cases against top military officers. After years of controversy, the verdict in the *Balyoz* case was finally pronounced in September 2012, followed by Ergenekon in August 2013. The verdics were harsh with many receiving life sentences, some of them multiple. What shocked public opinion the most was that many of those who were arrested, accused and convicted were only a few years earlier in the highest positions of authority, such as former Chief of General Staff İlker Başbuğ, former First Army Commander Çetin Doğan, and various air force and navy senior personnel. For the pashas, who until recently had been completely untouchable in Turkey, this was traumatic, but the whole officer corps seemed paralysed and demoralized by the long, drawn out trials and all the publicity.

In Turkey, the *Balyoz* and Ergenekon trials were and are very controversial. There is no doubt that underground ultranationalist networks existed within the state apparatus. Successive governments had frequently made use of the networks to do their dirty work, particularly in the early 1970s and 1990s. That many in Turkey deeply mistrusted the AKP and suspected it of having a secret agenda to turn Turkey into an Islamic state, is also a fact. Some of them would have preferred the army to take over. At the same time, it is also clear that the trials were used to silence outspoken secularist critics of the AKP and some of the evidence produced, especially in the *Balyoz* case, was very suspect. The courts at the time seemed hardly to be interested in finding the truth and to be working according to a pre-arranged protocol.

Whatever the truth, the AKP had reached its goal. The army was no longer an independent countervailing force against the elected politicians. It kept silent when, on 13 July 2013, ten years after it had first been announced, article 35 of the army's Internal Service Law (*İç Hizmet Kanunu*) was changed. This article, which claimed that 'the task of the Turkish armed forces is to guard and defend the Turkish fatherland and the Turkish republic, as described in the constitution', had always been the legal basis for military intervention in politics. Now the army's task was limited to the defence of 'the borders of the nation' and its duty to defend the republican order was scrapped. From now on, the army was solely an instrument of the government.

Fethullah Gülen and the 'Service'

In the court cases, the name of Fethullah Gülen's movement came up several times and, remarkably, on both sides. In 2001, Tuncay Güney claimed that Gülen had collaborated closely with Veli Küçük in the Ergenekon network. This is quite probable because, as we saw in Chapter 16, in the 1980s and 1990s Gülen had been quite close to Evren's neo-Kemalist state. On the other hand, many of the public prosecutors and judges in the special courts that handled the Ergenekon and *Balyoz* trials were themselves followers of Gülen. The reason for this lies in the rather special symbiosis between Gülen's *Hizmet* ('Service') movement and Erdoğan's *Milli Görüş* ('National Vision').

As we have seen, Gülen's movement had its roots in education, especially for poor but talented youngsters. The movement had grown primarily as a network of preparatory schools (*dershaneler*) at which children were prepared for high school. Later on, high schools, colleges and even universities were added to the network. The movement was extremely successful in spotting and shaping talent. Hence, 30 years after it started, it had built a large cadre of well-educated – and pious – economists, managers, lawyers and administrators. This was what the AKP needed most after its electoral victory of 2002. The party had the support of a large part of the population and an important section of the business world, but the judiciary, public prosecution service, police and public administration were still very much in the hands of the Kemalists. The party itself contained relatively few well-educated professionals because the support base of the AKP and the *Refah Partisi*, from which it was an offshoot, had always been a combination of small traders and producers and the mass of poor urban migrants. Thus, Gülen's movement and Erdoğan's party were made for each other. Many '*Fethullahcıs*' rose quickly within the party and, especially after 2007, acquired key positions in the judiciary, police and administration. Ideologically, this was not a problem, for the views of AKP and Hizmet on the desired direction of the country were not that different. They both favoured a combination of Islamic values with a capitalist free market economy and fast adoption of the most modern technology. The differences between them were of class on the one hand and strategy on the other. Erdoğan wanted to reach his goal – a deeply religious but at the same time rich and powerful Turkey – by acquiring political power through the ballot box. Gülen, however, entirely in the tradition of the *Nurcu* movement of which he was a part, preferred a gradual penetration of the state through the formation of new generations of well-educated Turkish Muslims.

In the years of symbiosis (2002–12) the Hizmet was able to strengthen its position considerably in the fields in which it had traditionally been active (education, media and business). The newspaper *Zaman* (Time) grew to be the largest in Turkey. The international network was also expanded enormously, primarily in Europe, the USA and Central Asia. Ultimately, Hizmet would become such a force that it started to be a threat to Erdoğan's own position, as we shall see below.

Consolidation of power

After 2007, of the three people who had founded the AKP in 2001, one was president (Abdullah Gül), one was prime minister (Tayyip Erdoğan) and one was president of the parliament (Bülent Arınç). Their party had won three elections in a row and a stable majority in parliament. The challenge of the political opposition, of the Kemalist civil society organizations and of the army had all been met successfully. The threat of a ban on the party by the constitutional court was (narrowly) avoided in 2008. With the active support of the president, all the appointments of top bureaucrats, provincial administrators, judges and public prosecutors that Sezer had earlier blocked could now be carried through. In other words, the AKP was now master of the house.

The internation situation did not pose a threat. Negotiations with the EU had reached an impasse, but for the AKP the EU had fulfilled its most important task, namely to function as a crowbar with which to dismantle the Kemalist state. From 2008 onwards, Europe was in the grip of a deep financial and economic crisis and fully occupied with its own problems.

It is therefore no exaggeration to say that the 2007–12 period was the golden age of the AKP. The first new opportunity for the party to seek the electorate's support arose with the local elections of 2009. On the one hand, these confirmed the AKP's dominance, for, with 39 per cent of the vote, it again was by far the biggest party. Nevertheless, 39 per cent was a loss of 2 per cent against the last local elections and 8 per cent compared with 2007. The CHP's share rose from 19 to 23 per cent and the MHP's from 14 to 16. The Kurdish DTP again did well in the southeast, but nationally it remained stuck at 5.6 per cent.

Erdoğan was disappointed, but still publicly interpreted the result as a vote of confidence. There are probably two explanations for the AKP's lesser result. On the one hand, Turkey escaped the financial crisis but felt the effects of the global economic downturn and unemployment rose sharply in 2008/9. On the other hand, in 2007 the AKP had been able to position itself as the party that defended the people against the authoritarian state and that polarization no longer played a role.

Unlike the ANAP in the 1980s and 1990s, the AKP did not suffer from a slow but continuous erosion of support. This was clear from the result of the 2011national elections. In the run-up to the elections, different polls showed an unusually wide spread, so quite a few pundits expected a change of government. However, when the results of the June elections were in, Erdoğan proved to have achieved his best result ever, with almost 50 per cent of the vote. The CHP continued its cautious upward trend with 26 per cent, but that was still far from its best results ever and it was especially disappointing because the new party leader, who in 2010 succeeded Deniz Baykal, now very old and damaged by scandal, had waged an imaginative and convincing campaign. The CHP seemed to have new energy. Possibly, for many Turks, voting for an Alevi Kurd from Tunceli was a bridge too far. The MHP, which had kept its old leader Devlet Bahçeli, a veteran of the radical right since the early 1970s, did badly with 13 per cent. This time, no fewer than 35 representatives of the Kurdish party managed to enter parliament as 'independents'. Nationally, they got 6.5 per cent of the vote.

The AKP's majority in the new parliament was slightly smaller than it had been before (through the vagaries of the Turkish electoral system) but it stayed solid. The opposition remained just as powerless as it had been in the previous nine years.

The AKP's power monopoly increased fears among secularist sections of Turkish society that the party would push through the Islamization of the country. Ever since the AKP's takeover in 2002, this had been a point for debate: was it really the broad conservative party that its leaders maintained it was, or was it a wolf in sheep's clothing, with a secret agenda to turn Turkey into an Islamic state? There was evidence for both arguments. On the one hand, the AKP government did not attempt to change the fundamentally secular political order. The Şeriat did not become a basis for legislation; polygamy was not allowed; common-law marriages by imams were not declared legal; and interest was not banned. New legislation introduced after the AKP took over the state machinery in 2007 tended to favour the executive, where before it had been designed to increase the power of the legislative, but this was more a question of power than religion.

On the other hand, Turkey's cultural climate underwent significant change. The political leaders were now all people who proclaimed themselves pious Muslims, and this created pressure in the civil service. Civil servants were increasingly expected to conform to the conservative religious norms of the party, something they could show by having their wives cover their hair, by fasting during *Ramazan*, praying and refraining from alcohol. Government offices and public spaces were given prayer rooms and an aggressive anti-alcohol policy was implemented, with heavy tax increases and restrictions on the times and places that alcohol might be sold. Increasingly, official receptions were dry. Campaigns were mounted against people kissing and flirting on public transport and against unmarried students cohabiting. With the state behind them, conservative Muslims increasingly felt free to impose their norms and values. The famous Turkish sociologist Şerif Mardin coined the phrase *mahalle baskısı* (the pressure of the neighbourhood) for this phenomenon and this term became popular among secularists.

Actual policy decisions apart, some of the AKP politicians' public statements made secularist Turks feel uncomfortable. In 2004, Prime Minister Erdoğan suggested that adultery should perhaps be made a criminal act and his justice minister said that women who had been raped would be better off marrying their rapists. The president of the national assembly, Bülent Arınç, repeatedly expressed his desire to turn the Aya Sofya into a mosque again and, in 2014, called for the reinforcement of public morals, singling out women laughing loudly in public as an

example of indecency. Prime Minister Erdoğan and other leading politicians repeatedly ridiculed the Alevi minority. All this gave important
sections of Turkish society the feeling that Islamization was a reality,
even if not through legislation. The AKP felt entitled to steer the country
in a different cultural direction because it saw itself as the representative
of the 'national will' in clear disregard of the fact that a majority of
Turkey's citizens had not voted for the party. This is, of course, a familiar
problem in Turkish politics, going back to the days of Menderes.

The changing cultural climate did not immediately signal the end of
the Atatürk cult. Veneration for the founder of the republic was too
closely intertwined with Turkish nationalism and national cohesion was
too important a factor for that to happen, but there was certainly a reorientation towards the Ottoman past. Not only did public interest in the
Ottoman past grow enormously in the 2000s (due mainly to popular films
and TV programmes), but the state also identified with the glorious, or
glorified, Ottoman past. This was evident from the names given to new
bridges, tunnels, schools and universities, as well as from the use of
(pseudo) Ottoman elements in the architecture of urban renewal projects.
Perhaps one sign that Atatürk's position would eventually come up for
debate was the sudden abolition, in September 2013, of the 'Pupil's
Oath', the formal proclamation of loyalty that Turkish schoolchildren
had been required to recite every school day since 1933.

The economic miracle of the AKP years
The AKP's electoral success between 2002 and 2014 is intimately linked
to the success of its economic policies, which improved the lives of most
Turks considerably. Kemal Derviş, in close collaboration with the IMF,
had used Turkey's deep financial crisis of 2001 to solve a number of
entrenched problems that were bugging the Turkish financial system. To
begin with, he pushed through legislation that made the central bank
independent of government policy and solely responsible for interest
rates and price stability, which made it difficult for opportunist politicians to influence its policies. The banking system was reformed. Banks
that were essentially broke were forced to close down or merge and state
banks were freed from the so-called 'duty loans' that could force them to
support politically inspired ventures even if they made no economic
sense. In exchange for IMF support, the government committed itself to
a fiscally conservative policy in which net expenditure (not counting
interest payments) would be kept below the tax revenues.

Many people feared that, when the AKP came to power in 2002, it
would revert to the populist financial policies of the 1990s, but it did not.
It stuck strictly to the policies agreed with the IMF. In addition, the

party's 2002 victory and consequent absolute majority in parliament gave Turkey political stability for the first time in 15 years. From 2004 onwards, a clear perspective of future membership of the European Union was added. As a result, the Turkish economy would be able to recover quickly from the collapse of 2000/1.

In 2001, the economy still contracted by 7.5 per cent, but in the years between 2002 and 2007 average GDP growth was about 6 per cent a year, driven essentially by rapidly growing investments in industry and consumer spending. The policies of the now independent central bank and government led to a substantial primary surplus and, as a result, inflation dropped from 55 per cent in 2001 to 10 per cent in 2005. This, in turn, allowed interest rates to be lowered and, as a number of new credit facilities were introduced in Turkey in this period, such as paying credit-card bills in instalments, the country witnessed a real explosion in consumer spending. The higher rate of economic activity meant more tax income for the state and, along with the IMF-induced very cautious budgetary policies, this meant that Turkey's sovereign debt, still over 100 per cent of GDP in 2001, gradually went down to an extremely solid 40 per cent in 2008. Turkey no longer had to borrow from the IMF and could pay off its outstanding loans. All these good macro data translated into an appreciable increase in the standard of living for the majority of Turkish people, even if this increase was largely based on private debt. The improvement was very visible in everyday life.[3]

The robust Turkish economy of these years had only two persistent weaknesses. The first was unemployment, which remained at around 10 per cent. That it remained so high was partly an after-effect of the population explosion of the late twentieth century, which meant that each year about 700,000 new people entered the labour market. This also explains why youth unemployment was much higher, at around 20 per cent. Even so, unemployment was held down by the unusually low percentage of women seeking work in Turkey – around 30 per cent compared with more than 70 per cent of males. This unusually low figure of course retards Turkish economic growth and development, but it also brings down the numbers registered as unemployed.

The second persistent weakness was, and is, the double deficit – that of the trade balance (which registers the difference between imported and exported goods) and the balance of payments (which also includes services and monetary transfers). Turkey had become an exporting country since Turgut Özal introduced his reforms in the 1980s, but although exports rose quite steeply between 2002 and 2008, that was not what drove the economy. Economic growth was driven by consumer spending and investments, by both the private sector and the state.

Together, consumer spending and investments led to an enormous growth in imports, so throughout the period Turkey had a double deficit. Between 2002 and 2008 the deficit on the balance of payments grew from 3 to 8 per cent of GDP. Such an extremely high percentage is generally regarded as unsustainable. If a country continues to spend so much more than it earns, it will eventually translate into a drastic devaluation of the national currency and a spike in inflation. That this was avoided in Turkey for a long time was only due to one factor – the foreign direct investment (FDI) that poured into the country.

Political stability, responsible budgetary policies, a fast-growing population of young consumers and the prospect of full membership of the EU gave foreign investors a lot of confidence. From 2004 onwards, they started to invest heavily in loans to the Turkish state, Turkish enterprises that were increasing their production capacity, and takeovers of Turkish companies. For European companies, Turkey was interesting for two reasons – as a market for the young population and fast growing consumption-oriented middle class, and as a production location with cheap labour close to the European markets.Manufacturing car parts and white goods such as washing machines and fridges was especially successful. Many company takeovers were in the still large state sector, which was now rapidly being privatized – ports, chemical plants, oil refineries, utilities, banks and airlines, as well as tobacco and alcohol monopolies. State land was also sold off on a large scale. Foreign direct investment, of which some 70–80 per cent came from Europe, created an inflow of hard currencies that supported the exchange rate of the Turkish lira. From 1 January 2005, the lira also visibly gained strength when the 'New Turkish lira' (*Yeni Türk Lirası* or YTL) was introduced. One YTL was worth 1,000,000 old liras. Nevertheless, the underlying problem of the persistent deficit meant that the Turkish economy and the Turkish lira remained vulnerable. Whenever foreign investors lost confidence, stopped investing or even retracted some of their money, there would be a sharp fall in the value of the lira and this happened several times. The first was in May 2006, when the currency suddenly fell by a quarter against the euro, but it soon recovered most of its losses.

The world financial crisis of 2008 also hit Turkey hard. Between mid-2008 and mid-2009 the economy contracted especially fast, in fact by more than 10 per cent in total. The lira fell by 15 per cent, consumption slowed down and investments dropped sharply. However, because Turkey had already thoroughly reformed its banking sector in 2000/1, its financial sector came through the crisis without the kind of problems that plagued the USA and Europe, where vast amounts of public money had to be used to save the banks that were considered to be 'too big to fail'.

The government and central bank reacted quickly and forcefully to the crisis by lowering taxes (in the case of the government), lowering the interest rate by nearly 10 per cent and massively increasing the money supply (in the case of the central bank). This stimulated both private consumption and investment, particularly in building projects, which compensated for the fall in exports and foreign investment. Consequently, the economy recovered quite fast after 2009 and, in 2010 and 2011, showed record growth of about 9 per cent per annum. These kinds of Chinese figures were only attainable through the artificial increase of the money supply and this led to an astronomical balance of payments deficit, which shot up to 10 per cent of GDP in 2011. A short but severe currency crisis that year led to a devaluation of the Turkish lira by some 20 per cent, which was yet another sign of the underlying vulnerability of the Turkish growth model. After 2011, economic growth slowed down to between 1 and 3 per cent, which is low for an emerging economy, but partly the result of a worldwide trend. With the crisis in the industrialized West slowly coming to an end and increasing signs that the Federal Reserve in the USA would be ending its 'quantitative easing' (namely printing massive amounts of dollars), investors withdrew their money from emerging markets and redirected it towards the USA and Europe.

As nearly always in Turkey, political crises tipped the balance, exposing the underlying weakness and causing a run on the lira. In this case, the culprits were the two crises of 2013 – Gezi in May and the confrontation with Gülen's movement in December. The central bank tried to stem the tide with draconic rate increases, but overall the lira lost some 60 per cent of its value against the dollar in 2013–15.

Overall, the economic legacy of the first 12 years of AKP government is definitely positive. The size of the Turkish economy, the GDP, doubled and the citizens' standard of living improved markedly. Per capita GDP, which at the start of the period was around 30 per cent of the European average, 15 years later stood at about 45 per cent (but of course, the EU took in 12 countries with lower than average per capita GDP in these years, something that affected the base for comparison). Government finances were solid despite huge investments in public transport, roads, railways, education and healthcare, which markedly improved the quality of life for most Turks. At the same time, the weaknesses of the AKP's development model surfaced repeatedly, most notably in 2006, 2012 and 2013: growth based on investments and consumption resulted in a permanent balance of payments deficit and made the country extremely dependent on the whims of foreign investors. The ready availability of foreign investment capital led to speculative 'bubbles', especially in the property sector. Keeping government finances solid while at the same time making huge investments also necessitated the privatization of state-owned companies and land. Hundreds of state-owned companies and institutions were privatized, which of course inevitably has to stop somewhere – once Turkey's family silver has all been sold then that hugely important source of income will dry up.

Another issue was that of the close ties between the government and party on the one hand and the business world on the other. Successful companies, if they are to stay that way, need good political connections, for which they are happy to pay, either directly to the party or through related foundations. Conversely, politically suspect companies, like the Doğan or Koç groups, could be and were hit hard by punitive taxation or exclusion from government contracts.

Finally, the model of hardcore capitalist development under the protection of the state had the effect of increasing social inequality, which, until the 1980s, had been relatively low in Turkey. This becomes clear when we compare the international index for economic growth with that for development. In the GDP index, Turkey climbed to seventeenth place overall, which means that only sixteen economies in the world were bigger. According to the United Nations 'Human Development Index', however, which also looks at health, life expectancy, education and gender equality, Turkey was sixty-ninth in 2014.

Middle-class resistance and a fracture in the ruling coalition

As in so many emerging markets, the building sector was the most important engine for economic growth in Turkey. In part, it owed its exuberant growth to Turkey's rapid population increase and extensive urbanization, but it was also actively stimulated by the AKP. In this, the Public Housing Administration (*Toplu Konut İdaresi* or TOKİ) played a leading role. In 2001, TOKİ took over the public housing fund that Turgut Özal had set up in 1984 – a fund kept outside the budget and financed through extraordinary levies. In the years that followed, TOKİ's powers increased significantly: it provided credit, did the valuations and became the main agent for large urban renewal projects. In 2003, TOKİ was placed directly under the prime minister's office, exempted from Ministry of Housing jurisdiction and given the exclusive right to privatize state land and properties. This made it very rich. In 2014, TOKİ's capital was estimated at 25 billion euros. Because it was neither a company nor a regular branch of any ministry, its financial dealings were not scrutinized in any regular manner.

New legislation in 2005 gave the various municipalities and TOKİ wide and vaguely described powers to change the zoning regulations for urban areas and to seize property. Armed with these new powers and the prime minister's protection, TOKİ became very active, especially in Istanbul and Ankara, and not only in the field of public housing. In collaboration with a new generation of developers with good political connections, such as Ali Ağaoğlu, countless shopping malls, multiplexes and sports facilities were built, as well as luxury apartments for the affluent bourgeoisie, often in the form of gated communities with their own security services, shops and swimming pools. Especially in Istanbul, urban renewal led to the gentrification of entire neighbourhoods, with old houses replaced or refurbished and their original residents forcibly removed and relocated, often very far from the city centre. This unchecked speculative building craze would spark mass resistance to the AKP's policies in 2013.

In May 2013, some of the tensions that had been building up in Turkish society for a decade exploded. The incident that sparked the explosion was minor. On 28 May, a small group of environmentalists started to camp out at the Gezi Promenade, a small park bordering Taksim Square in Istanbul. İsmet İnönü had commissioned the park in the 1940s, after an early nineteenth-century artillery barracks, which used to stand on the spot, was razed to the ground. The environmentalists were protesting against government and municipality plans to destroy the park (the last public gardens in that part of the city) to make room for a complex containing a shopping mall, apartments and mosque, in the style of the nineteenth-century barracks. On 30 May, the police intervened rather brutally and used teargas and water cannons to chase the peaceful occupiers away. Indignation over this unprovoked police brutality spread like wildfire over the social media and, in the days that followed, a massive protest ensued, not just in Istanbul but in a whole range of cities. The police again reacted very violently and some demonstrators died, which in turn led to ongoing escalation over the next fortnight.

The 'Gezi-movement' brought together many different groups and grievances. All sorts of organizations and communities that felt marginalized by the AKP's power monopoly joined it – environmentalists, of course, but also secularists, trade unions, Kurds, Alevis, women's rights activists, gays, socialists, communists and liberals. One characteristic of this protest movement was that it was clearly dominated by urban middle-class youth who, in their protests, targeted several AKP policies. These included the building boom that made all of Istanbul the property developers' target, the lack of respect for the environment and human rights, the exploitation of workers, the creeping Islamization of the public sphere, the social control mechanisms that the government promoted, police brutality and the regime's authoritarian tendencies.

Prime Minster Erdoğan was travelling in North Africa when the protests started to escalate and, on his return on 7 June, he insisted they be brought to an immediate end. While he was still abroad, other AKP leaders had called for reconciliation and dialogue, but Erdoğan opted for confrontation. He called the demonstrators 'vandals' (*çapulcular*) and unbelievers who had no respect for the 'national will' as expressed in the AKP's election victories. He saw the demonstrations as the work of conspirators and the demonstrators as puppets in the hands of mysterious international financial interests aiming to undermine Turkey's economy. He also targeted foreign media that reported on the unrest.

With his harsh, confrontational line, Erdoğan managed to mobilize his own supporters. Unremitting police brutality against wholly peaceful protesters did the rest and, by the end of June, the movement was largely crushed. Then the persecution of all those groups that had been involved – students, lawyers, medical doctors and journalists – started. Police officers responsible for the deaths of nine demonstrators (whose actions had been recorded on video) escaped prosecution. As in Cairo two years earlier, the Gezi movement had shown the mobilizing power of the social media. The government responded by temporarily blocking several social media in Turkey, most notably Twitter, and setting up a new Cyberspace Security Council.

Although people often compare Gezi with the Tahrir Square movement in Cairo in 2011, the similarities are superficial. While urban middle-class youths also initiated the Cairo movement and mobilization had also been largely through the social media, President Mubarak was eventually brought down by a broad coalition from left to right in which the Muslim Brotherhood played a decisive role. It alone was able to rally the urban proletariat, which in Turkey was not mobilized at all. The movement was essentially a coalition of urban, middle-class groups and minorities like Alevis and Kurds. The great mass of Sunni conservatives and the urban proletariat mostly remained loyal to Erdoğan.

During the May–June crisis, Fethullah Gülen adopted an unexpectedly conciliatory position from his headquarters in Pennsylvania by rejecting violence and calling for a fraternal dialogue. Reading between the lines, he was clearly condemning Erdoğan's hard line, which was yet another sign that the relationship between the two religious movements that had together dominated Turkey since 2002 – Erdoğan's 'National Vision' and Gülen's 'Service' – was deteriorating fast.

The first confrontation between the two had taken place in February 2012. During a large judicial inquiry into the Kurdish KCK, public prosecutors connected to Gülen unearthed evidence that, between 2009 and 2011, the chief of the National Intelligence Organization (MİT), Hakan Fıdan, had been negotiating with the Kurdish PKK on behalf of the Turkish government. For the Gülen movement, which traditionally had strong links with ultranationalist circles, this was tantamount to high treason. When the public prosecutors issued a warrant for Fıdan's arrest, the government immediately reacted and, that same day, parliament passed a law that exempted the MİT from prosecution and took the public prosecutors involved off the case.

Early in 2013, rumours appeared in the press about imminent government action against the Gülen movement. The Gezi events had laid bare the tensions and, in November, the government did indeed take steps. It announced that the state would take over the *dershanes*, the private preparatory schools and homework classes to prepare pupils for secondary or higher education. This was a direct attack on the Gülen movement, which owed its reputation and influence to these schools. It was from them that the movement selected talented pupils earmarked for careers as cadre members of the movement, Gülen's 'golden generation'.

Gülen called on his followers to resist these measures by the 'Farao' (Erdoğan) and soon enough the action started. On 17 December 2014, the media suddenly announced that a number of important members of Erdoğan's inner circle, including three sons of cabinet ministers and a number of business people, had been arrested pending an inquiry into corruption. The case turned on allegations of fraud at several large building projects and, mainly, on some shadowy and probably illegal transactions by Halkbank (People's Bank), a state bank with close ties to the AKP. Money that Turkey owed to Iran for the delivery of oil and gas had been used to buy gold in Africa, which had then been shipped through Turkey and Dubai to Iran. For Iran, this was a way of breaking the international financial boycott.

Erdoğan's government reacted furiously. Three cabinet ministers resigned, but the public prosecutors and police investigators who were involved were immediately taken off the case and transferred. In the weeks that followed there were constant leaks to the media of sound recordings of the private conversations of high-ranking AKP functionaries, including Erdoğan and his son Bilâl. The authenticity of the recordings was contested, but the picture that emerged from them was one of far-reaching corruption in the highest circles.

The government's counteroffensive took the form of massive transfers and demotions of police personnel with known Gülen ties and thousands were affected. In addition, an inquiry was opened into the origin of the taps. This showed that the political leadership of the country had been subjected to eaves dropping for a long time. While both parties were publishing evidence of the other side's misdeeds, Erdoğan mobilized his constituency. He depicted the corruption inquiry as a conspiracy

by a 'parallel structure' (*parallel yapı*), a state within the state that had
to be eradicated. Gülen was accused of having close ties with the United
States and Israel. Public prosecutors with Gülen sympathies reacted by
ordering gendarmes to open trucks destined for Syria and to have them
searched. A number of these turned out to be carrying arms and
munitions for the Islamic resistance in that country, apparently with the
connivance of the Turkish government.

Erdoğan beats off his assailants

In the spring of 2014 the tension in the country once more increased.
Tayyip Erdoğan convincingly won the municipal elections of March,
after an aggressive and intense campaign in which he denounced both the
liberal opposition and the Gülenists as conspirators and agents of foreign
interests. Before the elections, there was a lot of speculation among the
pundits about the number of votes that his rift with Gülen could cost him,
but with 43 per cent of the vote, the AKP actually did better than in the
local elections of 2009, although it did do 7 per cent worse than in the
national elections of 2011. With 26 per cent of the vote, the CHP equalled
its 2011 result and, at 18 per cent, the MHP improved a little. The big
cities of Istanbul and Ankara remained in AKP hands – Istanbul by a
wide margin and Ankara only just. The electoral map of Turkey once
again displayed its now familiar pattern – a fringe of CHP red along the
west coast and in Thrace, green in the southeast, which was dominated
by the Kurdish party (by now the *Barış ve Demokrasi Partisi* or Peace
and Democracy Party), and all the rest AKP yellow.

The elections showed that both the liberal-oriented, secular middle
class in the big cities in the west of the country, which had dominated the
headlines during the Gezi protests, and the Gülen movement, which had
conquered so many key positions in the state bureaucracy, were very
important social actors in qualitative terms. However, they were no
match for the AKP in quantitative terms. After the March elections,
Erdoğan did not take is foot off the accelerator – quite the opposite – and
the large-scale purges of the police and public prosecution service went
full steam ahead. On 10 August 2014, for the first time a new president
would be elected directly by the Turkish people and it was clear that
Erdoğan would be the AKP's sole candidate. Between March and
August, the prime minister remained on the campaign trail continuously
and, as in the December–March period, his campaign was not one that
depicted him as the president of all Turks, but one in which he mobilized
his own conservative religious following through aggressive rhetoric.
The local elections had taught the opposition parties that each of them
separately would not have a chance, so they put forward a joint candidate.

For two secularist parties, their choice was surprising – Professor Ekmeleddin İhsanoğlu, a Turkish historian born and raised in Egypt who, from 2004 to 2014, was secretary-general of the Saudi Arabia-sponsored Islamic Conference Organization. Ihsanoğlu was well respected, but he lacked political experience and was entirely unknown to the public at large. Erdoğan consistently put him down as '*ithal*' (imported) and '*monşer*' (from '*mon cher*' to infer an elitist person). The third candidate was the Kurdish party's – the young, charismatic human rights lawyer Selâhettin Demirtaş.

In the run-up to the elections the debate was not really about who would win, but about whether Erdoğan would gain the 50 per cent he needed in the first round. In the end he did win in the first round with 52 per cent of the vote, way ahead of İhsanoğlu at 38 per cent and Demirtaş at 9 per cent. Analyses of the election result showed that there were three reasons why Erdoğan was so successful. First, his own campaign, which had been going on since December, was extremely effective. With aggressive and self-confident speeches, in which he portrayed himself as the national will incarnate and the only one to defend Turkey against the conspiracies of its enemies, he motivated and mobilized his conservative constituency. Second, the CHP's choice of a candidate with a conservative Islamic profile, a kind of 'Erdoğan Light', was very unattractive, especially for the younger supporters of the party. They tended to stay at home. Third, a sizeable amount of traditional MHP voters opted for Erdoğan rather than for their own candidate.

The election result confirmed the paradox that had characterized Turkey over the last decade. On the one hand, this was the stability produced by the power monopoly of the AKP, which was rooted in the solid support of roughly half the Turkish population. On the other hand, the country was deeply divided. A number of important and increasingly frustrated minorities were essentially powerless in a political culture in which a simple majority in parliament was supposed to represent the will of the nation as a whole.

Inherited problems: the Kurdish question and Cyprus
When it came into power in 2002, the AKP government faced two problems that had plagued Turkish politics for decades – the Kurdish issue and the conflict over Cyprus. On both issues, Erdoğan's government showed a willingness to take courageous steps, more so in fact than any Turkish government of the preceding 30 years.

By 2002, work on a solution to the Cyprus problem, the so-called 'Annan Plan', had been going on for three years. Negotiations between the Cypriot government and the (internationally still unrecognized)

Turkish republic of Northern Cyprus under the direction of the United Nations had been moving ahead slowly. They had been broken off several times, but with EU membership of Cyprus becoming a realistic prospect, the pressure on both parties to reach an agreement increased. By 2004, a blueprint for a solution was on the table. It was not the direct result of negotiations between Greeks and Turks on the island, but a document drawn up by the staff of the UN secretary-general at the time, Kofi Annan. On 24 April 2004, it was put to a referendum, in both the north and south. The Turkish government wholeheartedly supported the Annan Plan and, consequently, it was accepted in the north by a wide margin. In the south, however, the Greek population rejected the plan by an even wider margin, primarily because it would allow Turkish troops to remain stationed on the island.

Therefore, it was a divided Cyprus that joined the EU in 2004, and this would create many problems in the relationship between Turkey and the EU. On the island itself, however, there was a thaw in relations between north and south. In 2005, a new president, Mehmet Ali Talât, a supporter of reunification, was elected in the north and in the south Demtris Christofias was elected in February 2008. He was also ready to make concessions and. over the next two years. there were negotiations that again raised hopes of a settlement. The restrictions on crossing the 'Green Line' dividing the island were relaxed. Unfortunately, this Cypriot Spring ended in April 2010 when the nationalist hardliner, Derviş Eroğlu, took over the Turkish zone.

An issue that became ever more important from 2011 onwards was exploration and exploitation rights for gas and oil on the continental shelf east of Cyprus. The Republic of Cyprus cooperated with Israel in giving out concessions to search for gas and oil deposits, whereupon Turkey also claimed the area as part of its own continental shelf and started to threaten military intervention. This development should also be seen in conjunction with the deteriorating Turkish–Israeli relations. Overall, the AKP government had invested a lot of prestige and goodwill in the Annan Plan, but had been unable decisively to influence developments on the island itself.

On the face of it, the situation pertaining to the Kurdish problem in the first AKP years seemed unchanged. PKK leader Abdullah Öcalan was sitting out his life imprisonment on the island of İmralı in the Sea of Marmara, but his authority within the PKK and its related organizations remained as strong as ever. From 2004, the armed conflict heated up again, with guerrilla attacks in Turkey and operations of the Turkish army on both sides of the Turkish–Iraqi border. From 2006, there was a steep increase in the number of bomb attacks in the big cities of western

Turkey. These were claimed by a hitherto unknown organization, the Freedom Falcons of Kurdistan (*Teyrêbazên Azadiya Kurdistan*), possibly a PKK offshoot.

The repression of Kurdish organizations continued unabated. In April 2009 several waves of arrests saw a total of 8000 people arrested for being members of the *Koma Civakên Kurdistan* (Union of Communities in Kurdistan or KCK), which the government regarded as a front organization for the PKK. Among the arrested were many writers and journalists, but also mayors and members of parliament. They were arrested under the anti-terror legislation. In the same year, the Kurdish party DTP was banned for pursuing separatist aims, after which its former members joined the new *Barış ve Demokrasi Partisi* (Peace and Democracy Party or BDP) in 2010.

While all this repression was going on, things were changing behind the scenes. On 29 July 2009, Interior Minister Beşir Atalay announced that the government was looking for an opening in the Kurdish stalemate and would come with a number of initiatives. In the autumn, the direction of these initiatives became clear. The government announced that restrictions on radio and television broadcasts in Kurdish would be lifted, that education in Kurdish would be allowed in private schools, and that the original Kurdish names would be restored to villages that had been given Turkish names (something that had occurred on a massive scale since the 1930s). The same, however, was not said for the originally Armenian villages. Kurdish refugees abroad who had lost their citizenship since the military takeover of 1980, could get it back and generally the administration of the country would be decentralized. In 2010, Prime Minister Erdoğan held a series of round table conferences on the reforms in the Dolmabahçe Palace, with all kinds of social actors (including people from the media, the worlds of art, culture and sports, and women's organizations), which were broadcast live on television.

These spectacular steps were not just taken unilaterally by the government. As mentioned earlier, it emerged during the KCK process in 2011 that the National Intelligence Organization (MİT) had been talking to PKK representatives on behalf of the prime minister, most probably in Oslo. Because of those talks, BDP members were given permission to visit Öcalan regularly in prison to receive his instructions for the negotiations. This was an extremely sensitive issue in Turkey, where for 30 years Öcalan had been depicted as a terrorist and mass murderer, but the AKP government stuck to its course and got Öcalan to support the peace initiative. The fighting continued, sometimes interrupted by truces, but so did the discussions between the state and PKK and, in the years 2012 to 2014, the contours of a settlement slowly emerged. On 21 March 2014, a mass of up to a million Kurds freely celebrated *Newroz*, the Kurdish New Year, in Diyarbakır surrounded by huge PKK flags and banners bearing Öcalan's portrait. BDP parliamentarians read a message from Öcalan, which would have been unthinkable a few years earlier.

The whole peace process, or the 'solution' (*çözüm*) as it was called in Turkey, was informal. Not until July 2014 did parliament pass a law that mandated the government to conduct negotiations with the PKK. The Kemalist and nationalist oppositions were left on the sidelines. They were too entwined in their tradition of thinking rigidly of Turkey as a unified nation-state to come up with any serious alternatives.

Strategic depth: a new foreign policy

Two themes dominated international relations in the AKP's early years. The first, as already described, was a sudden quickening in the pace of EU integration. That the EU decided to start negotiations in December 2004 and actually opened them up on 3 October 2005 was a great achievement for the government, in fact the fulfilment of a dream that successive Turkish governments had cherished for the past 46 years. At the time, nobody foresaw that the talks would soon be bogged down.

The other major event was, of course, the US invasion of Iraq in February 2003. In the initial planning of 'Operation Enduring Freedom' the Americans had counted on Turkish cooperation and scheduled a two-pronged attack – one from the south (Saudi Arabia) and one from the north (through Turkey). Turkey was a NATO member, but the invasion was not a NATO operation and, as in most countries, public opinion in Turkey strongly opposed the invasion. The new AKP government had only just been installed and, squeezed between ever-increasing American pressure and mass protests in its own country, it was at a loss over what to do. In the end, the Turkish national assembly refused to allow the Americans to move troops over Turkish territory and there was a consequent chilling of US–Turkish relations, which grew worse when the Americans arrested Turkish agents in northern Iraq and collaborated closely with the leaders of the Kurdish autonomous region in Iraq, Barzani and Talabani. Turkey watched developments with concern, for it feared that the increased autonomy and de facto independence of the Kurdish region could set off a chain reaction among Turkey's own Kurds. In 2005, relations between Turkey and the USA started to improve, but never regained the intimacy of the Özal and Çiller years.

During this period, it became increasingly clear that Turkey's foreign policy was undergoing a fundamental reorientation. Although Prime Minister Erdoğan emphatically supported this policy change, it was the brainchild of an academic, the political scientist Ahmet Davutoğlu, who was a member of the AKP's inner circle. In 2001, he had written a book that gave rise to a lot of debate in Turkey. It was called *Stratejik Derinlik* (*Strategic Depth*) and its main thesis was that Turkey had the potential to become not just a regional, but also a global player of the first rank, but that this potential was not being realized because of Turkey's one-sided Western orientation. Because, ever since the Second World War, Turkey's sole foreign policy objective had been to integrate with the West through NATO and the EU (and continued to be even after the end of the Cold War), it had been unable to exploit its 'strategic depth'. For Davutoğlu, this originally military term evoked the idea that, through its geographic location and historical legacy as successor to the Ottoman Empire, Turkey could become the natural leader of the Balkans, the Near East and North Africa – all areas that shared a common Ottoman past and civilization. Turkey would be able to use its economic strength and role as a democratic Muslim country as 'soft power' to bring about a new 'Pax Ottomanica' in the region. Once that had been achieved, it could become the voice of the region and a natural interlocutor for global powers like the USA and China. In Davutoğlu's eyes, a key precondition would be that Turkey had no serious conflicts with any of its neighbours (the so-called 'zero problems policy') and that it would actively engage in solving existing conflicts between neighbouring states.[4]

In 2003, Professor Davutoğlu was made special adviser to the prime minister with the rank of ambassador and was able to exercise real influence on Turkey's foreign policy. In 2009, he was appointed foreign minister, so could start to implement his own ideas and, for the first few years, the new policy seemed to be working. Many in the Arab world admired Turkey's economic success and the example it set as a democratically elected, moderate Islamist government. From 2008, Erdoğan started to gain personal popularity through his outspoken pro-Palestinian position in the conflict with Israel. Indeed, Turkish influence went even further. Turkish pop culture became influential in the Middle East, primarily through its popular TV series, and Turkish consumer goods and building contractors were exceedingly successful in countries like Syria, Iraq and Jordan. In 2008/9, ties with Bashar al-Assad's regime in Syria grew very warm and there was talk of joint military exercises. The ties with former Ottoman countries in the Balkans with partly Muslim populations (Kosovo, Albania, Macedonia and Bosnia) were strengthened. These countries all lacked investment and had difficult relations with neighbouring countries, so Turkey was a very interesting partner.

In December 2010, the 'Arab Spring' suddenly erupted and dictatorial regimes that had been in power for decades were brought down in Tunisia, Egypt, Libya and Yemen. Mass protests challenged Assad's dictatorship in Syria and the regimes in Jordan and Morocco had to introduce democratic reforms to forestall uprisings. Turkey seemed in an ideal position to profit. The opposition movements that had brought about the revolutions were generally dominated by moderate Sunni Islamists, like the Muslim Brethren in Egypt, who saw Turkey as an example to emulate. When Erdoğan visited Egypt, the masses in Tahrir Square hailed him a hero. His relationship with the new Egyptian president, Morsi, was intimate and warm. However, within a year, what for Turkey had seemed a very rosy picture, was now the exact opposite.

In Syria, Turkey used soft power and diplomacy in an attempt to force President Assad to make concessions, but was unsuccessful and, when civil war broke out there, the AKP identified with the Sunni resistance. It not only generously offered refuge to Syrian refugees, but also allowed a number of increasingly radical Islamist resistance movements to operate and receive supplies from Turkish territory. This naturally earned Turkey the enmity of the Assad regime (which, against all expectations, managed to hold onto power and even gradually reconquer the most important parts of the country in 2012/13). It also displeased Iran and the Shi'í-dominated government of Iraq. When, in July 2013, the Egyptian army toppled President Morsi, the representative of the Muslim Brethren, relations with Egypt also underwent a sea change. Prime Minister Erdoğan fiercely attacked the new Egyptian government and recalled the Turkish ambassador. The conflicts in Syria and Egypt tore the Arab world apart. Saudi Arabia emphatically supported the removal of Morsi, while Qatar (with its influential TV channel Al-Jazeera) sided with the Muslim Brethren. In Syria, both countries also supported different and competing opposition groups. Turkey mostly collaborated with Qatar and, in 2013, Saudi Arabia decided no longer to work with Turkey, but rather with Jordan in its support for the opposition in Syria. Five years after Ahmet Davutoğlu had become minister of foreign affairs, Turkey was largely isolated in the Middle East. Really warm relations existed only with the small ultra-rich princedom of Qatar and with Hamas.

Turkey's new activist foreign policy in the Middle East complicated its relationship with the United States, which, for the last fifty years had been the cornerstone of Turkish foreign policy, but which Turkey's refusal to allow American troops to cross into Iraq through Turkey in 2003/4 had damaged. After that, relations slowly improved, even if the very different positions of both countries vis-à-vis Iran remained a problem. To the Bush administration in the USA, Iran was part of the 'axis of evil' and the country, which was suspected of working on its own atomic bomb, needed to be isolated as much as possible. For Turkey, Iran was an important trading partner and source of energy.

When President Ahmadinejad was re-elected in Iran in 2007, and widespread protests against electoral fraud erupted in Iran and beyond, Turkey was the first country to congratulate him on his re-election.

When Barack Obama won the US presidential election in 2008, improving America's relations with the Islamic Middle East was one of his top priorities. His speech to the Islamic world in Cairo earned him the Nobel Peace Prize, more as an encouragement than remuneration for something he had actually achieved. He visited Turkey on his first international tour in April 2009 and declared that the US–Turkish relationship was a model for the kind of associations for which the USA strove.

Nevertheless, also under Obama, Turkish–US relations gradually cooled, partly because of Turkey's attitude to Iran. In May–June 2010, Turkey and Brazil, as temporary members of the UN Security Council, took the initiative in trying to find a solution to the nuclear conflict with Iran without first consulting the USA. Then, when the Security Council turned down their suggestion, the two countries were the only ones to oppose stricter sanctions on Iran. In 2013, it transpired that traders in Turkey, with the support of some cabinet ministers, had exported more than 200 tonnes of gold from Ghana, which they then sent to Iran to finance oil and gas deliveries.

Turkey–US relations suffered heavier damage from Turkey's volte-face with Israel. Friendship and cooperation with Israel had been just about the only constant factor in Turkey's role in the Middle East during the entire Cold War. Collaboration in the fields of technology, economy and defence had often been close and, although the Turkish population grew more sympathetic to the plight of the Palestinians in the 1980s and 1990s, this had never influenced the Turkish political elite. In the first years of AKP government, good relations with Israel continued while those with the Arab world, notably with Syria, improved. As a result, Turkey was able to play an active role as intermediary between Israel and Syria between 2007 and 2008 and, in fact, came close to a deal on ending the Israeli occupation of the Golan Heights. However, when, after repeated rocket attacks from the Gaza Strip, Israel decided to invade Gaza (operation 'Molten Lead'), the negotiations were abruptly broken off and the Turkish government turned against Israel. At the World Economic Forum in Davos in January 2009, a furious Erdoğan walked out of a panel discussion with the Israeli president, Shimon Peres, and UN secretary-general, Ban Ki-moon. However rehearsed this may have been, Erdoğan's gesture earned him a considerable amount of goodwill in the Arab world. A year later, Turkish–Israeli relations hit rock bottom when the Turkish Islamist Humanitarian Relief Foundation (İHH), which had close ties with Hamas, and possibly also with Al-Qaeda, sent a flotilla of ships to Gaza in an attempt to break the Israeli blockade. The Israeli navy stopped the flotilla and, in skirmishes on the largest ship, the Turkish *Mavi Marmara*, Israeli soldiers killed nine Turkish citizens. The expedition had not been Erdoğan's initiative – it originated in much more radical Islamist circles – but the indignation in Turkey was deep and Erdoğan made himself the mouthpiece of that anger. Since then, Turkey has had only minimal diplomatic ties with Israel and, in the conflicts around Gaza of 2012 and 2014, the Turkish government fully sided with Hamas,, even when that movement seemed to have no allies left in the Arab Middle East outside Qatar.

For Turkey's relations with the United States, the rupture with Israel was a disaster. Turkey did not only lose a lot of support in the American congress, but also lost the support of the pro-Israel lobbies that are so influential in the USA.

The relationship with the EU, which had enjoyed a real honeymoon period between 2002 and 2006, also cooled off. This was partly due to the Cyprus problem. In 2004, Cyprus was admitted to the EU, under great pressure from Athens and despite the EU having always said that it would not accept a divided Cyprus. Turkey found this very difficult to accept. It still did not recognize the Greek Cypriot government, so refused to admit Cypriot planes and ships. This in turn was unacceptable for the EU, which in retaliation halted negotiations on eight of the 35 chapters of the '*acquis communautaire*', the totality of legislation and regulations that together make up EU membership. Negotiations on other chapters continued, but at a very slow pace, much slower than for other candidate countries. The Turks found it hard to swallow that, in 2007, Bulgaria and Romania, countries that demonstrably were far behind Turkey economically and administratively, were admitted.

In the years after 2007, the European Commission's annual reports on Turkey became ever more critical. The main issues were freedom of the press, the independence of the judiciary and the rights of minorities. Attempts to reignite the negotiation process failed when Cyprus took over the EU presidency for six months in 2012 and Turkey halted all talks for that period.

A deeper reason for why the negotiations that had started with such enthusiasm in 2005 became bogged down so soon was that the enthusiasm on both sides dissipated rather quickly. On the European side, many countries, such as Austria, Hungary, Denmark, the Netherlands, Belgium and France, experienced a rise in nationalist and populist parties that opposed both further European integration and expansion. The deep financial and later economic crisis that enveloped Europe from late 2008 onwards, increased the support for these parties. Resistance to immigration in societies with steeply rising unemployment was fuelled by the fear of Islam that had already been on the increase since the attacks of 11 September 2001. In this climate, Turkey's accession was more and more seen as a threat and it became too hot for the European governments to handle. Unlike the populist parties, the governments continued to support Turkey's candidacy officially, but meanwhile were strongly inclined to delay it to some unspecified date in the future. The increasingly religious tone of the Erdoğan government contributed to the European unease.

On the Turkish side, the enthusiasm for membership also diminished quite fast. Ankara was well aware of the anti-Turkish and anti-Islamic rhetoric in European politics and the country felt it was being treated unjustly and unequally, especially when Bulgaria and Romania, with all their faults, were accepted as members. Europe also lost a lot of prestige in the great crisis of 2008–12, in which Turkey's next-door neighbour Greece could only be saved from bankruptcy through massive injections of European money. Turkey came through the crisis much better and, over the whole 2002–12 period, was one of the fastest growing economies in the world. Self-confidence increased and, by 2012, many in Turkey agreed with EU Affairs Minister Egemen Bağış when he said that 'the EU needed Turkey more than Turkey needed the EU.' One important factor was that by now the AKP no longer needed the EU to accomplish its internal agenda. The whole administration was solidly in the hands of the party and the army had been subjugated to the elected politicians.

Ten years after the decision to start negotiations and fifty years after the conclusion of the association treaty, the accession process seemed to have become a ritual exercise. It was in the interest of neither party to break off negotiations, but support for a process that would entail significant sacrifices on both sides if a common future were to be built was dwindling. In 2014, therefore, Turkey was, in essence, what it had been in 1914 and, to some extent, even in 1814 – a very important player on the fault line between Europe and the Middle East, not fully a part of either, or, alternatively, part of both. A comparison with neighbouring countries like Iraq, Syria and Egypt immediately shows the enormous strides that Turkey has taken in terms of economic strength, standard of living, quality of life, political rights and stability. However, a comparison with the countries of western and central Europe just as quickly reveals that Turkey still lags a considerable distance behind them in terms of liberal democracy, rule of law, press freedom (including the Internet) and social development.

Notes

Chapter 1
The Ottoman Empire at the End of the Eighteenth Century

1. For a useful overview of the problems one encounters when estimating the size of the population, see Donald Quataert (1994) 'The age of reforms, 1812–1914', in Halil İnalcık with Donald Quataert (eds) *An economic and social history of the Ottoman Empire 1300–1914*, Cambridge: Cambridge University Press, 777–98. The main problem is uncertainty about the average size of the Ottoman household. Adding one person per household leads to an increase of 5,000,000 in the total population.
2. Quataert, op. cit., 779.
3. Benjamin Braude and Bernard Lewis (ed.) (1982) *Christians and Jews in the Ottoman Empire*, New York: Holmes, 2 vols. Research based on local court records (*kadi sicilleri*), which have become increasingly popular over the last 20 years, often shows that Christians and Jews took their cases to the Ottoman *şeriat* courts.
4. Carter Vaughn Findley (1980) *Bureaucratic reform in the Ottoman Empire: the Sublime Porte 1789–1922*, Princeton: Princeton University Press, in its first two chapters gives an excellent description of the structure of the Ottoman ruling elite on the eve of the reforms of the nineteenth century. This passage is based largely on Findley's analysis.
5. This picture has been formed primarily by the statesman and scholar Ahmet Cevdet Pasha, whose historical writings became very influential. See Christoph K. Neumann (1994) *Das indirekte Argument: ein Plädoyer für die Tanzimat vermittels der Historie. Die geschichtliche Bedeutung von Ahmed Cevdet Paşas Ta'rih*, Münster: Lit, 108–21.
6. Carter V. Findley (1988) *Ottoman civil officialdom: a social history*, Princeton: Princeton University Press, 47, estimates the central state apparatus at 2000 clerks. That seems high, when compared with the official staffing numbers of the various departments that Findley also gives, but the 2000 may also include the overstaffing that is not visible in the official numbers.
7. Malcolm E. Yapp (1987) in his excellent introduction to *The making of the modern Near East, 1792–1923*, London: Longman, 40–1, makes a good case for such a low percentage.
8. Bruce McGowan (1994) 'The age of the Ayans, 1699–1812', in Halil İnalcık with Donald Quataert (eds) *An economic and social history of the Ottoman Empire 1300–1914*, Cambridge: Cambridge University Press, 714.
9. Dick Douwes (2000) *The Ottomans in Syria: a history of justice and oppression*, London: I.B.Tauris, 154–5. Douwes gives very detailed

specifications of the tax income of the district of Hama in the province of Damascus, which consisted of 40 different kinds of taxes.

10. These realities of late eighteenth-century warfare are described in Virginia H. Aksan (1999) 'Ottoman military recruitment strategies in the late eighteenth century', in Erik Jan Zürcher (ed.) *Arming the state: military conscription in the Middle East and Central Asia, 1775–1925*, I.B.Tauris, 21–39.

11. This at least is the proposition first put forward by Willam H. MacNeill (1964) in his *Europe's steppe frontier 1500–1800*, Chicago: University of Chicago Press.

12. McGowan, op. cit., 681.

13. See for example the contributions by Suraiya Faroqhi (for the seventeenth century) and Donald Quataert (for the nineteenth), in İnalcık with Quataert (eds) *An economic and social history*, Quataert has treated this phenomenon in several of his studies on Ottoman industry. Another example is Sherry Vatter (1995) in her 'Militant textile weavers in Damascus: waged artisans and the Ottoman labour movement 1850–1914', in Donald Quataert and Erik Jan Zürcher (eds) *Workers and the working class in the Ottoman Empire and the Turkish Republic 1839–1950*, London: I.B.Tauris, 35–57.

14. See Reşat Kasaba (1988) *The Ottoman Empire and the world economy: the nineteenth century*, Albany: SUNY Press, 18–23.

15. The spurious nature of the Russian claims is demonstrated in Roderick H. Davison (1990) '"Russian skill and Turkish imbecility": the treaty of Kuchuk Kainardji reconsidered', in his *Essays in Ottoman and Turkish history, 1774–1923: the impact of the West*, Austin: University of Texas Press, 29–50.

Chapter 2
Between Tradition and Innovation: Sultan Selim III and the 'New Order', 1789–1807

1. Stanford J. Shaw (1971) discusses the degree to which the Ottoman elite of this period was influenced by the West in his *Between old and new: the Ottoman Empire under Sultan Selim III, 1789–1807*, Cambridge, MA: Harvard University Press, 180–99.

2. Bernard Lewis (1961) *The emergence of modern Turkey*, London: Oxford University Press, 57.

3. Bernard Lewis (1953) 'The impact of the French revolution on Turkey', *Journal of world history*, 1 (1), 105–25.

4. Since the 1980s there has been a plethora of influential studies on nationalism published, but Elie Kedourie's (1960) *Nationalism* (London: Hutchinson), in my view is still the most interesting one for the student of the Ottoman Empire, even if it takes a very gloomy view of nationalism as such.

5. Reşat Kasaba (1988) *The Ottoman Empire and the world economy: the nineteenth century*, Albany: SUNY Press, 20–2.

6. Halil İnalcık (1964) gives an interesting analysis of the document in his 'Sened-i ittifak ve Gülhane hatt-i humâyunu', *Belleten*, 28 (112), 603–22.

Chapter 3
The Early Years of Sultan Mahmut II: The Centre Tries to Regain Control

1. The Kurdish emirates were suppressed gradually in the two decades following Mahmut II's destruction of the janissaries in 1826. The last important emirate to be subjected, in 1847, was that of Botan, which had its centre at Cizre and was ruled by the Bedirhan family, who would remain important Kurdish notables until this day. Cf. Martin van Bruinessen (1992) *Agha, shaikh and state: the social and political structures of Kurdistan*, London: Zed Books, 175–80 (original edition 1978).
2. Bernard Lewis (1961) *The emergence of modern Turkey*, London: Oxford University Press, 103, even describes Halet as 'a convinced reactionary', who hated anything European.
3. Matthew S. Anderson (1966) *The Eastern Question 1774–1923: a study in international relations*, London: Macmillan, 51–2.
4. Anderson, op. cit., 54.
5. Khaled Fahmy (1999) 'Conscription in Mehmet Ali's Egypt', in Erik Jan Zürcher (ed.) *Arming the state: military conscription in the Middle East and Central Asia 1775–1925*, 59–77. See also Khaled Fahmy (1997) *All the pasha's men: Mehmet Ali, his army and the making of modern Egypt*, Cambridge: Cambridge University Press. In Mehmet Ali's army, the officer corps consisted of 'Turks' (Turkish speaking Ottomans born in Anatolia or the Balkans), while the conscripts were Arabic-speaking Egyptians.

Chapter 4
The Later Years of Sultan Mahmut II: The Start of the Reforms

1. Enver Ziya Karal (1983) *Osmanlı Tarihi. V. Cilt, Nizam-i Cedid ve tanzimat devirleri (1789–1856)*, Ankara: Türk Tarih Kurumu, 137 (originally published 1947).
2. The expression 'Eastern Question' entered the international diplomatic discourse during the Congress of Verona in 1822. For a detailed treatment of the issue, see Matthew A. Anderson (1972) *The Eastern Question 1774–1923: a study in international relations*, London: Macmillan (first edition 1966). For an excellent short summary, see also Walter Alison Phillips's (1962) 'Eastern Question', in *Encyclopaedia Britannica*, Chicago/London, vol. 7, 861–8, based on the same author's contributions to the *Cambridge modern history*.
3. Erik-Jan Zürcher (1999) 'The Ottoman conscription system in theory and practice, 1844–1918', *International review of social history*, 43 (3), 437–9.
4. It is very difficult to find precise figures on inflation in this period, but the value of the most important Ottoman coin, the *kuruş* or piaster declined against the Venetian ducat from 8 to the ducat in 1800 to 45 to the ducat in 1834. The silver content of the coin dropped from 5.9 grammes to less than 1 gramme over the three decades of Mahmut's reign. (See Şevket Pamuk

(1994) 'Money in the Ottoman Empire, 1326–1914', in Halil İnalcık with Donald Quataert, *An economic and social history of the Ottoman Empire 1300–1914*, Cambridge: Cambridge University Press, 967, 970 and 975.

5. Kemal H. Karpat (1985) *Ottoman population 1830–1914: demographic and social characteristics*, Madison: University of Wisconsin Press, 21–2.
6. Ibid., 116.
7. Şevket Pamuk (1987) *The Ottoman Empire and European capitalism, 1820–1913: trade, investment and production*, Cambridge: Cambridge University Press, 19–20.
8. Ibid., 11.
9. Ibid., 149.
10. This is the most important conclusion of Reşat Kasaba's (1987) *The Ottoman Empire and the world economy: the nineteenth century*, Albany: SUNY Press.
11. Pamuk, op. cit., 40.
12. Ibid., 26.

Chapter 5
The Era of the *Tanzimat*, 1839–71

1. For the term *Tanzimat*, see Roderic H. Davison (1973) *Reform in the Ottoman Empire 1856–1876*, New York: Gordian, 42 (originally published by Princeton University Press in 1963); for the High Council, see Davison 1973, op. cit., 28.
2. Literally, the sultan's words were: 'The beneficiaries are the nation of Islam and the other nations among the subjects of our majestic sultanate without exception.' In the French version, which the Porte distributed, the reference to the nation of Islam was left out. See Davison 1973, op. cit., 40.
3. The Druze, or Muwahhidun (Unitarians) as they call themselves, were, and still are, an Arabic-speaking community in the Shuf mountains of the Lebanon and the Hauran region in southern Syria. They are followers of a 'secret religion' that is an offshoot of eleventh century Egyptian Ismaili Shi'ism.
4. Davison, 1973, op. cit., Appendix A, 413.
5. The introduction of conscription took a while. It was already discussed in Sultan Mahmut's final years and it was one of the promises of the Gülhane edict. New army regulations that included conscription were promulgated in 1843 and the draft, as basis for conscription, was instituted in 1848. See Zürcher (1999) 'Ottoman conscription system', 82.
6. A clear description, with a graph (p. 64), of the checquered history of the council can be found in can be found in Mehmet Seyitdanlıoğlu (1991) *Tanzimat devrinde Meclis-i Vâlâ (1838–1868)*, Ankara: Türk Tarih Kurumu.
7. Donald Quataert (1994) 'The age of reforms, 1812–1914', in Halil İnalcık with Donald Quataert, *An economic and social history of the Ottoman Empire 1300–1914*, Cambridge: Cambridge University Press, 855.

8. Ibid., 856–60 describes the conflicting evidence on the question of whether the land law was used by large landowners and tribal chiefs to expropriate small cultivators.

9. Stanford J. Shaw and Ezel Kural Shaw (1977) *History of the Ottoman Empire and modern Turkey. Volume 2, Reform, revolution and republic: the rise of modern Turkey 1808–1975*, Cambridge: Cambridge University Press, 86–7.

10. Davison 1973, op. cit., 144–7, 160–3.

11. Ibid., 132–3.

12. We have very little factual information about the degree of literacy in this period, but we can project backwards from the first census of the Republic of Turkey in 1927, which showed that even then only 10.6 per cent of the population could read and write. Although in the mid-nineteenth century literacy among the Christian minorities (which had all but disappeared by 1927) was much higher, the percentage of Muslims that could read and write was probably lower. See Orhan Cavit Tütengil (1980) '1927 yılında Türkiye', in *Atatürk'ün büyük söylevinin 50: yılı semineri. Bildiriler ve tartışmalar*, Ankara: Türk Tarih Kurumu, 56.

13. Şevket Pamuk (1987) *The Ottoman Empire and European capitalism, 1820–1913: trade, investment and production*, Cambridge: CUP, 28–9.

14. A comprehensive overview of issue prices, costs to the government and rates of interest is given in Christopher Clay's exhaustive study (2000) *Gold for the sultan: Western bankers and Ottoman finance 1856–1881*, London: I.B.Tauris, Appendix 1.

15. Ibid., 409.

16. Ibid., 69.

17. Davison 1973, op. cit., 100–2.

18. This currrent is described in detail in Albert Hourani's famous (1962) *Arabic thought in the liberal age*, London: Oxford University Press.

19. By far the best study of the Young Ottomans is still Şerif Mardin's (1962) *The genesis of Young Ottoman thought: a study in the modernization of Turkish political ideas*, Princeton: Princeton University Press, on which this account is based.

Chapter 6
The Crisis of 1873–78 and its Aftermath

1. Roderic H. Davison (1991) 'Mahmud Nedim Pasha', in C. E. Bosworth et al. (eds) *Encyclopaedia of Islam: new edition*, Leiden: E. J. Brill, vol., VI, 68–9.

2. Şevket Pamuk (1987) *The Ottoman Empire and European capitalism, 1820–1913*, Cambridge: Cambridge University Press, 14.

3. Christopher Clay (2000) *Gold for the sultan: Western bankers and Ottoman finance 1856–1881*, London: I.B.Tauris, 574.

4. Matthew S. Anderson (1966) *The Eastern Question 1774–1923: a study in international relations*, London: Macmillan, 184.

5. Robert Devereux (1963) *The first Ottoman constitutional period: a study of the Midhat constitution and parliament*, Baltimore: Johns Hopkins Press, 39.

Chapter 7
Reactionary Despotism or Culmination of the Reforms? The Reign of Sultan Abdülhamit II

1. Robert Devereux (1963) *The first Ottoman constitutional period: a study of the Midhat constitution and parliament*, Baltimore: Johns Hopkins Press, 126–7.
2. Ibid., 248–9.
3. That is the view of Shaw and Shaw (1977) in their *History of the Ottoman Empire and modern Turkey. Volume 2: Reform, revolution and republic: the rise of modern Turkey 1808–1975*, Cambridge: Cambridge University Press, 172–272.
4. Donald Quataert (1983) *Social disintegration and popular resistance in the Ottoman Empire, 1881–1908: reactions to European economic penetration*, New York: New York University Press, 96, describes how sailing vessels carried about 50 per cent of the total tonnage shipped to Istanbul in the 1860s and how that share dropped to 10 per cent by the end of the 1870s. In İzmir, the share of steamships, which was already as high as 80 per cent in 1872 went up to 95 per cent ten years later.
5. Orhan Koloğlu (n.d.) 'Osmanlı basını: içeriği ve rejimi', in Murat Belge (ed.) *Tanzimat'tan cumhuriyet'e Türkiye ansiklopedisi*, Istanbul: İletişim, vol. 1, 87.
6. In his book, *The well-protected domains: ideology and the legitimation of power in the Ottoman Empire 1876–1909*, London: I.B.Tauris, Selim Deringil (1998) gives a fascinating account of the way in which Abdülhamit instrumentalized Islam to strengthen the ideological basis of his regime.
7. About half of the total cost was covered from voluntary donations, not just from within the empire, but also from India, where the Central Committee for the Hejaz Railway, based in Hyderabad, was a very effective fund raiser. See Azmi Özcan (1997) *Pan-Islamism: Indian Muslims, the Ottomans and Britain (1877–1924)*, Leiden: E. J. Brill, 108–10.
8. Justin McCarthy (1995) *Death and exile: the ethnic cleansing of Ottoman Muslims, 1821–1922*, Princeton: Darwin Press, 15–18, 32–5.
9. Ibid., 91.
10. İlber Ortaylı (1983) *Osmanlı İmparatorluğunda Alman nüfuzu*, Istanbul: Kaynak, 67.
11. Şevket Pamuk (1987) *The Ottoman Empire and European capitalism, 1820–1913: trade, investment and production*, Cambridge: Cambridge University Press, 14–17.
12. Ibid., 66.
13. Donald Quataert describes this process of restructuring in his seminal chapter on Ottoman manufacturing in İnalcık and Quataert (1994) *An economic and social history of the Ottoman Empire 1300–1914*, Cambridge: Cambridge University Press, 888–933.
14. Justin McCarthy (1983) *Muslims and minorities: the population of Ottoman Anatolia and the end of the empire*, New York: New York University Press, 2.

NOTES 375

15. M. Şükrü Hanioğlu (1995) *The Young Turks in opposition*, Oxford: Oxford University Press, 74.
16. Ibid., 86.
17. Ibid., 32. For LeBon's ideas, which were very popular among the younger officers of countries as far apart as Romania and Tunisia, see Robert A. Nye (1975) *The origins of crowd psychology: Gustave LeBon and the crisis of mass democracy in the Third Republic*, London: Sage.
18. M. Şükrü Hanioğlu (2001) *Preparation for a revolution: the Young Turks, 1902–1908*, Oxford: Oxford University Press, 136–41.

Chapter 8
The Second Constitutional Period, 1912–18

1. Hüseyin Cahit Yalçın (1976) *Siyasal anılar*, Istanbul: Türkiye İş Bankası Kültür Yayınları, 3.
2. Yavuz Selim Karakışla describes the strike wave and its subsequent suppression by the Unionists in his 'The emergence of the Ottoman industrial working class, 1839–1923', in Donald Quataert and Erik Jan Zürcher (eds) *Workers and working class in the Ottoman Empire and the Turkish republic 1839–1950*, 19–34. As he shows in the chapter, the strikes were motivated by wage demands and demands for better working conditions. With one exception they were apolitical.
3. The episode is described in detail in Aykut Kansu (1997) *The revolution of 1908 in Turkey*, Leiden: E. J. Brill, 120–3.
4. There were 153 Turks, 53 Arabs, 27 Albanians and 40 Christians according to Kansu (op. cit., 239–40). Feroz Ahmad and Dankwart Rustow (1976) 'İkinci meşrutiyet döneminde meclisler 1908–1918', *Güneydoğu Avrupa aracturmaları dergisi*, 4–5, 247 gives a slightly different distribution: 142 Turks, 60 Arabs, 25 Albanians, 23 Greeks, 12 Armenians, 5 Jews and 5 Slavs.
5. Taner Akçam (1999) *Insan hakları ve Ermeni sorunu: Ittihat ve Terakki'den kurtuluc savacına*, Ankara: İmge, 122.
6. M. Naim Turfan (2000) *The rise of the Young Turks: politics, the military and Ottoman collapse*, London: I.B.Tauris, 243 (figures calculated by S. Karatumu in his *Türk Silahlı Kuvvetleri tarihi*).
7. Feroz Ahmad (1969) *The Young Turks: the Committee of Union and Progress in Turkish politics 1908–1914*, Oxford: Clarendon, 107.
8. Donald Quataert (1983) *Social disintegration and popular resistance in the Ottoman Empire, 1881–1908: reactions to European economic penetration*, New York: New York University Press, 121–45. See also Doğan Çetinkaya (2013) *The Young Turks and the Boycott Movement: nationalism, protest and the working classes in the formation of modern Turkey*. London: I.B.Tauris.
9. Erik Jan Zürcher (1999) 'Kosovo revisited: Sultan Reşad's Macedonian journey of 1911', *Middle Eastern studies*, 35 (4), 26–39. The number of Albanians attending was at least ten times lower than the 300,000 the Unionist press claimed.

10. Karl Klinghardt (translator and editor) (1927) *Denkwürdigkeiten des Marschalls İzzet Pascha: ein kritischer Beitrag zur Kriegsschuldfrage*, Leipzig: Koehler, 179.

11. Ahmad 1969, op. cit., 120.

12. In his *The rise of the Young Turks* (368–70), M. Naim Turfan propounds the thesis that two officers, Ali Fethi (Okyar) and Mustafa Kemal (Atatürk), had originally proposed the amphibious operation. His argument relies on a report, dated 4 February, written by these two on the landings. According to Turfan they must have used Gregorian instead of Julian (*Mali*, confused by Turfan with *Hicri*) dating by mistake; 4 February 1913 (Gregorian) would be equivalent to 22 January (Julian). This, however, is quite inconceivable for Ottoman officers (there are no other known examples). The argument must, therefore, be rejected, especially as the report also talks about the fleet being in the harbour of Gallipoli, where it went only *after* the landings had miscarried. In fact, the report was part of the recriminations among those responsible for the fiasco (cf. Erik Jan Zürcher, *The Unionist Factor*, 58–9).

13. Justin McCarthy (1995) *Death and exile: the ethnic cleansing of Ottoman Muslims, 1821–1922*, Princeton: Darwin, 159–61 gives a total of over 400,000 refugees.

14. The emergence of the Special Organization out of a losely-knit group of irregulars is described by Philip Stoddard (1963) in his unpublished Ph.D. thesis, *The Ottoman government and the Arabs 1911–1918: a preliminary study of the Teşkilât-I Masusa*, Princeton University, 52 ff.

15. An English translation of the treaty is found in Ulrich Trumpener (1968) *Germany and the Ottoman Empire 1914–1918*, Princeton: Princeton University Press, 28. Trumpener emphasizes the improvised nature of the agreement.

16. Trumpener, op. cit., 54.

17. Justin McCarthy (1983) *Muslims and minorities: the population of Ottoman Anatolia and the end of empire*, New York: New York University Press, 30, gives 600,000 as the most likely number. While McCarthy's interpretation of the Armenian problem is highly contentious, his estimates of the number of victims seem well founded.

18. I have based my summary of the Armenian question primarily on the work of Taner Akçam's (2012) *The Young Turks' crime against humanity: the Armenian genocide and ethnic cleansing in the Ottoman Empire*, Princeton: Princeton University Press, which summarizes his own and other people's recent research, on Donald Bloxham's (2005) *The great game of genocide: imperialism, nationalism and the destruction of the Ottoman Armenians*, Oxford: Oxford University Press, and, for empirical data, on Raymond Kevorkian's (2006) *La génocide des Armeniens*, Paris: Odile Jacob.

19. Kuşçubaşızade Eşref Bey, a prominent member of the Special Organization, describes the Ottoman Greek Orthodox as 'internal tumours' that needed to be removed (see Celâl Bayar (1967) *Ben de yazdım: Millî mücadeleye giriş*, vol. 5, Istanbul: Baha, 1572–82); the infamous governor of Diyarbakır, Dr Mehmet Reşit, as a choice between 'killing the disease AND the patients or

seeing the Turkish nation being destroyed by lunatics'. See Mithat Şükrü Bleda (1979) *İmparatorluğun çöküşü*, Istanbul: Remzi, 61. Bleda, the former secretary-general of the CUP, seems to agree fully.

20. The number is based on Robert Rhodes James (1965) *Gallipoli*, London: Batsford, 348, but computing casualty numbers for the Ottoman army in the First World War is very difficult. The Turkish government gives the official number of Ottoman casualties during the Gallipoli campaign as 251,000 (see Alan Moorehead (1989) *Gallipoli*, London: Andre Deutsch, 348 (first edition 1956). Edward J. Erickson (2001) in his book *Ordered to die: a history of the Ottoman army in the First World War*, Westport: Greenwood, 237, gives a substantially lower number, 165,000. The Australian war memorial and museum in Canberra puts the number of Ottoman fatalities at 86,692. Erickson gives 56,643. Possibly the difference is due to the exclusion of deaths from disease.

21. Ahmed Emin [Yalman] (1930) *Turkey in the world war*, New Haven: Yale University Press, 262. The numbers Yalman gives (and which are used by modern historians like Toprak) are based on the estimates of the Ottoman Public Debt Administration, which needed them to compute the compensation it was to pay to its employees.

22. Jehuda L. Wallach (1976) *Anatomie einer Militärhilfe: die preussisch – deutschen Militärmissionen in der Türkei 1835–1919*, Düsseldorf: Droste, 246.

23. Zafer Toprak (1988) 'Osmanlı Kadınları Çalıştırma Cemiyeti: Kadın askerler ve Millî Aile', *Tarih ve Toplum*, 9 (51), 34–8.

24. Celâl Bayar, op. cit., 1572–82; Erkan Şenşekerci (2000) *Türk devriminde Celâl Bayar (1918–1960)*, Istanbul: Alfa, 35–6.

25. Zafer Toprak lists them in his *Türkiye'de "Millî İktisat" (1908–1918)*, Ankara: Yurt, 1982, 363–4.

26. Yalman, op. cit., 151. The figures that Yalman gives (and that modern historians like Zafer Toprak have used) are based on the cost-of-living index drawn up by the Public Debt Administration to estimate what bonuses should be paid to its employees.

Chapter 9
The Struggle for Independence

1. Erik Jan Zürcher (1998) 'The Ottoman Empire and the armistice of Moudros', in Hugh Cecil and Peter H. Liddle (eds) *At the eleventh hour: reflections, hopes and anxieties at the closing of the Great War, 1918*, London: Leo Cooper.

2. Erik Jan Zürcher (1984) *The Unionist factor: the role of the Committee of Union and Progress in the Turkish national movement 1905–1926*, Leiden: E. J. Brill, 104–5.

3. N. Bilge Criss (1999) *Istanbul under allied occupation 1918–1923*, Leiden: E. J. Brill, 94–114. Criss builds on the story as told in in Zürcher (1984) *The Unionist factor*, 80 ff., but extends it considerably.

4. Tevfik Bıyıklıoğlu (1956) *Trakya'da millî mücadele*, Ankara: Türk Tarih Kurumu, 128.

5. The text of the National Pact is problematic in several respects. In the first place some authors talk about the area 'within and without the armistice lines', while others only mention the area 'within the armistice lines'. This is a fundamental difference and the specific demands of the pact seem to indicate that the maximalist version is authentic (after all: demands are formulated considering Western Thrace, Batumi and the Arab lands). In the second place, there is confusion about what binds the Ottoman Muslims. Was it 'origin' (*asıl*) or 'aim' (*emel*). Both versions are mentioned in the literature as early as the1920s. The confusion can only be caused by different readings of a *handwritten* text in Arabic script. In a printed text, the meaning would have been unequivocal. See Erik Jan Zürcher (2000) 'Young Turks, Ottoman Muslims and Turkish nationalists', in Kemal H. Karpat (ed.) *Ottoman past and today's Turkey*, Leiden: E. J. Brill, 170. See https://tr.wikipedia.org/wiki/dosya:misak-i_milli_beyannamesi.pdf for a picture of the original.

6. Ahmed Emin [Yalman] (1930) *Turkey in the world war*, New Haven: Yale University Press, 151.

7. Criss, op. cit., 29 ff.

8. Hüseyin Dağtekin (1955) 'İstiklâl savaşında Anadolu'ya kaçırılan mühimmat ve askerî eşya hakkında tanzim edilmiş mühim bir vesika', *Tarih vesikaları (Yeni seri)*, (1) 9–15.

9. Criss, op. cit., 100–1.

10. Kâzım Karabekir (1960) *İstiklâl harbimiz*, Istanbul: Türkiye, 391.

11. For an analysis of Lloyd George's attitude towards Venizelos and the Greeks, see Harold Nicolson (1934) *Curzon: the last phase 1919–1925: a study in postwar diplomacy*, London: Constable, 95–7.

12. Paul C. Helmreich (1974) *From Paris to Sèvres: the partition of the Ottoman Empire at the peace conference of 1919–1920*, Columbus: Ohio State University Press, 218.

13. Ali Fuat Cebesoy (1953) *Millî mücadele hatıraları*, Istanbul: Vatan, 72.

14. Mahmut Goloğlu (1969) *Sivas kongresi*, Ankara: Başnur, 73–4. Goloğlu also points out that the much higher numbers (up to 99) mentioned in some later studies are wholly unfounded.

15. Law 7 of 7 June 1920. See Gothard Jaeschke (1970) *Türk kurtuluş savaşının kronolojisi: Mondros'tan Mudanya 'ya kadar 30 ekim 1918–11 ekim 1922*, Ankara: Türk Tarih Kurumu, 106.

16. Law 2 of 29 April 1920. See Jaeschke, op. cit., 101.

17. A decision on the future status of the straits was left to a conference of riparian states, but it was stipulated that its decisions would not endanger Turkey's sovereignty. See Reha Parla (1985) *Belgelerle Türkiye Cumhuriyeti'nin uluslararası temelleri*, Lefkoşe (Nicosia): Tezel, 187.

18. Because of his legendary status among the Turkish left, the responsibility for Mustafa Suphi's murder has always been much debated. There is hardly any doubt that the local strongman in Trabzon, Yahya Kahya, was directly responsible for the murder, but who gave the order is an issue that has been

controversial: the government in Ankara, Enver Pasha's supporters or the Bolsheviks. Ankara certainly had the strongest motive and the Boslheviks could easily have prevented him from crossing the border in the first place (in the company of the Bolshevik emissary Mdivani).

19. Halide Edib [Adıvar] (1928) *The Turkish ordeal*, New York: Century, 91.
20. The reason for this was not that the British had become convinced of their innocence or despaired of building a case against them. It was simply that the release of the prisoners was a condition for the release of British hostages in Anatolia. The most prominent of these was Col. Alfred Rawlinson, the brother of General Sir Henry Rawlinson.
21. Michael M. Finefrock (1976) 'From sultanate to republic: Mustafa Kemal Atatürk and the structure of Turkish politics, 1922–1924', unpublished Ph.D. thesis, Princeton University, Appendix E.
22. Numbers taken from Justin McCarthy (1983) *Muslims and minorities: the population of Ottoman Anatolia and the end of empire*, New York: New York University Press, Chapter 7.
23. William Hale (1981) *The political and economic development of modern Turkey*, London: Croom Helm.
24. Ahmed Emin [Yalman], op. cit., 162–3.
25. Ahmed Emin [Yalman], op. cit., Appendix 2.

Chapter 10
The Emergence of the One-Party State, 1923–27

1. In interviews given to journalists in Izmit in early 1923 Mustafa Kemal promised the Kurds a degree of local autonomy and free use of their own language. See Doğu Perinçek (1993) *Mustafa Kemal Eskişehir – izmit konuşmaları (1923): ilk sansürsüz tam metin*, Istanbul: Kaynak, 104.
2. Erik-Jan Zürcher (1991) *Political opposition in the early Turkish republic: the Progressive Republican Party 1924–1925*, Leiden: E. J. Brill, 83. Mustafa Kemal gave an hour-long speech in which he called for stronger measures.
3. Robert Olson (1989) *The emergence of Kurdish nationalism and the Sheikh Sait rebellion, 1880–1925*, Austin: University of Texas, 125.
4. Mete Tunçay (1989) *T.C.'de tek parti yönetiminin kurulması (1923–1931)*, Istanbul: Cem, 169.

Chapter 11
The Kemalist One-Party State, 1925–45

1. Mete Tunçay (1981) *Türkiye Cumhuriyetinde tek parti yönetiminin kurulması (1923–1931)*, Ankara: Yurt, 308. Tunçay sees the 1931 party congress as a turning point because now a totalitarian model replaced the earlier efforts to work with a tame opposition. The 1931 congress was also the first to produce a more or less coherent ideological framework (the six principles of Kemalism). As in 1927, the party embraced the principle of unification, rather than separation, of powers.

2. An overview of the most important groups and figures can be found in Hakkı Uyar (1998) *Tek parti dönemi ve Cumhuriyet Halk Partisi*, Istanbul: Boyut, 99 ff.

3. Çetin Yetkin (1982) *Serbest Cumhuriyet Fırkası olayı*, Istanbul: Karacan, 208. Mustafa Kemal did this in reply to an open letter addressed to him by Yunus Nadi the editor of the newspaper *Cumhuriyet*.

4. Walter F. Weiker (1973) *Political tutelage and democracy in Turkey: the Free Party and its aftermath*, Leiden: E. J. Brill, 115.

5. The fact that many people who had supported him in 1930 later denounced him was especially galling. Osman Okyar and Mehmet Seitdanlioğlu (1997) *Fethi Okyar'ın anıları: Atatürk, Okyar ve çok partili Türkiye*, Istanbul: İş Bankası, contains a memoir on the episode written by Fethi Bey, which clearly demonstrates his anger and disappointment. Nevertheless, he and Mustafa Kemal remained on speaking terms until the latter's death in 1938.

6. Murat Belge (ed.) (n.d.) *Cumhuriyet dönemi Türkiye ansiklopedisi*, Istanbul: İletişim, vol. 2, 573 gives an excellent synopsis of the 'Menemen event', which is still part of secularist discourse in Turkey in the early twenty-first century. A very interesting analysis is also given by Hamit Bozarslan in his article 'Le mahdisme en Turquie: l'incident de Menemen en 1930', *REMMM*, 91–4, 297–320. According to Bozarslan there is no proof that the dervishes actually were Nakşibendis.

7. Walter Weiker, op. cit., 160–3.

8. Füsun Üstel (1997) *İmparatorluktan ulus-devlete Türk milliyetçiliği: Türk Ocakları (1912–1931)*, Istanbul: İletişim, 358–9. Üstel bases herself on François Georgeon's earlier work on the Turkish Hearths during the republic for this passage.

9. For a description and analysis of the German expatriate colony in Turkey during the Hitler era, see Sabine Hillebrecht (2000) *Haymatloz: Exil in der Türkei 1933–1945*, Berlin: Verein Aktives Museum.

10. Cemil Koçak (1986) *Türkiye'de millî şef dönemi (1938–1945)*, Ankara: Yurt, 17–19.

11. Andrew Mango (1999) *Atatürk*, London: John Murray, 524, basing himself on the memoirs of Hasan Rıza Soyak.

12. Selim Deringil (1989) *Turkish foreign policy during the Second World War: an 'active' neutrality*, Cambridge: Cambridge University Press, 56–7.

13. The question whether Atatürk was a dictator was always a sensitive one in Kemalist Turkey. Former party secretary Recep Peker touches briefly on the position of the 'leader' (*şef*) in his famous (1935) *İnkılap dersleri notları* (Ankara: Ulus, 65–6), but he avoids any discussion of dictatorship there. That the discussion remained on the agenda is shown by a curious booklet published at Güven (Istanbul) in 1949; this was A. Muhtar Kumral, *Atatürk diktatör müdür?* which consists of a selection of anecdotes and texts from Atatürk's life, purporting to demonstrate that he was not, in fact, a dictator. The booklet clearly forms part of the defensive reaction of the Kemalists when faced with the growing Democrat Party opposition in the immediate postwar era.

14. For the anti-veiling campaigns, see Sevgi Adak (2014) 'Anti veiling campagins and local elites in Turkey of the 1930s: a view from the periphery', in Stephanie Cronin (ed.) *Anti-veiling campaigns in the Muslim world*, Abingdon: Routledge, 59–85.

15. For an overview of all the attempts to change the Ottoman alphabet, see Hüseyin Yorulmaz (1995) *Tanzimattan cumhuriyete alfabe tartışmaları*, Istanbul: Kitabevi.

16. The most famous instance of a speech in new 'real' Turkish (*öztürkçe*) was Atatürk's dinner speech to the visiting Crown Prince of Sweden on 3 October 1934, which contained sentences such as '*Genlik baysal içinde erk surmenin gücü işte bundadır*', largely made up of newly invented words. Even those in attendance on the Turkish side could not make out its meaning. (Cf. *Atatürk'ün söylev ve demeçleri II (1906–1938)*, Ankara: TTK, 1959, 277–8.

17. Büşra Ersanlı Behar (1992) *İktidar ve tarih: Türkiye'de "resmi tarih" tezinin oluşumu (1929–1937)*, Istanbul: AFA, 203.

18. Gotthard Jaeschke (1951) 'Der Islam in der neuen Türkei: Eine rechtsgeschichtliche Untersuchung', *Welt des Islams Neue Serie*, 1, 74–6.

19. Michael Finefrock (1976) 'From sultanate to republic: Mustafa Kemal and the structure of Turkish politics 1922–1924', unpublished Ph.D. thesis, Princeton University, 313.

20. Uygur Kocabaşoğlu (ed.) (2001) *Türkiye İş Bankası tarihi*, Istanbul: İş Bankası, 112 ff.

21. William Hale (1981) *The political and economic development of modern Turkey*, London: Croom Helm, 43.

22. Hale, op. cit., 62. The index recovered slightly in the years that followed.

23. Hale, op. cit., 56.

24. Hale, op. cit., 69.

25. For a good recent discussion of the wealth tax, based on all the extant literature, see Rıfat N. Bali (1999) *Bir Türkleştirme serüveni (1923–1945): Cumhuriyet yıllarında Türkiye Yahudileri*, Istanbul: İletişim, 424 ff. See also Ayhan Aktar (2000) *Varlık vergisi ve 'türkleştirme' politikaları*, Istanbul: İletişim.

26. Deringil, op. cit., 191 (text of the second protocol added to the 'treaty of mutual assistance').

27. Ibid., 149.

Chapter 12
The Transition to Democracy, 1945–50

1. Hakkı Devrim, et al. (ed.) (1974) *Türkiye 1923–1973 ansiklopedisi*, Istanbul: Kaynak, vol. 2, 583. Ten years later the number was 216 (ibid., vol. 3, 962).

2. Max Weston Thornburg (1949) *Turkey: an economic appraisal*, New York: Twentieth Century Fund, 133.

3. The 1950 census of industry gives a total of 353,994 people working in 98,828 industrial establishments, but of these 96,626 were small and used less than ten mechanical horsepower (the equivalent of a light motorbike).

Richard D. Robinson (1963) *The first Turkish republic: a case study in national development*, Cambridge MA: Harvard University Press, 136.

4. An interesting analysis of the tensions creating disaffection with the CUP is given in Taner Timur (1991) *Türkiye'de çok partili hayata geçiş*, Istanbul: İletişim, 20 ff.

5. Baskın Oran (ed.) (2002) *Türk dış politikası: Kurtuluş savaşından bugüne olgular, belgeler, yorumlar, Istanbul: İletişim*, vol. 1 (1919–1980), 502.

6. These numbers are mentioned in Kemal Karpat (1959) *Turkey's politics: the transition to a multi-party system*, Princeton: Princeton University Press, 99. Thornburg, op. cit. gives slightly different percentages: 97 per cent smaller than 125 *dönüm* and 2.3 per cent between 125 and 1250 *dönüm*.

7. Karpat, op. cit., 164–5.

8. Timur, op. cit., 96 ff.

Chapter 13
The Rule of the Democratic Party, 1950–60

1. Frederick W. Frey (1965) *The Turkish political elite*, Cambridge, MA: MIT Press, 356 ff.

2. Feroz Ahmad (1977) *The Turkish experiment in democracy 1950–1975*, London: Hurst, 37.

3. Max Weston Thornburg (1949) *Turkey: an economic appraisal*, New York: Twentieth Century Fund, 149; James S. Barker et al. (1951) *The economy of Turkey: an analysis and recommendations for a development program*, Baltimore: Johns Hopkins Press.

4. Ahmad 1977, op. cit. 122–46; William Hale (1981) *The political and economic development of modern Turkey*, London: Croom Helm, 86–113.

5. Wikipedia actually has a very solid article on the topic: https://en.wiki pedia.org/wiki/Demographics_of_Turkey (accessed 5 April 2016), which for these data builds on the publications of the Turkish Statistical Office.

6. Alpaslan Işıklı (n.d.) 'Cumhuriyet döneminde Türk sendikacılığı', in Murat Belge (ed.) *Cumhuriyet dönemi Türkiye ansiklopedisi*, Istanbul: İletişim, vol. 7, 1828.

7. Hale, op. cit., 102.

8. Ali Gevgilili (1987) *Yükseliş ve düşüş*, Yassı Ada, 134 (with thanks to Socrates Petmezas and Vangelis Kechriotis).

9. Melek Fırat (2002) 'Yunanıstan'la ilişkiler', in Baskın Oran (ed.) *Türk dış politikası: cilt 1 1919–1980*, Istanbul: İletişim, 601.

10. A. Yücekök (1971) *Türkiye'de din ve siyaset*, Istanbul: Gerçek, 90.

11. In defending his decision to allow the prayer call to be recited in Arabic, Menderes made a distinction between the Kemalist reforms, which had taken hold (and should thus remain) and the ones that had been thought necessary in Atatürk's day, but had not taken hold. These could now be reversed without damage to the secular character of Turkey.

12. There were 717 dead, 167 missing and 5247 wounded. Figures from *Türkiye 1923–1973 ansiklopedisi*, Istanbul: Kaynak, 1974, vol. 3, 950.

13. William Hale (1996) *Türkiye'de ordu ve siyaset: 1789'dan günümüze*, Istanbul: Hil (translation of *Turkish military and politics*, London: Routledge, 1994), 95.
14. Uygur Kocabaşoğlu (n.d.) 'Radyo', in Murat Belge (ed.) *Cumhuriyet Dönemi Türkiye ansiklopedisi*, Istanbul: İletişim, vol. 10, 2743.

Chapter 14
The Second Turkish Republic, 1960–80

1. Translation of the full text of the proclamation in Walter F. Weiker (1963) *The Turkish revolution 1960–1961*, Washington: Brookings Institution, 20–1.
2. Weiker, op. cit. is fairly positive, but for instance Richard D. Robinson (1963) *The first Turkish republic*, Cambridge MA: Harvard, 268–70 is far more critical.
3. Mehmet Ali Birand (1987) *The generals' coup in Turkey: an inside story of 12 September 1980*, London: Brassey's Defence Publishers, 42–4.
4. The state security courts were reinstituted after the military coup of 1980 and they would play an important part in the suppression of Kurdish and Islamist movements in the 1990s.
5. Mehmet Ali Birand, op. cit, 84 ff.
6. Clement H. Dodd (1983) *The crisis of Turkish democracy*, Beverley: Eothen, 20.
7. Suzanne Paine (1974) *Exporting workers: the Turkish case*, London: Cambridge University Press.
8. The text of Mehmet Akif's rousing nationalist poem, which bore the title *İstiklâl Marşı* (Independence March) and the subtitle *Kahraman ordumuza* (to our heroic army), exudes strong religious feeling and a violent anti-Western sentiment. This is best expressed in these lines from the third stanza: 'My frontier is like my heart filled with belief. Don't be afraid, my nation!/ How can this one-toothed monster you call civilization ever strangle such a faith?' It is ironic that the fiercely secularist Turkish republic has had an anti-Western, Islamic poem for its national anthem for eighty years.
9. Alpaslan Işıklı (1836) 'Cumhuriyet döneminde Türk sendikacılığı', in Murat Belge (ed.) *Cumhuriyet dönemi Türkiye ansiklopedisi*, Istanbul: İletişim, n.d., vol. 7. Turkish trade unions often exaggerated their membership and reliable numbers are hard to find.
10. For a discussion of these bilateral agreements, see Çağrı Erhan (2002) 'Türkiye ile ABD arasındaki ikili anlaşmalar', in Baskın Oran (ed.) *Türk dış politikası: cilt 1 1919–1980*, Istanbul: İletişim, 556. According to Erhan, the exact number of agreements is unknown even today.
11. At first glance it seems strange that 60 years after the genocide a young generation of Armenians, who had been born after the Second World War, should become militants in the cause of their grandparents. For this, two explanations have been put forward, which do not necessarily exclude each other. In the first place, the civil war in the Lebanon, which pitted Muslims

against Christians, mobilized young members of Lebanon's large Armenian community. In the second place, the survivors of 1915 had spent all their energy on rebuilding their lives in their new country – primarily France and the United States. They managed to integrate so well into the new environment that they became fully French or American and that for the third generation the memory of the tragedy of 1915 ultimately was one of the few elements (alongside the Armenian church and Armenian food) that defined 'Armenianness'. The poet Peter Balakian (1998) gives an intimate picture of this process of rediscovery by an American–Armenian adolescent in *Black dog of fate*, New York: Broadway.

Chapter 15
The State of Kenan Evren and the Economy of Turgut Özal

1. In its 'Proclamation number one', the junta legitimized its action by referring to the duty the armed forces had under the Law on Internal Service (*İç Hizmet Kanunu*) to protect the republic. The key term in the proclamation is 'national unity and cohesion' (*millî birlik ve berbaberlik*), which was to remain the army's key political concept in the 1980s and 1990s.
2. Dodd, op. cit., 47.
3. Dodd, op. cit., 45.
4. Formally, even the rectors were appointed directly by the president of the republic.
5. Dodd, op. cit., 45.
6. In the polarized climate of the later 1970s the Hearths of the Enlightened became closely associated with the NAP of Alpaslan Türkeş and they agitated primarily against Ecevit and his RPP. Both Turgut and Korkut Özal were members of the organization in this period. Cf. Hugh Poulton (1997) *Top hat, grey wolf and crescent: Turkish nationalism and the Turkish republic*, London: Hurst, 179–81.
7. Poulton, op. cit, 184–5. After the 1980 coup, the leading members of the boards overseeing the media and higher education as well as the university rectors and education ministers were all members of the Hearths of the Enlightened. The influence of the synthesis in Turkish schoolbooks is shown convincingly in Etienne Copeaux (1998) *Türk tarih tezinden Türk– Islam sentezine*, Istanbul: Tarih Vakfı/Yurt.
8. In the 1980s and 1990s, this was a recurrent phenomenon. The Turkish legal system has been modernized and liberalized considerably, but there has often been a lack of synchronization between the changes to the different laws in force at the same time.
9. İsmet İmset (1992) *The PKK: a report on separatist violence in Turkey 1973–1992*, Ankara: TDN, 107 ff.
10. These 11 provinces together formed the 'Extraordinary Zone', known by its acronym OHAL in Turkey. From 2000 onwards the number of provinces in the OHAL was gradually reduced until it was finally abolished completely in November 2002.

Chapter 16
Years of Crisis (1994–2002)

1. That she could gain more seats with a slightly lower percentage of the popular vote is due to the peculiar election system in force in Turkey. Parties need to cross a 10 per cent threshold in the electoral district. Then they also need to cross a national threshold of 10 per cent. This can lead to strange results in areas with a polarized political landscape. Let us assume that there is a south-eastern district where the Kurdish party HEP (later HaDeP, still later DeHaP) gains 60 per cent of the popular vote and the Turkish ultra-nationalists (NAP) come in second with 25 per cent. All other parties poll less than 10 per cent. If the Kurdish party has regional, but not national support, it will not cross the national threshold. Its votes will be lost and the ultra-nationalists will take all seats (assuming it does cross the national threshold). In other words, the Kurdish nationalists will be 'represented' by Turkish nationalists in Ankara. If the NAP does *not* cross the national threshold, all the seats of the district will be allocated proportionally to those parties that do.

2. *Turkish Probe*, 10 October 1997, 248.

3. Increasing compulsory education by 60 per cent overnight created enormous problems with insufficient teachers, overcrowded classrooms and lack of teaching materials. Critics pointed out that this was also because Turkey still only spent 2.1 per cent of its GDP on education, a third of what Egypt, Tunisia or Jordan spent (*Turkish Probe*, 12 September 1997, 244).

4. *Turkish Probe*, 3 January 1999, 312.

5. *AK* in Turkish also means white, clean or transparent.

6. See *Turkish Probe*, 30 January 2000, 368 for an analysis of the movement and its history.

7. Mehmet Emin Yıldırım (2008) 'The Turkish economy between 1950 and 2000: policy and performance', *Philologiae et Historiae Turcicae Fundamenta V*, Berlin: Klaus Schwarz, 379–94.

8. *Mane pulite* (clean hands) was the name of a campaign conducted by Milan-based magistrates in Italy against corrupt links between the state and business. It had been triggered by the discovery of a rightist political–industrial network, which had been hatched inside the Masonic lodge *Propaganda Due* (P–2) and in which financial officials of the Vatican had also been involved.

9. 'Membership requires that the candidate country has achieved stability of institutions guaranteeing democracy, the rule of law, human rights and respect for and, protection of minorities, the existence of a functioning market economy as well as the capacity to cope with competitive pressure and market forces within the Union. Membership presupposes the candidate's ability to take on the obligations of membership including adherence to the aims of political, economic and monetary union.' (www.mfa.gov.tr/grupa/ad/adab/copenhagen.htm).

10. Turkey bought the two words 'without delay' by agreeing as a NATO member to the use of NATO facilities for the new European rapid intervention force (in which, as a non-EU country, it did not participate).

Chapter 17
Justice and Development (2002–2014)

1. An excellent source for the legislative changes in Turkey is formed by the 'Annual Progress reports' of the EU. (http://ec.europa.eu/enlargement/news_corner/key-documents/index).
2. A lot has been written about these investigations and trials. A good overview is: Gareth Jenkins (2009) *Between fact and fantasy: Turkey's Ergenekon investigation*, Washington and Stockholm: Silk Road Papers.
3. Economic data are often manipulated. A reliable source is formed by the yearly reports of the OECD, which can be accessed at www.oecdbook shop.org. Reliable data and good analyses (from a liberal, pro free market perspective) can be found in the archive of *The Economist*.
4. Ahmet Davutoğlu (2001) *Stratejik Derinlik. Türkiye'nin uluslararası konumu*, Istanbul: Küre.

Bibliographical Survey

Bibliographical survey

The following description of literature on the modern history of Turkey is intended to serve both as a survey of the sources that have been used in the writing of this volume and as a practical guide to further reading. It is largely confined to monographic material, which represents the 'state of the art' in this field. The titles have been arranged roughly according to the sequence of the subjects dealt with in the book, but many of the titles listed here are relevant to more than one period or subject. There are, of course, many more titles available, and the reader who wants to delve deeper into a particular subject is advised to consult the bibliographies of the books listed here. Works that have not been included are biographies (except for those of Atatürk), memoirs and novels, though it goes without saying that they, too, are often important to the historian. Books dealing exclusively with the Balkans or the Arab provinces of the Ottoman Empire have also been omitted.

Any student of Turkey who wants to get a systematic overview of recent publications can do no better than to consult the yearly *Türkologische Anzeiger* (Turkology Annual), which has been published in Vienna since 1975 (originally as part of the *Wiener Zeitschrift für die Kunde des Morgenlandes*) and covers books and articles in many languages.

General histories of modern Turkey

If the author and publishers of this book thought existing general histories of modern Turkey entirely satisfactory, this book would obviously not have been written. The situation is far from satisfactory; the supply of modern general histories dealing with the Ottoman Empire and Turkey in the last two centuries is meagre indeed. The classic work in this category undoubtedly is Bernard Lewis's *The emergence of modern Turkey* (London: Oxford University Press, 1961). Originally published in 1961 and revised in 1968, Lewis's book is a masterful and elegant treatment of the gradual intrusion of Western ideas into the Ottoman Empire from the sixteenth century onwards and of Ottoman/Turkish reactions. The strengths of the book are the author's breadth of vision and his extensive use of Ottoman and Turkish sources. His eye for the telling anecdote enlivens the story he tells. The main weakness of the book is that it is almost entirely a history of culture and ideas, with very little attention paid either to politics (as opposed to policies) or to socio-economic developments. Conceived in the late 1950s, even in its revised form the book is of necessity out of date and it bears traces of the strong belief in progress through modernization according to a universally applicable Western model prevalent in those years. Nevertheless, *Emergence* is a classic that every serious student of modern Turkey should read.

The other history of comparable size, Stanford and Ezel Shaw's *History of the Ottoman Empire and modern Turkey*, vol. II: *Reform, revolution and republic: the rise of modern Turkey, 1808–1975* (Cambridge: Cambridge University Press, 1977) has stood the test of time less well. The treatment of Stanford Shaw's recognized areas of specialization, the reigns of Selim III and of Abdülhamit II, is the strongest part. The book is a mine of data (which, however, are not always accurate) and its bibliographical essays are extremely useful as guides for further reading, but the text lacks coherence and the parts dealing with the last hundred years suffer from a marked Turkish-nationalist bias, which shows in the treatment of the Armenian and Kurdish questions, for instance. Like Lewis, the Shaws see the basic theme of modern Turkish history as a struggle between light and dark: modernizers and pro-Westerners on the one hand, religious reactionaries on the other. Much more recent is Carter Findley's (2010) *Turkey: Islam, nationalism and modernity* (New Haven: Yale University Press), which offers a very well-informed analysis of the subject. Like Lewis and Shaw, Findley sees the struggle between secular nationalists and Islamists as the underlying dynamic of Turkey's development, but unlike the older authors he sees the Islamist currents also as essentially modern and as offering alternative solutions for the problems that faced the Ottoman Empire and Turkey. In French, Hamit Bozarslan's (2013) *Histoire de la Turquie: de l'empire à nos jours* (Paris: Tallandier) is a good alternative.

Among smaller-scale general histories, Geoffrey Lewis's (1974) *Modern Turkey* (London and Tonbridge: Ernest Benn), first published in 1955 and thoroughly revised several times, should be mentioned. It is well written and dependable, with a strong emphasis on the republic's political history. Comparable in size is Roderic Davison's *Turkey: a short history*, 2nd edition, Huntingdon: Eothen, 1988 (first published by Prentice Hall, New Jersey, 1968). It covers the whole of Ottoman and Turkish history and is therefore much less detailed on the republican period than Lewis, while giving more information on the nineteenth century. For the second edition of 1988, a new chapter covering Turkey in the 1970s and 1980s was added, but the older chapters were left untouched and are thus out of date. The useful bibliography at the back has been added to rather than updated. Feroz Ahmad's (1993) *The making of modern Turkey* (London: Routledge) grew out of an essay on the role of the military in Turkish politics. Written by an acknowledged specialist on the twentieth-century history of Turkey, it is rich in detail and insights, but its perspective is staunchly Kemalist and in this sense it resembles that of Lewis and Shaw.

A very interesting and thought-provoking book is Çağlar Keyder's (1987) *State and class in Turkey: a study in capitalist development* (London and New York: Verso). A historical essay rather than a textbook, it proposes an interpretation of modern Turkish history from the perspective of the incorporation of Turkey into the capitalist world system (the dependency school). Hard to read in places for non-sociologists, the book is useful for the contrast it provides to the work of 'modernists' like Bernard Lewis, Stanford Shaw and Roderic Davison. A more recent and very original analysis of the process of modernization in the Ottoman Empire is offered by Cem Emrence (2015) in his *Remapping the Ottoman Middle East: modernity, imperial bureaucracy and Islam* (London: I.B.Tauris). In this work Emrence argues that modernization took on a distinct shape in the different areas of the empire (coastal areas, heartland and borderlands). A very different kind of study, but one which investigates the transition from empire to nation-state in a particular area (the eastern Black Sea coast) in a highly original manner is *Nation of Empire: the Ottoman legacy of Turkish modernity* by anthropologist Michael Meeker (2002) (Berkeley: University of California Press). It combines historical research with anthropological fieldwork.

In Turkey, the nationalist, secularist and modernist views of the Kemalist historians have long dominated the historiography of modern Turkey, as they have official historiography as expressed in textbooks for schools and universities. Over the last decade there has been a clear reevaluation of the Ottoman past and in the eyes of the now dominant conservative majority sultans like Mehmet II and Süleyman I, but also Abdülhamit II are now as much national heroes as Atatürk. This new take on history, which is reflected in textbooks, is just as nationalist as the older Kemalist tradition, however. Attempts to write textbooks on the basis of revisionist historical research, often with a Marxist approach, have blossomed since the 1970s. The most notable example is the four-volume *Türkiye tarihi* (History of Turkey), edited by Sina Akşin, especially the last two volumes, *Türkiye tarihi 3: Osmanlı devleti 1600–1908* (History of Turkey 3: the Ottoman State) (Istanbul: Cem, 1988) and

Türkiye tarihi 4: Çağdaş Türkiye 1908–1980 (History of Turkey 4: modern Turkey) (Istanbul: Cem, 1989). They take Turkish history to 1980. The series is a little lacking in coherence and the quality of the contributions by the many authors is a bit uneven, though on the whole quite good. A strong point is the inclusion of chapters on art and education, making it a really comprehensive history. A weak point is the lack of foreign source materials.

Readers able to read Turkish should certainly consult the two excellent historical encyclopaedias by Murat Belge (ed.) *Tanzimat'tan cumhuriyet'e Türkiye ansiklopedisi* (Encyclopaedia of Turkey from the Tanzimat to the republic) (Istanbul: İletişim, 1986, 6 vols); and Murat Belge (ed.) *Cumhuriyet dönemi Türkiye ansiklopedisi* (Encyclopaedia of Turkey during the republic) (Istanbul: İletişim, 1983, 10 vols). Written largely from a left wing or socialist perspective, they undoubtedly represent the state of the art of modern history writing in Turkey.

Two works, which are not strictly speaking general histories, should be mentioned as indispensable tools in their respective fields. Tarık Zafer Tunaya's (1952) *Türkiye'de siyasî partiler 1859–1952* (Political parties in Turkey) (Istanbul: n.p.) is a survey of political parties in Turkey and gives details of their personnel, programmes and history. It is still a standard reference work. A second edition, published in three volumes in the 1980s has more material but also more mistakes. Niyazi Berkes's *The development of secularism in Turkey* (Montreal: McGill University Press, 1964) is a rich intellectual history of Turkey, covering the last two centuries.

Incorporation and early attempts at modernization (1792–1908)

There are very few monographs on the condition of the Ottoman Empire on the eve of reform and incorporation in the late eighteenth century. For a long time H. A. R. Gibb and Harold Bowen, *Islamic society and the West: a study of the impact of Western civilization on Moslem culture in the Near East* (London: Oxford University Press, 1951–1957, vol. 1, parts 1 and 2 – the only parts published) was the classic account of the Ottoman Empire in the eighteenth century, but it has been severely criticized by younger generations of historians. For an example of this critique, see Roger Owen (1975) 'The Middle East in the eighteenth century – an "Islamic" society in decline: a critique of Gibb and Bowen's *Islamic society and the West*', *Review of Middle Eastern studies*, 1, pp. 101–12. Recently, the eighteenth century and especially the question of how far the changes of the nineteenth century were a continuation of an indigenous process rather than an effect of the impact of the West, have begun to receive the attention of historians. A trend-setting work in this respect was Thomas Naff and Roger Owen (eds) (1977) *Studies in eighteenth century Islamic history* (Carbondale: Southern Illinois University Press) but much of the best revisionist work in this field consists of regional histories, based on local archival material.

I found the introductory chapters of Carter Findley's (1980) *Bureaucratic reform in the Ottoman Empire: the Sublime Porte, 1789–1922* (Princeton: Princeton University Press) and his (1989) *Ottoman civil officialdom: a social history* (Princeton: Princeton University Press) particularly useful as guides in this field. Incorporating the relevant modern literature, these books devote attention to the reality of Ottoman society, thus avoiding one of the two most common pitfalls of the older historiography of the Ottoman Empire: over-reliance on central government documents, which leads to an emphasis on norms rather than on realities and on the state rather than on society.

A textbook on the eighteenth and nineteenth century history of the empire that incorporates many of the results of modern social and cultural history and emphasizes these rather than political developments is Donald Quataert's (2000) *The Ottoman Empire 1700–1922* (Cambridge: Cambridge University Press).

The classic study of the Ottoman Empire at the time of Sultan Selim III (and the French Revolution) is still Stanford Shaw's (1971) *Between old and new: the Ottoman Empire under Sultan Selim III, 1781–1807* (Cambridge, MA: Harvard University Press), the gist of which is also included in the above-mentioned general history by the same author. Discussions on the extent to which the ideas of the French Revolution had an impact among the Ottomans go back to Bernard Lewis's famous but controversial (1953) article, 'The impact of the French Revolution in Turkey', *Cahiers d'histoire mondiale*, vol. 1, no. 1, pp. 105–25.

For the reform policies of Sultan Mahmut II and the *Tanzimat* the above-mentioned books by Carter Findley are indispensable. The first volume contains institutional history of the changing bureaucracy, while the second is a social history of the members of that institution. In addition, Davison's *Reform in the Ottoman Empire 1851–1876* (2nd edition, New York: Gordian, 1973) is a thorough treatment of the second period of *Tanzimat* reforms, from the Reform Edict of 1856 to the constitution of 1876, concentrating on policy and administration. Davison was the greatest expert of his day on the nineteenth century modernization of the empire and a collection of his immaculately researched articles has been published as *Essays in Ottoman and Turkish history 1744–1923: the impact of the West* (Austin: University of Texas Press, 1990). Halil İnalcık's (1976) *Application of the Tanzimat and its social effects* (Lisse: Peter de Ridder, 33-page pamphlet, reprint from

Archivum Ottomanicum V (1973) pp. 97–128) was a pioneering effort in trying to gauge the actual impact of the reforms in the provinces (as distinct from the policy statements of Istanbul). This line has since been followed in a number of articles by different authors concentrating mainly on the Arab provinces and Arabic sources. Christoph Neumann's (1994) *Das indirekte Argument: Ein Plädoyer für die Tanzimat vermittels der Historie. Die geschicht-liche Bedeutung von Ahmed Cevdet Paşas Ta'rih* (Münster: Lit) is a very interesting analysis of how a leading Tanzimat statesman wrote the history of the preceding era to bolster the case for reform. It is illustrative of the reformists' way of thinking.

On the religious situation in the empire Frederick W. Hasluck (1929) *Christianity and Islam under the sultans* (Oxford: Clarendon, 2 vols) is still worth reading despite its age because of the extent to which it is based on the author's personal experiences. The most important Islamic minority within the empire, the Alevis and the related dervish order of the Bektaşiya form the subject of another old, but still unsurpassed book, John Kingsley Birge's (1937) *The Bektashi order of dervishes* (London: Luzac, reprinted in 1994). Birge describes the Bektaşi beliefs and rituals in great detail. The role traditionally ascribed to the *millet*s has been questioned in Benjamin Braude and Bernard Lewis (eds) (1982) *Christians and Jews in the Ottoman Empire* (New York: Holmes). Two more recent studies on Ottoman and Turkish Jewry are Stanford Shaw's (1991) overview, *The Jews of the Ottoman Empire and the Turkish Republic* (New York: New York University Press) and a particularly rich collection of articles, the results of a conference at Brandeis University in 1987, published by Avigdor Levy (1994) *The Jews of the Ottoman Empire* (Princeton: Darwin). This volume has much on the late nineteenth and early twentieth century, when the Jewish communities of the empire numbered 400,000 souls.

The important educational reforms of the nineteenth century (and indeed of the early twentieth century) form the subject of Osman Ergin's monumental but not entirely reliable (1977) *Türkiye maarif tarihi* (History of education in Turkey) (vols 1–5, Istanbul: Eser; originally published in 1943). Recently there has been a marked surge of interest in the educational reforms of the nineteenth century. On education in the Hamidian era one should read Benjamin Fortna's (2002) *Imperial classroom: Islam, education and the state in the late Ottoman Empire* (Oxford: Oxford University Press). A survey of the state of the art in English can be found in Mehmet Alkan's chapter 'Modernisation from empire to republic and education in the process of nationalism', in Kemal H. Karpat (ed.) (2000) *Ottoman past and today's Turkey* (Leiden: E. J. Brill). An attractive survey of the development of education in Turkish is Necdet Sakaoğlu's (2003) *Osmanlı'dan Günümüze Eğitim Tarihi* (Istanbul: Bilgi University Press). Recently there has been a remarkable upsurge of interest in the educational reforms of the Tanzimat and the Hamidian era. An overview in English of the 'state of the art' can be found in Mehmet Alkan's (2000) article 'Modernization from empire to republic and education in the process of nationalism', in Kemal H. Karpat (ed.) *Ottoman past and today's Turkey* (Leiden: E. J. Brill). An attractive recent overview of the development of modern education in Turkey (empire and republic) is to be found in Necdet Sakaoğlu (2003) *Osmanlı'dan günümüze eğitim tarihi* (History of education from Ottoman times to the present day) (Istanbul: Bilgi University Press).

The modernization of the army, which was the original impetus behind the whole reform movement, is treated in Erik Jan Zürcher (ed.) (1999) *Arming the state: military conscription in the Middle East and Central Asia 1775–1925* (London: I.B.Tauris). This is a collection of articles on the Ottoman Empire, Egypt and Iran. Unfortunately, there is as yet no equivalent for the Ottoman Empire to Khaled Fahmy's (1997) path-breaking study of Mehmet Ali Pasha's 'new model army', *All the Pasha's men: Mehmed Ali, his army and the making of modern Egypt* (Cambridge: Cambridge University Press).

A stimulating discussion of the history of the reforms is found in *İmparatorluğun en uzun yüzyılı* (The empire's longest century) (2nd edition, Istanbul: Hil, 1987) by Turkey's maverick intellectual historian İlber Ortaylı.

The importance of the Young Ottoman opposition movement is generally recognized by those interested in the cultural history of the Middle East and Şerif Mardin's (1962) analysis of the ideas of the leaders of the movement in his *The genesis of Young Ottoman thought: a study in the modernization of Turkish political ideas* (Princeton: Princeton University Press) is still the best treatment of this subject.

The short-lived constitutional regime of 1876, which seemed to fulfil the wishes of the Young Ottomans, is studied in detail in Robert Devereux's (1964) *The first Ottoman constitutional period: a study of the Midhat constitution and parliament* (2nd edition, Baltimore: Johns Hopkins).

The best survey of the extremely complex 'Eastern Question', which played such a large part both in the European chanceries in the nineteenth century and in the thinking of the *Tanzimat* politicians, is Matthew S. Anderson's (1972) *The Eastern Question 1774–1923: a study in international relations* (4th edition, London: Macmillan). A very well researched and innovative case study, telling the story of how the Ottomans eventually managed to defuse one of the most threatening aspects of the Eastern Question, the crisis in the Lebanon, is Engin

Akarlı's (1993) *The long peace: Ottoman Lebanon 1861–1920* (London: I.B.Tauris). For the Macedonian question, which would develop into the biggest headache for the empire between 1876 and 1912, we can turn to Fikret Adanır's (1979) *Die Makedonische Frage: ihre Entstehung und Entwicklung bis 1908* (Wiesbaden: Franz Steiner). An excellent recent study that emphasizes the conflicts between the Christian Balkan peoples rather than great power politics is İpek Yosmaoğlu's (2014) *Blood ties: religion, violence, and the politics of nationhood in Ottoman Macedonia, 1876–1908* (Ithaca: Cornell University Press).

The general tendency among historians to look away from the history of the central state and from politics and policies has led to a surge in the writing of economic and social history of the nineteenth-century Ottoman Empire. The standard reference work for the period up to the First World War is *An economic history of the Ottoman Empire 1300–1914* (Cambridge: Cambridge University Press, 1994), edited by Halil İnalcık with Donald Quataert. Despite its title, the book does not deal with the period up to 1450 or the urban manufacturing sector before 1600, but for the other subjects and periods it represents the state of the art. Halil İnalcık covers the period up to 1600; Suraiya Faroqhi the seventeenth century; Bruce McGowan the eighteenth; and Donald Quataert the nineteenth century. Şevket Pamuk has added a chapter on the history of Ottoman money. The last named author has also written *The Ottoman Empire and European capitalism, 1820–1913: trade, investment and production* (Cambridge and London: Cambridge University Press, 1987), which is required reading. Charles Issawi's (1980) *The economic history of Turkey 1800–1914* (Chicago: Chicago University Press) consists of a selection of primary texts with introductions, representing a fairly 'classical' approach, while Roger Owen's (1982) *The Middle East in the world economy 1800–1914* (New York: Methuen) represents a more recent current of historical thinking. Reşat Kasaba in his (1988) *The Ottoman Empire and the world economy: the nineteenth century* (Albany: State University of New York Press) redefines the role of the local Christian bourgeoisie. The same author also contributed to the collection of 17 papers (seven of which had appeared earlier) edited by Huri İslamoğlu-İnan (1987) *The Ottoman Empire and the world economy* (Cambridge: Cambridge University Press), which addresses a number of important questions on the basis of case studies and from the perspective of Wallerstein's 'modern world system'.

While on the subject of collections of congress proceedings, two others very much worth consulting are Jean-Louis Bacqué Grammont and Paul Dumont (eds) (1983) *Economies et sociétés dans l'Empire ottoman (fin du XVIIIe-debut du XXe siècle)* (Paris: CNRS) and Halil

İnalcık and Osman Okyar (1980) *Social and economic history of Turkey (1071–1920)* (Ankara: Meteksan), which also contains valuable material on different aspects of late Ottoman economic history. Some good examples of critical reappraisals of the old picture of uniform Ottoman economic decline in the nineteenth century are to be found in Çağlar Keyder (ed.) (1988) 'Ottoman Empire: nineteenth century transformations', *Review*, vol. XI, no. 2, Spring, Binghamton: Fernand Braudel Center, pp. 169–78), and particularly in Donald Quataert's (1993) *Ottoman manufacturing in the age of the industrial revolution* (Cambridge: Cambridge University Press) in which he convincingly demonstrates the adaptability of Ottoman manufacturing in the late nineteenth century. Quataert (1994) also edited *Manufacturing in the Ottoman Empire and Turkey 1500–1950* (Albany: State University of New York Press), which covers some of the same ground.

Jacques Thobie's (1977) *Interêts et imperialisme français dans l'Empire ottoman (1895–1919)* (Paris: Sorbonne), although dealing only with the later period, is an exemplary study. One older work, A. du Velay's (1903) *Essai sur l'histoire financière de la Turquie depuis le règne du Sultan Mahmoud II jusqu'à nos jours* (Paris: Arthur Rousseau) remains a standard work of reference for the financial history of the empire. The history of the Ottoman debt, the debt crisis and its solution is studied exhaustively in Christopher Clay's (2000) *Gold for the Sultan: Western bankers and Ottoman finance 1856–1881* (London: I.B.Tauris). In this story the Franco–British Imperial Ottoman Bank plays a pivotal role. Ethem Eldem has written up the history of the bank in his (1999) *A history of the Ottoman Bank* (Istanbul: Osmanlı Bankası).

Social history, in the sense of the history of the living and working conditions of the working class has only recently begun to receive attention. Donald Quataert, whom we have already met several times, is the pioneer in this field. His (1983) *Social disintegration and popular resistance in the Ottoman Empire, 1881–1908: reactions to European economic penetration* (New York and London: New York University Press) consists of a number of case studies of industrial and commercial development in the late nineteenth and early twentieth centuries, focusing on the social aspects. Donald Quataert and Erik Jan Zürcher (eds) (1995) *Workers and working class in the Ottoman Empire and the Turkish Republic 1840–1950* (London: I.B.Tauris) focuses on industrial workers and their organizations. The lowest rung on the ladder of Ottoman society, that of the slaves, is the subject of Ehud Toledano's (1994) *Osmanlı köle ticareti 1840–1890* (Slave trade in the Ottoman Empire) (Istanbul: Yurt, a translation of a Princeton University Ph.D. of 1980).

Demographic history is another relatively young field. The works used most widely for demographic data are Kemal Karpat's (1985) *Ottoman population 1830–1914: demographic and social characteristics* (Madison: University of Wisconsin Press), which essentially just lists numbers and gives little in the way of analysis, but is very useful for all that, and Justin McCarthy's (1982) *The Arab world, Turkey and the Balkans (1878–1914): a handbook of historical statistics* (Boston: G. K. Hall). The latter's (1983) *Muslims and minorities: the population of Ottoman Anatolia and the end of the empire* (New York: New York University Press) is the only attempt to reconstruct the population of Ottoman Anatolia from the Ottoman records. Armenian critics have fiercely attacked it. The same author's (1995) *Death and exile: the ethnic cleansing of Ottoman Muslims, 1821–1922* (Princeton: Darwin), although admittedly a one-sided story, focuses on an aspect of Ottoman history that is too often overlooked despite its vital importance (of the inhabitants of Turkey in 1923 almost a third had forced migration in their family background).

Sultan Abdülhamit's reign, which lasted from 1876 to 1909, has been inadequately documented. For a long time it was seen as a time of reactionary despotism and stagnation. Lewis was the first to call for a revaluation and to see it as the culmination of the *Tanzimat*. Shaw later took up this theme in articles and in the part of his above-mentioned history dealing with the period. A survey of the existing literature is given at the back of Shaw's book (pages 453–4) and in Jean Deny's (1954) article, 'Abd al-Hamid II (Ghazi) (Abdülhamid)', *Encyclopaedia of Islam*, 2nd edition, Leiden: E. J. Brill, vol. 1, pp. 63–5 (reprinted 1960). A very interesting recent study of the ideological bases of the regime and the way it tried to project its image at home and abroad is Deringil's (1998) *The well-protected domains: ideology and the legitimation of power in the Ottoman Empire 1876–1909* (London: I.B.Tauris).

The Young Turk opposition to Abdülhamit is much better catered for. Ernest Ramsaur's (1957) *The Young Turks: prelude to the revolution of 1908* (New York: Russell & Russell) has long been a classic, although it has now been superseded by Şükrü Hanioğlu's two-volume (1995 and 2001) history of the Young Turk movement in opposition: *The Young Turks in opposition* (Oxford: Oxford University Press) and *Preparing for a revolution: the Young Turks 1902–1908* (Oxford: Oxford University Press). Based on absolutely exhaustive archival research in many countries, these will surely remain the definitive studies of the subject.

The growth of Turkish nationalism during Abdülhamit's reign is treated in David Kushner's (1977) *The rise of Turkish nationalism 1876–1908* (London: Frank Cass).

The Young Turk era (1908–50)

The Young Turk revolution and the second constitutional period have been the subject of a number of excellent studies. The revolutionary events themselves are studied in Aykut Kansu's (1997) *The revolution of 1908 in Turkey* (Leiden: E. J. Brill), which should be read alongside Feroz Ahmad's older (1969) *The Young Turks: the Committee of Union and Progress in Turkish politics 1908–14* (Oxford: Clarendon Press). The latter is a detailed, but exclusively political, history of the years 1908 to 1913, while his (1985) *İttihatçılıktan Kemalizme* (From unionism to Kemalism) (Istanbul: Kaynak), a collection of articles, contains valuable material on the later period (1913 to 1918). The collection *'l'Ivresse de la liberté.' La revolution de 1908 dans l'Empire Ottoman* (Leuven: Peeters), edited by François Georgeon (2012), contains 23 articles that together constitute the state of the art on the revolution itself. Sina Akşin's (1987) *Jön Türkler ve İttihat ve Terakki* (The Young Turks and the Union and Progress) (Istanbul: Remzi), first published in 1980, is still the best all-round history of the second constitutional period, while his (1970) Ph.D. thesis, *31 Mart olayı* (The 31 March incident) (Ankara: Ankara Üniversitesi Siyasal Bilgiler Fakültesi), covers the crucial episode of the counter revolution of 1909 and gives valuable insights into the character of the Young Turk movement. Though suffering from an anti-Unionist bias, Hikmet Bayur's ten-volume *Türk inkılâbı tarihi* (History of the Turkish revolution) (three parts in ten volumes, 2nd edition Ankara: Türk Tarih Kurumu, 1983), first published in the 1940s, is still and no doubt will remain unsurpassed as a mine of information on the period. An important lacuna in the historiography of the second constitutional period has been filled with the appearance of Ali Birinci's (1990) study of the Liberal opposition, *Hürriyet ve İtilâf Fırkası* (Istanbul: Dergah).

The attempts of the Young Turks to establish a 'national economy' during the First World War have been studied by Zafer Toprak (1982) in *Türkiye'de 'Millî İktisat' 1908–1918* (The 'National Economy' in Turkey) (Ankara: Yurt). The prominent Turkish journalist Ahmet Emin Yalman covered the political and social developments of the war years, the events of which he was an eyewitness, in his (1930) *Turkey in the World War* (New Haven: Yale University Press).

As a result of the continuing identity crisis of Turkish society, the intellectual debates of the Young Turk era (which to an extent are still going on) are the subject of countless books and articles. Niyazi Berkes's *Development of secularism* mentioned above is one of the most important introductions. Other works that should be consulted are Hilmi Ziya Ülken's (1979) *Türkiye'de çağday düyünce tarihi* (A history of modern

BIBLIOGRAPHICAL SURVEY

thinking in Turkey) (2nd edition, Istanbul: Ülken), which gives separate introductions on all the more prominent thinkers; Taha Parla's (1985) study of the leading Young Turk ideologue, *The social and political thought of Ziya Gökalp, 1871–1924* (Leiden: E. J. Brill); Masami Arai's (1992) study, *Turkish nationalism in the Young Turk era* (Leiden: E. J. Brill), which consists mainly of a contents analysis of nationalist reviews of the Young Turk era; and Füsun Üstel's (1997) *Imparatorluktan ulus-devlete Türk milliyetçiliği: Türk Ocakları 1912–1931* (Turkish national-ism from the empire to the nation-state: the Turkish Hearths) (Istanbul: İletişim), which is a study of the main nationalist organization, should be mentioned, as should be François Georgeon's (1980) *Aux origines du nationalisme turc: Yusuf Akçura (1871–1935)* (Paris); and Şerif Mardin's (1969) excellent *Continuity and change in the ideas of the Young Turks* (Robert College, School of Business Administration and Economics Occasional Papers) and his (1964) *Jön Türklerin siyasi fikirleri 1895–1908* (The political thinking of the Young Turks) (Ankara: Türkiye İş Bankasi). Of the older works, Uriel Heyd's (1950) *Turkish nationalism and Western civilization* (London: Luzac), also about Ziya Gökalp and his ideas, is still useful. It contains a short but excellent biography of Gökalp. Heyd's former student David Kushner has given us a concise but solid overview of the beginnings of the nationalist movement in its primarily cultural phase in his (1977) *The rise of Turkish nationalism 1876–1908* (London: Frank Cass). The Islamist current is studied in Esther Debus's (1991) *Sebilürreşad: eine vergleichende Untersuchung zur islamischen Opposition der vor- und nachkemalistischen Ära* (Frankfurt am Main: Peter Lang). As is apparent from the title, this study is not limited to the Young Turk era. *The birth of modern Turkey: the Ottoman military and the march to World War I* by Handan Nezir Akmeşe (2005) (London: I.B.Tauris) gives us an insight into the ideological make up of the Young Turk (and Kemalist) officer corps, particularly their belief in the concept of the 'nation in arms'.

The way the Unionists handled the Macedonian question is the subject of Mehmet Hacisalihoğlu's (2003) thesis *Die Jungtürken und die makedonische Frange 1890–1918* (München: Oldenburg). The Balkan War in which the whole Macedonian issue culminated is studied in all its different aspects in a large volume edited by Hakan Yavuz and Isa Blumi (2013) *War and nationalism: the Balkan Wars, 1912–1913, and their sociopolitical implications* (Salt Lake City: University of Utah Press). For the strictly military history of the Balkan Wars we can turn to Edward Erickson's (2003) *Defeat in detail: The Ottoman army in the Balkans, 1912–1913* (Westport: Praeger).

As far as the military history of the First World War is concerned,

Turkey has its official war history, Fahri Belen (1963–1967) *Birinci Harbinde Türk Harbi* (The Turkish war in the First World War) (Ankara: Genelkurmay Harb Tarihi ve Stratejik Etüt Başkanlığı, 5 vols). Largely based on this and other Turkish military sources is Edward Erickson's (2001) *Ordered to die: a history of the Ottoman army in the First World War* (Westport: Greenwood). As a purely military history it replaces the much older but still interesting book by Maurice Larcher (1926) *La guerre turque dans la guerre mondiale* (Paris), which also gives the essential data. One important aspect of the war effort, the role of the German officers, is highlighted in Jehuda L. Wallach's (1976) *Anatomic einer Militärhilfe: die preussisch-deutschen Militärmissionen in der Türkei 1835—1919* (Düsseldorf: Droste) and in Ulrich Trumpener's (1968) *Germany and the Ottoman Empire, 1914–1918* (Princeton: Princeton University). This last-named book has now been complemented for the events of 1914 by Mustafa Aksakal's (2011) *The Ottoman road to war in 1914: the Ottoman Empire and the First World War* (Cambridge: Cambridge University Press). Aksakal confirms Trumpener's view that it was the Ottomans rather than the Germans that pushed for an alliance in 1914. The relationship with Russia is analysed thoroughly on the basis of documents from both sides by Michael Reynolds (2011) in *Shattering empires: the clash and collapse of the Ottoman and Russian Empires 1908–1918* (Cambridge: Cambridge University Press). The reasons for, and the effect of, the proclamation of jihad in 1914 form the subject of Erik Jan Zürcher (ed.) (2016) *Jihad and Islam in World War I* (Leiden: Leiden University Press). The Ottoman mobilization effort is the subject of a detailed and incisive analysis in Mehmet Beşikçi's (2012) *The Ottoman mobilization of manpower in the First World War: between voluntarism and resistance* (Leiden: Brill). War propaganda, an important element in the mobilization, is treated in Erol Köroğlu's (2007) *Ottoman propaganda and Turkish identity: literature in Turkey during World War I* (London: I.B.Tauris).

The Armenian question has been the subject of a heated debate for three-quarters of a century. A survey of the controversy is given in Gwynne Dyer's (1976) 'Turkish "falsifiers" and Armenian "deceivers": historiography and the Armenian massacres', *Middle Eastern Studies*, 12, pp. 99–107. Since 1976 the partisan efforts have not ceased and dozens of Turkish or Armenian sponsored publications have been produced. The most important work on the Armenian side, and the one that makes use of hitherto unused material, is that of Vahakn N. Dadrian. He has published the results of his research on the postwar Ottoman court martial's proceedings and findings in several places, but most comprehensively (in 1995) in *The history of the Armenian genocide:*

ethnic conflict from the Balkans to Anatolia (Providence/Oxford: Berghahn). From time to time Dadrian seems to explain the violence of 1915 as stemming from some innate bloodthirstiness in Islam or in Turkish culture. Dadrian's approach has been opened up to a Turkish readership by Taner Akçam, primarily in his (1999) *Insan hakları ve Ermeni sorunu: Ittihat ve Terakki'den kurtuluş savaşı'na* (Human rights and the Armenian question: from union and progress to the War of Independence) (Ankara: İmge), but he also adds to it original research of his own in German archives. The results of his research over the following decade have been made accessible in Akçam's (2012) *The Young Turks' crime against humanity: the Armenian genocide and ethnic cleansing in the Ottoman Empire* (Princeton: Princeton Universiity Press) that treats other minority groups as well as Armenians. For detailed information on what happened in the different localities in Anatolia, almost on a day to day basis, one should consult Raymond Kévorkian's (2006) monumental *Le génocide des Arméniens* (Paris: Odile Jacob), which is now also available in English: Kévorkian (2015) *The Armenian genocide: a complete history* (London: I.B.Tauris). In their attempts to explain the Armenian policies of the Young Turks, Fuat Dündar (2008) in *Modern Türkiye'nin Şifresi: İttihat ve Terakki'nin Etnisite Mühendisliği (1913–1918)* [The code of modern Turkey: the ethnic engineering of the union and progress] (Istanbul: İletişim) primarily looks at blueprints to homogenize the population, while Donald Bloxham (2005) in *Great game of genocide: Imperialism, nationalism and the destruction of the Ottoman Armenians* (Oxford: Oxford University Press) emphasizes the escalation and radicalization during the war.

The loss of empire is a theme that suddenly regained interest when the Soviet Union collapsed in 1990–92. This fall of an 'empire' rekindled interest in the way the continental empires had collapsed at the end of the First World War. Good examples of this genre are Karen Barkey and Mark von Hagen (eds) (1997) *After empire: multi-ethnic societies and nation-building: the Soviet Union and the Russian, Ottoman, and Habsburg Empires* (Boulder: Westview) but also two books that came out in 2001: Dominic Lieven's *Empire: the Russian Empire and its rivals* (New Haven: Yale University Press) and Aviel Roshwald's *Ethnic nationalism and the fall of empires. Central Europe, Russia and the Middle East, 1914–1923* (London: Routledge). L. Carl Brown (ed.) (1996) *Imperial legacy: the Ottoman imprint on the Balkans and the Middle East* (New York: Columbia University Press) has a different perspective and compares the successor states to the Ottoman Empire.

The postwar situation in Istanbul is the subject of Sina Akşin's (1983) *Istanbul hükümetleri ve millî mücadele* (The Istanbul governments and the national struggle) (Istanbul: Cem), which is a study of the policies of the sultan's government, and of Nur Bilge Criss's (1999) *Istanbul during the allied occupation 1918–1923* (Leiden: E. J. Brill), which focuses on the policies of the occupying powers.

The diplomacy of the postwar years, which led first to the Treaty of Sèvres and then to that of Lausanne, is the subject of Paul C. Helmreich's (1974) *From Paris to Sèvres: the partition of the Ottoman Empire at the peace conference of 1919–1920* (Columbus: Ohio State University Press), which looks at great power diplomacy, and of Salahi Ramsdan Sonyel (1974) *Turkish diplomacy 1918–1923: Mustafa Kemal and the Turkish national movement* (London and Beverley Hills: Sage Publications), which emphasizes the diplomacy of the Turkish nationalists. Stefanos Yerasimos (1979) *Türk–Sovyet iliykileri Ekim Devriminden millî mücadeleye* (Turkish–Soviet relations from the October revolution to the national struggle) (Istanbul: Gözlem) highlights the crucial relationship between the nationalists and the Bolsheviks.

The 'national struggle', the history of the nationalist resistance movement in Anatolia, is the subject of a vast literature. By far the most detailed work in the English language is Stanford Shaw's (2000) monumental *From Empire to Republic: the Turkish war of liberation 1918–1923. A documentary study* (Ankara: Türk Tarih Kurumu, 6 vols), which is based entirely on Turkish archival records. The most useful introductions in Turkish are M. Tayyib Gökbilgin's two-volume (1959 and 1965) *Millî mücadele başlarken* (At the start of the national struggle) (Ankara: Türkiye İş Bankası), which is based on archival material from the Ottoman government, newspapers and memoirs; and Selahattin Tansel's four-volume (1973–75) *Mondros'tan Mudanya 'ya kadar* (From Moudros to Mudanya) (Ankara: Başbakanlık Kültür Müsteşarlığı), which uses material from the archives of the Institute for the Study of the Turkish Revolution in Ankara. Sabahettin Selek's (1976) *Anadolu ihtilâli* (The Anatolian revolution) (6th edition, Istanbul: Cem) is an interesting attempt at revisionist historiography by a leading left-wing journalist, while Paul Dumont's (1983) short but excellent *1919–1924 Mustafa Kemal invente la Turquie moderne* (Brussels: Complexe) is also well worth reading. The transitional period of the regional 'Defence of Rights' movements is covered by Bülent Tanör's (1992) *Türkiye'de yerel kongre iktidarları (1918–1920)* (The local congress administrations in Turkey) (Istanbul: AFA). Erik J. Zürcher (1984) *The Unionist factor: the role of the Committee of Union and Progress in the Turkish national movement 1905–1926* (Leiden: E. J. Brill) is a study of the internal politics of the nationalist movement, concentrating on the continuity between the empire and the republic. L. Carl Brown's (1996) *Imperial legacy: the Ottoman imprint on the Balkans and the Middle East* (New York: Columbia) is an interesting and innovative collection of articles because it puts the Turkish postwar experience in a comparative perspective, something we need more of.

The purely military aspects of the independence war are the subject of a multi-volume history by the War History section of the general staff, like the one on the First World War.

The best scholarly biography of the founder of the Turkish Republic is Andrew Mango's (1999) well written *Atatürk* (London: John Murray), which uses all available published sources. The best of the popular biographies are Şevket Süreyya Aydemir (1976) *Tek adam: Mustafa Kemal 1881–1919* [The only man: Mustafa Kemal] (6th edition, Istanbul: Remzi, 3 vols) and Lord Kinross [Patrick Balfour] (1964) *Atatürk: the rebirth of a nation* (2nd edition, London: Weidenfeld & Nicolson). Aydemir had access to a number of collections of private papers while Kinross talked to many of Atatürk's surviving contemporaries. A. L. Macfie (1994) *Atatürk* (London: Longman) is much shorter – more a biographical essay than a complete biography – but its treatment of the subject is refreshingly critical.

Ali Kazancıgil and Ergun Özbudun (eds) (1981) *Atatürk: founder of a modern state* (London: C. Hurst & Company) is not a biography of Atatürk but a highly recommended collection of articles on his ideas and legacy. The same is true of Jacob Landau (ed.) (1984) *Atatürk and the modernization of Turkey* (Boulder: Westview). Şükrü Hanioğlu's (2011) *Atatürk: an intellectual biography* (Princeton: Princeton University Press) shows how the founder of modern Turkey was influenced by different early-twentieth century European intellectual currents. For those especially interested in Atatürkiana, Muzaffer Gökman's three-volume bibliography (1963–77) *Atatürk ve devrimleri tarihi bibliografyası* (Bibliography of the history of Atatürk and his reforms) (Istanbul: Millî Eğitim Bakanlıığı) lists some 10,000 titles in many different languages.

The internal opposition to Mustafa Kemal during the struggle for independence forms the subject of a thorough study based mainly on the minutes of the assembly, Ahmet Demirel's (1994) *Birinci meclis'te muhalefet: ikinci grup* (Opposition in the first assembly: the second group) (Istanbul: İletişim).

For the political developments of the early republic, the work to consult is Mete Tuncay's (1989) *T. C. 'nde tek-parti yönetimi'nin kurulması (1923–1931)* (The founding of the one-party regime in the

Turkish republic) (2nd edition, Istanbul: Cem), while the same author's (1991) *Türkiye'de sol akımlar (1908–1925)* (Left-wing currents in Turkey) (4th edition, Istanbul: BDS, 2 vols), which has been thoroughly revised and expanded since its first edition of 1967, is the standard reference work on the history of the political left (both before and during the republic). It can be contrasted with a well-known work by extreme right-wing author, Fethi Tevetoğlu (1967) *Türkiye'de sosyalist ve komünist faaliyetler (1910–1960)* (The activities of the socialists and communists in Turkey) (Ankara: Komünizmle Mücadele). Erik J. Zürcher (1991) *Political opposition in the early Turkish republic: the Progressive Republican Party 1924–1925* (Leiden: E. J. Brill) deals with the split in the nationalist movement and the suppression of political rivals to Atatürk after the Kurdish rebellion of 1925. On this insurrection and on the Kurdish problem in general the reader should consult the anthropologist Martin van Bruinessen's (1992) *Agha, shaikh and state: the social and political structures of Kurdistan* (London: Zed Books). The book is a revised edition of his dissertation of 1978. The other English-language book on the subject, Robert Olson (1989) *The emergence of Kurdish nationalism and the Sheikh Said rebellion, 1880–1925* (Austin: University of Texas Press) is interesting as a blow-by-blow account of the rebellion and for the insight it gives into British policy-making, but it is unreliable where Turkish history is concerned. For the history of the ruling Kemalist party in power one can look at Hakkı Uyar's (1998) *Tek parti dönemi ve Cumhuriyet Halk Partisi* (The single party era and the Republican People's Party) (Istanbul: Boyut). The Islamic current that developed into the most tenacious challenger of Kemalism is analysed in Şerif Mardin's (1989) *Religion and social change in modern Turkey: the case of Bediüzzaman Said Nursi* (New York: State University of New York Press), which is rich in new insights once one gets past the sociological jargon of the first chapter.

Many books were written in the 1920s and 1930s on Turkey's social, ideological and political transformation. Of these, some have retained their value as eyewitness accounts or as sources of information that have since been lost sight of. The following are particularly worthwhile: Elliot Grinnell Mears (ed.) (1924) *Modern Turkey: a politico– economic interpretation 1908–1923* (New York: Macmillan); Henry Elisha Allen (1935) *The Turkish transformation: a study in social and religious development* (Chicago: University of Chicago, reprinted New York: Greenwood Press, 1968); August Ritter von Kral (1937) *Das Land Kamal Atatürks: Der Werdegang der modernen Türkei* (2nd edition, Vienna: Wilhelm Braumüller); and Kurt Ziemke (1930) *Die neue Turkei: politische Entwicklung 1914–1929* (Stuttgart: Deutsche Verlagsanstalt).

Of course, there are also modern books on the Kemalist reforms. Hale Yılmaz (2013) *Becoming Turkish: nationalist reforms and cultural negotiations in early republican Turkey 1923–1945* (Syracuse: Syracuse University Press) focuses on the impact of the reforms on the local level, in everyday life. Andrew Davison (1998) *Secularism and revivalism in Turkey: a hermeneutic reconsideration* (New York: Yale University Press) discusses the supposedly secular character of the Turkish republic. Geoffrey Lewis (1999) analyses the language reform in a book with the telling title *The Turkish language reform: a catastrophic success* (Oxford: Oxford University Press).

The experiment with a tame opposition (which proved not to be so tame after all) in 1930 is described in Walter F. Weiker's (1973) *Political tutelage and democracy in Turkey: the Free Party and its aftermath* (Leiden: E. J. Brill), very much the work of a political scientist rather than a historian, but nonetheless useful for that. The period of one-party rule under Atatürk and İnönü has been ably described by Cemil Koçak in his (1986) *Türkiye'de millî şef dönemi (1938–1945)* (The national leader period in Turkey) (Ankara: Yurt) and Turkey's neutrality during the Second World War is the subject of Selim Deringil's well-researched (1989) *Turkish foreign policy during the Second World War: an 'active' neutrality* (Cambridge: Cambridge University Press), which takes a very sympathetic view of İnönü's policies. A less savoury aspect of the İnönü period, the discriminatory wealth tax of 1942 is put into context by Rıfat N. Bali in his (1999) *Bir Türkleşme serüveni (1923–1945): cumhuriyet yıllarında Türkiye Yahudileri* (A story of Turkification (1923–1945): the Jews of Turkey in the republican era) (Istanbul: İletişim), the best treatment to date of the way the nationalist homogenization of the republic affected the minorities. The pan-Turkist movement, which for some time during the Second World War and again during the cold war threatened to become a serious political force, is described, with its leading figures and publications in Jacob M. Landau (1981) *Pan-Turkism in Turkey: a study of irredentism* (London: C. Hurst & Company). A second (1995) edition, incorporating the changes brought about by the collapse of the Soviet Union is now available under the new title of *Pan-Turkism: from irredentism to cooperation* (London: Hurst). Mahmut Gologlu's five-volume (1968–71) *Millî mücadele tarihi* (History of the national struggle) (Ankara: private) and its sequel Mahmut Gologlu (1972) *Türkiye cumhuriyeti tarihi* (History of the Turkish republic) (Ankara: private, 3 vols) form a history of the entire period from 1919 to 1945; they are based on Turkish sources, notably the minutes of the national assembly.

An interesting and critical discussion of Kemalist ideology and its relationship with modernization and democracy is found in Levent Köker (1990) *Modernleşme, Kemalizm ve demokrasi* (Modernization, Kemalism and democracy) (Istanbul: İletişim). It can be read alongside Taha Parla and Andrew Davison (2004) *Corporatist ideology in Kemalist Turkey: progress or order?* (Syracuse: Syracuse University Press).

The postwar transition to multi-party politics and to economic liberalism is the subject of Kemal Karpat's (1959) *Turkey's politics: the transition to a multi-party system* (Princeton: Princeton University Press), the first serious historical study of the republic by a Turkish author in a Western language, written when the Democrats were still in power. Interestingly, at the end of his book Karpat recommends a number of reforms, which were implemented after the military coup of 1960 (which he did not foresee). On the same subject Taner Timur (1991) *Türkiye'de çok partili hayata geçiş* (The transition to multi-party life in Turkey) (Istanbul: İletişim) is a short but stimulating analysis of the transition period as seen from the political left.

A troubled democracy (1950–92)
Feroz Ahmad's (1977) *The Turkish experiment in democracy 1950–1975* (London: C. Hurst & Company) is a well-documented overview of the postwar period, using the Turkish media of the period and interviews with those concerned. It shows the signs of having been written at a time when Ecevit and his policies were still seen as Turkey's great hope for the future.

The blossoming of the relationship between Turkey and the United States in the 1950s reawakened interest in Turkey in America and gave rise to a spate of new publications. Some are still worthwhile for their first-hand descriptions of Turkish society. The following should, I think, be mentioned: Richard D. Robinson (1963) *The first Turkish republic: a case study in national development* (Cambridge, MA: Harvard University Press); Eleanor Bisbee (1956) *The New Turks: pioneers of the republic, 1920–1950* (3rd edition, Philadelphia: University of Pennsylvania); and Robert E. Ward and Dankwart A. Rustow (eds) (1964) *Political modernization in Japan and Turkey* (Princeton: Princeton University Press), one of the very few comparative studies of modern Turkey. Although not limited to the immediate postwar period, Frederick W. Frey (1965) *The Turkish political elite* (Cambridge, MA: MIT), an analysis of the background and the behaviour of the representatives in the Turkish national assemblies, devotes a lot of attention to the contrasts between the Kemalist and post-Kemalist assemblies.

The *coup d'état* that ended the decade of Democratic Party rule is described in Walter F. Weiker (1963) *The Turkish revolution 1960–1961: aspects of military politics* (Washington DC: Brookings Institution). It is a fairly mild treatment, which can usefully be contrasted with that of Robinson.

The 'second Turkish republic', the years between the two military coups of 1960 and 1980, is of course dealt with in several of the general histories mentioned above. This period of industrialization, rapid social change and increasing political instability is also treated in Kemal Karpat (ed.) (1973) *Social change and politics in Turkey: a structural historical analysis* (Leiden: E. J. Brill) and the almost identically named, but very different, Ergun Özbudun (1984) *Social change and political participation in Turkey* (Princeton: Princeton University Press). The first is a collection of articles, the second a monograph by a political scientist. Jacob Landau's (1974) *Radical politics in modern Turkey* (Leiden: E. J. Brill) is a useful but rather dry catalogue of the right- and left-wing radical groups active in Turkey in this period. These are also the subject of Otmar Oehring (1984) *Die Türkei im Spannungsfeld extremer Ideologien (1973–1980): eine Untersuchung der politischen Verhältnisse* (Berlin: Klaus Schwarz), which, however, deals only with legal groups, not with the illegal ones. Igor Lipovski's (1992) *The socialist movement in Turkey 1960–1980* (Leiden: E. J. Brill) is a useful study focusing on the Workers' Party of Turkey, but should be contrasted with the published memoirs of the protagonists of the movement, such as Mehmet Ali Aybar, Sadun Aren or Kemal Sülker.

The role of Islam in Turkish politics, perhaps the most hotly debated issue of all, is the subject of an insightful study by Binnaz Toprak (1981) *Islam and political development in Turkey* (Leiden: E. J. Brill) and of a collection edited by Richard Tapper (1991) *Islam in modern Turkey: religion, politics and literature in a secular state* (London: I.B.Tauris), which presents the results of a workshop held at London University's SOAS in 1988 and contains interesting articles on contemporary matters, largely from a social scientist's point of view. H. Wedel (1991) *Die türkische Weg zwischen Laizismus und Islam* (Opladen: Institut fur Türkeistudien) is a short but interesting analysis of the social and political role of Islam. A seminal anthropological study of the relationship between modernization and the growth of Islamist movements in Günter Seufert's (1997) highly recommended *Politischer Islam in der Türkei: Islamismus als symbolische Repräsentation einer sich modernisierenden muslimischen Gesellschaft* (Stuttgart, Franz Steiner). Two other studies that should be mentioned are Andrew Davison's *Secularism and revivalism in Turkey* (mentioned above) and Hakan Yavuz's (2003) *Islamic political identity in Turkey* (Oxford: Oxford University Press), which is very critical of Kemalist secularism. The growing self-awareness of the Alevi community has led to a plethora of publications over the last few years, mainly in Turkey, but one particularly interesting study by a foreign observer is Karin Vorhoff (1995) *Alevitische Identität* (Berlin: Klaus Schwarz).

Irving Schick and E. Tonak (1986) *Turkey in transition: new perspectives, 1923 to the present* (London: Oxford University Press) is an interesting collection of articles by leftist Turkish intellectuals who were banned from academic life after the 1980 coup. Another volume of articles well worth reading with reference to the period 1960–71 is William Hale (ed.) (1976) *Aspects of modern Turkey* (London: Bowker), which contains the results of a conference in Durham in 1973 and in which a number of prominent British Turkey watchers deal with a variety of topics.

The 'coup by memorandum' of 1971 is the subject of an excellent piece of investigative reporting by the later foreign minister İsmail Cem (İpekçi) (1972), *12 Mart* (12 March) (Istanbul: Cem). Turkey's political troubles in the late 1970s and the coup of 1980 are treated in George S. Harris (1985) *Turkey, coping with crisis* (Boulder: Westview Press), which also contains a useful selected bibliography. Clement Dodd's (1979) *Democracy and development in Turkey* (London: Eothen) examines the same period. As a purely political history (and analysis of the political system) it is rather one-dimensional in its treatment.

The 1970s saw a great outburst of anthropological studies by scholars such as Nermin Abadan-Unat, Fatma Mansur and Çiğdem Kağıtçıbaşı (among others), which fall outside the scope of this survey, but which are nevertheless very interesting for their focus on things like the Turkish village, the squatter districts, family life and the role of sex and gender in society.

Area Studies handbooks, which seemed to have gone out of fashion somewhat in the USA, flourished in Germany, with good examples being published by Werner Kündig-Steiner and, especially, Wolf Dietrich Hütteroth.

The economic history of the second republic is the main item in William Hale (1981) *The political and economic development of modern Turkey* (London: Croom Helm), which is stronger on the post-1960 era than on the earlier periods. The most authoritative treatment of the economy is Zvi Yehuda Hershlag (1988) *The contemporary Turkish economy* (London, Routledge), which takes the story beyond the coup of 1980 and the establishment of the 'third Turkish republic', while the same author's (1968) *Turkey, the challenge of growth* (Leiden: E. J. Brill) is still useful for the earlier period. The reports of the American investigatory teams, which visited Turkey in the immediate postwar era, are a mine of information on the then state of Turkey's economy: Max Weston Thornburg (1949) *Turkey: an economic appraisal* (New York: Twentieth Century Fund) and James S. Barker (ed.) (1951) *The economy of Turkey: an analysis and recommendations for a development program* (Baltimore: Johns Hopkins). A critical view of Turkish economic policies and of the IMF-induced stabilization programmes is taken in Berch Berberoglu (1982) *Turkey in crisis: from state capitalism to neocolonialism* (London: Zed Books). For those who can read Turkish, the books of economic historian Şevket Pamuk offer the best overview of economic developments, most particularly his (2012) *Türkiye'nin 200 Yıllık İktisadi Tarihi. Büyüme, Kurumlar ve Bölüşüm* (The two hundred-year economic history of Turkey. Growth, institutions and distribution) (Istanbul: Türkiye İş Bankası).

The 1960s and 1970s were also the years in which the labour movement came of age in Turkey. The best sources on the labour and trade union movements are the still unpublished Ph.D. thesis and a great number of articles in Turkish and French by Mehmet Şehmus Güzel, and Kemal Sülker's (1976) *Yüz soruda Türkiye'de işçi hareketleri* (The workers' movements in Turkey in a hundred questions) (3rd edition, Istanbul: Gerçek). Oya Sencer's (1969) *Türkiye'de işçi sınıfı* (The working class in Turkey) (Istanbul: Habora) has been very influential, but the data it gives should be treated with circumspection.

The phenomenon of large-scale labour migration of Turkish workers to western Europe since the early 1960s has given rise to a plethora of books and articles in the host countries, but there is little in the way of a general survey of the problem. The best-known book is Suzanne Paine (1974) *Exporting workers: the Turkish case* (London: Cambridge University Press), but it is now of course almost thirty years old and the character of the migration has changed radically since that period. The same problem of obsolescence applies to the best-known of Nermin Abadan-Unat's books on the subject, her (1976) *Turkish workers in Europe 1960–1975: a socio-economic reappraisal* (Leiden: E. J. Brill). However, Abadan-Unat has continued to publish on labour migration for the last 25 years and her books and articles are well worth consulting. Two more recent articles that give an informed discussion of the field are Rinus Penninx (1982) 'A critical review of theory and practice: the case of Turkey', *International Migration Review*, 16 (4), pp. 819–36, and Ercan Uygur (1990) 'Policy, productivity, growth and employment in Turkey, 1960–1989 and prospects for the 1990s', *Mediterranean Information Exchange System on International Migration and Employment* (MIES), 90 (4), a publication of the ILO in Geneva. Also from Geneva is Philip Martin's (1991) *The unfinished story: Turkish labour migration to western Europe* (ILO). Amazingly, I have been unable to find a single study of the social and cultural effects of labour migration (and remigration) on Turkey itself.

The important role of the military in Turkish politics has been studied in two seminal articles, Dankwart A. Rustow (1959) 'The army and the founding of the Turkish republic', *World Politics*, 7, pp. 513–52, which gives the historical background but does not foresee the military takeover less than a year away; and George S. Harris (1965) 'The role of the military in Turkish politics', *Middle East Journal*, 1, pp. 54–66 and 169–76. Both articles are of course relatively old and should be supplemented with newer material. A recent effort is a study by one of Turkey's leading journalists, Mehmet Ali Birand (1991) *Shirts of steel: an anatomy of the Turkish armed forces* (London: I.B.Tauris), which is based on interviews and is especially strong on the mentality and *Weltanschauung* of the officer corps. William Hale's (1994) *Turkish politics and the military* (London: Routledge) is both a historical overview and an attempt to put the Turkish experience with its military into a comparative perspective.

The foreign policy and foreign relations of the postwar republic have long received relatively scant attention for so strategic an area. The best introduction is probably Kemal Karpat (ed.) (1975) *Turkey's foreign policy in transition 1950–1974* (Leiden: E. J. Brill), which is a collection of articles. The crucial alliance with the United States is the subject of George S. Harris (1972) *Troubled alliance: Turkish-American problems in historical perspective* (Washington: American Enterprise Institute), while the relations with other Middle Eastern countries are treated in the rather superficial but useful Philip Robins (1991) *Turkey and the Middle East* (London: Royal Institute of International Affairs), for which no Turkish sources were used.

Turkey's difficult relations with the former Ottoman lands in the Balkans during the cold war form the subject of Erol Manisalı (ed.) (1990) *Turkey and the Balkans: economic and political dimensions* (Istanbul: MEBB), while the spectacular change in the relationship after 1990 is treated in Ebru Boyar's (2007) *Ottomans, Turks and the Balkans: empire lost, relations altered* (London: I.B.Tauris).

Clement H. Dodd (ed.) (1992) *Turkish foreign policy: new prospects* (Huntingdon: Eothen) is a very slim volume of essays that provide a good introduction to the problems and possibilities of Turkey's foreign relations, but there are now many other collections of articles dealing with Turkey's new geopolitical situation and the challenges it poses in French, German, English and Turkish. A comprehensive survey of the foreign policy of the republic from the beginning to the early twenty-first century is offered in Baskın Oran (ed.) (2002) *Türk diş politikası: kurtuluş savaşından bugüne olgular, belgeler, yorumlar* (Turkish foreign policy: facts, documents and opinions from the war of independence till today) (Istanbul: İletişim).

There is a lack of good monographic material on the period since the military takeover of September 1980, which itself is analysed in great detail in Mehmet Ali Birand (1987) *The generals' coup in Turkey: an inside story of 12 September 1980* (London: Brassey's Defence Publishers).

A few of the works mentioned above (such as those by Keyder, Schick, Oran, Pamuk, Boyar and Harris, and Hershlag on the economy) continue their story into the 1980s. Clement Dodd has written an extension to his *Democracy and development*, called *The crisis of Turkish democracy* (Beverley: Eothen, 1983), which was revised again in 1990. Frank Tachau (1984) *Turkey: authority, democracy and development* (New York: Praeger) is an analysis of the structures the military put in place after 1980. Short descriptions of the parties that came into being with the gradual political thaw after 1983 are given in Metin Heper and Jacob M. Landau (eds) (1991) *Political parties and democracy in Turkey* (London: I.B.Tauris). The prolific Metin Heper has also specialized in analyses of one of the most vexing problems of contemporary Turkey: the role of the state in society, witness his (1985) *The state tradition in Turkey* (Huntingdon: Eothen) and his (1988) book edited together with Ahmet Evin, *State, democracy and the military: Turkey in the nineteen eighties* (Berlin/New York: Walter de Gruyter).

The liberalization since 1989 has enabled writers in Turkey to write on the Kurds and their problems for the first time in more than 70 years. The result has been a number of publications, many of them highly partisan. An overview of recent developments, and especially of the role of the PKK, can be found in Michael M. Gunter (1990) *The Kurds in Turkey: a political dilemma* (Boulder: Westview). İsmet İmset's (1992) *The PKK: a report on separatist violence in Turkey 1973–1992* (Ankara: Turkish Daily News) is indispensable for factual information on the Kurdish guerrilla movement. Recently, an excellent and detailed overview of the problems the Kurds faced not only in Turkey but also in the neighbouring countries of Iraq and Iran has been published: David McDowell (1996) *A modern history of the Kurds* (London: I.B.Tauris).

Two books on the ideological developments of the most recent period in Turkish history that are well worth reading are Hugh Poulton's (1997) *Top hat, grey wolf and crescent: Turkish nationalism and the Turkish republic* (London: Hurst), which also contains much material on earlier periods; and Stéfane Yerasimos (ed.) (2000) *Civil society in the grip of nationalism: studies on political culture in contemporary Turkey* (Würzburg: Ergon), which caused an uproar in nationalist circles in Turkey. Hans-Lukas Kieser (ed.) (2006) *Turkey beyond nationalism: towards post-nationalist identities* (London: I.B.Tauris) is an important collection that reflects the optimism of the early 2000s.

The big changes of the 2000s (the takeover by the Islamist AKP, the spectacular economic growth of the early 2000s, the development of Istanbul as a global city and the fundamental reorientation of Turkey's foreign policy are still at the stage where they are primarily analysed in conference papers, articles and reports by think tanks, as well as in academic theses. Books that, each in their own way, offer good avenues to an understanding of the realities of Turkey in the new millennium are: Ümit Cizre (2007) *Secular and Islamic politics in Turkey: the making of the Justice and Development Party* (London: Routledge), Andrew Mango (2004) *The Turks today* (London: John Murray), Bill Park (2012) *Modern Turkey: people, state and foreign policy in a globalized world* (London: Routledge). *Muslim nationalism and the new Turks* (Princeton: Princeton University Press) by anthropologist Jenny White (2013) is probably the most sophisticated analysis of Turkey's now dominant cultural and political current. The economic development, with its successes and weaknesses is analysed with great incisiveness by Ziya Öniş (2013) in *Turkey and the global economy: neo-liberal restructuring and integration in the post-crisis era* (London: Routledge).

Hakan Yavuz has written an interesting study of one of the key players of the last 20 years, the preacher Fethullah Gülen: Hakan Yavuz (2013) *Toward an Islamic enlightenment: the Gülen movement* (Oxford: Oxford University Press), but we still lack good scholarly biographies of leading politicians. After Atatürk, İsmet İnönü and Celal Bayar have been well served by, respectively, Metin Heper and Camilla Dwalatschin-Linder, but while political parties in Turkey tend to be completely dominated by their leaders, we still do not have authoritative biographies of Menderes, Demirel, Ecevit, Özal, Türkeş, Erbakan or Erdoğan. Membership of the H/Turk discussion list, one of the many H (for history) lists can also be very rewarding for those seriously interested in Ottoman and modern Turkish history.

Biographical Notes: Some Important Figures in Ottoman and Turkish History

For the reader's benefit, biographical data on a number of important figures in the book are given below in alphabetical order. It should be remembered, however, that family names were only made compulsory in Turkey in 1934 and that until then they were the exception rather than the rule. Before 1934 people were known by their birth name or by the name they were given at an early age (for instance on entering school). They would often also have a surname denoting a special quality of the person involved or of his family. In addition, many of the leading figures held a title (*Bey* or *Pasha* in the case of bureaucrats and officers or *Efendi* in the case of *ulema*). To take an example, the first president of the Republic of Turkey was given the name *Mustafa* at birth and *Kemal* in primary school. To his fellow students he would be known as *Kemal* or *Selânikli Kemal* (Kemal from Salonica). From his graduation from the military academy until 1916 he was addressed as *Kemal Bey*, but when he was promoted to the rank of brigadier he became *Kemal Pasha*. After his victory in the War of Independence the surname *Gazi* (conquering hero) was often used. From 1934 onwards, he was officially known as *Kemal Atatürk* ('Father Turk').

Individuals are listed in Turkish alphabetical order, and each will be found under the form of his or her name most commonly used. For example, Ahmet Tevfik Pasha, the last grand vizier of the Ottoman Empire will be found under 'Tevfik', because in the years when he was a prominent diplomat and statesman everybody knew him as Tevfik Pasha. He lived just long enough to see family names introduced in Turkey, so shortly before his death he became Tevfik Okday. But nobody in Turkey remembers him under that name so listing him under 'O' would be a bit pedantic. To facilitate cross-referencing, '[Tevfik Okday]' is added to the entry. Persons whose main claim to fame is their activities after 1934 are listed under their new family name.

Dr Abdullah Cevdet (1869–1932). Born in Arapkır of Kurdish extraction. Graduated from the military medical school. Exiled to Tripolitania in 1896 for involvement in Young Turk movement. Escaped to Europe in 1897. Published the *Osmanlı* (The Ottoman) in Geneva. In 1899 accepted a diplomatic posting from the sultan. Dismissed when he started agitating for reform again. From 1904 published *İctihat* (Interpretation), first in Geneva, then in Cairo. After the revolution continued writing and publishing in Istanbul. Wrote and translated a total of 66 books. Known for his atheism. He was the first Ottoman to advocate adopting the Latin script.

Sultan Abdülaziz (1830–1876). Thirty-second Ottoman sultan and son of Mahmut II. Ruled from 1861 to 1876, when he was deposed after a *coup d'état*. First continued the policies of his predecessor, Abdülmecit, supporting the Westernizing reforms. After 1871 he sided with the conservatives, who leant on Russian support. First Ottoman monarch to visit western Europe (1867). Committed suicide after being deposed.

Sultan Abdülhamit II (1842–1918). Thirty-fourth Ottoman sultan and second son of Sultan Abdülmecit. Ruled from 1876 to 1909. In 1876 he succeeded his brother Murat V when the latter was declared insane. Introduced constitution and parliament in 1876 but suspended both less than two years later. Established autocratic rule, which became gradually more oppressive from the 1880s onwards. Supported the pan-Islamist movement. Remained on the throne for nine months after the constitutional revolution of 1908, but was deposed after the failure of the counter-revolution of April 1909.

Sultan Abdülmecit (1823–1861). Thirty-first Ottoman sultan, son of Mahmut II. Ruled from 1839 to 1861, continuing the Westernizing reforms of his father. During his rule the Porte replaced the Palace as the main centre of power.

Abdülmecit Efendi (1868–1941). Last caliph (1922–24), son of Abdülaziz. Supported the Nationalists during the War of Independence. Took his duties as a purely religious caliph (a novelty) very seriously. Was deposed and banned from the country in March 1924. From then on he lived in Switzerland and France. Known for his intellectual and artistic gifts (he was an accomplished painter).

Ahmet Rıza Bey (1859–1930). Son of a member of the first Ottoman parliament. Studied agriculture in France. On his return he was appointed

Director of Education in Bursa. Fled to France in 1889, from where he started a campaign for the restoration of the constitution and parliament. Published the main opposition organ *Meşveret* (Consultation) in Paris from 1895 onwards. He led the most radical nationalist wing of the *émigré* opposition (the Committee of Union and Progress), but his positivist convictions estranged him from many of his fellow agitators. After the 1908 revolution he was elected to the central committee of the CUP and to the presidency of the second chamber of parliament, but he did not wield any real power. In 1912 he was made a senator. After the 1918 armistice, he was involved in attempts to create a 'national congress'.

Yusuf Akçura (1878–1935). A Volga Tatar by birth. Deported to Tripolitania for his Young Turk activities while studying at the military academy in Istanbul. Fled to France and there graduated from the political science faculty in Paris. Contributed Turkish nationalist and pan-Turkist articles to opposition newspapers. Author of the pan-Turkist manifesto 'Three Types of Policy' (1904). Driving force behind the Turkish Hearth movement. Joined the nationalists in Anatolia. Elected to the national assembly continuously from 1923 to 1939. President of the Turkish Historical Society and professor of Turkish history at Istanbul University in the 1930s.

Mehmet Akif [Mehmet Akif Ersoy] (1873–1936). The son of a doctor of Islamic law, he learned Arabic and Persian, as well as French. Trained as a veterinary surgeon. After the 1908 revolution, he became interested in literature and published poems and articles. Taught literature at Istanbul University and at the same time gained fame as a preacher committed to pan-Islamic unity. In 1913 he left his job at the Directorate-General of Veterinary Affairs. Worked for the 'Special Organization' in the First World War, disseminating Islamic propaganda. Member of the first national assembly (and author of the new national anthem, the 'Independence March', in 1921), but left Turkey in 1926 because of the secularist tendencies of the republic. Until 1936 he taught Turkish at Cairo University. Died shortly after his return to Turkey in 1936.

Ali Pasha [Mehmet Emin Ali] (1815–71). Entered chancery as apprentice aged 15. Secretary at embassy in Vienna in 1835. Became a protégé of Reşit Pasha. Official translator to the imperial council. Secretary and later ambassador in London (1841). Seven times minister of foreign affairs after 1846. Five times grand vizier after 1852. Worked in tandem with Fuat Pasha on the formulation of the reform programme.

Kemal Atatürk [Gazi ('conquering hero') Mustafa Kemal Pasha] (1881–1938). Son of a low-ranking customs official in Salonica, he entered military primary and secondary schools there and in Monastir. Graduated from the military academy in 1904. After trying to found his own secret committee, he joined the CUP when he was posted to Macedonia in 1907. Member of the inner circle of Unionist officers. Played a prominent part in the Action Army of 1909. Seems to have belonged to Cemal Pasha's faction within the CUP. Served in Tripolitania in 1911 and in the Balkan War (1912–13). Military attaché in Sofia (1913–14). Gained fame through his defence of the Anafarta front in the Gallipoli campaign. Promoted to brigadier (and made a pasha) in 1916. Ended the war in command of the Syrian front. Returned to the capital and tried to establish himself in politics without success. Launched as the head of the national resistance movement in Anatolia, when the government appointed him inspector of the Third Army (eastern Anatolia). Elected president of the representative committee of the Defence of Rights organization at the regional congress in Erzurum and at the national congress in Sivas in September 1919. From April 1920 onwards president of the national assembly in Ankara. Brought together the regional resistance organizations into one national one, which he then proceeded to lead to victory in the war of independence (1920–22) against the Armenians, Greeks, Italians, French and British. During the years 1923–25 he established a power monopoly for his new party, the People's Party, and himself, taking over the remains of the Defence of Rights movement. Abolished the sultanate (1922) and established the Turkish Republic (1923) with himself as first president (1923–38). Embarked on an ambitious scheme of reforms aimed at modernizing and secularizing Turkey and building a new national identity. After his death his remains were kept at the Ethnographical Museum in Ankara until the completion of his mausoleum, where he was buried in 1953.

Nihal Atsız (1905–75). Trained as a military doctor. High-school teacher and assistant at the faculty of arts of Istanbul University. Banished to Malatya in 1933 for racist articles in the journal *Atsız* (Nameless). Promoted political pan-Turkism in the journal *Orhun* (Orkhon) he published there and in Edirne. Pan-Turkists such as Atsız were quite influential between 1939 and 1943 and again during the cold war. Tried and convicted of racism in 1944, but released in 1945. He influenced radical soldiers and politicians such as Türkeş.

Mehmet Ali Aybar (1910–95). Graduated from the Law School of Istanbul University in 1939. Went to France to study, but returned when war broke out. Lecturer in international law at Istanbul University (1942). Removed in 1946 for his political activities. In 1947, sentenced to three and a half years' imprisonment. Chairman of the Labour Party of Turkey, 1962–69. Elected to the national assembly in 1965. Resigned as chairman and left the party in 1969 as a result of the quarrel over his condemnation of the Soviet invasion of Czechoslovakia. Stood as a candidate for the Unity Party in 1971, but was not elected.

Talât Aydemir (1917–1964). Soldier. Made commander of the army academy in Ankara after his return from Korea in 1960. Active since the mid-1950s in plots against the DP government, but outside the country at the time of the May 1960 coup. Tried a military coup of his own on 22 February 1962. When it miscarried he was retired, but on 20 May 1963 he tried again. After some fierce fighting in Ankara, the attempt was suppressed. Aydemir was tried, convicted and executed in July 1964.

Bahaettin Şakir (1877–1922). Medical doctor. Worked with Ahmet Rıza and Dr Nâzim in Paris to revitalize the CUP. Edited the party newspaper *Şurayı Ümmet* (Council of the Muslim Nation). Although he never held an official political post after the revolution, he was one of the most influential of the Unionists. Member of the central committee, 1912–18 and chief of the political bureau of the Special Organization, 1914–18. Often seen as the man behind the Armenian deportations. Killed by an Armenian in 1922.

Celâl Bayar [Mahmut Celâl Bey] (1884–1987). Son of immigrants from Bulgaria. First made a career in banking, with the Deutsche Orientbank in Bursa. Joined the CUP in 1907. From 1908 to 1918 he was the responsible secretary (effectively the head) of the İzmir branch of the CUP. Worked in the 'Special Organization'. Helped to organize the nationalist resistance in İzmir and joined the guerrilla forces in 1919. Commanded the national forces in Bursa. Was elected to the last Ottoman parliament in 1919. Held several commissariats in Ankara during 1920–23. First director of the Business Bank in 1924, economic affairs minister 1932–37, and prime minister 1937–39. One of the founders of the Democratic Party in 1946. Third president of the republic 1950–60. Received the death penalty in 1961, but the sentence was commuted because of his age. Released following an amnesty in 1966.

Bekir Sami [Bekir Sami Kunduh] (1865–1933). Of Circassian extraction. Studied at the Galatasaray lycée and at the political science faculty in Paris. Worked first for the Foreign Ministry in several different embassies, then as governor of Van, Trabzon, Bursa, Beirut and Aleppo. Elected to the last Ottoman parliament in 1920. Joined the nationalists after the closure of parliament. Commissar of foreign affairs 1920–21. Resigned when the assembly rejected the compromise he reached at the London conference. Arrested after the discovery of the İzmir conspiracy in 1926 but released.

Mihri Belli (1915–2011). Graduated from university as an economist. Thereafter worked in the same department. One of the leaders of the outlawed Turkish Communist Party. Sentenced to seven years in 1954 because of his underground work. Came to the fore in the 1960s as the main exponent of the 'national democratic revolution', which held that a revolution in Turkey was possible only through the actions of a progressive elite. Left the country after the coup of 12 March 1971.

Behice Boran (1911–87). Trained as a sociologist in the United States. Taught sociology at Ankara University. Fired because of her contributions to left-wing periodicals. Sentenced to 15 years' imprisonment in 1950 for protesting against the sending of troops to Korea. Returned to writing and publishing in 1960. One of the founders of the Labour Party of Turkey in 1961. Ideologue of that party. Elected to the assembly in 1965. Secretary-general of the party in 1970. Succeeded Aybar as chairperson of the party in the same year. Sentenced in absentia to 13 years' imprisonment in 1971 after the banning of the party. Died in exile.

Ferruh Bozbeyli (1927–). Lawyer. Prominent member of the Justice Party. President of the national assembly, 1965–70. Resigned from his post and from the party in 1970, after he and 40 others had voted against the budget and forced Demirel to resign. Went on to found the Democratic Party (*Demokratik Parti*).

Mahmut Esat Bozkurt (1892–1943). Graduated from law school in Istanbul and completed his studies in Lausanne and Freiburg. When the Greeks occupied his native İzmir in 1919, he returned to the country and joined the resistance. From 1920 until his death in 1943 he served as representative for İzmir in the national assembly. Economic affairs commissar (1922–23) and justice minister (1924–30). Introduced the new (Swiss) family code in 1926. Held professorships of constitutional law and international law alongside his political positions.

Osman Bölükbaşı (1913–2002). Graduated from the mathematics department of the University of Nancy (France) in 1937. Worked as a teacher. Entered politics in 1946, when he became inspector-general of the opposition DP. Resigned from the DP in 1947 and together with Marshal Fevzi Çakmak founded the Nation Party in 1948. After 1950 was the party's only representative in the assembly. When the party was closed down in 1954, he founded the Republican Nation Party, from 1958 known as the Republican Peasants' Nation Party. After a bitter dispute, he broke with the party and founded the Nation Party once more in 1962, which was eventually reunited with the RPNP. When the party elected Alpaslan Türkeş party leader, he resigned from the party and for a third time founded the NP. In 1973 he retired from politics.

Hüseyin Cahit [Hüseyin Cahit Yalçın] (1874–1957). Graduated from the civil service academy. Thereafter had a career in education, while at the same time developing his writing skills. Already active as a writer and translator before the 1908 revolution, he came to the fore after it, both as a member of parliament and as editor of the daily *Tanin* (Echo), which had close links with the CUP. Deported to Malta in 1920. After his release edited the *Tanin* again from 1922 to 1925, supporting the reforms but opposing the authoritarian tendencies of the republican leadership. Arrested in 1925 and deported to Çorum. After his release he tried to make a living in business, but failed. Yalçın opposed the purism of the Turkish Linguistic Society after 1933. As a result, until 1943 he was in limbo, trying to survive on his publications. In 1943 he was elected to the national assembly and started the *Tanin* again. In 1948 he was made editor of the RPP party newspaper *Ulus* (Nation). Opposed the DP and was convicted and sentenced to 26 months in 1954.

Mehmet Cavit (1875–1926). Son of a *dönme* (crypto-Jewish) merchant from Salonica. Graduated from the civil service academy in 1896. Served as an accountant in different government departments. Director of a private college in Salonica. One of the earliest members of the Ottoman Freedom Society, which later merged with the CUP. Member of parliament for Salonica after the revolution. Several times finance minister and once minister of public works. Taught economics at the civil service academy and at the university at the same time. Fled the country in 1919. Involved in attempts to restart the CUP after the independence war. Executed in 1926 for his alleged role in the İzmir conspiracy. Close friend of Hüseyin Cahit.

Ahmet Cemal Pasha (1872–1922). Early member of Ottoman Freedom Society, later the CUP, when he was a major in the Macedonian army. Elected to CUP central committee after the constitutional revolution.

Prefect of Üsküdar (1909), governor of Adana (1909), Baghdad (1911). Prefect of Istanbul after the 1913 coup, of which he was one of the instigators. Minister of public works and of navy. Commander of Fourth Army (on the Sinai front) and governor of Syria during First World War. Fled to Germany in 1918. Served in Afghanistan as military adviser. Assassinated by an Armenian in Tbilisi in 1921.

Ahmet Cevdet Pasha (1822–1895). Statesman and scholar. Came to Istanbul in 1839, where he studied with leading *ulema*. Protégé of Mustafa Reşit Pasha. Together with Fuat Pasha, to whom he was particularly close, he produced the first modern Ottoman grammar in the 1840s. Served in many different educational functions. Made a vizier in 1865. Governor of Aleppo. As president of the 'council of judicial ordinances' from 1868 onwards, he was primarily responsible for the codification of Islamic law in the *Mecelle*. First justice minister of the empire. Thereafter again served in the provincial administration (governor of Bursa, Maraş, and Yanina) and in central government. In the last 20 years of his life he was justice minister five times, minister of education four times, minister of pious foundations three times, and minister of interior affairs and of trade once each. Author of the most important nineteenth-century Ottoman history, the ten-volume *History of Cevdet*, dealing with the years 1774–1826.

Marshal Fevzi Çakmak [Mustafa Fevzi Pasha] (1876–1950). Graduated from the military academy in 1898. Had a purely military career in the Ottoman army, ending the war as a full general. War minister in the pro-nationalist cabinets of Ali Rıza Pasha and Salih Pasha after the war. Joined the nationalists in May 1920. Member of the national assembly (1920–24). War minister and chief of general staff of the nationalists and, later, CGS of the republic until his retirement in 1944. Made a marshal after the victory on the Sakarya in 1921. Extremely conservative in military matters, he opposed the modernization of the armed forces. Joined the DP opposition in 1946 and stood as opposition candidate against İnönü in the presidential elections of 1946. Left the DP in 1948 to join the new Nation Party, of which he remained honorary president until his death.

Tansu Çiller (1946–). Born in Istanbul. Studied economics at the Bosphorus University in Istanbul. Received a master's degree from New Hampshire University in the United States and a doctorate from Connecticut University. Thereafter studied at Yale University for a short period. Together with her husband, built a fortune in the 1980s in banking and real estate. Was professor of economics in the Bosphorus University when Demirel persuaded her to go into politics in November 1990. In October 1991 she became minister of state (namely without a ministry of her own) for the economy. In June 1993 she was elected party leader of the PTP as successor to Demirel. This made her the first female prime minister of Turkey as well. Her coalition government fell in October 1995. After the elections of December 1995, she returned as vice-premier in a coalition cabinet with the MP. When that fell after four months in June 1996, she accepted becoming vice-premier to Erbakan in a coalition with his Welfare Party, which lasted for a year.

Süleyman Demirel (1920–). Born in a village in Isparta province. Trained as a hydraulic engineer. In charge of the dam-building programme under Menderes. After 1960 went into business, working for an American firm. Elected leader of the Justice Party in 1964. Prime Minister 1965–71, 1974–78, 1979–80 and 1991–93. Banned from politics in 1980. Led the Party of the True Path (PTP) from behind the scenes 1984–87, and officially thereafter. Ninth president of the Turkish Republic 1993–2002. Accomplished politician and public speaker.

Bülent Ecevit (1925–). Born in Istanbul, the son of a law professor who was also a member of the national assembly. Studied literature, but dropped out. First worked as a press officer for the government after the 1950 elections, worked at the RPP party newspaper *Ulus* (Nation). Studied journalism and politics in the USA. Elected to the assembly in 1957. Labour minister in İnönü's coalition cabinets of 1961–65. Created the legal framework for trade unionism in Turkey. Secretary-general of the RPP (1966). Launched the party's 'left-of centre' policy. Opposed the 1971 military intervention. Ousted İnönü as party leader in 1973. Prime minister in 1973–74 and again in 1978–79. Took the decision to invade Cyprus in 1974. Banned from politics in 1980. Efforts to reunite the political left in his Democratic Left Party after 1985 failed. Won 1999 elections. Prime minister until 2002, when his party, the PDL, was annihilated in the elections.

Enver Pasha (1881–1922). A leading member of the CUP from 1906 onwards. One of the 'Freedom Heroes' of 1908. Leader of the military wing of the CUP, especially after the coup of 1913, when he became a general and was appointed war minister. Carried out reorganization of the Ottoman army with the help of the Germans, to whom he was very close. Actively sought Ottoman participation in the war. Fled to Germany after the defeat of the empire in 1918. Thereafter tried to organize a worldwide Muslim revolutionary movement and to reestablish himself in Anatolia with Soviet support. When this failed in 1921, Enver, who had become a convinced pan-Turkist, went on to Central Asia, first with Soviet support but then to fight the Russians on behalf of Turkic nationalism. Died in a skirmish with the Red Army. Reinterred in Istanbul in 1997.

Necmettin Erbakan (1926–2011). Graduated from Istanbul Technical University as an engineer (1948). Studied in Germany. Taught at the ITU (as a professor from 1962). Came to the fore as president of the Union of Chambers of Commerce and Industry, where he was a spokesman for conservative small business. Elected to the assembly as an independent in 1969. In 1970 founded the National Order Party, which had Islamic fundamentalist traits. The party was closed down in 1971, and re-emerged as the National Salvation Party in 1973. Erbakan became vice-premier and minister of state in 1973, when his party joined the governing coalition with Ecevit's RPP. Served in the Nationalist Front cabinets of Demirel (1977). Banned from political life in 1980, he returned to head the Welfare Party after 1987. In the early 1990s his party became the biggest in Turkey, a trend confirmed by the elections of December 1995. In July 1996 he became the first Islamist prime minister of the Republic of Turkey. Resigned in 1997 under strong pressure from the army. Banned from politics in 1998.

Recep Tayyip Erdoğan (1954–) By far the most powerful politician in Turkey since 2001. The first important political leader to hail from the urban proletariat. He grew up in the poor migrant quarter of Kasımpaşa in Istanbul and was educated at a religious imam-hatip school. Then studied business economics at a vocational college that later became part of Marmara University and became active in the youth wing of the National Salvation Party (MSP) of Necmettin Erbakan. He worked in the municipal transport system IETT of Istanbul and for a time was a semi-professional football player. After the *coup d'etat* of September 1980 he was fired by IETT because if his Islamist sympathies and he went into the private sector. In 1983 he emerged as one of the leading young activists of the Welfare Party (RP). In 1989 and 1994 he stood as a candidate in the national elections, but his candidacy was declared void by the electoral council. As chairman of the RP in Istanbul he became mayor of the Istanbul metropolitan area after the party's election victory of March 1994 and gained an excellent reputation as an effective administrator. In 1999 he was convicted to four months in prison for Islamist agitation and lost his position as mayor. The RP meanwhile had been banned and re-established as the Virtue Party (FP). This lost the 1999 elections, after which the party split. The conservative old guard founded the Party of Happiness (SP), while younger cadres led by Erdoğan and Abdullah Gül founded the Justice and Development Party (AKP). Erdoğan became the party leader, but because of his prison sentence could not stand as a candidate in the elections of 2002, which the AKP won in a landslide. After a byelection in Siirt he was elected into parliament and immediately succeeded Abdullah Gül as prime minister. He served continuously as prime minister of Turkey until the summer of 2014, when he became the country's president. Over a 15-year period he consistently won all elections and referendums that were held and established an impregnable hold on political power. He oversaw both the economic boom and far-reaching democratization fo the early 2000s and the imposition of an ever more autocratic and xenophobic regime after 2012.

Nihat Erim (1912–80). Graduated from the law faculty in 1936. Thereafter studied in Paris until 1939. Taught at Ankara University (as a professor from 1942). Served as an adviser to the Turkish delegation to the San Francisco conference in 1945. Elected to the assembly in 1946. Served as minister of communications and vice premier in the cabinets of Saka and Günaltay (1945–50). Edited the RPP party newspaper *Ulus* (Nation) and its successors in the 1950s, but also served the DP government as an adviser on the Cyprus question. Served in the constitutional assembly of 1960. After the military intervention of March 1971 resigned from the RPP to head the 'above-party' cabinets (1971–72).

Kenan Evren (1918–2015). Graduated from military college in 1938 and from the military academy in 1949. Was made a general in 1964. Commander of the land forces in 1977. Chief of the general staff in 1978. Head of the junta that took over power in September 1980. Head of state and commander-in-chief, 1980–82. Elected seventh president of the republic in 1982 (with the adoption of the new constitution), in which function he served until 1989. Retired from the army in 1983.

Damat (Imperial son-in-law) Ferit Pasha (1853–1923). Ottoman diplomat and statesman. Married a daughter of Sultan Abdülhamit. Member of the Council of State. Made pasha in 1888. Entered senate in 1908. Leading member of Freedom and Understanding Party. Five times grand vizier after 1918. His policies were pro-British and anti-nationalist; hence had to leave Turkey in 1923 and died in exile in Nice.

Ali Fethi Bey [Fethi Okyar] (1880–1943). Joined the CUP in Salonica in 1907. Member of the inner circle and secretary-general in 1911. After falling out with Enver and leaving the army in 1913, he served as member of parliament, ambassador to Sofia and minister (1917). Formed the Ottoman Liberal People's Party in 1918. Interned in Malta by the British, he joined the nationalists on his release in 1922. Member of the assembly, internal affairs commissar and twice prime minister (1923 and 1924–25). Thereafter served as ambassador, except for three months in 1930 when, at Atatürk's request, he led the Free Republican Party. One of Atatürk's oldest and closest friends.

Turhan Feyzioğlu (1922–88). Of Circassian extraction. Graduated from the law faculty of Istanbul University in 1945. Professor at the political science faculty in 1955. Dean in 1956. One of the founders of the journal *Forum* in which he wrote articles critical of the DP government. Resigned when the government suspended him in 1957. Entered the assembly for the RPP in the 1957 elections. Rector of Middle East Technical University after the 1960 coup. Member of the constituent assembly and president of its constitutional commission. Education minister (1961); minister without portfolio (1961–62); vice-premier (1962–63). Resigned from the RPP in 1967 over its left-of-centre policy. Founded Reliance Party. Later moved farther to the right, joining Demirel's nationalist front coalition.

Fuat Pasha [Keçecizade Mehmet Fuat] (1815–68). Scion of a well-known bureaucratic family. Studied medicine and learnt French. Entered translation office of the chancery in 1837. Became a protégé of Reşit Pasha. Chief translator in 1838. First secretary in London, ambassador in Madrid. Translator to the imperial council in 1845. Five times minister of foreign affairs after 1851. Twice grand vizier (in 1861 and 1863). Collaborated with Ali Pasha in the reform policies of the 1850s and 1860s.

Ali Fuat Pasha [Ali Fuat Cebesoy] (1882–1968). Classmate and closest friend of Mustafa Kemal at the military academy. Member of CUP, but followed a purely military career. Made a brigadier (and hence a pasha) in 1918. Sent to Anatolia early in 1919, where he became one of the resistance leaders and a member of the national assembly. Commander of the western front (1919–20). Sent to Moscow as nationalist envoy (1920–21). One of the founders of the opposition PRP in 1924. Arrested after the İzmir conspiracy in 1926 but released. Was reconciled with

Atatürk before the latter's death and took up a seat in the assembly again. Minister of public works (1939–43). President of the assembly (1947–50).

'Ziya Gökalp' [Mehmet Ziya] (1876–1924). Born in Diyarbakır. Taught himself French. Studied at the veterinary college in Istanbul. Removed, imprisoned and exiled to his native town because of Young Turk activities. Lived there from 1899 to 1908. Founded branch of CUP after the revolution. Went to Salonica, where he was made a member of the central committee and started writing in the review *Genç Kalemler* (Young Pens). Taught philosophy at Istanbul University. Active in the Turkish Hearth movement. Introduced Durkheimian sociology to the empire and became the leading Turkish nationalist ideologue of the second constitutional period. Deported to Malta after the First World War. Worked for the nationalists in Diyarbakır and Ankara. Elected to the assembly in 1923.

Ragip Gümüşpala (1897–1964). Had a military career. Fought in First World War and was captured by the British in 1918. Joined the Anatolian resistance when he was released two years later. Played a prominent part in the suppression of the Kurdish insurrection of 1925. Served in several positions on the general staff (among them that of chief of army intelligence) until he was made a general in 1948. Commander of the Third Army at the time of the 1960 coup. Appointed Chief of General Staff in June 1960. One of the many high-ranking officers retired later that same year. Founder of the Justice Party in 1961 and its president until his death in 1965. Elected to the national assembly for İzmir in 1961. Played a major part in the reconciliation between the JP and the military.

Şemsettin Günaltay (1883–1961). Studied at the higher teacher training college and in Switzerland. Had a career in secondary education. Entered CUP. Was appointed professor of Turkish and Islamic history at Istanbul University in 1914. Dean of the faculty of divinity. Entered politics in 1915, when he was elected to parliament. Came to the fore after the armistice when he led students in nationalist protest demonstrations. Worked in the Istanbul nationalist underground. Member of the national assembly, 1923–54. Prime minister, 1949–50. After the 1960 coup became a member of the constituent assembly and, one year later, of the senate. Günaltay continued his scholarly career alongside his political one and published many works on Islam, of which he was a modernist interpreter.

Cemal Gürsel (1895–1966). Fought in First World War. Taken prisoner by the British in Palestine, 1918. Released a year later. Returned to Istanbul, but soon joined the nationalists in Anatolia. Completed his education at the military academy after the independence war. Made a general in 1946. Commander of the army in 1958. Retired by the DP government for writing a critical memorandum on 3 May 1960. Brought in by the conspirators to head the coup of 27 May 1960. After the coup he presided over the National Unity Committee. Ex-officio senator after the elections of 1961. Elected fourth president of the republic on 26 October 1961. Died in office in 1966 after spending seven months in coma.

Halet Efendi [Mehmet Sait] (1761–1822). Son of a judge. Had a successful scribal career under Selim III, culminating in an appointment as ambassador to Napoleon's France in 1802. Halet was considered the power behind the throne during the early years of Mahmut II's reign. Cautious and conservative, he protected both the janissaries and the Greek Phanariote elite. Finally he was exiled to Konya and beheaded on the sultan's orders.

Hamdullah Suphi [Hamdullah Suphi Tanrıöver] (1886–1966). Hailed from a family of pashas. After the 1908 revolution gained fame with patriotic articles and speeches. Professor of fine arts at the University of Istanbul. Founder of the Turkish Hearth movement in 1913. Until its closure 20 years later, he was the driving force behind the movement. Member of the national assembly from 1920 onwards. Commissar, and later minister, of education.

Dr Hüseyinzade Ali [Hüseyinzade Ali Turan] (1864–1942). An Azeri Turk born in Baku, he studied first in St Petersburg and then, from 1890 onwards, at the military medical school in Istanbul. There he was one of the earliest members of the original CUP. Had to flee to Azerbaijan, but returned in 1910 to take up a professorship at the military medical school. A prolific and influential pan-Turkist propagandist and theoretician.

İsmet İnönü [Mustafa İsmet Bey] (1884–1973). Graduated from the military academy in 1906. Joined the CUP while serving in Edirne (together with Karabekir) in 1907. Close to Enver. Served as chief of staff under Mustafa Kemal Pasha on the eastern front in 1916. Worked for the nationalist underground while serving at the war office in 1919–20. Moved to Ankara in April 1920. Was appointed commander of the

western front in 1921. Led the Turkish delegation at the peace negotiations in Lausanne. First prime minister of the republic (1923–24).
Prime minister again, 1925–37. Initiator of the statist economic programme in the 1930s. Succeeded Atatürk as president of the republic
(1938–50). Kept Turkey out of Second World War. Introduced multi-
party democracy after 1945. Leader of the opposition (1950–60), prime
minister again (1961–65). Leader of the opposition against the Justice
Party governments (1965–71). Resigned from the RPP in 1972. Although
widely known as İsmet Pasha, he was not a real Ottoman pasha, gaining
general's rank only when serving the nationalists.

Erdal İnönü (1926–). Elder son of İsmet. Graduated from the physics
faculty of Ankara University in 1947. Did his Ph.D. in California (1951).
Worked at Princeton (1951–52). Taught and did research at Ankara
University and Princeton (1958–59), Oak Ridge (1959–60) and Middle
East Technical University, Ankara, (from 1960 onwards). Rector of
METU in 1970–71. One of Turkey's leading scientists, he was one of the
founders of the Social Democrat Party in 1983. In 1991 he became vice-
premier as leader of the junior partner in Demirel's ruling coalition.

İzzet Pasha [Ahmet İzzet Furgaç] (1864–1937). Graduated from the
War Academy in 1887. Was made Chief of General Staff after the 1908
revolution. Succeeded Mahmut Şevket Pasha as minister of war in
1913. Served mainly on the Caucasus front during First World War.
Succeeded Talât Pasha as grand vizier in 1918. Served in several
cabinets in 1919–20. Though a patriot, he never joined the resistance
in Anatolia.

Kıbrıslı (Cypriot) Kâmil Pasha (1832–1913). Started his career as
translator in the service of the khedive of Egypt. Gained prominence as
a provincial administrator. Four times grand vizier after 1884. A
determined opponent of the CUP, he tried to crush it when he was in
power in 1912. Kâmil Pasha was known for his Anglophile tendencies.

Kâzım Pasha Karabekir (1882–1948). Son of an Ottoman pasha.
Graduated from the military academy in 1905. Joined the CUP in Edirne
in 1907. Had a purely military career, culminating in the command of the
Caucasian Army Corps with the rank of brigadier in 1918. Appointed
commander of the Ninth Army in eastern Anatolia in March 1919. His
troops formed the backbone of the national resistance movement.
Defeated the Armenians in 1920. Fell out with Mustafa Kemal over the
latter's monopolization of power and founded the Progressive

Republican Party in 1924. Arrested and tried in connection with the İzmir conspiracy in 1926, but released. Lived in retirement until he re-entered the assembly after Atatürk's death in 1938. Elected president of the assembly in 1946.

Vehbi Koç (1901–1996). Son of a Muslim merchant in Ankara. His father's business thrived during the First World War through Unionist protection. In 1926 Vehbi took over the business. In 1937 the head-quarters of the firm were transferred to Istanbul and the firm became a limited company. In the 1930s the company carried out large building projects for the government. From the late 1940s onwards, it began to import industrial products and to produce consumer products under licence. In 1963, the companies of the Koç group were brought together in a holding company, which was – and is – the largest industrial conglomerate in Turkey.

Refik Koraltan (1889–1974). A lawyer by profession, he served as prosecutor and police chief under the CUP. One of the founders of the Defence of National Rights organization in Trabzon in 1918. Joined the nationalists and entered the national assembly in 1920. Remained a member of the assembly until 1935 when he took up his administrative career again (serving as provincial governor). Re-entered assembly in 1943. One of the four founders of the Democrat Party in 1946. Assembly president, 1950–60. Sentenced to death in 1961, but the sentence was commuted to life imprisonment and Koraltan was eventually released under an amnesty in 1966. Within the DP he was prominent, but not powerful.

Fahri Korutürk (1903–87). Graduated from the naval academy in 1923. Served as naval attaché at several embassies. Became an admiral in 1950. Chief of the naval forces in 1957. In 1960 he left the navy and was appointed ambassador in Moscow, then in Madrid. Senator (1968) and sixth president of the republic (1973–80).

Fuat Köprülü [Mehmet Fuat Bey] (1890–1966). Descended from the famous family of grand viziers who ruled the Ottoman Empire during the second half of the seventeenth century. Studied law, but left the university without graduating. Studied literature, history and philosophy privately. Appointed lecturer of Turkish literature in 1913. Struggled to establish European scholarly standards in the study of literature and history. One of the founders of Turkology in Turkey (founding the Turkological Institute in 1924). While emphasizing the continuity

428 BIOGRAPHICAL NOTES

between older Central Asian cultures and the Ottoman–Turkish one, he opposed the more extreme nationalist historical theses. Entered politics (alongside his academic work) in 1934 when he was elected to the assembly. One of the four founders of the Democrat Party in 1946. Foreign minister in the first Menderes government after 1950. Resigned from the DP in 1957. Efforts to re-enter politics after the 1960 coup failed.

Sultan Mahmut II (1784–1839). Thirtieth Ottoman sultan and son of Abdülhamit I. After cautiously strengthening his hold on power between 1808 and 1826, putting his followers in leading positions and undermining the position of the notables, he dissolved the janissaries in 1826 and thereafter embarked on a programme of Westernizing reforms in all branches of the administration. Strengthened the hold of central government over the main parts of the empire but lost Greece, Serbia, Egypt and (temporarily) Syria.

Sultan Mehmet V [Reşat] (1811–1918). Thirty-fifth Ottoman sultan and son of Abdülmecit. Succeeded his elder brother Abdülhamit in 1909. During his nine-year reign left all power to the politicians, notably to the CUP, which tried to promote him both as a 'national' monarch and as caliph. Died before the end of the war. Minor poet.

Sultan Mehmet VI [Vahdettin] (1861–1929). Thirty-sixth and last Ottoman sultan, son of Abdülmecit. Succeeded his brother Mehmet V on 3 July 1918. After the armistice and the flight of the Unionist leaders, he tried to take the government into his own hands. Took a conciliatory line towards the Entente and opposed first the Unionists and then the Anatolian nationalists. Accepted the Treaty of Sèvres in 1920. Deposed in October 1922 after the nationalist victory. Left the country aboard a British man of war. Attempted to set himself up as caliph in the Hijaz. When this failed, he settled down on the Italian Riviera. Died in San Remo.

Ferit Melen, Ferit (1906–88). Graduate of the civil service academy. Had a bureaucratic career in the treasury department until he was elected to the national assembly for the RPP in 1950. He lost his seat in 1954, but regained it in 1957. Member of the constituent assembly in 1960. Finance minister 1962–65. Senator for the RPP at the same time. Broke away from the RPP over the left-of-centre strategy, together with Feyzioğlu. Joined the Reliance Party. Defence minister in the Nihat Erim cabinets of 1971–72. Prime minister 1972–73.

Adnan Menderes (1889–1961). Son of a landowner from Aydın. Fought in First World War. Joined the guerrilla war against the Greeks in 1919. Entered politics in 1930, as local chief of Fethi Okyar's Free Republican Party. Caught the eye of the RPP leaders and joined their party. Elected to the assembly in 1931. For 15 years served as a representative, at the same time studying law. The most vocal advocate of change in 1945 and one of the founders of the Democrat Party. Prime minister 1950–60, dominating the DP more and more and developing autocratic tendencies. Arrested after the 1960 military coup, tried, sentenced to death and executed on 17 September 1961 after a failed suicide attempt.

Ahmet Şefik Mithat Pasha (1822–84). Son of a judge. Entered office of imperial council as apprentice scribe in 1836. Made his name as efficient and progressive provincial administrator. Appointed president of the state council in 1868, but fell out with Ali Pasha. Grand vizier for three months in 1872. One of the initiators of the coup of 1876, which made him grand vizier again. Main author of the Ottoman constitution. Exiled to Taif in Arabia by Sultan Abdülhamit in 1877 and killed there on the sultan's orders in 1884.

Sultan Murat V (1840–1904). Thirty-third Ottoman sultan, eldest son of Abdülmecit. Known as a liberal, he was put on the throne in 1876 by the constitutionalists, but after 93 days his mental instability forced them to replace him with his younger brother Abdülhamit.

Mizancı (the Balance-man) Murat Bey (1853–1912). Born in Tbilisi and educated in Russia. Taught history at the civil service academy (*mülkiye*) in Istanbul. At the same time published the *Mizan* (Balance). After repeated problems with the censor fled to Egypt in 1895. Joined the CUP leaders in Geneva in 1896 and took over the leadership of the movement from Ahmet Rıza. Was persuaded by agents of Abdülhamit to return to Istanbul in August 1897, something from which his reputation never fully recovered. Exiled by the Unionists after the abortive counter-revolution of 1909.

Bayraktar (Standard-bearer) Mustafa Pasha (1750–1808). Son of a janissary from Rusçuk. Made a name for himself during the 1768 Russian war. Became the leading notable of Rusçuk with extensive landed property. Opposed Selim III's efforts to reduce the notables, but later grew close to the sultan and was given the title of vizier and the command of the Danube front in the Russian war of 1806. After the fall of Selim he rallied the opposition to the new regime and took Istanbul in June 1808. Put Mahmut II on the throne and took the initiative for concluding the 'Document of Agreement' between the sultan and the leading notables. Died in the janissary insurrection of November 1808.

Mustafa Suphi (1883–1921). Graduated from the Istanbul University law school and the political science faculty of the Sorbonne. Taught at teacher-training college. Deported to Sinop by the CUP because of his liberal leanings. Fled to Russia in 1914. After the October Revolution of 1917 he spread communism among the Turkish prisoners of war in Russia. Attended the first Komintern congress (1919) and founded the Turkish Communist Party in Baku in 1920. Drowned at sea by the nationalists (Trabzon, 1921).

Namık Kemal Bey (1840–88). Son of the court astrologist. Served in the translation office of the Porte, when he got to know Şinasi and started writing in the latter's newspaper. One of the founders of the Young Ottoman movement in 1865. Fled to Europe in 1867, where he edited the opposition newspaper *Hürriyet* (Freedom). Returned to Istanbul in 1870, but was exiled to Cyprus in 1873. In 1876 he was recalled to help draw up the constitution, but shortly afterwards Abdülhamit banished him again, this time to Lesbos. In his final years he served as governor of Lesbos, Rhodes and Chios.

Dr Selânikli Nâzim (1870(?)–1926). Member of the first CUP in 1889. Graduated from the medical school and studied in Paris. Together with Bahaettin Şakır, he revitalized Ahmet Rıza's CUP in Paris. Engineered the merger between the Salonica-based OFS and the CUP in 1907. After the revolution he became a member of the central committee and – until 1911 – secretary-general. One of the most influential members of the CUP inner circle. Joined cabinet as minister of education in 1918. Fled the country before the armistice. Executed in 1926 for his alleged role in the İzmir conspiracy.

Gazi (Conquering Hero) Osman Pasha (1832–97). From a poor Anatolian family. Served with distinction in a number of military capacities, but gained national fame with his defence of Plevna against invading Russian army in 1876. After the war, Osman Pasha served as *serasker* (commander-in-chief and war minister) for seven years. As Lord Chamberlain he was one of the most influential people in Abdülhamit's entourage.

Turgut Özal (1927–93). Born in Malatya. Graduated from the Istanbul Polytechnic as an electrical engineer. Studied economics in the USA.

Became technical adviser to Süleyman Demirel in 1965, and head of the State Planning Organization in 1967. After the 1971 coup he went to work at the World Bank in Washington. Worked in the private sector during 1973–79. Appointed to the cabinet by Demirel in 1979, with special responsibility for the economic reform package. Prime minister under the generals, 1980–82. Had to resign because of banking scandal. Founder of the Motherland Party in 1983. Prime minister, 1983–89. Eighth president of the republic from 1989 until his death.

Recep Peker (1888–1950). Trained as a military officer. Fought on different fronts during First World War. Thereafter returned to the academy to complete his education. Joined the nationalists in 1920 and became secretary-general of the national assembly. From 1923 onwards member of the assembly and, at the same time, secretary-general of the People's Party. Finance minister (1924). Interior minister (at the end of 1924) – resigned in protest over Fethi's moderate policies. Defence minister (1925), president of the assembly (1928), transport minister (1928–30). Strong proponent of authoritarian one-party system and statist policies in 1930s. Interior minister (1942–43). As prime minister (1946–47) he took an uncompromising confrontational line against the opposition, but had to resign when İnönü sided with the 'doves' in 1947.

Hüseyin Rauf Bey [Rauf Orbay] (1881–1964). Son of an Ottoman Admiral of Circassian stock. Naval officer, who became a national hero as commander of the cruiser *Hamidiye* in 1913. Served in the navy and as an Ottoman agent in Persia during First World War. Member of the Ottoman delegation at the Brest–Litovsk peace talks. Leader of the delegation that negotiated the armistice of Moudros. Went to Anatolia to organize national resistance in May 1919. Head of the nationalist group in the last Ottoman parliament (1920). Deported to Malta in 1920. After his return in 1922, commissar and prime minister of the nationalist government. From 1923 led the opposition in the PP against Mustafa Kemal Pasha and İsmet. Founded PRP in 1924. Accused of being the brains behind the 1926 İzmir conspiracy. Sentenced to ten years (*in absentia*). Lived abroad until 1936. Ambassador in London, 1942–44.

Mustafa Reşit Pasha (1799–1857). Son of a scribe. Started his career in the chancery as a protégé of his brother-in-law, Seyyit Ali Pasha. Ottoman ambassador in Paris and London. Minister of foreign affairs in 1836. Led the pro-British faction at the Porte and took the initiative for the trade treaty of 1838 and the reform edict of 1839. Six times grand vizier after 1845. Architect of the reforms of 1840s and early 1850s.

Prens Sabahattin (1877–1948). Born in Istanbul, a member of the imperial family. Moved to France with his father, Damat Mahmut Celâlettin Pasha, in 1899 and joined the Young Turks. As a follower of Edmond Desmolins he favoured minimal government and private initiative. Founded his own organization (Society for Private Initiative and Decentralization) in 1906 and so split the movement. Central figure in the anti-Unionist (but Young Turk) opposition after 1908. Arrested in connection with the murder of Mahmut Şevket Pasha in 1913. Exiled from Turkey in 1924 as a member of the Ottoman dynasty.

Haci Ömer Sabancı (1906–1966). Founder of the second largest industrial and trading conglomerate in Turkey. Only had a village education. Worked as a labourer in Adana (1918–26). Entered the cotton trade. Opened the first modern cotton gin factory in Adana in 1938. From then on, his business branched out into all kinds of sectors: textiles, oils, rubber and tyres and building. In 1947 he founded the Akbank, one of Turkey's leading banks. In 1967 his family businesses were brought together in the Sabancı Holding Company. After Haci Ömer's death, his son Şakip led the holding. Having close ties with the Özal family, his group expanded quickly during the liberalization of the 1980s, challenging the Koç group as the leading industrial holding in Turkey.

Colonel Sadık Bey (1860–1940). Graduated from the military academy in 1882. Taught at the academy. In 1907–8 led the CUP cell in the garrison of Monastir. Played a leading part in the revolution of 1908, but fell out with the CUP leaders soon after. Founded the Freedom and Understanding Party and the Saviour Officers who forced the CUP out of power in 1912. Had to leave the country after the Unionist coup of 1913 and lived first in Paris, then in Cairo. Returned after the armistice. Was banned from Turkey as one of the 150 undesirables in 1923. Lived in Romania for 22 years, refusing a pardon from the Ankara government, only returning when his name was cleared. Died on the night of his return to Turkey. A keen mystic and member of the Halveti order.

Küçük (Small) Mehmet Sait Pasha (1838–1914). Grew up in Erzurum. Moved to Istanbul and held a succession of positions in the bureaucracy of the Porte. His political career took off when he was made chief palace secretary after the accession of Abdülhamit, whose confidence he enjoyed. In 1877 he was given the rank of vizier and appointed interior minister. In 1879 he was appointed grand vizier for the first of nine times, three of them after the constitutional revolution of 1908. A prolific writer of newspaper articles and memoirs.

Sait Halim Pasha (1863–1921). Grandson of Mehmet Ali Pasha of Egypt. Born in Cairo and educated in Europe. Member of the council of state in 1888. President of the council of state and minister of foreign affairs in 1911. Succeeded Mahmut Şevket Pasha as grand vizier when the latter was murdered in 1913. Opposed the entry of the Ottoman Empire into the war but stayed on as grand vizier until 1916, when he resigned in favour of Talât and became a senator. Arrested by the British in 1919 and interned on Malta. On his release went to Rome, where an Armenian killed him. Prolific writer on social and Islamic matters.

Bediüzzaman (Marvel of the Time) Sait Nursi (1876–1960). Born in Nurs, province of Bitlis, son of a poor cleric of Kurdish extraction. Had a traditional religious education. Became an active member of the Nakşibendi dervish order. Went to Istanbul in 1896 and again shortly before the 1908 revolution. At first on good terms with the Young Turks, but after revolution joined the fundamentalist Muhammadan Union. After the counter-revolution of April 1909 he lived in the east for some years, but in 1911 he returned to Istanbul and seems to have entered the entourage of Sultan Mehmet V. During the First World War he served with the Special Organization as a propagandist. Russian prisoner of war, 1915–17. After the war returned and joined the Society for the Elevation of Kurdistan. Joined the nationalists, but broke with them in January 1923 over their secularist course. Arrested after the Kurdish insurrection of 1925. Deported first to a village near Isparta and then to Eskişehir (1935), Kastamonu (1936), Denizli (1943) and Emirdağ, near Afyon (1944). Released when the DP came to power in 1950. Arrested and tried many times for alleged political use of religion, but his ideas, expounded in a number of tracts collectively known as the *Risale-i Nur* (Message of Light), really revolved around a kind of Islamic moral rearmament, coupled with the adoption of Western technology and science. Acquired a large following in Turkey, which is still growing today.

Hasan Hüsnü Saka (1881–1960). Graduated from the civil service academy in 1908. Studied in France. Entered politics when he was elected to the last Ottoman parliament in 1920. After April 1920 he sat in the national assembly in Ankara. Member of the Lausanne conference delegation. Minister of economic affairs (1923), minister of trade (1924), minister of finance (1925). Foreign minister in September 1944. Represented Turkey at the San Francisco conference in 1945. Succeeded Recep Peker as prime minister in 1947, when İnönü withdrew his support from the hard-liners in his party. Saka remained in the assembly until the 1954 elections.

Şükrü Saraçoğlu [Mehmet Sükrü Bey] (1887–1953). After graduating from the civil service academy in 1909 he served as a teacher in secondary schools. During the First World War he went to Geneva to study political science. There, together with Mahmut Esat Bozkurt, founded a nationalist students organization. Returned and fought the Greek army in western Anatolia. Representative for İzmir in the second national assembly. Education minister (1924–25). Finance minister (1927–30). Founded Central Bank (1930). Justice minister (1933–39) and finally foreign minister (1939–42) and prime minister in the difficult years during and after the Second World War, 1942–46.

Refık Saydam [Dr İbrahim Refik Bey] (1881–1942). Graduated from the military medical school in 1905. Went on to study in Germany. Went to Anatolia with Mustafa Kemal Pasha in May 1919, as his chief medical officer. Left the army and took part in the congresses of Erzurum and Sivas. Elected to the national assembly in 1920. Health minister from 1923 to 1937. Minister of internal affairs (1938–39) and prime minister under İnönü (1939–42).

Selim III (1761–1808). Twenty-eighth Ottoman sultan, son of Sultan Mustafa III. Was interested in European ways and corresponded with Louis XVI of France even before his own accession. Tried to introduce a reform programme called 'new order' (*Nizam-i Cedid*), which consisted largely of traditional efforts to combat abuse but also contained a number of European-inspired innovations. His efforts to strengthen central authority over the notables failed, as did his attempt to replace the janissary corps with a modern European-style army. He was brought down by a janissary revolt in 1807 and murdered in 1808.

Zekeriya Sertel (1890–1980). Born in the Jewish community of Salonica. Graduated from the law school of Istanbul University and from the Sorbonne. Read journalism at Columbia University. Worked for the Turkish government after his return in 1923, but left in protest against the censorship rules. After having been involved in several other periodicals, he started publishing the *Tan* (Dawn) in 1936. Arrested many times for his leftist opinions. Tan's offices and presses were ransacked by a rightist mob in December 1945. In 1950, Sertel left Turkey, never to return. For most of his publishing life, Zekeriya worked in tandem with his wife, Sabiha, who had a similar background to his and espoused Marxism even more emphatically than her husband.

Ahmet Necdet Sezer (1940–). After graduating from the faculty of law, Ankara University, in 1962 had a career as a judge. Acquired an MA degree in civil law in 1978. Chief justice at the constitutional court from 1988. Elected tenth president of the republic in May 2000. Staunch upholder of the rule of law, which brought him into conflict with Ecevit and other politicians.

Cevdet Sunay (1899–1982). Soldier. Fought in First World War and was taken prisoner by the British in Palestine, 1918. After his return in 1920, joined the nationalists. Made a general in 1949. Chief of General Staff after the 1960 coup until 1966. Appointed to the senate in 1966 in order to make possible his succession to the presidency of the republic. Fifth president of the republic, 1966–73.

Dr Şefik Hüsnü [Şefik Hüsnü Değmer] (1887–1958). Studied medicine in Paris, where socialist and radical ideas influenced him. On his return founded the Turkish Workers and Peasants' Party and tried to spread socialism in articles in *Aydınlık* and *Kurtuluş*. Convicted for political activity, 1925, 1926, 1952. Spent the period 1929–39 abroad. Took part in sixth and seventh Komintern congresses. After his return he founded the Turkish Socialist Workers and Peasants' Party in 1946, which was closed down the same year.

Mahmut Şevket Pasha (1856–1913). Ottoman officer of Arabian descent. Commanded the Third (Macedonian) Army after the revolution of 1908. After the suppression of the 1909 counter-revolution he became war minister and commander of the First, Second and Third Armies. Replaced by the Liberals in 1912, he became grand vizier after the Unionist coup of 1913. Six months later he was murdered.

İbrahim Şinasi (1826–1871). Started his career as a clerk in the arsenal. Became one of Reşit Pasha's protégés. Sent to France for further education. In 1853 returned to Istanbul when he was appointed member of the education council. Enemy of Ali Pasha, who dismissed him after Reşit's death. In 1860 he started his own newspaper, which soon became a vehicle for criticism of the government. As a result, he had to leave the country in 1865. Mentor of Namık Kemal.

Mehmet Talât Pasha (1874–1921). Member of the first CUP in Edirne after 1890. Banished to Salonica when that organization was uncovered by the sultan's police in 1896. Founder of the Ottoman Freedom Society in Salonica in 1906. Most important civilian member of the CUP after the revolution. Representative of Edirne in all CUP parliaments. Minister of the interior (1913–17), grand vizier (1917–18). Fled to Germany in 1918. Assassinated by an Armenian in Berlin in 1921 because of his involvement in the persecution of the Armenians.

Tekin Alp [Moise Cohen, Munis Tekinalp] (1883–1961). Born in Seres, into an Orthodox Jewish family. Studied at the Alliance Israelite school and then at the law school in Salonica. Began to write articles in newspapers in 1905. Joined the CUP in 1908. Moved to Istanbul in 1912. Taught law and economics at Istanbul University, but made his living in the tobacco trade. An ardent Turkish nationalist in spite of his background and a prolific writer on Turkish nationalism and pan-Turkism, and on the national economy.

Ahmet Tevfik Pasha [Tevfik Okday] (1845–1936). Related to the Crimean royal family. Had a long and distinguished diplomatic career, culminating in the position of minister of foreign affairs from 1895 to 1909. He was grand vizier for one month in 1909 and four times between 1918 and 1922. Tevfik Pasha was the last grand vizier of the Ottoman Empire.

Alpaslan Türkeş (1917–1997). Born in Cyprus. Graduated from military college. Involved in pan-Turkist (and pro-German) propaganda during Second World War. Arrested in 1944, but released on appeal. Graduated from the military academy in 1954. Served on the general staff and with NATO. One of the main organizers of the 1960 military coup. Leading radical within the National Unity Committee. One of the 14 radical officers removed from the NUC in November 1960. Military attaché in New Delhi. After his return, he took over the leadership of the Republican Peasants' Nation Party in 1965. The party soon became the ultra-nationalist Nationalist Action Party, for which Turkeş sat in the assembly, 1969–80. Turkeş served as vice-premier in Demirel's Nationalist Front cabinets of 1974–1977. After the 1980 coup he was arrested and banned from political life. Re-entered the political arena in 1987.

Kemal Türkler (1926–1980). Dropped out of the law faculty of Istanbul University. Rose to prominence in the metalworkers union in Istanbul, of which he became the president in 1954. In 1967 Türkler was among the founders of the left-wing trade unions confederation (DİSK), of which he subsequently became the president. Murdered by right-wingers in 1980.

Suat Hayri Ürgüplü (1903–1981). Born in Damascus, son of one of the last Şeyhülislams, Hayri Efendi. Trained as a lawyer. Worked for the commission supervising the population exchange between Greece and Turkey (1925–29). Judge in Istanbul (1929–32). Entered the assembly in 1935. Minister for customs and monopolies (1943–46). Served as ambassador in Bonn, London, Washington and Madrid (1952–61). Senator (1961) charged with forming an above-party cabinet in 1965, which lasted until the elections later that year. Given the same charge in 1972, but resigned when changes to his cabinet were demanded. Retired from political life in 1972.

Kara (Black) Vasıf (1872–1931). Graduated from the War Academy in 1903. Rose to the rank of colonel, commanding a division. Member of the CUP before 1908. On the staff of the Action Army of 1909. Member of inner circle of Unionist officers. Co-founder of *Karakol* in 1918. Member of last Ottoman parliament and of the representative committee of the nationalists. Deported to Malta in 1920. On his return in 1922 helped to found the Second Group opposition. Tried but acquitted during the purges of 1926. Died (probably suicide) in 1931.

Ahmet Emin Yalman (1888–1973). From a *dönme* (crypto-Jewish) family of Salonica. Graduated from Columbia University. Lecturer in sociology and statistics in Istanbul (1914–20). Deported to Malta (1920–21). Founded the newspaper *Vatan* (Fatherland) in 1923, introducing a more modern American-inspired style of journalism. Arrested (and paper closed down) in 1925. Entered business life as an importer of American cars and tractors. For some time cooperated with Zekeriya Sertel at the *Tan*. In 1940 reopened *Vatan*. During the Second World War staunchly supported the cause of the Allies. Supported the DP after 1946. In 1952 narrowly escaped an attempt on his life by fundamentalists. Turned against Menderes in the lagter 1950s. Sentenced to 15 months in 1959. Ended his publishing career in 1962. Thereafter wrote columns, articles and memoirs.

Mesut Yılmaz (1947–). Graduated from the political science faculty of Ankara University (the *Mülkiye*) in 1971. Studied for MA in Cologne, Germany. Thereafter worked in private industry and in state enterprises. One of the founders of the Motherland Party in 1983. Elected as deputy for Rize. Minister of foreign affairs 1987–90. Prime Minister during 1991 and again in 1996. Leader of the liberal wing within the Motherland Party.

Ziya Pasha [Abdülhamit Ziya] (1825–1880). Son of a customs official, he entered the correspondence office of the Porte in 1842. In 1855 Reşit Pasha made him third secretary of the palace, but Ali Pasha sacked him after Reşit's death. Then he served as provincial administrator until he fled to France in 1867. In France he published opposition newspapers together with Namık Kemal. After his return in 1872 he served as a member of the state council. After the coup of 1876 he was appointed private secretary to the new sultan, Murat V, but removed from that post 24 hours later.

Index

454 INDEX